KATHERINE ANNE PORTER

A Life

JOAN GIVNER

A TOUCHSTONE BOOK
Published by Simon & Schuster, Inc.
NEW YORK

A Touchstone Book
Published by Simon & Schuster, Inc.
Simon & Schuster Building
Rockefeller Center
1230 Avenue of the Americas
New York, New York 10020
TOUCHSTONE and colophon are registered trademarks of
Simon & Schuster, Inc.
Designed by Edith Fowler
Manufactured in the United States of America
10 9 8 7 6 5 4 3 2 1
10 9 8 7 6 5 4 3 2 1 Pbk.
Library of Congress Cataloging in Publication Data
Givner, Joan, date.
   Katherine Anne Porter: a life.
   Includes bibliographical references and index.
   1. Porter, Katherine Anne, 1890-1980—Biog-
raphy. 2. Authors, American—20th century—
Biography. I. Title.
PS3531.0752Z64 1982 813′.54   82-10626
ISBN 0-671-43207-9
ISBN 0-671-50586-6 Pbk.

The author is grateful for permission to use excerpts from the following works:
"Katherine Anne Porter: An Interview" by Barbara Thompson from Writers
at Work: The Paris Review Interviews, 2nd Series. *Copyright © 1963 by
Paris Review, Inc. Reprinted by permission of Viking Penguin, Inc.*
The Collected Essays and Occasional Writings of Katherine Anne Porter,
*copyright © 1970 by Katherine Anne Porter. Reprinted by permission of Dela-
corte Press, Seymour Lawrence.*
Ship of Fools *by Katherine Anne Porter. Reprinted by permission of Little,
Brown and Company in association with the Atlantic Monthly Press. Copyright
© 1962 by Katherine Anne Porter.*
The Collected Stories of Katherine Anne Porter, *copyright © 1965 by
Katherine Anne Porter. Reprinted by permission of Harcourt Brace Jovanovich,
Inc.*
"Gerontion" *from* Collected Poems 1909–1962 *by T. S. Eliot. Copyright ©
1963 by T. S. Eliot. Reprinted by permission of Harcourt Brace Jovanovich,
Inc., and Faber and Faber, Ltd.*
"You, Andrew Marvell" *from* New and Collected Poems 1917–1976 *by
Archibald MacLeish. Copyright © 1976 by Archibald MacLeish. Reprinted by
permission of Houghton Mifflin Company.*
"Emily Dickinson and Katherine Anne Porter" *by Karl Shapiro. First appeared
in* Poetry *(April 1961). Copyright © 1961 by The Modern Poetry Association.
Reprinted by permission of the Editor of* Poetry.
Somewhere the Tempest Fell *by Josephine Herbst. Reprinted with the per-
mission of Charles Scribner's Sons. Copyright 1947, 1975 by Josephine Herbst.*
The Republic of Letters in America: The Correspondence of John Peale
Bishop and Allen Tate, *edited by Thomas Daniel Young and John J. Hindle.*

Acknowledgments

I have been most fortunate in having the good will and cooperation of my subject's family. In particular, Paul Porter, Katherine Anne Porter's nephew and the executor of her estate, has been a source of great strength and encouragement. I am grateful also to Ann Hollo-way Heintze and her family, to Breckenridge Porter and his family, and to more distant members of the Porter clan—Lady Bunton Terry, Mabel Kilpatrick, and Bebe Steves Rosser.

I am also grateful for financial assistance from the President's Fund of the University of Regina, the Canada Council, and the National Endowment for the Humanities. A fellowship at the Bunting Institute of Radcliffe College gave me working space, a forum for my ideas, and access to the Harvard Library facilities.

The great contributions of some people to this biography will be apparent from the story, in which they play important parts. They have provided information in interviews and letters, sometimes over a number of years, and have become valued friends: Erna Glover Johns, Kitty Barry Crawford, Mildred Koontz, Marcella Comès Winslow, the late Matthew Josephson, David Locher, the Reverend Raymond Roseliep, Rhea Johnson, Lieutenant Commander William R. Wilkins, and Barrett Prettyman, Jr.

The generosity of other scholars and biographers has been truly heartening. Lodwick Hartley gave me good counsel in weekly letters for five years. George Hendrick has been tireless in his efforts on my behalf and has allowed me to draw from the results of his own research; Thomas Walsh shared his knowledge of Mexico; Elinor Langer taught me to know Josephine Herbst. John Pomian, the biographer of Joseph Retinger, helped me to understand Joseph Retinger. Marya Fforde, Retinger's daughter, added to that knowledge and lent irreplaceable photographs of her father. David Levin, the biographer of Cotton Mather, taught me a great deal in his distinguished works and in informal discussions. The late Allen Tate gave information and invaluable suggestions, as did Alice Crozier, Joseph Weisenfarth, Gretchen Meiszkowski, and Margaret Neussendorfer.

Many people in Texas have taken an interest in my work and helped it along enthusiastically: Winston Bode, Maggie Mae Bode, Margarita Porter Folks, Maude Strawn (owner of the Cat Porter house in Kyle), Bobbie and Lex Word, Lady Bird Johnson, and the late Lon Tinkle.

This work owes a great deal to the following libraries and their staffs: the Regina Public Library; the University of Regina Library, especially the interlibrary loans and reference departments; the Humanities Research Center of the University of Texas in Austin; and the McKeldin Library of the University of Maryland, especially two custodians of the Katherine Anne Porter Room, Mary Boccaccio and Dr. Robert L. Beare.

A great many individual archivists and researchers have made important contributions. These include Christine Spilsbury, of the American Film Institute, and Sister Marguerite Brou, formerly of the Archives of the Archdiocese of New Orleans, who was responsible for the discovery of the circumstances of Porter's conversion to Catholicism and her baptism. Monsignor Anton J. Frank of Annunciation Church in Houston, Texas, provided more information on this subject; the diligence of Karen Hand Locher of the public library of Victoria, Texas, led me, after years of unsuccessful searching, to the Koontz family of Inez; Elsie White uncovered the certificate of Porter's first divorce; Claire Davenport researched the origins of the Skaggs family in Kentucky; and Amy Clendenning and my cousins, Norma Yates and Edward Barboza, all of Bermuda, contributed to the Bermuda part of the story.

My colleagues at the University of Regina have taken a lively interest in my work and have given their professional expertise. I am grateful to Burton Weber, Janice B. Moulton, Annabel Robinson, Orlene and Anatol Murad, Attila Chanady, Cesar Caviedes, J. K. Roberts, Marilyn Bickford, and Gertrude Bruce. President Lloyd Barber and Dean Cameron Blachford have provided support in a variety of different ways.

My editor, Erwin Glikes, believed in this book from the beginning and expertly steered it to its completion. Frances McCullough always gave sound advice and friendship. Marion Osmun made the final stages easier with her competence and good humor.

Professor Edward McVey of Huron College has for years read and commented on everything I have written. My husband, David Givner, has been unstinting of his advice and criticism. This book would not have been possible without his generosity and wisdom.

*This book is dedicated to
the memory of
Lodwick Hartley and
Robert L. Beare*

Contents

Katherine Anne Porter

Prologue

My life has been incredible, I don't believe a word of it."[1] Thus Katherine Anne Porter, using the words of a French courtesan, summed up her life. And she was right. Her long life spanned nine decades, and somehow she always managed to be present when the history of her time was being made.

She was born at the beginning of the last decade of the nineteenth century and grew up unfamiliar with electricity, automobiles, or airplanes. She learned to enjoy one after another of these revolutionary changes and lived to witness, finally, man's triumphant landings on the moon. Her presence at Cape Canaveral for the moon shot (she was eighty-two and covering the event for *Playboy* magazine) was typical of her capacity for gravitating always toward the center of historical events.

She grew up amid such vivid memories of the Civil War that she could say, "I am the grandchild of a lost war."[2] She lived through two subsequent world wars, nearly dying in the epidemic of influenza that swept the United States during the First World War. She lived in Greenwich Village during its time of transformation by the Volstead Act. She was in Mexico City during the Obregón Revolution ("I attended, you might say, and assisted at, in my own modest way, a revolution"[3]). She was in Berlin during Hitler's rise to power and her escort on at least one occasion was Hitler's henchman Hermann Göring. From Germany she went to Paris, and she lived there for four years before the outbreak of the Second World War.

For much of her life she roamed the world rootlessly, seeking a place in which she could feel at home. Finally she knew that America was her country and that she did not belong completely to the North or to the South. She settled at last in Washington, D.C., saying that she must live either "in a howling wilderness or a world capital,"[4] and there she became a frequent guest at the White House during the administrations of Kennedy and Johnson. "It tickleth me about my heart's rote," she said, quoting the Wife of Bath, "that I have seen the world as in my time."[5]

No less spectacular than the external panorama against which she moved was the inner drama of her own personal life. Her various metamorphoses were reflected in her physical transformation from a pretty dark-haired child to a kittenish adolescent, to a self-possessed young woman of the flapper era, her graying hair first bobbed in the daring fashion of the time and later caught in a bun at the nape of her neck. In middle life she finally emerged as a silver-haired, apparently ageless woman of striking beauty and presence. In each of these changing manifestations she was characterized by her large gray eyes, now dreamily unseeing, now focused with intense concentration; by her face, irradiated by her lively intelligence; by the dramatic gestures of her hands and by her memorable husky voice and the use she made of it.

Her skills as a speaker, whether she was addressing a packed auditorium or a single person, were legendary. Lady Bird Johnson found her conversation as flawless as her short stories.[6] The poet Raymond Roseliep described her as the most colorful conversationalist he had ever met because her image-making faculty was so alive.[7] Andrew Lytle, who knew her during her early struggles when she often did not have enough to eat, recalled going to her room and finding her lying face down on her bed. He remembered that she got up immediately and released "that wonderful flow of conversation which spoke as if it had been written."[8]

With that vivid personality matching her striking physical appearance, she had, not surprisingly, many affairs of the heart. She told Malcolm Cowley when she was approaching forty and before her last two marriages that (exaggerating a little) she had had four husbands and thirty-seven lovers.[9] There was rarely a time when she was not amorously engaged, and one of the most satisfactory loves of her life came along when she was in her seventies, and lasted almost to her death. This sphere of activity alone might provide the stuff of a biography, but for Porter it was never the predominant interest of her life. In *Ship of Fools* her character Jenny Brown is accosted by a gypsy fortuneteller who warns her that the man she is with is not her real man. Jenny replies, "There are going to be a lot of other things much more interesting in my life than this man, or any other man."[10] This is the voice of Katherine Anne Porter speaking loud and clear through her character.

Her emotional center, the one continuing thread of her life, was her work as an artist. Alice B. Toklas once spoke huffily of receiving a letter from Porter in which the phrase "as an artist I" was used several times.[11] Porter was well aware that such usage was not fashionable, but she defended it as a simple description of her occupation, just as one might be a plumber or a carpenter, and she used it with pride.

Her life was a variation on that theme so persistent in the history and literature of her country—the American Dream, the story of a man who starts life with nothing and reaches extraordinary pinnacles of fame and fortune. She belongs to the same tradition as Benjamin Franklin, Abraham Lincoln, Lyndon Johnson, and Jay Gatsby, who dreamed of what they wanted to be and never rested until they had transformed themselves accordingly.

Born in a log cabin, she was determined to succeed in the world through her own efforts. As a young girl she had a multiplicity of artistic talents and wondered which one to develop. She told her sister that what she really wanted was glory.[12] When she was twenty-nine she knew exactly what she wanted to do and she vowed solemnly to the same sister that one day she would write as well as anyone in America.[13] And she did that. For her work she received a rare combination of rewards. She gained popular adulation, material fortune (though this was the least of her aspirations), and critical acclaim. She was hailed as a brilliant stylist, a "writer's writer," and her work was compared with that of Hawthorne, Flaubert, and Henry James.[14]

Taking little pride in the distance she had traveled from her humble origins, she produced simultaneously with her stories another work of art. She transformed herself and her own personal history. In the place of Callie Porter, raised in poverty and obscurity, she created Katherine Anne Porter, an aristocratic daughter of the Old South and the descendant of a long line of distinguished statesmen. In this reincarnation she became one of the most celebrated personalities of the American literary scene, in demand everywhere for writers' conferences and lectures. She appeared on numerous platforms, elegantly gowned, furred, jeweled, and equipped with honorary degrees from several universities. With her magnolia skin, her velvety voice and white hair, she presented the perfect image of a southern belle, a member, as she styled herself, of the "guilt-ridden white pillar crowd."[15]

Both the impetus behind her literary work and the recreation of her own image had their root in the same source: her inability to accept the disunion between what life is and what it should be. She said: "My own habit of writing fiction has provided a wholesome exercise to my natural, incurable tendency to try to wrangle the sprawling mess of our existence in this bloody world into some kind of shape."[16]

Her disgust with the haphazard mess of ordinary life began in her early childhood. Even then she could not reconcile herself to life as one of four motherless children, raised on the bare bones of privation by an ailing grandmother. She had a disconcerting habit of running away from home and of giving assumed names to those who found her and tried to bring her back.[17] She early developed protective habits of fantasizing and she said that as a child her head was as full of fantasies as a hive of honey-making bees. She dreamed that she was a changeling who did not belong to her family, a highborn lady left there by some mischievous trick of fortune.[18]

Later the fantasies about her family produced some of her most successful fiction, the stories which lovingly evoke a mythical Old South which she had never known, and which was, in fact, indigenous to the eastern states rather than to Texas.

They revolve around Miranda Gay, one of three motherless children raised by a strong matriarchal grandmother, Sophia Jane Rhea. The grandmother, a member of a rich slave-owning family in Kentucky, had after her marriage migrated to Texas and there in the aftermath of the Civil War watched the family's fortunes decline. Widowed and in reduced circumstances, she raised her large family and tried to maintain her familiar way of life. The family lived in ample homes in the town and the country, and the former slaves remained in the household as devoted servants. The houses, full of books, old furniture, and family heirlooms, easliy accommodated the family, servants, and many visiting colorful relatives—dashing young cousins and impressive aunts and great-aunts.

Part of the fascination of Katherine Anne Porter was that her very presence seemed to confirm and authenticate the world of her fiction, and the stories she told about her childhood evoked a world as enchanting as that of her fiction. When Robert Penn Warren asked her to explain the sources of her story "Noon Wine," she wrote him:

> I was one of four children, brought up in a houseful of adults of ripening age; a grandmother, a father, several Negro servants, among them two aged former slaves; visiting relatives, uncles, aunts, cousins; grandmother's other grand- children older than we, with always an ill-identified old soul or two, male and female, who seemed to be guests but helped out with stray chores. The house, which seemed so huge to me, was probably barely adequate to the population it accommodated . . .[19]

When an interviewer asked about her past she described its cultural richness:

> Oh, we saw all the great things that came during the season, but after all, there would only be a dozen or so of these occasions a year. The rest of the time we depended on our own resources: our own music and books. All the old houses that I knew when I was a child were full of books, bought generation after generation by members of the family.[20]

When she was asked by a popular journal to give a description of her childhood Christmas she gave this idealized version:

> In my family, we children were given breakfast with a spoonful of the ritual Christmas-morning eggnog and then we were hustled off to church. We lived through the ordeal only for the sake of getting back to the waiting tree where the real treasures were stored. There was the little Lord Jesus asleep in the hay, just as we had been singing about Him, and there was the angel at the top of the tree, and between these two were the presents we gloated over—wary eyes quick to note favoritism but dazzled with the glitter; know- ing that Uncle Bill was dressed up like a fat old man with whiskers playing Santa Claus . . .
>
> Throughout the day everybody sang carols and danced and gave parties or went to them, and always with food and drink of an abundance and variety and richness like no other feast of the year. The children guzzled and ate right along

with the family, being given our jolly taste of Burgundy or Cognac or white wine or sherry or whatever was going at the time.[21]

To even her closest friends she spoke of dining on the plantation in a room whose paneling had been copied from the original paneling brought from England,[22] and she displayed as family heirlooms items she had purchased in antique shops.[23] Some of her friends developed a hearty skepticism about the stories of her life. Josephine Herbst (to whom she wrote about the paneling) said bluntly that she would not believe a word Porter said.[24] Others loyally maintained that her tendency to romanticize her own life was of little consequence because in her art she practiced the greatest truth an artist is capable of, a truth sometimes larger than living actually permits.[25] Many friends, like Glenway Wescott, learned not to expect straight biographical facts from her but to accept that the "story material" was somehow more characteristic.[26] He rightly discerned that her departures from strict literal truth were motivated by something more complicated than the simple wish to mislead or entertain and were somehow related to her fictional process.

She edited the story of her life as she might have shaped one of her short stories, rejecting certain experiences which she felt should not have happened and did not really belong to her and substituting others which seemed more appropriate. She rarely invented anecdotes out of thin air, but rather created around actual circumstances a tissue of fantasies which embroidered and transformed them and gave them back to her in a form she could bear to contemplate. As she reshaped the past, the more acceptable version took root firmly in her imagination. The real events were buried and if she was forced to look at them she reacted with something like panic. One of the most harrowing experiences she describes in her fiction is that of a character being ambushed by the memory of a horrible experience which has long lain dormant in the consciousness and suddenly, stirred by some accident, rises up in its full horror. Thus Frau Rittersdorf of *Ship of Fools* is strolling on the island of Tenerife when a scene from her childhood floats before her, as it must have done sometimes to Porter, and makes her almost unconscious with fright:

Frau Rittersdorf gathered up her things and walked away in a chill of horror as if a bony hand reached out of the past

clutching her coldly and drawing her again into the awful
wallow of ignorance and poverty and brutish living that she
had escaped oh barely-barely! The dirt-floored hut of her
grandparents, with the pigpens and the cattle stalls and the
chicken roosts all opening into the one room where the
whole family lived: the dull mean village cottage of her
shoemaking father and her seamstress mother, who felt they
had risen high in their world; their ambition for her to become a teacher in the village school—Oh, oh, oh, cried the
whole frightful memory, not only in the voices and faces of
those dead and gone people she had tried all these years to
forget, to deny; but the very animals, the smothering walls
and the dirt floors and the stinking shoe leather, the taste of
lard on the slice of sour bread she took to school with her—
the very bread itself, all rose again out of the deep pit in
which she had buried them, and one was as alive as the other;
in a terrible voiceless clamor they cried and lamented and
accused her, soundless as screams in a nightmare.[27]

Since the contemplation of her past was so fraught with emotional turmoil for Porter (she compared it with tapping the spinal
fluid, adding "and if that is a painful and gruesome comparison I
meant it to be"), it is not surprising that she never managed to write
a coherent autobiographical account. She said that she had been asked
to do so and that she could not do it because the "real" life had been
so hidden and internal.[28]

Predictably, her attitude to critics of her work who wandered
into biographical territory was one of fury. If, understandably, they
made errors simply through relying on her own accounts, Porter,
who read always with a pencil in hand, peppered the margins of their
books with furious remarks—"another bloody monkey mind,"
"bloody fool," "you god-damned fool" and, "God damn it *no!* Can't
you keep your grubby little paws off of our lives. You don't know
anything and you can't guess right so shut up."[29] If her outrage was
great when the critics erred, it was even greater when they found out
and printed accurate versions of experiences she rejected. Here she
angrily and flatly denied the facts.

Astonishingly, no one was more eager than Porter to achieve
immortality by having the story of her life told. To this end she
scrupulously preserved and accumulated the paraphernalia of her lifetime—photographs, souvenirs, mementos, correspondence, and the

most private documents. Only rarely did she destroy parts of letters which reflected an image of herself that she could not accept. She made a great effort to find a suitable biographer and to see that all her material was made available for the work.

In 1955, Edward Schwartz, who had completed a bibliography of her work, asked her about the possibility of doing her biography. She told him:

> I think your bibliography is a fine piece of work, and I am happy that it has been done. But I think the blood pressure of your interest is not really high enough for a biography. First place you haven't got a notion what you are asking for. Bushels of papers and letters, filing cabinets or note books and unfinished mss. The marginal notes on my books alone was undertaken, and given up in despair by a young friend. And think of the chronology! and the places I have lived or visited and the *reasons* for my being here. Friendships, love affairs, marriages . . . ideas of a life time, varying and changing and coming around again! And the genesis of stories, and how related to my experience . . . this and a lot more is what you undertake in an honest biography . . .[30]

There were greater difficulties than those she listed. Her lifelong habit of covering her traces and suppressing whole areas of her experience meant that only a systematic search through civic documents, church records, and old newspapers could bring to light her early experiences. Even that task, however, was less hazardous than the work of disentangling fact from fiction in the more visible parts of her life, for in the accounts given in autobiographical notes, essays, and interviews she resembles her own description of Mexico. She called it "this sphinx of countries which for every fragment of authentic history yields two riddles."[31] Perhaps more emotionally disconcerting than either of these tangible problems was the uneasy sense, inhibiting rigorous investigation, that the revelations about her life constituted some cruel kind of exposure.

In her eighty-sixth year, hearing of my work from Lon Tinkle, a Texas man of letters who had been book editor of the *Dallas Morning News,* and having read some of my commentaries on her stories, she appealed to me

> with a certain hope I have that you might be interested if I invited you to be my biographer and I know that we both

are well aware that this word is a weighty one that carries
heavy meanings. Too often I have seen writers who have
finished the history of a life, remarking that it was a twenty
year effort, and I myself have spent that length of time on a
mere novel: so I am well aware and have given full thought
to what I now am asking you to think over. . . .

This for me is an immensely important step and I
should be most grateful to you if you can accept the invitation to spend part of your life, your time, talent and energy
in this work.[32]

I accepted with little hesitation because, in spite of all the deter-
rents, I believed and still believe that the story of her life is important.
The interweaving of fact, fantasy, and fiction which confounds the
biographer is highly revealing for the literary critic. Porter once told
a group of students, "My fiction is reportage, only I do something to
it. I arrange it and it is fiction but it happened."[33] When the sources
of her stories are revealed it is possible to trace her method of shaping
them into fiction and thus gain a fresh insight into a writer's creative
method. In a broader sense, the uncovering of the sources of one
work after another makes it possible to reconstruct her creative life
and provide a unique and detailed portrait of an artist.

Finally, it should be said that this work is undertaken in the
conviction that what Porter concealed often reflects more to her credit
than to her shame, and that her actual life was more heroic than
anything she invented. Her steadfast determination, in the face of all
obstacles, to become a good artist justifies her own description of her
life as "this brave voyage."[34]

ONE

The Porter Family History:
Legend, Memory, Whimsy, and Applejack

The Porter family history is important to the record because it was inordinately important to Porter herself. She grieved that most of the members of the family she knew seemed to her totally lacking in distinction and dignity and she yearned to believe that earlier generations had been more distinguished. She tried to assemble a family tree and she spoke of it proudly in interviews and used it as the basis of her fictional family's history in such stories as "The Old Order" and "Old Mortality." Once an interviewer said to her, "It seems to me that your work is pervaded by a sense of history. Is that part of the family legacy?" Porter replied as follows:

We were brought up with a sense of our own history, you know. My mother's family came to this country in 1648 and went to the John Randolph territory of Virginia. And one of my great-grandfathers was Jonathan Boone, the brother of Daniel. On my father's side I'm descended from Colonel Andrew Porter, whose father came to Montgomery County, Pennsylvania, in 1720. He was one of the circle of George Washington during the Revolution, a friend of Lafayette, and one of the founders of the Society of the Cincinnati—oh, he really took it seriously!—and when he died in 1809—well, just a few years before that he was offered the post of Secretary of War, but he declined. We were never very ambitious people. We never had a President, though we had two governors and some in the Army and Navy, I suppose we did have a desire to excel but not to push our way to higher places. We thought we'd *already* arrived![1]

Her description was not, of course, completely true. But at the same time neither was it complete fabrication. It was the complicated mixture of truth and fantasy so characteristic of Porter's accounts of her life and so teasing to those wishing to disentangle fact from fiction. She did not actually grow up with a clear knowledge of her family tree, nor did she know much about her mother's side of the family, for her maternal grandparents were orphans, raised by people unrelated to them. Of her father's side of the family she heard many stories but these were anecdotes rather than historical accounts.

It was when she was in Paris in the middle of her life that she began to reconstruct her family tree. She said that her travels in Europe, Mexico, and Bermuda gave her back her own place and her own people and she told her father then that being in a foreign country had caused her to turn to her origins because she did not want to feel uprooted.[2] Unfortunately, when she began to reconstruct her family history her sources and methods were often unreliable. She looked up her family in genealogical dictionaries and guidebooks, but the fact that Porter and her mother's name, Jones, were very common seems to have given her no pause. She ignored her father's comment that the woods were full of Porters "about as thick as Smiths and Joneses,"[3] and she claimed Porters and Joneses wherever she found them, especially if they were people of distinction.

When she saw in Sylvia Beach's bookstore in Paris the letter from a young Texan named Willie Jones asking Walt Whitman for an autograph, she wrote home to ask if he was a relative.[4] She discovered a Cadwalader Jones of Virginia and wrote to ask her father if he was a member of her mother's family.[5] He thought not. Nevertheless she included in her genealogical sketches the fact that her maternal grandmother, Caroline Frost Jones, came from an old Charleston family.[6]

She found a John Porter and asked if he was the Uncle John her father had mentioned,[7] and when she came across a William D. Porter who was lieutenant governor of South Carolina about 1865, and who founded a school for sons of Confederate veterans, she wrote to ask if her Uncle Bill was not named for someone in the family and wondered if this man was a connection.[8] She was delighted when she found a listing of 1449 in the Paston Letters for a John Porter, landowner, connected with the Duke of Suffolk; she claimed him immediately and planned when she went to England to look up "the whole caboodle."[9] When she remembered someone looking down on the Porters as "rough and ready Kentuckians," she reminded her sister that one of their ancestors was listed in Hakluyt's *Voyages*.[10]

She supplemented her library researches by requesting information from an amateur genealogist in the family and by asking her father to write down all he remembered. Her sister warned Porter that their father had written a whole letter full of whimsy and applejack or whatever it was he was drinking. Nevertheless, when the letter came Porter was delighted and declared it "superb." She urged him to write more and told him, "Get yourself a softer pencil next time, honey! I will copy it out on the typewriter."[11]

Her father's name was Harrison Boone Porter and he had always said that he was descended from Daniel Boone. Porter had claimed the Kentucky pioneer as her favorite ancestor and included him in the autobiographical sketch she wrote for *Twentieth-Century Authors* in 1940. She told her father that Boone was originally a very old Flemish name, that there were many French Boones and wads and tons of them in England and still some Flemish ones flourishing. These were the original ones and the others were emigrants from Flanders who she guessed had moved out during the Hundred Years' War.[12]

It was a great disappointment to her to learn that she was not in the direct line of descent from Daniel Boone, and she substituted in his place his older brother Jonathan (although from time to time she could not resist reclaiming Daniel). Jonathan had the advantage that the record of his descendants was obscure, so that no one could contradict her. Thus her claim of connection to the Boones remained her undisputed and proud possession, although she declined an invitation to become a member of the large Boone Family Association.

Her Aunt Jinny Cahill of San Antonio told her that there were Pennsylvanians in two paternal branches of the family, and Porter thought this fact suddenly explained her affinity for Pennsylvania and the East, though she professed to be a little alarmed at the thought of having Yankee blood. "Let's hope that never gets out on us," she said, and added that she had nothing really against Yankees, it was just that she would rather see than be one.[13]

Eventually, with the help of her sister, she drew up a quasi-official version of her ancestors which she used with minor variations for the rest of her life. She copied out from congressional records the crest of an ancient Porter family in which sheaves of corn represented agriculture and three church bells signified loyalty, friendship, and honesty. The family motto was "Fear God, Honor the King."

Among her earliest ancestors on the chart, she listed a Porter descended in sixteen generations from a knight who accompanied William the Conqueror to England and whose family home was Wraxhill Abbey in Warwickshire; a Robert Porter who emigrated from Londonderry and settled in Pennsylvania; and his son Colonel Andrew Porter.

When Porter received the copy from her sister in 1956 she was delighted and said it was much more complete than her own copy. She told her sister to add to her account that their ancestor Colonel Andrew Porter was one of the group of officers closely associated with Lafayette and Washington who formed themselves into the com-memorative Society of the Cincinnati. She explained that they were named for that Roman Cincinnatus who advised his soldiers to go home and beat their swords into ploughshares. She admired the dream of that poor man, so high-minded and hopeful, and wondered what he would think of the "steerage-sweepings" that were running the country at the present time. She said that their "Grandpappy Andrew" was one of the founders and first officers of the Society of the Cincinnati and that membership is the only hereditary office in this country, from father to oldest son, like royalty. She said there were five of them very closely kin in every generation—Andrew Porter, David Rittenhouse Porter, his son Horace Porter (ambassador to France for eight years), William Sydney Porter (O. Henry), and herself, Katherine Anne Porter. She did not think it was a bad show-ing for one family who started out in Montgomery County, Pennsyl-vania.[14]

To people outside the family she affected an offhand attitude toward the whole business. When she reviewed a book on Daniel Boone in 1926 she said he had the disadvantage of being somewhat in the family and that "his coon-skin cap and God-fearingness" annoyed her.[15] She said that "poor" O. Henry was more known in the family for being a bank robber and that Horace Porter spent the whole of his time as ambassador to France looking for the bones of John Paul Jones.[16]

Unfortunately, the link between the son of Andrew Porter and Porter's great-grandfather was a false one and she was not connected to him or to any member of his family. Nor was she connected, except by the accident of her name, to O. Henry.[17]

While most of the genealogical connections she boasted did not exist, it was somehow typical of her method of manipulating facts that, while she conjured up imaginary links, she ignored some of the interesting ones which did exist. She was proved wrong in her assertion that there was no President in the family when Lyndon Johnson became President. Although neither of them was aware of it, they were connected through the Buntons, a distinguished Kentucky family who moved west and were among the pioneers of West Texas. Porter's uncle, Lucius Desha Bunton, and Johnson's grandmother, Eliza Bunton Ealey, were brother and sister.[18]

It is regrettable too that Porter never managed to collect information about the Skaggses, the family of her father's mother. She did have their names and some old daguerreotypes which she cherished, but she could find few facts and told her sister that they had sprung "full-panoplied into Kentucky pioneers without any previous history."[19] Her friends Caroline Gordon and Allen Tate, native Kentuckians, said that the Skaggses were all expert woodsmen and perhaps the description discouraged Porter, for she looked no further.

Her paternal grandmother was the daughter of Rhoda Bivens (Boone appears in some records instead of Bivens) Smith of Georgia and Abraham Moredock Skaggs of Tennessee. The Skaggses married in Warren County, Kentucky, and his occupation was listed in the 1850 census as "farmer." In the slave census of the same year his holdings were given as follows:

> 1 slave age 38 male
> 1 slave age 21 female
> 1 slave age 4 male
> 1 slave age 1 male[20]

In a census ten years later he was listed as "trader."[21] Local people remember that he helped his brother run the Skaggs mill and dam, about twelve miles east of Bowling Green. The brother's mill was a sizable operation and the house, which still stands, a substantial one. The will of Abraham's father, James Skaggs, also indicates sizable holdings of land and of slaves, suggesting that the family were landowners of means and not just average farmers.[22]

In 1849, when she was twenty-three and he thirty-six, Catherine Anne Skaggs married Asbury Porter.[23] In her essay "Portrait: Old South," Porter gave this description of her grandparents' wedding, which she placed "around 1850":

> Only a few years ago a cousin of mine showed me a letter
> from a lady then rising ninety-five who remembered that

wedding as if it had been only yesterday. She was one of the flower girls, carrying a gilded basket of white roses and ferns, tied with white watered-silk ribbon. She couldn't remember whether the bride's skirt had been twenty-five feet or twenty-five yards around, but she inclined to the latter figure; it was of white satin brocade with slippers to match.

The flower girl was allowed a glimpse of the table set for the bridal banquet. There were silver branched candle-sticks everywhere, each holding seven white candles, and a crystal chandelier holding fifty white candles, all lighted. There was a white lace tablecloth reaching to the floor all around, over white satin. The wedding cake was tall as the flower girl and of astonishing circumference, festooned all over with white sugar roses and green leaves, actual live rose leaves. The room, she wrote, was a perfect bower of south-ern smilax and white dogwood. And there was butter. This is a bizarre note, but there was an enormous silver butter dish, *with feet* [italics mine], containing at least ten pounds of butter. The dish had cupids and some sort of fruit around the rim, and the butter was molded or carved, to resemble a set-piece of roses and lilies, every petal and leaf standing out sharply, natural as life. The flower girl, after the lapse of nearly a century, remembered no more than this, but I think it does well for a glimpse.

That butter. She couldn't get over it, and neither can I. It seems as late-Roman and decadent as anything ever thought up in Hollywood. Her memory came back with a rush when she thought of the food. All the children had their own table in a small parlour, and ate just what the grownups had: Kentucky ham, roast turkey, partridges in wine jelly, fried chicken, dove pie, half a dozen sweet and hot sauces, peach pickle, watermelon pickle and spiced man-goes. A dozen different fruits, four kinds of cake and at last a chilled custard in tall glasses with whipped cream capped by a brandied cherry.[24]

The wedding may well have been a lavish affair for the young couple as well, as the Skaggses had some means. The census of 1850 shows Asbury Porter as having land at the value of $1,000 and the slave census shows him owning one seventeen-year-old female slave and a middle-aged male. The female slave was a wedding gift from

Catherine's brother, Harrison Skaggs, a New Orleans businessman who included among his transactions the buying and selling of slaves.[25]

Soon after the wedding, following the example of some of his brothers, Asbury Porter decided to sell his Kentucky land and move to Hays County in Texas, where, since 1840 when the Comanches were defeated in the battle of Plum Creek (later called the Cat Porter branch), land had been open for white settlement. The Kentucky land was disposed of for $1,000 and some time later Asbury Porter bought 368 acres for $765 in Hays County.[26] Porter has indicated in her stories that the family spent the interim period in Louisiana, and they may have done so, because this was a common procedure. Porter's father said he remembered the good sugar cane of Louisiana, but this seems unlikely as he would have been a baby in arms at the time.

They came to virgin land in Texas; the boll weevil had not yet arrived and all the farmers were prosperous. The soil in the rich blackland farming country was said to be so fertile that a walking stick planted there would sprout. Everything augured well for a good life for the Porter family, more prosperous than that they had left behind in Kentucky. But the year was 1857 and in three years the most devastating war in American history began.

Stories of the Civil War were a part of Porter's childhood. She heard accounts from her grandmother and from her father, who was three when the war started. Although there is no evidence in the Hays County records of any Porter taking part in the Civil War, her father told her otherwise. He said he remembered his father, well past the age of conscription (Asbury Porter would have been forty-six when war broke out), riding off with a double-muzzle shot gun across the saddle. He said that he had heard that General Fitz-John Porter, who commanded a division of McClelland's army at the battle of Antietam, was a second cousin of his father.[27]

One of Harrison Porter's early memories was of turning the grindstone for someone to sharpen weapons for the war, and he well remembered, as everyone did, the hardships of the times. His daughter wrote that the lack of coffee, sugar, and other staples had left him with a huge appetite for the rest of his life, though he did say that there was always plenty of cornbread, beef, potatoes, and sorghum molasses even if there was no coffee, sugar, or flour. Porter spoke of her grandmother parching a mixture of sweet potato and dried corn until it was black, then grinding it up and boiling it because her family couldn't get over its yearning for a dark hot drink in the mornings. But it was never called coffee, it was known as "That Brew."[28]

Harrison Porter said that his mother made blankets of wool from the backs of her own sheep and he had heard that a full company of Confederate soldiers was furnished with her blankets. A John Porter was buried on the battlefield of Mansfield, Louisiana, with one of Catherine Porter's woolen blankets around him in lieu of a coffin. A local man had told him that he was within ten feet of John when he died, and that another boy was carrying one of Aunt Cat's blankets when he was killed with Hood's brigade at Gaines' Mill, Virginia.[29]

After the surrender, Asbury Porter said, "When we raise a new crop of boys we must fight this whole thing over," and so he sent Harrison Porter and two of his brothers to military school. The old man died without ever having taken the oath of allegiance and never forgot Sherman's march of destruction through Georgia.[30]

Porter's father said that her maternal grandfather joined the army at the age of sixteen (this is unlikely since his daughter was born in 1859) and was a Confederate cavalryman for four years. He claimed that the best meat he ever tasted was a bacon rind picked up from a wagon rut after the cannons had rolled over it all day.[31] Porter used that anecdote in her "Portrait: Old South" but she transferred it to her Porter grandfather.[32]

Years later, when Harrison Porter died, his obituary was headed "Last Survivor of the Travis Rifles Dies."[33] The Travis Rifles was a militia unit organized in San Antonio to control the flood of carpetbaggers from the North, but it was also preparing to fight the war over again when the Confederacy got strong enough. That desire remained as dear to the heart of Harrison Porter as it had to his father, and it was, therefore, with some justification that Porter said she was the grandchild of a lost war and that her elders all remained nobly unreconstructed to their last moments.[34]

Soon after the war ended, Asbury Porter, either because he was engaged in land speculation or because he wished to relocate and reshape his holdings, sold his land at half the price he had paid for it. As a consequence, like many others at the time, the Porter family suffered a temporary reduction of means. He made good the loss fairly quickly and by 1871 had accumulated the few hundred acres which were to be his final holdings.[35]

Although Porter visited the site of her grandparents' farm in her later years, she was never sure whether its location was in Mountain

City or Buda, since the boundaries of the small towns of the area were changed and some disappeared entirely when the railroad was built. In fact, the farm was in a community then called Science Hall, as described in the *Kyle News* for April 20, 1928:

SCIENCE HALL COMMUNITY
by J. L. Andrews

In the year 1871, my brother, Whit Andrews, and I bought each one hundred acres of land just east of where Science Hall School House was afterwards built. Then there were few settlements between Science Hall and Lockhart. The only settlers were Lynches, Jimmy Goforth, Louis and John Franks, and Aunt Cat Porter. The county east began to settle rapidly and soon Rev. David Porter, a Baptist preacher, Tom Howe, W. W. Andrews and P. Allen bought land.

They all realized they needed a school and got together and decided upon a lot just west and adjoining my place. They built the house and I believe Mrs. Andrews named it Science Hall. The district was dissolved in 1926 and the territory divided between the Buda and the Kyle districts.

The special interest of the account lies in the designation of the Porter family simply as "Aunt Cat Porter." Was Asbury Porter so shadowy a character that no one noticed him? Was he ill, prematurely aged at fifty-seven, enfeebled? There is no way of knowing, for he remains a shadowy character, as he did perhaps to Porter, who in her fictional account has him die before the family settles in Texas. In her fiction, however, she describes him as a reckless young man, unreliable, careless with his wife's dowry, and ineffective in financial dealings, and she attributes the grandmother's strong character to the necessity of taking over when the grandfather proved ineffective.

In her story "The Old Order," which is based upon her family history, she has the character who represents her grandmother marry a second cousin of weak character:

. . . sometimes Sophia Jane saw in him, years after they were married, all the faults she had most abhorred in her elder brother: lack of aim, failure to act at crises, a philosophic detachment from practical affairs, a tendency to set projects on foot and then leave them to perish or to be finished by someone else; and a profound conviction that everyone around him should be happy to wait upon him hand and foot. . . . But the Grandmother developed a character truly portentous under the discipline of trying to change the characters of others.[36]

Later in the story Porter tells of the grandmother's hatred for men:

She could not help it, she despised men. She despised them and was ruled by them. Her husband threw away her dowry and her property in wild investments in strange territories: Louisiana, Texas; and without protest she watched him play away her substance like a gambler. She felt that she could have managed her affairs profitably. But her natural activities lay elsewhere, it was the business of a man to make all the decisions and dispose of all financial matters. Yet when she got the reins in her hands, her sons could persuade her to this and that enterprise or investment; against her will and judgment she accepted their advice, and among them they managed to break up once more the stronghold she had built for the future of her family. They got from her their own start in life, came back for fresh help when they needed it, and were divided against each other. She saw it as her natural duty to provide for her household, after her husband had fought stubbornly through the War, along with every other man of military age in the connection; had been wounded, had lingered helpless, and had died of his wound long after the great fervor and excitement had faded in hopeless defeat, when to be a man wounded and ruined in the War was merely to have proved oneself, perhaps, more heroic than wise.[37]

Like the grandmother of the fiction, Aunt Cat Porter was a hardy character who had been gently raised but whom circumstances had forced to work hard on the land and in the home. She had eleven children, lost two in infancy, and raised nine. There were three girls, Belle, Loula, and Annie, and six sons, Henry, William, Alpha, Harrison, Newell, and Asbury. Harrison Porter was the fourth child.

Since he was thirteen when the Science Hall school opened, his early education before he entered the military academy was probably at Mountain City, and an account in a local paper indicates the nature of that education:

The man who really made the school was Prof. John Edgar, a teacher of renown from Nashville, Tennessee. A large one-story school house, and a five-room residence for the teacher and family were built. (In 1868 the Masons added another story.)

This was the best school in this section of the state. Pupils came from different parts of the country and almost every home was a boarding house—the community spirit was strong and intellectuality ran high.

This school turned out good ranchmen, farmers, doctors, lawyers, and men of other vocations. It seems to me we have retrograded in our methods of teaching. That was an age of perfection in the "three R's" and the advanced pupils were experts in math and Latin.

The close of school was a great event in the community. All brought in dinner, spent the day and stayed to the night concert. Pupils were examined before the audience from the primer to university courses—no graded schools there.[38]

When Harrison Porter married he chose an equally well-educated young woman. Mary Alice Jones had grown up in nearby Luling County and was the sister of George Jones, who had married Harrison's sister Loula. Mary Alice had attended Coronal Institute in San Marcos. This school, founded in 1868 and named for its situation on the crown of a hill, was for fifty years the most popular Protestant school in southwest Texas. Both a boarding and a day school, it was coeducational, drew patronage from a large territory and, although the tone was chiefly Methodist, from all religious denominations.[39] That Mary Alice attended the school guaranteed good training, and that she was the valedictorian of her graduating class suggests intelligence above the average. Her valedictory address, "Does the Bible Teach Everlasting Punishment?" has been preserved among her daughter's papers.[40] After graduation she became a schoolteacher and also gave private lessons on the reed organ.[41]

Letters exchanged before the marriage show a certain literary bent in both partners. They are formal and full of ornate poetic flourishes. "Now as night has cast her sable mantle over this beautiful world and all nature is hushed into silence," wrote Alice in one letter.[42] (It was said in the family that Porter inherited her literary talent from her mother, but a cousin suggested that was because they couldn't think where else it might have come from.)[43] There is no indication of amorous interest but serious discussions of friendship. Alice wrote that when she called anyone friend she meant him to be as faithful as truth and true to the end, and warned Harrison that he would find in her a very stubborn friend, for friendship once acknowledged by her was never broken. They discussed their plans for the future and she asked his advice about taking a teaching position some distance away.[44] He wrote her in 1881 that his mother had decided to sell her Hays County land and that he had a contract to build part of the railway being constructed between Laredo and San Antonio.[45] When that work proved unsuccessful he returned to farming and proposed marriage to Alice. He had always thought that a man should not marry until he had at least $10,000, but he did it on about $500.[46]

Alice's parents had moved from Hays County to Indian Creek, near Brownwood, and it was there, when she was twenty-four and he was twenty-six, that Alice married Harrison Porter, whom she called "Hasson."[47] The ceremony was performed by an itinerant preacher named Noah T. Byars, who had been blacksmith and armorer for the Texian army and had later been ordained as a Baptist minister and helped to found churches in Waco, Washington-on-the-Brazos, and Brownwood.[48] It was in his house on March 2, 1836, that Texas independence was declared, and monuments to him stand today in Brownwood, only a few miles from the grave of Katherine Anne Porter, the famous daughter of the union he consecrated in 1883.

In the 1880s Indian Creek still had the character of a new frontier settlement, with some of the first families living in sod houses and others in rough log structures.[49] It would be a mistake to think of it as the quiet, pastoral paradise Porter later liked to imagine. The sale of liquor had been unrestrained in most of Texas since the days of the republic, and by 1879 the saloons in Brownwood were causing problems.[50] Noah Byars inveighed against "nightly revels, weekly fights and frequent murders," and one of the main thoroughfares was known as "Battle Row." Indian Creek itself had no saloons, but the village store stocked bottles of "pizen" for the cowboys from the nearby cowcamps.[51]

Harrison Porter told his grandsons of another kind of violence. On moonlight nights bands of Indians swooped down on the far-flung farms and stole horses. The farmers lay low in terror, but when daylight dawned they formed posses and went in pursuit of the Indians and, if they were lucky, they retrieved the horses.[52]

All the same, the community thrived. The land was good, the town grew rapidly and soon boasted an eight-room school and churches. Alice's parents and the Harrison Porters were among the founding members of the Methodist Episcopal church in 1886, and when a Sunday school was organized Harrison became the superintendent.[53] It seems in retrospect that he was influenced in his religious attitudes by his womenfolk. In one of the courtship letters he defended himself against Alice's charge that he had said he liked eggnog.[54] His oldest daughter, later commenting on his drinking habits, said that he left the stuff alone while he was raising the family and after that drank all he wished.[55] He also later abandoned his religious habits; it would seem that they were not the result of strong inner convictions.

The Porter house in Indian Creek was a simple two-room L-shaped log structure surrounded by a lovely garden and situated a few hundred yards from the carriage road in a grove of mesquite trees.[56] On two sides of the house there were orchards and below the house to the south, Indian Creek cut its way through rocky gullies to the Colorado River. There Miss Alice, as she was known in the community, often laid her baby on a blanket in the shade of some willows, under the watchful eyes of an older child, while she and her friends fished.[57]

Gay, the oldest girl, was the only one of the children who remembered Indian Creek, and she described to Porter the family's life there. She said that it was a place of great beauty and that they had good land with fine trees and fruits, and that Indian Creek itself, a branch of the Rio Blanco, ran through the yard. She described a wonderful orchard of peaches, pears, plums, and great pecan trees and in the yard a row of red roses, a row of chinaberry trees, and cedars. The picket fence was made in Kentucky paddock style and kept beautifully whitewashed, and the chinaberry trees were perfectly umbrella shaped. Porter came to claim the memory for her own and said that she would never get over her love for the place she knew where camellias and figs and gardenias (Cape jessamines) and peaches and watermelons and azaleas and honeysuckle all grew out in the open with a few lemon and orange trees.[58]

Gay also remembered that she would be sent to a neighbor to borrow fire when the back log went out in the fireplace, which was the only source of heat. She remembered her father roasting potatoes and popping popcorn and playing a fiddle and her mother playing the organ. And she remembered her mother sitting in the Methodist church wearing a black lace hat and a blue-and-white-striped dress of gingham made in a basque style and singing "Jesus is a rock in a weary land."[59]

Alice was loved by all who knew her, and especially by her young friend Cora Posey. Cora, like Alice, had attended Coronal Institute, and when she returned from San Marcos she found herself ostracized by the local girls, who, with the age-old resentment for those who go away to school, refused to speak to her even in church. Alice, ten years older and already a mother, sensed the younger woman's loneliness, came up from behind, and, placing her hands over her eyes, asked "Guess who?" They kissed and the friendship was sealed.[60]

The Harrison Porters already had one child when they arrived in Indian Creek. She was born in 1885 on the Porter farm in Science Hall, named Annie Gay for her father's favorite sister, given the childhood name of "Lady Gay," and later called "Gay." Two years after Gay came a son, Harry Ray. His name was later changed to "Harrison Paul" and he was known as "Paul." Like all the children he was dedicated to God and the Methodist Creed in the Indian Creek church. After Paul came a second son, Johnnie, and in 1890 tragedy struck the family for the first time. Johnnie caught influenza and died. Gay remembered her mother, heavily pregnant with her fourth child, sitting at the head of Johnnie's grave in the Indian Creek cemetery and staring into it without tears.[61] Shortly afterward, Katherine Anne Porter made her entry into what she called "this god-forsaken wilderness of lions, monkeys and snakes."[62] She was born on Thursday, May 15, 1890, her birth overshadowed by the death of Johnnie, and was named Callie Russell for a childhood friend of her mother's who had died young.[63]

During Callie's birth, Gay and her brother were sent outside to play in the orchard among the great clusters of purple and white grapes. Gay remembered that when they were called back into the house the mother turned back the blanket, saying, "Would you like to see my little tad?" and revealed a baby already different from the rest of the family. She was like a little newborn puppy, with black hair sticking to her head in damp waves and curls.[64] The dark curly hair was unusual in the fair-haired clan and later helped Porter fantasize that she was a changeling. She felt she had known from the cradle that she was different from the rest of the family.[65]

Still weak from the loss of Johnnie and the birth of Callie, Alice became pregnant again and on January 25, 1892, gave birth to her last child. She never recovered her strength and declined steadily. Local people talked of tuberculosis, but Porter insisted that her mother's death was caused by pneumonia complicated by bronchial problems.[66] She died on March 20 at the age of thirty-three just two months before Callie's second birthday. The new baby was named Mary Alice in memory of her mother and always called "Baby" by the family.

Reflecting on these events in later years, Porter felt great bitterness. She said that she had seen the house where she was born and in spite of the lovely garden that had surrounded it, it must at best have been desolate, built as it was facing north, the front door opening directly into the living room, and heated only by a little fireplace. She said it was no wonder her mother died of pneumonia after a winter childbirth in that house; she said the house was just such as was built at that time by men who had lost the art of building houses and never consulted the women about what they needed in a house; she said (erring slightly) that her mother had five children in just under seven years and that she died "under torture."[67] No doubt Alice was over-burdened with childbearing, but her husband's words suggest other reasons for her early death. He mentioned to Gay once that had her mother lived she would have been as exemplary as her Grandmother Porter "as far as her bodily strength would have permitted." In the same letter he spoke of the hardships of the early years, asking, "What could I have done in the drouth-stricken west with one of these stream-lined modern lip-stick pushers for a partner? Her lot was hard but she never complained nor blamed me for it."[68]

Alice was buried in the same grave by which she had mourned dry-eyed for her son two years before, and Harrison Porter raised over the grave a small marble monument under the live oaks in the little cemetery and bearing these words:

> Dearest Loved One we have laid thee
> In the peaceful grave's embrace,
> But thy memory will we cherish
> Till we see thy heavenly face.

The next November he gave his oldest daughter a picture of her mother inscribed with these words:

Gay: This is your mother. She is buried near Brownwood. It is a holy place for us all. You must bury me beside her. There I saw the star of all my earthly hopes go down in an endless darkness and there is no light in my heart even at noonday. In this strange twilight I try to trace the narrow road I must walk to reach this city of the dead and lie down in the long night beside my love. But this star is not extinguished altogether for it shed the rays of its purity and love over the waste landscape of my life, gave meaning to Nothingness and left memories that not time nor death itself can take away. Remember and love your mother my dear child.[69]

After Alice's death, Cora Posey, whom the Porters called "Cousin Cora," said she tried to take from Alice's hands the beacon light and pass on her sweetness of spirit and faith.[70] Porter sought Cora out and valued her all her life for her own qualities and for the link she provided with her mother.

In the years immediately after his wife's death, Harrison B. Porter could not bear to read the letters he and Alice exchanged during their courtship and because he wished to preserve some of them he asked Cora to sort them out. He instructed her to select certain ones for him to keep and certain ones for herself, and to destroy the rest. Parts of the letter he wrote on April 29, 1893, to Cora Posey reveal both his state of mind and his literary inclination:

The impression of that sweet life can only be erased when I am laid beside her. I honor you for the love you bore her and trust you in this because she loved you. How long she has been gone I cannot measure by the bitter anguish that has been mine, how long before the night hawk of death comes for me, I know not nor care not. I loved her better than my own life, aye, better than I did my God. And can it be that her corpse was thrown across my path to stop me. If that be so, I was mistaken, my faith was vain and I am yet in my sins. If I miss Heaven, I miss all, I hope for it but I have no evidence that I shall ever attain that happiness which it seems to me I ought to have for a season at least. If there is, after this turmoil, a halcyon period, a golden place somewhere "en vista" of the golden dawn, I know my spirit will seek hers there, though but a season. Hell thenceforth with the companionship of the Dragon of the Apocalypse will not torment me worse than the pangs that now rend me. There will, at least, be a feeling of certainty. Few men have had to bear what I have borne. In weakness I have been forced to carry the burden of Hercules. My little friend, God grant that you may never know sorrow as I have known it. Several of my family have gone out into the "unknown dark" sad enough, yet all this is as nothing compared with the illimitable system of worlds spread in the canopy above us.

She was a companion, confidante and friend, the Artist's masterpiece—He took it again unto Himself. My ruling passion, the single thought of my life as concerns the interminable beyond is where Alice is there may I be also. Is this treason, idolatry? How can I govern the faculties that God gave in possession of me.

I can only hope that somewhere, or somehow, as I travel the narrow vale midst these rugged craggs, I shall apprehend the golden thread, of mercy in the tangled web, and that the "woof and warp" of God's dealings with me, shall be clear "face to face" and not as "through a glass darkly" we shall know each other better.

Excuse I should have been brief. Seal them up and send to Kyle. Yes you may keep one or more if you like. I believe you the best friend Alice had there, if I did not you could not buy them. . . . They are dear to me, I know you have the ability to realize that and the heart to realize the confidence I place in you. Am sorry to trouble you thus, but I cannot, it were as the dropping of blood, drop by drop. Exercise your own judgement and select a few of these letters and such as you do not send or keep yourself, destroy. Happiness and prosperity and a peaceful exit from this land of shadows be your share is the wish of your friend.[71]

The death affected many lives. Cora Posey told Porter that she went into the empty house after her friend's death and was surprised to hear someone weeping like a soul in torment. Looking up she saw Alice's mother peering through the window. Porter said that story about the grandmother she never knew and was told so little about was the most tragically frightening thing she ever heard, not just because the children were nearby when all this happened but for the whole desolation and human loneliness in it. Later, after the death of her older son, Caroline Jones died in a "lunatic asylum."[72] Harrison Porter said that she grieved herself to death. Possibly she was in delicate health at the time of Alice's death, for there seems to have been no question of her taking care of the motherless family.

There was only one person to whom Harrison Porter could turn for help, and that was his mother. She was sixty-five years old, had been a widow for thirteen years, and suffered from the bronchial weakness that ran in the family.[73] Coincidentally she had, the day before Alice gave birth, lost in childbirth the last of her own three daughters, Belle Zorah Bunton.[74] She may well have been dismayed, after raising her own nine children, at the prospect of raising another family which included a two-year-old and a newborn baby. But Cat Porter was a determined woman ("genuinely effective" was Porter's description), aware of her Christian duty and not easily daunted. She went to Indian Creek just before Alice died, took care of the household, and later brought the family back to her home, 140 miles south in Kyle, Hays County.[75]

The town of Kyle had been established ten years earlier as a stop on the newly laid International and Great Northern Railway. The builder of the railway, finding no town between Austin and San Marcos, had purchased the gently sloping expanse of prairie to the east of the hill country from Captain Ferg Kyle and had engaged a surveyor to make plans for a town one mile square, with wide streets and a park the size of a city block. On an appointed day lots had been sold at auction under a group of live oaks and the recently widowed Aunt Cat had purchased a 110-by-115-foot lot on the corner of Groos and Center streets.

The entire community of Mountain City had then moved bodily to Kyle, and the population soon reached 500, including four doctors, two dentists, two blacksmiths, two painters, and a lawyer. There were twenty-five business establishments, among them a hotel, three general stores, a furniture store, and a livery stable. The railroad took over the function of the Old Chisholm Trail and the town became the heaviest cattle shipping point between San Antonio and Austin.[76]

To join his mother in Kyle, Harrison Porter had to give up his Brown County farm, and his method of disposing of his property added considerably to the family's economic difficulties. Years later Porter learned from the grateful purchasers that he lent them money without interest and gave them fifteen years to pay.[77] Whether this was motivated by generosity or simply by carelessness in his time of bereavement is impossible to say, but it suggests a family resemblance between father and daughter, for Porter was frequently to mismanage her own economic transactions in an impractical and generous way which she could ill afford.

Porter remembered almost nothing of the first two years of her life. She said that her earliest memory was of a journey she took at the age of two.[78] This may have been the journey from Indian Creek to Kyle in the spring of 1892, after Alice's death, or it may have been the return journey in November of the same year, when Harrison Porter came back to raise the monument over Alice's grave. And, surprisingly, Porter included among her early memories that of seeing the ghost of her little dead brother.[79] She also said that when she was two she knew that her mother was dead.[80]

She suffered all her life from melancholy and depression and often wondered if these states had their origin in the early tragedies she could not remember. She marked in a textbook the statement that what a child has experienced and not understood by the time he has reached the age of two he may never remember again, *except in his dreams.* When she read that early impressions received before people can talk sometimes manifest themselves later in an obsessive fashion, even though those impressions themselves are not consciously remembered, she wrote in the margin, "So my horror and pain here and now from that old terrible time."[81]

And yet Porter made a great effort to reconstruct the first two years of her life. She returned from France to make the pilgrimage back to Texas in the middle of her life and returned again when she was eighty-six. She kept her mother's picture at her bedside and made elaborate arrangements for her own ashes to be brought back and placed beside her mother's grave.

It was as if she were hoping that the years she could barely remember would erase the pain of the years she could remember, for with the move to Hays County began one of the most unhappy periods of her life.

TWO

Born to the Practice of Literature

To consider Katherine Anne Porter's childhood is to realize the remarkable nature of her achievement, for no writer can have grown up in more complete literary isolation.

Her regional uniqueness was a justifiable source of pride and she boasted of it quite shamelessly, especially to Texans. She told one Texas University professor:

> I happen to be the first native of Texas in its whole history to be a professional writer. That is to say, one who had the vocation and practiced only that and lived by and for it all my life. We have had a good many lately in the last quarter of the century perhaps and we have had many people who wrote memoirs and saved many valuable stories and have written immensely interesting and valuable things about Texas; and they are to be valued and understood. But I am very pleased that I am the first who ever was born to the practice of literature. . . .[1]

She might have added that it was a long time before anyone else from Texas gained a national or international literary reputation and even longer before another woman did.

She was less proud of her uniqueness in her own family, preferring to present herself as heir to strong literary and cultural traditions. Such suggestions are unfortunate, since they obscure what was greatly

44

to her credit—that she developed independently out of the utmost deprivation. Indeed, her career might confirm the theory that Sir Leslie Stephen expressed in his essay on Charlotte Brontë: "Great art is produced by taking an exceptionally delicate nature and mangling it slowly under the grinding wheels of the world."[2] The distance, however, which Porter traveled from the log house in Indian Creek and the dirt farm in Hays County was far greater than that traveled by the Brontës from the book-filled Yorkshire parsonage. It is appropriate, therefore, to examine carefully the confluence of circumstances which made possible Porter's achievement.

Like many another childhood, Porter's was a time of stifling and unbearable unhappiness. She said that she had forgotten her childhood home until she read of someone turning the slats of a window to darken a room. She had never seen such blinds except in her part of the country and the detail brought back a Proustian flood of agonizing memories. "You may not believe," she wrote, "that childhood is a terrible thing to remember. Wait till it reaches you in a flash."[3]

The main cause of misery in her early years was the death of her mother. This was tragic enough in itself, and Porter can have been spared few of the gruesome details during the two months that Alice lingered on her deathbed in the tiny two-room house. Even so, the agony did not end with the death, for that event brought in its train a whole series of related disasters.

First of all the family was uprooted from the pleasant surroundings of Indian Creek, where life had certainly not been affluent but was somehow orderly and agreeable. With the move to Kyle it suddenly became pinched, disorderly, and unharmonious.

For some reason, difficult to account for, the family was then plunged into real grinding poverty. Porter often puzzled over the family's desperate position at this time and could never completely understand what had happened. "How do I know what happened to the money, except that the land was gone?"[4] she asked in exasperation. All she knew was that there was no visible means of support.

Harrison Porter had disposed of his farm in Indian Creek in a way that yielded very little immediate income, and when he took his children to his mother, she herself was already in straitened circumstances. The records show that she sold her own land to a relative for a small down payment and a series of promissory notes which were never made good.[5] Again, there is no clear reason why she so divested herself. Did she, like Granny Weatherall in Porter's story, feel finished at sixty, make her will, come down with a long fever, and then abandon the idea of dying? Did she reason that her children needed the money and that she could subsist on very little? There is no means of knowing. Alice Porter had willed some land to her children and this was sold at once for the family's support, but it did not last long. Life was a hand-to-mouth existence, and if Harrison Porter took various jobs to help out, they were neither steady nor profitable enough to raise the family out of poverty.

As she grew up—and Porter was unusually precocious and sensitive—she became keenly aware of the degrading circumstances of her life. The most oppressive of these was the unbearably cramped living quarters. The grandmother, when she sold her farm land, had intended to live alone and had built on her lot in Kyle a small house, very suitable and pleasant for a solitary widow who might sometimes have family visits. It had a combination living and dining room, two bedrooms, and a small box room, each opening off the other with no connecting corridor. The place became badly overcrowded when it had to accommodate another adult with four children, and privacy of any kind was impossible. The grandmother kept her room and the others managed as best they could, sharing beds. Porter slept most often with her older sister, and when visiting members of the family arrived she occupied a pallet in the dining room.[6] There were beds everywhere, she later recalled, and when she visited the place years afterward she observed bitterly that the dreary little place was empty, full of dust, decayed, and even smaller than she remembered. She said simply, "I never lived there really."[7] But if she managed to dissociate herself mentally from her surroundings she did, in fact, live there for nine terrible years.

Poverty brought another affliction almost as great as that of the squalid living conditions. Of all the sources of humiliation during her childhood none was more painful to Porter than the state of her clothing. Her clothes were impeccably clean and repaired but so old and shabby that well-meaning neighbors often tried to help out by sending over cast-offs. Porter was mortified and never recovered from the shame of being an object of charity. In later years she could recall with exact clarity and use in her stories the disgust the family felt in their reduced circumstances.

"It's just charity," says Mrs. Whipple in "He," "that's what we've come to, charity! I certainly never looked for this."[8] And again,

"Why can't we do like other people and watch for our best chances? They'll be calling us poor white trash next."[9]

When she grew up nothing was more important to Porter than to be well dressed. Even if she was living meagerly as she learned to write, it was clothes rather than food or housing that had priority and she constantly astounded her friends by her impulsive sprees of buying clothes far beyond her means. "If I get a little money," she exulted, "I must always have clothes,"[10] and when she got a great deal of money she spent lavishly on clothes and jewels, preferring, when she had the choice of purchasing a fine house or some emeralds, to buy the emeralds.

In her childhood she learned lessons she never forgot about the effect of poverty and misfortune and the attitude of other people to the downtrodden and suffering. She felt that the family was regarded with pity and contempt and that even the death of the mother was, in some obscure kind of way, a disgrace. Later, in "The Leaning Tower," she used what she learned and she early developed the habit of dwelling on the unspoken feelings of those about her and of trying to understand and express her own inarticulate, troubling emotions. Like her Miranda character she developed a social sense like a strong set of antennae.

The effects of such poverty and social discomfort might have been mitigated if Porter had been a member of a warm and supportive family, but no such consolation was offered to her. The family, and especially her father, added considerably to the misery of her childhood.

One of the obstacles to presenting an accurate portrait of Harrison Boone Porter is his daughter's ambivalence toward him. She struggled all her life, unsuccessfully, to understand him, and her puzzlement is reflected in the many contradictory statements among her papers. Often a comment which explains his motivation will have "No, no, no, how wrong I was" scribbled over it years later.[11] Her perplexity is understandable, for this key figure in her life is enigmatic. He was evidently endowed with gifts well above the average. His letters show intelligence and sensitivity and there is abundant evidence of his physical attributes in photographs and verbal descriptions. In appearance he was impressive—tall, slender, and strikingly handsome, with an assured bearing and pleasant manners. And yet his character seems to have belied the impression he gave. He was a man of no substance, ineffective in his personal relationships, incapable of finding steady work and looking after his family. As he grew older and more aware of his own deficiencies, his character deteriorated. Always vain and irascible, he became hostile, violent, and uncontrolled.

The complete collapse of his will to live and work apparently began with the death of Alice. In the family he was generally explained as a "one-woman man" who had been crushed by the death of his wife.[12] As such, he was regarded as an unusual phenomenon, for many women of his generation, like his wife and three sisters, died in childbirth. Their husbands ordinarily mourned briefly and then set about the practical task of finding new wives who would care for the first family and raise additional ones of their own. Perhaps, indeed, Harrison Porter was disarmed for such action by a morbid sensitivity, or perhaps a fastidious moral conscience prevented him from ever shedding the guilt of his wife's death. He told his daughter that men were terrible, really terrible.[13] Porter said that his gloom was so heavy that it seemed to darken the very air around him, and she called him a will-less, inert, depressing man.[14] Even forty-two years after Alice's death, he became visibly agitated and physically ill when he visited her grave.[15] And in the years immediately after the death he made a cult of Alice's memory, telling beautiful and romantic stories about her. The children touched the relics with awe and Porter said the story of her mother's death made a sore spot all her life, for she had died too young and too hard a death. The widower treasured all her possessions, her dresses, locks of hair, bits of jewelry, pictures, gloves and shoes, and displayed them to the children as heirlooms. At the same time the children learned early not to broach the subject, for the father's grief belonged to him alone and they could neither share nor lighten it.[16] He blamed himself and the children for the loss of Alice and told them bluntly that he wished they had never been born. Porter realized how deeply he meant what he said.[17]

All the same, there are many signs that depression was not caused by his widowhood so much as aggravated by it. In their courtship correspondence Alice urged him to set aside his "mantle of gloom" and assured him that it was not in keeping with his "joyous nature."[18] On another occasion she felt the need to reassure him when he accused himself of ruining other people's lives. (There was mention of an engagement which he had broken off.)[19] And even before 1892 his attempts to make his own way in the world were conspicuously unsuccessful. When he turned to farming after the railway venture failed, it was Alice's father who provided the land and his mother who furnished his home. Porter herself believed that his nature had always been difficult and that he had made Alice's life as miserable as he made the children's. In a picture of her mother she remarked the tension of the mouth and tightly clasped hands (features not in fact very noticeable) and saw them as the result of her marriage to an exacting, self-absorbed man, handsomer than she and with a vicious temper.[20]

It is inexplicable why an intelligent, well-educated man of impressive appearance should have retreated into hopeless self-pity, ceased to work and provide for his family, and in his last years have become paranoid and almost mad. Both Porter and her brother all their lives feared that they might have inherited something of his nature. Porter said:

> What did he make of his life? I have never seen a more terrible example of apathy, the mere almost unconscious refusal to live, to take part, to do even the nearest most obvious human thing, which was to take care of the children left to him. He began with a good lively mind, wonderful looks, spirits, the kind of man who would have been welcome anywhere he wished to go. But he discovered absolutely not one glimmer of talent for anything, not a trace of a capacity for attention and direction of his energies, no imagination; and as he grew older his vices got possession of him, rages and resentments and petty mischief-making among his children and all the evils that can inhabit the idle motiveless mind . . . My God, what a waste! Let me tell you, I have turned in hope to other strains in my ancestry, for I have sometimes felt myself under a curse with such a father; I had to find in other sources the courage to outlive and outgrow him. . . . But what a hundredth anniversary note for him! I must leave him to rest in peace and not look into that grave again.[21]

She described him as loving confusion, hatred, and cross-purposes, and as being the only person she knew who slandered his own family —both children and grandchildren. (Her brother described his insults as "soul-searing."[22]) She said he had a murderous temper which he never tried to restrain and which crashed over everything and broke what it touched. He nagged perpetually and desired to be loved, praised, believed in, and deferred to without ever having done anything to deserve such respect. He demanded that the children be adults in their behavior and capacities and remain helpless in their obedience. He was given to violent outbursts of hatred and he always wanted to kill someone. Years later, when he died, she said she felt only relief, as if a beautiful white silence had fallen in all the places where he breathed such fury and bitterness.[23]

Porter knew that she had been fundamentally affected by her relationship with her father. She said that she had tried to love him but could not and that his affection frightened her because it was based on incomprehensible motives and was likely to change for inexplicable reasons. She longed for a stable affection on which she could depend during the successive upheavals that attend all growth and hers more than most. But while she craved his love, he doled out his preference by whimsy to whichever daughter he decided was the prettiest.[24] (For his son he seems to have had simply a steady, unwavering hostility.) For a time Porter was the main object of his attention (it can hardly be called love) because she was the prettiest of his daughters. But soon she had a formidable rival in her younger sister, who was blond and plump and won first place in his esteem. Porter's rejection on such grounds made her, even as a child, attach inordinate importance to physical beauty, and at the same time made her uneasy about her own attractiveness.

Many of the anecdotes which have survived about her childhood reflect her preoccupation with physical beauty. A young cousin remembered a lesson in nail care from Callie, who showed her how to use a towel to press back the cuticle as she dried her hands.[25] The sister who shared her bed remembered the time that Callie put herself on a regimen of eating an onion a day (in bed) because she thought it would make her beautiful. To a childhood friend Porter wrote years later:

> I remember your hands and ears, no doubt because my own hands were always thin and flat and a little grubby, into garden dirt and every kind of outdoor climbing and picking and handling animals, objects, all the fascinating natural world. My ears were, and are, too large: I wanted them rosy, discreet, like yours.[26]

She said that the friend was her ideal of beauty and she remembered her as tall for her age always, with thin shell-pink skin, really live, shining, *long* golden hair, bright pure-blue eyes.

Her father's neglect left her with an insatiable hunger for masculine admiration and a sense of uneasiness in the presence of other women who might deflect attention from her. And there was always something unbalanced and feverish in her relationships with men. Her habit was to fall in love deliriously and at first sight with a handsome appearance to which she wedded a character of her own imagining. Inevitably the object of her love failed to match her high ideals and her rapture turned swiftly to revulsion.

In her choice of lovers she typically gravitated to men who were married, homosexual, or in some other way disqualified from providing the stability she sought. Regardless of her own advancing years, she formed relationships with men around thirty—Harrison Porter's age during her growing years—and many of her partners resembled him in appearance. They were often conventionally good-looking men with fair complexions, for her father's tawny coloring remained her ideal in masculine beauty. It is reflected in descriptions in her fiction, like that of Adam Barclay in "Pale Horse, Pale Rider": "He was wearing his new uniform, and he was olive and tan and tawny, hay-colored and sand-colored from hair to boots."[27]

While Porter acknowledged that her dealings with men had been impaired by her disastrous experience with her father, it was not in the way suggested above. Her interpretation, typical of her irrational, almost superstitious thinking in certain areas, was that girls whose fathers did not take care of them got a curse on them and other men sensed that they need not take care of them either. She said that if she had not been so starved for love she would not have squandered her energies and time in the futile search for it.[28]

Since she lacked any effective parental model during her formative years, it might be expected that Porter's sense of identity would be weak, her image of herself a tremulous and uncertain one. This weakness manifested itself in the fantasies about herself that she never outgrew. If as a child she dreamed of being an orphan and a changeling, she never relinquished that habit, always giving unreliable accounts of her family and experiences and even distorting and misrepresenting her accomplishments. Deeply unsure of herself, she was morbidly sensitive to criticism and demanded from her friends an almost fanatical devotion and loyalty.

At the same time, the absence of parental models produced some unexpected benefits. Harrison Porter's wasted life was a powerful negative example which increased her own determination to do something with her own life, to "amount to something."[29]

The absence of her mother was also a factor in her success, for Porter grew up in a time and region in which the sexual roles were strongly polarized. Careers for women were almost unthinkable. They might write a little or play musical instruments but such accomplishments were to be practiced only for the delight of their families. Porter's mother, who was a skilled musician, used her talents in her home and in the Sunday school. She, in fact, fulfilled perfectly the role of Angel in the House, which Virginia Woolf argued so eloquently must be killed before a woman can become an artist. All who knew Alice remembered her gentle, accommodating nature and her ability to create domestic harmony even with such a volatile husband as Harrison Boone Porter. Porter's older sister, who well remembered her mother, herself became such a domestic angel, living for her children, happiest when she was tending her house and garden, and working outside the home only because difficult circumstances compelled her to do so. Porter herself, with her mother's exemplary life as a model, reinforced by society's expectations of women, might well have become such a person. Since she never knew her mother, however, she never felt compelled to play the traditional feminine role and she had from the beginning developed a strong sense of vocation, of wanting to be something in her own right. Her childhood companions remember spending hours during the long cricket-whirring summer days helping Callie decide what she wanted to be —sometimes a nun, sometimes a writer, and most often an actress.[30]

She naturally dreamed of marrying, raising a family, and having a domestic life, but it was much in the way that the men of her time did. She no more planned to be a wife and mother first than they would have aspired to be husbands and fathers first. When she thought of having a home, she saw herself as the chatelaine, strong and independent, running the show, and not as a supportive helpmate providing a basis for the life work of someone else. Thus the death of her mother, while it was a personal tragedy which ruined her childhood, became an asset in her development as an artist, the basic necessity for which was that she become a free and independent woman.

Virtually bereft as she was during her growing years of any strong parental figure, Porter naturally looked elsewhere for influences. The greatest of these was the grandmother whose importance in her growth she later acknowledged by adopting, with a minor spelling variation, her name. The most beneficial effect of Catherine Anne Porter on her granddaughter was to convey a sense of a woman's being independent, effective, and totally in control of her world. Her energetic presence was a vivid contrast to the passivity of her son as it had been to that of her husband, whether or not he was immobilized by his war injury. Possibly Aunt Cat's domineering presence had a paralyzing effect on the men about her, for Porter said that after Harrison Boone Porter joined his mother's household in Kyle he was treated as a kind of elder child in the family. Porter records in her fiction the contempt for men felt by Sophia Jane Rhea, the character modeled on her Grandmother Porter.[31] She seems not to have considered the possibility that it was the grandmother's own powerful personality that actually caused the passivity of the men in the family, but her world in both her fiction and her actual life perpetuated the early impression of a capable woman yoked to a weak man.

All anecdotes, both true and apocryphal, reinforce the same impression of Aunt Cat. She was strong-willed, uncompromising, and firmly convinced of her own infallibility. Any intractability on the part of the granddaughter was seen as the natural inheritance from such a grandmother. In her granddaughter's words, "She belonged to a generation who all talked and behaved as if the final word had gone out long ago on manners, morals, religion and even politics."[32]

Cora Posey remembered hearing that when some flowers failed to arrive for a social occasion, Aunt Cat drove at a gallop to Austin to fetch them and the minute she arrived home the horses dropped dead.[33] Perhaps the story was apocryphal, for Porter scorned it, saying that Cora was senile when she told it, and added that her grandmother was kind to animals.[34] She did not, however, deny the energy or determination which the story suggests.

Other residents of Kyle remember Aunt Cat's intransigence in church matters. The Baptist and Methodist congregations joined for services in the church building they shared, but the Baptists preferred to have their own communion. One story has Aunt Cat leaning across two communicants to get her share, announcing loudly that she was as much a child of the Lord as anyone else.[35]

On another occasion, there was some consternation in the church when the members of the Mexican colony attended a revival meeting. The congregation mistrusted them because they spoke Spanish, ate strange food, and were Catholic in an iron-bound Protestant region. When the deacon asked them to leave, Aunt Cat was furious and led the Porters out of church in the wake of the Mexicans.[36]

While she was a highly moral character, notorious for her good works in the community (in spite of her poverty, tramps and derelicts were often directed to her doorstep), her rectitude was forbidding. One of her brothers said that if God were anything like his sister thought he was, he wanted no part of him,[37] and local children, seeing her gaunt frame and shrunken face, were afraid of her and afraid to go to her house. The playmates of the Porter children never ventured beyond the front porch. She was extremely pious and Porter said she ground the fear of God into the children's very bones, while they were too young to protest.[38] She was puritanical, disapproving, and repressive. Dressed in the black of perpetual mourning, she thought that red was associated with sin and the devil, and Porter said that in her early years she thought of the devil as a creature dressed in red with long nails who lived in her grandmother's closet.

Aunt Cat believed that it was her duty to be a stern, methodical disciplinarian, and she made a point of raising her children as she herself had been raised. She rarely indulged in full immersion in a bathtub, preferring instead a discreet pitcher of water in the bedroom. Similarly, she considered it shameful for the children to be naked at any time and they were hastily bundled in towels when they bathed.

In middle life Porter posed narcissistically for nude photographs by her husbands and lovers. Not only did she have the pictures taken but she sometimes sent them back home to her family, flaunting perhaps her liberation from Aunt Cat's strict standards as much as the beauty of her body.

One of Porter's earliest memories was of telling a visiting clerical gentlemen when she was six that she wished to be an actress.[39] Aunt Cat was so mortified that Callie was taken out at once and ceremoniously and awfully beaten. Other forms of discipline were less ceremonious and more impulsive. She recalled, "I'd never been harmed in my life by anybody except my grandmother, who would box my ears from time to time—she didn't really box them, she used to slap me in the face, smack, like that, and made me so damn mad that I'd wish she were dead for hours at a time."[40]

While the effects of Aunt Cat's repressive puritanism were deep and lasting, they did not become apparent until much later. In her childhood the grandmother, for all her faults, represented the only source of security she had. She said later that the one dependable thing in her childhood was the wrath of her grandmother.[41] If that seems an oddly grudging kind of praise it must be remembered that in a world of uncertainty, even anger, if it is constant, can be a greater

source of security than love which might at any moment be withdrawn. Porter also, in her later years, praised her grandmother in
many essays and interviews. Perhaps she came to realize how difficult
it had been for Aunt Cat, afflicted as she was with the bronchial
troubles, grieved by the loss of her three daughters, oppressed by
hard work and poverty, to raise another family, in which the father
was an added burden rather than a support.

Besides feeding, clothing, and instilling moral and religious principles in her granddaughter, Aunt Cat provided one additional and
unlikely function—she laid the foundation for Porter's literary gifts.
These talents Porter sometimes explained by saying that she came
from a long line of storytellers and had listened all her life to articulate
people.[42] The statement bears examination because, while Texas is
notoriously the home of the tall tale, the sensational and amazing
anecdote, the telling of tall tales would seem out of character for the
grandmother. In the first place storytelling was suspect in strict evan-
gelical circles and children were taught that it could lead to untruth
and transgression. Accordingly, when Porter exercised her imagination in childhood games she was punished for such wicked tendencies.
She was particularly fond of reproducing the story of the burning of
Joan of Arc, either with miniature figures or with herself as the central
figure tied up according to her own instructions by her playmates.
Aunt Cat took the most disapproving view of such games and saw
them as signs of morbidity and wickedness in her granddaughter.[43]

Nevertheless, the grandmother found her own kind of solace in
storytelling and yarning of a most imaginative kind. Mortified as she
was by her reduced circumstances and by the pity of her neighbors
and sisters, she harked back constantly to the better times she had
known, recalling her own childhood and youth and the early lives of
her daughters. Her favorite subject was her youngest and best-loved
daughter, Annie, who had made a good marriage to a dashing young
man from West Texas who owned a string of racehorses. She had
traveled with him to racecourses all over the country, even going as
far north as Saratoga Springs. Abruptly tragedy struck, for she survived only four months after her marriage and died away from home
of a mysteriously ill-defined illness. Porter said that when she was
growing up the memory of this aunt, Annie Gay, was kept as vivid
in the house as if she had never left it.[44] Later she used the story, in
"Old Mortality," basing Aunt Amy on Annie Gay and Gabriel on
her uncle, Thomas Gay.

Thus Aunt Cat instilled in the little girl a passionate interest in her family, and, like her grandmother, Porter took comfort in knowing that her family had once had dignity and position and had not always been in its present pitiful state. All through her childhood she was preoccupied with the family, feeding on its history and watching with hungry fascination for evidences of former distinction in the present. Later, the family's past, imaginatively recreated, became the subject of some of her most successful stories. Aunt Cat also laid the foundations for Porter's sound storytelling technique, for, being a deep-rooted moralist, she did not tell stories merely for their entertainment value but cast them with sharply pointed morals, each tale having "shape and meaning and point."

Lacking parents she might emulate, and fed by her grandmother's zest for the family, Porter watched visiting members of it with eager curiosity. Her sharp ears caught every inflection, her sharp eyes every gesture, as she fixed her attention upon them, and long after they left the house she thought and fantasized about their lives, especially when, in contrast to her own, they were successful and colorful.

Most of the relatives failed to measure up to her expectations and she remembered them as a mean, selfish, godforsaken lot who descended on Sunday and ate up all the fried chicken. She said that no one hated his relatives as much as she did. There was, she said, a broad streak of highwayman or pickpocket in the family. Jewelry would disappear and accusations of theft would be hurled back and forth. Once Gay was accused of stealing a ring. Perhaps this accounts for Porter's use of the theft of a precious object as a recurring motif in her fiction. She said that her grandmother never trusted her sister, Aunt Eliza, with anything portable, edible, wearable, sellable, or just plain keepable.[45]

Occasionally, however, a living relative did live up to the grandmother's stories of earlier generations. Such a one was the daughter of her late aunt, Belle Bunton, named Laredo for the place where she was born and always called Lady. Cousin Lady had come all the way from West Texas to finish her education at Coronal Institute in San Marcos. With her smooth black hair and magnolia skin, she provided Porter with a vision of what beauty in a woman should be. She was also accomplished, a graceful horsewoman and a lover of poetry and music. Fifty years later Porter would recall in exact detail the words that were spoken during her cousin's weekend visit to Kyle. She recalled that Lady fanned herself with a palm-leaf fan and said, "Oh,

I'm so hot I'm about to melt." Porter remembered the very look of her grandmother's face and the tone of her voice as she said, "Don't say hot, child, say warm." She remembered that Lady talked excitedly about hearing Paderewski for the first time—and after talking about the wonders of his playing she added, "And oh, what beautiful hands! The most beautiful hands I ever saw except . . ." Then she stopped and looked down at her own, and turned them and moved the long smooth fingers and never finished the sentence.[46]

Thirty years later Porter's sister read this description in "Old Mortality":

> When Cousin Isabel came out in her tight black riding habit, surrounded by young men, and mounted gracefully, drawing her horse up and around so that he pranced learnedly on one spot while the other riders sprang to their saddles in the same sedate flurry, Miranda's heart would close with such a keen dart of admiration, envy, and vicarious pride it was almost painful.[47]

She wrote in the margin of her copy, "Lady Bunton."[48]

The impression made by the schoolgirl, Lady Bunton, however, was as nothing compared with that made by another relative, only a little older than Lady but already married.

Harrison Porter's younger brother, Newell, was a worldly character who traveled frequently between San Antonio and New Orleans and who had amassed a great deal of money by gambling. At the age of thirty-seven he had married a tender-looking, beautiful young girl from Mississippi, who being an orphan had spent most of her life in a New Orleans convent. Newell and his wife sometimes visited Aunt Cat, and these visits soon became the highlight of young Callie's life. Her attitude to Aunt Ione was one of complete hero worship. The nineteen-year-old matron had a great many airs which impressed her young niece. She called her guardian "Guardie" and her husband "Hubbie," and she asked her nieces to call her "Tante Ione." When Aunt Cat was trying to bed down a houseful of guests, Tante Ione refused to help matters by spending the night apart from her "hubbie." Porter said later that Newell and Ione were the only relatives she could bear and that they "shone like bonfires in that naughty world."[49]

Besides her impressive manners Tante Ione had other attributes, among them a beautiful wardrobe of clothes and some very fine jewelry. She carried with her a jewel case full of diamonds. Most of these she did not generally wear but she sometimes entertained the family in the evening by putting them all on at once—two necklaces, three bracelets, three sets of earrings, and a cluster of brooches. These came from her grandmother, her mother, and an aunt or two, and she had more in the vault at the bank which her "guardie" insisted she could not expose to the random life of travel she had taken on. The only piece she wore regularly was the five-carat engagement ring which her husband had given her. She had no use for any gem except a diamond, and she expressed something like derision for colored stones—emeralds, rubies, and above all pearls. Porter found this difficult to take politely, since her birthstone was an emerald and she had the impression that no jewel was more beautiful, more elegant, or more lucky. Her sister was a ruby by birth and her father and brother were pearls, though none had ever seen a ruby or an emerald up close, or a diamond until Tante Ione came along. Harrison Porter had inherited a set of fine old pearl shirt buttons and cuff links but these he had not worn since his wedding ceremony.[50]

Besides her fine clothes and jewels, Tante Ione entertained her young nieces (it is hard to imagine Aunt Cat as part of her admiring audience) with enchanting stories of her life. She told about the convent in New Orleans where she had been obliged to wear a little shift for modesty when she bathed. It had floated on the bath water like a lily leaf, but she had never realized how truly delightful bathing could be until she discovered she didn't have to wear a shift in the bathtub. She told of the Mardi Gras celebrations she had seen in New Orleans and of her marriage to Newell and how shocked her guardian and aunts had been at her choice of a worldly man so much older than herself. Leaning on her hand listening to these stories and gazing dreamily at Tante Ione, Callie thought she would have given anything to have such experiences. And even when Tante Ione was not present, Callie spent an inordinate amount of time dreaming about her aunt's life, imagining what it was like and fantasizing that her own life might become so exciting. When she wrote "Old Mortality" she had Miranda Gay, exactly like Tante Ione, elope from a New Orleans convent to marry. But long before she wrote the story, Porter developed the habit of using the stories of Ione Funchess to embellish her own life story. She told friends who knew nothing of her early life that she had eloped from a New Orleans convent when she was sixteen and had married a man much older than herself who shut her up.[51]

Porter watched her childhood acquaintances with an attention much more intense than that inspired by mere curiosity. By drawing on their lives in her fantasies and annexing their experiences into her own biographical record she tried to compensate for the disappointments and insufficiencies of her life. Later she used their stories in her fiction, and eventually the boundaries between their lives and hers, between the fiction and the fact, became blurred.

One person on whom she trained her sharp eyes was a little girl her own age who lived just across the street from the Porter house. Erna Schlemmer was Porter's closest friend during her childhood and remained her friend to the end of her life.

The Schlemmers, like the Porters, had four children, three girls and a boy. There the resemblance between the two families ended, for the family life of the Schlemmers was as comfortable, orderly, and affectionate as that of the Porters was disagreeable.

Mr. Schlemmer was the owner of the village mercantile store, which he had built up into a prosperous business with seventeen employees. He bought land prudently, increased his holdings steadily, and was known as the business genius of the town. The family lived in an ample home, cared for by devoted servants, and taught before they entered the village school by a governess who lived in the house.

The family had the additional interest of being European. The father, Nicholas Schlemmer, had come to the United States from Germany in 1870. He was intelligent and enterprising, quickly mastered the language, and prospered as surely as Harrison Porter failed. On one of his return visits to Germany he met at a music festival the young woman who became his wife. Wilhelmina Schlemmer, while not as Porter believed a countess, did come from a distinguished family, proud of its coat of arms. She was attended by her faithful maid, Elise, who insisted on accompanying her mistress to Texas even if she had to pay her own fare. Elise spent the rest of her life with the family, becoming the children's nurse and then in turn maid to them.[52]

The family's way of life was, even in Texas, very European. Mrs. Schlemmer had grown up in England, had an English accent—which she tried to modify so as not to seem odd to her neighbors—and always served tea at four. Mr. Schlemmer had a well-stocked cellar of imported wines and wine was always served at the meals to which Callie was sometimes invited. The children spoke German and French and even the son studied music. The house was full of music and books. Erna had her own pony and an elegant riding habit. Every two years the family made the journey back to Germany to visit relatives. These holidays left Porter lonely all the long dull summer and she was only barely mollified by the colored postcards which arrived from places like Wiesbaden and Bremen.[53]

Porter said later that she and Erna were set apart from the other children by a "quality of observingness" and she thought they shared certain qualities of the imagination.[54] Erna remembered the relationship differently. She certainly granted Porter the "quality of observingness" but beside it she felt like a lesser light, "a pale shadow." She recalled feeling ordinary and dull beside her friend's vivid personality and wondering why Callie chose her as a friend. When she read "Old Mortality" she wrote:

> . . . little Miranda at once became Callie that dearest friend of my childhood. I'm afraid I wanted to brush Aunt Amy out of the way and get on with what Miranda did and thought and said. . . . Why you ever loved me I don't know —I was such a pale shadow beside your vivid personality. We were so strictly reared and such an undemonstrative family I think I was secretly rather astonished that you should be fond of me.[55]

She long remembered how Callie's schemes and games enlivened her childhood. Once, for instance, Callie had the idea of placing an old cigar box on the fence near the Schlemmer privy and the two used it as a mail drop for the notes they exchanged. Callie signed hers "Witch" and instructed Erna to use the name "Fairy."[56]

At other times Callie was a ringleader in the most literal sense, for the arrival of a circus in the neighborhood would inspire her to organize the other children into doing daredevil bareback riding stunts on the Schlemmers' patient mules and large white hogs, or performing dangerous trapeze tricks in the Schlemmer loft. There she instructed them how to dangle and jump recklessly, until Mrs. Schlemmer came running out in alarm to put an end to such dangerous games and sharply rebuke Callie for leading Erna into mischief.[57]

Toward the end of her life Erna wrote:

> Did I ever tell you about the time Callie startled me so when she asked *me* to write a story and let her illustrate it. I can still see us in a crowd of school children just set free for the

afternoon. We must have been about 11 or 12. She was quite in earnest and I know she could have done some drawing in excellent form. I must have just turned in a good essay or something but I never even thought of trying. And, by the way, that copy of Dante Callie read was in our "parlor"— sacred of sacred rooms—I remember when I read it (it was illustrated with very terrifying drawings etc.) I wondered and worried over what in the world Harpies were. They were awful looking women in the illustrations. Of course I didn't have sense enough to look in a dictionary. I'm sure Mama never knew either Callie or I had slipped in and read it.[58]

Erna was the first in a series of friends who were important to Porter for providing something beyond mere companionship. They all helped her develop by showing her a glimpse of a life much richer and fuller than her own. They fanned her ambition and made her determined to acquire their advantages.

The friendship with Erna also brought a certain amount of confusion. Porter has claimed that her sense of social injustice was born when Aunt Cat protested the discrimination against the Mexicans at the revival meeting, but, while that undoubtedly made an impression, her sense of injustice was much more personally engaged in her consciousness of the wide gap between the affluent Schlemmers and the deprived Porters.

The reaction to the injustice she witnessed, however, was not straightforward but complicated, for it did not escape Aunt Cat's disapproving eye that there was some irony in seeing the recently arrived Schlemmers prosper while the long-established Porters sank into poverty. Nor was she one to keep to herself her contempt for these people as foreigners, tradespeople, and barbarians. Porter absorbed something of this opinion and she maintained to the end of her life, and in the face of all contrary evidence, the belief that the Porters had been aristocratic landowners and the Schlemmers mere tradespeople who "had no culture."[59] In her story "The Leaning Tower" she has the father of Kuno, a character based on Erna, seem curiously undignified in his shop, as he follows people around trying to sell them things. By contrast, the farmer is a dignified person on horseback or striding the fields in his big boots or riding on the cast-iron seat of a plow.[60] The long-range result of this confusion was that all her life Porter wavered in her class identification, now agitating on behalf of downtrodden, exploited people, now speaking proudly of belonging to a slave-owning, aristocratic class.

The immediate effect of this ambivalence was to add to the discomfort of poverty and unhappiness at home the insecurity of a chaotic view of the world. The extent of her alienation is captured in a description she wrote of a recurring childhood dream. She dreamed that she was in a crowd, sometimes in church, of silent, motionless people, almost faceless, never friendly, sometimes indifferent with the kind of indifference that could turn to hostility—at least mutely censorious, inaccessible. She said that she never saw in a dream then or later any person or even animal that was friendly toward her; the figures of her dreams were always deeply, quietly threatening or full of sinister indifference and shrewd, enigmatic evil.[61]

The pressure of such alienation might well have been psychologically devastating, and Porter always listed among her personal liabilities "an unstable set of nerves." She told friends years later, "I was an unhappy restless child, and have no pleasant memories. . . . But it certainly does not matter, for my unhappiness was not from my circumstances but from within myself."[62]

Notes in the books in her library suggest that she thought of herself as not merely "restless" but emotionally disturbed in childhood. In her copy of Grasset's *The Semi-Insane and the Semi-Responsible* she underlined this set of symptoms: ". . . the most advanced neurasthenia and incredible sense of smell, a feeling of presences, intuition of others' thoughts, mad agonies and disturbances without cause." "That's me, from my first memory," she wrote in the margin, "except I think I had causes." In the same text she marked two other passages:

> The psychoanalyses of individuals have taught us that their earliest impressions received at a time when they were hardly able to talk, manifest themselves later in an obsessive fashion, although those impressions themselves are not consciously remembered.[63]

To this she added, "So my horror and pain here and now from that old terrible time. KAP 16 August 1949."

> Neurosis in children is very common . . . *often overlooked,* regarded as a manifestation of *bad behaviour or naughtiness* and

often subdued by *the authorities in the nursery*. From childhood on they draw attention to themselves by their precocity, their quickness in taking hold of everything and understanding it, and at the same time by their whims, their headstrong ways, their cruel instincts, their violent and convulsive attacks of anger.

She wrote in the margin, "Alas! myself?"

There were so many areas of pain and conflict in her childhood that her assessment of herself as seriously disturbed seems very plausible. And yet there were among the disasters certain positive elements not present in lives of luckier people in her time and place. The unpleasantness of her outer world caused her to turn inward and develop remarkable powers of imagination. Poverty and social embarrassment gave her a fierce determination to obtain for herself the comfort and respect enjoyed by her more advantaged friends and relatives. Most important, the absence of strong parental models freed her from conformity to a traditional way of life and allowed her eventually to be completely herself.

THREE

Adolescence: The Old Order Changeth

In Porter's life the demarcation of the adolescent period was sharper than in most. The death of her grandmother when she was eleven abruptly ended her childhood, and her marriage when she was sixteen just as abruptly thrust her into womanhood. The intervening years were among her most painful, for just as her mother's death nine years earlier had plunged the family into chaos, so once again death shattered whatever remnants of stability had remained. Her childhood was sealed off as it began by the loss of the one person around whom her world revolved, and to the painful anniversary that darkened each winter was added another in the fall of the year. Porter's health was ever afterward imperiled at these times, affected perhaps as much by deep emotional scars as by climatic changes.

In spite of all this trouble (perhaps because of it) no other period yielded so richly to her fiction. It was thirty years before she achieved full control of her métier, and when she did so, she found her most successful material in reshaping and reordering the experiences of these five years. From them she created the short novels "Old Mortality" and "Noon Wine," and the short-story sequence "The Old Order."

Apart from the suppression of the younger sister who had supplanted her as her father's favorite, Porter based the characters in "Old Mortality" and "The Old Order" on those of her actual family. She also faithfully reproduced certain events, notably that of the death of the grandmother, which she had closely witnessed. Porter was the only one of the immediate family who saw Aunt Cat's death, for she was with her on a trip to West Texas when it happened.[1] Two of Aunt Cat's sons, Asbury and Bill, lived in Marfa and El Paso, and it was a rare treat for Porter to accompany her when she went by train to visit them. The journey to the bandit-infested West was long (around 500 miles) and adventurous, the more exciting part being the crossing of the precarious-looking bridge that spanned the Pecos River.[2] When they arrived in Marfa, Callie and Aunt Cat stayed in Asbury Porter's adobe house. It must have been a rough place, for Porter long remembered hearing her Aunt May plead for curtains in the windows and her uncle scorn the idea as a foolish waste of money.[3] He was not so successful in resisting his mother's ideas and she immediately began to make changes to his property. In "The Old Order" Porter describes Sophia Jane Rhea's activities when she visits a son in West Texas:

> The son had long ago learned not to oppose his mother. She wore him down with patient, just, and reasonable argument. She was careful never to venture to command him in anything. He consoled his wife by saying that everything Mother was doing could be changed back after she was gone. As the change included moving a fifty-foot adobe wall, the wife was not much consoled. The Grandmother came into the house quite flushed and exhilarated, saying how well she felt in the bracing mountain air—and dropped dead over the doorsill.[4]

The fictional account closely follows the actual events. Aunt Cat had been busily supervising the Mexican Indian farm hands all day long in the hot sun, and at the end of the day she came indoors, removed her summer straw hat, and stood in the hall confused and blinking, her face suddenly like parchment. Porter, alarmed, called out to her but she seemed not to hear and toppled and fell. Someone rode the five miles to bring a doctor, and the family, realizing that she was dying, grouped around her bed, her son saying distractedly, "Mammy, don't tell us you're going to die."

"Azzy, of course I'm going to die," she replied, and with everyone in tears around her she gave instructions for her own funeral. At some point in the evening the presence of the eleven-year-old girl was noticed and she was sent off to bed.

The next morning she was told, "Wake up, your grandmother's

dead," and sent along, barefoot and in her shift, to see the body. Two days later she made the journey home, bringing her grandmother in her coffin to Kyle, where a large crowd met the train.

The grandmother was buried in the newly founded cemetery five miles from town, and the funeral was an impressive one. Mourners came from seven counties and the first people to reach the cemetery had to wait two and a half hours, singing and praying throughout the long hot afternoon, for the last Negroes to arrive.[5] Since the Porter girls had nothing to wear for such an occasion, Erna Schlemmer's mother made sashes to disguise the shabbiness of their dresses.[6]

The next day the San Antonio paper carried the following obituary:

> Kyle, Texas, October 4th.
> Mrs. C. A. Porter who died at Marfa, Texas on the 2nd inst., was buried here today. Mrs. Porter has been a resident of this vicinity for 50 years and was well known in this county. She had been a life-long member of the Cumberland Presbyterian Church. She leaves seven sons and many friends.[7]

The body of Asbury Porter, brought from the family cemetery in the country, was placed beside his wife's and a joint headstone was raised over them, rather more elaborate than those on the surrounding graves, and bearing for an epitaph the single word "Reunited." When she wrote about her fictional family, Porter described the transfer of the grandfather's body as an act of possessiveness on the part of the grandmother:

> After the grandmother's death, part of the land was sold for the benefit of certain of her children, and the cemetery happened to lie in the part put aside for sale. It was necessary to take up the bodies and bury them again in the family plot in the big new cemetery where the grandmother had been buried. At last her husband was to lie beside her for eternity as she had planned.[8]

Aunt Cat's death, like their mother's, brought in its wake a whole series of disasters, and once the excitement of the funeral had passed, the awful realization of their loss was borne in upon the children. If Harrison Porter had had little inclination to work for the family's support before, his mother's death certainly did not provide any incentive for him to do so, and he sank deeper into hopelessness and depression. Porter said that after Aunt Cat's death her father made "no reasonable effort to pull them out of the hole they were in and let them go to rags and almost to death."[9]

In addition, the grandmother's fixed outlook on the world, her fundamentalist religion, her unwavering system of values, no matter how strict and repressive they were, had been the one constant in the confusions of the years before. A friend later said that Aunt Cat made the Porter girls "walk the straight and narrow path" and that later Porter rebelled against her strict way of life.[10] It is true that she rebelled in the most predictable and standard ways against her grandmother's code. She became an avid and skillful card player, she loved dancing and drinking and led a sexually uninhibited life. All the same, her attitude was not one of straightforward rebellion but was a complicated ambivalence of the kind most destructive of emotional tranquillity.

It is, of course, not unusual for the rejection of a rigid system of beliefs, which answers all questions and leaves little room for uneasy doubts and uncertainties, to be replaced by a system completely different but equally rigid and inflexible. Porter, accordingly, while rebelling against her grandmother's creed, craved a similar fixed doctrine and eventually worked out one for herself in which right and wrong, villains and saints, were clearly recognizable and distinguishable from each other and in which Evil was a recognizable entity and there was no gray middle ground.

Although she ventured to criticize her grandmother, she reacted with fury when the grandmother's point of view was criticized by anyone else. When, for example, she read a master's thesis in which the student criticized the character and outlook of Sophia Jane Rhea, she wrote angrily to the writer. She asked if the rejection of a Christian and moral idea of life by the lowest elements of society proved that system to be evil and corrupt, and she said that the whole argument of the thesis was "so netted with personal prejudice against the traditional Southern social system" that she would not even try to answer it.[11]

There was, of course, no reason why the grandmother's philosophy of life or religious teaching should have passed away when she died. That it did so was the work of Harrison Porter. At this time he added to his general fecklessness an even more cruel blow—he set about stamping out systematically all that the grandmother had inculcated, so that if Porter had earlier felt that she was torn between two adults, the conflict was intensified by the death of one of them. She remembered her shock and horror when her father bluntly refuted the dogma of the virgin birth, telling her that there was only one way for babies to come into the world and that was by the natural way.[12]

Exactly when Harrison Porter's rejection of orthodox religion occurred is not known. Certainly his faith had seemed strong in his married days, when he was the superintendent of the Indian Creek Methodist Church Sunday School. Perhaps his agnosticism developed gradually as an underground rebellion against his mother's teaching in the days when he and his children lived with her. If it did, he waited until her death to express it, and it is hard not to see his sudden undermining of the faith of his bereaved children as a cowardly and malevolent act. Naturally in the course of a lifetime each child reacted differently to such contradictory religious experiences. Paul remained very devout and moral, and to the end of his life could not bring himself to tell a lie. He instilled in his own children the lesson that "whoever tells a lie, flies in the face of God and shows fear of man."[13] Gay changed one religious denomination for another and, in the face of personal tragedies in her later life, turned to spiritualism.

Of herself, Porter said that after her grandmother's death she had on the subject of religion alone ten years of conflict ahead of her.[14] Her estimate was conservative, for she never really resolved the conflict and for most of her life wavered, torn between her grandmother's faith and her father's agnosticism.

This then was a period when her world fell completely apart and she was in a single blow deprived of any sense of family dignity, material security, or religious certainty. Moreover, the uncertainties of the period were considerably aggravated because they coincided with the internal physical changes which inevitably attend the onset of adolescence. The interaction of all these areas of painful uncertainty in her short story "The Grave" well illustrates Robert Penn Warren's statement that "Katherine Anne Porter's fiction remains, perhaps, the best source of biography in the deeper sense."[15]

"The Grave" is set in the country and takes place just after the death of Miranda Gay's grandmother and the removal of the grandfather's coffin from the family graveyard to the new public cemetery. One paragraph, written for the story but omitted from the final version, describes the three children going into a part of the land which they no longer own to pick some of the fruit from the trees the grandmother planted and their bitter humiliation as the present owners of the land allow them to do so out of unmasked pity for them:

They puzzled over the loss of land, over the sale of the finest orchard where grandmother had planted her favorite peaches. Even the empty cemetery was no longer theirs. They felt like trespassers. . . . The summer after the grand-mother's death, they remembered her Indian cling peach trees in the orchard that was now sold. The three of them went boldly, walked into the orchard and filled their baskets with the fruit as they had done the summer before. The woman who owned the orchard saw them from her vege-table garden nearby. She and her husband had been renters, sharecroppers but in twenty years' time they had saved enough money to buy the first old house the grandmother had built, and her first beautiful orchard. She came running towards the children, waving at them and calling. They were frightened . . . but stood their ground. . . . The woman came panting up, a little fat person with red cheeks, a tiny smiling mouth; she called out to them: "Wait a min-ute, children!" Maria, standing with her basket on her arm, stammered a little, her chin shaking, but she said firmly enough, "We wanted some of our grandmother's Indian cling peaches." The woman said, "Why of co'se you did, honey. Why I should say so. Jes' help yose'f and whenever you want any more, you come right back and get 'em! I just come over to help you pick the good ones . . ." And they had to stay and pick and pick, sweating with shame and prickling with anger. She loaded them down, and found a dozen more every time one of them hinted that they didn't want to take all she had, and it was time to go.[16]

In the final version she simply describes the contemptuous attitude of the country people to the family:

It was said the motherless family was running down, with the Grandmother no longer there to hold it together. It was known that she had discriminated against her son Harry in her will, and that he was in straits about money. Some of his old neighbors reflected with vicious satisfaction that now he would probably not be so stiffnecked, nor have any more high-stepping horses either. Miranda knew this, though she could not say how. She had met along the road old women of the kind who smoked corn-cob pipes, who had treated her grandmother with most sincere respect. They slanted their gummy old eyes side-ways at the granddaughter and said, "Ain't you ashamed of yoself, Missy? It's against the Scriptures to dress like that. Whut yo Pappy thinkin about?" Miranda, with her powerful social sense, which was like a fine set of antennae radiating from every pore of her skin, would feel ashamed because she knew well it was rude and ill-bred to shock anybody. . . .[17]

Against this unsettled background Miranda Gay is described, the first incident of the story showing her awakening sense of her own sexual identity. In tomboy fashion, she is following her brother Paul, who likes shooting rabbits and birds. As they wander about they come across the recently emptied family graveyard on the part of the land which has been sold, and they explore the cavity which until recently housed the grandfather's coffin. In it they find a wedding ring and the screw head of a coffin, which in shape resembles a dove. Paul is delighted to possess the coffin screw and Miranda the golden ring. When she places it upon her thumb she becomes suddenly aware of her ragged and grubby appearance and longs to be prettily dressed and scented and to be reclining in suitably female fashion in a wicker chair.

Following hard upon this incident comes another one much more unsettling because it focuses her attention not on the external trappings of being a woman, but on the physical implications. Paul shoots a rabbit, and when he slits open its skin he reveals an interior full of fetal young. The sight seems to Miranda to confirm something she has sensed for a long time but has not articulated fully, and the knowledge makes her tremulous and uneasy. The brother swears her to secrecy about the sight:

"Listen now. Now you listen to me, and don't ever forget. Don't you ever tell a living soul that you saw this. Don't tell a soul. Don't tell Dad because I'll get in trouble. He'll say I'm leading you into things you ought not to do. He's always saying that."[18]

In the story Miranda keeps silent. She has no wish to tell about the frightening sight. The actual events on which the story was based diverged from the fiction at this point. Porter did, in fact, tell her father what she had seen and the brother received a savage beating.[19] Whether the exposure of the brother was motivated by vindictiveness or carelessness, it constituted an act of betrayal the recognition of which cannot have escaped her. She was always troubled by any act of betrayal, and her deliberate or accidental betrayal of her brother and his suffering as a consequence must have added considerably to her sense of horror at the entire incident. That it did so is confirmed by the fact that, after the story was published, her brother reminded her of what really happened and she was furious and unbelieving.

The rabbit incident is powerful enough to stand alone as a complete story, but Porter adds another dimension by placing it in the context of Miranda's whole life and showing that the effects of this small event are neither trivial nor transient and that the past is not easily sloughed off. She tells of Miranda walking years later through the marketplace of a strange city in a strange country when a Mexican Indian vendor shows her a tray of dyed-sugar sweets. Suddenly the sights and sounds converge to bring back to her mind, from where it has long lain buried, the memory of her brother and the rabbit. The memory horrifies her and the horror reinforces the frightening nature of the incident and shows the capacity of past experiences to lie dormant and make a sudden unexpected ambush.

The story is one of Porter's most popular ones, frequently anthologized and endlessly explicated. Students of her work have commented on the grave image which links the episodes and underscores the connection between life and love and death. They have continued to explore the suggestions of such objects as the coffin screw shaped like the dove of Venus (symbol of earthly love) and the womb-grave of the dead rabbit. While their efforts have been useful, such exegesis stops short of explaining the impact of the story, showing what even Edmund Wilson admitted—that the task of uncovering the source of power in Porter's stories is a baffling one.[20] But when the story is seen against the events of her life it becomes apparent that the power derives from the compression of so much intensely felt experience. The experiences were not only compressed but their meaning contemplated over a long period of time, from their happening in 1902 to the time the story appeared in 1934. Porter described something of this process in a letter to Josephine Herbst:

I believe we exist on half a dozen planes in at least six dimensions and inhabit all periods of time at once, by way of memory, racial experience, dreams that are another channel of memory, fantasy that is also reality, and I believe that a first rate work of art somehow succeeds in pulling all these things together and reconciling them. When we deliberately ignore too much we make a fatal mistake.[21]

The most significant change that Porter made in her reshaping process was the improvement of her family's social and material status. Her fictional family lives in reduced circumstances but they are the kind that might be described as "genteel poverty." Although there is little money and the family homes are somewhat dilapidated, they are, nevertheless, large, ample, impressive, and maintained by the faithful family retainers, former slaves.

In the fiction, the life of Miranda Gay revolves around three spacious family homes:

The summer house was in a small town a few miles from the farm, a compromise between the rigorously ordered house in the city and the sprawling old farmhouse which grandmother had built with such pride and pain. It had, she often said, none of the advantages of either country or city, and all the discomforts of both. But the children loved it.[22]

The farm is described as having great secretaries full of books, sets of Dickens, Scott, Pope, Milton, Dante, and Shakespeare, and Dr. Johnson's Dictionary.[23] Outside are extensive orchards and fields with cabins housing a colony of former slaves and servants. The town house is equally ample and also surrounded by gardens. From a vantage spot in the side garden the women of the family can supervise the household:

In the summer the women sat under the mingled trees of the side garden, which commanded a view of the east wing, the front and back porches, a good part of the front garden and a corner of the small fig grove. Their choice of this location was a part of their domestic strategy. Very little escaped them: a glance now and then would serve to keep them fairly well informed as to what was going on in the whole place.[24]

These houses, which became the homes she described in her biographical record, were transformations of the three Porter homes.

These were the little house in Kyle where the family lived during the school year and also a house on a strip of land in the country which the grandmother had retained when she sold her farm. Visitors recall it as a bleak, treeless, undesirable place with a small one-story shack.[25] Porter herself described the country house as a "back-country shed of a house surrounded by a pretty garden."[26] One feature of the farm was that it adjoined the grandmother's original land, which was now owned by a family of former sharecroppers whose fortunes had risen as the Porters' declined.[27] It was a further mortification to Porter that these people, who in her grandmother's time had been inferiors on the social scale, were now in a position to make the Porters the object of pity and charity.

There were no Negro servants attached to the household in Porter's childhood, but one former servant sometimes visited. She was Aunt Jane, who had been a wedding present to Aunt Cat and had remained for years as wet nurse to her children and cook for the family. During Porter's childhood she lived in San Marcos and sometimes dropped by to chat with Aunt Cat. In a letter to her sister Gay Porter recalled these occasions:

> Aunt Jane would say as she came in "yassuh, I'se jes gotta see my chillen now and then" and would go to the kitchen and delight our souls with some good cooking for several days. But Dad would mutter under his red moustache "another ham and side of bacon for Jane to carry off to those black bastards," referring, of course, to Jane's numerous off-spring and the off-spring of the off-spring.[28]

It was Aunt Jane on whom Aunt Nannie Gay of the fiction was based.

One unhappy experience of these years was turned into the short novel "Noon Wine," which many of Porter's admirers consider her strongest work, and in which Lady Bird Johnson saw the tragic impact of the great Greek myths in a place "where the outcome was even bleaker and less hopeful."[29] At one time Harrison Porter decided to relocate the family and needed somewhere to leave his younger daughters. Since travel was expensive, he took only Gay along to help him. Harrison Porter had two cousins, Ada Skaggs Bentley and Ellen Skaggs Thompson, both of whom lived on farms in the area. Ada was so willing to accommodate homeless children that her house was often called "the orphan's home." He might have left the girls with her, but he was already in her debt for a loan, and demurred for that reason. He left them instead with her sister Ellen.[30]

Ellen lived on a small farm near the former Porter holdings just outside Buda. Her family consisted of her husband, Gene, her two sons, Clay and Herbert, a black cook called Cindy, and a hired man called Mr. Helton. The farm itself was a combination chicken, dairy, and cotton farm from which the eggs and butter were sold to the Deaf Institute just south of Austin. The house was small and company meant that somebody, perhaps the visitors, had to sleep on pallets perhaps in the combination dining room–kitchen. For entertainment there was a phonograph, and a stereograph with pictures to look at. The most pleasant part of the place was the yard, which was full of roses, asters, jasmine, and mulberry and fig trees.[31]

Ellen Thompson was an invalid during these years, and while the nature of her illness was not known, members of the family remember that after the death of her husband she was able to work hard in the fields. Gene Thompson himself was an easygoing and even-tempered man whose teasing sometimes annoyed his nieces. One recalled his joke that if her mouth got any larger her ears would have to be set back.[32]

It is easy to see that Porter would find much to displease her at the Thompson place. The cramped conditions must have been annoying and she can have had little patience with Eugene Thompson if he teased her as he did the others. But the stay there was disturbing for another reason—it caused her to reassess the quality of her own family and the atmosphere of her family life, for not only did the farm closely resemble the Porter farm but Mr. and Mrs. Thompson closely resembled her own parents.

No one, of course, could have described Harrison Porter as even-tempered and jocular, but he did have exactly the same kind of pride which Porter in the story attributed to Mr. Thompson. Pictures of Harrison Porter in profile show him, like Mr. Thompson, holding his neck so straight that his features are aligned with his Adam's apple. He chewed tobacco all his life,[33] even when he smoked a pipe at the same time, and his disinclination for work might well have been described in the words used for Mr. Thompson:

All his carefully limited fields of activity were related somehow to Mr. Thompson's feeling for the appearance of things, his own appearance in the sight of God and man. "It don't *look* right," was his final reason for not doing anything he did not wish to do.

It was his dignity and his reputation that he cared about, and there were only a few kinds of work manly enough for Mr. Thompson to undertake with his own hands. Mrs. Thompson, to whom so many forms of work would have been becoming, had simply gone down on him early.[34]

Mrs. Thompson is not unlike Alice Porter, a gently reared girl, well educated enough to teach school but physically delicate. While the general disorder of her circumstances for the most part drags her down and defeats her, she can, when the occasion presents itself, rise to it. When she has a hired man she knows how to address him with exactly the right amount of condescension, complimenting him on a job well done, on playing a pretty tune, and inquiring about his preferences in food:

> "They'll be needing something to eat," said Mrs. Thompson in a vague friendly way, "pretty soon. Now I wonder what I ought to be thinking about for supper? Now what do you like to eat, Mr. Helton? We always have plenty of good butter and milk and cream, that's a blessing. Mr. Thompson says we ought to sell all of it, but I say my family comes first. . . . We usually have cornbread except on Sundays," she told him, "I suppose in your part of the country you don't get much good cornbread."[35]

Her newly acquired manner even carries over to her husband, and she addresses him in much the same way when he returns from the saloon, which she delicately calls "the hotel."

> "You smell like a toper, Mr. Thompson," she said with perfect dignity. "I wish you'd get one of the little boys to bring me in an extra load of firewood. I'm thinking about baking a batch of cookies tomorrow."[36]

In comparison, Mr. Thompson is rough and noisy in his speech and clearly not of the same social standing as his wife. (It must be remembered that Ellen Thompson's mother was a Skaggs and she was not, therefore, entirely one of those described by Porter as the "Plain People.")

Critics have responded in various ways to the depiction of the Thompson family. Mark Schorer took the portrayal of the plain people to be a rare departure from the description of Porter's own aristocratic milieu, and he praised it as a sign of her versatility: "Let us observe . . . Miss Porter's remarkable skill in moving into a kind of life that was not hers and into a point of view that was completely alien to her own, to Miranda's."[37] Many have seen the portrait as a harsh exposure of ignorant, dangerous people. Among these were the Thompsons and the Skaggses, who thought the author should be sued.[38] Porter herself on the other hand regarded her characters with indulgence, saying of Mr. Thompson that he "was not an evil man, he was only a poor sinner doing his best according to his lights, lights somewhat dimmed by his natural aptitude for Pride and Sloth."[39] One critic, more attuned than most to the nuances of local speech, has seen the relationship between the Thompsons as a gentle, teasing, affectionate one, the only portrayal of a happily married couple in the whole of Porter's fiction.[40]

In contrast to the diversity of opinions about the characters, critical opinion has been unanimous in its praise of the wealth of vivid detail in which the Thompson farm is described, and there has been speculation on how Porter achieved such remarkable clarity. In answer to such speculations she set herself the task of trying to separate the various strands of her experience which made up the story, and the result was a fine essay, "Noon Wine: The Sources." It was this task which she described as being "as gruesome and painful as tapping the spinal fluid."[41]

The events which made up the plot presented no difficulty. She took these from an incident or series of incidents which happened in the community and which were so sinister that they remained in the memory of local residents for a long time. One incident was a murder and the other was of a murderer touring the neighborhood with his wife, begging his neighbors to believe in his innocence.[42]

It was when she tried to explain the setting and the characters and her own intimate knowledge of them that Porter became embarrassed. At this point she embarked on a series of elaborate digressions in which she described the beauty of the countryside, Miss Cora Posey's quaint feeling that people who stayed in hotels had "lost their raising," and other charming anecdotes.[43] All these allowed her to circle her subject and skirt the edges in order to avoid making the one simple statement that would have explained everything: "This was my place and these were my people." The only person to whom she could admit their closeness was her sister Gay, who knew the Thompsons. She wrote to her at the time she wrote the essay:

> The only thing in that piece that is not fact as I remember it, or fiction as I explain it to the reader, is the name of Gene Thompson. I kept the Thompson name in the story but not the Christian name. Thought the descendants might see it. But I call this kind of concealment just tact, not fibbing.[44]

In the essay she twice disclaims all kinship with the Thompsons:

> Let me give you a glimpse of Mr. and Mrs. Thompson, not as they were in their lives, for I never knew them, but as they have become in my story. . . .
>   The woman I have called Mrs. Thompson—I never knew her name . . .[45]

Her circumlocutions had at least one virtue. As always when she was creating a fantasy world, she wrote her finest lyrical prose and produced an essay which has become a favorite anthology piece, especially in textbooks such as Cleanth Brooks and Robert Penn Warren's *Understanding Fiction,* which tries to show how fiction is written.

That Porter wrote the story at all reflects her desire to recreate her familial background, and that she chose from all her stories to probe the sources of this one shows her need to understand her relationship to her early environment. The fact that she came so close and yet could still not acknowledge her relationship to her own place and her own people suggests her fatal ambivalence on the subject. She could not identify with her family and yet she craved a sense of identity. She was alienated in the most basic sense and spent years of her life in a vain quest for a place and people. In the end, she came to suspect that the place and people could exist only in her fantasies and in her fiction. This conclusion was expressed in her favorite Chinese proverb, one which, for a short time, she used as the title of her novel: "The land that is nowhere, that is the true home."

During these years which yielded so richly to her art, one more experience contributed a greal deal, not in providing the substance of fiction but in preparing her to be an artist. At this time she acquired her only useful formal academic training. It was brief in duration, but the choice of institution could not have been more fortunate and it says much for Porter's initiative that she went there at her own behest.

Hardship had sharpened her determination to succeed in the world, and she spent more time than ever trying to decide what she "wanted to be." She seems to have been the only member of the family who had plans for any kind of future. Gay had a beau and was vaguely satisfied with life. Paul thought he would join the navy as soon as he was old enough, and Mary Alice was still a child who enjoyed romping about the farm.[46] After much thought and many discussions with Erna Schlemmer, Porter decided that the stage rather than the convent was to be her destiny, and she begged her father to allow her to go to San Antonio and train as an actress.[47] The one advantage of his own fecklessness was that, while he did little to help his children, he did little to oppose them either. Farming the strip of land that remained from Aunt Cat's original property was not very profitable, he didn't much like Kyle, and he saw no reason why they should not move fifty miles to San Antonio, the Bexar County seat, especially since someone in the family owned a house there which they could rent. His only stipulation was that, if Callie went to train as an actress, Gay should go along with her as a kind of chaperone. It was arranged, therefore, that when Gay graduated from the Kyle school, the family should move to San Antonio.

The Kyle house was sold for only $10, a sum which suggests that part of the proceeds was used to discharge a debt or pay a mortgage.[48] There was little money left over for day-to-day expenses and Harrison Porter solved the problem of his immediate expenses by borrowing $200 from Ada Bentley, who willingly gave him the money and did not complain even when the loan was never repaid.[49]

Porter was eager to get to the city, as she had begun to think that country life was "tacky" and to long for electric lights,[50] paved sidewalks, and theaters and shows. Possibly her only regret at leaving Kyle was that she had to part from Erna Schlemmer. In the memory book Erna had received for her twelfth birthday she wrote this standard memory-book verse:

> Dear Fairy,
> When the Golden Sun is setting
> O'er the Western Sea
> When of others you are thinking
> Will you sometimes think of me?
> Very lovingly
> Witch (Callie Porter).[51]

Even if Callie had not moved away the two would have been separated at this time, for Erna's father was appointed soon afterward to the Consular Service in Mannheim, Germany. For the next two years the family lived in Wiesbaden and Heidelberg and Erna attended a boarding school in Wiesbaden, where she learned French, English, German, and also dancing from a former prima ballerina in the Kaiser's theater.[52]

Erna's new home probably seemed no more foreign to her than San Antonio seemed to Callie, because the strongest impression there was its Mexican atmosphere. Later Porter traced her love of Mexico and her familiarity with it to the early days in San Antonio, when it was full of political exiles from Mexico.[53] She thought the Mexican quarter itself was a slum and described the city as a shabby Spanish town full of muddy streets and plaster houses with red-tiled roofs. The young girls could not walk alone downtown because there were at least three saloons, real sties, to every block. There was a rough red-light district and also a fashionable area around San Pedro Avenue.[54] The Alamo was a ruin which anyone could have bought (in 1903 Texas patriot Clara Driskoll pledged her fortune to buy a thirty-day option on it), and Porter remembered it as a place for picnicking.

The house the family rented was near Woodlawn Lake. It was an 1880-style house which retained vestiges of its former elegance—gilded woodwork and moldings, fancy wallpaper, imitation Spanish leather in the dining room, and beaded curtains.[55] All the same, the family did not live well, and Porter remembered their cook as a horribly dirty old woman.[56] Before long they could not afford to keep the house or rent another and moved into a small apartment. Cora Posey, visiting them from Indian Creek, described them as living "a somewhat Bohemian life."[57] Since she habitually described the family in the best possible terms, her guardedness in this instance suggests that she was a little shocked at the disorder in which they lived. Such a conclusion is supported by the many expressions of disgust which Porter used over the years for the depths to which her father let them sink after the grandmother's death.

Harrison Porter's wisest move at this time was to use some of the money borrowed from his cousin to buy one year in a good school for the children. Aunt Cat would have turned in her grave at the thought of Callie's becoming an actress, but she might well have approved the choice of the place at which she was to learn her trade.

The Thomas School, a small private establishment near Woodlawn Lake, had been founded a year or so earlier by Professor Asa

Thomas, who had been the first graduate and later principal of Alice Porter's old school, Coronal Institute. He must have known the girls' mother, and perhaps this fact rather than the school's proximity to their house influenced their choice. Professor Thomas in his years at Coronal Institute had built up a fine reputation as a teacher and an administrator. He had, however, a strong personal philosophy of education and wished eventually to have a school of his own. For this purpose he moved to San Antonio with his second wife, a teacher of languages and bookkeeping, and purchased a three-story brick building on the outskirts of the city. The Thomas School was advertised as Christian and nonsectarian, but like Coronal Institute it had a strong Methodist flavor. Many of the students were boarders but local girls could ride the trolley car to school. The Porters as day girls were able to avoid the $400-a-year boarding fees. Nevertheless they had a tuition fee of $30 and fees for extras such as music and dancing lessons, which somehow they managed to afford.[58] The expensive uniforms could be purchased in San Antonio for $35 and these consisted of navy blue pleated skirts, white blouses with sailor collars, and mortar board hats which, Porter thought, made them look like little doctors of philosophy.[59]

When Porter asked one of the teachers why they wore uniforms she was told that the purpose was to prevent any girl from being better dressed than the others. The answer did not satisfy her, since she said by their modest standards everybody knew whose family had money and whose had not and it was abundantly clear the Porters were poor.[60] Once again she was in a situation calculated to make her feel different and inferior, and it is little wonder that she erased the school experience from her memory.

Not surprisingly, she was a poor student. First of all, though the Thomas School was not excessively strict by the standards of the time, it was stricter than the Kyle school and clearly a free spirit like Porter was uncomfortably confined by all the rules. She said that her books were taken away when it was discovered that she did not know her multiplication tables and that her grades in every subject except English were Ds and she never won any of the medals which were handed around liberally as rewards for hard work.[61]

This continued to be a time of inner turmoil, for the geographical move from the area in which the family had lived for two generations made her feel deracinated and increased her sense of the family's disintegration. She brooded constantly on the subject, and because her childhood had been nourished by her grandmother's stories of the family's better times, her present rootlessness and loss of family connections mortified her. Professor Thomas, whom the students affectionately called "Fessor,"[62] took it upon himself to instruct them in religion and Bible history. His favorite passages were Matthew 7:12 and John 3:16, and he said there was enough in these verses to carry any student through this life and land her in the better world.[63] Porter was struck by another passage: "Do men gather grapes of thorns, or figs of thistles? Even so every good tree bringeth forth good fruit; but a corrupt tree bringeth forth evil fruit."[64]

For her this had a meaning quite separate from its religious connotation. She said that when she heard that passage a deep shudder went all through her, as if all the dust of the dead quivered and communicated with her flesh. She felt terror because she did not want her family to die and disappear and she felt that she belonged to a generation that had been left stripped and homeless. She thought that there had been times in the past when her family had split apart (when they left Europe and then again after the war) and she hoped that they would strike roots and come together again and regroup as they had before. She made a point of seeking out her San Antonio relatives, especially the descendants of her grandmother's sister Eliza. These were the Myers and the Cahills, whom she encouraged to tell stories of the family's past as her grandmother had done.[65] In her fiction she later celebrated the solidarity of the family, and the biblical image of the fig tree is a recurring one as well as a title in her family chronicles.

Added to all these problems was a new one. The craving for love which had never been satisfied in her childhood was now intensified by her own sexual development and different social situation. She now met a number of boys, quite different from the country boys she had known in Kyle and on the farm, and she herself, plump and strikingly pretty, with long black hair, was very attractive to them. She described herself at the time as "vain, self-conscious and mad for love." She said that she was boy crazy but afraid of boys and sex because she had been taught to be.[66]

It was a gauge of Professor Thomas' common sense that he provided opportunities for the girls to meet in carefully controlled circumstances with young men of suitable backgrounds. For this purpose dances and parties were arranged with the boys from the nearby military academy, the Peacock School, which unlike the Thomas School has continued to the present time. The girls drew their partners' names out of a hat and then were allowed to promenade on a well-lit balcony and have refreshments. There was music and dancing and party games.[67]

In preparation for these occasions the girls were given detailed instruction. Porter remembered being trained in formal good manners, including deep curtsies. She also practiced the art of backing out of a room gracefully while managing a long train, by having a length of old curtain attached to her belt. She used these memories in *Ship of Fools* when she described Mrs. Treadwell dancing with one of the young officers:

> "If you are uncertain whether you are at the proper distance," her dancing teacher told her earnestly, "mentally raise your right arm crooked at the elbow, straight out from your shoulder, and if it barely touches your partner's chest, rest assured you are entirely correct. If your partner seems to be encroaching, simply hold yourself away firmly but gracefully without losing step until he takes the hint. And remember this, if he is a gentleman, he *will* take the hint. If he does not, then you will not dance with him again. . . . "
> This voice from the pre-Flood era of her youth so delighted her, its ghostly sound drifting through endless spaces of forgetfulness, she turned upon her partner a dazed tender smile. . . .[68]

In spite of the vigilance of the chaperones, the students from both schools attended the Travis Park Methodist Church and invariably a group of boys would be waiting under the elms to smile as the girls boarded their street car back to the school. The more daring ones passed notes, especially at the Empire Theater on Saturdays, where the Peacock boys sat in the row behind the Thomas School girls.

As might be expected, Porter was among the more daring, and as a day girl she had more freedom than the boarders. Ten years later, in the spring of 1914, a letter that earned her a dollar from the *Chicago Tribune* gave a version of one of the sequels to the Peacock School dances:

How Did He Propose?

Brother Spoiled a Romance.

Dear Miss Blake: We were coming home from a dance on a brilliant moonlight night, picking our way very carefully along a narrow trail around a little lake near my home. He was a shy lad and I was a shy girl, so conversation languished until he mustered up enough courage to slip an arm around my waist and stammer some incoherent thing about loving me, asking me to marry him as soon as he graduated in June etc., when, without warning, a heavy hand seized him by the back of the collar and tossed him into the lake, which was pretty deep there.

I turned with a squeal of fright to behold my very big and very proper brother, bristling with rage at what he termed the "impertinence" of any man who would dare embrace me.

"Proposal!" snorted brother, "you just wait until you're out of school before you think of proposals. Come right along home with me this minute." And he marched me away forthwith, leaving my discomfited gallant to flounder out of his predicament as well as he might. "He'll never, never come back," I wept loudly to my unsympathetic relative. And for a fact, he did not!

KAP

In spite of distractions, disturbances, and miseries, Porter learned a great deal at Professor Thomas' school. She did manage, as she had planned, to study drama, and her teacher—she said they were always taught by people who were supposed to have drunk at the fountainhead[69]—was an ancient actress who was impressed enough with Porter's ability to suggest that she gain experience by acting with the summer stock company which formed in Electric Park in the summer. At the end of her year at the school Porter acted with them for six weeks and enjoyed the experience.[70]

She also prepared for her vocation by taking singing lessons, and the musical education offered by the school formed the basis of her lifelong interest in music. To the end of her life she could quote her own treatment of an Italian song she learned while studying voice when she was fourteen:

> O dry those tears, and calm those fears,
> Love will be faithful tomorrow!
> Oh sing your song the whole day long
> Life was not meant for sorrow—
> Forget your pain, and love again—
> Love will be merry tomorrow.[71]

Many of the students who attended the Thomas School were ranch girls, and Professor Thomas knew that most of them, for financial and other reasons, would remain for only a year before returning to isolated rural homes. Since this one year at the school would be for many, as it was for Porter, their only academic training and perhaps their only exposure to cultural experiences, he tried to make it as rich and full as possible. The result was not always happy, as many a ranch girl returned to the farm to be ever afterward restive, her head turned by memories of concerts, theaters, poetry, and music for which there was little opportunity in her life. Porter, however, relished everything. She loved the Tuesday morning concerts given by the Ladies Musical Club of San Antonio which the girls attended. And in her last years she described them to a reporter: "Violas, cellos, second violin, every kind of fiddle there was those ladies played. Almost half of them played and half sang. Oh how I loved those Tuesday musicals."[72]

More than the amateur performances she loved seeing the professional ones. Of these there were a great many, for every actor, actress, singer, pianist, and violinist of note stopped in San Antonio on national and international tours. Porter was fascinated by the big stars with their special trains or at least their own private cars, gaily decorated and embellished with their names, and the Thomas School girls could go to any of the concerts for twenty-five cents.

In later years Porter sometimes complained about the strangely ornamental education she had been given, saying that when she went into the world, supposedly grown up, she was totally unequipped and as ignorant of the world as it was possible to be. She knew nothing of practical matters or domestic jobs and could not cook or sew, but she had been trained in singing, elocution and acting.[73] It was, however, the one year of training at the Thomas School in nonpractical subjects that contributed most to her life's work. She often boasted about her early knowledge of Shakespeare. She was probably exaggerating, but former students of the school have testified that any student who stayed there for a year learned by heart long passages from Shakespeare. Professor Thomas stressed rote learning and the students filled notebook after notebook with Shakespeare's sonnets and speeches from the plays. While he discouraged "light reading," he did encourage the girls to read widely, and the school library was well stocked with the classics.

Porter appreciated her early introduction to literary classics and thought her education superior to that of later generations. She told her nephew when he was in college, "I agree with your teacher that you should read Milton and Keats now, which seems strange to me at your age, because I was mumbling around in them when I was ten years old, and had learned all of Shakespeare's sonnets by heart when I was twelve."[74]

She was habitually inaccurate about dates and it is probable that the reading experiences she mentioned took place at the Thomas School rather than the one at Kyle. But she never gave Professor Thomas or his school any credit for her education, and if she ever mentioned the school it was with irritation that her presence there should be known. She said it was odd "that someone with a wish for privacy should come to this point where there is a rumor that I once went to school in a thoroughly dinky girls school by a lake in the deep suburbs in an unknown area that I was completely unconscious of and which had no definite place in my life."[75]

The long-range benefits of the Thomas School were great for both girls. They used their training for teaching jobs, and Gay, later in her life, supported herself and her children by doing bookkeeping and other office work. The immediate benefits, however, were less apparent and it must have seemed that the expense of the education was scarcely justified. Perhaps because she was too young and inexperienced, Porter was not able to realize her ambition to find work as an actress and had to look elsewhere. While Paul was in the navy and Mary Alice was in school elsewhere, the father and the two older girls remained together for a time, and it fell to the girls to find some way of supporting the family.

FOUR

That Preposterous First Marriage

In view of her poverty, homelessness, and lack of family life and love, it was perhaps inevitable that Porter should have been tempted to escape as soon as possible into the imagined security of marriage. Her beauty and vivacity made it easy for her to do so. At fifteen, when she met her first husband, she had reached her full growth of five feet two and was at the height of her youthful beauty. The year before, a San Antonio photographer had used her as a model for a photographic competition. His entry, which won a prize, shows Porter plumper than in childhood, kittenish and winsome, with thick curly black hair falling over her shoulders.

Unfortunately, the youth and charm that made it easy for her to find a husband quickly also ensured that her choice was a hasty and unwise one. Years later she told her sister that she did not think often of her first marriage because she could not afford to.[1] In contrast to the extensive use she made of her painful adolescence, she made little reference in her fiction to her first marriage and suppressed it as much as possible from the biographical record. She told one interviewer who asked about it, "I have no *hidden* marriages, they just sort of slip my mind."[2] She refused to mention the man's name to friends and interviewers and she reduced the length of the marriage to a few years. Actually it lasted nine years, seven of which she spent living with her husband, and was far longer than any subsequent marriages. Even before it ended she had begun to substitute for the facts other versions which seemed more appropriate to her.

She later told Erna Schlemmer that she had joined a traveling theater company in San Antonio and gone with it to New Orleans, where she had become a star. She said that she was playing the role of Lydia in *Ben Hur* when a member of the audience fell in love with her and persuaded her to marry him.[3] She told another friend that she and her sisters had been in a San Antonio convent and she had slipped away from the convent and married, dressed in a white crêpe de chine dress the three sisters had combined allowances to buy.[4] More often she annexed to her personal history a chapter from the more colorful history of her aunt, Ione Funchess Porter. She said that she had eloped from a New Orleans convent to marry a rich man, much older than herself, "who had shut her up."[5]

The actual circumstances of what she called "that preposterous first marriage"[6] were fairly humdrum, its preposterousness lying more in its ordinariness than in anything sensational, and the events leading to the marriage took place not in Spanish San Antonio or French New Orleans but in the more ordinary Texas towns of Lufkin and Victoria.

Victoria, in fact, for all its nineteen saloons, unpaved streets, and superficial resemblance to other small Texas towns, had a colorful history which gave it a distinctive flavor of its own. It was the center of a rich cotton-growing and ranching area and some of the homes were palatial. There was an opera house with a seating capacity of 500; the city streets were well lighted and regularly graded and graveled, and the hitching posts around the square were kept in good repair; there were spouts on the downtown buildings so that passersby were not sprayed with rain water. The residential streets were pleasant, tree-shaded thoroughfares with well-proportioned white frame houses.[7]

The place was already familiar to Harrison Porter from his railroad building days before his marriage, for then it had been the headquarters of Joseph Telfener, the dynamic Italian count who had engineered the building of the New York–to–Mexico City railroad. When his girls left school, perhaps it occurred to him that it might be an easy move, just 116 miles from San Antonio and a convenient place for them to earn a living. The father himself was not able to find employment befitting his dignity, but being supported by his children then or later did not hurt his pride and seemed quite satisfactory to him. He found accommodation in a rooming house on Juan Linn Street and rented a room nearby in which the girls could offer lessons in the arts they had learned at the Thomas School. An advertisement appeared regularly in the fall of 1905 in the *Victoria Advocate:* "Misses Porter, studio of music, physical culture and dramatic reading, 107 Santa Rosa Street 27."

For her work the younger of the two Misses Porter wore a gray dress with long full sleeves, cut in an Empire line and shirred from the waist, but so short that it caused something of a scandal among the respectable ladies of the community. Miss Pridham, who owned the rooming house, was a daughter of a former mayor of the city and very respectable, but she was also broad-minded and she approved of the younger Miss Porter, who now called herself Katherine Russell and liked to be called "K.R." K.R. often obliged the Pridhams and their other guests by entertaining them with songs and dances.[8]

Besides its regular residents, the Pridham house had a changing flow of guests from the ranching families of the surrounding area who stayed there when they came into town for business and pleasure. Among these were the members of the Koontz family, who often drove the fifteen miles by horse and buggy from their ranch in Inez. It was on a visit to the dentist that nine-year-old Mildred Koontz first saw Katherine Porter. She never forgot seeing her come downstairs in the short gray dress on her way to work in the rented room on Santa Rosa Street. Mildred thought she had never seen anyone so tiny and "cute." The other Koontzes found K.R. equally delightful, and when she expressed an interest in their farm she was immediately invited to visit. As it happened, another resident of the rooming house was a close friend of Mrs. Koontz and she and K.R. went out to Inez together for the weekend.

The Koontz place was a large ranch which had been founded in 1890 by Mildred's father, Henry Clay Koontz. He was born in Matagorda and was of Swiss descent. Porter seems to have overlooked this fact, for when she scoffed at Texas Germans she included the Koontzes in her scorn. Orphaned at an early age and left to fend for himself, Henry Koontz had developed strong habits of thrift and industry. He built up a successful mercantile business on the Arenoza Creek and later was postmaster at both Arenoza and Inez. When he founded the ranch it was on an extensive scale, with lands extending over both communities and into Victoria itself. In spite of its great wealth, the family's life was unpretentious, centering upon home and church. They were devout Catholics and the church in Inez relied upon their support. For all their plain way of life, it cannot have escaped Porter's sharp eyes that the family was very prosperous indeed. Years later she would sneer at German meals as characterized by abundance rather than elegance, but at this time the necessities of life had not come so easily that she was disposed to criticize the Koontzes' copious meals or their frank enjoyment of them. The family's life seemed very warm and comfortable.

There were eight Koontz children, most of them grown and away from home. When Porter was there, the twenty-year-old son was visiting from Louisiana, where he was working as a clerk for the Southern Pacific Railway Company. John Henry was a serious, bespectacled young man of medium height (five feet ten). He had finished his education with a year at St. Edward's School in Austin and, like all the children of H. C. Koontz, was industrious, prudent in financial matters, and steady. No doubt his steady qualities were initially attractive to the more temperamental Katherine and a reassuring contrast to her father. Witnesses described their meeting as "love at first sight."

Since the Porters had few possessions, they could move easily, and in 1906 the advertisement for the music studio no longer appeared in the *Victoria Advocate*. The father and two daughters moved east to Lufkin, near the Louisiana border, and meetings between Katherine and John continued, made easier by the move. The courtship was brief; soon after their first meeting and just a month after Katherine's sixteenth birthday they were married. The ceremony was a civil one, but in keeping with the Porters' faith it was performed by Ira Bryce, a Methodist minister. It was a double wedding, for at the same time Gay Porter married T. H. Holloway.[9]

After the wedding, Katherine and John returned to the Koontz ranch on a honeymoon visit and were warmly received in spite of various misgivings. Mildred Koontz, whose admiration for Katherine was boundless, was nevertheless put off by seeing her "loving up John something terrible." The Koontzes, for all their close family affection, were not demonstrative people, and besides that, John was Mildred's favorite brother and she was frankly jealous. On one occasion when Katherine was fondling her new husband Mildred turned in annoyance and embarrassment to leave the room, only to be told by her sister-in-law, "This is the way it's gonna be from now on all our whole lives, so you'd better get used to it." When the young couple left for Louisiana, the *Victoria Advocate* for June 27, 1906, carried the following item in its "Inez News":

John Koontz, son of our postmaster, H. C. Koontz, at present with the S.P. Ry at Lafayette, La., paid his parents a visit
accompanied by his bride who was formerly Miss Porter of
Lufkin, Texas. They left yesterday for their home. We wish
the young couple all the happiness in this life.

John's parents were not pleased by the marriage, and Porter,
sensing their disapproval, believed that they considered her "a little
gold-digger." The family, however, thought with some justification
that the marriage was undesirable because both partners were too
immature and inexperienced to embark on a lasting relationship. In
the event, the unsuitability of the match became apparent much earlier
than even the most skeptical observers might have predicted.

Fifty years later, Porter, an inveterate observer of anniversaries,
made some of her rare commentaries on her first marriage. She told
her sister Gay that she had passed the fiftieth anniversary a whole lot
better than she did the first. On another occasion she said that "that
filthy J.H." should have been killed for what he did to her and complained that her family just stood by and let it happen.[10] To her
nephew she wrote this account:

Today—this is just for you—is the fiftieth anniversary of
that fatal day, the first serious disaster of our lives, when
Gay and I were married in a double wedding and which of
the two men were the most ignobly inadequate in mind, or
feeling to anything in human life, it would be hard to say. I
can only say in my own defense that I saw through my
monster in a very short time, and I did manage to shake him
off before he had broken my life really to bits, as he wanted.
. . . If we had had a father to care for us, and protect us a
little, we would never have taken that dreadful step. But we
were really quite desperate, and of course, things came out
as they do when you take any step in desperation.[11]

She had a lifelong habit of describing her former husbands and
lovers in very severe terms and often used the word "monster" for
them. In the case of John Koontz the divorce petition which was filed
at the end of the marriage, countersigned by Koontz himself, lends
some weight to her accusations:

Plaintiff says that after their said marriage and while they
were residing at Houston, Harris County, Texas, that defen-

dant threw plaintiff down a stair way of their home, breaking her right ankle and severely wrenching and lacerating
her right knee; that thereafter in the month of July, 1909,
while still residing in the City of Houston, that defendant
struck plaintiff in the temple with a clothes brush, knocking
her down and rendering her unconscious for a space of three
hours; that thereafter in May, 1912, while plaintiff and defendant were residing in Corpus Christi, Nueces County,
Texas, defendant struck plaintiff with his fist, causing her
great physical pain:

That on many occasions during their married life defendant while in a state of extreme intoxication used to and
concerning plaintiff in the presence of many people vile and
opprobrious epithets subjecting her to disgrace and humiliation.

Plaintiff further says that in addition to all of the matters
hereinbefore complained of, defendant abandoned her and
lived in adultery with five different women at different periods of time between March, 1907, and February 25, 1913.
Plaintiff says that she knows the names and whereabouts of
each of said five women but asks permission of the Court to
be permitted to omit their names from this petition.[12]

On the other hand, allowance must be made for the fact that
some exaggeration may have been necessary to expedite the legal
proceedings, since divorce at that time would not have been granted
on slender grounds. And it must be mentioned in defense of John
Koontz that nothing in his subsequent career suggested violence or
excess. When he remarried he lived the rest of his life quietly as a
devoted husband and father. Even Porter in one interview said of
him: "There was nothing wrong with him—he just wasn't the man
for me, and I had no business bolting off with him. He was rather a
nice man—I know that now—but I didn't like him and that's no
foundation for a marriage."[13]

It seems quite likely that the two young people, both totally
unprepared for marriage, drawn together for the most unsubstantial
of reasons—physical attraction and, on Porter's side, a desperate need
for financial and emotional stability—found themselves swiftly disappointed and pushed each other into outrageous acts. Porter was
little more than a child and it is easy to imagine her annoying her
husband by coquetting with other men, taking from them the atten-

tion she so badly needed. Moreover, she had a fatal ambivalence, never to be resolved, in her attitude toward any husband. She craved the protectiveness and support that she never had from her father and at the same time she was disposed to be independent and dominant as her grandmother was. If her disinclination to be a domestic angel eventually allowed her to become an artist, it certainly disqualified her as a wife in her time and place.

In addition, there was a more profound area of discomfort. From the very beginning Porter's sexual development had been troubled. She had seen at very close quarters the relationship between childbirth and death. Later she had been thrown into an agony of self-doubt by the transfer of her father's admiration to her prettier younger sister. She had been raised by the puritanical Aunt Cat, and as she approached puberty she had suffered from the absence of anyone who could give her the slightest sexual instruction. (Gay was a little older but she was both too uninformed and too inhibited to give coherent information.) The marriage to John Koontz was one more step in this series of sexual misadventures which had undermined her confidence in herself as a woman.

Porter has said that she refused to consummate her first marriage. Since the marriage lasted for nine years and Koontz was a healthy young man who subsequently married and had a child, this seems improbable. It is likely that the marriage was consummated, whether she refused or not. Her description would seem to be a dramatization of the situation and perhaps a way of saying that she was unable to respond sexually. Her vocabulary at that time did not contain such words as "orgasm" and "frigidity"; nevertheless she must have had a keen awareness of her inability to find any pleasure in sex. Her sense of failure was aggravated furthermore by her discovery that she was not able to bear a child. She was not only frigid but barren. To understand the full weight of this disappointment, it is necessary to look at the marginal notes in her books. These show how closely linked her idea of femininity was with fertility. (After all, Aunt Cat had been remarkable for her fertility.) Whenever Porter saw references to penis envy, she was highly indignant. She noted that women were the childbearing sex, that they had wombs instead of penises, which were highly significant comments in view of her own childlessness.

It seems likely, then, that her first marriage reinforced her feelings of sexual confusion and her distaste for sex. It also prepared the way for a lifetime of painful relationships with men, most of them erratic and humiliating. Her strong words about Koontz, that he was criminal and should have been killed for what he did to her, should be read in this context. The divorce certificate too might be read in metaphorical terms as indicating that this first marriage was a brutalizing experience from which she never completely recovered.

Perhaps she drew indirectly on her memories of it when her character Mrs. Treadwell, in *Ship of Fools,* recalls her failed first marriage:

> Well, well, she said, drawing in her head, Life has been in fact quite disagreeable if not sordid in spots. If anybody called me a lady tramp I hope I should not have my feelings hurt. Nasty things have happened to me often and they were every one my own fault. I put myself in their way, not even knowing they were there at first. . . . Was I really ever married to a man so jealous he beat me until I bled at the nose? I don't believe it. I never knew a man like that—he isn't born yet. It's something I read about in a newspaper . . . but I still bleed at the nose if I am frightened enough at anything.[14]

If the nature of the abuse to which Porter was subjected is open to question, the immediate collapse of the relationship is not. It was a difficult, abrasive marriage and there was every reason why it should have been so, for, apart from their immaturity, the two partners were as temperamentally incompatible as it would be possible to be. John's skills were in business, bookkeeping, and mathematics, his goal to advance in the world of business. She despised commerce of any kind and was interested only in the arts. He was a careful manager who budgeted prudently and was saving money to buy a house. She loved pretty clothes and jewelry and was a reckless spender, given to shopping sprees, impulsive purchases, and spurts of generosity toward her family.

All the same, the idea of terminating the marriage was such an extreme move that neither partner considered it, and Porter, no doubt, thought herself permanently trapped in a degrading, restricting situation. She yearned for some kind of escape and her longings took on an artistic shape. She loved Lafayette, in the heart of the Cajun country, and she sought out native artists and tried to learn from them. Her lifelong interest in folk art began at this time, and ten years later when she was working as a journalist she described the artists of the area:

> The so-called Cajuns, a corruption of the word Acadians, in Louisiana, have weirdly attractive songs of their own, mostly bergerettes of musical value. These probably came by way of France or Spain in old days but have the negroid tang in them, and so might be termed American.
>
> The negro and Indian tunes are poignantly real, as are the songs of the cowboys. These last are always deeply emotional, filled with the melancholy of those who live in vast spaces. They are as primitive as the howl of a wolf, actually partaking of this quality of tone at times. The howl of a wolf is a magnificent thing. We have heard them run scales as true and even as a coloratura soprano could produce, thru a full two octaves.[15]

She still retained her love of the theater and took a great interest in the troupes which passed through the town. She may have found some way to become involved in their performances, because years later she could vividly recall the exasperation of a theatrical troupe stranded by rain in Lafayette on Christmas Day.[16] She also tried to organize another little school, and the following advertisement appeared for a short time in the local paper: "Mrs. J. H. Koontz. Teacher of Elocution, Physical Culture and English. Residence near F. O. Broussard's Grocery, Convent St."[17]

After two years there was a sudden change in the rhythm of the Koontzes' life, for in the fall of 1908 the Southern Pacific Railway laid off ten clerks and among these was John Koontz. He decided to go to Houston, a move which did not please Katherine, and there he found a job as a clerk in a firm of wholesale greengrocers. One advantage of the move was that they could easily take the train to Inez and spend weekends enjoying country life on the ranch, hunting and riding and walking.

They had been settled in Houston only a few months when the ranch itself underwent a sudden change through the unexpected death of the head of the family. Henry Koontz was a robust and energetic man, in his early sixties, who had never had an illness in his life. One winter night when he had a cold, a sudden storm blew up and he went out to look after his cattle. The cold turned to pneumonia and, before long, his life was in danger and his children were summoned from everywhere. John rushed home on the first train and Katherine followed on a later one. The event marked a temporary truce in the marriage, because even she, whom circumstances were quickly hardening, could not help sympathizing with someone grieving for the death of a loved one. She long remembered a moment of closeness when John held her in his arms and she realized, perhaps for the first time, that he was having "just as tough a time" as she was in the troubled marriage.[18] Later Henry Koontz died and was buried in the cemetery on the ranch. For Porter, it was one more in the series of bedside vigils, sudden deaths, and funerals in bleak country cemeteries, and perhaps this particular one was in her mind when she described the death scenes in "The Jilting of Granny Weatherall" and "Holiday."

Soon the Koontzes' life resumed its usual pattern, with John and Katherine coming to Inez on weekend visits. Katherine liked Mildred Koontz best of all and enjoyed the younger girl's admiration, feeling that she was fulfilling the same role in Mildred's life that Ione Funchess had in her own. She even gave Mildred an opal ring one Christmas, the same gift that Tante Ione had given Gay Porter years before. Apart from Mildred, she no longer cared for the other members of the family and often brought her own friends along for the weekend, until the senior Mrs. Koontz protested that she liked seeing John and K.R. there, but not large numbers of their friends.

The young Koontzes moved as frequently, if for different reasons, as the Porters had done, and in 1912 they took rooms with John's married sister and her husband and two children on Chenevert Street in Houston.[19] John was busy building a pleasant little house in the Woodland Heights area, and during the construction it was convenient to live with the Hasbrooks. The two families took all their meals together. Katherine quite liked Beatrice Hasbrook (the only member of the family who called her "Katherine" instead of "K.R."), but the proximity of so many members of John's family annoyed her. She resented particularly that she and John could be heard by everyone in the house when they engaged in their frequent noisy quarrels. The closeness of the families exacerbated the problems of the marriage because each developed a strong dislike of the other's family. John's family thought that Katherine was too generous to her sisters, for whom she often bought clothes, charging them to the account that John had set up for her. They began to think she was flighty and no longer troubled to keep silent in their disapproval of her. Beatrice Hasbrook was critical of Katherine's dressmaking endeavors and, when she examined the hurriedly run up but wonderful-looking dresses, said they were terrible on the inside. She also commented on the affected voice Katherine used when she answered the telephone. For her part, K.R. found the Koontzes limited and unimaginative in their outlook. "Oh, that narrow-minded family I stumbled into," she told a reporter years later.[20]

Another disappointment was her continued childlessness, a sorrow aggravated by seeing other members of the family producing fine babies. When her sister Gay in Dallas had a daughter in December 1912, Porter left immediately by train to see the baby, the first of that generation in the family and named Mary Alice for Porter's mother and younger sister. The new aunt was enchanted: "She was ten days old and had the most beautiful little shellrose pink face I ever saw, with tilted, enormous grey blue eyes, and little fluffyduck feather hair, and the longest blackest eyelashes you ever saw on a baby."[21] Porter sat by the crib for hours adoring the infant. She never tired of watching her, and once again her tendency to compensate for her own unsatisfactory circumstances by fantasizing came heavily into play. She dreamed about the baby's life and imagined that she, whom Mary Alice would call "Tante," would guide the child to a great future. She pretended to herself that she and not Gay was the mother, and when the time came for her to return home she could hardly bear to leave the baby.[22]

Beatrice Hasbrook had two pretty daughters, and Porter was very attached to the younger one, Mary Koontz, whom she called "Baby Koontzey." She loved to play mother, dressing Baby Koontzey and taking her out, proud of their good-looking appearance together and delighted when they were mistaken for mother and daughter. She even had her photograph taken in a decidedly maternal pose with the child but she disliked the result. She took the picture to the photographer and complained that it made her eyes look "starey." The photographer said that he could do nothing and that she actually did have eyes like that. The Koontz family agreed that she had wild, "starey" eyes and she was even more angry.

Since the marriage was troubled so deeply and variously from the very beginning, the wonder is not that it ended but that it should have lasted for nine years, seven of them spent living together. Practical considerations no doubt prevented an early flight. Divorce was an unthinkable step, and the more ordinary course of going back home was not possible, since Porter had no family home to return to.

The factor which precipitated the end of the marriage was that in 1912 Porter began to have a taste of freedom. Although John had built the little house, Inglenook, in Woodland Heights, he was now promoted to traveling salesman, a position which took him further afield. For a time he was assigned to travel out of Corpus Christi, and the two moved for a period of some months to the Tourist Hotel there. Although the place was a squalid apartment over a shoe store, her new surroundings had many attractions for Porter. She could make her way about very easily because the city had a modern mass transit system. She grew to love Corpus Christi for its beautiful situation at the foot of a bluff overlooking a bay with islands and legends of buried treasure, and she liked the exotic atmosphere which the Mexican population gave to the city.

Moreover, she soon discovered that she had an old friend nearby. She read in the paper of a thriving automobile agency established two months before. The owner was Glover Johns, the husband of her childhood friend Erna Schlemmer, and she lost no time seeking her out. Again Porter was reminded of her childlessness, for Erna was now the mother of an eighteen-month-old son, Glover Johns, Jr. And once more, as in childhood, Erna seemed effortlessly to possess all the ordinary ingredients for happiness which so eluded Porter—a harmonious family, a pleasant house and garden. Nevertheless, the friendship resumed as warmly as ever, and Callie (Erna could never manage to call her anything else) was a daily visitor at the Johns home. Since the Koontz apartment faced west it was unpleasantly hot, and she gladly took refuge at Erna's cool house on the beach. The two spent the summer sunbathing and swimming, both of them long remembering the porpoises which would appear suddenly beside them as they swam.[23] Porter incorporated her memory into *Ship of Fools,* giving it to Jenny Brown, who says:

> "I remember once I was swimming far out in the Bay of Corpus Christi, on a beautiful day, and I was coming towards land again, and a whole school of porpoises came straight at me, oh they looked like mountains rising and dipping in the waves, and I thought I might die of fright; but they just divided around me and went on, sweeping out to the Gulf of Mexico. And I was suddenly very happy and thought, 'Oh, this is the pleasantest thing that ever happened to me!' "[24]

Porter, however, was not simply idle at this time, for the pleasant surroundings and the solitude during her husband's absences stimulated her restless, ambitious nature. She had already tried to write poetry and one of her poems had been published in a trade journal to which John subscribed.[25] Now she tried to work on short stories, and she finished one, "The Opal Ring," in which she described the theft of a precious object.[26] She was not only writing; she was also, for the first time, reading modern literature. She was led to it by her discovery of a most unusual and interesting bookstore, the Corpus Christi Book and Stationery Company,[27] which she later described:

> I read Gertrude Stein's *Tender Buttons,* for sale at a little bookshop with a shoeshine stand outside; inside you could find magazines, books, newspapers in a half-a-dozen languages, avant-garde and radical and experimental; this in a Texas coast town of less than ten thousand population but very polyglot and full of world travelers.[28]

Not only did the solitude stimulate her creativity but it allowed her to reassess her marriage. Perhaps the best indication of her mood is in the story "Holiday," which is based on a visit she made with her sister at the time to a German farming family.[29] The first paragraph of the story conveys her emotions in the last part of her unsatisfactory marriage:

> At that time I was too young for some of the troubles I was having, and I had not yet learned what to do with them. It no longer can matter what kind of troubles they were, or what finally became of them. It seemed to me then that there was nothing to do but run away from them, though all my tradition, background, and training had taught me unanswerably that no one except a coward ever runs away from anything. What nonsense! They should have taught me the difference between courage and foolhardiness, instead of leaving me to find it out for myself. I learned finally that if I still had the sense I was born with, I would take off like a deer at the first warning of certain dangers.[30]

Once she faced the fact that her marriage was "trouble that did not belong to her" she hardened her resolve to run from it "like a deer." She confided her plan to Erna, who was thoroughly shocked. She was, however, tactful and sympathetic and suppressed her disapproval. Porter talked all summer long about her ambitions and plans, and when the two parted at the end of the summer in front of the automobile agency on the corner of Mesquite and Laguna streets, they were both full of emotion. They wondered when they would meet again, and Erna felt just a slight twinge of envy at the thought of Callie's going off alone with plans to do great things. As a parting gift she gave her a good-luck pin engraved with the message "from F.F.E. to F.F.C."—from freckle-faced Erna to freckle-faced Callie.[31]

Such understanding and support was not forthcoming from members of her own family and naturally not from the Koontzes. John's family found it hard to understand her defection and, being apt to see events in tangible terms, believed that financial matters had provoked the final crisis. They recalled that John had opened charge accounts at various stores and that, while his wife was free to use them, he had been shocked by having them overdrawn and used not only by her but also by her family. Finally he closed the accounts, and they thought this action caused K.R.'s departure.

For a long time the Koontzes knew nothing of her whereabouts. Mildred Koontz, who lived in Inez all her life and, like her father, ran the post office, always wondered what happened to her lively sister-in-law, but she was in her eighties when she found out. John Koontz quickly remarried. His second wife, Mabel Mason of Houston, was no rival to her predecessor in beauty or vivacity but she was a good homemaker, a loyal wife and mother. It is possibly a measure of John's grief over his failed marriage and perhaps of his genuine love for his first wife that he insisted, when he remarried, that no one ever question him about Katherine or remind him of her in any way. His new wife and his family respected his wishes and the subject was never broached. If he ever saw pictures in the papers or read in magazines of a writer called Katherine Anne Porter and connected her with his former wife, he gave no indication.

Harrison Boone Porter, whose limitations as a father and provider did not modify his high standards for female behavior, was so disgusted by his daughter's flight that the relationship between them never recovered. Years later, when his pride in her literary success was mentioned, she said that it was difficult for her to resume a relationship which ended years ago. She said that during the very critical years of her life her father was "quite indifferent to her fate or to her living."[32]

And what of Porter herself? Did she feel any regret at leaving the members of the family whom she had loved—Mildred Koontz, Beatrice Hasbrook, Baby Koontzey? A friend eloquently described Porter's ability to shed one life completely and take up another:

> She doesn't wait for death to effect transformation. Every now and then she stops being what she is and becomes something else. In some secluded corner of the world, she spins a cocoon and presently comes out more brilliantly colored, with longer, swifter wings. She leaves her old life there in a tree, dry and forgotten and dead, and something she had put forever behind her.[33]

In response to these words, Porter wrote, "Romantic and nice, but not true. I carry my whole life within me, all that matters, and have left nothing but debris of it behind me."[34] In her fiction she has described with feeling the pain of dying friendships, the irreparable loss of severed relationships, the sense of being divided into fragments and having lost parts of herself in every place she traveled, in every life hers had touched.

Perhaps the most important legacy of Porter's time with the Koontz family was her conversion to Catholicism. Describing the religious conflicts of her early years she said that she cried, dramatized her struggles, questioned priests and prayed because they told her to.[35] She had ample opportunity to talk with priests at the Koontz home because there was usually one in residence. There being no rectory in the parish of Inez at that time, the priest lived at the Koontz house, which stood conveniently beside the church. It was not, however, in Inez that she was instructed and baptized but in Houston, perhaps because she preferred the priest she found there. He was Father Thomas Hennessy, the pastor of Annunciation Church and by all accounts a remarkable person. Irish by birth, he had come to the United States, married the daughter of a Baptist minister, and been ordained in the Catholic Church after he was widowed.[36] This varied background must have made him especially sensitive to Porter's problems. She took instruction from him and was baptized on April 5, 1910, with her sister-in-law, Beatrice Hasbrook, as her sponsor. Porter never forgot Father Hennessy, and to the end of her life, when she read what seemed to her to be misrepresentations of Catholic dogma, she wondered "did my good Sister Borgia or Fr. Hennessy tell me wrong?"[37]

There were many aspects of Catholicism which appealed to Porter. In the first place, it provided the security of her childhood faith without recalling any of the disagreeable memories associated with it. There was none of her grandmother's repressive morality; no long list of prohibitions against dancing, drinking, card playing, or other activities that she enjoyed; there were no wild scenes of unleashed emotion such as she witnessed at revival meetings.

On the other hand, there was a great deal that appealed to her aesthetic sense. She loved the dramatic qualities of the Mass, the beauty of the liturgy, the sound of the church music and the Latin words. She liked the atmosphere of the churches, with their ornate windows, high altars, intricate vestments, and she was moved by the symbolism inherent in word and gesture. It is possible that Father Hennessy's instruction not only prepared her for entry into the Church but also laid the basis of her future literary techniques.

She was particularly interested in the saints and began reading saints' lives. Later she collected every version she could find of the lives of her favorite saints, Joan, Ursula, and Theresa of Avila, and of her own patron saints, Anne and Catherine of Siena. Her indispensable bedside text, replaced numerous times during her life, was *The Confessions of St. Augustine*.

There were, of course, many aspects of church dogma which offended her, and her disagreements are understandable in view of her natural tendency to dissent. She was not likely to be an orthodox Catholic any more than an orthodox anything else. Being strong-willed and independent and very conscious of being deprived, as a married woman, of certain rights, she had become by now a vocal feminist. She berated her brother when he spoke disparagingly of his girl friends and she was a strong advocate of woman's suffrage.[38] Accordingly, she was sensitive to the Church's attitude to women and quick to resent, then and later, the antifeminist tendencies of the Church Fathers and of individual priests whom she met.[39]

She hated St. Jerome, thought he would have been a very successful thug, and deplored his statement that death came through Eve.[40] Usually she blamed the Church's attitude to women on its Jewish origins and said that the Adam and Eve myth was a wild, silly story about a Jewish God which neglected to say why God created male and female if he meant to have only two people in the world.[41] Of St. Paul's attitude to women she said that he began as Saul and that the idea of sex as evil was a Jewish poison foisted on Christianity.

She thought that contempt for women had been the great evil of the Jewish influence upon Western religion. In her marginal notes she observed that her opinions were so heretical that she would never have survived the Inquisition and that it was only an accident of her birth date which prevented her from burning at the stake. When her views did coincide with orthodox Catholic ones, she would preface her comments with the remark that it pained her to agree with the Holy Office on anything.[42]

In one matter, however, she was quite consistent. Even when she wavered in her ability to believe in God, she never wavered in her preference for Catholicism over every other religious creed. She usually kept a rosary beside her bed, and on the many occasions when she hovered near death she received the last rites of the Catholic Church. Catholicism was the faith of her fictional family and she indicated that it was the religion of her actual family until assiduous researchers established that Porter's parents and grandparents were Methodists and Presbyterians. She never regretted her decision to convert to Catholicism and said at the end of her life that no other religion had ever attracted her.[43]

All in all, her attitude to religion, her deep need to believe and her equally deep skepticism, formed another area of ambivalence in her character. It is a strange feature of her life that she was able to take on the religious coloration of the environment in which she found herself. Close friends who were themselves nonbelievers, like her niece, found it difficult to believe that she ever took religion seriously.[44] In the company of nuns and priests, on the other hand, she was very devout and they never questioned her strong faith. When she was in Corpus Christi three years after her baptism, Porter showed no signs to Erna Schlemmer of her new faith, or of any faith, for that matter.[45]

Perhaps the most accurate apprehension of her delicate balance between skepticism and faith was that sensitivity recorded by Flannery O'Connor half a century later: "When she asked me where we were going in Europe and I said Lourdes, a very strange expression come over her face, just a slight shock as if some sensitive spot had been touched."[46]

By the time she was twenty, then, the religious pattern of Porter's life was established. She was baptized Catholic and she never considered any other creed, but her rhythm of turning to the Church and leaving it had already begun.

Another of the compelling patterns of her life was established at the same time. It was a negative act but none the less important for being so. What Porter learned was to strike the courage, remarkable in a woman of her time, to shed all the bonds that prevented her from being free and independent and able to discover herself. In her fiction she has well expressed her understanding of this need to throw off the restricting ties. Miranda in "Old Mortality" articulates her determination:

> She was sick to death of cousins. She did not want any more ties with this house, she was going to leave it, and she was not going back to her husband's family either. She would have no more bonds that smothered her in love and hatred. She knew now why she had run away to marriage, and she knew that she was going to run away from marriage, and she was not going to stay in any place, with anyone, that threatened to forbid her making her own discoveries, that said "No" to her.[47]

Porter said that she had eventually developed a "severity of rejection"[48] she would not have believed herself capable of. This first flight when she was twenty-three years old was the beginning of that severity and an important step on the long hard road to the realization of what she thought of at last as her "destiny."[49]

FIVE

The Ungodly Struggle

Writing about the late beginnings of Victorian women writers, the feminist literary critic Elaine Showalter says:

> . . . simply finding out and making clear to themselves what they should do with their lives was a more difficult and time-consuming process for women than for men. Making up educational disability added years to their apprenticeship, as did the subtle battles for independence within the nuclear family.[1]

The next few years of Porter's life exemplify this statement. She had gained her independence—not in a subtle battle but in a single bold stroke—and now she had to decide what to do with it. Since she was not well educated and not qualified for any profession, it was perhaps inevitable that she should gravitate again to her childhood ambition of becoming an actress. The work appealed to her love of make-believe and fantasy, and it satisfied her desire to be always in the spotlight. Moreover, silent movies were becoming popular and offering huge rewards of fame and fortune to those who starred in them. She was now more beautiful than ever, mature enough for substantial roles, and able to convey an air of great self-confidence. Accordingly, she decided to go north to Chicago and try to break into one of the big movie studios there.

It was a daring move—she called it later "my wild dash into that wilder world"[2]—and she must have started out with some trepidation. Her letters home, however, only show her exulting in her new adventures. On St. Patrick's Day, 1914, she wrote of the journey by Pullman to Chicago and of arriving in the huge railway station there. She wrote of spending her first days in a friend's luxurious apartment which had the extraordinary comforts of steam heat and running water, and of exploring the city.[3]

After a time she found an apartment of her own and apparently it was not luxurious, for she gave no details. Once settled there, she began to look seriously for work by making the rounds of the movie companies. Her first interview was with the manager of the Essanay Picture Company, who talked with her for a full seven minutes. He promised her work as an extra and maybe a permanent place. She felt optimistic afterward but, all the same, went round to other companies. The Selig Polysepe people promised her a position in May and she discovered that the Advance Company paid better than the other two. Eventually she settled for the Essanay Company and was placed on the "guaranteed list." This meant that they called her when they needed her to work as an extra and paid her three dollars a day. Soon she was telling friends to look out for her in movies. Her first appearance was in big two- or three-reel features called "From Out the Wreck." The friends were instructed to look hard because she was just a cabaret habituée with little work to do. The other movie was a full-length one, *Song in the Dark,* which was released June 6. Again she had a small part in a crowd scene.[4]

Gradually the excitement of the new work faded. It was not just that she was not an immediate success and that she was given only bit parts, but the work was far more difficult than she had imagined. She told Erna Johns that if she wanted to succeed and make all her friends proud of her she had to take good care of herself. She had to live quietly, sleep ten hours each night, and protect her nerves, because on work days she came home ready to cry with nervous exhaustion and could not believe that she could be so broken up in such a short time. She was now relieved that the work was not regular because on work days she had to be at the studio already "made up" by 8:30 A.M. Once there, she was on her feet constantly, working under green mercury lights that "sapped my life," and bombarded with a great noise and confusion of people chattering and directors shouting through megaphones. At one point a sprained ankle added to her discomfort. On days off she rested, washed her hair, massaged her face, manicured her nails, pressed "waists," slept and ate, knowing that after another day on the set she would look once again as if she had been snatched through a sausage grinder.[5] Clearly she was becoming aware of her great liability—the constitutional frailty that made her buckle under physical or nervous stress. After six months she gave up the work and returned to Texas.

Later she decided that the whole episode did not really belong to her and should not have happened. She tried to erase it from the record and gave fanciful versions, like the following two, of her reasons for going to Chicago:

> And at twenty-one I bolted again, went to Chicago, got a newspaper job, and went into the movies. . . . The newspaper sent me over to the old S. and A. movie studio to do a story. But I got into the wrong line, and then was too timid to get out. "Right over this way, Little Boy Blue," the man said, and I found myself in a courtroom scene with Francis X. Bushman. I was horrified by what had happened to me, but they paid me five dollars for that first day's work, so I stayed on. It was about a week before I remembered what I had been sent to do; and when I went back to the newspaper they gave me eighteen dollars for my week's non-work and fired me.

> In 1912 I went to Chicago at the age of 22 and having to earn a living and thinking that being a writer newspaper work was the nearest thing, I went to the Chicago Tribune and the City Editor, I've forgotten his name, consented to see me and I asked for a job. He . . . hired me at 15 dollars a week and sent me to the Essanay studios to get a story about the moving pictures and what they were doing. In those days the newspapers asked the studios for stories and news instead of the studios having publicity men getting stories in the newspapers. Quite a change, no? I thought this was rather nice because I had never been to moving pictures much because . . . in my place in life and my upbringing they were very low things, respectable people didn't attend and I hadn't seen anything at all at that time. It was four years before I saw two pictures and they were very good and very strange and I remember them today.[6]

She was fond of saying that the only experience of the time which really belonged to her was that she went to see *The Playboy of the*

Western World with the original Abbey Players, Frank Fay as the Boy, Sarah Allgood as the Widow Quinn, and Synge's affianced bride, Maire O'Neill, as Pegeen Mike.[7]

Of her decision to quit, she said years later:

> I stayed on for six months—I finally got to nearly ten dollars a day—until one day they came in and said, "We're moving to the coast." "Well, I'm not," I said. "Don't you want to be a movie actress?" "Oh, no!" I said. "Well, be a fool!" they said and they left. That was 1914 and World War I had broken out, and so in September I went home.[8]

Nearer the time she told a much more exciting story. She said the leading lady of the studio was enamored of the star, Francis X. Bushman. He, however, was paying attention to Porter, so that the lady became violently jealous and Porter, fearful for her safety, left before she was physically harmed.[9]

There can be little doubt that, whatever the cause, returning home so soon after her brave start must have given her a shattering sense of failure. She felt that she had accomplished nothing, did not know what to do next, and that time was slipping away from her. True, she was still only twenty-four, but she said when she was sixty, "I felt more decrepit at twenty-four than I ever have since."[10] In retrospect she might have seen that the experience did, in fact, yield some results, but she never took stock of what her excursions into the theater, then and later, gave to her art. Eventually one of her great literary assets was the ability to dramatize the psychological, internal action of her stories. She also drew on her theatrical experiences when she read her stories, and she became much sought after as a performer on the university lecture circuit. It is possible, too, that the work in Chicago contributed something quite specific to her short-story technique.

While she claimed not to remember or have been much interested in the movie *Song in the Dark,* she did on one occasion at least give a fairly detailed account of it. It seems likely that if she was in it, she not only did her scenes several times in rehearsal but went to see it a number of times. It is worth noting that the plot of *Song in the Dark,* described in *Moving Picture World,* has a structure similar to the one she would use in short stories like "The Grave." It consists of two episodes dealing with different experiences but thematically linked by the controlling image of blindness:

> It was only natural that Angela and Richard should become engaged. They were children together and had lived for one another. Their love was the true and undying love, that had been born to live forever. Angela loved nature, and when a bird vendor stopped her on the street one sunny afternoon she unhesitatingly purchased a canary and asked the man for a card, that she might recommend him to her friends. Angela was awakened by the singing of the canary, and could not understand why the bird should be so free-hearted and merry at that late hour. Her discomfiture was genuine, when she discovered that the bird was blind, and the next morning found her at the bird vendor's home, seeking an explanation. She learns that all the birds are blind—that they are blinded on purpose—that they sing better thus—and that it is easier to sell birds that have excellent singing quality. She becomes furious to think that such an inhuman act could be inflicted upon the innocent creatures, and has the vendor arrested; her brother, George, a promising young attorney, prosecutes the case and the Italian vendor is flogged in court.

> The day had been set for the wedding. Their new home to be was in readiness. Angela meets with an accident, which costs her eyesight. Would Richard continue to love her— would he forget that he had asked her to become his wife. The loss of her eyesight was nothing compared to the infinite love she bore in her bosom. He was all and all to her. The dark hours spent in the lonely room with the canary as her only companion helped to cheer her at times and she wondered why he was so happy. She was blind—never to see God's light again. The bird had long forgotten that it had ever seen the light and he chirped on merrily, in time making Angela forget her affliction. The newspapers printed an article and the vendor, seeking communion, begged her forgiveness on his knees. His heart softened and he prayed that she might get better. One evening, as the bird sat on his perch, singing gaily, she stole softly down the carpeted stairs, into the living room. Richard was there playing chess with George. Angela found her way to the piano and as the strains of music reached Richard's ear, he whispered, "'Tis Angela," and he crept softly to her side, and said, "It is I who am blind. I love you."[11]

In the fall of 1914, Porter, as it happened, had little time to brood about past failures or future plans, because she was urgently needed at home. She had visited both sisters before her journey north and neither of them had been very happy. Baby, in Beaumont, had recently married and was pregnant, ill, and dispirited. The two had sat around for hours discussing the "dear dead past, the equally dead present and the apparently dead future."[12] Now when she returned, Baby had a son. Porter still yearned, as she had in childhood, for her family to show some signs of distinction. Since it was clear now that her own generation would not do so any more than the previous one had, she transferred her hopes to the next generation of children just being born and made elaborate plans in her mind for their education and future. She had strong opinions about naming them and she chose for Baby's son the name Breckenridge.[13] She could not stay long to cheer up Baby and help with Breckenridge because her older sister's predicament was far more serious.

Gay, with two-year-old Mary Alice, was living in Gibsland, a small country town in Louisiana, and expecting a second child at any moment. Her situation was desperate because her husband, who had turned out to be a philanderer, had once again "run out on her." Gay's marriage reinforced considerably Porter's theory about the curse that falls upon girls whose fathers do not take care of them. Her hatred for Gay's husband was boundless and she said he was the only person she ever seriously planned to kill. In the emergency she rushed to help out and remained with Gay during the birth. She said later that it was among the personal tragedies of her life and she remembered with horror the terrifying ordeal in the small, poor house in midwinter with only a country doctor in attendance. The baby was born with a broken arm and Gay was "torn to pieces."[14] On this occasion Porter seems to have manifested all the resourcefulness of Aunt Cat herself. She nursed Gay, looked after both children, and, when she was able to leave them in the care of an old woman, went off to earn money for their support.

Because no jobs were forthcoming in the small town, Porter made herself a costume and went out on the Lyceum Circuit giving performances of songs and poems. She traveled within a radius of Gibsland and came back as quickly as possible to look after Gay and the children. The costume she wore was a long red dress with a medieval style of headdress, which she thought appropriate since most of the songs in her repertoire were of medieval origin. Since her recent experiences had heightened her feelings about the irresponsibility of men and the vulnerability of women, it is perhaps not surprising that her songs reflected her feminist sentiments. One of her favorites, by an interesting coincidence, was the Scots ballad from which Virginia Woolf took her personae when ten years later she wrote her feminist tract, *A Room of One's Own*.[15] "The Three Maries" tells the story of the four handmaidens of Mary, Queen of Scots, all also named Mary. One of the young women bears the child of the Queen's husband, drowns it, and is convicted of infanticide. For her sins, she hangs from the gallows in Edinburgh town. Porter always walked to the front of the platform, told the story, and then sang the ballad with its haunting refrain:

> Last nicht there was four Maries,
> The nicht there'll be but three;
> There was Marie Seton, and Marie Beton
> and Mary Carmichael and me.[16]

For an encore she often sang "Oh, Careless Love," and discovered that people particularly enjoyed this verse:

> Oh, when my apron strings was low
> He followed me through wind and snow,
> But now they rise up to my chin
> He goes right by and won't look in.

She said that was something the audience really understood and that they yelled with laughter.[17]

With characteristic enthusiasm Porter threw herself wholeheartedly into the work. She was touched to see how much her performances meant to the country people and long remembered how eagerly they came in all kinds of weather. In cold and rain they came in rough mule-drawn wagons, accompanied by their children because there was no one to leave them with. She said she could hardly bear to see the downtrodden women sitting and listening and rocking their babies, and tiptoeing out with them if they would not stop crying. The people were so starved for beauty that they absorbed every word and afterward came up to the platform to finger her dress and ask where she found such material and such a dress. She told them, "I made it, and you could too."

When she was a child, Porter's ability to sink herself completely into some game and then suddenly lose interest and abandon it had puzzled Erna Schlemmer. Porter never lost that tendency, and in the spring she abandoned her fans on the Lyceum Circuit and decided it was time to do something else. A further reason to quit was that her sister not only could manage without her but had also annoyed her. Gay's husband had returned and she had actually allowed him to move back into the house. Moreover, Gay refused to call her new baby Paul, which Porter considered a good family name, but called him Thomas after his father. Porter's only regret in leaving was that she had to say good-bye to Mary Alice, whom she adored and on whom she pinned her hopes for the family's future. The little girl was beautiful, clever, and devoted to her aunt, but it was time for Porter, once more, to summon her "severity of rejection" and leave.

There were no ambitious bids for fame this time, and no daring journeys north. She went only as far as Dallas and tried to find office work there. All the same, her intention to start a new life is reflected in her step, taken on her birthday, to divorce herself from John Koontz. She went to Mike Lively, a prominent Dallas attorney, and he drew up the necessary papers. She included in her request that the name Katherine Porter be given to her. John Koontz in Corpus Christi signed the affidavit to confirm her account of his misdemeanors, happy that he would now be free of financial obligations to her. When she first requested support payments he had promised to send her $50 a month, but he had not fulfilled this promise. Nevertheless, he had a tidy bookkeeper's mind, disliked owing money, and in addition wanted to marry again. The divorce was granted on June 21, 1915, a day after the ninth anniversary of the wedding.

Taking stock of her life at this time, Porter recognized that she had had more than her share of setbacks, but at least she was her own person again and completely free to do as she pleased. Sometimes in later years, when she reached level ground after being submerged, she cautioned herself to mention the fact in a whisper, lest the Furies, hearing, should descend again. Such a warning might have been appropriate at this time, for it did seem that the Furies were waiting at every turn to pounce. They dealt their severest blow so far.

No doubt the work at the movie studio, followed by the hard winter on the Lyceum Circuit, with not enough food and rest, had weakened her and she became ill. She had always suffered from the bronchial trouble that ran in the family and it was probably no surprise when, in the fall, she coughed and grew feverish. On this occasion the diagnosis was horrifying, for the chest X-rays revealed that she had tuberculosis. A salesman friend of the Koontzes greeted her in a Dallas hotel shortly after she received the news and she told him that she was not going to be alive much longer.[18] She not only feared for her life but had no money for treatment and no one to look after her. Her only recourse was to enter one of the dreaded charity hospitals or "pest houses" for the tubercular. These were overcrowded, dirty places, which provided little treatment and simply accommodated the dying during their last months.

There she was placed in a ward full of the shriveled bodies of women dying slowly with almost no care at all. She had always started the day with the strong coffee she loved, but here there was neither coffee, tea, nor fruit, nor much food of any kind. The patients were fed on dry bread and thin soup, just enough, she recalled later, to help them die a little more slowly. The staff were lazy, sodden, overweight people who sat by the fireplace and did nothing. Years later she wrote a description of this experience to Lon Tinkle. She remembered it as the most unbelievably wretched time of her whole life and wondered how she managed not to lose her nerve completely and to survive. The horror of gruesome people in charge of helpless dying creatures haunted her to the end of her life.[19]

The only member of the family who was solvent was Paul, still in the navy. Although his wages were not very large and he was saving them in order to marry and return to civilian life, he never refused to help. He had been contributing his tobacco allowance to his father for years, and when Baby's husband died he helped to support her and eventually adopted and raised young Breckenridge. Now, hearing of his sister's illness, he managed to send her an allowance so that she could leave the charity hospital and find a better place. For a time she lived in one of the rooming houses for the tubercular. Then, in the spring of 1916, she was admitted to the recently opened Carlsbad Sanatorium in West Texas, a few miles from San Angelo.[20]

Here she was once again in a large ward of forty women, but, quite unlike the Dallas hospital, the Carlsbad sanatorium was a pleasant, well-kept place.[21] It had a competent staff, modern, airy buildings, and lovely gardens maintained by an Englishman called John Bull. Former patients described its atmosphere as resembling that of a college campus.[22]

For Porter it may even have fulfilled some of the functions of an institution of learning. She had a great deal of time to spare, since all activities that called for exertion were forbidden. Reading might have filled her time but there were no books. The place had no library and the magazines which visitors brought were read to tatters. Porter claimed to have read each magazine so thoroughly that she even memorized the advertisements.

In this forced idleness the chief occupation was talking, and it was Porter's good fortune—or perhaps her determination to learn—that she found a woman who taught her a great deal. Kitty Barry Crawford was unusual for her time because she was a career woman, one of the first newspaperwomen in Texas. She had a B.A. degree from Kidd-Key College in Sherman, Texas, was a skilled musician, and was much interested in literature and writing. After graduating from college she had been a reporter on the *San Antonio Express* and in that capacity had visited Mexico very often. She was older than Porter, and the mother of a little girl. She had married a fellow reporter on the *Fort Worth Telegraph* and together they had founded their own paper, the *Fort Worth Critic*. Before she contracted T.B., Kitty had contributed two columns to the paper, "This Week at the Theater" and "This Week at the Hippodrome," and she also covered art, music, and social events.

The two quickly became friends and spent the next months talking across the bed of the young woman who lay between them. Porter learned all about Kitty's work and, in turn, told about her own experiences. In the large ward the two always had an eager audience for their discussions, and this may explain why Porter's stories of her life to Kitty were among the most extravagant she ever gave. Decades later, scholars and critics of Porter's work discovered Kitty and she became the unintentional source of much erroneous biographical information.

Porter told of her elopement from the convent to marry, and of the jealousy of the leading lady in the Chicago movie company, and of a marriage she had made in Dallas soon after she divorced her first husband. She said that she had met and loved a young Englishman who had begged her to marry him. She had done so to comfort him before he was sent back to England to join the army. The marriage had not been consummated and she returned to Mike Lively to ask him to annul the marriage. He had been amused to see her again so soon but had annulled the second marriage, telling her, "Boy, you're a fast worker." Subsequently she said that the young man had been killed on the battlefield and that his family wrote to her but were unable to help her financially. She said that before she became ill she had worked as a reporter for the *Dallas Morning News*. Like many others, Kitty soon learned that while Porter loved to talk of her life she was very quick to resent any questions, and that she liked to preserve the air of mystery her stories generated. Kitty had no reason to question the veracity of any of her friend's accounts and she concluded:

> Of one thing I am very sure. Katherine Anne came of a very fine family. Her childhood friends in Austin and San Antonio and elsewhere were prominent people. There is no fiction about these circumstances. She really is of "Old Southern" descent. She had been beautifully brought up with exquisite manners and taste in clothes.[23]

Although she was not actually present, another young woman loomed importantly in Porter's life at this time and became a third party in her discussions with Kitty. She was to play a later part in Porter's life and also to become a notorious, infamous woman, accused of treason to the United States after the Second World War. Her name was Jane Anderson and she had been Kitty's roommate in college and had remained devoted to her afterward. When Kitty's daughter was born she was named for her mother's colorful friend. Jane had gone to Kidd-Key with a very unusual background. Her mother had died when she was born, and after some years with relatives in Atlanta she had joined her father, who was sheriff of Yuma, Arizona. She had lived there with a Mexican housekeeper, lonely and isolated, waiting for her father's homecomings to turn the house into a scene of noisy parties.[24]

When Jane appeared at Kidd-Key College, Kitty was immediately fascinated by her appearance and thought her, as many did, the most beautiful girl she had ever seen. Jane had too few credits to graduate but she proved (it was to become the standard comment of all who met her) as brilliant as she was beautiful and distinguished herself in French, music, and English literature. After graduation she went to New York, married the musicologist Deems Taylor, and became a newspaperwoman and a writer of short stories which appeared in *Harper's Weekly*. For her stories she drew on her unusual background in the Arizona desert and they had a somewhat exotic

cast. They were well-written but melodramatic stories of dying prostitutes, or young women left to die and nursed back to health by the
love of good men.[25]

There were certain parallels, which Porter cannot have failed to
remark, between herself and Jane. They were the same age and at the
same time had left their husbands and embarked on new, exciting
careers. Porter had gone to Chicago and Jane had gone to Europe as
a war correspondent. Jane's success, however, had been meteoric. In
London she had turned many heads, including that of Lord North-
cliffe, the owner of the *Daily Mail*. She became a fearless reporter,
going to France and to the battlefront and the trenches exactly like
her male counterparts. When a zeppelin raid over London killed a
hundred women and children she called a taxi and was swiftly on the
scene. When the zeppelin was shot down and dying men were strewn
about in someone's pasture, she borrowed a nurse's uniform so she
could get close to the scene.[26] Not surprisingly, she suffered a reaction
to so much horror and became ill with what she called "a bad case of
war nerves." For her recovery she was invited to stay with Joseph
Conrad and his wife. Conrad, calling her "the dear Chestnut filly,"
wrote about her to a friend: "We made the acquaintance of a new
young woman. She comes from Arizona and (strange to say!) she has
a European mind. She is seeking to get herself adopted as our big
daughter and is succeeding fairly. To put it shortly she's quite yum-
yum."[27]

The two young women at Carlsbad followed Jane's life with the
greatest interest. The clippings she sent of her newspaper articles from
the *Daily Mail*, her long letters describing the London air attacks, the
landing of the zeppelin, and her visit to the Conrads were read to
shreds and committed to memory even more than the stray magazines. In addition, when Kitty's husband sent packages of fruit he was
asked to include copies of Jane's stories so that Porter could read
them. It seemed to her that such work—journalism and traveling and
writing—was even more exciting than acting and she began to wish
that she too could be a reporter. She wished also that, instead of
having spent her life in cities and small towns in Texas, she had had
experiences like Jane's which would lend themselves to short stories.
In any event, she was developing a strong idea of what she would like
to do with her future, if she regained her health.

When she left Carlsbad, Porter was not strong enough for a
demanding full-time job, but she found a perfect interim solution—a

job which would provide some income and still allow her to complete her cure. She was admitted to Woodlawn Hospital, in Dallas, as part patient and part assistant, with the job of looking after the tubercular children there. She immediately formed the group into a little school, which she called "Academy Oaks," and began to teach them so they could keep up with their healthier counterparts. The books and curriculum were those of the public schools adapted to the special needs of the sick. No desks were used and lessons took place outdoors under the live oak trees on the sanatorium grounds. Porter adapted folk dances to require less exertion than usual and filled the children's wards with bright colors.[28] Disobedient children were punished by not being allowed to attend classes and having to remain in bed. When Porter was not teaching she rested and ate well. Her weight soared to 120 pounds and her health and spirits improved still more.[29]

Having made friends with some of the staff members of the *Dallas Morning News,* she persuaded one of them to write up her story for the paper. She was paid $8 for the story but the real benefit was a deluge of gifts and clothing and money from the people of the city. By December 21 she had received $67.50 in cash alone. She wrote jubilantly to her sister comparing the present well-being with the misery of the Christmas two years earlier. She was happy for the children in her care, for her family, whose circumstances were now easier, and for herself. She apologized that her own presents were small and late and said that she was receiving more presents than she deserved. One friend had given her a bottle of her favorite La Bohème perfume and a mysterious benefactor whom she did not name had given her a robe, slippers, and a heating pad. She said that he was very proud of her work with the children and had told her she was the most talked of person in Dallas. She said that they were immensely good friends and loved each other very much but that it was a strange affair, all told. She said that she was selfish and that he was the kind who gave everything and asked nothing in return, looked to see that she was warm, well clothed, and happy, and that she never had a man love her like that. She had seen him only twice since coming to Dallas but they talked on the telephone and he brought her the peace of mind which she had needed all her life. Above all he believed that she had the fiber of greatness and never let her forget it.[30]

The newspaper account of her school had carried the caption:

WHAT ONE WOMAN IS DOING TO HELP CHILDREN

TUBERCULOUS LITTLE ONES ARE TAUGHT
WITH SKILL AND THOROUGHNESS
BY ONE WHOSE SOLE COMMENT WAS "I LOVE THEM"

These words, the pictures of Porter with the children, and the account of the school make it hard to believe that she left Woodlawn without some heartache, but perhaps, once again, she summoned up the severity of rejection necessary to the fulfillment of her destiny. On the other hand, the episode of the Christmas gifts had ended unhappily and possibly this had soured her on the place. She told her sister that people had come from headquarters and taken away all the offerings brought for the children, and that her objections had caused a scandal.

No matter how she felt about the school she had established, she was strong enough in the spring of 1917 to leave and she was eager to do something different. She wished now to become a journalist and writer, like Jane Anderson and Kitty. When she talked to reporters from the *Dallas Morning News* she tried to persuade them to help her find work there, and she told her sister that she had been promised a job. To her disappointment the job she coveted on the famous newspaper did not materialize. She often told later of applying for a newspaper job and having an interview at which the editor was shocked to find that the applicant, K. Porter, was a woman. When he recovered from the shock, he turned her down on the ground that she had no previous experience. She objected that she never would gain experience if she were refused work for that reason, but the editor was not persuaded.

She returned for a visit with Gay and was happy to spend time with little Mary Alice, and she waited until the fall to begin her career as a journalist. Then she got her start through her friends, the Crawfords. They had confidence in her ability and were ready to give help and assistance if she needed it. Moreover, they needed someone to undertake the job that Kitty was not yet strong enough to do.

Kitty's illness was more severe than Porter's and her recovery was slow, but she was back home with her family in Fort Worth. Porter moved in with the Crawfords and took over Kitty's columns on the *Critic*. She was introduced to readers on September 15, 1917, with a photograph and the following description:

The exuberant young person above is Miss Katherine Anne Porter, late from the staff of several prominent newspapers. She has come to Fort Worth to devote her young life to THE CRITIC. Miss Porter likes things which many people consider frivolous and of no consequence—Society and the many small factors which go toward making life pleasant and interesting are among her hobbies. She also originates beautiful stories for children.[31]

A year later, when she was working on another paper, Porter inserted in one of her reviews a paragraph which suggests the extent of Kitty's help in the beginning:

Kitty Barry Crawford, herself a writer and critic of sorts, from whom we drew inspiration in the old days, sends us the following protest: "I have been silent a long time on the subject of your critical delinquencies, but feel that I can no longer remain so. You draw a living wage for writing about the 'drammer,' giving yourself over to airs and sarcasms as to who can or cannot build a play, anyhow. Yet never in the course of months have you made use of such current and recognized terms as jejune, rococo, decadent, jeune fille, bienséance, motivation, bijou or picaresque. As for dichotomy, I doubt if you know its meaning." (Righto.)[32]

For several months she wrote up society notes and theatrical performances for the *Critic*, and her work is entirely characteristic of one described as liking things which others thought frivolous and inconsequential. Her reviews were fairly lighthearted and any play or musical show which depicted "Cupid's career from beginning to end" was treated with indulgent amusement. In a way this was appropriate to the circumstances, for Fort Worth was badly in need of light entertainment. The city was a ferment of military activity, with thousands of soldiers stationed on the outskirts training for service in Europe. As fall turned to winter the weather became cold and rainy and many of the soldiers fell ill with stomach ailments, pneumonia, and contagious diseases. The military hospitals were inadequate for such emergencies and many of the sick soldiers were housed in makeshift tents in cold, miserable conditions. The people of Fort Worth rallied to help, and Porter became active in civic affairs, joining the Red Cross Corps, which immediately appointed her publicity chairman. Many of her articles in the paper, like the following, promote the work of the Red Cross Corps and the Hospital Visiting Corps, which did "cheer up work" at the Camp Bowie Base Hospital:

Even three years ago what society girls studied the problems of immigration or pure food, or tenements or clean milk for poor little neglected babies? Which one of them dreamed of giving a fixed portion of her time to a certain work, reporting at headquarters and taking her orders like a little soldier? Yet here they are deep in war work doing their bit courageously. As one of them said only yesterday, "It is bigger than I am all this. But I couldn't let go now. I don't know how I used to fill my days! And even when the war is over I don't think we can ever go back to living entirely for ourselves alone. Wouldn't it be dull and empty?" And wouldn't it though?[33]

Before Christmas she reminded readers that the girls of the Social Service Club's Cheer Fund would be selling red-white-and-blue tags on the downtown streets, so that everyone could have a part in giving a happy Christmas to the soldiers in the Camp Bowie Base Camp. Her stories on a planned benefit bridge tournament brought many prizes from local merchants and a large crowd to the tournament itself.

She was glorying in her new career and the popularity she had gained among the Crawfords' friends and the soldiers who came into the city. She was not only working hard as a journalist but also doing volunteer work. In addition to all this, she kept up an active social life, attending all the dances at the Texas hotel where regular exhibitions of ballroom dancing were given. Evidently she had forgotten, or was too caught up in the excitement of bustling about to remember, that she had twice before impaired her health by overwork and lack of rest. She was, however, reminded of it very suddenly when she became ill again and had to be sent home to her family in Beaumont. Her one consolation during this period of convalescence was that she could see her sisters' children—Breckenridge and T.H. and, above all, her favorite, Mary Alice, who was now five and a half.

Kitty was still making a slower recovery than her family wished, and so her husband decided that she should move from Fort Worth to the more favorable climate of Denver, Colorado. She hoped to enter a hospital there in the fall, and while she waited for a bed she stayed in one of the many boarding houses for the tubercular. It was here that she received a visit from her old friend Jane Anderson, who was just home from Europe. Jane had a number of writing assignments for which she was under contract and she needed a place to stay while she worked. She looked around Denver and decided that she liked it well enough to spend the summer there. She quickly found a summer cottage, called Watson Lodge, which was bolted to the side of Cheyenne Mountain near Colorado Springs, and decided to take it. It was expensive but commodious and she soon made plans to finance it and fill it. She took the lease to Kitty and asked if she would pay a share as well as paying half the salary of a housekeeper. Kitty agreed, and once they were settled in, Jane sent for her latest lover to join them. He was Gilbert Seldes, a young Harvard graduate whom she had met in England and accompanied back to the United States on the *Rochambeau*. When the ménage seemed a little uncomfortable, she solved the problem by writing to Porter, about whom she had heard a great deal from Kitty. She told Porter that Kitty was lonely and very devoted to and dependent on Porter, and begged her to join them. Porter needed little urging because, apart from her niece, she found her family depressingly dull and broken-down. She was fascinated by the idea of meeting Jane, becoming her friend, hearing about her experiences in Europe, and learning more about her work. The only obstacle was money, because Porter had spent what she earned from the Crawfords as quickly as she got hold of it. Once again she approached her brother, telling him that Colorado would be much better for her health than Beaumont. He was very burdened with his own family and Baby's son, but he agreed to give Porter a sum of money to contribute as her share of the housekeeping expenses at Watson Lodge.[34]

The meeting with Jane was a disappointment, and Porter soon discovered that neither Jane nor Gilbert Seldes had much interest in talking to her. They looked down on her and made it clear that they considered her uneducated and untraveled. She was unusually subdued in their presence, watchful and silently resentful. Her only revenge was to beat them at card games. She was an excellent player and always won, but they soon grew tired of being constantly beaten and stopped playing with her.

Porter did not appear to advantage beside Jane, whose beauty was of the particularly striking kind that drew attention and caused flocks of admirers to surround her. Kitty described her as "queenly, triumphantly beautiful, and with a veneer of international sophistication." She described Porter, on the other hand, in this way:

She was beautiful but not of the classic type. She was average in height, slender and graceful. Luminous gray eyes dominated her face but her nose was insignificant and decidedly retroussé, her mouth too large in her wide, almost flat face. It was her manner, confident, assured, and the questioning glint of humor in each glance that marked her personality.[35]

In spite of her still impressive appearance, Jane was no longer admirable in other ways. The fact was that she had returned from Europe a changed person. Her reckless search for adventure had exposed her to too many terrible sights and she was broken-down in the way that many were who survived the trench fighting of the First World War. Possibly her war experiences only aggravated disturbances which were present from her unstable childhood, but the effect was alarming. She lived in a constant frenzy of activity, unable to rest and be calm. She was always planning trips to Denver and rushing off as far away as San Francisco and Los Angeles. (She had decided she wished to be an actress.) Messengers brought telegrams, cables, special letters, and there was a great deal of long-distance telephoning. Even short periods of calm unnerved her and her nerves fluctuated wildly. At times she was entertaining, even brilliantly amusing, but at other times she was morbid, oversensitive, and easily upset. She did little work on the writing for which she had contracted, but spent most of her time with Gilbert Seldes. She spent the first hours in his bed each night and afterward returned to her own bed, took barbiturates for her "war nerves," and remained sedated until noon the next day.

For a time Porter enjoyed hearing Jane's stories about the Conrads and about her war experiences, and she was interested in Jane's ambition to be an actress, but eventually she grew to dislike her thoroughly, and she especially disliked hearing Jane praising everything European. Her resentment was voiced the next year in her thinly disguised account of Jane in her journalism:

There was a lady once a very lovely person with a great ambition to be an actress; and she went away to Europe to study for several years. When she returned she was no better actress than she had been, but she talked constantly of Europe, of the drama, the art, the society, the traditions and rich backgrounds of culture abounding there. She contrasted this with America and its uncouth ways. She never failed to use the word "crude" when describing us. No matter what

the subject in hand might be, it invariably came back to the
manners of this country, and its crude state as regards all
that made the life of this lady worth living. We learned to
hate her fervently in a short while and our hate far exceeded
any love we had ever known.[36]

The summer was not a success. Kitty became seriously upset by
Jane's disturbances, the final outrage being her appropriation of the
whiskey that Garfield Crawford had brought along in case of an
emergency in his wife's health. Jane and Gilbert took the liquor out
on to the mountain and drank it. Jane also refused to pay her share of
the household expenses, and finally Kitty was so worn out that she
went away and spent two weeks in a hotel. Porter, with nowhere else
to go, remained at the lodge until Jane left and Kitty returned. Then
the two spent a happy two weeks together with Kitty's four-year-old
daughter, Jane Anderson. The little girl liked Porter as much as she
hated "Big Jane," who had ignored her completely. Porter told little
Jane the charming stories which she had told her own niece, Mary
Alice, and to Kitty's dismay she also taught her the Cucaracha song,
with its endless verses about a poor cockroach.

Neither Kitty nor Porter ever saw Jane Anderson again, and the
friendship ended there. She did not, however, quite disappear from
their lives, for she and Porter were later rivals for the love of the same
man, and much later Jane's notorious exploits during the Second
World War, which led to her being tried and exonerated as a traitor,
were reported in the international press.[37] Porter's fascination with
Jane found its way into the fiction, so that Jane, who married a Spanish nobleman and became the Marquesa de Cienfuegos, contributed
something to the character of La Condesa in Ship of Fools.

In retrospect, Porter referred to the situation on the side of Cheyenne Mountain as a "kettle of snakes" and to Jane as a reckless adven-
turess. In her story "St. Augustine and the Bullfight" she took as her
theme the devastating effect of reckless adventuring for its own sake,
and she quoted Yeats's remark that the man most to be pitied was he
whose adventures had outrun his capacity for experience. Porter
began her story with a paragraph describing an experience of her own
on Cheyenne Mountain.[38] She does not mention Jane in the story,
but, all the same, it was Jane she thought of as she contemplated her
theme. It must have been brought home to her that Jane's experiences,
which she envied so much, had ended in just this: that Jane was no

longer capable of feeling any but the most violent shocks and that she had no capacity for feeling anything for her friends or her lovers.

Porter's interest was not merely casual. Jane's career had for some time now provided a model that she had aspired to. She wondered if she too, in her hunger to see and experience everything and her ability to free herself from undesirable human ties, might not end by feeling nothing, being unable to relate to anyone. She had, after all, disentangled herself from her father, her sisters, and her husband; there was really only one person left whom she loved without qualification, and that was her little niece, Mary Alice.

She hoped that her past setbacks and her future experiences would not harden her, but even if they did, she was more determined than ever to succeed so that no one could look down on her as ignorant and untraveled. Her goals were now well defined. She wanted to find a job as a journalist, to write stories, and to travel as far as Europe. The first goal was soon achieved. She was delighted to be given a job on a Denver newspaper, the *Rocky Mountain News,* which was just as good as the *Dallas Morning News,* and at the end of the summer, while Kitty went into Agnes Memorial Hospital and little Jane returned to Fort Worth, she settled into her job and found a place to live in a Denver rooming house.

SIX

Death and Rebirth in Denver

Her achievement would have seemed incredible four years earlier. She was now a reporter, not on a small-town newspaper but on a big-city one with a large circulation and a strong reputation. Besides that, she was so adept at the job that she soon became one of the most popular writers in the city, amazing her colleagues by the speed with which she dashed off her columns. The only drawback was that the paper paid her a mere $20 a week, so that she had to budget strictly to afford the clothes and perfumes she loved.[1] She managed characteristically by stinting on food and surviving on a diet of coffee, doughnuts, and cigarettes. Her battle for her health had not made her cautious and she was already smoking a great deal.[2]

Her success did not completely satisfy her ambitious nature, and soon after she started work on the *Rocky Mountain News* she was planning to go further afield. She asked an acquaintance on the *Houston Chronicle* for a letter of recommendation to support her application to join the Red Cross. The letter was written on October 4, 1918, but it was already too late, for once again the Furies were hovering in the wings.

The atmosphere of the whole country in the fall of 1918 was bleak. The calculated hate campaign against Germans at home as well as abroad had reached a crescendo and resulted in fearful hysteria about acts of domestic sabotage such as germ warfare and poisoned water supplies. (Like many long-established German families the

Schlemmers suffered cruel social persecution. Under the pressure of this torment, Porter's childhood neighbor Mrs. Wilhelmina Schlemmer lost her health and died of a massive heart attack at the age of fifty-eight.)[3]

Besides the poisonous emotional climate there was a more tangible danger, one that was foreshadowed in the title of a new book which appeared on the library shelves that year. This was Blasco-Ibáñez' *The Four Horsemen of the Apocalypse,* which suggested that along with Conquest, War, and Famine there was a fourth menace, Pestilence. The full realization of the association of war and pestilence came in late 1918, when the plague of influenza spread rapidly across the United States and the women who had been rolling bandages for the soldiers turned their attention instead to making gauze masks to trap the germs supposedly put into the air at home by German spies. Church services and public meetings were canceled and places of entertainment closed.

For the second time in two years Porter's life was threatened by a deadly illness, and it looked as if another attempt at a career was doomed to failure. She contracted influenza, and her case coincided exactly with the epidemic's rise and fall in Denver. When all the public places were closed in the first week of October she was already ill in her rooming house at 1510 York Street. The hospitals were filled to capacity and it was very difficult to find beds. Her situation became desperate when her terrified landlady threatened to put her out of the house. No hospital bed was available and she had nowhere to go. Once again friends sprang to her assistance. Porter herself said that the city editor of the newspaper managed to get her into the county hospital,[4] but Kitty Barry Crawford said that she appealed to one of her own doctors, who was head of the emergency committee for flu patients.[5]

All accounts of the subsequent events coincide. By the time she was admitted to a hospital there seemed little hope that she could survive; she ran a fever of 105 for nine days. Gay Porter Holloway rushed to Denver and talked daily on the telephone with Kitty, both of them expecting to hear news of the death every day. The *Rocky Mountain News* set up the obituary and the Porter family made arrangements for disposal of the body. Harrison Porter, who had taken little responsibility for his daughter's well-being in the past years, now said that her body should be taken to Brownwood and buried as near to her mother as possible.[6] One Sunday afternoon she was left behind screens to die, and Gay Porter told Kitty that as a last resort she was having a special Mass said for her sister. At the same time a group of young interns in white coats looked at Porter as she lay dying in the corridor of the crowded hospital. They decided to give her an experimental shot of strychnine. Miraculously, it worked, and she began to fight her way back to life. Gay called Kitty to tell her the news that Porter's temperature had returned to normal.

The frantic series of events cannot have lasted more than two weeks, and yet it assumed in Porter's imagination an importance quite beyond its length. She saw it as a crucial episode in her life and as the moment in which her desire to be a good writer and a good artist crystallized:

> It just simply divided my life, cut across it like that. So that everything before that was just getting ready, and after that I was in some strange way altered, ready. It took me a long time to go out and live in the world again. I was really "alienated," in the pure sense. It was, I think, the fact that I really had participated in death, that I knew what death was, and had almost experienced it. I had what the Christians call the "beatific vision," and the Greeks called the "happy day," the happy vision just before death. Now if you have had that, and survived it, come back from it, you are no longer like other people, and there's no deceiving yourself that you are. But you see, I did: I made the mistake of thinking that I was quite like anyone else, of trying to live like other people. It took me a long time to realize that that simply wasn't true, that I had my own needs and that I had to live like me.[7]

There had, of course, been dramatic reversals in her life before this, even brushes with death and recoveries. Why this particular one should so have caught her imagination invites speculation. Perhaps her closeness to death and the suddenness of her recovery convinced her, at last, that, despite all blows, she was somehow indestructible. Perhaps the fact that so many of the ceremonial occasions in her life had been funerals had left her an interest in the trappings of death that amounted to necrophilia. Perhaps the experience of her childhood religion had impressed upon her the importance of being "born again," or perhaps the experience formed the perfect symbol in her mind for the transformation she felt necessary before she could become an artist. Whatever the reason, the experience became central to her biographical record and also the subject of one of her most successful short stories.

The crucial incident of the story is Miranda Gay's romantic attachment to a young soldier from Texas who is soon to be posted abroad. He has come into Denver to spend a brief leave before going to the battlefront. When Miranda becomes ill he looks after her, brings her medicine and food and helps her to get into the hospital. When Miranda recovers she is suddenly stricken by the news that the soldier contracted influenza and died of it. She feels that she infected him and that she was the cause of his death.

Neither Gay nor Kitty Barry Crawford met the young soldier, but after her recovery Porter told Kitty that he was a young Englishman. The fictional accounts as well as those given to friends and interviewers all agree that the affair was unconsummated, although they vary in the amount of involvement between the two young lovers.

After she saw the televised version of the story, in which Dorothy McGuire played Miranda, Porter told Gay that the young soldier was someone who happened to be living in the same rooming house, whom she did not know at all, but who looked after her for three days before a doctor and a bed could be found for her. She said he nursed her and gave her medicine and came in three times every night to see how she was. They did not shed tears and carry on hysterically as portrayed in the screen version, but laughed, joked, and sang together, and only kissed one time, when he lay down beside her at the end, tired out, and they fell asleep as innocently as two babes. Ten days later, while she was unconscious in the hospital, he died of influenza. She said that she could not forget this and it was terrible that he should have lost his own life and saved hers. She said that she felt directly responsible, for he was a big, healthy fellow who lived out of doors and need never have come into contact with the epidemic at all.[8]

Over the years the versions changed slightly and she indicated that the man was in fact known to her and that they had been engaged in a youthful love affair before she became ill. In 1956 she told the *Denver Post*:

"I was quite young during World War I in Denver and I had a job on *Rocky Mountain News*. Bill, the city editor (the city editor of her story is named Bill), put me to covering the theaters. I met a boy, an army lieutenant. . . . Our time was so short and we were much in love. But we were shy. It was a step forward and two steps back with us . . . I was taken ill with the flu. They gave me up. The paper had my obit set in type. I've seen the correspondence between my father and sister on plans for my funeral. . . . I knew I was dying. I felt a strange state of—what is the Greeks called it?—euphoria. . . . But I didn't die. I mustered the will to live. My hair turned white and then it fell out. The first time I tried to rise to a sitting position I fell and broke an arm. I had phlebitis in one leg and they said I'd never walk again. But I was determined to walk and live again, and in six months I was walking and my hair was grown back."

"And the boy, Miss Porter?"

"It's in the story." At the sudden memory she fought back tears—and won gallantly. "He died. The last I remember seeing him. . . . It's a true story. . . . It seems to me true that I died then, I died once and I have never feared death since. . . ."[9]

In 1969 she gave this version to the *Baltimore Sun:*

He was so patient with me, those nights when I was sick and delirious, getting me things and always just sitting there. When I would wake up he would be there, sometimes with his foot propped up. After I went to the hospital he sent me two dozen roses and a note. They took the roses away from me because they said flowers used up oxygen. And the nurse read me the note, and I could hear that she was reading but I couldn't make out the words. And that was all. He died. And no one seems to think that was important, and it was one of the most important and terrible things that ever happened to me.[10]

Toward the end of her life she spoke of him as the one person she had really loved and with whom she might have had a lasting happy relationship. When she was seventy-one and living in Italy she visited the room in which Keats died. She found the experience moving and said that she had never felt such a living sympathy with a dead person before, "except with Alexander—the Adam of my World War I story." She said consistently in her later years that his name was not Adam Barclay as in the story but Alexander Barclay.[11] (The name is that of the translator into English of Brandt's *Ship of Fools.*)

In the story, Adam is an insubstantial figure, completely lacking the vivid details and turns of phrase that usually animate the characters based on people whom Porter knew. He is an idealized saintly person whose features are obscured because he usually appears in a flash of light or surrounded by an aura of brilliance. Moreover, Porter was not a shy young girl but a twenty-eight-year-old divorcée for whom unconsummated love affairs were unlikely. It would seem safe to conclude, therefore, that if a young man did help Porter in the early stages of her illness, he was a casual acquaintance and not a suitor or lover. Later, when she replaced the actual circumstances with fictional ones, the more satisfactory literary version probably erased the original one and became the only version she remembered. The lifelong devotion to the young man, which was so dear to her heart, should properly be seen as the love of a writer for a favorite character, the love of an artist for the created object. There is, therefore, an ironic truth in her assertion that he was the one man she could have loved. A statement made when she was seventy-nine suggests that others saw the irony of the situation.

"And except for the fact that it didn't happen quite as fast as I say, it was just like that, the dream and everything," Miss Porter remembers now, still—two husbands, a career and half a century later—still in love with him. "I always thought it was so funny that he should have died and I should have lived, because I was small and not particularly strong, and he was big and magnificent looking. And I trusted him so. I had absolute faith in him. I remember saying to a Spaniard in Mexico once that Alexander was the only man I could ever have spent my life with. And he replied, 'Just think, now he can never disappoint you.' And I suppose if there is anything at all good about it, that's it, but it does seem an awfully high price to pay to keep one's illusions, doesn't it?"[12]

Whatever her relationship with the young soldier, "Pale Horse, Pale Rider" contains an important central truth, a piece of "biography in the deeper sense." Porter describes her character, Miranda Gay, as being emotionally changed when she emerges from her experience of the war and the plague.

The nature of the change was not apparent to observers. Porter did, of course, take some time to recover from the phlebitis, and she had broken her arm in a fall. All her hair fell out and she had to wear bandannas to cover her baldness. And she was tired and strained. When she was released from the hospital she went to stay with Gay and remained with her through the Christmas holidays. Her chief joy at this time was once again in being with her little niece, reading to her, telling her stories and teaching her songs. She particularly enjoyed a shopping expedition during which she helped Mary Alice buy a Christmas gift for Gay.

She returned to Denver early in 1919 to resume work on the *Rocky Mountain News* and was now promoted to drama editor, in charge of the whole theater section and required to write numerous play and movie reviews and editorial columns. Her colleagues at this time describe her as strikingly attractive and as a dramatic kind of person who had an air of mystery about her. When she talked she did so with great animation, using theatrical gestures and flashing her large gray eyes, and all the men fell in love with her. One of her female colleagues describes her as a "glamorous figure whom I worshiped," the epitome of southern femininity and a person to be looked up to. She dressed very attractively and in good taste, mostly in gray. She wore gray and black hoods which covered her glistening black hair, and she was so glamorous and intriguing that passers-by would stop and take a second look, particularly because she constantly talked with her hands and her eyes.[13]

Clearly Porter was full of energy at this time. Besides filling her new position as drama editor, she was busy with several other activities. She wrote an advertising column, "Let's Shop with Suzanne," a job which provided an extra source of income and required her to visit local clothing stores. The style of these columns is quite unlike that of her serious journalism. Possibly she was imitating the mannerism of the advertisements she memorized in the boring days in the Carlsbad Sanatorium. Even so, her language is so affected and exclamatory that it seems more like parody than imitation. She adopts the persona of a Frenchwoman, using (sometimes inaccurately) the fragments of French that she was learning at the local branch of the Alliance Française:

> Next to being a bride is being a graduate; n'est-ce pas? And this week I saw, oh! so many fluffy little creations made just for those dear little girls who have finished school. Dresses betucked and beruffled, with long sleeves and short but al-

ways full and flowing. Sashes and bows that clamor for attention, dear little rosebud bouquets that nestle close and are happy with their wearers. . . .

I am—oh! such a busy little girl. I was almost afraid that I couldn't get to you this week, but here I am. And each Sunday now I shall have such interesting things to tell you of the "pretties" that I find in the shops. There are really some lovely ones in Denver, mais oui! and you will surely want to know what they are showing. I am a splendid shopper, too. Certainement.[14]

She also joined the recently formed Little Theater, throwing herself wholeheartedly into the productions, and supporting the Little Theater Movement in her newspaper column:

In this country the Little Theater idea, of which the Denver organization is an integral part, will soon become the great medium of artistic expression for young painters and singers and dancers and mimes, who will come there, each with a passionate dream locked in his soul, to offer their gifts to the world. Away with the boarding-school-miss attitude toward art, the amateur state of mind toward life, the squeaking, mouselike fear of thinking in terms of breadth and depth. Then speak your thoughts out boldly, to the stars, as if you knew your soul were immortal.[15]

She was a cheerful participant in lighthearted fund-raising ventures for the Little Theater, playing "Tipsy" in an Omar Khayyam pageant.[16] She acted in a number of productions, and when she wrote the review of a performance of Oscar Wilde's *The Happy Prince,* she singled herself out for special praise:

Miss Katherine Anne Porter was the little Swallow with birdlike voice and the grace of a wheedling swallow who flew out over the city to do the Prince's bidding and at last, dulled by the winter, died at the foot of the statue. . . . Her dancing and posturing were lovely.[17]

This particular production had momentous consequences for her. She wore for the part a blue costume which was the most beautiful one she had ever had. She attracted a great deal of attention, won several admirers, and found herself, as Jane Anderson had the summer before, the center of a group of admiring "beaux." Among these was a handsome young architect whose wife had fallen ill, as Porter had in the fall, and who had not recovered. Parke French, recently widowed and left with a baby son, was active in the Little Theater and was serving as managing director. When he saw Porter in the bird costume he fell in love with her, began an urgent suit to make her his wife, and managed to persuade her to become engaged to him. As the engagement had to be kept secret until a decent period of mourning for his wife had elapsed, Porter wore her great diamond engagement ring on a chain around her neck. She was not displeased at the need for secrecy, since it permitted her to enjoy the attention of her other admirers, and her only worry was that she felt nervous in the possession of such a valuable jewel. Moreover, she was not at all sure that she really wanted to marry Parke French and become a Denver socialite.

She seemed outwardly, then, completely active and cheerful, but in fact she was changed emotionally, and it is in her reviews that the change is most clearly reflected. These are characterized by a moral earnestness which is in striking contrast to the flip tone of those written the year before in Fort Worth. The year before she had said: "We can't have too much vaudeville for the soldier boys, and the Byers management is giving us the best—clean, original, with plenty of comedy."[18] In early 1919 she was extremely critical of vaudeville in particular and of frivolous entertainment in general. She wrote disapprovingly of the crowds who flocked to see a group of scantily clad dancing girls and neglected entirely a war hero's account of his experiences:

An average audience faced the soldier who had lived thru the most profound experiences ever offered to humanity on this sad earth; and there they sat, looking calmly ahead, while the aviator told them a few unattractive truths about themselves, the Bolsheviki and kindred evils. When we came out of this theater, the crowd on the other side of the street had extended half way down the block on either side of the magic portals. All to glimpse six scampering chorus girls inadequately clad! Forgive these slightly ironic smiles —it was amusing.

A study of their faces under the sharp sidewalk lights revealed a really serious appreciation of art, so to speak. That is, they seriously wished to be present when the parade started. Some of them wedged in, and the disappointed ones were still there, augmented by several hundred additional devotees of the drama when the lucky ones wended forth late in the evening, wearing surfeited cat-and-cream smiles. There was nothing scandalous in the whole affair save the mental atmosphere. That was somewhat suffocating we admit.[19]

She had also shed her illusions about the quality of the plays and had no hesitation in voicing her scorn for them. Whereas in the *Critic* she had been happy to accept the career of Cupid as subject matter for drama, she now rejected it in favor of more serious themes. She scorned the inevitable happy endings, mocked the subject matter (love presented as an "ethereal affair ending sedately at the altar with an exchange of vows," and marriage as a "long roseate picnic"), and she attacked the weak plots.[20]

Nor did she single out individual plays alone for criticism. She condemned the whole of the drama of the day. In one review, answering those who bewailed the deterioration of theatrical standards, she wrote that she doubted if the theater was ever the pillar of the fine arts. Rather she believed that it had always been "cheap and callow or else bombastic and hideously untrue to life and art."[21] In a review of *The Man Who Came Back* she said categorically that she considered modern drama to be a "slander on life, on art, on—pardon the stodginess—on morals,"[22] and she rejected its facile optimism:

Most of us care little for art, and are terrified of life. So, therefore, our moral truths must be doled out to us in sugar pills of sentimentality. We cannot endure to see people being punished for wrongdoing or dying in the last act. We must be cheered up and slapped on the back and assured that everything is for the best in this best of all possible worlds.[23]

A review of June 1919 presents her opinion of the drama in summary:

Of plays and books, especially those of the current season, there is not much to be said. Flaccid and flavorless most of them are; the plays have been a wearying procession of saccharine he-and-she affairs, or a coarseness that passes for comedy and a brutality that is meant for strength. The plots

creak in both books and plays, the long arm of coincidence
is being fairly snatched from the socket half the time.[24]

It is apparent from Porter's descriptions of the simpering heroines and stereotypical heroes and villains that the theatrical fare of
the time consisted mainly of crude Victorian melodrama. But what is
interesting is that while she objected strenuously to the plays she did
not question or reject the basic characteristics of melodrama itself.
The form, in fact, was completely acceptable to her. (That this should
have been so is not surprising when the polarities of her childhood
world are remembered.) She accepted, for example, the polarization
of good and evil and the division of characters into saints and sinners.
In an untitled editorial on the villains of stage and screen she mocked
the exaggerated, unconvincing, stereotypical appearance of the usual
villain, but she did not question the existence of the villain himself:

> Screen villains are for the most part basely (sic) untrue to
> life. They have no respect for the police and very little for
> the neighbors. They make scenes in hotel lobbies which is
> in very bad taste and always openly persecute the heroine,
> which is bad judgment. . . .
>   The screen villain's clothes are usually all wrong and his
> moustache deceives no one. Yet he is not without interest in
> many respects, tho' after attending a series of pictures we
> have an uncanny feeling that we are meeting the same man
> again and again in varying disguises.[25]

She went on, having dubbed him "Every Villain," to trace his trail of
crime in his various manifestations as a tall, dark, mustached man, as
a blond, balding type in a business suit, as a middle-aged impresario,
and as an aesthete. Her amusing descriptions show that she objected
not to the concept of the villain but to the quality of the villains being
presented.

In the same review, one that is especially revealing of her attitudes, she said that she had a "longstanding fascination with the psychology of villainy." She then modified the statement, explaining that
the real villain deserves some admiration because, after all, "it takes
imagination and real nerve to become a real first-class sinner." In
another review she expressed the opinion that a sinner is more interesting than a saint probably because "he is often a trifle more sincere."

As a result of her recognition of the positive qualities to be found in villains, her attention moved from the villain to the virtuous, passive heroine, and it was on this figure that she eventually heaped all her scorn and contempt. She felt that the attempt to pass off such a feeble person as the receptacle of virtue was not only bad art but also, in her own phrase, a "slander on morals." Many reviews, like the following one of George Broadhurst's *The Woman on the Index,* express her impatience:

It must be true that Broadhurst wrote the role of Sylvia Angot, the heroine—the deadly virtuous deeply wronged creature who spent a great deal of valuable time concealing her past from her highly respectable husband. None but a Broadway playwright could cast such a sickly halo around the head of a straw woman. "Look," says he, "look, how this saintly woman is being wronged by everybody in sight, and see how pure she is. Look at this husband who must never, never know or he would turn from her in horror." And he proceeds to build up a tissue of bogus, near crimes, wherein he tangles the lady, and sets her to work concealing a past that she wouldn't need to conceal if she had a grain of intelligence. But, of course, she hasn't, or she wouldn't be the heroine of a Broadway drama.[26]

The shift of Porter's attention from the villain to the saintly heroine was not a temporary change of focus but a permanent one, and her attitude toward the virtuous heroine eventually formed the cornerstone of her moral philosophy. The main tenet of this philosophy was that the evildoers are not the most reprehensible people of the world because at least they have the courage of their convictions. Nor are they the most dangerous people, since they can be easily recognized. The people who really need to be watched are the so-called innocents who stand by and allow others to perpetrate evil. Porter was to express repeatedly the opinion that the innocent bystanders allow the activity of evildoers not merely because of fear and indifference but because they gain vicarious pleasure from seeing others perform the wicked deeds which they themselves wish but fear to perform. She came eventually to see passive, virtuous people as guilty of promoting evil even when they do not consciously do so.

This theory about the relationship between saints and evildoers and their collusion in evil became her lifelong gospel, the subject of numerous informal talks, the message she preached from political platforms, the basis of her interpretation of current events, the foundation of her literary criticism, and the theme which informed all her fiction.

Over forty years later, when *Ship of Fools* appeared, she gave an account of the events of the twentieth century which illustrated its theme:

> . . .the collusion in evil that allows creatures like Mussolini, or Hitler, or Huey Long or McCarthy—you can make your own list, petty and great—to gain hold of things, who permits it? Oh, we're convinced we're not evil. We don't believe in that sort of thing, do we? And the strange thing is that if these agents of evil are all clowns, why do we put up with them? God knows, such men are evil, without sense—forces of pure ambition and will—but they enjoy our tacit consent.[27]

Within the novel the theme is stated in a crucial discussion which takes place at the captain's table of the *Vera*. The guests are discussing the activities of the Spanish dancers and one of the passengers expresses the opinion that they are "dangerous criminals." The captain of the ship disagrees because "it takes a certain force of character to be really evil."[28] His remark has the special interest of being almost word for word what Porter wrote in her 1919 editorial on the villains of the Denver stage. The ship's doctor elaborates on the captain's statement:

> "I agree with the Captain it takes a strong character to be really evil. Most of us are too slack, half-hearted or cowardly—luckily, I suppose. Our collusion with evil is only negative, consent by default you might say. I suppose in our hearts our sympathies are with the criminal because he really commits the deed we only dream of doing."[29]

She not only acknowledged the unchanging nature of her point of view but took pride in it, saying after the publication of *Ship of Fools*, "It's astonishing how little I've changed: nothing in my point of view or way of feeling. I'm going back now to finish some of the great short stories that I have begun and not been able to finish for one reason or another."[30]

In later years when she spoke of her theme she said that it developed out of her observation of the disastrous events in pre-Nazi Germany, but that those events would have meant nothing if she had not witnessed similar events before that in Mexico.[31] The journalism that she wrote in Denver, however, makes it clear that her theme predated her visits to Mexico and Germany and emerged when she was reviewing theatrical productions in 1919.

What she acquired at this time was to be of the greatest importance to her as a writer, for she considered her "theme" or "message" the raison d'être of all her fiction. When she was praised as a stylist, she said she was furious, because the important thing was not the style but what she had to say.[32] The philosophy which provided her theme was also, however, one of the greatest factors in limiting her work. Her view of a world peopled by villains, victims, and people of dubious virtue allowed her characters little scope for growth and change. In fact she could not imagine characters with the capacity to develop, and she was never able to create them. Within the confines of the short story this weakness hardly mattered. It was when she tried to write a novel that she had to find a way to substitute for characters unable to mature in the way traditionally required of the novelist. But the struggle with the novel was far ahead. In the meantime she had taken her first major step as a writer. She was now in possession of a theme and a point of view.

Porter herself never acknowledged and probably never realized how much she gained at this time from her journalistic experience. If she had been aware of it in 1919 it would probably have yielded her little satisfaction, because her last days in Denver were overshadowed by disaster which, once again, struck without warning and from the direction she least expected.

A full account of what happened has survived in a series of descriptions which Porter wrote a few years later when she was trying to use the experience in a story. While the details may be shaped and arranged, the actual events have been verified by others.

One summer night in July she was suddenly overcome with a growing apprehension and premonition of disaster which grew to a state of panic. Without understanding why, she fell about the floor in paroxysms of grief and terror and finally heard herself say that she must go home. Having made that decision she set her alarm clock so that she would wake early and, exhausted by her frenzy, fell asleep. It was noon when she woke, having overslept the alarm clock, and she found a telegram pushed under her door which told her that her little niece, Mary Alice, had died of spinal meningitis. Later she received a letter, unaccountably delayed, which told her of the child's illness. It said that Mary Alice wanted her aunt to say a Mass, as the child had done for Porter earlier in the year, and that she was putting all her faith in the efficacy of this Mass. It added considerably to Porter's grief and guilt that she had not been able to fulfill the child's dying request.[33]

One of the first people Porter met after the news arrived was Kitty Barry Crawford. Kitty, now out of the hospital, was coming down a Denver street when she saw Porter walking along haltingly, looking ill and lost, her face white and drawn. When Kitty approached her, she fell into her arms sobbing, "My little niece—oh, Kitty, she died."

Porter sent roses for the child's grave but she did not go home, then or for many years. She made plans to visit her sister but said that she would not have the courage to go to Mary Alice's grave.[34] The plans she made were never carried out, and it seems likely that her grief over the loss of her niece had a part in her long years of separation from her family. For years afterward she said that summer was darkened by the approach to the terrible anniversary of the death, and she thought she suffered from it more than her sister, who still had one child and was expecting another. For all that, Gay was deeply upset and turned in her trouble to spiritualism. Porter rebuked her sister and told her that spiritualism was a superstition for darkened minds, like a belief in witchcraft and a personal devil.[35]

She told Gay that she was cutting herself off from a very lovely experience by her spiritualism and related how she herself was coming to terms with the loss. She said that Mary Alice came to her once as she lay in bed and she moved over to make room for her. Another time when she was sewing she felt that there were two people in the room. She also made the following poem to commemorate the child.

Poem for Dead Mary Alice
It is quiet enough now in the house where she lay,
Watching the lattice of window vines swaying in the
    sun;
Saying, "Oh, dearly, dearly I love the light of day
And all the growing things that flower or run."

It is quiet enough now at window and on stairs,
And not again will she lift up her arms and smile and
    say,

"Oh dearly do I love the dress the summer garden
    wears,
And dearly do I love the light of day."[36]

She never quite got over the loss and all her life tried, without much success, to write a significant literary memorial to her niece, just as Virginia Woolf wrote her versions of her father's Mausoleum book to lay the ghosts of her brother and her parents. The most Porter managed was "A Christmas Story," a description of the shopping expedition she had taken with Mary Alice in December of 1918. This was published by *Mademoiselle* in 1958 and reprinted in a gift edition for the magazine staff and their friends. The same story, with drawings by Ben Shahn, was republished in 1967 by the Delacorte Press. When she sent a copy to a friend in 1974, she inscribed it as follows:

I learned long ago from the life and death of this child how
deathless love, and faithful memory, can be. She has lived in
my life for more than half a century, a perpetual spring of
joy that has helped me to live—
But why was she taken away?[37]

The impact of Mary Alice's death, much like Porter's own near death from influenza, is not completely explicable. Porter tried for years to probe the sources of her grief and find some meaning in the whole experience, but she never came to terms with it. Her prolonged struggle and failure to write a story about the incident suggests that she never fully understood the sources of her grief or all the reasons for her reaction. The loss did, however, seem to provide the final step in the change and alienation that was complete by the end of the summer of 1919.

One person who was not sympathetic to Porter's grief was her fiancé, Parke French. He was jealous and bitter about her unconsolable sadness and told her she was morbid to be wallowing in misery. His attitude caused an estrangement between them and Porter felt afterward that she had been saved from an unhappy marriage.

All year Porter had been saving up money in an old shoulder-length evening glove and her aim was to use it to go to New York. At the end of the summer she felt that she had learned all she could at the *Rocky Mountain News,* and after all the sad experiences she longed to get away from Denver. Kitty was going home to Fort Worth and

Porter decided to travel with her, visit her own family, and then make the long-planned journey to New York. When she left for Texas there was no visible sign of her inner grief.

Garfield Crawford had reserved a drawing room in a Pullman car so that Kitty, little Jane, and her nurse could travel in comfort. They were besieged at the station by Porter's admirers, who squeezed into the drawing room carrying flowers. They kissed her and refused to leave until the last possible moment, and when the train finally pulled out Kitty looked out and saw them all running down the platform after it, waving handkerchiefs.

In Fort Worth Porter changed her mind about seeing her family and went directly to New York. She wrote her father that she was sorry their lives had grown apart, but that she had known from the cradle that fate would not do the usual thing with her. She said all her life so far had been a hideous, blind, mad struggle to break her shell and achieve her destiny, and just now she was beginning to see that she was right and had not been deceived by that inner conviction. She was sure that she was an artist, a little deformed by her battle and a little weakened by the long, grinding resistance, but a living creative force, just the same; she had not been fooled.[38] To her sister she wrote that she had done very well in Denver and had made a good name for herself. She added that she was going away now and that one day she would write as well as anyone in America.[39]

SEVEN

Greenwich Village and Mexico City:
A Very Growing Season

Porter's intuition that another break from her old life was necessary to the realization of her destiny was a sure one, as was her choice of Greenwich Village as her destination. She said later, "It was a very growing season for me . . . and I would not have missed being there just when I was there for anything."[1]

Her first year of residence in the Village—she was to live there intermittently throughout the twenties—coincided with a turning point in the history of the United States. The Volstead Act, which changed the character of the country in general and of the Village in particular, went into effect a few months after she arrived. Shortly afterward two Italian immigrants, a fishmonger and a shoemaker, were arrested for murder and thus began a case which lasted for seven years and became the rallying point for the many forces dividing the country. Porter eventually became heavily involved in the Sacco-Vanzetti affair, but in the early days she was more taken up with the gathering momentum of her own life.

In Greenwich Village she found herself for the first time among artists and Bohemians who lived for their work and were restrained by none of the conventions of ordinary society. The atmosphere was completely congenial to her temperament and she quickly adapted to her new surroundings. When Parke French, her Denver fiancé, pursued her, she had no hesitation in sending him on his way, tossing his engagement ring down to him from her apartment window.[2]

She had by this time set up housekeeping in a second-floor-front flat at 17 Grove Street, and her apartment reflected her new way of life. She never tired of describing its charms in her letters home:

> I suppose I must have yammered about my purple furniture until you are all weary of it, but I must tell you once more how it looks. Think, I have been three months getting into the devilish place but as it stands now, with the last thing bought irrevocably, my studio room is arranged thus—dull blue crash curtains, couch cover to match, piled up with pillows in vermilion, green, orange, rose, black and purple. The fireplace is black, and across the room, between two windows stands a tall old-fashioned black mirror, that reflects the fire. My desk, chair, a tall hall chair and a drop leaf table are painted purple. A deep steamer chair is black with green cushions. The rug is dull blue, round woven fibre. The floor is black, and the walls are pure white. I have a tea table furnished with every color of pottery under heaven, blue, rose, gray, black, and, oh, my books are there, and I have two Holbein prints on the wall. There is a tiny dressing room, and a wee bath, and a kitchen the size of a closet, all fixed up in yellow crockery (the kitchen) and its a plumb satisfactory house. The great lovely joke being that, finished and done, the thing has cost me just $155 but it does seem as if I am forever buying something for it. But now half a dozen more things, and I am finished. And it is the sort of place I love. I don't really like ready made furniture—I snooped around second hand shops and picked up funny looking things and painted them and gosh, its grand! The wilder the place looks, the dearer it is to me![3]

Even with her keen eye for bargains she soon exhausted the money saved up in the evening glove and had to find some means of support. In this she tried to follow the advice of Deems Taylor, the musicologist and former husband of Jane Anderson. During a visit to Denver he had told her not to waste her time on journalism but to find a well-paying job that would leave her enough time and energy to do her own work.[4] Accordingly, she found such a position in the publicity department of a movie company, but soon her own competence earned her a promotion to a more challenging and demanding job. She was made publicity manager and transferred to the Select Studio in East Orange, New Jersey. The advantage was an increase in salary, the disadvantage that she had to spend three hours a day traveling on subways, ferries, and streetcars.[5]

Later she spoke disparagingly of this work, advising young writers to do anything in preference, even "hashing in a restaurant."[6] At the time, however, she threw herself wholeheartedly into the job as she had done in Denver. One sample of her work has survived in the *Motion Picture Magazine* for October 1920, and it shows a precision of language and other qualities not usually present in such journalism. It is an account of an interview she did in Los Angeles with the popular actor Charles Ray:

> As he spoke I studied his rugged, sturdy face, with its extraordinary frankness and clean, friendly lines. His hair and eyes are dark—many who have seen him only in pictures imagine him to be fair-headed and grey-eyed—and he is immensely deliberate in speech and action. He carves out each word carefully, speaks thoughtfully, his diction somewhat hesitant at times.
>
> When he turned and caught my eye, he must have seen the naive admiration registered therein, for he turned away again, a slight wrinkle on his brow. Well, any healthy man hates hero-worship, and it must be particularly dreadful to one whose pet horror was being a matinee idol. He is not a gusher, this young man, but a deep well.
>
> I began to understand more fully that Ray's portrayal of the country youth is the highest form of mimetic art. He literally assumes the character as a garment and casts it off again at will. In everyday life he is of a spick and spanness in attire, like the famous gentleman who once stepped out of a band box.[7]

The distinction of her work resulted in another job offer, and for a time she thought of becoming a feature writer for Charles Ray, whom she considered the least objectionable of all the stars she had met. The job was almost arranged when she backed out, realizing that, however well it paid, such work was not for her. It was, after all, her "artist work" she lived for, and, although it would not keep her in shoe-latchets, it was bread and air and sleep and joy to her. The rest of her activities, she said, were just a gray background for her to flame against.[8]

Her "artist work" had received a new impetus through the circle of friends she had recently made, artists and writers and journalists of far wider experience than those she had known in Fort Worth and Denver. Among them were Ernestine Evans, who worked for the *Christian Science Monitor;* Rose Wilder Lane, Laura Ingalls Wilder's daughter, who had come East from Los Angeles; Bessie Beatty, the editor of *McCall's* magazine; Gertrude Emerson, who had traveled in the Orient and now worked for the *Asia* Publishing Company; and the illustrators Berta Hoerner and Elmer Hader.[9]

Most of these people worked for magazines with a national circulation, and Porter began to do likewise, although she later erased this work from her record and was firm in designating as her first story one she published three years later: "I published my first short story in 1923. . . . That was a real battle, and I was thirty-three years old. I think it is a most curious lack of judgment to publish before you are ready."[10]

In fact, she published a number of stories in 1920. She had always loved telling stories to children and appropriately three of her earliest stories were for children. She signed a contract to write twelve in all to appear in *Everyland,* a children's magazine of world friendship run by the Interchurch World Movement. The plan was that they would be illustrated by Hoerner and Hader and eventually published in book form. She was excited about the volume and intended to dedicate it as a memorial to the niece who had so loved her stories.[11]

Only three of the stories appeared, and perhaps Porter consigned them to oblivion because they were fairy stories and, besides that, retellings of existing stories. Nevertheless, they give a clear indication of the stage reached in the slow evolution of her talent, and even though she preferred to retell myths and legends rather than invent her own stories, her choice of material is consistent and very revealing.

The January story, "The Shattered Star," a whimsical explanation of the Northern Lights, is the story of an Eskimo girl who is stolen by Moon People.[12] She lives among them and learns all their magic, so that eventually she is able to steal their three precious possessions and take them back to her own people. Her people, however, have forgotten her; they reject both her and the gifts. She flings the gifts in all directions and they fall into the sea and sky, causing the curious effects known as the Aurora Borealis. The story published in February, "The Faithful Princess," is an account of a princess who insists on marrying her first love in spite of the opposition of the gods.[13] The March one, "The Magic Earring," tells of a clever princess who finds and rescues her bridegroom after he is stolen by a wicked fairy queen.[14]

Certain recurring motifs in these stories reveal Porter's perennial preoccupations. She had fantasized from childhood that she was a changeling and two of the stories describe people who are stolen by strange beings. She was often drawn to talented people and absorbed their skills and knowledge until her expertise exceeded theirs. The same two stories describe women who learn the magic art of others to such a degree that they outwit the original possessors. Two of the women in the stories go out, as she had done, among strangers. Each story contains the presence of a hostile supernatural force, a malignant kind of deity. Perhaps the most striking similarity is the marked, and probably unconscious, feminist bias. Each story features a strong, resourceful female character contrasting with a weak, ineffective male. When the female character is abused she acts swiftly and effectively to assert her rights. The theme reflects Porter's own childhood world, dominated by her forceful grandmother, in which her father played a subsidiary role. It is the reverse side of the theme that had developed out of her annoyance with the Denver theatricals and their monotonous portrayals of weak, passive women, and it became the thematic pattern of the stories she wrote in the next years—"María Concepción," "The Cracked Looking-Glass," and "The Jilting of Granny Weatherall."

Even when she wrote for adults, as she did after she abandoned the children's stories, Porter chose again the same thematic material and maintained her rootedly feminist orientation. "The Adventures of Hadji: A Tale of a Turkish Coffee-House" appeared later in the year in *Asia*.[15] It is the story of a dim-witted man, Hadji, who grows restive with his intelligent but aging wife and becomes embroiled with another woman. He is not able to interpret the cryptic messages of his new love and relies on his wife for their interpretation. His wife makes possible the pursuit of her rival until the moment when the lovers meet. At the rendezvous, when they are arrested and thrown into prison, the faithful wife intercedes with a trick that frees them, sends her rival on her way, and earns her husband's admiration. His fatuity is emphasized by the ritualistic misogynistic comments running throughout: "There is an old saying among the Osmalis, O Company of the Faithful, that from a woman nothing is to be had but foolishness and vexation. . . . Besides, O Company of the Faithful, when did truth ever come from the mouth of a woman?"[16]

The four stories provide an exact measure of the stage Porter had reached by the time she was thirty. They show her already in possession of many of the components of her mature talent. Evidently the journalistic writing had profited her more than it had harmed her, for she had become a fluent and graceful prose stylist. She acknowledged

Chapter Twenty of *Indian Myth and Legend,* by Donald A. Macken-zie,[17] as the source of her February story. A comparison of this story with its source shows that she knew how to organize her material so that it had shape and point and meaning. Perhaps most important, the stories show that the world view and the theme that were to inform all her work were fixed.

Why then was she taking so long to fulfill her promise and achieve the full mastery of her art? It seems that she lacked (or imag-ined she lacked) a body of material that she considered worthy of being used in fiction. What she imagined "the proper stuff of fiction" to be can be surmised from the four stories she *did* write. She seemed to think that an exotic setting, highborn characters, and exciting ad-ventures were needed, and that so far her untraveled, humdrum life had yielded her no such experiences. After all, she had lived her entire life in Texas.

In her own estimation, her experiences could not compare with those of her writing friends, Jane Anderson, Gertrude Emerson, and Ernestine Evans, with their adventurous excursions to Europe, Rus-sia, and the Orient. The nearest Porter had come to foreign experience was her contact with the Mexican community in Greenwich Village. Kitty Barry Crawford had worked as a reporter for the *San Antonio Express,* which maintained a Mexican bureau, and she had often gone to Mexico City to work or to spend holidays. She believed that her stories about Mexico had aroused Porter's interest. Porter, on the other hand, said that her early years in San Antonio accounted for her interest and that later, when she came to the Village, "there were all these charming young Mexican artists." Among them was Tato Nacho, who played the piano in a Village cabaret, and Adolpho Best-Maugard.[18]

Best-Maugard had invented a system of drawing based on an-cient Mexican designs from buried cities, mostly Mayan and some done by Aztec and other tribes, and she spent many hours listening to him. He proposed that she should get out a book on his system in English, and, amid all the other projects she had on hand, she at-tempted that too.

Eventually she turned it over to someone else, and when it was finished it influenced a whole generation of Mexican children, who used it in learning to draw and paint.

When the Diaghilev ballet with its galaxy of stars came to New York, Best-Maugard managed to interest Pavlova in doing a Mexican ballet. It was to be a simple romance set in Xochimilco and based on three of the most attractive Mexican dances. He asked Porter to do the story and Castro Padillo the music, which was based on popular dance tunes and compositions of his own. Best-Maugard himself started painting the scenery. He worked throughout the spring and summer of 1920 in a big loft near Broadway, and Porter spent hours watching him work and listening to him expounding his theories. For Porter, the outcome of all the work was disappointing. Pavlova loved the result and performed the ballet in various places over the next three years, putting on a great triumphant performance in Mexico City in 1923. She was not, however, able to perform it in New York because paper scenery was banned there as a fire hazard. Porter took friends to the theater hoping to see her work and discovered that her name was not on the program and that the Mexican ballet was excluded from the repertoire.[19]

In spite of her disappointment with the ballet, the experience had some positive results for Porter. She had learned a great deal about Mexican history and folklore and, more important, had gained the confidence and respect of some influential Mexicans. As a result she was offered a job with the *Magazine of Mexico,* a new promotional magazine backed by a group of rich American bankers. The great advantage of the job was that it required her to visit Mexico for material.

She was jubilant. Here at last was the opportunity for travel outside the boundaries of the United States; when she asked her father for the records necessary for her passport, she told him that she intended henceforth to travel outside the country every year of her life.[20] Her expectations of high adventure were fulfilled even before she reached Mexico, for when she changed trains in San Antonio (a quick visit to the restored Alamo gave her a sense of doubling back on her tracks) and boarded the train for Mexico City, it was like an armed camp, full of soldiers with their families and camp followers. When she got off the train one evening in Chihuahua and looked at the roof, she saw bayoneted rifles silhouetted against the sky, and smoke rising from the hot braziers of what resembled a militarized kitchen. Traveling on through the war-ravaged land, she saw the charred ruins of the old hacienda mansions and, in the large towns, whole buildings which had been leveled by cannon fire or burned by the peons. The walls of most of the buildings were densely pocked with bullets and plastered with slogans: VIVA LA REVOLUCION/MUERTE A LA TIRANIA/

PAN, TIERRA Y LIBERTAD. She was told, "We're having a little revolution down here," but she was not dismayed and her chief discomfort was that the coffee ran out before she reached Mexico City.[21]

In fact, the Mexico to which Porter came in 1920 had been in a state of revolutionary upheaval for nearly a decade, ever since the thirty-five-year dictatorial rule of Porfirio Díaz had ended. The ousting of Díaz, instead of bringing justice and prosperity to the masses, had been followed by a long series of conflicts. One emerging leader after another had died, some brutally murdered—Francisco Madero, Victoriano Huerta, and, earlier that same year, Venustiano Carranza. All over the country bandits and various political factions warred against each other.

But at last it seemed that a period of stability and peace might be hoped for. Alvaro Obregón, the current president, had been chosen in September in a free election and many of the dissidents were ready to accept him. Zapata was dead and his followers were inclined to be at peace with the central government. That other colorful and powerful bandit, Pancho Villa, had quietly retired to a hacienda near the Chihuahua border.

Porter felt the full force of the national optimism, because she arrived in Mexico City in time to take part in the celebrations surrounding Obregón's inauguration on December 1. She described him later as a ludicrous figure on that occasion, so drunk that he was draped over his podium like a rag doll and surrounded by generals in well-tailored foreign suits that were pulled out of shape by concealed weapons.

In a matter of months, the hopeful mood would dissipate and she would watch that too. It did not take long for the regional revolutionaries to become once again dissatisfied with those in power and for factional fighting to break out again and for the radicals and Catholics to clash.

But in the beginning Porter shared the hopes of the new administration and took an active part in the program of reforms in education and the arts, instigated by José Vasconcelos, the Minister of Education. Under his leadership, hundreds of teachers were employed to go like missionaries into the villages to teach the rudiments of reading, writing, arithmetic, diet and sanitation. Painters returned from fighting at home or studying abroad and formed a Syndicate of Painters, Sculptors and Intellectual Workers. Headed by Diego Rivera when he came back to Mexico in July 1921 and whom Porter met on a later visit when she ground paints for him and listened to him discuss his political and artistic theories, the Syndicate set up scaffolds and began painting huge murals that glorified the revolution and the people of Mexico. These were exciting times and she was not inclined to return quickly to New York.

As it happened, Kitty Barry Crawford and her daughter had arrived in New York just as Porter was preparing to leave. They took over the Grove Street apartment and the feeding of the pet ringtail monkey, Porter's latest acquisition, which lived in a cage on the landing. In Mexico City Porter set up another apartment at 20 Calle del Eliseo, in what had formerly been a ballroom, and this she furnished sparely with tables and chairs she bought at the National Pawn Shop. Thus established, she threw herself into the life of the city, her eager curiosity involving her in many situations and many people's lives.

As usual, she undertook a surprising number and variety of activities. Many of the Americans in Mexico City were employed as teachers and she was soon pressed into service as a teacher of dancing at the girls' high school, the Lerdo. She also had writing assignments apart from the work which was her chief source of income and the justification for her presence in Mexico. She had promised Ernestine Evans that she would send her some articles for the *Christian Science Monitor,* and she was still trying to finish an ambitious project she had undertaken some months before at the behest of Gertrude Emerson, ghost writing an entire book.

This was a novel based on a formless manuscript written by a woman who had married a Chinese student and gone to live with him in China. She had three children there and had just adapted herself to his way of life when he accepted an ambassadorial post in the United States. As they were traveling there he died of influenza. The exotic setting appealed to Porter, and she went to Ann Arbor, where the woman lived, took down her story, and brought it back to New York to finish. As she worked on it, however, the task grew distasteful. She could not sympathize with the young woman's subservience to her husband and her willingness to obey him in everything. Porter said later that she undertook the work in all good faith and innocence and that it could not have been more false because the woman had no idea what had happened to her. It was also the longest work that Porter had ever done, and the size of the task weighed on her. She had told her sister in the summer that the "novelette" was 12,000 words long and it nauseated her to look at it. Since it was not finished when she left for Mexico, she took it along,[22] and finished it in time for publication the following year.

In Mexico City it grew even more irksome to her to be working on someone else's fiction, because she had at last found the one remaining ingredient necessary for fiction of her own—a substantial body of material. It was all around her in the places she visited, the people she met, and the situations she was drawn into, and she set to work to record everything. She said later, "I listened to everybody and set down an amazing quantity of what I heard and saw. I was young and very eager to learn about the affairs of the world and the time I lived in."[23] But she rejected the idea that she had systematically gathered material. Soon after she left Mexico she wrote, "I cannot say 'I gathered material' . . . there was nothing so mechanical as that, but the process of absorption went on almost unconsciously, and my impressions remain not merely as of places visited and people known, but as of a moving experience in my own life that is now part of me."[24] And many years later she remarked, "I've had a great difficulty persuading young people who want a beginning in what they call a literary career, that we don't begin it as a literary career. We begin it as a vocation, and you don't go looking for material."[25]

The copious notes among her papers on this early period in Mexico, however, give credence to the notion that she was methodically collecting material for her own fiction. And in finding a form for her fiction she was influenced more by the novel she was ghost writing than she would have willingly admitted.

The novel, *My Chinese Marriage,* was in four sections,[26] and it occurred to Porter that she might use a similar pattern for her own novel based on the people she was meeting. These were colorful characters from very diverse groups, for as an American she was naturally drawn to the group of foreigners of all nationalities who had converged on Mexico City. Some of these were impecunious like herself and many were active in the revolution. Others were from a different milieu altogether:

> I had Revolutionist friends and artist friends, and they were gay and easy and poor as I was. This other mob was different: they were French, Spanish, Italian, Polish, and they all had titles and good names: a duke, a count, a marquess, a baron, and they all were in some flashy money-getting enterprise like importing cognac wholesale, or selling sports cars to newly rich politicians.[27]

Through Adolpho Best-Maugard she was also readily accepted into the community of Mexican artists like Manuel Gamio and Jorge

Enciso. She met David Siqueiros at a party and formed a special affinity with Siqueiros' wife. Her natural sympathy was not with the successful politicians and rich foreigners but with the outlaws; she said that her favorite people were the bandits. She made notes for a Mexican novel divided into two parts: "A Book of Men" and "A Book of Women," the first to consist of "Four Portraits of Revolutionaries" and the second of four descriptions of their female counterparts.[28]

To this end she gathered material on such characters as Felipe Puerto Carillo, a handsome Mayan Indian who was a *diputado* (congressman) from the state of Yucatán. She met him soon after she arrived, and he took her rowing on the lake in Chapultepec Park and to the Salón Mexico, where he taught her all the latest dance steps. (Later he was assassinated by a group of military officers who feared he might become president of Mexico.)

Another character who fell under Porter's scrutiny was Robert Haberman, a California lawyer of Rumanian Jewish descent. He had come to Mexico City with his Swedish wife, Thorborg, a journalist for the newspaper *El Heraldo*. He worked as a pharmacist and taught school but his real purpose was to smuggle guns for the peons of the Yucatán to use against their oppressors. In this he was closely allied with Carillo.

But more than any of these she fixed her attention on Joseph Hieronim Retinger, whom she met at the banquet after Obregón's inauguration. There over champagne he told her the story of his life. After their first meeting they met regularly and Porter recorded every word he spoke in his clean and precise English.[29] His story interested her for two reasons. One was that it was entwined with that of her old acquaintance Jane Anderson, the other that Porter herself had fallen in love with him. She said that she remembered every word he spoke not because she willed to remember (she wished she could forget) but because his words became a definite part of her life the moment they were spoken. She thought he was the most attractive man she had ever met. Pictures of him at the time show him as having a gaunt physique, a somewhat simian face, and lank, unruly hair. He certainly does not look handsome but he was a brilliant talker and enormously well informed. He told her about his native Cracow with its immense sound of bells, and about Ghenghis Khan, and he gave his opinions on the different races and countries he had known. He had attended the Sorbonne and studied psychology in Munich, and had lived in England, where he had been a close friend of Joseph

Conrad. His tragedy was centered in his belief that he had betrayed his country and his ideals by falling in love with the beautiful unattainable Jane Anderson. It was true that his friendship with Conrad and his marriage had both disintegrated because of his association with Jane, and it was perhaps through her also that he had been forced to leave England and later the other Allied countries. Calling him "De Rhett," Porter planned to write the story of his life. The story was never finished but she used her notes on Retinger for Tadeusz Mey, a character in "The Leaning Tower," which she wrote twenty years later.

The two became lovers, but the love affair did not for long increase Porter's happiness or her self-confidence. Described by his daughter as a person of weak sexual drives, Retinger seems to have been a less than passionate lover. In this area as in others, he preferred intrigue and complicated situations. Porter was in any case less concerned with physical than with other kinds of gratification. What she most craved was adoration, and she described in one note the keen pleasure of being in the arms of one man while another burned with jealous rage. She was gravitating to men who, instead of providing the adoration she craved, confirmed her doubts about her own worth. Retinger was hopelessly embroiled with Jane Anderson, talked of her constantly, and was full of schemes to meet her again.[30]

Surrounded as she was by dynamic, flamboyant characters with massive egos, Porter still found time to pay earnest attention to one person who possessed no colorful attributes.

She was Mary Louise Doherty, a midwesterner ten years younger than Porter who had a degree from the University of Wisconsin. From there she had gone to New York, studied economics at the Rand School, and made friends among the Communists. Porter later spoke scathingly of Mary's Communist tendencies: "She was trying to be a Communist and she really didn't know how and she'd never seen a real Communist: she had seen a few that had gone to Russia during the early days and had come back with wormy little books called *The Red Dawn,* don't you know, *To the Barricades* and so on."[31] But despite Porter's scorn, Mary was a genuine Mexicophile, devoted to the welfare of the country, and her conversion to communism sprang from her deep concern for the oppressed people. Her purpose in going to Mexico was to help the working women organize themselves into labor unions. She arrived later than Porter and the two met through the Habermans. Porter found in Mary a supportive friend such as she had had in Kitty Barry, someone who was in no way competitive with her or a sexual rival. Mary taught English several days a week to Indian children in the village of Xochimilco several miles south of Mexico City. Porter often went there, drawn by her friendship with Mary and also by her fascination with the place, which was the setting for the ballet on which she had worked with Best-Maugard the year before.

If Mary Doherty was not inherently as interesting as some of Porter's other friends, she did in spite of herself—perhaps it was inevitable in Mexico at that time—get drawn into some highly dangerous situations. Porter described the social atmosphere in which they moved:

> We used to have a kind of a beautiful old palace of blue tiles that had been turned into a kind of restaurant or café and it was all crowded with us together there in the evening and you know we'd have one drink around—anything you liked —everybody smoked what he wanted. I didn't pay any attention to people smoking marijuana. I didn't want it for myself, never thought about it, and we'd have one drink of something, you know like Tequila, perhaps, and then after that we'd sit nursing cups of coffee and we'd talk until four o'clock in the morning sometimes and sometimes those young men—they were very talented and good and some of them very good artists—and all kinds you know . . . they were worth having, worth keeping. And they would get up and say well all right we're off. And what they meant was they were off to join the troops and they expected to have a battle that next morning or the next day and some of them never came back and you know, I would say goodbye to the last, shake hands with them and sometimes never see them again and the time would come when someone would tell me what had happened to them. And that was the way—the atmosphere in which we lived.[32]

The friends who were not killed in battle often found themselves in jail, and Porter and Mary visited them as they languished on army cots in hot little cells. The women carried baskets of fruit, reading material (whodunits were in great demand), cigarettes, marijuana, and sleeping pills.

Living in such a situation inevitably had its dangers. One tragic accident involved a young man who demanded more than the usual small amount of sleeping pills. He was persuasive in his pleas and, having wheedled an excessive amount of sedatives, took the whole lot and died.

This incident later became part of the story "Flowering Judas," but when readers asked Porter about the source of the character of Laura and her role in the death of Eugenio, Porter's responses varied. Sometimes she said that Laura was a composite of "five different young women of whom I was not one." Many years later, she said in a tearful scene that it was she who had handed over the pills and caused the death—a situation that very likely would have dramatized her deepest fears about herself: namely that she inadvertently brought death to anyone she cared about.[33] More often than not, however, she said that Mary Doherty was the model for Laura, and it seems likely that because of her gentle, compliant nature, Mary would have let herself be persuaded by the young man to give him the pills. She was in any case horrified by his death and told Porter of a nightmare she had subsequently in which the young man appeared before her and accused her of killing him.

On another occasion Mary became the object of the unwelcome attentions of a fat half-Indian, half-Italian revolutionary called Yudico. He had deserted his wife to spend his evenings singing sentimental songs to Mary. One evening Mary asked Porter to come along and chaperone her. Porter willingly did so, being most amused at Yudico's annoyance and triumphant when she outstayed him.

What drew Porter's attention steadily to Mary was her resemblance to the passive, virtuous women of the Denver stage. Porter thought of her as a secular nun, who never became sexually involved with any man but devoted herself to one cause after another and to one man after another "as a kind of virgin office-wife."[34] Porter could not understand the feminine submissiveness and easy acquiescence which led Mary always into the service of someone stronger than herself.

Porter planned for many years to form the experiences of this time into a novel. It was listed in her "works in progress" over the next decade under such titles as "Thieves' Market" and "Many Redeemers," and sometimes privately she called it "Historical Present." The novel never appeared but various parts of it were published as separate stories, and one of the most successful of these was "Flowering Judas." In this story she linked the episodes of Mary's courtship by Yudico and that of the young man who died in prison. She worked the story into the thematic pattern she had developed in 1919, showing that by remaining passive Laura was drawn into serving the evil ends of her suitor Braggioni and that she was more guilty than he for the death of the victim. Laura is unable in her conscious, waking life to face up to her guilt. Instead she has a nightmare, and it is only in her dream that she approaches any understanding of the implication of her actions.

For the dream that concludes "Flowering Judas," she used not the dream Mary had confided to her but an experience of her own during a party in Cuernavaca with Moisés Saenz and other friends. The party took place in an old colonial house on a cobbled street overlooking a ravine. When Porter arrived she walked onto the patio and looked out over the low terrace wall at the ramshackle *jacales* of two squatter families who occupied the lowest level of the rocky arroyo at least a hundred feet directly below. The precipitous drop made her slightly dizzy.

The purpose of the party was to experiment with smoking marijuana, and Porter with her eager curiosity was ready to sample *"la yerba encantadora."* Her reaction to the drug was alarming, perhaps because her emotional instability made her unusually susceptible, but more likely because she was given some strong adulterated form of marijuana. Certainly the effect was beyond the ordinary. She felt herself transported to another dimension, as if the room and all its furniture were detached from its normal rectangular boundaries and were floating freely within itself. She felt that she was floating, moving about in slow motion, not quite touching anything she reached for. She thought that other people seemed to be moving in trances, talking in a soft deliberate manner so that each syllable they spoke came forth separately and apart. Most alarming of all, when she looked at one of the men in the room, without any warning she felt that she could actually see his thoughts whirling around inside his skull, little levers and springs and tiny cogwheels busily ticking away inside a glass dome. She turned and slowly looked around the room and saw that everyone else had a clear transparent crystalline skull with mad-whirling mechanisms which went faster and then slower as the conversations ebbed and flowed. Turning to the first person whose brain had been so exposed, she noticed that his little cogwheels had come to an abrupt halt even though his lips were still moving. She found she could no longer bear the sight of all the frightfully exposed brains and went out on the terrace.

There she experienced a relaxed euphoria and, looking beyond the terrace wall, saw thousands of shimmering stars caught in the sharp angular branches of a dead and leafless jacaranda tree; and she felt the strong urge to walk out into the dark sky, fully confident that she could defy the law of gravity. She walked across the terrace and reached the wall, which had at first seemed to recede from her, and had started to climb over when someone restrained her.[35]

In her story she described her character's dream landscape:

Laura takes off her serge dress and puts on a white linen nightgown and goes to bed. She turns her head a little to one side, and reminds herself that it is time to sleep. Numbers tick in her brain like little clocks, soundless doors close of themselves around her. . . .

Without a word, without fear she rose and reached for Eugenio's hand, but he eluded her with a sharp, sly smile and drifted away. This is not all, you shall see—Murderer, he said, follow me, I will show you a new country, but it is far away and we must hurry. No, said Laura, not unless you take my hand, no; and she clung first to the stair rail, and then to the topmost branch of the Judas tree that bent down slowly and set her upon the earth, and then to the rocky ledge of a cliff, and then to the jagged wave of a sea that was not water but a desert of crumbling stone. . . . She saw that his hand was fleshless, a cluster of small white petrified branches. . . .[36]

It is both a literal description of her own marijuana-induced hallucination and a haunting and poetic climax to the story.

In the spring of 1921, however, all the disparate experiences which would eventually be woven into the story remained separate and unconnected. In fact, Porter made little progress with any stories at this time, since her active life precluded work. The only writing she managed was some essays which eventually appeared (unsigned) in the *Christian Science Monitor* and in Carl Van Doren's *Century* magazine. In some of them she described the accelerating violence of the time. For example:

Uneasiness grows here daily. We are having sudden deportations of foreign agitators, street riots and parades of workers carrying red flags. Plots thicken, thin, disintegrate in the space of thirty-six hours. A general was executed today for counterrevolutionary activities. There is fevered discussion in the newspapers as to the best means of stamping out Bolshevism, which is the inclusive term for all forms of radical work. Battles occur almost daily between Catholics and Socialists in many parts of the Republic.[37]

She spoke knowledgeably, for many of her own friends were heavily involved in the turmoil. Robert Haberman was in hiding and he and Yudico were polishing their weapons for battle. Angel Gomez was planning to blow up churches and spent hours on his knees before the *tilma* of Our Lady of Guadalupe. Retinger managed to inject his own personal complications into the situation by making a dangerous journey to the United States, ostensibly to see his brother but really to meet Jane Anderson. Since he had no American passport his undertaking involved a risky smuggling venture. He managed to reach Washington, D.C., and see Jane, but on the way back he was arrested and thrown into jail, first in St. Louis and then in Houston. He sent desperate telegrams to Porter asking her to help raise his bail. This she did and he was eventually freed and able to return to Mexico City. Porter still loved him, but she was beginning to see that he was not a reliable person on whom she could build hopes for her future. She was forced to conclude with Gilbert Seldes, Retinger's rival for Jane's affections, that he was a born intriguer who preferred pieces of secret information to straightforward dealings: "He is utterly without responsibility of any kind, and obsessed with a sense of the dramatic."[38]

With such friends it was inevitable that Porter herself should fall under suspicion. She was accused of being a Bolshevik and for a time was on the proscribed list, fearing arrest or deportation and having in readiness a speech prepared for the police when they came to arrest her.[39] Eventually she could stand the tension no longer. She left Mexico City and tried to get back to the United States. This was not a straightforward matter either, as she had spent all her money as fast as she earned it and did not have the means to travel out of the country.

For help she turned once again to her old friends the Crawfords in Fort Worth. Kitty was now back with her husband, having been able to stand the Grove Street apartment no longer than a week. She had been constantly disturbed there by Village friends who, unaware that Porter had left the country, would gather on the sidewalk below the window, throw gravel, shout for her to come down, and threaten to come and pull her out if she didn't appear immediately. Between the friends and the pet monkey she had had a difficult time and had fled first to Connecticut and eventually back to Texas. When Porter appealed for money, Kitty persuaded her husband, somewhat against his will, to send the train fare, and Porter, thin and worn out, arrived shortly afterward in Fort Worth.[40]

She was heartsick at leaving Retinger and exhausted by the events of the past weeks, but she had a large portfolio of material and the Crawfords' white frame house on the quiet street was a good place to recover. She found in the house next door to the Crawfords' a large attic workroom so that she could write in peace.[41] Now, at last, it seemed she had everything necessary for the full and triumphant realization of her art. She had practiced her craft until she could write beautifully; she understood how to organize a story; she had a mass of material for fiction; and now, finally, she had the time and solitude for writing.

And yet, she was still unable to finish any of her stories. She did a fragmentary mood piece called "In a Mexican Patio" and offered it to Garfield Crawford for the oil journal he was publishing, and she wrote another story which the Crawfords admired, but neither of these was published. Kitty, who knew her friend very well, thought she was much more interested in day-to-day active life and social events than in her writing. She said later:

> In my opinion she rarely worked hard to create something, such as a story or a book. . . . What she has mainly striven for is the opportunity to *be* something and *do* something as she goes along.
> When she does write she writes with expert artistic precision, but mostly very quickly because she wants to haste away, or stay where she is if she likes for the time to be there, and needs money to do so.[42]

Kitty had some grounds for her conclusions because Porter did easily allow herself to be distracted by numerous activities. She needed money as usual and she took a job working on Garfield Crawford's *Oil Journal* for $50 a month. Also, as she had done in Denver, she wrote an advertising column for the Fort Worth paper, this time called "Let's Go Shopping with Marie."[43] Kitty herself was involved in a fund-raising venture to organize a T.B. sanatorium in Fort Worth and Porter's help was enlisted in this too. She undertook the job of publicity chairman. In addition to these paid jobs she also found another interest.

At this time a young Fort Worth actress, Rosalind Gardner, with her brother, Hunter Gardner, had founded a Little Theater.[44] The first performance took place soon after Porter's arrival, in a large barn on the Gardner property, and Porter and Kitty were in the audience. Afterward they went backstage to greet the performers and Porter was invited to join the company. Thereafter she appeared in all the plays that were performed that season. Hunter Gardner, recently divorced, fell in love with her and hoped to marry her.[45] She could not take him seriously as a suitor but she did enjoy the attention, and she acted opposite him in a number of plays. Her first part must have pleased her, for its theme (a strong woman triumphing over a weak man) was one of her favorites and it was from this role that she named the persona of her advertising column:

> "Poor Old Jim" is a farce in which Roscoe Carnrike keeps the house roaring during the entire length of the play. Katherine Anne Porter, as Marie, his wife, and Hunter Gardner, as Paul, the doctor, complete the cast. Jim likes his club, but his addiction for alcoholic refreshment is leading him to the grave. Maria and Paul "frame" him when he comes home "dead drunk" one morning. They pretend that he is dead, and that his spirit has returned. They lament his death and a clever plot is unravelled, much to the delight of the audience, who are in convulsions most of the time. Jim returns to his wife and is cured of his alcoholic inclinations.[46]

In December she played Columbine to Hunter Gardner's Harlequin in a production of *The Wonder Hat*. As in Denver, her participation in the plays brought a crowd of admirers. Little Jane Anderson Crawford remembered that their home was crowded with young men waiting to escort Porter, that she always wore beautiful clothes and shoes with very high heels, and that she always seemed to be dashing in to change and rushing out again.[47]

After six months, when the Little Theater season ended, Porter, having regained her health and equanimity, realized it was time once more to leave Texas. Her preference was to return to Mexico for a reunion with Retinger. She still loved him and had made one long journey to Laredo for a rendezvous, but she had no illusions about his

feelings for her. He was still involved with Jane Anderson and, although he wrote Jane angry letters and stormed about her, Porter
recognized his feelings. When he sent her a copy of one of his letters
to Jane, she told him:

> Do you think it tactful to ask your latest mistress to mail for
> you a love letter to your former one? For even if you did not
> intend it to be one, my dear, my dear! one does not write
> such a letter of hate until letters of love have proved hope-
> less. And above all, one does not write letters of this sort to
> a woman for whom one is merely indifferent, as you claim
> to be.[48]

As it happened, the choice of destination was taken out of her
hands. She had no money, having again spent her journalism pay as
quickly as she earned it, and had to ask the Crawfords. Garfield
Crawford refused to give her the fare to Mexico. He would provide
her fare only if she went to New York, where she would have reasonable job prospects and the opportunity to publish her stories. She was
bitterly resentful of his interference, but she took his advice and went
to New York.[49] When she wrote to her sister at this time she was less
optimistic than before about her art. She wondered if she would ever
have the strength to realize her dream.

Her dream had now taken on a very specific form. At Christmas
in Fort Worth she had read an issue of *Century* and told Mary Doherty
that it was her aim to one day publish a story in that family magazine.[50] When she arrived in New York she took one of her essays to
the editor and it was accepted for the July number. It was an account
of the political situation in Mexico called "Where Presidents Have No
Friends." She was pleased, but what she really wanted was to have
her fiction accepted there. Buoyed by the acceptance of the essay and
more conscious than ever that time was running out, she set to work
with a fierce determination to write a good story.

When she had arrived in New York City she had once again gone
to Greenwich Village, this time to a well-known rooming house run
by Madame Katrina Blanchard at 75 Washington Place. It was known
as the "House of Genius" because of Madame Blanchard's sympathy
for creative artists, and it bore on the outside wall a plaque to the
memory of Alan Seeger. Here she went into hibernation and worked
on a story:

I got a big crusty roll with butter and a cup of coffee and sometimes an orange in the morning so I could start the day and then I'd hold out as long as I could and then go down to the corner and get myself a hot dog or a hamburger and a banana. I always had a banana because I'd been told it was nourishing.[51]

She said that she lived like that for seventeen days and seventeen nights while she wrote her first story. For her material she chose an anecdote told to her by an archeologist friend. She had met in Mexico City an elderly archeologist named Nivens who owned a shop there in which he sold the objects he found in his dig outside the city. Porter was a frequent visitor to his shop and took notes for a story about him. The story never appeared, but many years later she used her notes for an essay called "The Charmed Life."[52] Besides visiting Nivens' shop she sometimes visited him at the dig, and once when she was there she sat down on a mound of skulls and looked about. She saw nearby a spread of pepper trees and a wall of organ cactus enclosing an adobe house. Beside the house a woman was making tortillas. The smell was so tantalizing that Porter asked to buy one, knowing well that the rules of hospitality would make it necessary for the woman to offer one, and indeed she offered three. Porter described the woman to an interviewer:

> Aside from her instant generosity, there was a certain natural grace in the way she offered to feed me, an inherently gentle manner that would have shamed some of the so-called ladies I have seen here and there. Moreover, she was a genuine beauty. Her brown eyes were almond-shaped and vaguely oriental, her glistening black hair pulled severely back into a long single braid that reached her slender waist, and her finely-wrought features were unbelievably classic, I said to myself, the very essence of fine beauty. Several hours later, I tried to capture that impression in a rambling paragraph in my notebook but could find no words adequately to describe her.[53]

On a subsequent visit she saw the woman delivering her husband's lunch and also bringing the old archeologist some live fowl. She had slung the chickens over her right shoulder so that half of them fell upon the flat of her back and the rest dangled across her breast. In spite of the squirmings and fluttering of the live chickens she moved gracefully and with instinctive serenity. When Porter admired the woman's queenly manner the archeologist told the story of how she had killed her rival. She had been barely eighteen when she married, and her husband had soon afterward run off with a fifteen-year-old sweetheart. After the two returned the woman ignored them until the sweetheart's baby was born. Then she went into action:

> On a bright sunny afternoon when most of the villagers were at work or taking a siesta, she stealthily crept into her husband's second home and stabbed his young sweetheart to death. She stabbed her at least twenty times and "left her looking like a sieve," according to Mr. Nivens. Apparently no one saw the murder, but several neighbors saw María coming home with the week-old baby gently held in her arms. That evening two policemen, who had been summoned by Juan, visited every house in the village but failed to get one scintilla of evidence concerning the gruesome crime. There was a complete conspiracy of silence, a strange and eerie sense of justice well done. Juan moved back to his old home, and María Concepción accepted him without a murmur of reproach.[54]

The theme was her favorite one—a strong, queenly woman who is wronged and who by her own exertion and resourcefulness avenges herself and sets her world in order. But Porter added another moral dimension by making her story, "María Concepción," reflect the outrage she had expressed in her essays at the oppression of the Mexican Indian, whom she felt to be the life of the country. In "The Mexican Trinity" she asked if any country had as many enemies within its own gates as Mexico did; she described how Mexican capitalists united with American capitalists to oppose the revolutionaries, and how the Catholic Church united with the Protestant to subjugate the Indian and acquire his land. The country was dominated by a triumvirate of powerful forces, those with land and oil interests and the Church. In her essay on the Festival of Guadalupe she described the Indians, exploited and afflicted, turning with groping hands and blinded eyes from the good earth toward the vast and empty sky, hoping for some miracle to solve all their wrongs.[55]

María Concepción of the story is such an Indian, converted to a Christianity which is alien to her culture and to her nature. For her livelihood she is meagerly paid by a foreigner who is unearthing the relics of her historical past. She has been married in the Church and is to have a baby when her husband deserts her because he prefers the pagan charms of another free spirit to his wife's respectability.

María, however, is not like the straw women of the Denver stage against whom Porter wanted to cry out, "Why don't they stand on their feet?" She avenges herself and sets her world to rights. When her husband returns with his mistress and a baby just after María Concepción has lost her own baby, she attacks her rival with a butcher knife, kills her, and takes the baby for her own. In doing so, she regains the affection of her husband and the admiration of the towns-people, and she lives happily ever after.

When Porter spoke later, as she often did, about writing this short story that she designated as her first, she was apt to make the circumstances as sudden and unexpected as the conclusion of a good horse race:

> When I was finished with it I didn't know what to do with it. I mentioned it to George Sill who was the art director of *Century* magazine and he said, "Why [don't] you come down to the *Century* magazine and I'll introduce you to Carl Van Doren" who was the editor. And so I did and Carl took it and looked it over right before me and said, "I think you're a real writer" and I just went out walking on air. I never said anything about money at all.
>
> And the next day George Sill himself came down in person on the bus, to Washington Square and handed me a cheque for $600. I was launched!
>
> I said to George, "I didn't realize there was money in this" and he said, "You might have hurried up a little if you had."[56]

She may have simplified and dramatized the actual details, but she was right in seeing the acceptance of "María Concepción" as a momentous occasion in her career. She was, indeed, launched. She had fulfilled her dream, realized her promise, and there seemed no reason why she should not follow this triumph with a series of similar ones. She had mastered her art and she still had all her unused Mexican material. All she had to do was hibernate a little longer and write out her stories.

EIGHT

Getting Ready to Be a Writer

Porter had traveled far and overcome many obstacles by the spring of 1922. At thirty-two she had defined her goal, learned her craft, gathered her material, and finished a good story. To people of other temperaments it may be surprising that she should have lost her momentum just now and not regained it for five years.

Her failure to fulfill expectations became legendary over the last part of her lifetime, and many observers thought she was self-indulgent or lazy. Marianne Moore called her the world's worst procrastinator.[1] The explanation is rather more complicated than that. There were a number of factors that predisposed her always to leave the desk, the typewriter, the work in progress, and bolt.

She had had from childhood a short interest span, which nothing in her training or education so far had helped her to overcome. The kind of perseverance she had developed had prepared her to move forward through a series of upheavals and jolts but had not prepared her for long, uneventful hours of working doggedly at one task.

The diversion that most often took her from her work was a love affair, and it hardly needs explanation that a beautiful woman in her early thirties should drop everything and embark on one amorous adventure after another. It should be remembered, however, that Porter's need for love was far beyond the ordinary, a desperate compulsive need inspired by the nagging, ever present sense of her own deficiencies. Every new love affair held the promise of alleviating her sense of sexual failure, her failure to bear a child, to inspire and keep the love of a man of some substance. Each one failed, and reinforced her feelings of rejection, but she never stopped hoping. Although she eventually decided that there was something in her life more important than a man, it took her many years to reach that conclusion, and she never did resist the temptation to abandon her work and throw herself single-mindedly into one more affair.

During the next few years another temptation cropped up regularly in the form of reasons, invitations, and excuses for her to rush off to Mexico. Here again something more was involved than her irrepressible love of a jaunt. Mexico had yielded her richest store of material so far and she felt that it could be mined for more. Still unaware that there were rich sources of story material in her past, she could not afford to turn her back on this important one.

Perhaps the most fundamental of all the factors in her loss of creative energy at this time was the deep-rooted doubt about herself and her work that ran like a powerful undertow beneath the overconfident surface. Her exposure to clever, well-traveled and well-educated people who wrote fluently, talked brilliantly, and produced effortlessly was a constant threat. She hesitated to challenge their ideas and rival their efforts. She thought she could do as well as they did but she was not sure, and her uneasy balance between confidence and self-doubt made her a ready prey to distraction. Thus she had a great many internal forces to overcome before she could surge forward again.

Two of her greatest temptations came together to cause the break in her progress in 1922—the promise of a resumption of her love affair with Retinger joined with a job in Mexico City. A telegram arrived from Retinger urging her to come at once to Mexico because she had been appointed by the president of Mexico to help organize an exhibition of Mexican folk art for a tour of the United States. She was to be paid $800 and her immediate presence was necessary. The telegram arrived on March 21 and she went immediately, this time by boat.[2]

In Mexico City she again became part of a happy working relationship with her old friends in the artistic community. She and Adolpho Best-Maugard were the oldest in a group of young artists that included Xavier Guerrero, the principal organizer of the exhibition, Manuel Lozano, Carlos Mérida, Manuel Gamio, Jorge Enciso, and, youngest of all, the talented, witty caricaturist, eighteen-year-old Miguel Covarrubias. Together they assembled 80,000 objects of the most beautiful Mexican art and even hauled in the enormous Chac-Mool known as the Mayan Bacchus.[3]

Porter's specific task was to set up all across the United States galleries in which the exhibition could be shown, and to prepare a catalogue to go along with it. She did careful research and, aided by Retinger and other friends, wrote a historical survey of Mexican art that expressed the aesthetic philosophy of the group.

All her close friends were involved in the discovery of their country's Indian heritage, and, not surprisingly, the catalogue reflected their enthusiasm. She refuted the idea that "Mexican art" began well under foreign influences and later degenerated into a mere meaningless peasant art, and she asserted instead that the "alien aristocratic" influence was a catastrophe. The strength of Mexican art (and by implication, all art), she said, was in its native roots: ". . . if the artist were removed from his fructifying contact with his mother earth, condemned daily to touch instead the mechanics and artifices of modern progress, he might succumb, as do the aristocratic arts, each in turn, to the overwhelming forces of a world turned dizzyingly by a machine."[4] And she pointed out that the life of the Mexican was bound to his home place, to his beloved earth; that no matter how far away he went, nor how long he stayed in foreign places, he would inevitably return to *"mi tierra,"* his own earth.

Her work on the catalogue gave Porter her first exposure to a coherent, consciously articulated aesthetic philosophy, and she was profoundly affected by it. Ever afterward she incorporated her ideas on Mexican art into her own aesthetic theory, expressing frequently, in her discussions of her own work, the opinion that the artist must draw his strength from his roots and from his familiar world.

This opinion was, of course, directly contrary to her own method of working, and she was aware of the ironic fact that she had turned her back on her own native territory and deliberately sought her material in a foreign country. Perhaps others commented on this paradox, for soon afterward she wrote an essay for *Century* magazine, "Why I Write About Mexico," explaining her use of "exotic" material.[5] She argued that Mexico was not really a foreign country to her. She had visited it as a child, had been familiar with Mexican communities in the Texas towns of her childhood, and had lived in San Antonio when it was full of Mexican exiles. Her main reason for writing about Mexico, she said, was that it was her "familiar country" and she summed up her attitude to her subject matter in this way:

"The artist can do no more than deal with familiar and beloved things, from which he could not, and, above all, would not, escape. So I claim that I write of things native to me, that part of America to which I belong by birth and association and temperament."[6]

But if her work on the catalogue yielded something permanent to her artistic credo, its immediate effect was less salutary, for in spite of her spirited public justification of her choice of subject matter, she was left with grave doubts about her work. In other ways, too, the outcome of the exhibition was unfortunate. The United States government, which did not recognize Obregón's regime, labeled the show "political propaganda" and refused to let it into the country. It remained on a railroad siding for two months, until it was finally declared a commercial enterprise, duty was paid, and it was sold to a private dealer in Los Angeles. All those who had worked on it were bitter and disillusioned. Porter, returning alone to New York, was "as bitter as gall that politicians could have been allowed to do so much destruction, so much damage; that international politics, and oil and finance could ruin art."[7]

Of the exhibition she said, "That was a defeat if ever I saw one." The fact was, however, that the abortive exhibition was simply the last in a series of ventures undertaken with wild enthusiasm only to end in disappointment. She may have learned something from them but they had taken away far more than they had yielded, and looking back over the two years since her arrival in New York she could see that she had not accomplished a fraction of what she had intended and that her time and energies had been squandered.

Simultaneously, her beliefs in many other areas were being eroded, and she began to feel in her political commitments a sense of misdirection like that which had affected her artistic life. She had been passionately enthusiastic about the Mexican revolution in its early stages but many of the young idealists whom she had truly admired, like Felipe Carillo, had been killed. In their place, those who had grabbed control seemed to her to be self-indulgent opportunists. Her disaffection with the Mexican revolutionaries extended to the Communists and other political activists in the United States. She could still say confidently that her political bent was to the left, but her experience with the exhibition made her think that all political parties were made up of corrupt self-serving people who were basically hostile to the arts and who would use artists for their own purposes.

She was also ready to make another fundamental change in her life style. She had lived for two years freely and adventurously among young Bohemians and artists and she had at last tired of her casual way of life. It had been just over ten years since she left her first marriage. At thirty-two she realized that if she ever wished to settle down and have a family she must waste no more time. The desire for a normal domestic life, and particularly for children, was rising again.

Consequently, when she met Charles Sumner Williams, a steady man, a Harvard-educated bachelor exactly her own age, she was quite receptive to his overtures. He was an ardent suitor, and when Porter demurred slightly at the idea of settling down as the wife of a businessman he was ready to give up his job and embark on an "experiment in living." Porter at this time wanted to get away from the city and settle down in the country, perhaps on a small farm. She was tempted by his offer, but just then she was asked to go to Mexico and gather material for an issue of the *Survey Graphic* magazine. She was away just long enough to gain perspective on her relationship with Williams, and when she returned she told him bluntly that it would not work. He was bitterly disappointed and wrote sadly to ask how as a rejected suitor he should act when they met at the homes of friends.[8]

Porter herself had some misgivings about ending the relationship, and she remembered Williams affectionately for the rest of her life as representing the best chance she ever had for a stable, economically secure domestic life. When she was nearly seventy and he had been dead for years she recalled with nostalgia that he was one of the nicest men she had ever known, that he had good breeding, good money, a true appreciation of her work, and that he had wanted to marry her. She said she had been just too self-centered and busy with her own affairs to pay proper attention.[9] In actual fact, she often gravitated toward "nice" men with good careers but she never found them irresistible and her interest soon waned. Perhaps too these conventional men with the potential to be good husbands and fathers were more sexually motivated and threatening than most of the men with whom she formed associations.

Porter's next lover was a type much more threatening to her equilibrium than Sumner Williams. He was Francisco Aguilera, a twenty-two-year-old Chilean, widely traveled, well educated, fluent in four languages, with degrees from the University of Chile and Indiana University. Darkly handsome and with a great deal of facile charm, he was now at Yale, studying for a Ph.D. and working part-time as a Spanish teacher.

He appealed immediately to Porter, satisfying a hunger in her that went deeper than any sexual need or wish for domestic security. This was her craving to be sought after, admired, wooed, and showered with attentions and love tokens. Moreover, she was still in many ways the child for whom there was never a party or a surprise present and whose birthday passed unnoticed.

Aguilera was adept at courtship and no one could have provided more of the romantic gestures she loved. He praised her extravagantly, exaggerating his devotion and her desirability. He serenaded her on his guitar, and when he was absent he sent messages and poems. The distance between New Haven and New York only added to the excitement of meetings and departures. There were rendezvous at a country farmhouse; visits by her to New Haven, where she stayed at the faculty club and had her visit written up in the social column of the local paper; weekend visits by Aguilera to New York. When he called her apartment "our enchanted medieval castle" she was not inclined to laugh, for she was delighted by the fantasies he wove about her name, her home, and particularly about their future together.[10]

When they were separated after their first meeting, he headed one letter "3rd day of the New Era." For their exchange of letters they bought writing paper with their monograms printed in the same pattern, and at the end of one missive he experimented by adding "Aguilera" to her name.

It is often assumed that a lover so skilled in the external gestures must be lacking in serious intentions, and in this instance the popular notion proved correct. It would, indeed, have been surprising if Aguilera had intended to marry at this point in his university career, and especially to a divorcée nearly twelve years older than he, whose sexual habits were rather casual. Before long he was trying to disengage himself with the same adroitness that he had used in wooing her. Suddenly he was overwhelmed with work, messages between them went astray and plans to meet became confused. Finally he told her that he could no longer endure being a steady tourist in the United States and intended to return to Chile to write poetry.[11]

He did not, of course, leave the country, but the affair was clearly ended. The loss of Aguilera and the collapse of her dreams of marriage reactivated all the rejections of her early life, and she was not only emotionally devastated but physically ill. She was not exaggerating when she told her sister that she "had suffered a great deal from love, or from the impossibility of finding an adequate substitute."[12] In some notes for a story she described her main character, based on herself, as "convalescent of a love affair that had not ended in marriage, or rather had not ended at all but had been bitterly, disastrously broken off." Thirteen years later, when she came across his letters, she scribbled on the envelope, "From Francisco Aguilera the silly fraud—but I was deceived by him all the same! 1937."[13]

The incident contributed to Porter's art one small but enduring legacy. After she wrote her "Miranda" stories, critics assumed that she had taken the name of her fictional heroine from *The Tempest*. She explained to one critic that her actual source was not Shakespeare but Aguilera:

> Once a long time ago I had a very romantic (though fickle) Spanish beau. I received a letter from him beginning: "Ariel to Miranda: Take this slave of music for the sake of him who is a slave to thee!" I haven't got Shelley (it is Shelley, isn't it?) by me, so I can't write the line with the proper stops, but this is the way I remember it. . . . Well, it was all fox-fire and soon over, but just the same, that is why the young woman (and the child) named Miranda represented me, or rather the observer, in those stories you know. All this happened several years before I published a book, and surely nothing could have been more ephemeral and unimportant, yet from that far-off episode I took my alter-ego name which now I can never abandon—and there is no reason why I should since it is, in meaning and origin, exactly appropriate to that character![14]

It may have been all fox fire but for Porter it was not soon over. Instead it took her months to recover from the blow, and it is possible that the affair left her not only physically debilitated but also pregnant. She often spoke to intimate friends of miscarriages that she had suffered, and she even mentioned being in the care of a midwife.[15] During the months after her separation from Aguilera she announced to her close friends that she was pregnant and discussed the possibility of abortion, but finally said she had decided to have the baby. While she wrote to Genevieve Taggard that she had never carried a baby to full term and had doubts about this one, she seemed gradually to grow more confident.[16] In November she said that the child's name and sex were already chosen.[17] She planned to have a daughter and to give her the name Miranda, which Aguilera had used in happier times. In mid-December, however, she wrote Taggard that the baby had been born prematurely on the second, had been dead half a day before it was born, and had been a boy.[18]

Although the letters sound very convincing, it must be remembered that Porter could always make her dreams and fantasies sound authentic. Clearly she wanted desperately to have Aguilera's child just as she wanted to be his wife, but there remains some doubt whether her desire produced an actual or an imagined pregnancy. A friend who met her daily during the fall of 1924 learned only later that she had been pregnant; he had noticed no sign of it himself.[19]

During this desolate period she could not bear to live in New York with all its recent memories, and she moved to Windham, Connecticut, where her friends John and Liza Dallett had rented a farmhouse. There she was part of a small community of artists, among them her old friend Miguel Covarrubias, who was living with a dancer. Many of her friends returned to the city at the end of the summer, but Porter decided it would be better for her health and her work if she stayed in the farmhouse. Before long, however, the isolation and loneliness proved unsettling to her shattered nerves, and she moved from North Windham to an inn in the village of Windham itself. There she continued to rest and to write.

As often happened, she started many more stories than she finished. One story begun at this time, picked up often over the years and never finished, was "Season of Fear," an account of her terrifying experiences in the lonely farmhouse. She wrote descriptions of a fear that affected even the dogs and cats and of her own terror when one of the dogs started to have fits.[20]

Another story which remained uncompleted for decades but eventually was published was "Holiday," based on a visit to a German farm in Texas which she had made when her long marriage to John Koontz was about to end. Her present desolation recalled the emotional distress of the earlier time and the farmhouse recalled the Texas farm, but she was not yet ready to write about her own experiences. Although she wrote Taggard on November 14 that she had "finished Holiday" in a "bath of bloody sweat,"[21] when she reread it she did not feel that it was satisfactory. She wrote three versions of the ending and set it aside indefinitely.

The only story she did finish and publish was "Virgin Violetta," a rendering of someone else's story. On her first visit to Mexico City she had met the Nicaraguan poet Saloman de la Selva, and had listened with disgust to his story of the mean and deliberate seduction of a young girl. As with "María Concepción" her final version contained much more than the original story. She drew on her knowledge of the life style of the aristocratic Spanish upper class and the story became another in her series of "fragments, each touching some phase of a versatile national temperament, which is a complication of simplicities." It appeared in *Century* magazine in December 1924.[22]

That month she returned to New York and lived quietly with the Dalletts for a time while she recovered her health and established her life once more, supporting herself partly by writing book reviews for the *New Republic* and the *New York Herald Tribune*. And eventually —it was inevitable that sooner or later she should do so again—she married.

Around this time a familiar figure to the women of the Art Students' League in New York was Ernest Stock, a twenty-five-year-old Englishman who had worked for a firm of interior decorators and subsequently decided to be a painter. For all his current Bohemian affectations, Stock was very much like the men Porter had previously recognized as too staid to make her happy. In fact, he was considerably duller than Parke French, Hunter Gardner, and Sumner Williams, but his dullness was not immediately apparent to Porter or to the other women he married. His English accent, public-school education and service in the Royal Flying Corps, which he talked about frequently, all gave him a deceptive air of distinction. He was, moreover, very good-looking: one woman remembered him from the war years as "devastatingly handsome," especially in his RFC uniform. Porter found him particularly attractive because in coloring and stature he resembled her father. Stock was slender and tall, crisp-looking, with reddish hair and a debonair mustache.[23] He was eager to be married, and since Porter had no hesitation it was quickly done and they moved to the country. There they joined a congenial group of artists and writers who had settled in Merryall Valley, Connecticut. Among them were Nathan Asch and Robert Coates and their wives, and Josephine Herbst and John Herrmann. The Stocks occupied an old farmhouse owned by Genevieve Taggard and her husband, Robert Wolfe. At first the place seemed idyllic and Porter wrote enthusiastic letters to Taggard.

She said that all the fullness of green and bloom which Taggard had predicted had come true and that she was perfectly happy. She loved the house and the garden was in full bloom, the lilac bush in full leaf. Rain would come and then a wind and then clear sunshine.

The house was gay and clean and Ernest was making wing chairs out of boards. They were eating bean soup at night, fresh milk in the morning, they had white paint to do the kitchen and she was full of plans for the garden. She picked pails of dandelions and made wine which the others found "as subtly intoxicating as champagne." Asch found an old waffle iron and made waffle feasts with maple syrup; someone else cooked pork roasts studded with garlic.[24]

She had accumulated notes for three stories she was trying to finish. One was inspired by accounts she heard of the former occupant of the Wolfes' farmhouse, a rich Irish widow who had done nothing to improve the farm but who had caused something of a scandal with her pier-glass mirror, her big carved bed, and the young boys she adopted for no good purpose. One of the young boys had suddenly gone mad and after that incident she walked off and never showed her face again in the area.[25] The story fascinated Porter and she thought of calling her version of it "St. Martin's Summer," for the false season of warmth that comes in November after the first chill. Later she preferred the title "Dark Rosaleen in Connecticut."[26]

She also picked up again her notes from the terrible lonely time she had spent two years earlier in the North Windham farmhouse and thought again of making them into a story called "Season of Fear."

Most of all she still longed to write a story that would be a lasting memorial to her niece. She wrote a version that yoked together two incidents, the death of Mary Alice and something that happened in Merryall Valley when Ernest was away in New York. One day the woman who came to clean brought along her little daughter. The child was wearing a white veil against the dust and Porter, enchanted with her, lifted the veil and asked her name. The girl replied that her name was Alice. Porter linked this incident to the death of her little niece seven years earlier and intended to write about the struggle to come to terms with her grief. She meant to call the story "A Vision of Heaven by Fra Angelico" and to use as the central image a picture by Fra Angelico of a circle of angels. The epigraph to the story was to be "I will show you sorrow and the ending of sorrow."[27]

Somehow she could make no progress with the stories. She said that while there were not the distractions in the country which she had found in town, there were, nevertheless, troublesome things that provided an excuse for her nervous inability to settle and grind. She admitted that she had no alibi and was tired of hearing of frustrated geniuses, and refused to call herself such a thing. She knew that when the will to say one's say was powerful enough nothing could stop it for long. She had to acknowledge that the trouble lay in her and no one else and she was losing hope, denied the bright fantasy of blaming her unproductiveness on other people.[28]

The chief obstacle to her productiveness was her husband. It did not take Porter long to realize that his charm was very superficial and that he was a naïve, humorless, and indecisive man. He had no real vocation, no occupation, and his desire to be a painter was based neither on training nor on natural talent.[29] By the end of the summer she was calling him "Deadly Ernest." Later she claimed that she based her short story "Rope" on this summer of listening to the quarrels of the other couples—the Wolfes, the Asches and the Herrmanns, but actually the story contains more of the Stocks than the others. One detail suggests her continuing disappointment at her inability to have a child.

> He wanted to know what of it? And did she realize she was making a complete fool of herself? And what did she take him for, a three-year-old idiot? The whole trouble with her was she needed something weaker than she was to heckle and tyrannize over. He wished to God now they had a couple of children she could take it out on. Maybe he'd get some rest.
>
> Her face changed at this, she reminded him he had forgot the coffee and had bought a worthless piece of rope. And when she thought of all the things they actually needed to make the place even decently fit to live in, well, she could cry, that was all. She looked so forlorn, so lost and despairing he couldn't believe it was only a piece of rope that was causing all the racket. What *was* the matter, for God's sake?[30]

By the end of the summer Ernest was annoying not only his wife but everyone else. Eight years later Josephine Herbst published her own story of the Stocks' marriage and left a graphic account of Ernest's fecklessness. It appeared in the *American Mercury* in January 1934 with the ironic title "A Man of Steel." She described Ernest's refusal to do his part of the household chores, his jealousy of Porter's ability to hold an audience spellbound with a story, and his resentment of her loving recollections of a past in which he had no part. He often drank too much and became maudlin and self-pitying, particularly on the subject of his war wound. Herbst's story also contains a descrip-

tion of the acute sense of sterility which the breakdown of this marriage, her failure to have children, and her inability to work had
produced in Porter:

> It sometimes seemed as if her stillborn baby that had never
> breathed was the realest of all to her. He had had arms and
> legs, a perfect thatch of hair, everything for living except
> life. Why hadn't he lived? Why had everything she loved
> withered and died to her touch? She got up off the dampish
> ground and went around to the back. The black cat mewed
> and stretched, arching his back as he came toward her. Even
> he had worms in spite of the eggs and olive oil and the
> vegetables that she pampered him with. She petted him now
> and he rubbed himself against her still mewing. If she had a
> dog it would get fits, a horse, it would break a leg, a bird, it
> would die of the pip. A kind of cursed black doom seemed
> on her like a mound.[31]

Porter said that the creative power in her was almost quenched
and that she was strangled speechless and could not say why. She
knew, however, that the only happy and productive parts of the past
months were during Stock's absences in New York, and she realized
once again that she must free herself from the prison of marriage. The
final outrage was her discovery that he intended at the end of the
summer to return to the city without paying his bill at the local
grocery store. As from her first marriage, she resolved to avoid arguments and recriminations by slipping away without warning. Early
one morning while Ernest was still sleeping she rode in a milk truck
to the station and caught the train to New York. There was a brief,
angry scene when Ernest arrived one day in an abusive mood and
took back all the little gifts he had given her, but she managed successfully to disentangle her life from his.

Porter once confided that she had contracted gonorrhea from her
first husband and been obliged, as a result, to have a hysterectomy.[32]
She sometimes transferred events from one marriage to another, and
it seems likely that if such an incident occurred, it was the result of
her association with Stock. She was ill after she left him and, although
she herself denied it, it was rumored that she had gonorrhea.[33] Moreover, Stock had infected someone else not very long before. Such an
ugly experience may explain why she erased her second marriage so
completely from her memory.

There can be little doubt that the loss of her uterus, so central to her sense of feminine identity, was traumatic. She handled the situation as she did many other painful experiences—with pretense and pose. Although her family knew of the operation, she concealed it from her lovers and husbands. She went through the motions of menstruation, acquiring monthly toilet articles, using them, and sometimes mentioning them in letters to her sexual partners during separations.

For all its crippling effect on her life, the flight from Stock, like the flight from Koontz thirteen years earlier, was another major step in her progress. This time Porter freed herself not only from the marriage but from the illusion that she could find happiness in marriage. She had now had two disastrous unions and knew that she would never have a child. It was many years before she succumbed again to the temptation to marry. In the meantime she contented herself with casual lovers, like the Mexican painter Ruffino Tamayo. Such associations were brief, unlikely to lead to deep involvement, and left her free to concentrate her energies on her work.[34]

While her relationships with men had always diverted her from her writing, her friendships with women had often had the opposite effect. Many of her women friends were gifted artists and writers and the prospect of their accomplishments made her long for similar success. Before she married Stock she had formed a friendship with Elinor Wylie, an established poet who combined a striking appearance with considerable literary talent. By leaving her first husband in a scandalous and widely publicized elopement, Wylie had gained a reputation as a *femme fatale*. When Porter knew her she had left her second husband and was planning to marry William Rose Benét. While he tried to reconcile his family to the marriage, Wylie and Porter spent Thanksgiving and other holidays together, eating in Italian restaurants, drinking wine out of teacups in speakeasies, making toast and singing Scots ballads together by the fire in Porter's apartment. Apart from her poetic gifts, Wylie was a dramatic storyteller and managed to make the story of her life, with its many love affairs and attempts to have a child, poignant and fascinating. One anecdote which gained some currency was that Wylie had come to Porter's door saying she intended to kill herself and Porter was the only person she cared to say good-bye to. Porter included the story in her list of people who tried to win her sympathy by threatening suicide. She said that she simply replied, "Well, good-bye, Elinor," and closed the door. She later sneered at Wylie's posturing, which she thought covered her "simple, utilitarian, banal feelings" and "tinny emotions," and she thought that Wylie was popular because she represented for her admirers "their wistful notions of romance."[35] It is possible, however, that from Wylie's stories about herself Porter gained her first hint of how such personal experiences might be turned to fictional use. She was scornful always of personal exploitation in the works of other writers, and yet her own most successful works were those based on her personal experiences.

Less notorious in her personal life but equally attractive and talented was the poet Genevieve Taggard, who also became Porter's friend. Porter herself turned again to writing poetry and since Taggard not only wrote poetry but edited a little poetry magazine, *Measure,* Porter submitted her own work for possible acceptance. Her timidity about her work comes out in the notes which accompanied her submissions: "If you like it, print it. If not, darling, don't trouble . . . I expect you to be severe with me . . . as you remember, that time when you told me you could be cruel with me because I am strong, I told you I liked that because it fostered in me the illusion of strength."[36]

Taggard accepted a poem, "Requiescat" (changed from the original title "Last Choice"), and Porter was pleased when Burton Stevenson asked to reprint it in his *Home Book of Verse.* When he wrote to her for some biographical information, including her birth date, Porter said that she had given him "the latest possible date on which I could possibly have been born."[37] That date was 1894, and it was the first appearance of an error that was long perpetuated. But if Porter thought she was beginning a career as a poet she was disappointed. Taggard did not like subsequent submissions and Porter admitted that she was really a prose writer. She wrote to Taggard: "You aren't to trouble about the poems. I don't, my amazement was not when you decided they weren't good enough, but when you thought they were. I am not a poet, and shall write no more verse: it is far better you sponsor someone who is, and will give cause, as you say, to rejoice later on."[38]

Although she did from time to time write poetry she never, after the mid-twenties, considered herself anything more than a "Sunday poet."[39] She sometimes regretted that she had destroyed all her early poetry, but what has survived suggests that she was correct in deciding that her talent lay elsewhere. And yet her early interest in writing poetry, like her early interest in the drama, imparted something valuable to her art, for it was from the poetic, lyrical grace of her prose that its quality derived.

Later in the 1920s she met other liberated and productive women in the apartment house which was her home after she left Stock. The house on Hudson Street (a former headquarters of the Hudson Dusters, a West Side gang that preceded the big mobs of prohibition) was called by its inhabitants Casa Caligari or Caligari Corners after the great horror film. Visitors to the place said that it housed the three most talkative women in New York—Katherine Anne Porter, Caroline Gordon, and Dorothy Day. Herbst gave this account of the place:

> Creaking up the stairs you half expected to see a skeleton wag from the ceiling, but instead, a door opened on the second landing to a view of a child strapped to a high chair while it gobbled its bowl of bread and milk. It was Dorothy Day's little daughter, a rare sight, for children were few and far between for our generation. When you came to Katherine Anne's room the prospect opened surprisingly to a domestic pavilion with gingham curtains at a window, a flowering primrose, a small cookstove with a coffeepot sizzling away, a gray cat on a cushion in a child's rocking chair. Her footing was as precarious as the house was shaky, but she could make light of it, wittily tossing the jacket of a book she had reviewed into a waste paper basket or pinning up the jacket of Holger Cahill's *Pagan Earth* with a drawing by John Sloan in a place of honor. She was promising herself to do a review of the book but she never got around to it. . . .
>
> Porter invested in a chair with a delicate frame and a striped upholstery of blue and lilac veined satiny material that gouged a hole in her "capital" bigger than what remained.[40]

Dorothy Day had already published a novel, *The Eleventh Virgin,* and was at work on another which she provisionally called "No Continuing City." She was an extremely spiritual woman who had converted to Catholicism and who tried to join her religious faith to her commitment to communism. Porter was more sympathetic at this time to communism than to Catholicism, but somehow the combination did not appeal to her and there was a coolness between Porter and Day (Porter was closer to Delafield Day, the more conventional and less talented of the sisters) which in later years became outright hostility. In the early days, however, Porter was interested in Day's writing and offered to help her find a publisher for "No Continuing City." The novel never appeared, but Porter used its title in the epigraph to Part III of *Ship of Fools*.

Porter was much more fundamentally sympathetic to Caroline Gordon, a young woman of trenchant wit and sharp intelligence. Her father had been the classics master in a private school for boys and Gordon, the only girl admitted to the school, had gained there a first-rate classical education. She was from Kentucky and fiercely proud of her southern heritage. Porter called her "an unreconstructed South-erner, if ever I saw one."[41] Gordon was married to the poet Allen Tate, and through them Porter met other members of the talented group of poets who had formed the "Fugitive Group" at Vanderbilt University in Tennessee, among them Andrew Lytle and Robert Penn Warren. Warren became one of the most durable of her lifetime friends and she recorded the impression he made when she first met him:

> I saw him first when he was 21, a poet born who was grow-
> ing from one form to another, those of his friends knew
> even then that he was taking off on a long journey—at that
> time I happened to see a portrait drawing of John Keats
> when he was about 20, 21—a fine thin black line profile,
> spare and perfect—It could easily have been a portrait of
> Robert Penn Warren. He had brilliant flaming gold-red hair,
> and a skin fire-white, like a lighted frosted lantern—a most
> beautiful head of a young man.[42]

The chief benefit of her association with this group was that they caused her to change her attitude to her southern background. She began to see that it was not a liability but something in which she might take pride. It was still a few years before she reached the point of thinking it might be a literary asset.

Important as these friendships were, the most important to her personal and literary growth was the bond she formed with Josephine Herbst. The two had come to New York at the same time and had moved in the same circles, but the friendship was sealed during the summer they spent together in Merryall Valley.

Herbst came, like Porter, from a poor family, but hers was a close-knit one with deep bonds of affection and respect uniting the parents and the four girls. The family had moved to the Midwest from Pennsylvania, and the mother, who had a cultivated eastern outlook, constantly encouraged the girls' interest in literature, and told them stories about her own family, the Freys, who had moved from Switzerland to Pennsylvania.

Although the family was unable to provide formal education, Herbst through her own efforts had attended various colleges and finally earned a B.A. degree from the University of California at Berkeley. In addition to educating herself and reading widely she had lived and traveled a great deal in Europe. There she had met John Herrmann, an American writer eight years younger than she, and they eventually married.[43]

Unlike Taggard and Wylie, Herbst was a homely woman whose unprepossessing appearance was emphasized by her negligent attitude toward dress. She was also a veteran of struggles and losses more debilitating and less glamorous than the sensational love affairs of Wylie and Taggard. Under the strains of her early life she had developed a forthright courage and a strong moral and political consciousness. She was politically radical, and although never actually a member of the Communist party, she was more than a mere "fellow traveler." Also like Porter, she was struggling to establish herself as a writer, and although her talents were considerable, she had published so far only a few short stories.

Perhaps the biggest factor in the friendship was Herbst's tremendous admiration for Porter. Allen Tate thought that Herbst's admiration amounted to hero worship, that she "waited on her hand and foot" and "carried her around."[44] Certainly the description of Porter in Herbst's fiction and her use of Porter's experiences seem to suggest some kind of romantic fascination.

In her novel *Rope of Gold,* Herbst incorporated the incident of the stillborn baby into the life of her autobiographical heroine, Victoria Chance:

> She was a lucky woman to have Jonathan and she could have wished nothing better for her baby boy than that he had grown up the spit and image of him. She bowed her head on her knees; the light wiped out of the skies. Lord, how it sent a knife to her very spine; he would be almost as that picture of Jonathan as a baby on the dresser upstairs, sitting in the sand with his eyes all squinted up from the sun. A

woman with her life before her and the world full of troubles and work to do has no business thinking of what's over and done with, but the past had a way of tolling, like some bell. It could bring you to a dead stop in the middle of the day. . . . It did seem, though, that losing her baby was a sign she should have something of her own to do and be.[45]

For her part Porter was loyal to Herbst, but she had from the beginning rooted reservations about her work. Herbst's radical political convictions informed her writing, and it was not leavened by the delicate sensitivity, the poetic grace that Porter's possessed. Eventually the divergencies of style, temperament, and point of view broke the friendship, but at first the differences seemed inconsequential. When Herbst began her first novel during the summer at Merryall, Porter described it to Taggard:

Jo began her book about two weeks ago, and read us about fifty pages last night: a good beginning, she has uncanny insight into the petty motives of drab, starved people: she makes a sort of surface dissection of a very third rate little family dissolving under the strain of small town disgrace. Her style is plain and severe: she elects to write of something she knows too well and despises. Some day I hope we will find something in the life of this country we all know so well to love, and write about that. We will make better books.[46]

It was perhaps Porter's reservations about Herbst's method which made her, when she reviewed the novel, *Nothing Is Sacred,* on its publication two years later, speak of it with praise but in a style that was, for her, unusually pedestrian:

It is a short book, the sentences are short, the words are simple, and still the prose has poetic grace and style. It is not angular, spare, stark, dry or any of the more kindly synonyms for jerky dullness. It is beautiful and full with the fullness of a perfect economy and final choice of phrase. It is all in one piece from beginning to end, and must be read line by line, or you will miss something important to the story.[47]

A year later she reviewed Herbst's second novel, *Money for Love,* and this time her reservations were much more outspoken. She spoke of Herbst going after "poor lost middle western human nature with a kind of cold detached ferocity that makes my hair rise" and ended with the following summation:

> No. These people are more interesting in this book than they were before, or could be again. They are fascinating in a fearful way, because a good artist, perfectly in command of her method, has for her own mysterious reasons chosen to assemble them: her lack of human pity is her own business. She has made a fine job of destruction. What, precisely, is she trying to kill?[48]

When Porter compared herself with Herbst—as with Day, Wylie, Taggard, and Gordon—she felt peculiarly unproductive. Most of them had husbands, children, and significant publications which were helping them establish literary reputations. She, on the other hand, was older than most of them—now approaching forty—alone, childless, and with little to her credit aside from book reviews. She had done a great many reviews for the *New Republic* and the *New York Herald Tribune* and some of them were excellent. Among these were the review of Covarrubias' book of caricatures, *The Prince of Wales and Other Famous Americans,* and her reviews of the poets she admired—Taggard and E. E. Cummings. She enjoyed reviewing her friends' work but, on the whole, reviewing wearied her. She said that every bore under God's heaven went to Mexico and wrote a dull book and she got it from the *Herald Tribune.* She vowed to quit playing Mexican expert—the fizz was all out of it.[49]

At the same time, there were gains. She must have realized that she could do as well as the other women. She was as clever as they were and the reviews reveal her as an astute judge of literature, well aware of the weaknesses of those who were producing more than she was. Once again her ambitions were reviving and she began to move again toward realizing her full potential. By the beginning of 1927 she was ready to undertake an ambitious literary project, and perhaps her later statement about her long periods of inactivity applies to these years:

> All this time I was writing, writing no matter what else I *thought* I was doing, in fact. I was living almost as instinctively as a little animal, but I realize now that all that time a part of me was getting ready to be an artist. That my mind

was working even when I didn't know it, and didn't care if it was working or not. It is my firm belief that all our lives we are preparing to be somebody or something, even if we don't do it consciously. And the time comes one morning when you wake up and find that you have become irrevocably what you were preparing all this time to be.[50]

NINE

The Foreign Land of Massachusetts

Whel she returned to serious work again, Porter did not, as might be expected, write fiction, but chose instead a new genre—biography. This may have been suggested to her by her southern friends, many of whom were, if not actually writing biographies, preparing to do so. Allen Tate published *Stonewall Jackson: The Good Soldier* in 1928 and *Jefferson Davis* in 1929, and Andrew Lytle published his first book, *Bedford Forrest and His Critter Company*, in 1931. For these writers biography proved to be, in the words of Robert Penn Warren, "a step towards fiction," but clearly it was very much in the air, and it was bound up with their loyalty to the South.[1] Porter's approach differed slightly. Biography appealed to her because she had not yet found her true subject matter and still preferred to go outside her own experiences and use someone else's story for her writings. Nor was she attracted to a character who figured in southern history; she chose, instead, the seventeenth-century New England theologian Cotton Mather. Her choice of a male character seems a striking departure after her series of strong women, and his New England background seems geographically odd for a woman from Texas whose "familiar country" was supposedly Mexico. The discrepancy, however, between the previous themes and the current ones was more illusory than real, for her interest in Cotton Mather was the natural outgrowth of preoccupations rooted in her southern childhood.

Although Porter said publicly that her part of Texas was an iron-

clad Protestant region still untainted by "petty middle class puritanism" and that "the petty middle class of fundamentalists who saw no
difference between wine-drinking, dancing, card-playing and adultery had not yet got altogether the upper hand,"[2] in private she admitted that it was "poxed with teetotalitarians who seemed to hold
that every human activity except breathing was a sin."[3]

The atmosphere affected her profoundly and she was haunted
always by her childhood memories—by the tangible devil, whom she
thought of as a creature dressed in red who lived in her grandmother's
closet[4]; by the revival meetings with the "singing and praying and
shouting and tears and sacred joy" and the mourners' bench for re-
pentant sinners.[5] She remembered one old lady (could it have been
Aunt Cat?) who came from the meetings so overwrought that she
used to throw the silver candlesticks around.[6] Such occasions left
Porter with a deep interest in mass hysteria and became her touchstone for political and religious frenzy. When she watched a Hitler
rally in Berlin, she said it reminded her of a Methodist revival meeting.

That Cotton Mather's name was somehow associated with her
early memories is suggested by a description on the book jacket prepared by her overoptimistic publisher:

> In this biography of the sternest and strangest of our New
> England figures, Miss Porter has given us an astounding
> picture of religious ecstasy and righteousness, contrasted to
> an unbelievable strain of bigotry and superstition, of cruelty
> and implacable retribution in the name of the Lord. As a
> story of the New England conscience, as a narrative of the
> Salem Witchcraft, and as a study of a pious and bigoted
> figure, this book—which treats the subject in the modern
> biographical manner—is an important document.[7]

More specifically, Porter traced her interest in Mather to a moment in her childhood when her sister showed her a picture in a
schoolbook of a Puritan wearing a wig and told her, "That man
caused witches to be burned."[8] Mistakenly Porter assumed that such
activity was part of Mather's story, and in one of her descriptions of
the book she compared with the religious revivals of her own day
what she called "his witch-burning orgies."[9]

Such orgies had long fascinated Porter. When at the age of seven she reproduced the scene of the burning of Joan of Arc as it was pictured in storybooks, she had tied up twigs in the classic faggot shape, made a cardboard scaffold, and assembled white scraps of drapery and cornsilk for the figure of Joan herself. When everything was completed, she set fire to the twigs and watched excitedly as the whole creation went up in flames. Her playmates recalled another version of the game, in which they were instructed to tie up Porter herself for a simulated burning. The grownups saw these games as a sign of something morbid and perverted in her nature and she recalled that they forbade them and stopped them with humiliating punishments.[10]

It was not long after she embarked on her research that Porter discovered that Cotton Mather never caused anyone to be burned, and ever afterward she claimed to be long weary of explaining to the "New Ignorami" of criticism that no witch was ever burned in New England or anywhere else in America.[11] Nevertheless, the connection between her interest in women in general, witches in particular, and the life of Cotton Mather is apparent from her early outline of seven chapters of the book. Two are devoted to witch hunts, two to Mather's wife Abigail, and one to the rebellious Anne Hutchinson, who was expelled from the New England colony. (Porter was so interested in Hutchinson that she planned to write a biography of her after the book on Mather was completed.)

When, in 1927, she had a little outline of her book, Porter took it to the New York publishing house of Boni and Liveright and there managed to convince Horace Liveright of its worth and of her own ability to finish the work in time for the two hundredth anniversary of Mather's death the next year. He offered her an advance of $300 so that she could finish the research and deliver the manuscript in the fall of 1927.[12] Delighted to be thus set up financially, she went to Salem, Massachusetts, to work in the Essex Institute. The choice of that location was not an obvious one. The library there contained none of the rich primary material on Mather which was housed in other archives nearby. But she was motivated by the same interest which led her to the subject in the first place, for the library contained rich primary material on the Salem Witch Trials.

Furthermore, Salem is very rich in the atmosphere of its historical past. It is a somber town, especially in the late fall and winter, full of dark old buildings, many of them monuments to past scenes of persecution and superstition. Since Porter was intensely sensitive to her surroundings, the choice of a place so rich in the atmosphere of the subject she was working on was a wise one which augured well for the progress of her task. (Perhaps also the gloomy aura of Salem evoked the atmosphere of her childhood, darkened as it was by her grandmother's thin-lipped disapproval and her father's depression of spirit.)

She took lodgings in a rooming house, Barstowe Manor, at 26 Winter Street, overlooking the Salem Common, and soon she was comfortably settled in the routine of scholar and researcher, going each day the short distance from Winter Street to work in the quiet book-lined rooms of the Essex Institute. The work, however, did not go as well as she expected.

This was her first attempt at a subject requiring scholarly research, and she soon began to experience the frustrations attendant on such work. First among these was a total lack of cooperation from her subject's family. When she wrote to Cleveland Mather for permission to examine his collection of Americana, she was refused. When she approached another Mather he replied facetiously, saying that he had made a point of knowing nothing about Cotton Mather but had the impression he was a very wicked fellow. When she needed a photograph of her subject and wrote to a descendant who owned one, he told her his picture was spurious and that he had a friend who owned one. From the friend Porter received what she described as the "most courteous and involved refusal" she had had. This, she said, put her in a mood to slaughter not only the memory of Cotton Mather but all his kin and descendants, and she began the book in such a fury that it was three years before her anger cooled enough to allow her to see her subject clearly.[13]

Another problem was that of ordering the vast amount of material on the subject. She said there was too much material and the subject was "too well-documented." Years later, in a review of George Willison's *Saints and Strangers,* she spoke feelingly of the work involved in such a study:

> Don't miss the notes; and you will also do well to take a look at the selected bibliography, if for no other reason than that you will think twice before rushing into an enterprise like this. In spite of the easy reading, this is a work of long-suffering scholarship. As a student of the period, having read more than two thousand "items" on that and related subjects, I assure you that when you have read it, you will know

all you need to know, now or ever, about that group of early American settlers now called the Pilgrim Fathers.[14]

Vocal as she was on the subject of these initial frustrations, there existed an obstacle, far more serious than these technical details, inherent in the subject itself. It was recognized by Nathaniel Hawthorne, who said that none of the nineteenth-century writers who had dealt with Mather had succeeded in treating him with the sympathy and love that made him live on the page as a human being rather than a phenomenon to be analyzed. It was recognized by Mather's latest biographer, David Levin, who confessed that he had not managed to love his subject but he had learned to understand why others loved him and to admire and respect him as a writer and as a man.[15] Levin has written perceptively of the problem of treating fairly a character who is such a useful emblem of puritanical faults and who falls easily into the kind of stereotype which is appealing and perhaps necessary to the modern mind. He has fully understood the challenge Mather offers to the biographical vocabulary of a hostile age and seen that the man lends himself not so much to character portrayal as to caricature.

For Porter, who had selected Mather as a subject precisely because he seemed to her a villain, and who intended to portray him as such, this problem simply did not exist. If it had been suggested to her she would have dismissed as unconscionable the idea of toning down the severity of her portrait. Her world was peopled with saints and villains and it was her resolute moral conviction that any attempt to explain, understand, and arrive at a sympathetic view of the villains amounted to the most criminal kind of collusion between writer and character. Her characters were always shaped and trimmed to her preconceived scheme. Such shaping was difficult enough when she was dealing with fictional characters whom she could control at will, but it was considerably more difficult when she was writing about historical characters. She had prejudged Mather and was predisposed to depict him as an absolute villain, but inevitably certain shadows appeared. A tension developed in her mind, so that part of her began to incline to a sympathetic view while another part morally resisted such sympathy as weak-minded and sentimental. She told Herbst that when she came to the death of Cotton Mather it was all she could do to stop feeling sorry for the selfish beast, but she managed to resist it by keeping her mind fixed on the image of Martha Corey swinging by a rope from a tree limb on Gallows Hill. That, she said, stopped her sympathies from getting sidetracked and kept them on the right object.[16]

The existence of such a fundamental cleavage in her attitude to Mather naturally hampered her work. For anyone else it might have caused a final and fatal block, but Porter's particular brand of obstinacy made her struggle on with the task. She managed to complete a number of chapters, three of which were published in little magazines several years later. In these she selected some of the more dramatic episodes in Mather's life and related them with wit and grace. She described the young Mather and the hazing he suffered at the hands of his schoolmates, the attempts he made to exorcise the devils which had afflicted a group of children, his part in the trial and hanging of a woman accused of witchcraft, and finally the part he played in the death of his wife (Porter described him as "praying" Abigail to death). In spite of the stylistic mastery, entertainment value, and many other virtues of her chapters, Mather does emerge as a caricature and her work contains numerous distortions and inaccuracies. Her description of Mather as an insufferable child prodigy illustrates both her virtues and her weaknesses:

> When he was three years old, he could read and spell, and his serious education began in the free school of Mr. Benjamin Thompson. Family legend contends that he was an apostle from the first, and stammer or no, he began at once to lead his schoolmates in prayer. At playtime he preached little sermons to them. The feebler wits of the school listened and were impressed, but sturdier spirits made fun of him, poked him and pinched him when the masters were not by, and gave him the joy of suffering for his principles. Increase Mather liked to believe that his child was a saint at three years, and resented the treatment he received. He encouraged him in his unutterable priggishness, and soothed his vanity by explaining that persecution was the fate of good souls in a wicked world.[17]

David Levin has pointed out the mistakes in this account:

> The factual errors in this paragraph are astonishing. Miss Porter reduces the age at which Mather wrote prayers for his schoolmates from seven or eight to a monstrous three; she invents sermons to replace the rebukes that his own

account mentions; and she attributes joy to a state of mind which Mather himself confesses that he had been unable, even with the help of his father, to see as cause for joy.[18]

In 1927, while Porter was persevering with her unwieldy body of material on Mather and feeling painfully conscious that the blood pressure of her interest in the subject was dropping rapidly, there came an occasion which provided the perfect justification for her to take a break from her work. It was not, this time, an invitation to Mexico, but a chance to fight in a deserving cause against injustice and prejudice.

When Porter spoke retrospectively of the Sacco-Vanzetti case, she said that she had followed it closely from the beginning and, on each of her returns from Mexico, had gathered more information and given money. It was true that she was in New York when Nicola Sacco and Bartolomeo Vanzetti were accused in 1920 of a brutal murder in the South Braintree suburb of Boston. It seems unlikely, however, that she was aware of it then, since only gradually did American artists and intellectuals see the case as relevant to their own lives and start to organize acts of protest. Sacco and Vanzetti were sentenced to death in 1921, and by the spring of 1927, as appeals continued to be made and denied, people rallied in great numbers to the cause, urging the innocence of the victims and protesting the prejudice against them as anarchists and foreigners which had dominated the case. Huge protest demonstrations were organized outside Charlestown Prison in Boston. It was natural for Porter to become involved at this stage. Many of her friends were taking part, and in Salem she was very close to the action.

In later years the protesters were accused of having been present chiefly to find grist for future conversations in literary gathering places or copy for their writing. The many literary accounts of the trial which did appear subsequently suggest that the accusation was not without foundation, and the fact that Porter took copious notes throughout the proceedings makes it likely that this was part of her own motivation. She herself described her attitude as one of naïve helpfulness, simply "as one wishing to help, a confirmed joiner in the fight for whatever relief oppressed humanity was fighting for."[19] In *Ship of Fools* she drew on the experience and shaped it to the dramatic needs of the novel. Her description of Jenny Brown, however, does not suggest serious commitment to the cause:

1   2

Katherine Anne Porter's parents, Harrison Boone Porter (1) and Mary Alice
Jones Porter. (2) In this photograph of her mother, Porter saw signs of strain
that she believed were the result of having endured a marriage to an exacting,
self-absorbed man. She said of him, "I have sometimes felt myself under a
curse with such a father." His neglect left her with an insatiable hunger for
masculine admiration; his wasted life increased her determination to "amount
to something." (3) Callie Porter (far right) at eighteen months, with her
brother Harry Ray and sister Annie Gay. Porter seems to have been the only
member of her family who despite the grinding hardship and poverty of their
life in Texas had any hopeful plans for the future.

3

COURTESY OF BRECKENRIDGE PORTER

4

5

(4) Porter at fifteen, a year before she married John Henry Koontz (5). This marriage, her first and longest, lasted nine years. Thereafter she rarely mentioned it to anyone, although several years later she still referred to Koontz as "that filthy J.H.," who should have been killed for what he did to her. The unhappy marriage was further burdened by Porter's disappointment over her inability to bear children, a fact she never quite accepted. She had herself photographed in a maternal pose (6) with her niece, Mary-Koontz Hasbrook ("Baby Koontzey"), and was delighted by the occasions when they were mistaken for mother and daughter.

6

TWO PHOTOS:
COURTESY OF
MARY-KOONTZ LOWERY

7

8

In Erna Schlemmer Johns (7), whom Porter had known since childhood and whom she visited in 1913 (8) when her marriage to Koontz was nearing an end, Porter found not only a lifelong friend but also her earliest ideal of beauty and the first of many friends who provided her with a glimpse of a life richer and fuller than her own. (9) Through Kitty Barry Crawford (right), a newspaperwoman whom she met in 1916 while recuperating from tuberculosis at the Carlsbad sanatorium, she learned of the work of Jane Anderson (10). Both Crawford and Anderson influenced Porter in her desire to be a writer and journalist. Later, Anderson became Porter's sexual rival and eventually the basis for the character of La Condesa in *Ship of Fools*.

9   10

THE DALLAS MORNING NEWS

Surrounded by a Group of little tots she was photographed as she led them to one of their favorite haunts

A Sufferer at One Time Herself, She Devotes Her Regained Health and Energy to the Helpless Boys and Girls at the Tuberculosis Sanitorium.

This lot of young sters enjoyed be ing snapped

Miss Porter is an enthusiastic fresh-air fan.

11

Porter had a deep-rooted didactic impulse and a natural penchant for teaching. At fifteen, she taught dancing and dramatic skills; much later she taught in Mexico and in many universities in the United States. But one of her most gratifying teaching experiences was at the Academy Oaks school for tubercular children (11), which she ran after leaving the Carlsbad sanatorium and which in December 1916 was written up at her request by the *Dallas Morning News*.

12

13

COURTESY OF MARYA FFORDE

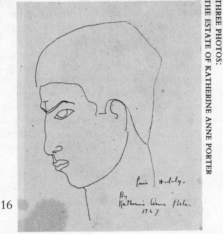

14

15

16

In search of broader, more exotic experiences to write about, Porter was "running back and forth between Mexico and New York all through the '20s." In Mexico, she met and had an affair with Joseph Retinger (12), who later became the model for Tadeusz Mey in "The Leaning Tower." But while she found rich material in Mexico, much of her actual writing during this period was done in New York, where she lived in a number of Greenwich Village apartments, one of which was on Gay Street (13), ca. 1923. Among Porter's lovers was Francisco Aguilera (14), a young Chilean studying at Yale when Porter met him in 1923. He appealed to her craving for admiration and praised her extravagantly, but the affair, she said later, was "all fox fire and soon over." Porter referred to her second husband, Ernest Stock (15), ca. 1926, as "Deadly Ernest." The marriage was short-lived and all but erased from her memory. As she said of John Henry Koontz, "I have no *hidden* marriages; they just sort of slip my mind." In 1928, Porter told her sister that she narrowly escaped marrying a man sixteen years younger than she. She called him "Hidalgo" (16) because of his aristocratic disinclination for helping with domestic tasks, and although his true identity is not known, the information she gave about his occupation, age and appearance suggests that he was the talented caricaturist Miguel Covarrubias.

17

(17) Hilgrove—the Bermuda house that Porter rented for four months in 1929 while recovering from a serious illness following her affair with Matthew Josephson—became the Porter ancestral home in her fiction and biographical record. Extremely important to Porter's personal and literary growth was her friendship with Josephine Herbst (18), though later differences in the two women's literary styles, as well as moral and political points of view, split them apart. Josephson (19) was another important influence when he and Porter became lovers in 1928. At his wife's insistence, Josephson ended the affair, but Porter sought him out and begged to be his mistress, saying, "I am willing to accept any terms. I have never done this before." In 1930, Porter (20), again in poor health, went back to Mexico to recuperate and write. Her health improved, but as usual her work was continually interrupted by her active social life, which included Eugene Dove Pressly (21), who was to become her third husband and the model for the character of David Scott in *Ship of Fools,* and Hart Crane (22). She later spoke of the marriage to Pressly as the "blind alley we used to live in, if it could even be called living," but her seven years with him were in fact the happiest and most productive of her life. Porter's friendship with Hart Crane, however, ended abruptly after a bitter argument in 1931, a year before his suicide.

18

19

20

21

22

(23) Porter at the height of her literary powers, as photographed by George Platt Lynes in 1933.

24

TWO PHOTOS:
THE ESTATE OF KATHERINE ANNE PORTER

25

(24) Porter in Paris in 1934, by now transformed into a white-haired *Grande Dame*. Here she is seated at one of the many pianos and harpsichords that she never learned to play, using them instead as stage properties in the domestic settings she designed for herself. Soon after she returned from Paris in 1936, Porter went to Texas to see her family for the first time in fifteen years. The long-delayed reunion with her father (25), pictured here during the family visit to her mother's grave at Indian Creek, was ostensibly a happy one, although when he died some years later, she did not attend his funeral.

GEORGE PLATT LYNES

26

A languid Porter (26) basking in the evident attention of Monroe Wheeler and the less evident adulation of her fourth husband, Albert Erskine (center). It was not until their wedding in New Orleans that Erskine, then twenty-six, learned that Porter was nearly fifty. Porter herself said that this last marriage ended on the day it began and described their first summer together as a "long season of rain, terrible heat and suffocating unhappiness."

27

MARCELLA COMÈS

28

Porter with Allen Tate (27) in Washington, D.C., 1944, the year she met Charles Shannon (29). Her brief liaison with Tate several years earlier had by this time been virtually forgotten and outlasted by a deeper friendship. Charles Shannon, however, became "the love of a lifetime," the one man with whom she might have found lasting happiness had he not been married. Through the Tates, Porter met and for a while lived with the artist Marcella Comès Winslow, who painted this portrait (28). It shows Porter at 54, still strikingly beautiful, but with an unmistakable air of sadness. After four failed marriages, she knew that domestic happiness was not for her, and although *The Leaning Tower and Other Stories* appeared at this time, she had not written anything of substance for the last four years. Porter's ambitions for the younger members of her family often made her a difficult aunt. For her nephew Paul (30), she had literary aspirations and hoped that her own talents might be manifested in him. While he did have a number of artistic skills, he chose a more practical way of earning a living in business. Porter was extremely disappointed and said that it "was a sheer curse to be an aunt," but nevertheless depended to the end of her life on Paul's help in practical matters.

29 30

31

32

33

34

Porter in 1947 (31 and 33) by George Platt Lynes. (32) (From left to right: Porter's niece Ann, her new husband Walter Heintze, mother Gay Porter Holloway, Porter, Donald Elder.) When in 1950 Ann decided to marry Walter Heintze, Porter was livid and warned against "getting another worthless cad," which Walter was not. On the back of this wedding photograph, Porter indicated her proprietary feelings toward Ann: "Mother of the Bride"—apparently meaning herself and not her sister Gay. (34) Porter attracted numerous literary disciples, one of whom was William Goyen. In 1951 they had an affair, but in the end Porter understood the hopelessness of their relationship.

35

(35) In 1952, Porter was invited—along with André Malraux, William Faulkner, W. H. Auden, Stephen Spender and others—to attend the Congress for Cultural Freedom in Paris and was chosen to speak for the official American Delegation, which included James Farrell, Robert Lowell, Glenway Wescott (pictured above on Porter's right) and Allen Tate. She later joined the anti-communist organization, though in the past she had sometimes indicated that her political leanings were to the left. (36) Thirty-one years after Porter traveled to Germany on the S.S. *Werra,* the novel based on that voyage was triumphantly published. *Ship of Fools* was a stunning popular success which brought her fame and fortune. Both were increased when the movie *Ship of Fools* was made with its international cast of stars. (From left to right: Vivien Leigh, Simone Signoret, Jose Ferrer, Lee Marvin, Oskar Werner, Elizabeth Ashley, George Segal, Jose Greco, Michael Dunn, Charles Korvin and Heinz Ruehann.)

36

To Barrett
With love
1966
Washington, D.C.
Katherine Anne

37

Porter often laughed at her academic regalia as "another cap and gown to put away for the moths." All the same, she was proud that she, who never entered a university until invited there to teach, should have received so many honorary degrees. She presented this picture of herself (37) in her University of Maryland robes to Barrett Prettyman, whom she met in the 1960s. Prettyman (38) talks with Robert Penn Warren at one of Porter's Twelfth Night parties.

38

TWO PHOTOS: AL DANNEGER

(39) Porter on her eighty-fifth birthday, College Park, Maryland.

She believed warmly and excitedly in strikes, she had been in many of them, they worked; there was nothing more exciting and wonderful than to feel yourself a part of something that worked towards straightening out things—getting decent pay for people, good working conditions, shorter hours—it didn't much matter what. She had picketed dozens of times with just any strikers who happened to need pickets, and she had been in jail several times, and really, it was just a lark! She didn't stay long, anyway. Somebody always came from a mysterious Headquarters with plenty of money, so it was out on bail for everybody and back to the line. She had never held with those hotheads who advised her to bite policemen and kick them in the shins. She had heard gruesome stories of police brutalities to working women, really on strike, on the picket line and in jail, and knowing what she did about people, she could believe it. But she was glad to say she had got along very amiably with her policemen, all of them. She always made conversation and tried to convert them on the way to the station, and they were always quite polite, or at least decent, and impervious. They also knew what they knew and what they believed, and if this picketing stuff wasn't against the law, it ought to be. "And yet," she said, "some of them were quite nice!"[20]

All the same, Porter's interest in the case was related to the theme about which she felt strongly. She called it "another and terrible example of an American witch hunt" and saw her attendance there as an active protest against political hysteria and injustice, exactly parallel to the protest she was making in her biography.

The other protesters included such friends and acquaintances as the Australian poet Lola Ridge, John Dos Passos, Paxten Hibben, Michael Gold, and Helen Crowe, and people she disliked, such as Edna St. Vincent Millay and Dorothy Parker. The police allowed them to march once or twice and then closed in and made the arrests they invited. Porter was arrested repeatedly by the same pleasant blond policeman and placed in a cell. She recalled that the cell was terrible and that no books, papers, cigarettes, or lights were permitted. But she was never held overnight and was always released before dinnertime. When she was not picketing and getting in and out of jail, she copied out on her typewriter the letters of Sacco and Vanzetti. And when she was not doing any of these things, she made detailed notes of all that went on around her—the conversations she had with the policeman and the reactions of the journalists, the leaders of the various protest groups, and all those concerned with the case.

. On August 23 the two men were to die at midnight. Porter went to Charlestown Prison and stood with the crowd watching the light in the tower, which would flicker at the time of the electrocutions. Although police on horseback galloped about with pistols, clubs, hand grenades, and tear-gas bombs, charging anyone who stepped beyond a certain point, the crowd was mostly quiet. They simply stood with their faces upturned to the light which would fail at the moment of death. Porter recalled the scene:

> For an endless dreary time we had stood there massed in a measureless darkness, waiting, watching the light in the tower of the prison. At midnight, this light winked off, winked on and off again, and my blood chills remembering it even now—I do not remember how often, but we were told that the extinction of this light corresponded to the number of charges of electricity sent through the bodies of Sacco and Vanzetti.[21]

She described the night as one of perpetual remembrance and mourning, the moment as one of strange heartbreak. Like many of her most moving experiences, this was transmuted into her fiction.

Glenway Wescott has spoken of Porter's struggle to capture Miranda's experience with death in "Pale Horse, Pale Rider." He helpfully suggested that she simply write a page "about your inability to recede, your impotence to write. Eternal curtain, blinding effulgence!"[22] Eventually Porter solved the problem of describing Miranda's death and return to life. She took the little flickering point of light, so indelibly fixed in her imagination at the Charlestown prison, and used it as the image of Miranda's facing life: "This fiery motionless particle set itself unaided to resist destruction, to survive and to be in its own madness of being, motiveless and planless beyond that one essential end. Trust me, the hard unwinking angry points of light said. Trust me. I stay."[23]

It was ten years before she wrote that description, but at the end of her few days in Boston she had many pages of notes. She intended to turn the material on the case into a publishable work, but she found it was as intractable as the material on Cotton Mather and for exactly the same reasons. Over the years she made several attempts to finish her account of the case, and finally, after fifty years had passed, she succeeded. She called her essay "The Never-Ending Wrong," and when it appeared as a book in 1977 the reviews were mixed. One reviewer felt that it was an inconsequential work which told too little about the case and too much about how the writer felt "on every occasion of human betrayal."[24] Only Porter's friend Eudora Welty pointed out the close thematic link between the essay and the fiction.[25] In fact, the theme of the essay is exactly that of her stories and her novel, the arrangement of characters in the triangle of villain, victim, and not-so-innocent hero/heroine that appears in all her work.

The villains of "The Never-Ending Wrong" have the porcine, complacent traits of the villains of her stories and her novel. They are Governor Fuller, Judge Thayer (who is reported to have said while playing golf, "Did you see what I did to those anarchistic bastards?"), and the judges who preside over the trial of the picketers and who are described as follows:

> . . . three entirely correct old gentlemen looking much alike in their sleekness, pinkness, baldness, glossiness of groom-ing, such stereotypes as no proletarian novelist would have dared to use as the example of a capitalist monster in his novel. . . . The gentlemen regarded us glossily, then turned to each other. As we descended the many floors in silence, one of them said to the others in a cream-cheese voice, "It is very pleasant to know that we may expect things to settle down properly again," and the others nodded with wise, smug, complacent faces.[26]

Arrayed against these representatives of corrupt authority are all those who wish to help the victims and protest their unfair trial. There are the journalists, who gain good copy from the scenes of high emotion when the victims' families appear, and there are the Com-munists. On close inspection both these groups turn out, like other of Porter's blameless characters, to be conspiring to the same ends as the villains. One of the journalists gloats that he has arranged the whole show. When Porter expressed a wish that the victims might be saved, she was horrified to hear the Communist Rosa Baron say, "Why, what on earth good would they be to us alive?"[27] Some critics felt that Porter's essay greatly exaggerated the role of the Communists in the Sacco-Vanzetti protests. She was at the time disenchanted with communism, but her main reason for focusing on the Communists was that she was shaping the events to her own world view. As with the Cotton Mather material, she found hard facts and real people almost impossible to manipulate and her final version is flawed by numerous factual errors.

The end of the protest was unheroic for Porter. There was a quick trial in which the lawyers and the judge connived to get all the protesters out of town as quickly as possible. They were fined $5 for "loitering and obstructing traffic" and set free. Once on the sidewalk again, an officious committee member pressed railway tickets to New York into their hands and told them to go to the station and catch the next train.[28]

Porter took advantage of the offer to return to the city, visit friends, talk about the events of the past weeks, and enjoy a reunion with the Mexican artist who was her current lover. In her letters she calls him "Hidalgo" because of his aristocratic disinclination for helping with ordinary domestic tasks. The information she gives, however, about his occupation ("the famous caricaturist"), age, and appearance all suggest that he is Miguel Covarrubias.[29] The reunion was not untroubled because she had to resist his arguments that they get married. Six months later she told her sister that she had narrowly escaped making another unfortunate marriage, this time to a man sixteen years younger than she. Her escape was effected, in this instance, by her return to Salem, where she hoped to finish her book on Cotton Mather. But once again that task proved difficult.

As she felt herself dangerously losing the momentum of her work and slipping back into inactivity, she became despondent and did some serious soul searching. Her old feelings of self-doubt and sterility were reactivated, and, looking back over her life, she wondered if she had not been corrupted irreparably by the bad habits of her father and the grownups who raised her. She had been critical of them and rebellious, but it seemed now that she had never criticized with discrimination, nor had she rebelled against the really damaging conditions. She thought she had been lazy and egotistical and had taken naturally to the examples of inefficiency and arrogance she had seen around her. She felt that she had thought too much about a career to buckle down and make one. Her sexual impulses constantly led her into situations over which she had no control and she allowed all sorts of people to trespass on her personal life because she was too timid to fight back and too lazy and indifferent to put up the battle she knew was necessary if she was to hold her proper ground. She thought too that she harmed others, encouraging them by her weakness, allowing them to encroach more and more on her life and time, and doing nothing until drastic emergency methods were necessary. It seemed to her that her life was a long process of aimless drifting.[30]

Having disentangled herself from two unsatisfactory marriages and many love affairs, she had vowed to remain free from such involvements, but once again the relationship with Covarrubias had become complicated and painful. He constantly begged her to marry him and live with him, and yet when they did live together, they were paralyzed with misery. By remaining in Salem she at least put some distance between them, but she dreaded facing the situation when she returned to New York. And so she stayed in Salem, frustrated and unhappy, and making little progress with her main task.

Her time, however, was not as wasted as the stagnation of the work on the biography might have indicated, for her life in Salem was producing some interesting side effects. One advantage was that the distance from the stimulating social and literary circles of New York afforded her the kind of solitude which she bore with great unhappiness and yet which had always the most beneficial effect upon her work. After working alone all day at the institute, she returned to long empty evenings at Barstowe Manor. During this time she wrote long letters to her family and friends, and told Josie Herbst that solitude and long evenings were all she needed to turn her into a copious letter writer.[31] Thus began her lifetime's habit which developed into a minor art and contributed much to her major art of writing fiction.

It was not simply the solitude that fostered certain developments. In the brooding, morose atmosphere of Salem she was also absorbing a powerful literary influence. Whenever she left the house she was reminded of Nathaniel Hawthorne, the Salem native whose statue dominated the town's main thoroughfare. If she went toward the wharf she could not miss the rusty wooden house with seven acutely peaked gables facing toward various points of the compass. If she went by the Custom House she was reminded of Hester Prynne of *The Scarlet Letter*. If she went to the Old Burying Point (her interest in graves and graveyards often drew her there) she could read the headstone of the writer's ancestor, John Hawthorne, who had presided at the witch trials. The interest aroused by all these places caused her to read, or read again, the works of Hawthorne, and she read with special interest the story that featured the subject of her own work, Cotton Mather.

Chance could not have found a writer whose point of view, moral outlook, and whole imaginative disposition were more in tune with her own, and who could better help her to find her own way. Like her, Hawthorne imagined a world peopled by saints and sinners and like her he focused less upon them than upon the virtuous people who coldly promoted the workings of evil. His great interest was in the egotistical saints, the high-minded sowers of discord like Chillingworth and Hollingworth. Robert Penn Warren discerned the similarity between the two writers when he wrote that, like Hawthorne, Porter "presumably believes in the sanctity of what used to be called the individual soul. She may even go as far as Hawthorne does in 'Ethan Brand' and elsewhere in regarding the violation of this sanctity of the soul as The Unpardonable Sin."[32] Porter's words on the death of the poet Hart Crane suggest her closeness in this to Hawthorne: "His parasites let him commit suicide. He made such a good show and they had no lives of their own, so they lived vicariously by his, you know. And that of course is the unpardonable sin."[33]

With literary influences and physical circumstances thus conspiring together, Porter turned again to short stories which began to form in her mind, and she finished three. One of these was a reminiscence of her childhood which she called "The Fig Tree" and sent to *Harper's Bazaar*. It was not accepted and was not the story which eventually bore that title, but it seems likely that it was an early or even final version of one of the stories of her childhood, perhaps "The Circus" or "The Grave," both of which contain echoes of Hawthorne. At the end of "The Circus," the grandmother's remark that "the fruits of their present are in a future so far off, neither of us may live to know whether harm has been done or not" expresses a thematic preoccupation present throughout Hawthorne and described in similar words at the beginning of *The House of Seven Gables:*

> . . . the act of the passing generation is the germ which may and must produce good or evil fruit in a far-distant time; that together with the seed of the merely temporary crop, which mortals term expediency, they inevitably sow the acorns of a more enduring growth, which may darkly overshadow their posterity.[34]

In "Alice Doane's Lament," his story in which Cotton Mather appears, Hawthorne describes not only the relationship between present and earlier generations but also the relationship between present and past within the living memory of one character. His description of a character's being suddenly confronted with an early buried memory anticipates Porter's description of Miranda's being ambushed by her past in "The Grave: "I know not what space of time I had thus stood, nor how the vision came. But it seemed to me that the irrevocable years since childhood had rolled back and the scene that had long been confused and broken in my memory, arrayed itself with all its first distinctness."[35]

Two stories written at this time were published. These were "Magic" and "The Jilting of Granny Weatherall," and their completion was a significant achievement because they show that she was at last finding her own subject matter and establishing some control over it.

She based "Magic" on a tale she heard from a black maid who had worked in a house on Basin Street in New Orleans. Although it was again someone else's story she shaped it deftly to her own use. It is a dramatic monologue by a maid who, hoping to relax her mistress as she brushes her hair, tells the story of a villainous madam who cheats and bullies the prostitutes in a New Orleans brothel. The point is that the madam's activity is made possible by those around her— the male clients, the police, and the cook—who do nothing. Not only are these people as guilty as the one who perpetrates the violence but so too are the woman and the maid who relish the story. The woman sniffs scent (the detail is intended to suggest her desire to hide the unpleasant realities), stares at her blameless reflection in the mirror, and urges the storyteller on whenever she pauses. Lest there be any doubt about the equation in guilt between both madams and both maids, they resemble each other so closely as to invite confusion. When the storyteller describes the cook of the brothel it might well be herself she is describing: ". . . she was a woman, coloured like myself with much French blood all the same, like myself always among people who worked spells. But she had a very hard heart, she helped the madam in everything, she liked to watch all that happened."[36]

The point is not made sufficiently clear nor is it dramatized quite effectively, and the story, therefore, falls short of being a masterpiece. All the same, it is a first version of the theme, the passive promotion of evil by innocent people, which would run through her works in a steady unbroken line until it reached its fullest expression in *Ship of Fools*.

In the other story, "The Jilting of Granny Weatherall," Porter described again a strong female character surrounded by unreliable men. Ellen Weatherall's first lover jilts her at the altar; her husband dies and leaves her to manage the land and raise the children by herself; and finally an inconsiderate God calls her to an untimely death before she is quite ready. Granny's personal weakness is that when her first lover jilts her she does not give way honestly and naturally to her anger, but suppresses it so that it undermines her whole life.

Porter said she drew on several "Granny" figures for her story, but the central matriarchal character which finally emerges owes more to her own grandmother than any other.[37] Like Aunt Cat, Granny is totally effective in managing her life without men. She runs the farm, raises her young children, and dominates their lives when they are grown. The sorrow of her life is the loss of her favorite daughter, who dies in childbirth, and her hope for her life after death is that she will be reunited with that daughter. The strength of the story is the power of the "felt experience," which is present always when Porter draws on her own past and her familiar childhood world of central Texas.

The fact that her work had undergone a special kind of flowering was not immediately apparent to Porter. In the first place, her literary progress, often more apparent in retrospect than realized at the time, was so hidden and internal that she had little confidence in what she had done, and left it to friends to submit her stories to literary journals. Josephine Herbst admired "Magic" and sent it to Eugene Jolas' *transition,* and its appearance in this avant-garde magazine of international standing marked a significant advance over *Century*.[38]

Even if she had realized fully what Salem yielded to her, it might have done little to mitigate her hatred of New England. She had long had strong reservations about almost every aspect of the place. She scorned the architecture, comparing the colonial churches with their pointed steeples to dogs with their tails held up in the air. She disliked the cuisine, and once when she made for "certain folk here approximately human" a Creole dinner which had disastrous results, she spoke wryly of her guests:

I borrowed the kitchen of an acquaintance and gave them crayfish gumbo, celery stuffed with butter, Roquefort cheese and French dressing and a baked chicken bursting with pure chestnuts and almonds. Cocktails full of New Iberia tabasco, paprika, horse radish and chili sauce. Well, every member of the party except me spent the next day in bed with acute pains in the tum. The ghosts of a lifetime of pale New England boiled dinners rose and did frenzied battle with the foreign spices. But wouldn't you think systems nourished on fried apple pie could sustain anything? Not at all. I heard with glee that they all damn nigh perished.[39]

Her dislike of the place was confirmed during her unhappy fall of 1927 and early winter of 1928, and years later, when she wrote a biographical account of Henry James, she began by painstakingly denying the rumor, started by Carlyle's reference to Henry James the elder as "your New England friend," that the family was touched by the New England spirit, "which even then was spreading like a slow blight into every part of the country."[40]

She therefore packed her bags and left the rooming house, which she now called "a graveyard of mouldering corpses"[41] and returned to New York. Once there she made some fundamental changes in her life. She terminated the relationship with Hidalgo and found a full-time job. Self-supporting and free from emotional entanglements, she gathered her energies for her own work.

TEN

The Fabulous Year

Porter had often before built up an impetus in her work and disentangled herself from a burdensome relationship, only to rush headlong into another love affair that caused emotional turmoil and obstructed the work in progress. There seemed no reason now to expect anything different and, sure enough, the pattern repeated itself. This time, however, there was an important variation— the man was a practiced judge of literature who recognized her talent and encouraged it.

When she returned to New York, Porter, having exhausted the advance on the biography and needing funds to support herself while she worked on her short stories and finished the book, took a routine job as copy editor at Macaulay and Company, a new publishing firm. Besides providing a source of income, this job precipitated her into the arms of her next lover. The year was 1928 and the man was Matthew Josephson.

Josephson has left a graphic account of his impressions of her:

> A small woman, she bore herself with great poise, was low-voiced, soft-spoken, and full of old-fashioned airs and graces that made her seem very different from the New Woman one saw in New York at this time, who habitually wore the "dead-pan" expression then in vogue. Katherine Anne also had much wit, and soon won many friends among the members of my own circle. Like some of them, she too had experienced an interesting phase of "exile" though in revo-

lutionary Mexico instead of Europe, and this subject was very much on her mind. At first we enjoyed only oral versions of her stories; they were reminiscences of her early life in Texas and Louisiana and of her years in Mexico. Her way of telling them was fairly "mesmerizing," as Edmund Wilson once remarked; we often expressed the wish that she would write them down. She would begin:

> Today is the 105th birthday of my name grandmother. She died when I was ten years old. When I remember that indomitable woman . . .

There would follow an unforgettable portrait of a crusty, humorous, and hard-swearing lady of the Old South.[1]

He lost no time in getting the relationship onto a less professional footing by inviting her out to dinner. It was arranged that he should pick her up at the home of the novelist Holger Cahill, who at that time was a museum official and later, during the Roosevelt era, national director of the W.P.A.'s Federal Arts Project. When he arrived Matthew found Cahill entertaining a young woman who looked about sixteen and impulsively he invited them to come along to dinner and then to Harlem afterward for dancing. Matthew, although happily married, was an unabashed philanderer and he planned to enjoy the "esprit" of Porter, while at the same time contriving to sleep with the younger woman. As it turned out, Porter's considerable charm triumphed and it was she whom he escorted home. Once there, he resisted being dismissed at the street door and pleaded successfully to be allowed inside.[2]

At the time Matthew was in a buoyant mood because his biography of Emile Zola, which Macaulay had published, had just been chosen by an important new book club and promised to earn him several thousand dollars in royalties. His night on the town had been a lighthearted celebration and his conquest meant less to him than it did to Porter, who expected him to prove his nocturnal ardor by returning promptly the next morning. It was, in fact, several days before he called again, and he was astonished to find her storming. In addition to his failure to reappear, she was upset by the discovery that he was not only married but the father of a small son.

"What does this mean?" she cried with fine dramatic effect. "I will not be a homebreaker . . . And little children too."

Breaking up his home was the furthest idea from Matthew's mind, but neither did he plan to relinquish Porter so easily, and he reacted accordingly, hanging his head and using his considerable poetic skill to describe the "inexplicable affinities that drive people together." Taking his cue from Joyce's *A Portrait of the Artist as a Young Man,* he told her that she reminded him of dreams he used to have of one like her with great, sad, dark eyes, who touched him, pulled him to her, and who had suffered much. His approach was totally effective: her anger was assuaged and the affair continued gaily for some time.

The early fall of 1928 was a heady time for Matthew. His biography of Zola appeared, was favorably reviewed in the *New York Times,* and was widely acclaimed. His wife was expecting a second child and, taken up with domestic concerns, left him time to spend with his interesting and charming mistress. Porter, for her part, was desperately in love. She had, of course, been so very often before, but this time there was a difference.

Not only was Matthew tall, slender, and strikingly handsome (Hemingway said, "If I looked like Matty, I wouldn't need to be a writer"[3]), but his character comprised some traits rarely found in combination. Porter's previous partners had reflected the ambivalence of her social attitudes, some being conventional well-bred men with successful careers, like Sumner Williams and Parke French, and others, in contrast, being volatile artists and revolutionaries. In Matthew she found for the first time a rare and happy blend of both types. He led a steady, well-organized productive life, and yet felt himself, with some justification, to be an infidel in the temples of respectability.

In addition to this versatility of temperament, he had considerable literary experience. A native of Brooklyn, he had graduated from Columbia and afterward traveled in Europe, becoming an intimate of the Surrealist painters and poets. Most of the books that marked his distinguished literary career were still in the future, but he had already published a volume of poetry, had edited the experimental magazines *Secession* and *Broom,* and was now a contributing editor of *transition.*

His editorial experience prepared him to recognize at once the distinction of the work Porter showed him and she responded eagerly to his enthusiasm, telling a friend that "his first interest is in my work, which is a gorgeous novelty! From a man I surely never had that before. It's terribly important."[4]

She had made the same remark about Sumner Williams and would make it of many of her future lovers, since it expressed not the actuality but some elusive quality she craved. In later instances it was often inappropriate, but when applied to Matthew it happened to be true. She assessed quite correctly the value of their association to her work.

Years later, she was asked what she thought of Hemingway's remark that a writer writes best when he's in love. She would not, of course, permit herself to agree with anything that sounded so romantic and unprofessional. She replied:

> I don't know whether you write better, but you feel so good you think you're writing better! And certainly love does create a rising of the spirit that makes everything you do seem easier and happier. But there must come a time when you no longer depend upon it, when the mind—not the will, really, either—takes over.[5]

In the fall of 1929, with Matthew as her Muse and mentor, she was experiencing just such a rising of the spirit as she described. With his encouragement, she set aside the biography of Cotton Mather and worked on her short stories. Matthew recorded that she worked with an intense concentration in a tormented way, as if using autohypnosis to find language that conveyed her meaning.[6] The description coincides with her own. She said, "My work is done at a subterranean level and fragments of the work come to the surface. I record them as they come up."[7] And again:

> Sometimes an idea starts completely inarticulately. You're not thinking in images or words or—well, it's exactly like a dark cloud moving in your head. You keep wondering what will come out of this and then it will dissolve itself into a set of—well, not images exactly, but really thoughts.[8]

She said she would capture the fragments at first in total incoherence and it would sometimes be years before they assumed their final form.

She asked Matthew to criticize her work unsparingly but, although he was usually a severe critic, he had only admiration for the fragmentary sketches, and he exhorted her to finish them. She trusted his judgment and allowed him to send "The Jilting of Granny Weatherall" to *transition*. Being in love was a powerful stimulant to learning and she profited from Matthew's broad knowledge of modern literature. She absorbed all he told her of contemporary European movements and discussed the essays he was writing for *Broom* and *transition*.

They talked for hours about the book on which he was preparing an essay for *transition*. It was *The Education of Henry Adams,* a work that was almost a textbook for the twenties.[9]

There were in the relationship so many areas of mutual respect which might have provided the basis of a lasting relationship that it is tempting to speculate that this one association might have worked. In the event, there was no opportunity to test its durability and it became simply one more in the series of rejections she suffered throughout her life. The ending was precipitated by Hannah Josephson, who learned of the affair and told her husband that he must choose between his wife and his mistress.

If this ultimatum, which signaled the end of his convenient enjoyment of both wife and mistress, disappointed Matthew, it certainly presented no dilemma, for there was little doubt in his mind about which woman he would choose. At twenty-seven he was very conscious that Porter was more than ten years his senior. Not only was Hannah much younger than Porter but she had certain maternal qualities which made her more satisfying to Matthew as a sexual partner.[10] Sexually, he found Porter unsatisfactory because of her self-consciousness and excessive use of perfume. Even Porter had been astonished at his infidelity, and one day when she saw Hannah wheeling her baby carriage in the street, she had told him, "But your wife is so very pretty, so young, how was it that you wanted me?"[11]

The fact was that Matthew had been immersed for the past few years in the life of Zola and had succumbed to the occupational hazard of biographers, that of identification with the subject to the extent of patterning his own behavior on that of his hero. Porter herself sensed something of this, if not at the time, at least later. She told him, "When I first knew you, you were just emerging from the Zola period, when a literary man should engage in battles for the right and keep a mistress. . . . I suffered a good deal because you *would* model your relations with me on literature."[12]

This being so, it was only as a mistress and never as a wife that Matthew had thought of Porter. She found him a uniquely satisfying blend of conventional spouse and romantic lover but he was quite satisfied to have the two roles compartmentalized. At the same time he was immensely impressed by her talent, and his chief regret in losing her was that he would relinquish his role as her literary guide. What he struggled to do, either consciously or unconsciously, was to relinquish her as a mistress but keep her dependent upon him as a protégée. He recorded in his diary how she sought him out and begged to be his mistress: "She said, 'I am willing to accept any terms. I have never done this before.' She was in his arms weeping while he looked out past her through a window feeling very uncomfortable and feeling himself a heel."[13]

Matthew was not by any means obtuse, but he was self-indulgent in his relationships with women, and quite unable to resist situations that gratified his ego. Only this can explain his insensitivity to the pain he caused by resisting Porter sexually and withdrawing his love but continuing the friendship, wooing her with gifts of books and with letters in the poetic vein which had proved so effective in seducing and appeasing her at the beginning of the relationship. Porter later complained that he had treated her cruelly and his friends reproached him, saying that she was a fine woman, in poor health, with a lot of courage, and that it was a shame to make her suffer. He was astonished to learn that she said he had treated her cruelly and, to the end of his life, professed not to know what this meant.

The pain and humiliation stayed with Porter a long time and years later found expression in the description of the love affair of Dr. Schumann and La Condesa in *Ship of Fools*. The heartless doctor, much as Josephson did, refuses to be disloyal to his wife and torments La Condesa with his high-minded attentions:

It would be a blameless charity which could call for no explanation, could be carried on at a distance, and his wife need never know. He thought of his wife with habitual fondness, of her known strength, always the same, her unexpected and constantly changing weaknesses and whims. She was the center, the reason, and the meaning of his marriage, around which his life had grown like an organism; she was not to be disturbed for anything. He would make his reparations for the wrongs he had done, in silence, as part of his penance. Dr. Schumann, soothed, eased, felt himself blissfully falling asleep in the divine narcotic of hope, and relief of conscience.[14]

Nearer the time, the experience found its way into the story "Theft," and it was a masterpiece, the most nearly perfect story she had written so far and one which showed her in complete control of her métier. The theme was the one she had used in "Magic," the dangerous apathy of the apparently innocent. The central character is a nameless woman, a writer, no longer very young, who lives in New York. She allows various people to take advantage of her, borrowing sums of money and treating her discourteously, and instead of resisting she takes pride in her unaggressive, unmaterialistic nature. Two incidents, however, make her question her motivation. A former lover writes to terminate their friendship and the janitress of her apartment building brazenly steals her purse. The striking similarity in the two incidents is that both the lover and the janitress deftly switch the blame to the woman herself. She realizes at last that she is indeed guilty since her indifference had invited their crimes. And there is the further indication that she is more guilty than they because she is responsible not only for her own loss but for their moral decline.

The difference between this and the earlier stories lies in her use of experiences which are very personal and which actually happened. The letter in the story, for example, is one she had received from Josephson: ". . . thinking about you more than I mean to . . . yes, I even talk about you . . . why were you so anxious to destroy . . . even if I could see you now I would not . . . not worth all this abominable . . . the end."[15] Such actuality of detail was to be a feature of all her later fiction and an aspect of her technique which she often tried to explain: "You see, my fiction is reportage, only I do something to it. . . . And that's very hard to explain—that's the one thing you can't explain to a person who isn't a natural born fiction writer."[16]

In this story she also achieved complete mastery of the lyrical style for which she became celebrated, capable of great virtuosity and yet always held in restraint and never overworked. The story opens in a low-keyed prosaic way, but as the climax approaches and the woman's thought processes quicken, it soars to a poetic intensity which makes it completely arresting and dramatic. That it should be so is a feat, since the subject matter is so psychological and internal.

The dramatic and moral impact of the story is reinforced by a discreet use of symbolism. The characters' biblical quotations and blasphemies take on a special significance, as do the woman's purse and the cup of coffee which goes cold on the table during her moment of self-revelation. The only bold stroke is that the woman who steals the purse is graphically depicted as a devil as tangible as that which Porter once believed lived in her grandmother's closet. She has red eyes which flash fire, a coal-blackened face, and she is stoking up a fiery furnace. While the symbolism effectively emphasizes the moral point, the description is entirely plausible on the literal level since the woman is a janitress. Such symbolic naturalism became an inherent part of Porter's method.

If Porter's experiences of the time provide insight into the story, the fiction in turn is no less illuminating of the life. The story's implication that the girl should have resisted those who abused her reveals her misgivings about releasing her hold on Matthew. That she wondered if she should have clung to him more resolutely is borne out by letters to Becky Crawford, a new but already intimate friend. Mrs. Crawford had no mixed feelings on the subject; she wrote Porter that if she had succeeded in binding Josephson to her the outcome would still have been disastrous and she would have been blamed for anything that went wrong.[17]

The story also shows one of Porter's obsessions. She often said, especially after she became successful, that she had never been associated with anyone who had not tried to use and exploit her in some way. At the time of the story, although Matthew had hurt her and another friend refused to pay a debt, she was surrounded by many friends ready to leap to her help. Josie Herbst, observing this, remarked bitterly that because she looked like a strong woman no one ever sprang to her rescue, whereas Porter looked fragile and vulnerable.[18] Porter herself, however, never fully appreciated the help she received.

At this time Porter had a devoted circle of friends—among them Josephine Herbst, Susan Jenkins Brown, Andrew Lytle, and, most active in protecting her, Becky Crawford, whose husband, John, was a novelist and worked for the *New York Times*. Porter said she was often comforted by the warmth and generosity of Becky, whom Matthew Josephson described as a "big warm-hearted river of a woman," overflowing with warmth and kindness.[19]

It was Becky Crawford who came to the rescue when, in the late fall and early winter of 1929, Porter became seriously ill. The exact nature of the illness, like so many of Porter's illnesses, is difficult to determine. She certainly had influenza and bronchial problems and T.B. was suspected. At the same time, it seems likely that the disappointment with Matthew sparked the old cycle of loss and rejection and aggravated the physical trouble. This time she was prostrated, and all her friends were seriously worried. There was a meeting of those concerned, including Matthew, and, with Becky as organizer, a sum of money was raised to send her to a warmer climate. Becky Crawford at first favored sending her to a sanatorium, but finally it was decided that she should go to Bermuda, a resort very popular just then with easterners in general and Porter's circle in particular. Since a group of her friends were holidaying there, the problem of accommodation was solved and Becky Crawford undertook to manage the financial arrangements. Porter set sail in early March, seen off by Andrew Lytle, and feeling as if she were going into exile.

The speedy nature of her recovery would suggest that the basis of her troubles was emotional, because on the trip her health problem disappeared with dramatic suddenness. In fact, she improved almost as soon as she was on the boat. She said that at first she lay in her bunk on the *Avon* more dead than alive, but after twenty-four hours she staggered up on deck, had a whiskey and soda, and looked with delight at the approaching island rising from the blue sea and dotted with white and coral houses.[20]

Another version was that she arrived on Bermuda in the middle of winter and found it a cold and depressing place.[21] That, however, seems to be the less authentic variation on the theme of her arrival in Bermuda; most accounts indicate that a swift recovery of body and spirit took place.

She had always experienced an unreasonable excitement when she arrived in a new place, as she had on arriving for the first time in Chicago, New York, Mexico City, and Salem. Such changes of scene seemed always to offer the possibilities of shedding problems and making a new beginning.

In Bermuda this sense of excitement and adventure was heightened. In the first place, the beauty of the island was much more satisfying to her aesthetic sense than New York and Chicago. She wrote ecstatically of the blueness of the sea, the mildness of the climate, the richness of the vegetation: "I am across the road from the bluest clearest sea, in the world—if it were the Aegean it could not be bluer, I envy no man his sea in whatsoever part of the world; and so, alas, I am like any other contented animal, I have no history."[22]

She wrote Josephine Herbst that for once in her life she had got precisely what she wanted and that she could not soak up enough of the peace and solitude and silence: "I was never so happy, never so straight in my mind, never so hopeful in all my born, foolishly optimistic life. Even if it lasts only a month, still, there you are! a month! I had never dreamed of so much."[23]

It did last longer than a month, thanks largely to the continued efforts of the Crawfords. The weekly checks for $50 from them continued to arrive on schedule and by April she had received $325. Porter also managed to augment that amount by doing various kinds of hack work. She rewrote a translation of the life of Peter Brueghel and earned something from that. She contributed a part of the play *Carnival,* which ran in Boston, but it folded after a month and she earned nothing there.

When she first arrived she had joined Delafield Day and her husband, Franklin Spier, and Thorborg Haberman, now separated from Robert and living with someone else. This group of friends was renting a large house, Sunnyside, in Shelley Bay, and Porter moved in, contributing to the rent and occupying one of the many empty rooms, which she set up as a workroom in the hope of completing the biography of Cotton Mather.

By the end of April, however, the friends had all returned to New York, Sunnyside was no longer available, and she had to look about for another place. Again all occasions seemed to conspire toward the flourishing of her art, and the house she found, while too big and impractical for one person, suited a deep inner need. She described it, again to Herbst, ecstatically:

> I have changed my house, this one was rented from under my footsoles, but Josie (whisper for fear the demons might hear me) my luck has changed. I found another, twice as beautiful, on a terraced hill with a garden, fully furnished, ten rooms and two baths, house of white stone with green latticed porches overlooking the sea, for $25 a month until January 1st. That is because the season is dead. I have a woman who cooks and washes and cleans for me $3 per week.[24]

The house was Hilgrove, the ancestral home of the Hollis family, who had been shipwrecked on the island around 1600 when they were on their way to Virginia. It had been built in the middle of the nineteenth century by Captain Hilgrove Hollis, father of the present owner. It was a spacious home of about seventeen rooms, but it was impossible to estimate accurately the cluster of half-rooms, pantries, closets, dressing rooms, and storage rooms. It consisted of three stories, with the first floor high off the ground. Along the two upper stories were long verandas with balustrades of wooden scrollsaw work, where Porter set up her table overlooking the bay and wrote.

Inside the house there was an accumulation of eggshell Spode china, thin silver, and old family portraits and furniture heavily carved with fruits and flowers. There was a well-stocked library, and she described her browsing there as "botanizing" because one of the Hollis girls had married a botany professor and they often used the house in the summer months. A study had been added on the ground floor to house their sea catches.[25]

Hilgrove was surrounded by spacious gardens. There were terraces on three levels, as well as a ten-acre wood, two rose gardens, a small banana grove, and a tennis court. There were rustic retreats and bowers and little stone steps running everywhere. Porter had limes for her sloe gin rickeys, and pomegranates for her breakfast from the garden trees. Across the road from the house was the sea, and she could dive from a cliff into the water and swim whenever she wished.

She described her daily routine:

I have been experimenting with the Elijah-Raven motif, and it comes in beautifully. If a little boy shows up with fish, why, we have fish, and if he doesn't we don't. The same with everything else. I take what God sends to my door, and the meals come around approximately on time, because the time is when they come around, if that is at all clear. In the morning, I get up at five or six IF I didn't sit up too late the night before. If I did, I get up about nine. I make myself three lovely cups of coffee, and I wander around in the dewy garden while I drink it, rambling in now and then to fill the cup. Then if I have oranges I take orange juice, and if I don't, I eat bananas, or if no bananas, a pawpaw, and if nothing, why then, nothing. After a while if I feel like it I eat bread and butter, or mush and milk. Then I go to work. Around two o'clock the maid comes up and invites me to come down and see what she has pulled together for lunch. It's apt to be almost anything, like cabbages and cucumbers, with a piece of good wholesome fish, or a slice of bacon, with a mango. I swallow it gratefully, come up and lie down for a siesta, get up at four, take a cold bath, a cup of tea, and go to work. About ten or eleven at night I go down and raid the ice-box.[26]

She filled all her letters with vivid descriptions of her delight in the place:

Tonight it is raining very gently, my yellow and white kitten is playing with the crumpled sheets of paper on the floor, I hear crickets outside and all up and down the valley, a perfect silence. I don't have the slight crinkle of the nerves I sometimes got in the country in Connecticut. Here is a truly friendly entirely safe place, it is only a little island, and I am not really alone. You know the sea is companionable now. Have I stayed away from it for so long? I know that everyone raves to sea sickness about the blue clear water here, but it really is a miracle, I can lie flat and watch the coral and the sea-anemone and sea-urchins and sea cucumbers and star fish and the many colored fishes. I don't get tired of the colors and the flowers. I can't soak up enough silence and quiet and peace. Now and then I go out in a sail boat. Every day I swim. . . . This may never happen to me again, but it's happening now and I shall never hope for more than I have if this state is so good for me. For once, for absolutely the first time in my life, I have somehow got precisely what I wanted, at the right time on bearable terms and it's grand to discover that I really did want it and am happy in it![27]

Lovely as it was, the place assumed a greater importance than an idyllic retreat in which she could regain her health and have time and leisure to resume her work on *Cotton Mather*. The island lies on approximately the same latitude as South Carolina, and, accordingly, has a climate similar to that of her native Texas. It is a place where the extreme heat of the summer months is paralyzing, where the colors have a sharp clarity, the vegetation is lush, day and night arrive with dramatic suddenness, and hurricanes and squalls blow up without warning.

In 1929 the life of the island happened also to resemble that of the Old South. There were spacious homes reminiscent of the plantation homes of the South, sustained by black servants with close ties to the families for whom they worked. Social occasions were marked by formality, affluence, and graciousness.

Hilgrove itself was just such an ancestral home as she might have wished for and dreamed of when her grandmother told stories of her family's past. On the other side of Bailey's Bay was another of the homes of the Hollis family, Cedar Grove, not so stately as Hilgrove itself, more of a comfortable, sprawling family dwelling.

Porter absorbed every detail of the climate, the houses, and the leisurely, gracious life of the Hollis family. She was especially impressed by a young niece of Hilgrove's owner, Miss Amy (Amy was a family name and this niece was one of several), who was an excellent horsewoman. One day Miss Amy came riding by Hilgrove leading another horse. Seeing Porter at work on one of the balconies she called out to ask if she wanted a mount and to invite her to come along for a canter. Porter declined the invitation—she had work she must do— but the vignette of the lovely young horsewoman set up reverberations that would have astonished Miss Amy.[28]

True, she was working hard at *Cotton Mather,* but something more interesting began at this time to take shape. In later years she talked of her time outside the United States in such places as Mexico, Bermuda, Spain, Germany, Switzerland, and Paris and concluded that "my time in Mexico and Europe served me in a way I had not dreamed of, ever, besides its own charm and goodness: it gave me back my past and my own house and my own people—the native land of the heart."[29]

This happened for the first time in Bermuda, where the physical setting and the quality of the family life at Hilgrove combined to give her back her own family's life—not as it really was, but recreated imaginatively as it should have been. The past memories and the present surroundings harmonized so well that she combined the two scenes to create the fictional background of Miranda Gay. So successful was the grafting of Porter's own childhood onto the Bermuda setting that the resulting fiction supplanted the actuality and yielded a vision of her own past which she never relinquished.

When Andrew Lytle found a pleasant home in the South she told him, approving his name for it, "If ever I have one I'd like to call it Cedar Grove after our old one."[30]

Although it was many years before most of the stories were written, one was completed when she left the island. This was "The Fig Tree," in which she describes the Gay family's journey to their country home, Cedar Grove. When they arrive in the country Miranda is disturbed by the sound of the tree frogs. The particular kind of Bermuda tree frogs are a feature of the island found nowhere else. They are winged, miniature frog-like insects which make a sound described by the islanders as "gleep gleep" but by Porter in the story as "weep weep." Finally Miranda's fears are allayed because, like Miss Amy of Bermuda, she has a botanizing aunt who sets up a telescope on the roof of the henhouse and who explains the source of the noise which haunts the little girl.

When the other stories were finished, they contained exact descriptions of places on the island. One photograph of Porter, taken at Hilgrove, shows her reclining in a chaise longue in the kitchen garden at one side of the house. Her memories of sitting in this place inspired her description of the vantage point taken in "The Old Order" by Aunt Nanny and the Grandmother, so that they can supervise the activities of the whole family:

> . . . the women sat under the mingled fruit trees of the side garden, which commanded a view of the east wing, the front and back porches, a good part of the front garden and a corner of the small fig grove. . . . They had never found out who stole the giant pomegranate growing too near the fence. . . . They never saw Maria climbing trees, a mania she had to indulge or pine away, for she chose the tall ones on the opposite side of the house.[31]

At the time of her thirty-ninth birthday she took stock of her life once again. She told Herbst that she was thirty-five—a slight deception but a surprising one since their relationship was characterized by unusual frankness and honesty—and added that she had no lover and could not imagine finding another. She didn't wish to go on having affairs of varying degrees of intensity, full of upsets and miseries, which left her feeling as if she had "just got out of a hurricane" with her life in her hands.[32] What she wanted was to write two novels and go to Europe or the other way round, and to have a whole lot of books—all the books she hadn't read, all those she had read and wished to read again.

She even began to feel better about Matthew and wrote reassuring letters on the subject to Becky Crawford:

> But really, Angel, he is a dear, he is full of generous interest, and as he said to me once: "I represent myself badly and I swear it's because I'm timid!" Besides, we are honestly in love with each other, and there's nothing to be done about it, handicapped as we are by a whole elaborate system of compulsions and restraints, vague but powerful moral convictions and fool notions of conduct. To say nothing of hideous expediency. So I think of him gently as you can, he is really sweet, or I am the worst mistaken woman in the world.[33]

About Matthew: I really believe—its very hard to know exactly what is happening to you at the moment it's happening—but I'm out of the immediate excitement enough to get some idea—that psychologically I'm in pretty good order. Evidently the crisis passed at the first of the year, I don't know how I got hold of myself, but certainly I did: there was nothing to stop me but a sense of responsibility to myself and to him and to the plans and the work of us both, and then, besides, there was my whole life with its relations and associations, and his; and where before, many times, I have plunged and broken my bones, I was always able to heal: but this was more serious, I had a perfect intuition that if this ended in disaster, I was done for, for good and all. Maybe my fear cut me off from something that was more important than anything I may have saved by rejecting it, but I shall never be able to know what it was, now. But one thing happened new: I had always had great respect for the dignity, the importance and the permanence of other people's life plans, their feelings, their human relations that are developed with such pains, so much investment of energy and hope. And suddenly, almost for the first time, I also respected my own. This life that I wasted so carelessly was worth something to me, and I wished to keep it as intact as I could. And in this way it would also be worth more to other people: in short, I woke up and grew up, and I think it was a little late, my dear and lovely Becky.[34]

Around the same time she wrote hopefully about the completion of the biography:

Darling I've got a book too. Honest to God. It leaves here hot or cold on the first of June. I can't bear to read it, and wish I'd never started it, even now that it's finished I can't get warmed up to it any more. It's taken too long, there have been too many breaks in it. My copying and editing simply degenerated into a plastering job, trying to conceal the cracks. I should have written it red-hot in the mood I was in at first. But I'll say this: it's got everything in somehow, and it has got some lively moments.[35]

Ever afterward Porter spoke of her Bermuda sojourn as a time of idyllic peacefulness and complete solitude. Periodically she tried to recapture the same situation by making retreats to isolated hotels. In fact, her solitude in Bermuda was neither complete nor appreciated. After she moved from Sunnyside to live alone at Hilgrove she entertained the Crawfords, who came from New York to be her house guests for a time. And she made every effort to entice other guests. She invited friends such as Andrew Lytle, Helen Black, Hedwig Perry, and the brother of Delafield Spier. She tried to lure out her family, inviting her father and offering to adopt for the summer her six-year-old niece Patsy. When her invitations were not accepted she was disappointed and lonely,[36] and by July she could hardly wait to return to New York. She wrote to Josephine Herbst:

> Ah, Josie, God knows the heart in my buzzum beats sympathetically when you say you are tired of flowers and sunshine and whatnot. This island is so rotten ripe it simply wears me down. It simply sprawls and festers in the heat. . . . If you hear me complain of the cold in New York next winter, I hope you remind me of Bermuda in July. But Hullabaloo my hearties I'm booked to sail out of here the last week in September.[37]

When she sailed home at the end of the summer it was in a spirit of relief and thankfulness.

In June she had written to her publisher asking for an extra $250 to be added to the second advance of $300 she had received. She promised to send two chapters every week until *The Devil and Cotton Mather* was finished around August 1. Liveright sent the money and also sent dummies of the book and its jacket. She thanked him for the money and sent the two promised chapters but was horrified by the jacket. She told friends that the binding was very nice—a decent clerical black with pale orange lettering—but the jacket was blatant and vulgar beyond all words. She thought it misrepresented the book and looked like a circus poster. She also thought that at four dollars the book was too expensive. The biography was dedicated to Becky Crawford and she was amused to see Becky's good German-Jewish name, Edelson, sitting up in "Old English script, prayer book type."[38]

For all her promises, however, she could not finish the book. No more chapters arrived at the publishers after the first consignment and she remained stuck at the eleventh chapter. In September she wrote asking Liveright to stop announcing the book, saying that she could

not finish because of the demands of her other work. She thanked
him for his patience and said she hoped he was encouraged enough
by what he had seen of the manuscript to be patient a little longer.
Puzzled, he replied immediately:

> Naturally, I am surprised, shocked and chagrined to learn
> that there is as yet no definite date from you for the delivery
> to us of the balance of the manuscript of *The Devil and Cotton
> Mather*. Can't you give me some sort of idea when we will
> have the book? Can't you say that we will surely have it for
> publication in the Fall of 1930.[39]

Porter's reply has not been preserved, but his plea was not persuasive. The germination of a number of stories helped to harden her
resolution to set aside the biography, and she gave all her attention to
her fiction. In November her story "Theft" appeared in *Gyroscope,* a
mimeographed quarterly edited by Yvor Winters and Howard Baker.
Although it was a small publication which ran for only four issues
and whose subscribers never exceeded 180, many of them were leading literary figures and it was the most prominent little magazine since
The Transatlantic Review and *transition*.[40] Matthew Josephson persuaded her to make a collection of her stories and send them to his
new publisher, Harcourt, Brace. One of the young editors, Charles
A. Pearce, after reading the manuscript, exclaimed that it sounded
like something out of the classics; Josephson assured him that the
work was her own but would become a classic in future.

Besides working on the stories, Porter had taken up again the
Mexican material from 1920 and which she had made intermittent
attempts to shape into a novel, provisionally called "Thieves' Market." Out of this work emerged something that she had not consciously planned.

Porter often said that she wrote her stories in one sitting,[41] a
statement that seems dubious in view of the many drafts of stories
written over periods of ten or twelve years. And yet it was a paradox
that, while a story might simmer for a decade, when she was ready
to make the final version she would strike it out in one sitting with
little reference to her notes. This happened in the winter of 1929,
when she was living with the Crawfords, at 74 Orange Street in
Brooklyn.

The first month she was in Bermuda she had heard that Stanley
Moore, the young man to whom she had lent her apartment, had

attempted suicide and was in a hospital. The superintendent of the apartment building was kept in the dark about this, but Thorborg Haberman, to whom the apartment belonged, had Moore give up the place. Porter asked Becky Crawford to take over her furniture— including such items as a plum-colored chair, a Mexican chest which she wanted sealed because it was full of manuscripts, a white bookcase, an armchair, a red ladder-back chair, and the bed—and some linen and kitchen things. Thus the apartment at 74 Charles Street was vacated, and when Porter returned from Bermuda she had moved into a spare room in the Crawfords' large house.[42] They were happy to have her as a paying guest and willing to wait for the money. One evening they asked her to join them for a game of bridge as usual, and were surprised when she refused and went to her room saying there was something she must do.

She had just realized that two episodes in her Mexican material belonged together and were in themselves a complete story with the same theme which in a spare form she had used in "Magic" and "Theft." One episode was the account of the fat, sentimental revolutionary whose unwelcome attentions had made Mary Doherty ask Porter to chaperone her on the evening he serenaded them on his guitar. The other was the story about the young man in prison who had managed to obtain more than the usual harmless amount of sleeping pills and had killed himself. Porter also remembered the dream in which the young man appeared and accused her of killing him.

Porter named the revolutionary "Braggioni" and made him, like all her villains, a complete caricature. He looms in the story like a grotesque Easter egg in shades of purple and yellow. A hideous creature with the eyes of a cat and the paunch of a pig, he embodies each of the seven deadly sins. In contrast to Braggioni is the young, innocent victim, Eugenio. But once again the focus of attention is on neither of these characters but on the supposedly innocent girl who promotes Braggioni's wickedness by not resisting him and who is responsible for the death of Eugenio. This time she is drawn in greater detail. She has a name, Laura, and both her motivation and the implications of her actions are explained. Like the girl of "Theft" she has developed a principle of rejection:

> . . . the very cells of her flesh reject knowledge and kinship in one monotonous word. No. No. No. She draws her strength from this one holy talismanic word which does not suffer her to be led into evil. Denying everything, she may

walk anywhere in safety, she looks at everything without amazement.[43]

The implication is that if Braggioni is a self-serving, self-indulgent villain he has not always been so. Once he was a young idealist in both politics and love. It is Laura and those like her who have caused him to change from idealist to opportunist, and the main focus of the story is on her and upon her motivation. She neither loves nor opposes Braggioni because she is basically indifferent to him as she is to most people.

Her indifference and alienation are caused by her loss of the Catholic faith of her childhood and her inability to replace it with the worship of social progress and machines of those around her.

Porter's strength was not in showing growth and change in her characters, and in any event such a method was more appropriate to the novel than the short story. But she made a spontaneous discovery of a method of suggesting all the ramifications of the situation. As the story was nearing completion a pattern of symbolism appeared to her, not imposed upon the story but implicit in it, an extended use of the symbolic naturalism she had used in "Theft."

She remembered the Judas tree in the little Mexican patio where Mary Doherty lived, and it suggested to her the story of the arch betrayal of all time, that of Judas Iscariot.

The Judas tree also suggested the lines in T. S. Eliot's poem "Gerontion," a description of spiritual aridity and betrayal:

> . . . In the juvescence of the year
> Came Christ the tiger

> In depraved May, dogwood and chestnut, flowering judas,
> To be eaten, to be divided, to be drunk
> Among whispers . . .

And she thought of the epigraph Eliot used for his poem, from *Measure for Measure,* a play also closely related to her theme:

> Thou hast nor youth nor age;
> But, as it were, an after-dinner's sleep,
> Dreaming on both.

Above all she thought about the source of Eliot's description of the dogwood and flowering judas in Henry Adams's account of the eastern springtime. It had been just over a year since she read and discussed *The Education of Henry Adams* with Matthew, and she remembered now the chapter, "The Dynamo and the Virgin," in which Adams compared his feelings on seeing the forty-foot dynamo in the great exposition with those of an early Christian contemplating the Cross. The chapter suddenly seemed highly relevant to Laura's sense of being stranded between the lost religion of her childhood and her inadequate faith in the machine.

With her title Porter brought all these works to bear on her theme, and the rich superstructure of symbolism lifted the story onto a new plane and marked a great step forward in her art. She may not have been fully aware of the achievement but she was exhilarated by her night's work and did not wait for dawn to send it off. At one thirty in the morning she was standing on a snowy, windy corner putting it into the mailbox to Lincoln Kirstein, the editor of *Hound and Horn*.[44] The story was "Flowering Judas" and it made her literary reputation.

ELEVEN

Farewell to Mexico

Several of Porter's friends had been trying for some time to help her get a collection of her stories published. Matthew was one of the most active and in June 1929 he had written to his own publisher, Harcourt, Brace:

> Certainly it would be a good idea to get Katherine Anne Porter authoring for you. For some years she has been one of the bright "promises" of the surrounding scene. Her short stories have really caused underground admiration and murmur. Sometimes I have thought that instead of translating, which she can do very easily, she ought to write her book of her life in Mexico during the revolution. . . . Well you ought to correspond some more; find out about her experiences. I recall having proposed the idea of working her Mexican stories together into one subjective book. Her particular writing gifts I can hardly think of anybody here as exceeding. She used to be a friend of Elinor Wylie. Many people who know her, like Cowley and Allen Tate, have a great respect . . .[1]

The publishers, not having been exposed to Porter's charismatic presence, were less enthusiastic than her friends. She later claimed that Harcourt was hostile, Brace lukewarm, and another member of the company, "a little worm" called Raymond Everitt, determined to block publication.[2] Certainly it required a concerted effort, in the form of an epistolary attack by such friends as Caroline Gordon, Allen Tate, Edmund Wilson, and Yvor Winters before the book was accepted.[3] Even then three of the stories submitted were excluded ("Virgin Violetta," "The Martyr," and "Theft"), and a limited edition of 600 copies was planned containing only "María Concepción," "He," "Magic," "Rope," "The Jilting of Granny Weatherall," and the title story, "Flowering Judas."

Porter said she was humiliated beyond words by the expense of the book and the whole limited edition racket, which merely meant that the publisher did not wish to take a chance on her. She said that no one earned anything from the book except the publishers and that she got only $100.[4] (Since she was not an admirer of William Faulkner, it would have been little consolation to her to know that Harcourt, Brace in the same year turned down his manuscript of *The Sound and the Fury*.)

All the same, in spite of the somewhat unsatisfactory publishing arrangements, "a book is a book," as she often said later. *"Quand je serai lancé,"* "When I am launched," was a phrase always on the lips of the hopeful young writers of the twenties. Surely she could now consider herself truly launched. Her supporters were all the bright, promising writers of the day, her publishing house was a prominent New York one, and her stories were very well written. She had every reason to feel triumphant.

Her failure to do so was largely due to the continued disappointments of her personal life, and chief among these was still the loss of her relationship with Josephson. Time and distance had not lessened her infatuation and he was the first person she wanted to see when she came home. He was to meet the boat when she docked, an arrangement which was apparently compatible with his promise to Hannah to end the relationship. It was a cruel blow that instead of finding Matthew at the quayside Porter was handed a telegram reminding her once more that his family came first:

> MISSED YOU. BITTERLY DISAPPOINTED. ERIC GRAVELY ILL.
> FORGIVE WRITING.
>
> MATTHEW [5]

This humiliation was followed by others. Once Harcourt decided to publish her collection, the Everitts gave a party in her honor. Again it should have been a triumphant occasion, her finest hour. Matthew was invited, and for the party she fashioned an evening dress out of a beautiful old gown and managed to make it look very elegant. She was stunned, however, when Matthew arrived at the party with Hannah on his arm. Hannah was even more attractively dressed than her rival, and her youthful bloom accentuated Porter's age and the strained appearance which ill health had given her. Porter was too shocked to hide her dismay and lost control completely. She drank too much at dinner, and later, when the party moved to Harlem for dancing, she made crude and obvious advances to Matthew, pleading with him as they danced together to take her back. The situation was quite apparent to the rest of the group, for Porter stormed noisily around, and later Helen Everitt apologized to Matthew and said she had had no idea of the relationship between them or she certainly would not have invited them together.[6]

Since her return from Bermuda, Porter's life had become increasingly chaotic. She may have found its tenor in keeping with the general social atmosphere, for the fall of 1929 and early winter of 1930 was a time of violent upheavals and distortions. In October the stock market crashed, causing havoc in many lives. Two months later the literary community was stunned by the suicide of the young poet Harry Crosby. Shortly before Crosby's death, Porter, with a number of friends, went up to Sherman, Connecticut, to celebrate the birthday of the painter Peter Blume. The party became a strange Walpurgisnacht, with heavy drinking and many comings and goings and pairings off. People disappeared into the woods and others went in search of them.

For Porter the evening was the culmination of a whole series of disasters. There are various accounts of what happened to her and, while they are somewhat contradictory, most indicate that she was attacked by Robert Coates, a gifted but maverick writer who had returned four years earlier from a period of residence in Paris. Those closest to Porter at the time—Josephson and Susan Jenkins Brown, whom Porter had met in Greenwich Village—believed that Coates raped her and that, as a result, she required hospital treatment.[7] Josephson (who believed she was, in his words, *"enceinte"*) later reported that her friends once again raised the money to defray hospital expenses and that he approached Coates for help. Coates refused a contribution, saying that she had been with numerous men and he was not convinced that he had caused the problem. Malcolm Cowley, an admirer of Coates's work and a sympathetic observer of his general conduct (he described him as "romantic by disposition, almost nympholeptic"), thought that Coates had not committed rape but had managed, in the process of making love vigorously to a consenting woman, to break her ribs.[8]

Months of crises predictably broke Porter's health again; all the old bronchial problems recurred, with T.B. once again suspected. In the early months of 1930 Josephson had an almost fatal accident, but by this time Porter was too much overwhelmed with her own problems to grieve for his. He was preparing to leave for Europe with his family when there was a fire in the apartment house where the Josephsons lived. Instead of leaving the building swiftly, he tried to rescue his books and papers and was nearly burned to death. At Bellevue Hospital he was covered with layers of tannic acid which blackened as it dried, and it was feared that if he survived he would remain horribly disfigured. When he asked to see Porter she refused to go and merely told Herbst that he was not expected to live.[9]

When he was better they met by chance at a friend's home and he reproached her mildly for not visiting him. She replied that she could not bear to see him because she had heard he was completely disfigured. Then, turning on Hannah Josephson, she said with dramatic emphasis, "Why did your wife let you go back into the fire?" as if Hannah had unconsciously wanted him killed. He thought she was imagining quite a fantastic plot and explained that it was entirely his own fault that he had rushed back to save his manuscripts. She seemed strange and remote and very detached about the whole experience and said she had resigned herself to the idea that he would die. They parted coolly.

Porter was advised once again to seek a warmer climate and her thoughts turned to Mexico. She wanted to finish the long-planned novel, "Thieves' Market," and since it was set in Mexico, she thought that being there might expedite the task. Becky Crawford did not favor the Mexico plan, mainly because she was reluctant to have her friend so far away. Nevertheless, she helped by persuading a rich man, "not Otto Kahn but someone like him," to provide an income of $90 a month until the end of the year.[10] The relationship with the Crawfords cooled at this time because Porter resented Becky's opposition to the journey to Mexico. No amount of generous help could ever erase her resentment against unwanted "advice," which she always construed as "interference."

Susan Jenkins Brown, on the other hand, did favor the plan, found the money for the fare, and, as many other friends did, gave a farewell party for her. All the parties gave Porter a sense of something coming to an end. Her air at the time was one of summoning courage in the face of death. But, as always, when she set sail in late April on the S.S. *Havana* for Mexico, she had the feeling that once again she was embarking on a new life.

In her first days in Mexico, Porter experienced the improvement in health and euphoric raising of the spirits that she had felt when she went to Bermuda. The place excited her not only for its present beauties but for its past memories. She went out again to stay in Xochimilco, where Dorothy Day was now living with her daughter in a beautiful Indian shack. Porter took photographs and described the place as the location of Laura's teaching in "Flowering Judas."[11] She went with Carleton Beals and his wife to the floating gardens and rejoiced in the beauty of the place. She floated through the canals and saw the brightly decorated boats drifting about. She went to Cuernavaca and admired the bright red berries of the coffee plants, and she went to Chapultepec Park and remembered how ten years before she had gone boating there with Felipe Puerto Carillo.

When Dorothy Day returned to the States, Porter found an apartment on Calle Ernesto Pugibet, and there experienced a great renascence of her nest-building instincts. The place had four rooms scattered around an inside balcony, a roof for sunbathing, and a room for an Indian servant. She bought a pink overstuffed parlor set at the National Pawn Shop and enough potted trees and ferns to make the balcony look like a garden. Not only the house but the whole city delighted her. She wrote ecstatically of the beautiful weather, the good Spanish wines, the Mexican food, and the walks through the flower markets: "You simply emerge drunk and indescribably happy after walking between the stalls loaded to the ears with fresh bouquets. My Eufemia comes in every morning with a bunch of flowers on top of the basket."[12]

The place might have been as conducive to creative growth as Bermuda, inspiring an imaginative recreation of her experiences during the twenties as Bermuda had inspired a recreation of her childhood. Porter, hoping desperately that it would be, worked on her novel, parts of which were already written. Unfortunately she made little progress and the reason is not hard to find.

The difference between Mexico City and Bermuda as work

places was that Mexico City was not an island. In both locations she was tempted by all the usual distractions—her love of an active social life, her desire to be chatelaine of an establishment in which she could plan delightful social occasions, her fondness for cooking and gardening and interior decorating. In Bermuda she had known few people. Of the scores of friends and relatives invited to enjoy the amenities of Hilgrove only the Crawfords had accepted. In Mexico City, on the other hand, she had many friends, and those who were invited to visit from the United States came in large numbers. There was rarely a time when she did not have a house guest. The friends she saw most often were Mary Doherty and a young man who became Porter's next lover and a few years later her husband.

As she approached her fortieth birthday she had written her usual stock-taking letter to Josie Herbst reminiscing about affairs of the heart:

> My one or two real love affairs were always something that dropped on me like a bolt in the midst of poverty, illness and the exact middle of a piece of work, and love, for me, has been rather more as if I were a bundle of wheat going through the threshing machine than anything else. When I came through, I was clean winnowed.[13]

In spite of the elegiac note she was on the brink of one of her most durable relationships.

A few days after she wrote that letter, she was sitting at Chole's restaurant with friends when a young man, slightly drunk, tottered up in search of Dorothy Day. He noticed Porter, doffed his ten-gallon hat, gave a histrionic bow, and staggered away.[14] Eugene Dove Pressly was a twenty-seven-year-old native of Denver, employed as a secretary for the Crane Foundation but more interested in writing. He was attractive, intelligent, inclined when sober to be brooding and silent, and as reclusive as Porter was gregarious. Most of her friends disliked him, considering him undistinguished and unworthy of her. It was said that he would escort her to parties, sit silent all evening, and later remember and record all that was said. To Hart Crane he seemed dour, puritanical, and most like a YMCA secretary. While Crane's interpretation of "puritanical" must necessarily be open to question, his impression is supported by the portrait of David Scott in *Ship of Fools*. This character, based on Pressly, is dour, disapproving, and equipped with what his partner describes as a "Quaker con-science." Certainly Pressly seems to have had a suspicious, hostile nature but from the beginning his devotion to Porter was absolutely unwavering. (His loyalty was one of a number of traits he shared with Porter's father, both being described as "one-woman men.") At an early meeting when she mentioned her plan to go to Europe he said quickly, "Oh, don't go!"[15] She was charmed, and their lives were from that moment inextricably bound together. All the same, this was for Porter no *coup de foudre*. Gratified as she was by the young man's admiration, she was not so euphoric that she abandoned her work and forgot her troubles.

Her chief problem was that she was too tired to work. She said that she felt she must rest and sleep in the hope that the next day she would really be able to work, but she rarely mustered her energies sufficiently to do so. The main reason was that she engaged in too much social activity. She shopped and sewed to furnish her house, arranged large dinner parties, and constantly entertained visitors from the United States. Moisés Saenz, the Minister of Culture, tried to help by offering his house in Taxco as a place of retreat and Porter went to look at it. She saw at once that the place was unsuitable and stayed only one night before returning to Mexico City. The excursion to Taxco did, however, yield one tangible result, for on the road she saw an unforgettable scene. An Indian man and woman were engaged in a life-and-death battle, killing each other with knives and stones, blood gushing from the wounds in their stomachs and breasts. She was at once horrified and fascinated by the sight, which gave her a deep premonition of disaster, and she made brilliant use of it in *Ship of Fools* to describe Jenny Brown's nightmare:

> During the first month after she began to live with David, she had gone by bus from Mexico City to Taxco, to look at a house there. At the noon of the burning bright day they had slowed down in passing through a small Indian village with the little thick-walled windowless houses sitting along the road, the bare earth swept before each door. The dust was bitter to taste, the heat made her long for sleep in a cool place.
>
> Half a dozen Indians, men and women, were standing together quietly in the bare spot near one of the small houses, and they were watching something very intensely. As the bus rolled by, Jenny saw a man and a woman, some

distance from the group, locked in a death battle. They swayed and staggered together in a strange embrace, as if they supported each other; but in the man's raised hand was a long knife, and the woman's breast and stomach were pierced. The blood ran down her body and over her thighs, her skirts were sticking to her legs with her own blood. She was beating him on the head with a jagged stone, and his features were veiled in rivulets of blood. They were silent, and their faces had taken on a saint-like patience in suffering, abstract, purified of rage and hatred in their one holy dedicated purpose to kill each other. Their flesh swayed together and clung, their left arms were wound about each other's bodies as if in love. Their weapons were raised again, but their heads lowered little by little, until the woman's head rested upon his breast and his head was on her shoulder, and holding thus, they both struck again.

It was a mere flash of vision, but in Jenny's memory it lived in an ample eternal day illuminated by a cruel sun, full of the jolly senseless motion of the bus, the deep bright arch of the sky, the flooding violet-blue shadows of the mountains over the valleys; her thirst; and the gentle peeping of newly hatched chickens in a basket on the knees of the Indian boy beside her. She had not known how frightened she was until the scene began repeating itself in her dream, always with some grotesque variation which she could not understand. But this latest time, she had been among the watchers, as if she were at play, and the two narrow white-clad figures were unreal as small sculptured altar pieces in a country church. Then with horror she saw that their features were changing, had changed entirely—the faces were David's and her own, and there she was looking up into David's blood-streaming face, a bloody stone in her hand, and David's knife was raised against her pierced bleeding breast. . . .

In her relief at waking, and her melancholy in remembering that time when she had been enchanted with David and had believed in their love, she almost wept.[16]

This passage was the only benefit of the Taxco trip, and for a while she resigned herself to working amid the distractions of Mexico City.

In the early stages of her relationship with Pressly, Porter was still writing frequent letters to Josephson. Many of them were in the spirit of an extended lovers' quarrel, with recriminations for past injuries and present imagined slights:

> When I first knew you, you were just emerging from the Zola period . . . Later, remember, you were the man of action warring single handed against great cities. Later when you feared I might stubbornly keep on being in love with you when the occasion that called for me had passed, you wrote that "our emotional feats" were of no consequence compared to the realistic businesses of life such as running a household, begetting young and writing books. We were to be machines, I remember distinctly, functioning with hair's breadth precision. I wasn't deceived then, dear Matthew, and still I'm not when you decide that we must all be romantic rather than decorous. One might be both if one's nature was such? I think it means merely that you have found someone or something new to play with, and this point of view may be for the moment useful to you? You are like a good golfer who chooses just the right club to hit the ball in a certain way.[17]

Since she later destroyed all traces of this relationship in which she was spurned, his reply has not been preserved, but it may be surmised from her reaction to it:

> You do wrong to be so angry with a friend who loves you as I do, and you mustn't burst into abuse, elegies and eternal farewells regularly as you do whenever I forget myself and take the liberty of writing to you as frankly and freely as I do to other persons. Why cannot you grant to your friends the freedom you give yourself of criticism and comment. And as for MY rhetoric? I am being continually humbled and confounded by the complicated brilliance of your style. It wasn't acid and brimstone—not at all these. I was in an excellent but I see now foolhardy humor. And it wasn't pretty of you—I can't say graceful, for that word is gradually being destroyed for me—to answer by a general flight under cover of such words as psychosis, vengeance, vomiting, spewing—oh, come now, Matthew. You'll have to do better than this. I did not mean to insult you; I was perfectly aware I was writing a provocative letter, but it was not a bitter one. But this has happened before. You have written

frightfully wounding things to me, or have said them. And then I answered with edged words, and you were grieved and astonished and wounded, and wounded that I was wounded—and yes, really, to flee is one answer for such persistent wronging of the human heart.

Let me answer your thousandth farewell with the thousand and first. But I do not mean it and you need not. Am I among all your friends to be the only one not permitted to quarrel even a little with you, and make it up again. . . .

Out of this well-renovated bosom of tenderness I send you my affection. In the hope that Mr. Rousseau will make a fine book. Better than The Portrait, and The Portrait was better than Zola . . . and remember what we thought of Zola.

Above all, no more good-byes.[18]

Ten years earlier, when Joseph Retinger showed her an angry letter he had written to Jane Anderson, she had told him plainly that, no matter what he thought, it was a love letter, since one didn't write such letters until all else had failed. Her words now applied exactly to her letters to Matthew.

Soon after she arrived in Mexico, her book of short stories appeared to very enthusiastic reviews, mostly by critics who were also her friends. Porter thought she was fortunate to have fallen into such good hands, but her sensitivity to slights ran along with her enjoyment of adulation. She was annoyed to learn that Josephson, of all people, had written the blurb for the jacket. He had called her a member of the younger generation of writers, and she wrote him tartly that she had been a member of that generation once and had not the strength to go through it again.[19]

It was a measure of her lukewarm response to Pressly that she was also highly susceptible to other men at this time. There was one Jacobo with whom she exchanged "a coupla dozen burning looks and a few amusingly childish hand squeezes" before deciding that fidelity was her best bet if she wished to keep Pressly.[20] And on the whole she did wish to keep him, for she valued his loyalty and his protectiveness. When her money ran out, he gladly supported her, and her remark that he prevented her house from being "a desert of howling jackals" suggests that he exercised some control over her unruly social life. Unfortunately, it was not enough to prevent chaos.

One guest from New York was Porter's old friend Liza Dallett, with whom she had lived in Windham, Connecticut, in 1924. Porter went to endless trouble preparing a room with mats, rush chairs, yellow curtains and matching bed covers, but the visit was a seven-week nightmare. Liza was now separated from John Dallett and, according to Porter, talked constantly and hysterically so that Porter could neither sleep nor work. When she finally left, Porter was in bed with tonsillitis and a high fever.[21]

Peggy and Malcolm Cowley, finding themselves temperamentally incompatible, journeyed to Mexico for an amicable divorce. Porter thoroughly enjoyed their visit, but not all her guests were so pleasant.

She also found a new distraction. She had always loved music and wanted to study it seriously, and now found a willing teacher in the painter Pablo O'Higgins. He gave her lessons for six weeks, teaching her the principles of harmony and explaining the system of balance and weight in getting tone, and showing her how to read music. He set her firmly in the middle of third-year music and left her to practice, which she did by "staggering through six Bach preludes and a capriccio by Scarlatti." She bought a wreck of a piano which she had repaired so that it tinkled a little, and she hoped to have it completely restored. The piano, made in 1820 in England, was bought for forty-five dollars from the grand-niece of the first owner. She described it as a rosewood miniature grand with pedals but only seven octaves, the first type after the spinet and clavichord.[22]

She was also doing essays and reviews for the New Republic, solicited by Malcolm Cowley in his capacity as book editor. He accepted her work, put it into shape, and gave tactful explanations to salve her pride. When she sent in "Leaving the Petate," an essay based on her maid's conversation, Malcolm said it was universally liked but judged too long and he was condemned to do the amputation.[23]

Early in 1931 she struggled to review two books by Kay Boyle, *Plagued by the Nightingale* and *Wedding Day and Other Stories*. Of the stories she wrote Herbst:

They are gorgeous but I feel as you do about Faulkner—there is something a little off somewhere in this talent or it may be it is just that she is a little shrill and noisy because she isn't quite certain. . . . I hope Kay Boyle gets over her toughness that is just a thin layer over what seems perilously like apple-sauce beneath, and that the inner fibre strengthens and warms a little.[24]

And of the difficulty of writing the review she said:

> I have fiddled all around it, trying to do that girl justice, and I am having a hard time. I have read her poems long ago, and some of these stories, and she is gorgeous and irritating, and sharp as a whip and mean as the devil, and a vitality that is like a sock on the snoot. I like her immensely but there are some things to be said against her. And that is the trouble. It is almost impossible to get her disentangled from her work, she has the kind of personality that *is* her work, and comes very near sometimes to simple self-exploitation, that is the bane of too many literary women and some men.[25]

When she finally sent in the review, Malcolm Cowley told her it was embarrassingly long but so good that he could not bear to cut more than two sentences, just to keep the blue pencil in practice. He also rearranged her sentences and told her that she never was a great hand at building tight brick paragraphs, but the people who could do that would be lucky if they could write as well as she.[26]

Porter praised Boyle for writing of love "not as if it were a disease or a menace, or a soothing syrup to vanity, or something to be peered at through a microscope, or the fruit of original sin, or a battle between the sexes, or a bawdy pastime," but as one who believed in love and romance—not the "faded flower in the button hole" but love so fresh and clear it came to the reader as a rediscovery in literature.[27] When the review appeared on April 22, Kay Boyle was delighted and wrote to her reviewer saying that every sentence Porter had ever written made her want to shout and wave and cry. Boyle remained Porter's staunch admirer and friend, although later Porter changed her mind about Boyle and told a critic in 1952, "How I was deceived in this talent—it rotted very early. But it *was* talent."[28]

One of the reasons for writing reviews was, as always, money. She had a cash advance from Harcourt for her novel, but no matter how much the publishers advanced and her friends raised it was never enough. She quickly spent any money that came along, so that when unforeseen expenses arose there was another financial crisis. In February of 1931 her standard of living became considerably more lavish when she left the Mexico City apartment and moved out to the suburb of Mixcoac.

The move naturally disrupted her work and she must have justified the disruption carefully, deciding that the house in Mexico City was too noisy and lacking in air and was bad for her health. She needed more spacious surroundings and the solace of a garden and flowers such as she had had in Bermuda. Although she did not say so openly, perhaps she hoped too that the surroundings would cause a rise in her creative energy. Certainly the place she chose resembled Hilgrove in its spaciousness of rooms and gardens. It was a ten-room place with endless galleries, a roof to ramble on, and a beautiful garden with a fountain, fruit trees, and a small swimming pool. There were baths and ovens and dressing rooms and servants' quarters all on the grand scale of a prosperous Mexican family of fifteen. She could afford the house because Pressly and Mary Doherty were moving in with her, planning to commute by train to their jobs in the city. Each person was to have a bedroom and sitting room and share living and dining rooms, and among the three of them they had enough furniture to fill the place. Both Porter and Mary were taking their servants and Mary was also bringing an assortment of animals —cat, dog, bird, and two goldfish.[29]

By March, Porter had gone through the usual hard work of straightening out and was settled in a huge, sunny room upstairs. In her letters she described what she could see from her desk:

> . . . a square of roof to the east with bougainvillaea climbing all around it, looking down into a garden full of honeysuckle, heliotrope, white and purple flags, dame de noche (a small greenish cluster of flowers that gives a beautiful perfume at night), a wall covered to the top—nine feet—with blooming pink geraniums (the modest pot plant!), a tree with gorgeous bell-shaped flowers which smell like a cross between magnolia and jasmine, two pomegranate trees, a scattering bed of violets, mint, a salt cedar far from its native land, roses red and white, an apricot tree, lace ferns—other things I can't remember until I look again. Everything is in bloom or full of fruit.[30]

The front and back gardens had orange, zapote, fig, cherry, and avocado trees loaded with fruit, all mixed up with rosebushes, woodpiles, a henhouse and a mess of loose building stone in the corner.

There was also an outdoor menagerie, consisting of a brown hen called Trinket with two gray chickens, two "grand turkey ladies" called Madame Grundy and Blanche of Castille, and four ducks which paraded solemnly quacking around the pool all day. The younger pair were named Kuku and Koko, the older Missy and Mister, and the former kitten, Ixiquintla, was now a mother. There was a yellow kitten and a black puppy, both of whom thought, as she did, that they were in heaven.

When she had exhausted the subject of the charms of her house, garden, and menagerie, she wrote about changes of weather and climate:

I wish I could describe to you the mornings here. Usually there is rain in the afternoons, the nights are freezing cold, but the mornings are blue and clear with heavy sleepy shadows and the sparkle of water on the leaves. We take a dip in a tank of ice water about 11 o'clock, bake in the sun, put the kittens out in their baskets, pick up the alligator pears that have fallen during the night, explore for ripening figs, walk around to see how much the plants have grown during the night. The birds sing and flutter and the pigeons parade along the walls, the butterflies and lizards are almost tame. I cannot take my eyes from the sight of the world at these times. Then about three o'clock the big sulky thunderheads roll up, a high wind trembles the branches of the ash trees, the rain begins. I fly to see that the little fellows around the place are under cover, then put on my red jacket and settle down in the house. This morning I picked a bouquet for the table: heliotrope and honeysuckle, pink and climbing geraniums and Spanish jasmine. Yesterday it was red roses, tomorrow it can be oleanders and pale bluish grey vine flower, with fern. And the day after, huge white bell flowers that smell like gardenia or the little pale green sweet-by-night that smells like tube roses and cinnamon mixed. The sweet smells around here would send you off your head.[31]

Clearly the place was proving to be inspirational and perhaps she did not regret the time she spent describing it. She told a friend once that "writing *real* letters in which you really *said* something" was the best form of creative writing that she knew of.[32] All the same, her epistolary efforts did nothing to advance her task in hand—the novel. She was still determined to finish it, especially when in April she learned that she had earned a Guggenheim fellowship and could now make plans for her long-postponed trip to Europe. The grant was only $2,000 but she thought that would keep her in Europe for some time. She determined to finish her book by September 1 and leave for Europe in October.[33]

In the middle of moving she had reorganized her novel completely. She had given it a new title, "Historical Present," and she said she would, if necessary, "tear out my gizzard" to make the deadline.[34] She did not, however, do much work, and the house proved to be her chief obstacle. The household was larger by two people than Hilgrove, and even when there were no invited guests the three of them made a party which prevented much work. Pressly loved good food, Porter loved to cook, and they both enjoyed drinking and did so copiously. She reported to Josephine Herbst and John Herrmann:

> I have reduced it to a formula. All day, I am sober as a crow. I work on the novel—and not until six o'clock do I break down and take a little cocktail or a sloe-gin rickey or a Black Strap Rum punch, and then with supper I have three or four modest glasses of red wine and then a little cognac to top it off, and there is the evening, all ablaze. I will *not* give up wine and such for I consider it part of living, but I do give it up for the time that I am working.[35]

The pleasant surroundings stimulated Porter's love of entertaining and the descriptive letters and invitations which flew to the U.S. brought more results than she anticipated. Her father planned to visit and had to be hastily discouraged, as did Kitty Barry Crawford.[36] Porter fretted about her unfinished work but the dinner parties continued. She celebrated her birthday by entertaining Moisés Saenz, who gave her a beautiful silver rosary. She gave dinner parties for the Russian movie director Sergei Eisenstein, who was in Mexico to make the movie *Que Viva Mexico;* for Eugene Jolas, the editor of *transition;* and for Carleton Beals (who inspired her story "That Tree").[37]

By far the biggest interruption to her work was the arrival of Hart Crane in April. She had known him only slightly in New York but they had many friends in common and she admired his work. He came out to Mixcoac, liked the house and garden, and decided to move in. Most of his friends were well aware that he had changed from a heavy social drinker to a problem drinker whose drunken exploits were already legendary, but in Mixcoac his drunken scenes exceeded any previous ones.

Porter thought the problem was that he had come to Mexico steeped in the legend of Mexican homosexuality and in happy anticipation of a freer love life than was possible in the United States. She said that although homosexuality was commonplace among the Indians, it was not practiced on the crude scale he expected. He got madly drunk every night and brought home policemen or youths he picked up in the street. She guessed they accompanied him out of curiosity and she never saw the same one twice. Her room was above his and she heard people prowling about all night long. Money disappeared, and if she needed to go to the bathroom she would run into strange men, drunk and buttoning up their trousers, as they stumbled out.[38]

A crisis came when he fell in love with the fourteen-year-old carpenter's apprentice who was building some bookshelves for Porter, and tried to snatch him from under the nose of his father. Crane brought the lad to the house and, when she refused to have him for dinner, grew drunk and boisterous and accused her of being an evilminded creature who could not understand the nobility of his emotions. When he was sober he apologized tearfully and she explained that his sexual life was his own affair but as she would not be an accomplice in the seduction of a fourteen-year-old girl, she would not let a man seduce a fourteen-year-old boy in her house if she could help it.[39]

Characteristically Crane would begin talking in an ordinary voice, saying that he knew he was destroying himself as a poet, that the life he was leading was blunting his sensibilities and he could no longer feel anything except under the most violent and brutal shocks. He would invoke the memory of other artists who lived excessively —Baudelaire, Marlowe, Melville, and Blake. As he grew really drunk he would shout and weep, shaking his fist and banging the table until she was ready to jump out of her shoes with fright. He talked constantly of suicide and once ran from the room and rushed to the roof shouting that he was going to throw himself off. The roof was only one story high and Porter called out anxiously that he would only hurt himself. Immediately he began to laugh, the tension was broken, the crisis averted, and he climbed down an apricot tree. [40]

Often he would go into town to ramble from cantina to cantina picking up lovers, causing fights and ending up in jail. Once after a night in jail his skin was breaking out because he had been chewed by bedbugs and lice. Worrying that he might have contracted some venereal disease, Porter cleaned out the bathroom with Lysol. This infuriated him and he accused her of treating him like a leper.

Porter found that when he was sober she could talk to him and half pretend that nothing had happened, but Pressly, who had a horror of homosexuals, hated him and became an icicle. Once Pressly bribed a policeman not to arrest Crane, but afterward told him that if he kept Porter awake another night he would not stop any policeman who wanted to arrest him. Porter told Pressly angrily that that was not altogether necessary, but she was glad he had said it. [41]

The household was relieved when Crane moved to his own house around the corner, but he was still near enough to cause trouble. Once, high on tequila, he climbed over the roofs from his house to hers and descended howling with delight. She was terrified and locked herself in the bathroom.

The final and well-publicized break came soon afterward. Hart Crane's account was that he had invited Porter and Pressly to dinner and made extensive preparations but they failed to arrive. He felt that the ignored invitation was a calculated insult devised mainly by Pressly. Porter did not mention the dinner in her account but did describe his arrival at her gate later that evening, drunk and shouting. He demanded to come in, pleading with her, "Katherine Anne, I am a poet and you are a poet, let me in." At the end of her patience, she refused to let him in. [42] Then he broke into monotonous, obsessed, dulled obscenity, his only language when he reached a certain point of drunkenness. She found his voice at such times intolerable, a steady, harsh, inhuman bellow which she said "stunned the ears, and shocked the nerves and caused the heart to contract." In this voice he cursed separately by name the moon, and its light, the heliotrope, the heaven tree, the sweet-by-night, the star jessamine, and their perfumes. He cursed the air they breathed together, the pool with two small ducks huddled at the edge, and the vines on the wall of the house. "But," said Porter, "those were not the things he hated. He did not even hate us, for we were nothing to him. He hated and feared himself." [43]

The immediate problem was resolved when Crane's father died on July 6 and he left Mexico immediately, but by this time Porter's health had been seriously affected. Crane bitterly resented being blamed for her ill health and unproductiveness. He said that she had been in Mexico for a year before he arrived and had not written one paragraph of the book she intended. She was encumbered with a menagerie of animals, a regular stockyard, and spent hours talking to them far more than she ever did in his company. He thought she was not happy and was constantly in a nervous flutter and talked to herself more than others and was a puzzle to many of her old friends before he arrived. He thought there was a tendency among her friends to sentimentalize her ill health and exaggerate her delicateness. He thought her health problem was gout caused because she and Pressly had been sampling all the best wines. And he resented her letter writing, saying that she wrote every scrap of news about his behavior to their friends in New York, and that all his relationships were impaired on that account.[44]

There was some truth in what he said. She did, in fact, have an attack of gout in early June and wrote amusingly about it. Her vanity was flattered at finding she had such a "high falutin" hereditary disease and she reported, boasting a little, that the doctor asked if any of her ancestors belonged to the nobility. She was advised to give up smoking and drinking and she complained that she "missed her dear old T.B. which allowed [her] to smoke, drink [herself] under the table, and eat a rare steak every day if [she] could get it."[45]

And both she and Pressly had been garrulous on the subject of Crane's misdemeanors. It was Pressly's reports to Eylor Simpson, secretary of the Guggenheim Foundation's Mexican Selection Committee, that caused Crane to be censured by the foundation's secretary in New York. Porter had not only written detailed accounts to friends but had also taken notes, possibly intended for inclusion in her "Book of Men," on the various stages of his drunkenness, recording in the first stage the false sweetness of his eyes, in the second the fraudulent distinction of the head held too high, the chin lifted disdainfully, in the third the brawling, gluttonous, flabby mouth vomiting filth, and in the final stage the raving and utter falling apart. In view of her own activity, it is ironic that she should have laid the blame for his suicide a year later at the door of his friends: "He made such a good show and they had no lives of their own, so they lived vicariously by his."[46]

Considering her nervous, overwrought state it is not surprising that she resented her other guests too, but she could not stem the flow of visitors she had encouraged. Peggy Cowley came again. Achilles Holt spent a few whole days swimming and drinking and relaxing, as did Lallah Rogers and Dorothy Day. Porter wrote Caroline Gordon that Dorothy Day would hang around and try to pick quarrels and Porter could not make her understand that she did not quarrel on slight grounds and would never have enough in common with her to quarrel on serious ones.[47]

Years later Porter spoke with bitterness of certain literary friends, for whom she had no jealousy and who she had assumed were not jealous of her. She had subsequently been amazed at her own simplicity in not recognizing their bitterness and resentment of her. In this group she included Dorothy Day, adding, "She gave up writing and took to being a saint and I don't know what she says or thinks about anything now."[48]

She wrote Dorothy's sister Delafield that Dorothy disliked her very much and toward the end was so unfriendly that she could not approach her about anything. She regretted it, because she was so fond of Della and didn't know how she had offended Dorothy and thought it was very mysterious. In spite of Porter's professed puzzlement, she and Day were so temperamentally opposite that enmity between them was not surprising. Porter wrote in one letter:

About Dorothy? Does she keep her ingenuous convert fanaticism? Such a strange end for her! But religion is necessary at certain crises to certain temperaments. It gives a solid foothold. But never for me. And I am always amazed when I see a grown person deliberately embrace a religious life.[49]

Retrospectively, Porter wondered at the people who had crowded out to Mixcoac, some uninvited, and who she felt then and afterward had a veiled hatred for her. She puzzled at why she was not able to defend herself against such "a curious swarm of plagues," people who were nothing to her and yet who swarmed out, eager to enjoy the place, pretending they liked her and yet inexplicably hostile and malignant, unable to conceal their malice and determined to leave a little drop of poison on everything they touched. The description— so close to that of her childhood dreams—suggests the paranoia always ready to flare up when her health deteriorated.

The remaining months of the summer were terrible, and she brooded not only about her unwelcome guests but about the political atmosphere. She said that Mexico was the God-sent stamping ground for every kind of disguised banditry and that the whole country was menaced from within and without. Her novel's title suggests that she already understood this situation, but it was only when she was on the spot that she realized the extent of the corruption. She had always felt indignant about homosexuality, and she thought the political group a vast network of gentlemen who gave lads good jobs in return for their favors; every political appointment and benefit seemed to be ruled by this principle. She was also disgusted at seeing corrupt politicians prospering in the new social organizations while the Indians remained as poor as ever. In particular she resented the foreign entrepreneurs who were raising the price of works of art while the native craftsmen gained nothing from their skills.

Amid all this unpleasantness she found a respite of three days when she visited the Hacienda Tetlapayac in the state of Hidalgo, where Eisenstein was working on his movie. The visit was not an apparent success since filming was suspended because of cloudy weather, Eisenstein's illness, and the accidental shooting on the set of one of the actors. But many of Porter's old friends were there and she spent the time talking with Castro Padilla, Adolpho Best-Maugard, and the Russian assistants, Alexandroff and Tissé. She thought she might do a piece on the visit with the names changed.[50]

When the story appeared, it was a summation of all her feelings about Mexico. Her other stories had each dealt with a single aspect of the place. "María Concepción" had explored the plight of the Indian on whom an alien religion had been imposed; "Virgin Violetta" had described the life of the Spanish upper class; "Flowering Judas" the revolutionary movement; "The Martyr" the new arts; and "That Tree" the foreign journalists who flocked in large numbers to Mexico City. In the account of her visit to Tetlapayac she brought together all the strands of Mexican life. When Eisenstein wanted a symbol for all the varied elements in Mexico he cast about and decided on the serape, the striped blanket with contrasting violent colors, to represent the violently contrasting cultures. Porter found an effective symbolic pattern similar to the one she had used so effectively in "Flowering Judas." This was the hacienda itself.

It is first of all a pulquería, and the changeless basis of this primitive occupation is closely associated with Indian life:

> . . . pulque-making had not changed from the beginning, since the time the first Indian set up a raw-hide vat to fer-

ment the liquor and pierced and hollowed the first gourd to draw with his mouth the juice from the heart of the maguey. Nothing had happened since, nothing could happen. Apparently there was no better way to make pulque.[51]

The hacienda is permeated with the smell of the pulque, a nasty smell suggestive of rotting human products, a detail which intimates that the life of Mexico is being undermined by the oppression of the Indian, whose rich artistic heritage should be assimilated. Instead, the Indian remains exploited, his willing refuge in superstition and narcotics making him an easy prey. For this reason the pulque has a menacing character and is described as "corpse-white":

> All over Mexico the Indians would drink the corpse-white liquor, swallow forgetfulness and ease by the riverful, and the money would flow silver-white into the government treasury.[52]

The fresco depicting the discovery of pulque is described in detail and shows the Indian's ability to transform his superstitious veneration of the liquor into a work of art:

> The walls were covered with a faded fresco relating the legend of pulque; how a young Indian girl discovered this divine liquor, and brought it to the emperor, who rewarded her well; and after her death she became a half-goddess. An old legend: maybe the oldest, something to do with man's confused veneration for, and terror of, the fertility of women and vegetation.[53]

For the Spanish overlords who are interested neither in the production of pulque nor in works of art, the hacienda is a feudal manor and as such represents the Spanish occupation, alien to Mexico in its origin, anachronistic in its present form, and surviving only by exploitation of the native. Each member of the Spanish family of the story is ineffectual in his attempt to adapt to the modern world. The old grandfather lives in retreat in the farthest patio, the son, devoted to speed and machines, lives in a constant frenzy of purposeless activity.

The intellectual class is represented by Carlos and Betancourt, based on Castro Padilla and Adolpho Best-Maugard.[54] Betancourt with his anomalous mixed background fits in nowhere; he takes refuge in cynicism and in a complicated esoteric "Way of Life" drawn from a careful choice of the doctrines from several schools of oriental philosophies. Carlos is more human and the narrator defends him against Betancourt's charges of failure by saying that he has done a good day's work in his time and is not finished yet.

The use of the hacienda as a movie set makes it a microcosm of the Mexico on which various foreigners converge. The Russians, whose nation has been important to social change in Mexico, have no human involvement with the country. They are technicians interested only in producing a perfect movie. Kennerly, the representative of the worst kind of American, is interested only in making a lucrative movie.

The hacienda in its capacity as a movie set also dramatizes the ineffectiveness of the revolution, which has changed the names of many things with a view to an appearance of heightened well-being for all creatures. The movie is set in 1898, but as Andreyev points out, when he shows still shots of the film, nothing has changed, a fact which embarrasses those in charge of Mexican propaganda who are assigned to assist the movie makers.

The central event is the shooting of one of the actors and the characters all respond predictably, according to what they represent. The feudal overlord is outraged that one of the peons he owns is put in prison. Betancourt says cynically that the dead girl would have had no decent life anyway; the other artist composes a gently romantic song to her. The Russian technicians regret that they did not capture the killing on film and the American business manager regrets the loss of money.

The story, however, is not simply a comprehensive picture of Mexico. One of the few stories written in the first person, the emphasis is upon the narrator's relationship with the country, and her attempt to find a place where she can live and work. Her final word on the hacienda, "I could not wait for tomorrow in this deathly air," is also, in this last Mexican story, her final word on Mexico.

For all its air of disillusionment with Mexico, her story "Hacienda" was one of her most substantial. That fact, however, provided little satisfaction in the fall of 1931, because the story was then merely a pile of notes. It would be many drafts and three years later before it reached its final form. Her sense of its potential did nothing to alleviate the sense of despair she felt at the end of her seventeen months in Mexico.

Later she spoke of this period in terms of the utmost horror, saying that for months afterward she felt as if she were convalescent from a nightmare. It was true that she had come through some trying times. There had been far too many unruly house guests, with Hart Crane's tempestuous visit as the final outrage, but there was a stronger reason for her feeling that she was completely broken in body and spirit, as if she had been attacked by an army of bloodsuckers. The real truth was that she was desperate because of her failure to write. In 1929 she had reached a peak of achievement in her art. From there she thought she should have gone on to crown that success with a novel. Her supporters, her publisher, and she herself had expected no less. Instead of doing that, she spent seventeen long months unable to write even a short story. She must have wondered if her career was finished, and it is little wonder that she blamed everyone but herself and felt impotent, panicky, and feverish.

In this mood she made her final plans to leave for Europe, and her last days in Mexico were as painful as the previous months. When she closed up the Mixcoac house she was appalled by the speed and thoroughness with which her friends dismantled everything and carried off her possessions.

A farewell party lasted until four in the morning and she rose after only two hours' sleep determined to travel by day and see the mountains through which the railway wound to Veracruz. But the fog shut out the valleys and she had to sit, miserable from a hangover, on an upright bench seeing nothing.[55]

In Veracruz a storm blew up at three in the morning and thunder crashed like falling skyscrapers; lightning struck the elevator just twenty feet from her room, like a bomb bursting in her face.[56] In spite of all mishaps she and Pressly boarded the S.S. *Werra* on August 22, intending to disembark in France, for which purpose the Mexican agent said they could get visas in any port.

TWELVE

The German Experience

Decades later, when it was abundantly clear what the German trip had yielded, Porter called it a "God-sent opportunity."[1] Sometimes she even spoke as if her journey had been part of a calculated plan, telling Erna Glover Johns, "I went to Germany instead of France on your account on my first European trip."[2]

In fact, her choice of a German ship and a German city as her destination was purely accidental. Ever since 1919 her plans to go to Europe had habitually miscarried, but they had finally come to fruition with the Guggenheim fellowship. Between the announcement of the award and her departure, as her life became chaotic and her state of mind more unstable, her decisions became completely erratic. One problem was that she and Pressly disagreed on which country they should head for. Porter longed to go to France, most particularly to Paris, while Pressly, a hispanophile, wanted to go to Madrid, where his knowledge of Spanish would help him get an embassy job.[3]

Finally they chose the German ship S.S. *Werra* because it was leaving from Veracruz and because it was cheap. (Porter described it as a tramp steamer disguised as a passenger boat.) At first Porter thought they might save money by traveling steerage (there was no second class), but she finally decided to pay the $180 for a shared first-class cabin. Although the ship was going to Bremen, Porter understood that it would be an easy matter to obtain visas en route and decide later where they would disembark.[4]

Somehow the uncertainty about their future and disagreement

about their destination was symptomatic of the whole relationship. They quarreled constantly and their life together fell into a pattern of irritability, incessant bickering, and heavy drinking. Porter said sadly that they could never bear to be sober together.

In spite of the abrasive nature of the relationship and the restiveness Porter felt at Pressly's constant presence, the association had already lasted far longer than any other, and Porter had grown dependent on Pressly for emotional and practical comfort.

When Josephine Herbst complained that she had learned of the association only from their mutual friends, Porter replied that she had been superstitiously afraid of mentioning it until they had been together for one year. Her explanation was perhaps more an excuse than a reason, but since Herbst had asked, she wrote a description of Pressly. Like many of her epistolary versions of situations, it was highly colored and idealized. Her lover acquired the following attributes:

> . . . quiet, extremely balanced, not very easy to know, and so far as I can discover doesn't care much about anybody except me.
>
> He is a Communist but not a party member, has no ambition. He has been the same person 24 hours a day for one year and he loves me so steadily and infallibly I can hardly believe it.
>
> He has worn through my fits of nerves, my depressions, my illnesses, my general hellishness with a kind of superhuman patience and friendliness, if those words could half express the solid rock of love and goodness that simply never lets down for even half a minute. I haven't been able to work but it is not his fault . . . now that my allowance has stopped he takes care of me.
>
> He has a realistic tough mind, a little too inclined to dismiss things not perfectly clear cut. I think this is his youngness—he is only 27. The one quality I value above everything in love—or any other relation—is loyalty. I never had it from a man—sometimes it was physical infidelity, sometimes that worse thing, a moral disloyalty founded on fear and distrust and vanity.
>
> This boy has the gift of being able to stake himself on his beliefs, and there is an indescribable grand dignity in the way he simply takes for granted the things that should go with love, and mostly don't.

I am older than him by just ten years and it's all very well now but not 10 years from now. Besides I don't like a domestic life because I have to keep hours and engagements and have always a sense of responsibility for my moods and my time. All the little adjustments and compromises that he takes with such perfect calm very often give me a pain and a grievance that is as acute as it is. Yet, if I can pull through and manage to live for a respectable length of time with any man, this is the one. It would be a real victory for me over my really deep feeling that I do better to live alone. Yet already we are so grown into each other there is no possible reason not to go on.[5]

Of the twin attributes that Porter longed for in a partner, an interest in her work and a willingness to look after her, Pressly satisfied only the second. He admired her work but resented her absorption in it and eventually formed the habit of drinking while she wrote. He did, however, look after her devotedly. He was willing to support her when her money ran out, and, as she said to Herbst, his devotion never wavered or wandered to other women.

Pressly was also youthful and handsome. Photographs of him at the time show a striking profile, accentuated by his receding hairline, with a delicately shaped nose. He was better educated than Porter but not really her intellectual equal. His chief fault was his passivity, his lack of fire. In contrast to her lively personality and garrulousness he seemed silent and dull. When friends asked, "Why doesn't he say anything?" Porter would laugh and say that she did all the talking.[6] The friends considered him pleasant enough but dull. In reality he was less pleasant than they gave him credit for being, and was often suspicious of and hostile to those who befriended Porter. Eventually his lack of assertiveness became the trait which irritated Porter most of all, but in the beginning she seemed to find his easy acquiescence to all her plans acceptable. Perhaps his similarity to her father explains a great deal about this curious relationship.

What she contrived, consciously or unconsciously, was a kind of compromise. She tried to retain his loyalty, support, and love without being irritated by his continual presence. Consequently the journey on the *Werra* was something of a relief because as an unmarried couple they were obliged to take separate cabins, and once on board she began to enjoy herself. Even if she was slightly oppressed by Pressly's presence and the uncertainty about both their destinations, she responded as always to the excitement of the voyage and the stimulation of new surroundings.

Soon she told Caroline Gordon, to whom she decribed the journey in a log which she wrote daily, that she was having the loveliest time of her life. She slept long hours, enjoyed the huge German meals, and worked on deck, typing away as the whole life of the ship revolved around her.[7]

One of the focal points of *Ship of Fools* is the abrasive relationship of Jenny Brown and David Scott, which is based on Porter's own relationship with Pressly. There is, of course, shaping of the material so that the fictional pair are not exact counterparts of Pressly and Porter. Jenny and David in the novel are young and there is no large age difference between them. They are graphic rather than literary artists and David considers Jenny's work much inferior to his own. This was certainly not true of Porter and Pressly, because Porter insisted that, even if Pressly did try to write fiction, she was the artist in the family because she had been doing it longer.

But the incessant quarrels which flare up uncontrollably, despite the pair's efforts to get along amicably, are probably a record of the real couple's constant bickering. Possibly they more closely represent the end of the relationship than the early years, when presumably there were more harmonious times.

One source of antagonism between Jenny and David, which sounds like an authentic rendering of the relationship between Porter and Pressly, is David's frank skepticism about the truth of Jenny's stories. When she talks excitedly about a lightning stroke which hit the elevator shaft in a hotel and nearly knocked her out, he protests the memory "coldly, doubtfully." "You never told me this before," he said.[8]

The only reference to Pressly in Porter's letter to Caroline Gordon mentioned his jaundiced attitude to the world. As they neared the Bay of Biscay Porter wrote, "Gene just popped in with the stewardess bringing me my four o'clock coffee, gave as his opinion that this was a fearful looking place—no one can accuse that lad of over-enthusiasm—and said we were starting across the Bay of Biscay tonight."[9]

In spite of the quarrels, the relationship of the fictional pair is presented more positively than that of the other inharmoniously matched pair on board, for Jenny and David, even if their exchanges deteriorate into fights, always begin again hopefully:

"Pig's knuckles, David darling," said Jenny Brown, restoring his private particular name to David Scott.[10]

"Let's be real tourists this once," said Jenny angel to David darling.[11]

"David darling," said Jenny, "let's be tourists again."[12]

"David," said Jenny, as they touched their cocktail glasses together. "Salud, David darling!"[13]

At the end of the novel, as all the passengers disembark, Jenny and David make a final reconciliation:

> "Here we go talking again," said David. "Let's think of something pleasant."
> "You think of something, David darling," said Jenny, "something wonderful."
> David leaned with great discretion and a very straight face and whispered, "Tonight in Bremen we'll sleep in the same bed for a change." Jenny made a slight purring sound at him, and he watched her face grow radiant.[14]

Since all previous attempts at reconciliation have failed, it seems likely that this will also fail.

One of the factors which pleased Porter about life on shipboard was her realization that in the chance-gathered people there was probably a short story. She told Caroline Gordon:

> We have everything on board. A woman who may have a baby before we get to Bremen, a new-born one who came aboard when he was two weeks old, a little dying man who sits curled up on his pillows and coughs all day, a hunchback, a woman who weighs nearly four hundred pounds, and a beautiful Spanish bride with her devoted bridegroom —married the day we sailed from Vera Cruz. She is a lovely creature, as romantic looking as the princess in a fairy tale, with the grace and silence and naturalness of a fine wild animal. She sits and walks all day with her long hand lying loosely in his, smiling and dazed. He is the most utterly happy looking person I ever saw, with an irregularly featured sensitive face. . . . They are really something to see. They do not dance, nor wear paper hats, nor drink, nor play

cards, nor grin. If I ever saw two persons walking in Eden, it is now.[15]

Porter was immediately aware of the symbolic and microcosmic possibilities of the ship, with its hierarchic arrangements—the captain on the bridge, the 876 ("exactly") third-class passengers below deck, and the division of the passenger list into seven nations. Forty years later, when the events of the voyage appeared as *Ship of Fools,* the novel provided a rich hunting ground for symbol hunters and analogy seekers, who speculated endlessly on the significance of the ship's name, *Vera,* that of the port of departure, "Vera Cruz," and the hierarchic arrangements of the ship, with the captain on the bridge and the 876 steerage passengers below. But, consistent with her statement that she never invented a symbol, the novel adhered very closely to the actual facts.

In her letter she described the passengers who most interested her and who were later to form the basis of the characters of *Ship of Fools.* One of the steerage passengers became two characters in the novel, the cherry-shirted man and Herr Baumgartner:

> There was down there a huge fat man with a purple face and watermelon pink shirt, who got on at Vera Cruz. He had a voice like seven fog horns, and he roared and sprawled and guzzled beer and sang in a voice that drowned out the brass band and I think everybody looked forward with terror to so many weeks shut up with the noise. His wife and child came on at Habana, and he has been mute ever since, sitting around drooping like a grief-stricken elephant. Now and then you can see wife lecturing him, coldly, calmly, patiently. He never says a word.[16]

Another character who caught her attention was a little hunchbacked man with dry hair and a shriveled face who wore very gay neckties. On party nights he put his paper hat over one eyebrow and then sat on deck all evening with his head between his hands, eyes closed, listening to the music. There was a Spanish zarzuela company, a kind of musical comedy troupe, on its way back to Spain after the usual failure of hopes in Mexico City and Havana, and a large number of Germans. These Porter described as Herr Doktors, Herr Professors, and Herr Engineers with "typically German Frauen, vast, bulky, inert, with handsome heads and elephant legs, who drink beer all day long, swallowing a steinful in two drinks, smacking their lips and saying 'Ja, Ja!' "[17] Her cabin mate was a hefty Swiss girl whose father had for thirty years been a mining engineer in Torreón, Mexico.

At one point she was watching the teeming mass in the steerage section when she found herself next to a young man. She reported the incident to Gordon in some detail:

> As a young oculist from Texas, on his way to Vienna for a special clinic of some kind, commented: "It isn't as if they were dirty Bolsheviks." I was so startled by this remark, as a voice from the prehistoric times of the world, that I asked involuntarily, "Where are you from?" It seemed, Austin, Houston, Corpus Christi, Texas. Still, so help me, they are talking that way in Texas. I got him located by swapping names with him for a while, and it isn't as if he were an ignorant hulk. He represents a great part of whatever enlightenment that place has to offer. "They don't deserve their hard luck," he said. "It isn't as if they were dirty Bolsheviks."[18]

The young oculist is the basis of one of the most unpleasant characters of the novel, William Denny, who also owes something to Porter's first husband, John Koontz.

Another character who interested her enough to merit a paragraph of description was the ship's doctor:

> The ship's doctor is an old Heidelberg student with a grand hooked nose, a fine head, and two sabre scars across his cheek and forehead. He walks like an officer, and stands at attention apparently, for half an hour at a time, gazing at the water with the kindest, most serviceable pair of tan eyes you can image: they are almost maternally sweet and good. I went to him for help, having broken out with that dangerous tropical disease known as heat rash. All over I was a welter. He gave me a lotion he had mixed for himself, being, he said, a martyr to heat rash. It worked like a charm. Was there anything else he could do for me? No, I was in perfect health otherwise. "You do not look like a tough voman," he told me, "but it is possible you are very strong inside," and he tapped the front of his tunic. I said I thought I was fairly tough inside. He told me cheerful little anecdotes about his wife, like me a tough voman who did not seem

so. She would insist on raising chickens, and they grew so tame they wandered all through the house, so that often she exhausted herself chasing them with a broom. He himself has a bad heart, and may drop dead at any time, but not, he hopes, until once more he can see that voman chasing herself with a broom after those chickens.[19]

The character who most fascinated Porter was a Cuban woman about fifty years old with short, curled white hair and a smooth waxy face. She was slender and had been a tremendous beauty but now her mind was unhinged. She backed people into corners and talked for two hours at a time making strange desperate gestures, thumbs turned in flat to the palms. As she talked she leaned forward and peered at the person as if she were communicating some dark important secret. She told everyone that her husband had been killed fighting for the revolution in Cuba and that her sons were fugitives. Her eyes were very bright and dry and she talked in a crying, complaining voice about her sons who were lost and the government officials who laughed when she went to plead with them not to persecute her children. Porter learned that she had never married and had no children, but had been active in helping the revolutionary students and was being exiled to Tenerife. Cuba was her murdered husband and the students her children.

There was a gang of university students on board going to Gijón, on the Bay of Biscay, because their university had been closed. They founded a Cucaracha Club, with the Cuban woman, whom they called La Loca (the Madwoman), as president, and they escorted her around, dancing, prancing, mimicking her, and singing the noisy song with endless verses about an unfortunate cockroach who cannot run because she lacks feet and cannot buy marijuana because she has no money.

The woman would smile at them and make a speech, her hands dancing a ballet: "My sons were students who defied the government, and they were right. Youth must defy governments, even though it means persecution, exile, death. The young must not throw away their beautiful lives being stupid and living like half-dead things— leave that for an old woman."[20] Then she would make a grand old-fashioned bow. Sometimes the students danced with her and afterward she would stand talking, one hand under her breast, the other stroking her flank, a "perfectly appalling" expression on her face.

Porter recorded in great detail not only the characters but scenes.

One night she stayed up until after midnight watching the Asturians on the deck below. A drunken man was improvising verses on any theme or word the people gave him. He would mutter to himself for a few minutes and then break into a long cry, sing his verse, and wind up with a slow, flat-footed dance step. After midnight these activities ended, the participants fell asleep, and Porter was moved to see all the shouting, singing, swearing Asturanos "lying in the pious attitudes of well-disposed corpses." They lay on their backs, their hands clasped on their breasts, feet crossed, and with an occasional muffling white sheet giving the look of "a cheerful morgue" to the whole deck.

At Tenerife she and Pressly went ashore and she was struck by three sights: the camels going loaded through the streets in company with burros; friars fat and lean of two orders, black and brown, slapping through the streets in old-lady shoes and porkpie hats; and the milkwomen in short black dresses, bare legged, their heads swathed in black shawls with little round hats secured at the back by an elastic band under their knots of hair, carrying great flat trays loaded with battered milk cans. She liked their charming half walk, half run, with rigid head and shoulders and wildly swaying hips.

They found a café, El Quita Penas, where they sampled Canary wines from the great barrels along the wall—Málaga, Muscatel, Malvasía, Madeira; the island's cognac, Tres Copas; and an orange liqueur something like Curaçao—and ate a huge Spanish lunch. Afterward they hailed a very small horse-drawn vehicle and drove in state to the foot of the gangway, arriving just as it was about to rise.

As they passed the Isle of Wight, Porter was charmed by the sight of a little castle standing in the greensward, surrounded by a small wood and grass that came down "neatly shaven to the lip of the sea."

Her notes were mostly made at random and incorporated into the letter-log, but one of her descriptions did suggest a story to her. It was an account of a little piglike man dancing to Strauss waltzes, and she gave it the provisional title "Wiener Blut." The story never appeared, but the description was incorporated into *Ship of Fools* as the portrait of Herr Rieber twirling and pirouetting to the music of "Tales from the Vienna Woods," with the rhythm of the sentences echoing the rhythms of the music.

As the boat approached the European mainland, the disagreement about their destination solved itself. First of all, the captain declared that he would not stop at Boulogne, and, second, she learned that no French consulate would grant visas to people in transit. In fact, the boat did stop at Boulogne in the middle of the night, but she was carried helplessly on to Bremen.

She was not totally despondent at the idea of seeing Germany. If she had not gone there on Erna's account exactly, her interest in the country had been aroused long ago by Erna's stories about her travels there. Now she would have the opportunity to compare her childhood images with the actuality. More recently she had heard a great deal about Germany from Josephine Herbst, who had spent a year in Berlin in 1922. Furthermore, the political situation into which she was heading, as she had sensed on the *Werra*, was highly volatile. Her presence there was quite consistent with her habit of arriving on the scene when history was being made. The five months she spent in Germany were in the middle of the period during which Hitler rose to power. Just a year before she arrived, his Nazi party, hitherto the subject of ridicule, had proved itself a force to be reckoned with by winning 106 seats in the Reichstag. A year after she left, Hitler came into power as Chancellor. The year of her arrival, 1931, was the country's *annus terribilis,* a time of most desperate hardship. Unemployment had passed the five million mark and there was such a shortage of fuel and food that Chancellor Brüning was known as the "hunger dictator."

Porter was not equipped to understand completely the political implications of the situation. In the first place, her knowledge of the historical events leading up to the present situation was much less than Herbst's. Nor could she understand the language well enough to speak to people on the streets, listen to the radio, or read the newspapers. When she met important figures like Johannes Becker, editor of the Communist newspaper *Rote Fahne,* she had to ask someone to act as interpreter.

Nevertheless, she was an acute observer and there was much to make a visual impact on her. The unemployed were everywhere and the signs of famine and poverty highly visible. Street violence was growing and there were frequent clashes between the Nazis and the Communists. Goebbels, the Nazi leader in the Berlin area, was already organizing marches and parades, and attacks on Jewish businesses and synagogues. As she had quickly recognized in Mexico and on the *Werra,* there was rich material all around her that might some day be shaped into fiction. She recorded her impressions very carefully and later yoked them very successfully onto her retrospective understanding of the political events.

Eventually she claimed that she began writing at once to newspapers in the United States to warn them about Hitler and what would happen:

> When I was in Berlin, I did have experiences and I wrote to places like the *Nation* and *New Republic* and I tried to tell them what was happening. You see, I knew instantly, the minute I put my face in the place and saw Hitler going along in that great six-wheel wagon of his down the street, standing in the middle while people went right up to him throwing rose petals and violets and confetti and screaming at him with hysterical joy. I stood there and I knew—I went through five revolutions in Mexico—what was happening. But I couldn't get any editors in this country to take anything from me. I was not a newspaper reporter. I was not a woman known for her political views. Even if I knew what I was saying and even if I had proof, it was hard to make anyone listen.[21]

Her letters from Berlin, on the other hand, show that she was more interested in sightseeing and arranging her own life than in political analysis.

When they arrived in Bremen, she and Pressly went with a group of young officers to the famous Rathskeller, enjoyed the good wine and food, stayed overnight, and set out the next day for Berlin.[22] Once in Berlin, they took two rooms in the Thüringer Hof, a small hotel, on Hedemanstrasse, for the first month. Porter disliked the cold climate and was a little troubled about its possible effect on her health, but she said she preferred it to the combination of warm climate and human vacuum she had found in Mexico. She liked Berlin's concerts and exhibitions and it seemed a blessed relief to be fed and to be in a room with nothing to do but work and no responsibility for keeping a house.[23] Clearly her few months as chatelaine in Mexico had, for the moment, exhausted her enjoyment of domesticity.

After a month she found more suitable lodgings in a *pension* on Bambergerstrasse and settled in for the winter, saying she could go no further and must stay in one place and work. Her move solved the problem of Pressly's oppressive company, because he left for Spain, the only place where he knew the language well enough to qualify for a job.

Porter expressed her early impressions of Berlin and her feelings about Pressly in a poem, "Bouquet for October," later called "After a Long Journey." The poem contrasts the chill city of Berlin with the warmth of Mexico, but focuses mainly on the chill which has fallen on the two lovers:

> This is not even a timely season for our love—
> Kisses freeze in our mouths, our arms enfold by habit
> Talking columns of stone; yet we do not talk of love,
> Our love, or say again, once more, once and forever
> As if it were for the first time and the last time, a long
>   farewell:
> "I love you."[24]

She had a strong sense that their relationship was doomed, and an incident which happened as they looked at places to stay seemed to foreshadow the ending. They were inspecting a *pension* when Pressly touched a cheap souvenir of the Leaning Tower of Pisa. It crumbled under his touch and Porter, mortified, cried out in great anguish, "Why must you touch things? Why must you always touch and destroy things?"[25]

Although Pressly's departure made it easier for her to work, she felt acute dismay at seeing him go, and remained during the whole of her time in Berlin ambivalent both about him and about the idea of marriage. In her loneliness she had extended crying jags and wrote long daily letters to him, sometimes as long as twenty pages of single-spaced typescript. When she did not hear from him she wrote, "I almost lost my poor feeble mind when I didn't get a letter from you."[26] In his absence she was already beginning to idealize the relationship, endowing it with a perfection it lacked when Pressly was present, and she wrote not only to him but about him to Malcolm Cowley and Josephine Herbst.

Meanwhile she worked on her projects. Even though her letter writing was time-consuming, the solitude was productive and certain tasks were accomplished. The poem was finished and sent to Kenneth Burke to be appraised and placed where he thought appropriate.

It appeared early in 1932 in the winter edition of William Carlos Williams' *Pagany*. She worked on the material she had gathered at the Hacienda Tetlapayac and an early version of "Hacienda" was completed. She described it as not fiction but very exact reportage and said it took the form of a story only because of the way events happened. In its earliest form it was less detailed and less polished and the tense wavered uneasily between historic present and past. She had intended it for the *New Republic* as an essay similar to "Leaving the Petate," but when it ran to 4500 words she sent it instead to *Scribner's*. It was rejected there and she sent it on to *Virginia Quarterly Review*, where it appeared in October 1932. Caroline Gordon tactlessly reported that it was probably accepted because she and Allen Tate had told the editor, Stringfellow Barr, that he would bring "lasting obloquy" on the magazine if he did not print something by Porter,[27] a piece of information which did little to bolster Porter's confidence in her work.

Although her claim that she was sending warnings about Hitler to the United States was false, she was writing for the *New Republic*. As before, she was doing book reviews at the request of Malcolm Cowley, and difficulties arose when Cowley refused to print her unfavorable review of Stuart Chase's *Mexico*. She had expressed outrage at Chase's recommendation that Paca Toor (the writer Frances Toor) be kept on by the government. She felt that Chase had no powers of discrimination and confused good people like Moisés Saenz and Manuel Gamio with those she considered hacks, like Bill Spratling. Cowley tried to explain that she could have said the same things and he would have published the review if she had gone about it in a different way—for instance, if she had adopted a more-in-sorrow-than-in-anger tone, praised what Chase had written in the past and then said "but . . ." She could have been merciless if only she had been polite.[28]

She was not mollified and wrote angrily to say that she realized it was devilish bad form to be angry about anything and to have deep feelings, but she had been hopping mad when she wrote the review. She added that looking back she realized she was just getting over the shock of the Hart Crane visit and that her accumulated angers and nervous irritations had driven her to the point of wishing to repay brutality with brutality. Stuart Chase's book had been only a small straw but it was the last in a great number and she had socked it to him. She had seen his attitude as representing all the evils which made Mexico uninhabitable for her.[29]

The episode marred her relationship with the *New Republic*, and in spite of all his previous kindnesses she never forgave Cowley, speaking of him with derision ever afterward: "Poor Malcolm Cowley was never anything but cold oatmeal from the neck up, and even warmed with likker it is still oatmeal. I wouldn't trust him for even the simplest insight or memory of anything."[30]

Cowley had also sent her Virginia Woolf's *The Waves,* and she tried but failed to review it. She lamented to a friend that she did not write fluently and *The Waves* was giving her fits; her piece was in the shape where she looked at her pile of notes, observations, sentences, all of which broke off at the point where the idea she was trying to express died on its feet. It would take her at least two days to pull it into 1500 neatly strung words which came within a mile of what she wanted to say. She added that her determination to be perfect sometimes cramped her style. She wanted to be a bit more helter-skelter but didn't "know how to go about it."[31] And after that, although she needed the money they brought in, she stopped doing reviews.

By fall her long letter to Caroline Gordon was going the rounds of their friends in the States. When it reached Malcolm Cowley and he praised it she was indignant, interpreting his praise as typically masculine condescension. She wrote to Gordon:

> The log was written without pains, hastily from day to day as you saw it: women are, as you know, fabulous letter writers. It has been supposed (by men) to be their ideal form of literary activity. Malcolm wrote that you sent him fragments and "Darling," says he, "Your masterpieces are your letters" for which cheerfully I could have throttled my good friend Malcolm. . . . Even if it is true (God forbid!) somehow there was an echo of cheerful masculine voices down the centuries saying, "On his mother's side also our hero inherited some gleam of literary talent, for she was a writer of delightful letters." Now, I do not despise good letters, indeed, I love them, and if I write one now and then, I am glad of it.[32]

As usual, the main achievements of the time were the ones that were not immediately apparent, and these were the stories which were begun and set aside to be finished triumphantly many years later. She complained that "Wiener Blut," begun on the S.S. *Werra,* had joined half a dozen stories she began but could not finish until some flash came to clarify them. She also began "Promised Land," an account of the crossing from Veracruz to Bremerhaven, but put that aside too. Near the anniversary of her niece's death in early December she picked up again the story "A Vision of Heaven by Fra Angelico," which she had begun in Connecticut in 1926, and wrote a long first version, again giving it the epigraph "I will show you sorrow and the ending of sorrow."

She had developed the habit of taking careful notes on any situation which might produce a story or novel, and she continued to do so undeterred by seeing bales of notes accumulate while no works of fiction resulted from them. At this time, just as she had recorded the people on the *Werra,* she began to make notes of all the people in the *pension,* her landlady and her fellow boarders. She had chosen the *pension* because its owner was a Viennese woman who could understand Porter's inadequate French. She was Rosa Reichl, a charming and touching hostess, whom Porter described as fifty years old, with a fine little china figure and skin and hair like roses and spun silver. Saying she would remember her as one of the best things that happened in Berlin, Porter mentioned the pitifulness of Rosa's perpetual mending of worn linen and patching of shabby old furniture, and her stories of better times. She displayed pictures of her younger self wearing Paris clothes and driving fine horses.[33]

In spite of the sympathy she felt for her, Porter found her constant fussing attentions wearisome. Rosa spent two hours every morning cleaning Porter's room, and Porter was horrified to find her papers tidied and arranged. When she went to the bathroom Rosa rushed in ahead to see that everything was in order and when she came out went in again to see that nothing had been disarranged. Porter paid slightly more than the other guests and therefore received some extras such as afternoon coffee, which Rosa served in a brown-glazed coffeepot that was "seated upon a plate and wearing a red knitted skiing bonnet lined with silk and padded with fleece."[34]

Porter, afflicted with insomnia and a chronic cough, liked to drink wine at night and was embarrassed when Rosa found her cache of wine bottles, which seemed very many and very empty for so short a time. Rosa scolded her and said that if she wished to buy wine she should ask her advice on where to buy it. On another occasion Porter met Rosa as she was carrying in a bottle and felt obliged to ask her to share it. Rosa brought a silver tray with a lace cloth and two small glasses, ceremoniously proposed a toast, and, to Porter's dismay, drank only one glass. She complained of all this in her letters to Pressly and told him that she smuggled out her monthly toilet items so that Rosa would not find them.

From Rosa, Porter learned about the other guests. There was a young Dalmatian student called Herr Bussen, a Pole, Herr Mey, and a military gentleman who objected to the noise of her typewriter. She learned about Herr Mey's untidy bathroom habits and Herr Bussen's bringing milk into his room and drinking it like a baby. Of her fellow boarders Porter felt she knew Bussen best, for she occupied his room while he went on a visit to his native Dalmatia. She also noted a conversation with him when they met in the hall one day. He asked if Rosa abused her as much as she did him and Porter said that, on the contrary, Rosa had been kind to her, otherwise she would have left. Bussen replied that she received preferential treatment because she was a foreigner and paid more, and that Rosa was a terrible woman who insulted him for an hour every day and then went and insulted Herr Mey. The conversation made Porter melancholy because he was a gentle-faced young fellow trying to finish his studies on too little money.[35]

Porter also befriended a music teacher in the apartment above and for a few pfennigs an hour was allowed to use her piano. When the woman, Frau Hildesheimer, came to visit Porter, Rosa bustled her out before long, telling her, "It is time for you to go now," and explaining to Porter, "She is a Jew and I don't want her to feel she can just come into this house when she likes."[36]

At the same time Porter was developing an interesting social life outside the *pension*. She had been told by friends to look up Herb Klein, a young correspondent for the *Chicago Tribune*. When Pressly had left she did so, and found him living with his mother in rooms at 27 Rankestrasse close to the Gedächtnisskirche (Memorial Church) near one end of the Kurfürstendamm. He recalled his impressions:

> She visited us . . . not once but several times. She was charming, animated, full of late literary gossip, not un-touched by name-dropping. We had some very pleasant af-ternoons and evenings. I remember her dancing Cuban or Brazilian style, with appropriate movements of her scarf, around the living room put at our disposal by the Bermanns.
>
> We also went about together somewhat in various parts of Berlin. I was moved to show her some poetry I had written. Her comments were favorable but by no means over-enthusiastic. She was an amusing companion, full of anecdotes and observations.[37]

Klein remembered her attitude toward religion, especially her telling him, "We are groping around in the dark, like in a cellar, with only the feeble flame of our reason to aid us. And along comes the theologian and blows out the light."[38] And he was enthralled by her readings from the copy of Archibald MacLeish's poems that she carried around, remembering particularly her fondness for these lines from "You, Andrew Marvell":

> And here face down beneath the sun
> And here upon earth's noonward height
> To feel the always coming on
> The always rising of the night

In December of 1931 the German Communist party celebrated the thirteenth anniversary of its founding by holding rallies all over the country. Several were held in the densely populated Berlin area and Porter attended one of these with Herbert Klein. She made detailed notes, as usual, and later incorporated them into a letter to Herbst. She reported that the streets were patrolled for two blocks around in every direction by policemen on foot and on horseback, and riot wagons were drawn up about a dozen to the block. When the gates were closed, a hundred ticket holders (Porter among them) were denied entrance. She said the others had paid 80 pfennigs each, which they could not afford, and many had walked for miles in the sharp, damp cold, and their faces were so despairing you could see they had no resistance left in them except this quietude. They were real proletarians, pale from inadequate diet, from the constant cold and the lack of work. They went away quietly with the brutal-looking policemen stretched in a moving wall behind them. When the meeting ended, the Communists came out very quietly, but the police provoked a stampede and arrested sixteen of them. The police were dangerous-looking, hard as nails, in fighting trim and heavily armed, so that resistance would have brought on a massacre.[39]

It was pleasant to have an admiring, handsome twenty-four-year old escort on her outings in Berlin, and Porter told Klein that she wanted to stay in Berlin for his wedding, scheduled for early 1932, when his fiancée was to arrive from the United States. Soon, however, Porter attracted the attention of someone far more unusual than her young countryman. This was an important member of the Reichstag, Hermann Goering. She met him soon after Herbert Klein introduced her to Sigrid Schultz, chief correspondent of the *Chicago Tribune* and a famous hostess who entertained constantly in her West Berlin studio garden apartment. It was said that more nobility, politicians, and just plain common folk were received at her formal dinners and luncheons and *Bier Abends* than anywhere else in Europe.

As the new bureau chief, Miss Schultz had been eager to meet members of the government, and she described her own contact with Goering:

> When the Nazis won their first big election victory, I sent one of my assistants to the Reichstag with orders to find a deputy who had the kind of manners one could tolerate. He picked Goering who accepted my invitation to a lunch at Pelzer's if I allowed him to bring along his adjutant, which I naturally did—with my assistant acting as my "adjutant," we had no trouble making Goering talk—his line was the same as that quoted by Miss Porter as far as the Jews were concerned, but he would only trot it out after he had enjoyed a good number of drinks. In the early 30's he still helped a number of very rich Jews, the banker Goldschmidt, for instance, in order to please the actress he was courting. He also was in the habit of mentioning the death of his wife in a mournful tone, but that did not prevent him from courting one of Berlin's better known actresses assiduously nor did it prevent his future wife, Emmy Sonneman, from spending hours in the Reichstag waiting for him.

She also described the circumstances of Porter's meeting with Goering:

> Yes, I remember that Miss Porter attended one of the more formal dinners in my Berlin studio . . . together with Goering and his "adjutant" Milch. The latter held a high post in the Air Ministry during the war. . . . At the time of the dinner I was the correspondent-in-chief of the *Chicago Tribune* for Germany and Eastern Europe, and used to entertain many politicians and diplomats to collect news from them. Miss Porter was introduced to me by one of our young countrymen who got their start as correspondent by serving on my rather big staff—Herbert Klein. Since she was really beautiful, I invited Miss Porter to several dinners to give a more festive tone or whatever you want to call it to the party —and it was clear right from the moment that Goering saw her that he was fascinated by her looks and determined to try his luck with her, together with Milch.
>
> My recollection is that she had only one nightclub celebration with Goering after my dinner. And rumor had it that she was disappointed about his failure to reinvite her. I say "rumor" because I never saw her again after that dinner.

NOTE: It was quite natural for people who attended a formal dinner during which they enjoyed each other's company to leave together and go to some club or continue their acquaintance. Everything at my house was "tout à fait comme il faut," and given Miss P's beauty Goering's interest was comprehensible.[40]

Some years later, when she was living in Paris (still well before the outbreak of war), Porter described her meeting with Goering in a letter to Herbst. Porter remembered that he was in a softened, sentimental mood, mourning the death of his wife. He told Porter that she was too beautiful and too sensitive to be about the world by herself and that being a writer she must not forget to be a woman. She told Herbst there was a great deal of this nonsense, the kind that usually made her want to stick out her tongue. But she liked him and told him that her whole trouble as both a writer and a person was that she was too much a woman. He liked this reply so well that he kissed her heartily, "smack, smack, smack on the cheek." Porter really wanted to talk politics with him and eventually did get him onto that subject. He told her that the Jews must learn to be good Germans or they must go, and he boasted that after Hitler came to power there would not be a Jew left in Germany in any position of power. Porter said later that she knew she was not receiving any confidences; he was talking to her because she was a writer and might record his statements. At the end of the evening he took her home and embraced her at the door like a big bear.[41] Rosa was thrilled to know that Goering's car had stopped at her door, and thereafter Porter felt that the house was hers.

That Goering did in fact try to arrange a second meeting is proved by the existence among Porter's papers of a note about a phone message which Herr Bussen took and tried to transcribe into English:

12^{42} 17 XI

Mr. Von Gehring had belled you now.
He would against bell you, this
afternoon between three and four
a clock.

Bussen[42]

The outcome of the phone call is not known, although one of the "Notes on Writing" in Porter's collected essays refers to a December meeting in a Berlin café with a "Von G" (in her letters she refers to Goering as Von Goering), and suggests that there were other meetings.

A later version has Porter standing Goering up and leaving Berlin without seeing him again. She told an interviewer that she returned home one evening in the early months of 1932 and found a note pinned to her pillow: "Herr Goering was here at five o'clock and waited until six. He was quite annoyed."[43]

Over the years Porter's accounts of her association with Goering became more and more exaggerated. Benefiting from hindsight after the war, she credited herself with having discerned his dangerous nature, sometimes had herself meeting Hitler as well as or instead of Goering, and sometimes described her impassioned tirades against one or both. Apparently unaware of Sigrid Schultz's work in alerting the United States to the danger of Hitler, and knowing nothing of her background (her father was the Norwegian-American artist Herman Schultz), Porter, calling her "Sigrid Somethingorother," said that she was raised in the United States of German parents and described her as "indeed a beautiful woman—treacherous, devious, fiendishly clever and always scheming—but a real beauty nonetheless. Hitler and his sordid clique could not have hoped for a more attractive ally." And she reported herself as emboldened by champagne cocktails and saying of Hitler, "He's nothing more than a common criminal. . . . That man—unless he's checked right now—will cause serious damage to this country and to all of Europe. You simply can't do business with him."[44]

Decades later the following version appeared in the *Washington Star:*

> Even in Berlin, when I met all those people . . . the one I talked to most was Goering. It was at this little party and we just sat by the fire and discussed Germany and he explained to me what they were going to do to the Jews and I said, "Well, you know, I wonder how you dare to do it because it's never done any good and it doesn't suppress them. It does do great damage to the country. Look what happened to Spain. Nobody has ever prospered harassing the Jews. They are rooted and they are going to stay and I don't see what you have against them." He said the time had come to clear out the degenerate forces in the country. "We've got to restore that good clean German blood," he

said. I argued with him a little bit that they had pure blood by this time. I could say with confidence that I was a mixture of British, Scotch, Irish and Welsh. We're all the whole white race. Well, no one ever listens to me except in conversation. It makes me so furious. I was in a place—in Germany —and I knew what was going on and I couldn't get anyone to let me tell it. I just stopped trying.[45]

A curious light is thrown on Porter's state of mind at the time by a letter she wrote to Pressly the day after Herr Bussen transcribed Goering's telephone message. She had mentioned in an earlier letter that her cough was "astonishingly much worse" and that she intended to drink a bottle of red wine and get a sound sleep. Now she reported a crisis. The T.B. had flared up again and a new spot had appeared on her left lung. Any prospects of leaving Germany that they had discussed were now out of the question. She speculated that she had been infected in Mexico by Peggy Cowley, who was ill with something that sounded like T.B. Porter said she thought her own trouble had begun in Mexico about four months before, when she began to suffer with her nerves and lose weight.

She had seen a doctor and he had put her on a regimen of non-smoking and rest and good eating—fresh cream, butter, chocolate, and all foods to make her fat. She must not smoke and the only part of the program she liked was the two glasses of red wine she had to drink at bedtime. A tonic of twenty drops three times a day was prescribed to make her hungry but it merely made her vomit. She said that they had discussed a change to a warmer climate, but decided against it since the upheaval of moving would be too much for her. She was concerned about the possibility of Pressly's having been infected and warned him to eat well, keep warm, and look after himself. She also reassured him that she had survived many T.B. scares and was not overwhelmed, especially as the doctor said that of the two classified types of T.B. she had the second, more hopeful kind.[46]

Porter's health was never good at this time of year, and it seems more than likely that she should have had bronchial trouble in November in Berlin and that there should have been a recurrence of what she described as the "ptomaine poisoning" or gastric disorder that also flared up briefly about twice a year. On the other hand, it seems unlikely that if the T.B. were diagnosed as she said, she would have remained in Rosa Reichl's *pension*. Furthermore, Herbert Klein, with whom she spent much time, did not remember her ever being confined to the house with an illness. He is quite certain that he never heard a mention of T.B., and that Porter's social life was not in the least curtailed. She continued going to her German lessons, visiting museums and galleries, and accepting invitations. While Porter went to no more of the small formal dinners at Sigrid Schultz's studio, she was asked to larger gatherings. She went there on Christmas Day and met English and German politicians and journalists.

But by the end of December another change was occurring in her thinking. From all the records Goering seems to have disappeared from her horizon, but she was writing in a bitter, critical, anti-Semitic vein about Herbert Klein. She was no longer eager to stay on for his wedding and wrote Pressly that there was something sinister about Jewish family feeling.

Once again she was acutely lonely and depressed:

> I cannot explain a curious imprisoned feeling I have . . . as if some invisible fetters were on me and I could never move freely. It's because partly, I do not really use my time; and so am weighted with terrible undischarged obligations. There is a vicious circle out of which I cannot come. . . . It comes of my long habit of poverty and worry during which I tried to work.[47]

She had for a time after Pressly's departure had some hopes for a pleasant stay in Berlin, but now all these had collapsed. Herr Goering had lost interest, and, even if she found him unpleasant in certain ways, she seems to have been flattered by the attentions of such a prominent person and disappointed by his failure to pursue her. The friendship with the Kleins ended badly, and ill feeling on both sides lasted long after she left Berlin. Herbert Klein described what happened:

> KAP was interested in getting some clothes and accessories. My mother, whose German was rather more adequate than KAP's (she had only a smattering, as I recall), went along to help her shop. A rather good dressmaker had been doing some work for my mother. KAP apparently liked what she saw and had my mother take her to that seamstress. KAP ordered a dress or some other garment requiring fittings and construction "from scratch."

Some days or weeks later I found that KAP had left Berlin. Rather hastily, it seemed. Shortly thereafter my mother received an appeal from the seamstress. KAP had not paid her for the garment nor—again I rely on memory after so many years—cancelled it, nor called for it. The woman was stuck for the time and materials. What could my mother do to help her? From somewhere I obtained an address that I was told would reach KAP at one of her next stops. I wrote to her explaining the plight of the seamstress and asking her to do the right thing; namely, pay what had been agreed.

An answer came from KAP, quite annoyed and resentful. She had no intention of doing any such thing. The dress she asserted had not been coming along the way she wanted it anyway. I can't recall whether my mother finally paid the woman all or some of the debt, since she (my mother) had, in effect, vouched for KAP.

You may perhaps understand from that rather shabby sequence of events of the early 30's why I could not feel surprised that KAP had gone about telling listeners she had met Adolph Hitler, or that she had been longer in, and deeper into, Berlin and the ominously-moving German political situation than she had, in fact, been or could have been.[48]

With the collapse of other social relationships, it must have seemed to her that once again her best bet was fidelity to Pressly, and she began to make arrangements to join him. At the same time she carefully recorded some of her disturbing dreams, and these suggest acute anxiety about her relationship with him. One of these was very much like the menacing dreams of her childhood.

In her dream she was in a crowd gathered for a religious purpose. Some man was either murdered or put to death legally and she went to the place where he was and saw that it was a lake, dark and evil-looking. At the bottom lay several bodies, two of them women clasping newborn babies. One was in a kind of current, her arm waved back and forth, and the newly dead man lay nearby, with a heavy cross of flowers weighing him down. And then her sister Alice came up with another baby on her arm and a very censorious look such as Porter remembered when she was displeased. She did not know what she was angry about but it seemed that the anger was against her and that the baby she carried was Porter's. She put him down on the grass and they sat talking and Porter was happy about the baby. She thought the dream very sinister—mysterious and portentous.[49]

She recorded in detail another sinister dream from November 1931, and fifteen years later she wrote in her notes, "This dream is very clear to me now and has been for more than ten years":

> Gene and I were together in some kind of arid strange place I did not recognize or particularly notice. In some way that I cannot now remember, though it seemed clear in the dream, we came into possession of a minute lively monkey, small enough to lie comfortably in the palm of my hand. We were delighted with him and he became fond of us at once. We were playing happily with him, and he was like a small kitten. I tickled his belly and he smiled and curled up happily. I began to think of what he should eat and how we could feed him, for our situation was for some reason very unsettled, we did not know just where we were going or what we should do next, and I couldn't seem to arrive at any place where we could find food for the monkey. I kept worrying because he was thirsty and needed milk (this something to do with a monkey belonging to a friend of mine long ago who used to drink milk from a cup with both hands like a child). Our wanderings became very confused, but they seemed to be taking place somewhere in the Orient or a desert except for one small glimpse when we were in an automobile and for another moment in the garden at Mixcoac. The monkey was gradually failing of starvation, but I could not find anything that he needed: I kept thinking of fruit and milk and small dry bread sticks, but I could not even find water for him. But he was altogether loyal and faithful and behaving like a tender child to us, would be very vicious and bit whoever tried to pet him. I had to detach his teeth from several people—notably Lisa, who kept trying to persuade him away, and a young man whom I did not recognize, but who at times was in the party. The dream ended I do not remember precisely how or when, except that my uneasiness was growing and the monkey was shrivelling up and lying in the palm of my hand almost perfectly still and silent. It was a very anxious and unhappy dream and very hopeless.[50]

Somehow the dreams suggest something more complicated than a wavering between terminating an unsatisfactory relationship and her reluctance to let go a youthful, handsome admirer whom a year's habit of living together had rendered dearly familiar. They suggest twin anxieties—that someone she loved might die or receive a sentence of death, and that some defenseless creature placed in her charge might die through her negligence.

Although she was deeply troubled, she decided, as the year turned, that she could no longer live without Pressly, and she made plans to join him in Spain. It seemed to her a confirmation of the wisdom of that decision when she was accosted one day in Berlin by a beautiful gypsy woman, greasy, grimy, and with a red rag knotted around her neck, who said, "Wait I have something to tell you. You have been very unhappy (unglücklich) here, it is not the place for you. Your man is unhappy too, but he loves you, you are very much loved. You are going to make a journey soon, you are going to a country better and more beautiful than this, and you will be happy and your man will be happy too. This is going to be your fabulous year (literally Fabelhaft Jahr) and you will live a long time and have what you want. You are lucky but you do not know it. Stop thinking about death, for you will live to be more than eighty years old and you will have a beautiful (schön) life." The gypsy struck her mood and her past so exactly that she chose to believe the future the woman predicted. Her heart was so lifted, Porter wrote, that she wished that woman luck too, because she deserved better than she had for having the imagination to say exactly what was needed.[51]

Porter was thus mentally prepared for a reunion with Pressly, when another event happened to upset once again the delicate balance of her feelings. On her last weekend in Berlin an old friend arrived from the United States. He was Robert McAlmon, another writer who was to give an account of Berlin in the early thirties. He immediately looked up Porter and insisted that she join him in a night on the town. Porter wrote Pressly that his idea of a good time was to get noisily drunk. This he did and they were turned out of several places. What she failed to mention to Pressly was that McAlmon was accompanied by a young friend, William Harlan Hale, who had just written his first novel. Hale was at once attracted to Porter and the two enjoyed each other's company, deploring the fact that she was leaving and planning to be married. They hoped to meet again and promised to write to each other. It was William Hale who saw her off when she left Berlin, who occupied her thoughts on the journey, and to whom she wrote immediately and affectionately when she arrived in Paris.

When the six months of her German experience are seen in the context of her whole life, it is apparent that this was another of the rich periods in its yield of fictional material. It provided the substance for the short novel "The Leaning Tower" and the novel *Ship of Fools*. At the same time, by a strange paradox, no other period of her life reflects so much to her personal discredit. When full account is taken of her treatment of the dressmaker, the anti-Semitism of her criticisms of the Kleins, her slanderous untruths about Sigrid Schultz, and her opportunistic treatment of Pressly, it forms a dismal record of cheating, lying, slander, and malice.

The full extent of her malice—the misrepresentation of Sigrid Schultz, for example—revealed itself much later, but it does seem that at the beginning of her fifth decade Porter had developed a greater ruthlessness, a deeper alienation, than had been present before. Perhaps, as she had explained to Cowley, the accumulated angers and nervous irritations had driven her to the point of wishing to repay brutality with brutality.

THIRTEEN

Paris, Madrid, Basle, Paris:
Once I Followed a Husband
All Over Europe

Porter always claimed to have fallen in love with Paris "on sight and without reservation,"[1] which she said was the only way she could ever fall in love. The description of her way of falling in love was quite accurate, but her letters suggest that her love object at this time was completely human. When Bill Hale wrote from Berlin, expressing his desire to see her before he departed for England, she replied, "And you and you, Bill, my dear, why are you not in Paris, or I in Berlin, or both of us in London, or anything but this? It's been too long."[2]

In Paris she stayed on the Left Bank, at the Hotel Malherbe on the Rue de Vaugirard, and crammed as much activity as possible into her brief stopover. Her stay was extended by a brief illness which prevented her traveling further but did not apparently curtail her social round. She visited Jimmie's Bar, the Dôme, the Select, the Coupole, the Cluny Museum, Sainte Chapelle, and Notre Dame, where she lighted a candle to Bill Hale's long life and happiness. She went to the Caveau Rouge des Oubliettes and the Baths of St. Julian the Apostate, and attended a *bal musette* on Ash Wednesday. She spent some time with Eugene and Maria Jolas, Ford Madox Ford, Sylvia Beach, and Caresse Crosby, Harry Crosby's widow.[3] She even found time to visit a dressmaker and repair the loss of the Berlin suit by having a beautiful red dress made by a former cutter for Lanvin.

She described all these events in gay letters to Bill Hale but perhaps she suspected that he was not someone she could count on in her plans for the future, for eventually she packed her bags, took along John Skelton's poems as a traveling companion, and resumed her journey to Madrid, where Pressly had ready for her a wedding ring and an apartment.

Somehow the fling with Bill had unsettled her resolve to marry Pressly and she could not bring herself to carry out her plans. The reality of the situation caught up with her; panic set in and she had a complete collapse. She reported that she behaved like an old-fashioned capricious woman, went to bed, cried for eleven hours, changed her mind, and returned to Paris. The reason she gave: she intended never to live in Madrid while there was Paris.[4]

She was not able, however, to sever her ties with the faithful Pressly and he accompanied her back to Paris. There she was distraught and fretted about financial and other troubles but afterward she reassured him that their time together had been happy and that he had been wonderfully patient with her. When she saw him off at the station they were both barely sober and very desolate. She wrote him immediately that once again she had the "Gene's-Gone-Away-Again-Blues," but she added that after Berlin she had learned there was no point in crying and fretting.[5]

At the same time she wrote gleefully to Bill Hale that she had escaped marriage and had mistakenly blamed on Berlin a heaviness of heart that in reality "was simply mine because I had got myself engaged."[6] Bill replied that it was great news that she had not succumbed to the absoluteness of marriage and told her that he thought she had been intent on getting married the day she left Berlin. Somewhat ingenuously he added that he would like to fathom the things that brought about her change of mind. Was he being deliberately unaware that he had figured in her decision? She wrote him, "Yes, I will see you in London. Yes, you will see me in Paris! Yes rather! We shall see one another all over this blessed, this unaccountably cheerful world! There are no limits to the things we might do, the places we might go, are there?"[7] She told him she had found a place to live near the Hotel Malherbe. It was "an attickish kind of room in a small hotel, modest beyond description, in a wing over a court." There she was able to use the typewriter and play the piano at all hours without fear of disturbing anyone. He said that he would come over by the first balloon, burst in on her, and play her piano.

Eventually he did arrive in Paris and they had gay times going to parties and to the races and meeting for lunches and dinners. Sometimes she cooked dinner for him at her apartment.

In April, Pressly returned to Paris for a leave before he took up another foreign service post in Basle. It presented something of a problem for Porter to have both her admirers in town at the same time. Illness saved the potentially embarrassing situation and she wrote Bill Hale that she could not meet him because she was in bed with influenza. She said that she was using the time profitably by studying the racing form and preparing to attend Auteuil, Longchamps, or St. Cloud with him later and pick winners. By April 20 she announced that she was "emerging little by little" and suggested that they meet for supper.

The illness, for all its expediency, was not merely a way of coping with the presence of Hale and Pressly, but may in part have been caused by the emotional stress of being caught between them. At the end of Pressly's visit she had to enter the American Hospital at Neuilly with a case of pneumonia and once again the suspicion of T.B.

While she was in the hospital a tragic echo from her past reached her. The news came that Hart Crane, traveling with Peggy Cowley on the *Orizaba* from Veracruz to New York, had jumped to his death. She was filled with a frightful sense of loss and waste and horror at the form his death had taken, and at the same time she couldn't help feeling relief that the incurable sickness from which he suffered was over for him.

Gradually it dawned on her that there was no point in counting upon Bill Hale in her future plans. He planned to return to the United States and, while he would have been quite happy to have her come along as a companion, he was evidently not contemplating marriage with a woman twenty years older than himself, no matter how charming she was. Porter finally caught his mood and tried to respond in kind, making light of the vagueness of his arrangements to meet her and of his tendency to borrow money. Nevertheless, her disappointment comes through in one of her last notes to him:

Dear Bill

When you bolted throwing kisses my woman's intuition told me we had seen the last of each other for this day.

By all means write me a note, but no more engagements to be merry! I am too tired, too full of changing plans and uncertainties, let's continue to be as gorgeously vague as we have been; it's more in character and therefore more entertaining.

La Dette might mount even another note without bank-rupting the Guggenheims. This modest boast is for them, not for myself. Why are we always so delicate about money? Please don't squirm my dear, my favorite debtor. I shall take no mortgages out on you!

With my love
Katherine Anne[8]

It might have been expected that, with his rival thus disposed of, she would be ready to resign herself to the faithful Pressly and settle down with him. Letters continued to fly back and forth between them and he urged Basle upon her as having an excellent mountain climate for her health. She still held back, hesitant to leave Paris and the new circle of friends she was beginning to form. Some of the people she had met when she first arrived had not become friends. She said that Caresse Crosby took a "nasty little spite" to her.[9] Djuna Barnes, then and always, considered Porter a "vulgar little woman,"[10] and Porter now took a dislike to Eugene Jolas. She did begin, however, to enjoy three people she met through Ford Madox Ford—Glenway Wescott, Monroe Wheeler, and Barbara Harrison. She told Pressly of engage-ments with them and wrote, "I shall be pleased to go to all three, for I want to keep up some kind of easy relationship with such people, who are busy with their own lives and can't waste time any more than I can. But when I have free time I should enjoy spending it with them, or the Fords."[11]

Porter had met Ford Madox Ford a number of years earlier, when he was living in New York and Caroline Gordon was his secretary. She was happy to renew the friendship in Paris and at first liked his new companion, the Polish painter Janice Biala. While his pompous English manner was not to Porter's liking, she was impressed by his reputation as "the dean of novelists" and by his prestige as editor of the *Translantic Review*. Probably she felt that he might help her as he had many young artists. This feeling was reinforced when he sug-gested that she do translations of some French songs to be published in a volume by Harrison of Paris, the small firm run by Barbara Harrison and Monroe Wheeler. Porter loved the idea and selected her songs carefully from a period of about six hundred years; there was to be one song of a kind—a Carol, a Ballad, a Complaint, a Legend, a Brunette—and each one was to be representative of its kind. This book would be a medley of the familiar, the famous, the popular, the obscure, the almost lost, and she chose first for musical beauty and next for poetic and historic interest.

Someone translated the songs for her and she made them into rhymed verse translations, following the French syllable by syllable so that she preserved the original rhythms and, at the same time, managed to make the English versions singable. The French versions were to be printed facing the English and she planned to give informative and entertaining accounts of the authorship or origin of each song.

Ford's relationship with his protégées, especially when they were attractive women, was often exploitive. Jean Rhys, in her novel *Quartet,* left an incriminating account of her experience with Ford, prefacing it with the epigraph:

> Beware
> Of good Samaritans—walk to the right
> Or hide thee by the roadside out of sight
> Or greet them with the smiles that villains wear.[12]

Porter needed no such warning. She had ample experience with demanding benefactors and was wary of Ford's condescension and soon annoyed by him. In the early period in Paris, one particular source of annoyance was his determination that she should solve his and Biala's practical problem of subrenting their apartment while they were in the South of France.

She told Pressly that Ford had been her *bête noire* since she arrived and that she had been interviewed five times about the apartment. Each time the Fords reduced the rent until finally they offered to let her have it free. Porter still objected, since she would have to move her piano again and hire a *femme de ménage.* Ford told her very irritably that it was notorious that she did not know how to manage her life and should be taken care of. She replied yes, a great many people had thought so and had interfered in her life and she did not intend to let it happen again. The last straw in the whole business was the news that the Tates were to arrive in Paris in July and that Ford was planning, without having consulted any of the three, for them to occupy the apartment together.[13] Possibly, since he had first known them when Porter was living in the same house with the Tates in New York, there was some justification for his assumption that they were compatible. All the same, the incident foreshadowed the kinds of disagreements which caused Porter's final break with Ford and Biala. At the beginning, however, she resisted their interference and amicable meetings with them continued.

Unlike Porter's relationship with Ford, which began warmly and later cooled, her relationship with Wescott, Wheeler, and Barbara Harrison began with misgivings and little hint of the close and important lifelong friendship that would develop. She spent the evening she met Monroe Wheeler talking to him without knowing who he was. Later she went out to visit Barbara Harrison at her house in Rambouillet and was delighted with the place. She had seen it pictured in a magazine the year before and had clipped the article. She was even more charmed when she saw the house itself, and she understood immediately that Barbara Harrison was a very wealthy woman indeed.[14] It was she, in fact, who provided the funds for the press, Harrison of Paris, while Monroe Wheeler provided the expertise that helped produce the fine volumes. She became even closer to Wescott and Wheeler when, a few years later, she married Glenway's brother Lloyd. Barbara Harrison also became Porter's patron, and her friendship and financial help were finally to be rewarded with the dedication of *Ship of Fools*. A timid, humble person, she was fearful of giving offense, touchingly eager to help Porter, and too modest to offer the advice that had often accompanied material help and antagonized Porter.

About Wheeler and Wescott, Porter at first had strong reservations. She reported to Pressly that she rode back from Rambouillet with Wheeler and was put off by his constant name dropping and his preoccupation with the famous and titled acquaintances who were so important to him but not to her.[15] When she attended their parties she wondered why they were sad and stiff. She thought that both Wescott and Wheeler went everywhere and saw everything and were so informed that they spread at the edges. Pressly agreed with her and, when he heard of their going off to Italy, remarked that he could see the whole gang very elegantly voyaging about Europe, trying oh so hard to be serious about it, to get a realistic viewpoint and show they'd had some sort of gut reaction and failing, of course, miserably.[16] His continued suspicion, as Porter grew to appreciate them, was typical of their differing attitudes to the friends she made. Porter came to enjoy Westcott's and Wheeler's courteous good manners and friendly interest in her.[17] Pressly said their good behavior was the kind that came from the ruling passion to get on well in titled and moneyed society. He said that the ones born to it could do as they liked, but people like Wescott and Wheeler had to watch their step.[18]

Certain of Porter's reservations never entirely disappeared. She said soon after they met that she had observed Glenway Wescott on social occasions and had concluded he was an inveterate trouble-maker. She described him then as a completely, boldly, successfully, genuinely wicked person and said that he had made an art out of making mischief and keeping it at a boil with inexpressible hidden movements of constant intrigue.[19] At the end of her long life, after years of friendship, she wrote in her own copy of her Collected Essays, "I have had several poisonous implacable enemy-friends in my long life, but Glenway is the tireless wakeful one."[20]

When they first met in Paris, Wescott, although ten years younger than Porter, had ten years of solid achievement behind him —two volumes of poetry (his first published by Monroe Wheeler in 1920), a collection of short stories, Good-bye Wisconsin, which had been critically acclaimed, and two novels, The Apple of the Eye and The Grandmothers. He was at the peak of his powers and hard at work. Harrison of Paris had published his story "The Babe's Bed" and "A Calendar of Saints for Unbelievers," and Fear and Trembling, a book of essays, appeared in 1932. Like Porter's, Wescott's childhood had been unusually bitter. He had been raised on a Wisconsin farm and his early life had been soured by the hostility of a father who despised his effeminate, artistic son. The conflict between them caused Wescott to leave home at an early age and lead a wandering, unsettled life with various relatives. Finally he entered the University of Chicago on a scholarship. There he met Monroe Wheeler and the two began a friendship which, although not without its own bitterness and tur-moil, was very durable. Like Porter, Wescott had nearly died in the 1918 influenza plague, and like her he had been attracted to Catholi-cism for its historical and aesthetic associations.[21]

Besides the pleasure of having friends who shared her back-ground, provided financial patronage, and published her work, Por-ter's relationship with the three had an even more immediate function in her life. She was at this time undergoing a personal transformation. Previously she had been a youthful, vivacious person with her hair pertly bobbed or held in a bun at the back of her neck. Now she was emerging as a grande dame, a mature femme du monde, with a wardrobe of haute couture clothes and with her hair, now turning white, ele-gantly coiffed. All three helped to form her taste and shared her ideas of elegance and chic. The two men liked and encouraged her new style and were not in the least self-conscious about seeming affected or precious. Moreover, they played the roles of courtiers, forming an adoring entourage for her.

When Matthew Josephson came back to Paris two years later, he noticed the change in Porter immediately, thought it was ridiculous, and understood their part in it: "It was only years later in the days of her fame that I found she had changed and was playing a role suited to what she conceived to be her public image. She would have these pansies sitting at her feet as if she were a bronze monument, deferent, reverent, genuflective."[22]

Allen Tate also placed Porter's transformation at this time, for he wrote in 1941:

> There has been a wonderful change in her since I first knew her, even since about 1932, and I don't think it means anything good. She has become a Great Personage, and my experience of this sort of transformation convinces me that it signals, in her as in others, a weakening of the creative powers. . . . And finally, I think some of her friends of the epicene order are very bad for her: they do nothing but flatter her, and while the flattery seems to be coming from men, it lacks the necessary element which would keep it in the right perspective—sex.[23]

And James T. Farrell referred to Glenway Wescott as "The Captain of the Guard," the guard being Porter's guard of honor.[24]

Basking in such admiration, busy with her work for Harrison of Paris, and liking her new self, Porter was naturally not eager to leave the capital. She did, however, yearn for sexual companionship and eventually this made her think again of marrying Pressly. Finally she set aside her desire for an emerald wedding ring and decided that for ease of traveling together and for their own privacy they should be married. She packed her trunks once more and joined Pressly in Basle, writing Josephine Herbst that she had finally disposed of Gene's only rival, which had turned out to be a city.[25]

Once again the wedding failed to take place, but this time Porter did not bolt back to Paris. She settled comfortably in the Krafft Hotel overlooking the river Rhine and enjoyed the summer, making regular weekend excursions into the countryside around Basle. She said that they had made many plans and had many dreams the year before and only one had come true—this was their vow to walk in the Black Forest, and it proved just as delightful as they had hoped. They took the train to Abrucke and went on by Reichspost to Mittratt and from there walked through wood and valley to Todmoos. The next day they went by foot through the deep woods with leafy mold underfoot and sunlight streaking out on hilltops with open valleys below, drinking from springs and wading in streams. They crept into the bushes and made love because they felt so happy, drank a bottle of white wine, and went on. Another time they went up to the Feldsee and on to Lake Titisee and then to the Schluchsee and down to St. Blasien.

Porter thought that Catholic south Germany must be the gentlest, loveliest place in the world, the people calm and friendly, with perfect human dignity, and every foot of it a garden spot. She wrote to Herbst that it was the happiest thing that ever happened to her, walking through this part; she felt that the gentleness was a novelty because she had lived so much of her life in violent dangerous places where the idea of death was always at her elbow.[26]

It was a curious comment to make in the very place where Hitler's greatest support was being mustered. But although the countryside was peaceful, Porter did notice signs of strife. She saw Hitler placards and swastikas scattered all along the road, and in almost every town she ran into Hitler meetings. In the evenings, when she sat on her hotel balcony drinking Rhine wine, she heard the young Hitlerites singing on their way to meetings.

Back in Basle at the Krafft Hotel, Porter found herself able to work again. There were not the social distractions of Paris, although for two days Ford and Biala visited. She wrote in her notes:

Ford and Janice came through for two days. I'm glad, for they were both in better spirits and were so pleasant my rage and fury and uncharitableness towards them vanished. I had hoped never to see them again, but now I feel rather friendly towards them; mostly towards Ford, who is after all just what he is: but Janice is a "little soul" no doubt about it, one of those designed, in the Catholic faith, for devotion to Therese of Lisieux, petty and small grained and incapable of growth. But something touching, too, in that dryness and thirstiness and little sharp-edged nervousness. She has the kind of eye that can pick out every smallest fleck on the surface, but sees nothing of the whole design, nor of anything underneath. During the two days they were here, literally I never heard her speak one decently perceptive or friendly thing about one living being. . . . It would end by annoying me if I had to stay around her but blessedly I do not.[27]

She managed to take up her writing again. Pressly was occupied with his work and her days were her own. She completed her French song book, her story "The Cracked Looking-Glass" had been published by *Scribner's* in May, and her early version of "Hacienda" was accepted by the *Virginia Quarterly Review*. She was happy in her surroundings, not lonely and not feeling completely sterile. Slowly she was recovering the equilibrium she had missed for the past two and a half years.

In November the rhythm of her life changed again, for Pressly was posted to the headquarters of the International Peace Conference in Geneva. Porter had been working fairly well, not finishing stories exactly, but having ideas for them, and she was reluctant to interrupt the creative flow. She therefore decided to remain behind at the Krafft and Pressly joined her for weekends. During the week letters went back and forth as usual, often concerned with the question of Pressly's future. He disliked his job and was thinking of resigning and going to work for the Communist party. Porter, assuming that her fate was inextricably bound with his, discouraged him. She said she would go along if he decided to but she knew they would both end up being secretaries and the same people would still be out of work and she would be doing propaganda for revolutionary magazines. She said she wanted to write novels, not to have to cut and distort her natural shape to fit some political platform. Temperamentally she and Gene were bound to get on the inside and learn all the ragged little secrets, and if he had ever worked alongside the Communists as she had, he would understand this.

Without intending it and perhaps without even recognizing what was happening, Porter had achieved a situation not unlike that of her five months in Bermuda. Basle was not as beautiful nor was the climate so favorable, but once again surroundings and solitude came together in such a way that her creative energies were released and some important stories began to form in her mind.

She worked a little on "A Vision of Heaven by Fra Angelico." She also worked on the story of Amy, which had been inspired by her stay in Bermuda and which was now divided into three parts: 1)

Introduction to Death: the Beginning; 2) Midway This Mortal Life; 3) Beginning Again: the End.[28]

But something else was happening that she had not calculated. The place itself, rather like Salem, was eliciting a response. Although the climate was very different from that of Texas, there was something in the atmosphere, in the background, in the connection with Calvinism, and in the emotional tenor of the place that evoked the constricted atmosphere of her childhood. She thought again of the South, and, as in Berlin, her observation of the scenes of the city brought back contrasting scenes from her childhood. She watched an old beggar on the bridge by the hotel vying for a spot with an artist, and simultaneously she remembered traveling in a train in central Texas and seeing a small boy bitterly humiliated by a chamber pot which was wedged accidentally on his head. She remembered conversations from her childhood as she had watched men slice chewing tobacco and discuss its qualities. Now she thought of a part of the South that she had barely touched on in the story "He." This was the actual South of her childhood—Calvinistic, poverty-stricken, and pregnant with violence. She thought particularly of the bitter experience thirty years earlier when she had unwillingly spent the summer on the Thompson farm outside Austin, and she wrote a long account of that place, an account that formed the basis of the story she later called "Noon Wine."

She never fully understood the process by which this happened, but when asked about the dialogue in "Noon Wine" she recalled her childhood reaction to the conversations of her neighbors:

> I often wondered what they found to say to each other, day in day out year after year; but I should never have dared go near enough to listen profitably; yet I surely picked up something that came back whole and free as air that summer in Basel, Switzerland, when I thought I was studying only the life of Erasmus and the Reformation.[29]

One letter to Pressly shows how her political preoccupations inform her story:

> Let me add that politics in themselves are not very satisfactory to me as a basis for explaining the human predicament; there are too many elements besides calling for attention: the nature of man in whatever climate, situation, age or social state is my concern. Take my Mr. Hatch since in evil-doing

he enjoys a sense of power—a man whose nature inclines him towards evil-doing.

Place him as A a rich employer; B as a powerful reactionary politician; C as a labor leader; D as a social reformer. My argument is that you would still have Mr. Hatch, with his powers for evil working in a wider field (and that he would have an evil influence in any case). That is roughly what I am driving at. One does not change the nature of the individual by changing his economic or social status. One only more or less shifts the level and the opportunities for expression of his fundamental self.

I am opposed to the belief that the mere adoption of a set of ideas, no matter how good the ideas may be, is any cure for the innate flaws of the individual. He merely takes his own nature with him, and can adapt and use to his own purposes no matter what situation or argument. It accounts for the comparative failure of all movements towards human improvement: a good half of the adherents to any cause are motivated by hopes for personal revenge, personal expression, personal justification. The formerly oppressed behave with criminal cruelty to those they gain power over. This seems to me to be no sort of step forward. . . . There is always Mr. Hatch to contend with, and he will always find a Mr. Helton to abuse. A cause is more often weakened and destroyed by its adherents and followers than by its avowed enemy in the opposite camp.[30]

Neither "Noon Wine" nor the Amy story was finished; both were set aside for a third story inspired by her surroundings. As she looked out at the Swiss mountains she was reminded of her experience in Denver, Colorado, in the last months of the First World War, and she began the story that would eventually become "Pale Horse, Pale Rider." All these stories rested in her mind for the next four years.

Meanwhile, as fall turned to winter, Porter began to feel dissatisfied with Basle. She continued to enjoy the comforts of the Krafft Hotel and the friendship of the owners, who sometimes took her out for drives into the surrounding country. They were the Lutz family, whose women were huge monolithic figures with thick legs, solid mounds of flesh.[31] Later they appeared in *Ship of Fools* as the parents of Elsa Lutz, Jenny Brown's cabin mate. But she grew lonely and depressed and began to turn against Switzerland. She said the Swiss in general tried to get every penny they could from foreigners and she thought they had the worst manners she had seen in Europe. They were not merely rude but blunt and utterly lacking in any kind of personal attractiveness; they were shaped like tubs and put their chins in the plates when they ate:

Ah, not for nothing is a fork a gabel, and a spoon a loffel, and a knife a messer, in the onomatopaeic German tongue.
They luffel their soup, and gobble their meat, and mess their food generally.[32]

To console herself she spent hours by herself telling fortunes with playing cards, and it looked as if she were once again going to lose her creativity and start on another period of loneliness, despair, and disorientation.

Happily, events conspired to keep her on course. At the end of November Pressly was offered a position as secretary to the First Secretary at the American Embassy in Paris. Moreover, it was a permanent position; he was ready to take the job and know where he was to be for the next few years. Ecstatic, she threw her playing cards into the Rhine and hurried off to Paris, saying she preferred the bleak Malherbe on the Seine to the comfortable Krafft in Basle.[33] Pressly joined her in Paris on December 12.

Porter did genuinely love Paris better than any other place, even when it was cold, drizzling, and gray. She often tried to analyze her fondness for it, saying that it was not for all the obvious reasons—the American bar life, the pretty clothes, the people, the theaters, the art shows and music—and decided it was because she could live there unself-consciously as an artist.

Once they were settled where they most wished to live, there seemed no reason to postpone the marriage. Porter wrote her sister before the wedding:

This Saturday week I am going over to the Mairie and marry Eugene Dove Pressly. We have known each other for nearly three years—so it is nothing sudden. In fact, he is the same young gentleman I almost married this same time last year, thought better of it, and have changed my mind again, because it becomes obvious as time goes on that neither of us will settle down or do anything until this is arranged. He is private secretary to the First Secretary of the American Embassy here, has a life appointment to the foreign service, will take exams for the diplomatic service soon, and then, we hope, get a better job. He is very intelligent, and charming and mum as an oyster and ten years younger than I am.

He comes from Pennsylvania, is of very good old Quaker and Presbyterian stock, pure Scotch and English descent.[34]

Years later she added a marginal note to this description: "Gene told me only of his father's side—on his mother's side he was German, *half German!* and behaved like it at last."

There was some delay, caused this time by the French bureaucracy, and they spent a frustrating time running from one office to another to arrange visas, certificates, passports, and other documents. Finally they were married on Saturday, March 18, 1933, at eleven in the morning at the Mairie of the sixth arrondissement, with Ford Madox Ford and Janice Biala as their witnesses.

Biala sang all morning in a soft whisper "Safe in the Harbor of Marriage," and Ford's little daughter brought along a bouquet of heather tied with a blue ribbon. All the suitable ceremonies were observed. A very grand old gentleman with pointed whiskers and a red ribbon across his chest spoke "the fatal words," shook hands with them, wished them well, and gave them a small brochure on the care and feeding of infants with space on the back to record the births of a round dozen of young. Afterward the party went across to the Deux Magots and sat on the terrace in splendid sunshine drinking champagne at high noon. That evening Ford gave a party in his studio and about twenty-five people came and danced until three o'clock, sometimes in the courtyard under a full white moon.

The ornate and impressive wedding license bears a number of signatures besides those of Ford and Biala, because Porter had some friends, like Josie Herbst, sign when they visited Paris later. At the time she wrote Herbst that the wedding was one of the pleasantest and gayest she had ever seen and she had had no idea one's own could be such fun.[35]

Thus, by the time Porter was forty-three, many kinds of wandering were at an end. She was no longer geographically adrift, lonely, unsure of her talent. She was living exactly where she wanted to live. She was married and, since Pressly was at the embassy all day, she had some command of her time. She had a respectable number of publications and a great deal of material for future ones. All she had to do was stay in this situation long enough to write them.

FOURTEEN

Paris

The next three years of Porter's life were an extraordinary flowering. Later she described what was happening:

> I didn't begin to feel contemporary, or as if I had come to my proper time of life, until just a few years ago. I think after I went to Europe—Europe was the place for me, somehow, Paris the city, France the country. From there I got a perspective and somehow without a struggle my point of view fell into clear focus, right for *me,* at any rate; and what other rightness is there for the individual?[1]

Why it should have been so has been partly suggested. She was very much stimulated by the excitement of *la vie Parisienne,* and at the same time she was drawing strength from the most stable domestic arrangement she had ever had.

The Presslys settled down to married life in a small top-floor apartment, "a kind of roomy birdcage,"[2] at 166 Boulevard Montparnasse. They had to climb six flights of stairs to reach the apartment but it had the advantage of a fine view into the garden of a convent which had been there since 1551. Porter's romantic childhood interest in convents had never left her, and she spent hours contemplating the activity of the nuns below her window. Her reveries found their way into her fiction. Part of "Old Mortality" is set in a convent, and Mrs. Treadwell in *Ship of Fools* includes the following in her memory of Paris:

I wonder if that Catholic society in Montparnasse still gives dowries to poor but honorable girls in the parish. I wonder if the little novices who used to climb ladders and go to the top of the apple trees to pick the apples—in that old convent garden under my window—oh I wonder if they have grown sober and sad living on greens, and apples and prayer?[3]

Soon after they had settled in, Porter received a letter from her convent-educated aunt, Ione Funchess Porter. Newell Porter had lost most of his money and was working for a railway company in California. Did it give Porter satisfaction to reflect on the changes in their fortunes? The glamorous Tante Ione, who had set such a standard of elegance, was now an ordinary middle-aged California housewife, while she, Callie, was Katherine Anne Porter-Pressly, a writer, a married woman, and a resident of Paris. When she replied to the letter, Porter said depreciatingly that they led a very quiet domestic kind of life, walking in the Bois de Boulogne on Sunday mornings, sitting on café terraces drinking beer in the late afternoons, occasionally staying up late to watch the vegetable trains come in and afterward eating onion soup at Les Halles.[4] It must all have sounded very exotic to Tante Ione.

The one problem with Porter's domestic life was that she was living in very confined quarters with Pressly, and even though he was at the embassy each day, it was difficult for her to find the privacy and solitude necessary to her work. Ford Madox Ford provided a temporary solution to the problem. He was finishing his autobiographical novel *It Was the Nightingale,* and he enlisted Pressly's help with the typing. When it finally appeared Ford acknowledged Pressly's help and apologized for impinging upon his domestic life:

During all these months, you as Benedict, should have been squiring Katherine Anne Porter-Pressly to Maxim's, or the Moulin Rouge, or the Chat Noir. . . . I see a smile of polite irony come over your diplomat's inscrutability: but what do I know or care about the transportive night life of the Ville Lumière today!—Instead you have rushed home from your embassy at the day's end and have spent the hours with Katherine Anne poring over my indecipherable script. It is a scandal and I a real scoundrel to have let you do it. . . . Youth and beauty should be better served though the sky fall in on the manuscripts of all novels.

But there is this: Whilst you sat quiet at home Katherine Anne has written some more of her exquisite short stories. Thus what youth, beauty and the night club lost on the fugitive swings, Literature has gained for her roundabouts that are eternal.[5]

Porter was gratified by the dedication of Ford's book and proudly wrote her family to look up the book in the library because Ford's words were "pretty damn swell."[6] They were in fact absurdly affected and pompous, and Porter recognized this and laughed about it to Herbst, especially at Ford's promotion of Pressly to a position of some importance in the diplomatic corps. She said he made Gene sound like an ambassador at least. In spite of her amusement, she herself in later years similarly promoted her husband, and at the time she was thoroughly annoyed when Glenway Wescott maliciously mocked the dedication. There was still no great affection between Wescott and his friend's husband.

A temporary truce was established between Ford and Biala and the Presslys, and the two couples spent Christmas of 1933 together; Ford used the younger couple as the model for his pair of lovers in his novel *Vive le Roy,* in which the young American artist Cassandra Mather is a portrait of Porter.

Inevitably Biala's pettiness and Ford's bossiness became unbearable, and when the French song book, which Ford had arranged, was finally published Porter let the dedication go by default rather than dedicate it to him. Not only did she find him personally tiresome but she could not respect his work. Already she had arrived at the opinion she expressed later, when she was asked if she considered *The Good Soldier* one of the fifteen or twenty greatest novels in English produced in the twentieth century:

I simply don't think so. Sorry, I have read this novel several times—Ford gave me an inscribed copy in Paris years ago— and I have always thought it had great interest but it is a breathless over-heated frightfully sentimental style. Ford was a wonderful technician, a real master, but he lacked the mysterious something that makes the great artist. However, he looks pretty good beside the Beuchners and Capotes and McCullerses and almost any of the corresponding grade in the English school. No, that's not really fair to him. He must be compared with serious writers—and by that standard,

there is something important—a sense of the truth? a knowledge of love?—lacking in him.[7]

In any event, Porter was widening her circle of friends and many of
them were more congenial and interesting than Ford.

When she first arrived in Paris, Porter had gone to Sylvia Beach's
bookstore, introduced herself, and brought messages from friends.
The two women had liked and admired each other and meetings
continued, which later included Beach's friend Adrienne Monnier and
Pressly. Beach and Monnier were appreciative dinner guests at the
Presslys' and the Presslys enjoyed the soirées at the Rue de l'Odéon.
In 1956, when she learned of Monnier's death, Porter recalled these
evenings and remembered "the sparkle of life in *everybody* present,
which you two could always bring out."[8]

One evening Porter was in the bookstore when Ernest Hemingway came in. Sylvia had just announced that she wanted the two best
modern American writers to know each other, when she was called
away to the telephone. The lack of rapport has been described by
Porter:

> Hemingway and I stood and gazed unwinkingly at each
> other with poker faces for all of ten seconds, in silence.
> Hemingway then turned in one wide swing and hurled him-
> self into the rainy darkness as he had hurled himself out of
> it, and that was all. I am sorry if you are disappointed. All
> personal lack of sympathy and attraction aside, and they
> were real in us, it must have been galling to this most famous
> young man to have his name pronounced in the same breath
> as writer with someone he had never heard of, and a woman
> at that. I nearly felt sorry for him.[9]

In the winter of 1933–34 the Josephsons were in Paris and Matthew sent a pneumatique to ask if they might meet. Porter had several
meetings alone with him and once the Josephsons both came to the
Presslys' version of tea (Riesling and cheese). The meeting was memorable for Porter's dramatic account of Hart Crane's scene at her gate
in Mexico, which moved Hannah Josephson to tears. Later the Josephsons passed the story on to Crane's biographer and Porter was
furious at what she read. She said:

> I like the Josephsons, they are quite all right, but you must
> know by now that they have no sense at all of reality, i.e.

any means of understanding first-hand human experience. They are very unreal people, and you cannot expect them to have a feeling about the things that happen to them or other people if they have no literary precedent.

The incident in the garden would impress them: I saw them being impressed as I told the story, and half a dozen other episodes which to my mind were more important and revealing went over their heads completely. . . . They had only the basest kind of curiosity and desire for vicarious excitement. They are not fitted to be told the truth about anything and I should never have talked.[10]

During these years Porter had the satisfaction of seeing a large portion of her fiction come to fruition. As well as writing new fiction, she reworked the first version of "Hacienda," which had appeared in the *Virginia Quarterly Review*, and produced a finished version twice the length of the original.

Harrison of Paris was eager to follow up the French song book with another of her works and was delighted to have "Hacienda." The press imprint survived a transatlantic journey to New York and the book *Hacienda* appeared in the United States in December 1934. Wheeler contracted with the printers Haddon Craftsmen, in Camden, New Jersey, and chose a twelve-point Baskerville italic type, Arnold English unbleached pure rag paper, a binding of claret balloon cloth with apple-green slip covers. The price for this luxury edition was $3. Many reviewers had reservations about the story, but Porter said she was not really troubled because she did not take reviewers seriously when they praised her and now did not do so when they dispraised her. But she did not like her book being reviewed along with three others in the *New York Times,* and said she thought there was something about a beautifully made book that aroused antagonism in the "faded calico souls of certain little people."[11]

Donald Brace had visited Paris in the fall of 1933, talked with Porter, urged her to finish the Mather biography, and discussed plans to get the contract away from Liveright. He also wanted to bring out a new edition of *Flowering Judas,* and contracts for both books were drawn up. When *Flowering Judas and Other Stories* appeared in 1935, Porter was gratified that the book was not a "limited edition" and that it now included "Theft," "That Tree," "The Cracked Looking-Glass," and "Hacienda."

Two of Porter's friends, Robert Penn Warren at the *Southern*

Review and Allen Tate at the *Virginia Quarterly,* were eager for short stories and quick to publish what she sent them. "Circus" appeared in the *Southern Review* and "The Grave," "That Tree," and "Two Plantation Portraits" in the *Virginia Quarterly*.

Not only was a great deal appearing in print, but Porter was full of plans for more work. Many of the stories that had appeared she regarded not as finished complete works but as fragments of novels. (She was astonished when "The Grave" was accepted as a story in its own right.) *Cotton Mather* was a perennial headache and she wanted desperately to work on a novel whose first section she called "Legend and Memory" and which was a recreation of the story of her family from the time it settled in America.

She was also working on new stories, one of which she had promised to Schumann Rare Books of Detroit. An early title was "The Never-Ending Wrong" and a later one "The Man in the Tree." Although the central event was a lynching, Porter insisted that it was not a lynching story since the killing was done before the story began.

The story concerned a white family, the same or similar to the one that eventually appeared as the Gay family of "Old Mortality" and "The Old Order," and there were several black servants who had been with the family for years. The counterpart of the Miranda character in this story is sometimes called Gabriella and sometimes Courtenay and she has an older sister called Maria. The counterpart of Nannie Gay is Nannie Bunton, and it is her grandson, Hastings Bunton, named for Gabriella and Maria's grandfather, who has been lynched.

The boy has been accused of rape by a sluttish white woman who runs a fruit stand and whom ordinarily any white man can have for a dollar. The townspeople seize on her lying testimony as revealed truth because it affords them a pretext for violence. But the real focus of the story is the dilemma of the white family, who feel a blood guilt for the crime and the effect of it upon their relationship with the servants. Old Nannie suddenly reveals a deep hatred which she has harbored all her life for the white people to whom she has seemed to be mother, nurse, and friend but still a slave and black. The little girl who is the central character fears the murderers around her who periodically go mad with blood lust, but she has no fear of the blacks, even when the young ones are restive and rebellious.[12] As the second title suggests, the story made the victim into a Christlike figure; it was concerned with the need to kill, find a scapegoat, and later rationalize and justify murder. The notes indicate a story with Porter's usual theme—an innocent victim, a villain of evil life, and the other characters in various ways abetting the villain. It would seem to have been a thickly textured story of black and white lives intertwined and, among all the unfinished stories, one of those that nearly reached completion, but it was set aside for *Cotton Mather*.

This was in some ways the happiest time of Porter's life, and looking back she considered it so. But her literary and personal triumphs were accompanied by a deterioration of her relationship with Pressly. She was driven to distraction by his constant presence, especially since he was drinking more than ever and, when she worked, drinking gloomily by himself. She was desperate for some time alone, and in the early months of 1934 she was so ill that her friends realized she needed a rest. Barbara Harrison had gone to Davos for her health and Monroe Wheeler had gone along to keep her company. They wrote Porter that she had been too long shaking off her last cold, urged her to join them for two or three weeks of complete rest, and sent her the fare and $100 advance on her story. Monroe Wheeler came to meet her en route and escort her for the last part of the journey. He informed Pressly after a day or two that a full examination had revealed severe bronchitis but no T.B.

Porter wrote Pressly from Davos that she would have died if she had not got the rest and that she had made up her mind to commit suicide.[13] She said she had wanted badly to do so and yet fought the notion all the time. Pressly was quick to accept the responsibility for any problems between them and told her she was such a grand kind of person that he believed any adjustments and rounded edges should be on his side.[14] This time the letters between them were neither so long nor so frequent as in other separations, because they had agreed that she should work when she was not resting. Barbara Harrison persuaded her to stay until the revised version of "Hacienda" was finished, and to accompany her to the Salzburg Festival at the end of May to hear Mozart and Beethoven.

When Porter returned to Paris she tried to improve matters by looking for a larger place, and eventually the Presslys moved into a pavilion at 70 *bis* Rue Notre Dame des Champs, formerly occupied by Ezra Pound. It had six rooms on three floors, two baths, and central heating. There was a little closed garden full of shrubs with ivy-covered walls, and across from the garden was a huge atelier with a fireplace and two rooms above.[15] She had the top floor of the atelier to herself and set up there the new noiseless typewriter Gene had given her for Christmas.

Porter wrote her friends glowing reports of her new home, but added soberly that they must not be deceived by her enthusiasm; it was really not a gorgeous house, just a little country cottage set down in the middle of Paris. All the same, it pleased her more than any place she had lived in since Bermuda, and it rented for less than the smallest improved apartment. The icebox was "as big as a truck" and sat just outside the kitchen door in a kind of shed with black oilcloth hung in front. In rainy weather she had to get under the oilcloth and grope in the dark cave.[16]

The move provided only a temporary improvement in the domestic situation, and after a few months she was once again desperate for solitude and freedom from Pressly's brooding presence. In 1935 he was due for a leave of some months and she persuaded him to go alone to the United States so that she might have some time of Bermuda-like solitude. He was reluctant to leave her but was finally persuaded and set off alone.

In the United States he missed her desperately. When he visited his family in Denver he talked about her constantly, wrote long letters to her, and read her letters over and over again, sometimes to his family. It seemed that the trip was more a banishment than a holiday. He counted the days impatiently because every day was one less before he could return to Paris, the house and garden, the cat, Skipper, and his wife.[17]

He cannot have been pleased to learn that, while he had sacrificed himself to ensure a period of solitude for his wife, Josephine Herbst had arrived in his absence. Porter received her as a house guest because of their ten-year friendship and also because Josie was deeply unhappy over marital problems. Her visit dismayed Porter, however, both because she resented the distraction and because her attitudes had changed over the past two years and had diverged considerably from those of Herbst. Porter wrote Pressly that she really liked Josie, who was an old friend and in great trouble, but it horrified her to see someone of Herbst's mind and heart going for communism. She said that Herbst was trying to get a German Communist refugee into the United States and was trying to use Porter as a sponsor. Porter felt that Josie was unscrupulous and would use her name even without permission, and even when she knew that doing so would endanger Pressly's embassy position. She compared Herbst unfavorably with

Wescott, Wheeler, and Barbara Harrison, who were angels of light and civilized feeling, bringing nothing but "gayerty and goodwill."[18]

There were times during Herbst's visit when the two different sets of friends were entertained at the same time, and Porter, as hostess, had the difficult task of trying to make them merge harmoniously. In her novel *Somewhere the Tempest Fell,* Herbst includes a scene closely based on one of these occasions. The three "glittering young men" are Wescott, Wheeler, and their friend the photographer George Platt Lynes:

It was in Paris, in June or July of 1935, that I first met Johns. He showed up one evening in the beautiful walled garden of an American woman living there. We were sitting in the early dusk, before dinner, drinking a delicious white wine, while she tried to ease the tension that threatened to split the evening between her other three guests and myself. I had never met the three rather glittering young men before but they were friends of each other and devoted friends of our hostess. They had managed to make me only too conscious that I was nobody they had ever heard of before, and therefore, a Nobody, and though their conversation was filled with references to people in the art world I knew perhaps better than they did, they had the air of simply talking Greek before a barbarian. I was sore inside myself, not only on account of them, but because they reminded me that if I had followed my earlier impulse, I might be writing about the arts myself. It sounds strange to talk about it now for it faded away as so many things do, yet even as I write some of the excitement comes back that was so real then. I sat brooding about the work I had turned my back on while the three bright boys chattered on about subjects, that, their manner clearly implied, could not possibly interest me. Our hostess was so charming and the look she gave me so intimately pleaded, that I simply strung along with the talk, getting what amusement out of it I could. It seems one of the young men had two old ladies as patronesses and had only that afternoon escorted these ladies to the Louvre. He retold the adventure with much hilarious detail as to the old ladies' rubbery legs, little poodles and fat coachman. One of the other young men interrupted with a detail concerning the divorce of a famous Spanish painter and was just launching into a description of a dinner, in which the wife to be divorced had broken out in a tantrum, when the door to the gate in the garden buzzed and our hostess went to answer it.

She came back leading Johns by the hand. I had never seen him before, but the other three guests had apparently met him and rose to shake hands, rather indifferently. . . .

The three bright boys continued to chatter away, quite as if it didn't matter, and implying that nothing mattered except their own little secret society to which they graciously admitted their hostess. They had now turned to a trip two of them had just made to Italy and back, in a big open car, the better to enjoy the fine countryside. Johns woke up.

"How was Italy?" he asked sternly.

"Beautiful as always. It is always ravishing, perfect, but we had the most wonderful luck with weather, with everything."

As if he had not heard, Johns repeated, "How was Italy?"

"Oh, clean, neat, wonderful. One thing you have to credit Mussolini. He is really doing a first-rate job of restoring all the fine old things. He's salvaged old treasures that were ready to crumble. In Paris, if it weren't for American money, they'd let the whole business slide."

"How was Italy?" repeated Johns impatiently. Our hostess broke in lightly but a trifle nervously. "Why don't you ask Mr. Snow? He lives there."

I got to my feet. Now I was enjoying myself. I meant to rub the noses of the three bright boys into it. "You mean the people, the life," I said, as if I were about to tell the friend of the patient, who has been put off by indifferent nurses, the worst possible news. "It is bad. . . . I am a privileged foreigner, living off my privileges. The best of them are jailed, broken, intimidated or have escaped. If they aren't dead. But they might all be good people only now they are bewitched. . . ."

His eyes crinkled. He didn't make a sound but he looked as if he were about to burst into a huge laugh. Looking at each other, in the deepened twilight of the garden, we recognized each other, as if, unexpectedly, we had met in darkest Africa.[19]

The passage suggests that Herbst thought Porter was more sympathetic to her than to the glittering young men, and possibly Porter's ability to adapt herself to the company in which she found herself concealed from Herbst her real attitude. In fact, ever since she came to Europe Porter had been moving away from Herbst's political point of view to a more aesthetically oriented one. Her feelings were well summed up in a letter she had written earlier to Bill Hale:

> The Vanity Fair job sounds as cheerful a thing as one could wish in these quite confusing times. It isn't exactly the next step towards serious writing but heavens! it's a job! As between the Vanity Fair point of view, and the New Masses, I should hate to have to choose, there is still another territory on which I feel more at home. Literature isn't social criticism, except by inference, but it isn't altogether decoration either, or something to play with. I think Vanity Fair and the New Masses both miss the point badly. But Vanity Fair is more amusing and not so dangerous. It has the deadly sureness of slickness, smartness, and the light touch, and actually I despise it; I do not despise the New Masses, far from it: but in the end it is more harmful than V.F. could ever be.[20]

In spite of their long friendship, and in spite of the tragic collapse of Josie's marriage to John Herrmann, Porter was not disposed to confide to her friend her own marital difficulties. She had stopped being frank with Herbst about her love affairs. Now she bewailed Pressly's absence, said that he seemed more absent with every passing day and she was counting the days until his return.[21]

Finally Herbst left, Pressly returned, and all the same problems resumed. In an effort to distance herself from him, Porter now planned to visit the United States herself. She set off in the spring of 1936, heading first to Boston to visit Herbst. Perhaps she also hoped that she might strike the necessary inspiration there to finish *Cotton Mather*. As usual when there was a great distance between them, she began to miss Pressly and wrote long, frequent letters telling him so. When she read John Buchan's *Oliver Cromwell* she mistranslated his dedication, "Conjugi dilectissimae laborum studiorum gaudiorum consorti," writing in the margin, "Most delicious wife, laborious student, and gaudy companion." She wrote Pressly that she was lonely and wished there were someone who shared her sense of humor.[22]

Escape from Pressly was not the only or even the compelling reason for Porter's journey to the United States. In spite of her other errands—visits to publishers and friends, attempts to finish *Cotton Mather*—the focal point of her trip was a pilgrimage back to her family and her native state.

She had not been home for fifteen years, not since the death of Mary Alice Holloway. She had promised to go, even made travel plans, but at the last minute she had always canceled her arrangements. Now, after her time in Europe, she felt sufficiently reconciled to her past to face it again.

She was, of course, a different person now, in appearance, experience, and accomplishment, and she must have seemed a stranger to her family when she arrived in her Paris clothes with her white hair, husky voice, and muted accent. Her sisters were somewhat awed, and the younger generation, their children, regarded their aunt almost with reverence. She now commanded, in her own right, the adulation that Wescott and Wheeler had taught her was her due.

Family had always been inordinately important to Porter and she had yearned for such a homecoming, but, besides the emotional reasons, there was a practical reason for her visit. She had been researching her family history while she was in Paris and using it in the fiction she was carrying in her mind. Two of the stories which had been lying fallow since their inception in Basle were set in Texas, and she hoped that being in the location of the stories might help her finish them. She knew that her surroundings often worked wonders on her creative efforts and so did her friends. Caroline Gordon wrote her, "I am glad you are wallowing in family after years of exile. It should be particularly valuable to your kind of writer."[23]

Less dazzled by her family than they were by her, she said that the best of the lot was her brother Paul, who was perceptive and intelligent. Her father was as contentious as ever, still the dissenting voice in every gathering, stomping around in the morning pulling the covers off people to wake them up. Her sister Gay, who had been involved in spiritualism and astrology since the death of Mary Alice, she thought lived in a fog of self-delusion and self-pity. Her other sister, Baby, she thought was equally beyond human appeal and felt tenderness only for her bulldog. Porter was appalled by her kissing the dog and telling him, "I do love you, you sweet good thing," with such a look as Porter had never seen her give to any other living thing.[24] Baby told Porter that the dog was a thoroughbred and had thoroughbred instincts, that three times when she was near to dying he had been the only one who understood, and that she loved him more than any other living creature. Porter wrote all this to Pressly and later used her impressions to describe the relationship between the Huttens and their beloved bulldog, Bébé, in *Ship of Fools*.

The most important part of this visit was a family pilgrimage to Indian Creek. They drove 340 miles and stayed at a tourist camp in Brownwood. The next morning the women bought flowering plants and took them to the country cemetery for their mother's grave. Harrison Porter found all this emotionally draining. He had been exhausted and stayed late in bed after they arrived at the tourist camp. Walking into the cemetery he indicated a tall, narrow blue stone and said, "It is there." Porter walked straight to it and without hesitation sat down beside the long, shallow, neglected grave and began to dig a pit to set the growing plants. She could not explain her feelings, except that it was as if she had come into a very familiar, not unhappy place, where she belonged and was known, and that the grave was the center of life, not death, and there was nothing to grieve for.[25] She wrote an early version of her poem "Anniversary in a Country Cemetery" and buried it in the grave:

> This time of year, this year of all years, brought
> The homeless one, home again,
> To the fallen house and the drowsing dust
> There to sit at the door—
> Welcomed, homeless no more.
> Her dust remembers its dust and calls again
> Back to the fallen house this restless dust,
> This shape of her pain.[26]

From the cemetery they drove to the house where they were born and came to the big gate of a rambling, shabby old place. Two tired-looking women in their mid-forties came out, remembered them, and insisted on giving them dinner. They said that the place did not look as it did when the Porters lived there. It had been beautiful then; now the pecan grove and the vineyard were gone. They told Porter that their papa would have been ruined if her father had not given them fifteen years to pay for the place. Her father looked suddenly as if he were about to cry. They went to the river and gathered colored stones and walked all over the land. Porter was amazed at finding these people in the very center of roaring, progressive Texas. They seemed like survivors from several generations past. She gave them some green sunglasses as she had several pairs, and she took a picture of her father standing under an oak tree he had planted. Back at the tourist camp her father said that he did not want to go on to Kyle and San Antonio and they agreed that the trip was finished. They set out for home, and she felt an extraordinary lightness of heart all the way.

From Houston she went to New York to visit Monroe Wheeler, Glenway Wescott, and Barbara Harrison, whom she had left to the last because she wanted to see them and enjoy them unhampered by other worries. They had returned to New York in late 1934, and with their departure from Paris began a correspondence which lasted nearly to the end of the lives of all four.

While she was away Porter had given every impression of being impatient to be back with Pressly. She couldn't wait to see him and have him admire the new sleepwear she had bought. She wondered if she should come by the embassy as soon as she got to Paris, or if he should meet her train, or if he wished simply to come home and find her there.[27]

Unfortunately this eagerness did not long survive the actual meeting, and she had not been home long before all the old grievances against him revived. The main problem was his uncertainty and indecision about his future, and no doubt Porter found this all the more unbearable because her childhood happiness had been so destroyed by her father's indecision. Pressly thought he might be transferred and did not know where he might go or where he wished to go. He dreamed vaguely of Istanbul, Lima, Madrid, or even London. Finally he decided that he would resign the dull secretarial work and return to the United States and Washington to see if he could find a more appealing job, perhaps as a newspaperman. Porter's visit to the United States had reconciled her to living there once again and she was quite happy at the prospect of returning home.

Although they went back to the United States together in October 1936, the marriage was slowly but surely disintegrating. They quarreled and fought incessantly. One reason for Porter's nervous irritability was that three stories which had been simmering in her mind for years were now at the point of being written down. As she had hoped, her visit to her own place and her own people had done its work. She had made piles of notes on the stories over the years, but she no longer needed them because the stories were so familiar and complete in her mind. All she needed was the time and solitude to sit down and write them out uninterrupted. If she had been frustrated before because she was not able to work well, she was now irritated because her creative powers were at their height and she knew that if she did not write it might be years before she would be ready again. She also knew that if the moment passed she might never be ready again.

FIFTEEN

Pennsylvania, New York, Louisiana, Texas

Not surprisingly, the return crossing to the United States was stormy for Porter and Pressly. Their hostility erupted into constant noisy quarrels, and it was this journey which informed the descriptions of Jenny and David's relationship in *Ship of Fools*. By chance they happened to meet Matthew Josephson soon after they arrived. He was astonished and amused at their rowdy shouting and fighting, and also a little disturbed to notice a side of Porter he had not remarked before and which had perhaps not existed before. He described it as a kind of cold malevolence, a "mean streak."[1]

It was clear once more that if Porter was to do any work, the Presslys must part, at least temporarily. Gene therefore went to Washington to look into job possibilities, and Porter, at Carl Van Doren's suggestion, went to the Water Wheel Tavern in Doylestown, in Bucks County, Pennsylvania. There were other reasons for this choice besides its relatively secluded location. She was hoping to find a place to live, and her researches into the Porter family history, having revealed early Pennsylvania connections, recommended the state to her as one in which she might strike roots. She intended to look around for a house while she was there. Also, if she became lonely she could visit Herbst, who had a permanent home in nearby Erwinna.

Her choice of place was fortunate. She liked the inn and its air of respectability, industry, and thrift soothed her. The atmosphere was very like that of the Krafft Hotel in Basle, where four years earlier she had begun the stories she was now trying to finish. The resemblance between the two places gave her a sense of continuity and she quickly settled into a routine. She worked in complete solitude, taking her meals in her room during the day and emerging only in the evening for a bourbon in the bar followed by dinner. Immediately after dinner she bathed and slept in preparation for another long working day.[2]

The strict routine and the isolation were exactly what she needed, and she finished her stories, in about seven days each. "Noon Wine" "took the bit in its teeth, galloped past the 21,000 word mark," and was finished by November 7. Her method was to write straight through as well as she could, go over it again, make a final copy, set it aside, and go on to another story. When she finished all the stories she intended to go through all of them, making corrections with a pen, then go over them again in proof for "last-minute repentances." She wrote Wheeler that she could not explain her present steady energy even though she had had fits of it before, but that it was the best thing in the world while it lasted.[3] By mid-November three of the stories were almost finished and, allowing herself a day's rest, she went for Thanksgiving dinner with Herbst.

The occasion was not pleasant, perhaps because interrupting her work made her nervous, and she was happy to return to her cloistered life. Her one indulgence was still her pre-dinner drink, and in the fall of 1936 the cocktail hour was enlivened by news reports of the romance between Edward VIII of England and the American Wallis Simpson. Porter followed the news with great interest, heard the King's abdication speech on radio, and was greatly moved by the infinite loneliness in his voice. She also heard on the radio such songs as "Pack Up Your Troubles in Your Old Kit Bag," which reminded her of the oppressive atmosphere of the First World War and helped her recapture the mood of "Pale Horse, Pale Rider." She now had nine stories in her mind and was confident that she would finish five of them by January.[4]

She then started "Promised Land," a story based on her crossing from Mexico to Germany in 1931, but perhaps because her impetus had weakened and perhaps because this material was more intransigent, the work did not go quite as smoothly.

Sitting in the bar listening to the King's abdication speech, she made an important decision about her own life. She decided that she must have permanent freedom and solitude if she were to work, and that she could no longer be married to Pressly. She thought that he too would get along well alone. He was a competent writer, knew English, Spanish, and French, and was an expert researcher; she thought he might do good work for one of the Luce publications.[5] She wrote immediately to ask him for a divorce, and felt a tremendous sense of relief and lifting of the spirits as she went out to mail the letter.[6]

The decision was easier made than carried out, for Pressly, in spite of all the difficulties of living with Porter, did not want to be separated from her. He came rushing to Doylestown as soon as he received the letter, to plead with her to resume the marriage. With his arrival all literary productivity ceased.

In later years Porter described the last months of 1936 as the most wonderful of her life, but added that her creative flow was soon disrupted by her husband. But even if Pressly had not arrived, there seems little chance that "Promised Land," which took twenty-five more years to grow into *Ship of Fools,* could have been contained in short-story form and finished in a week. And it seems unfair to blame Pressly for an injurious effect on her art. If his presence had at times been abrasive, he had at least provided her for seven years with domestic stability and financial support.

Uncertain of where and how she wished to live, Porter now embarked on a course very similar to that of the years before Europe and Paris. It was a period of distraction and dislocation—which included many changes of scene, many journeys, another disastrous marriage, and only a few, sparse literary accomplishments.

She returned with Pressly to New York. She had decided against Pennsylvania as a place to live because she was angry with the local real estate people and with Herbst. The uncomfortable Thanksgiving visit had been the culmination of years of resentment against her old friend. She wrote to Pressly just after the holiday:

> Josie came back for Thanksgiving, and it was pleasant. It's true she has an awful voice, and it's no good trying to deny it, she has a very underbred nature. . . . Her road manners, the way she screams at other drivers, because she is a stupid driver herself, her real, immediate reactions of envy and hatred toward almost anyone who has the slightest good fortune or talent or beauty, her positive lack of any generosity . . . I keep determinedly not noticing, but in the end

one has the feeling of being with a serving girl who has managed by some freak of will and imagination to lift herself to a plane above herself, but is not always able to stay there.

This is only to you, darling. It cannot be escaped. I have known her for years, and I never said this, or even let myself admit it, until now. . . . If you had her in the kitchen, she would cheat and steal and break crockery to show you she was as good as you were, until you'd have to fire her and then would find the silver gone. . . . And she is not really of degenerate origin. It is that that I can't understand. Dishonesty is entirely without caste, it takes various forms according to opportunity, that is all, I believe. But her really *bad manners*—they are in her blood and bones, and *low* bad manners, not the high sort. There is a caste in manners, both in the good and bad kind. You can tell as much about the breeding of a person from his rudeness, as from his courtesies.[7]

The Presslys arrived in New York in time for Christmas and it was a thoroughly miserable one. Christmas Eve was spent wrangling about their marriage and the rest of the time house hunting. They finally found an apartment for $60 a month on the first floor of 67 Perry Street and for the moment put aside all plans for a divorce. As soon as they had settled into the dark little apartment, Porter collapsed with a severe attack of flu and stayed in bed for ten days.[8]

The problems which had attended the past year of the marriage did not disappear, and chief among these was Gene's inability to decide what to do and where to live. He considered journalism, ranching in Colorado, and returning to the foreign service. Porter berated him for his indecision and blamed her miserable state of tension on him: his carelessness with her life had been ruinous and his capacity for doing nothing was "neurotic to a dangerous degree."[9]

Finally he decided on the foreign service, and she saw him off on April 1 to a post in Venezuela. They did not meet again for several years, and never again as husband and wife. At their parting, Pressly was heartbroken and Porter felt a blessed sense of relief.

If marriage could have worked for Porter with anyone, it would probably have been with Gene Pressly. In spite of his lack of ambition and worldly success, he was always ready to give her everything he had, even to the point of scrimping on food when he was in Madrid so that he could send more money to her in Germany.[10] She still concealed from him the fact that she had had a hysterectomy, but apart from that he had few illusions about her. He knew her family background, her weaknesses, her physical disabilities, and her exact age—and the knowledge made no difference. He told her (and meant it) that he would still love her even if she got to weigh a ton.[11] He could even endure her changing moods and towering rages. In addition, he was completely faithful, a trait she valued highly in spite of her own lack of it.

On her side, this relationship had never been a grand passion, but it was the nearest she ever came to combining her conflicting desires for a family life and the solitary existence she considered necessary to her art. For most of seven years they had lived together, sharing the routine and trivial concerns of their daily lives, and these had been Porter's most productive years.

She had often been ready to shed Gene's physical presence—on the S.S. *Werra,* in Berlin, in Basle, by escaping to Davos, by sending him to the United States and later going there herself while he remained in Paris. All the same, it seems possible that he was not sexually aggressive, and was therefore more acceptable as a sexual partner. In the descriptions of Pressly as David in *Ship of Fools* the word "cold" is frequently used. Like Pressly, David is engrossed in himself, too self-conscious to dance, inhibited, and very much embarrassed by Jenny's free behavior, as this incident shows:

> "Amparo told me I had no money, no man, and nothing here," and unself-consciously as a cat washing itself, Jenny slapped herself high up on the inner thigh. David turned instantly so bright a scarlet his eyeballs flushed too, and he said quite desperately, "Jenny *angel,*" with such violence the words sounded like a curse, "do you ever think how you *look?*"[12]

Yet in the novel's catalogue of sexual encounters the relationship of Jenny and David alone suggests hope for happiness when the book ends with both of them thinking with pleasure that they will be able to sleep in the same bed when the ship docks in Bremen.

She never openly acknowledged Pressly's contribution to her work, but at the same time she never tried to disclaim this marriage or erase it from the record. She referred to it not merely because so many of her friends knew of it but because there was nothing in it that made her want to cringe at the memory. There was nothing violent, degrading, or destructive. Gene never became "that monster" but simply "my Paris husband."[13]

Her belief that he had prevented her from working was confirmed when she wrote a new story just after he left for South America. Based on a family's quarrels which she overheard through the air vent of the Perry Street apartment, it was eventually published as "A Day's Work." Her relief, however, was short-lived, for once again Pressly tried to return to her. Eight days after he left he wrote that the Venezuela job was not to his liking, that he missed her desperately, wanted more than anything to be near her again, and intended to be back in July.[14] This prospect threw her into turmoil, for she knew that the marriage would never end if he kept returning, and that she would not have the heart to dismiss him from her life if he came back to New York. Consequently she decided to leave the city and not come back until he had left for another overseas assignment.[15]

The visit to her family the year before had been a reasonable success and she planned now to return to Houston. Once there she and her father and Mary Alice undertook another pilgrimage to places where she had grown up, this time to San Marcos and Kyle. She wrote to Erna, apologized for not stopping to visit her in Austin and added: "Mary Alice, my father and I visited the dreary little place at Kyle, empty, full of dust, decayed, smaller even than I remembered it. I had no feeling at all. I never lived there really, and have not any memories that I cannot bring up, look at, and put away again calmly."[16]

She visited the Kyle cemetery to look at graves and found an astonishing number of her own generation there, people she had forgotten until she saw their names again. She said it seemed very natural that they visited the graves and not the living people, except for a few stiff-necked old-timers. In San Marcos they stayed at the Vogelsang camp and attended an Old Settlers' reunion at which she spoke, introduced as "the littlest Porter girl, the curly-haired one." The visit was marked by a calm acceptance of her past. She saw houses and gardens and children who had once been herself, and she had no regrets and no wrenchings of the heart for any part of the past. Everything had "moved back and taken shape" and was "something whole and finished," and she could look at it "with complete detachment except for a pleasurable sense of possession."[17]

In this calm state of mind she might have settled down for a summer of work in Houston, but an interruption came along in the form of a telegram from Allen Tate and Caroline Gordon, urging her to join them at a writers' conference at Olivet College, in Michigan. Delighted at the prospect of enjoying some human sociability and literary conversation, she hurried off immediately.

She had known the Tates since the mid-twenties. Over the years they had corresponded frequently and had reunions in New York and Paris. The friendship was one of her most flourishing. They admired her work, gave practical suggestions for its publication, and also encouraged her sense of identity as a southern aristocrat. In addition, a letter from Allen Tate to Porter indicates that they had had a brief love affair, which Caroline never discovered.[18] After their time together, which Tate called a "beautiful escapade," he wrote Porter to say that while he found it hard to reconcile himself to the fact that it was over, he was nevertheless both afraid and grateful that the experience would last him for the rest of his life. He also said that he had begun a poem the minute he returned home. He enclosed a copy of "The Buried Lake," his poem addressed to the "Lady of Light." Confident of Allen Tate's sexual and literary admiration, Porter trusted his judgment and never considered his interest in her patronizing or interfering. She enjoyed the Tates' company at Olivet in the summer of 1937, and when they invited her to return with them to their recently acquired plantation home, Benfolly, in Clarksville, Tennessee, she gladly accepted. They drove back through West Virginia and Virginia, stopping for sightseeing in Mount Vernon and visiting Kenmore, a famously beautiful house that had belonged to Allen Tate's ancestors.[19]

The Tates were very hospitable and their home (as described in Caroline Gordon's novel *The Strange Children*) was always full of guests, many of them writers. Cleanth Brooks and his wife arrived from Baton Rouge, Louisiana, while Porter was there, and twenty-year-old Robert Lowell, who had been at Olivet, came to sit at Tate's feet and learn the older poet's craft. Because there was no room in the house, Lowell lived in a tent in the garden. And another student, six years older than Lowell, arrived from Baton Rouge on his way to visit his family in Memphis. He was Albert Russel Erskine, an M.A. candidate and business manager for the *Southern Review*.

Erskine had been enthusiastic about Porter's work from the time it first came in to the review, and when one story was read at an editorial conference he had been so enthralled he read it over and over.[20] Now he was equally enthralled by the writer herself, beautiful, silver-haired, and sophisticated after her years of residence in Paris.

For her part, Porter was enchanted by her young admirer. His appearance was that of Adam in "Pale Horse, Pale Rider," and later she recalled her first sight of him:

> Last time I saw your eyes, they were a light tawny tan with quite definite green spokes around the pupil, and little occasional flecks, mustard color, the whole effect being of a very pleasant and of course I thought perfectly beautiful hazel. And your hair at times was a kind of polished tan or leather color, edging towards straw at the temples and neck, and in the light it was just a mixed, bright straw blond. And your complexion was a fine sunburnt olive.[21]

The two sat talking together and wishing the others would go to bed, and after everyone else retired they remained on the gallery talking in the moonlight (it was a full moon) until four in the morning. Only Allen Tate in his room off the gallery lay awake listening through the open window to everything they said and thinking they ought to go off to New Orleans together and have an affair.[22]

When it was time for Porter to leave Benfolly, she had changed her mind about returning to New York and decided to go instead to New Orleans, where the Brookses offered to help her find an apartment. By the middle of September she was settled there and all her belongings in New York had been packed by Pressly and sent on. This arrangement was financed by a $400 loan from Monroe Wheeler, to whom she explained her predicament. She told him she had been kept in suspense by Gene all summer and then he suddenly packed up her household and sent it to her to receive collect; her expenses had been high, she must take the possessions when they arrived or lose them, and she needed all her books and music around her.[23]

She was thus settled on the top floor of an old apartment building, the Pontalba, which overlooked Jackson Square. To the right of the square was St. Louis Cathedral and the Cabildo Museum and to the left the French Market and the wharfs. She had an attic room forty feet long with windows opening on three sides, with a bath and a little kitchen on one side. She had apparently got over her anger at Herbst because she wrote her regular progress reports, saying she was in an attic that might be appropriate for a beginning artist and it seemed odd that she who never liked *la vie bohème* could afford only attics. Her rent was $30 a month. She was able to move to a better apartment in the same building after a reporter and photographer discovered her and wrote her up in the paper. The coverage had two practical results. The manager of the apartment building found her better accommodations and she was suddenly swamped with invitations to literary gatherings, including a tea for J. B. Priestley.[24] She had arrangements with several magazines which would amount to $15,000, and she could easily fulfill all these commitments if only she remained quiet and worked. That, of course, was the most difficult thing for her to achieve.[25]

In the early fall she made another visit to Houston, this time to attend the wedding of her nephew, Breckenridge. She told Herbst that weddings could be very pleasant, so long as one was not the victim.[26]

Her relationship with the editors of the *Southern Review* continued to be friendly and she went to Baton Rouge for a weekend with the Brookses. With Mrs. Brooks she visited St. Francisville and saw the plantation homes there. She reported that the people she met were the pleasantest, best-mannered and simplest in the world and added that she knew that was boasting because they were hers, not exactly hers, but she had people just like them in other parts of the South. She said she had begun to doubt their existence, the truth of what she knew, and the visit confirmed her in her belief in them.[27]

Although she was disappointed that she could not make more money by selling her work to well-paying magazines like *Harper's,* she was pleased to have her work accepted by the little magazines. "Noon Wine" was accepted by *Story,* "Old Mortality" and "Pale Horse, Pale Rider" by the *Southern Review.* Also, at the request of the editors of the *Southern Review,* she was making her debut as a critic with an article on Katherine Mansfield. She said she was finding it difficult because, while she admired Mansfield, she loathed her slimy crowd of friends. Once the critical essay was finished, she planned to return, after a nine-month interruption, to "Promised Land."

Pressly by this time had left New York to take a foreign service position in the Soviet Union, and although they had agreed not to exchange many letters, he insisted on sending her $100 a month.[28] She told him in early October that she was working hard and had taken vows of poverty and chastity and hoped the latter would come as easily as the first.[29] Poverty usually came of itself, especially when she was not producing very much. Solitude and chastity were a little more difficult, and in this instance her vow was very soon broken, for the week after she wrote the letter, Albert Erskine took the bus from Baton Rouge to New Orleans and they spent their first weekend together. When he left, Porter was rapturously in love and wrote him in a dazzle of joy. She said she missed him fearfully, as if she had known him all her life, seen him every day, and suddenly found him gone.[30]

In spite of missing him, she resisted the temptation to move nearer to him and remained in New Orleans working doggedly at "Promised Land," writing him every day and going each evening across the street to mail the letter in front of the cathedral. He broached the subject of marriage, but she told him that although she loved him she knew that if they tried to live together they would be miserable.

Her assessment of the situation was accurate, as she must have known when she recalled her past experiences of marriage and considered the great age difference between herself and Erskine. And perhaps, if the two had continued to live in close proximity, common sense would have prevailed. But a separation of some months occurred during which absence and loneliness did their work and overcame reason.

Both left Louisiana in December 1937 to spend Christmas with their families, Erskine with his in Memphis and Porter with hers in Houston. Gay Porter Holloway drove to New Orleans and brought her sister home. Harrison Porter was now eighty and still lived alone in a little house on a strip of land near Brownsville. He cultivated the land with the help of a patient mule named Kit, and he worked off the accumulated frustrations of a lifetime by "beating hell" out of the mule. He joined the family party in Houston for Christmas and Porter told Erskine that he had reverted to type, drank two fingers of bourbon before breakfast, had a goatee and mustache, and looked the perfect example of an antebellum colonel.[31] His daughters planned to have him photographed as a museum piece and his vanity was much flattered at the prospect. Porter described Christmas as a crowded family affair, with parties and open houses. She said that she badly missed Erskine. When he raised the subject of marriage again, she began to weaken and told him she had thought there was no possibility that they might be married, but that now she thought "it might be so" and she was glad it was so and "wished his wish" with all her heart."[32]

Soon after she had agreed to marry him, however, she told him that she had become ill and could not return to Louisiana. As when she had told Pressly in 1931 that she could not join him in Madrid, she wrote Erskine in a tone of brave optimism describing the seriousness of her illness and her determination to survive. She told him that her left lung was affected and that she had a fever. She was remaining in Houston because she needed a warm climate and had a doctor there who understood the family weakness. She said she had been much more ill before, when she was at Davos, and had recovered and had a good life since then, and she hoped to recover once more.

Erskine, naturally distraught by the serious nature of the illness, called and said he would come and visit. She was quite firm in resisting that suggestion, saying that it was something she could never explain and that it would simply not do. She always reacted with panic to the idea of any of her friends visiting her when she was with her family and rejected the prospect of anyone meeting them. But this time there may have been an additional reason for her refusal to receive him. The fact was that the health problem she had described as critical was not outwardly recognizable as such. Her family, in fact, never remembered that she was ill at this time.[33]

Her various conflicts are understandable. Common sense and experience must have urged the realization that another marriage with anyone would not work. With a man so much younger it was even more likely to fail. At the same time, she was in love with Erskine and desperately wanted to keep her young lover. Equally desperately she wanted to recapture the creative energy which had now been in abeyance for a whole year.

Remaining in Houston, claiming illness, writing love letters, promising to return when she was well and meanwhile working on her stories, was the best interim solution. She settled down, therefore, for a winter of work in Houston, renting a house near Gay's home. This she furnished simply, with a bed and a writing table that consisted of a long piece of wood set upon two saw horses. Visitors saw her smoking incessantly and working hard, while the rejected pages scattered on the floor around her table piled up, but they did not recall that she was ill.

While she was living in Houston she saw much of her family. She spent time with her sisters and enjoyed each one separately, but since there was some hostility between them, she could not spend time with them both without feeling torn. She also got to know her young nieces and nephews. Her favorite was Gay's daughter Ann, with whom she went cycling. While she was there Ann made her debut as a dancer. There was a record crowd in the audience and wonderful writeups in the paper, but nothing could console Ann for the fact that she was not chosen to dance the leading role.

Mary Alice's son, Breckenridge, used to drop in with his new wife. He was in the Houston police force and his political views naturally diverged sharply from those of his aunt. She spoke of taking part in protest movements in Mexico and the eastern states and of joining the Bastille Day processions in Paris. He was disgusted and on the side of the officers of the law. She, in turn, deplored his opinions and the friendship did not last long.[34]

More devoted than either Breckenridge or Ann, although Porter never realized the extent of his devotion, was her brother's son, named, like his father, Harrison Paul and called Paul. He was seventeen, sensitive and intelligent, and the one member of the family whose aspirations were closest to those of his aunt. He was interested in music, art, and writing and like her had a multiplicity of talents. He thought she was wonderful and asked her questions about music and advice about what he should read. She was flattered to have such an admiring disciple, but she happened to have many others, for she had placed an advertisement in the paper, and formed a creative writing class.

The class met on two afternoons a week and the students came surging across the porch like a cavalry charge. She realized what a mob of lonely, hungry human beings could be discovered in a place like Houston. She had twenty-nine students, of whom one or two were interesting, an average she considered not at all bad. One homesick Irish girl, who spent her time reading the Irish writers, came and talked about everything. Another student was an expert ornithologist, an old lady who had tagged 5,000 geese; she knew all about birds and bird sanctuaries and the systematized slaughter of game.[35]

When she was not writing, teaching, and visiting with her family, Porter spent her time writing long letters to Erskine. Nothing could have been more calculated to make her forget experience and reality and put her in the frame of mind for marriage. She always idealized relationships when the other person was not present, and when she wrote about any situation she lost her sense of proportion and began to romanticize, exaggerate, dramatize. In this instance a very dangerous element entered into the correspondence. The two started tentatively at first and then more seriously to make plans for the house they would build if they ever did marry. At this her resistance crumbled completely, for, if there was anything she craved, it was a home of her own in a settled place. She wavered sometimes in her decision to marry, saying that her doctor had forbidden it, but they went ahead and made concrete plans for a home. The house they planned, The Cares, was to be in the Ninth Ward of East Baton Rouge Parish, and designs for the house and plans for the garden flew back and forth between Baton Rouge and Houston.[36]

Not surprisingly, she began to talk once again of the marriage as a reality, and as spring approached her mood became cheerfully optimistic. In March 1938 she learned that she had been awarded a renewal of her Guggenheim for another year, beginning at any date and giving her $2,000. She had $2,000 worth of work arranged for, her health had improved, and she stopped fretting that she could not finish "Promised Land." She felt that the title was developing a nasty symbolism of its own, and when she gave an interview to the Houston paper she described her work in progress as a novel called "The Land That Is Nowhere." She had an orgy of burning manuscripts because she wanted to be rid of all irrelevant odds and ends, and she was astonished by how useless much of her writing seemed to be. It seemed to her that she had served an apprenticeship, was now at the journeyman stage, and would one day be a master.[37]

By the end of March she had stopped her writing class, bought a very high-style dress in gun-metal gray with a pearl-gray jacket, "suitable for a wedding," had sought a divorce from Eugene Pressly, and was ready to return to Louisiana and marry Albert Erskine. The final days in Houston were full of happy activity. The divorce from Pressly became final on April 9 and she set April 19 as the date of her wedding to Erskine. The packers came and packed up all her possessions.

On Saturday, April 16, Erskine drove to Houston, sending telegrams all along the route. He stayed overnight in a hotel, helped with the final packing, and the next day drove his fiancée to Baton Rouge. He met none of her family, but Porter's adoring seventeen-year-old nephew, Paul, watched from a corner as they left, curious about the man his aunt was marrying but fearing to arouse her anger by intruding.[38]

In Baton Rouge, Porter stayed in Erskine's apartment while he occupied the Warrens', two doors away. On the first day they got the marriage license and had blood tests, and the next day, Tuesday, April 19, they went to New Orleans and were married, with Robert Penn Warren and his wife, Cincina, as witnesses. Porter described the notary who married them as a typical Jewish papa who repeated several times that it was not too late to call the whole thing off, looking anxiously at Albert and reproachfully at her, as if she were not the one who should have been warned and rescued.[39]

No marriage can have been based on slighter knowledge. The partners had known each other for eight months, but during that time they had spent only a few weekends together. The letters had served not to deepen their knowledge of each other but to obscure it. Porter refused to take stock of the age difference between them and Erskine did not even know how old she was. He had thought she was approaching forty, and when he found out, during the marriage ceremony, that she was nearly fifty, he was horrified. This was a moment of the deepest humiliation for her and she never quite got over it. Long after they were divorced and when he was almost fifty she wrote him reproachfully, saying that she hoped no one would ever inflict that particular suffering and humiliation on him. She said she had paid dearly for her recklessness in not feeling her advanced years as she should have done.[40] Erskine was not the only person shocked by the discrepancy in their ages. Caroline Gordon and Allen Tate, hearing of the result of the meeting at Benfolly eight months before, were dismayed. And casual acquaintances, seeing the pair together, naturally assumed they were mother and son. Porter was mortified when a clerk in a store told Erskine that "his mother" had picked up their purchases.[41]

The marriage was a total and unmitigated disaster, and she knew it to be so on the day it began. She said it ended on the day they were married and the rest was just appearances, the first summer together being a long season of rain, terrible heat, and terrible, suffocating unhappiness.[42] There were violent rows in which Erskine would vent his rage by driving at terrifyingly high speeds. Porter, if she was beside him, would fear for her life. And all the while they were wishing each other dead or separate, the wedding gifts and hearty good wishes kept creeping in—bitter, ironic comments on a former state of mind and feeling.[43]

One source of conflict had developed even in the correspondence before the marriage, when Porter mentioned that she was committed to attend the Olivet writers' conference again. Erskine opposed the plan, not liking the idea of a separation and saying besides that he considered such conferences dishonest. Porter stood her ground, insisting that she had given her word to attend, that she needed the fee and would enjoy seeing her friends. She also insisted on her own right to make the important decisions about her work, saying firmly that there were many questions to do with her writing which he could not solve for her.

Erskine agreed with none of her arguments and she said later that he had the executive temperament; he thought and even convinced her that he was right about everything. She said she had never been so bossed in her life as in the early days of her marriage to him. In spite of that, she was as strong-willed as he and nothing stopped her from doing as she wished. Years later, when she read in her copy of Simone de Beauvoir's *The Second Sex,* "A lover who has confidence in his mistress feels no displeasure if she absents herself," she wrote that she never knew one like this, that her absences for her professional work became sources of her lovers' deepest grudges and resentments. "I was the one who felt no distress because I was the lover and the believer."[44]

If in the spring she had been eager to attend the conference, she was even more determined to do so after the marriage. Her reason was an old familiar one—she wanted to get away from her husband. But there was another reason. It had taken her years to achieve the acclaim that had come to her recently and she felt her success nowhere so much as at writers' conferences. She loved being at Olivet, and in the summer of 1938 she was applauded when she walked into the room, whether she was to perform or not. She was pampered, petted, given breakfast in bed, "handed around on a lettuce leaf," and she relished such attention and care. She read "Hacienda" for her first performance and took part in a round-table discussion with William Troy, Léonie Adams, and Ford Madox Ford. What she dreaded most was an hour's talk on the short story, but she fell back on Henry James, who she thought had left an excellent testament for helping out at conferences.[45] Near the end of the conference she was exhausted and feared she might become ill, but the time apart had made her feel some of her old affection for Erskine. When she heard that he too was feeling ill, she worried about his health and thought that perhaps she had not been feeding him enough.[46]

When they were together again, however, the old hostility resumed and the fall and winter were as painful as the summer had been. Years later she remembered Christmas 1938 as a terrible time, hideous for the whole world as the threat of war loomed, and for her because of her destroyed personal life. All the same, when she wrote her usual Christmas letter to Erna Johns it was in a note of sprightly optimism that belied all her troubles. She said that this Christmas had a special tone about it that she liked very much, and she told of her marriage, saying that she and her husband had been married eight months after they met. She said the delay was caused by her former husband's being stationed in Moscow so that the divorce came through only three days before the wedding. She said that they had been "living happily ever after" for eight months and had every hope of continuing so. She described her husband as a good editor and beginning to be a good critic. Remembering Erna's interest in music, she mentioned that Erskine loved and understood music and said that he was charming, amiable, and extraordinarily good-looking. "What more could a woman want?" she added.[47]

Erna was now a grandmother and Porter told her that she herself was not without honor in the next generation, because her niece, Anna Gay, whom she thought of as her daughter, was a ballet star. The tone of her letter indicates not so much a desire to mislead Erna about the state of her life as an inability, which she once confessed to Glenway Wescott, to talk about difficulties when she was in the middle of them. When she was desperately unhappy her letters sometimes became fictional exercises in which she described life not as it was but as it should have been, a deep-rooted habit that she had carried over from childhood.

During the marriage, as the problems of the relationship intensified, she wrote glowing accounts of her life and her husband to Glenway Wescott and Monroe Wheeler. She described Albert as a wonderful sort of person to be around. He was working steadily at two jobs, with the *Southern Review* and the Louisiana University Press, and at the same time writing his M.A. thesis and learning Anglo-Saxon for his Ph.D. orals. Such an example, she said, was a spectacle from which she hoped to draw some moral support.[48]

In the summer she told about the house they were building and described all the shrubs and flowering trees in the garden. When in the fall of 1938 Erskine became ill and they moved to an apartment on America Street for the winter, she seemed happy with that too. In November she said the weather was heavenly, with warm slanting sunshine and high restless soft winds, such as one felt sometimes in

Paris in June or July. Twenty miles away were the most wonderful oaks in the world, and the boats on the Mississippi bawled lonesomely all night long with Old Man River rolling along just on the other side of the levee. She said she could put out her hand and feel enormous quantities of emptiness, something she felt in Mexico but never in the East or Europe.[49]

If she was making little progress on her fiction during this time, she did have the satisfaction of seeing in the spring of 1939 the three stories she had written in Doylestown, Pennsylvania, published by Harcourt, Brace in one volume: *Pale Horse, Pale Rider: Three Short Novels*. The praise could hardly have been higher. Ralph Thompson wrote in the *New York Times* that although she had been called a brilliant stylist she had nothing like a "manner" and no stylish preciosity. "Her work . . . is of unmistakable quality, simple in pattern, substantial, honestly moving."[50] In the *New York Herald Tribune*, Lewis Gannett called her one of the greatest American writers.[51] Paul Rosenfeld told readers of the *Saturday Review of Literature* that she moved in the illustrious company headed by Hawthorne, Flaubert, and Henry James.[52] Clifton Fadiman said in the *New Yorker* that she shared with Hemingway and a mere scattering of other writers both the will and the ability to create by suggestion,[53] and Glenway Wescott, in a *Southern Review* article entitled "Praise," compared "Noon Wine" to *Paradise Lost*.[54] Wallace Stegner, not even an acquaintance at the time, but a discriminating and nonpartisan critic, wrote in the *Virginia Quarterly Review* that she was one of the surest and most subtle craftsmen now writing.[55]

Her public appearances were gratifying as well as financially rewarding. Often she read her own works, but even speeches no longer daunted her. She said she had completely overcome her horror of public speaking and it was managed so tactfully that she felt she was simply carrying on a kind of conversation with anyone who liked to join in and ask questions. She spoke at the women's colleges Vassar and Bryn Mawr that spring, and that summer, Erskine's objections notwithstanding, she went to Olivet again. Everywhere she was "a drawing card in the most New Yorkish sense of the word."[56]

It was by now an established pattern for her hard-won literary successes to be undercut by disappointments in her personal life, and this time was no exception. If the literary triumphs were the greatest yet, so were the disasters.

In the spring of 1940, Porter and Erskine acknowledged that they could not live together. Porter wanted a divorce but Erskine, not quite ready for a complete break, persuaded her to agree to a separation. She was crushed by the collapse of the marriage, both as another failure and rejection and also because it made her feel rootless again. She did not know where to go when she left Louisiana.

Her rootlessness was intensified when the reconciliation with her native state, achieved after a long estrangement, was suddenly destroyed. In 1939 the Texas Institute of Letters, founded in 1936 for "The Promotion and Recognition of Literature in Texas," announced its first award for the best book by a Texas writer. *Pale Horse, Pale Rider* had been in the running and seemed a certain winner, since no other author had achieved Porter's national stature. When she learned that the prize had gone to J. Frank Dobie for *Apache Gold and Yaqui Silver* because of the "indigenous nature" of his subject matter and because he was not only a native but had remained in Texas, she was convinced once again that Texas was no place for her.

Over the past years, to her personal griefs had been added the burden of world disasters. She had said in the fall of 1939 that she had been listening to war reports on the radio and playing bridge with the Brookses when she had extraordinary premonitions of disaster, "the steady sound to usward of evil, no winged chariots either but iron hooves," which induced in her a "last will and testament state of mind." When France fell on June 14, 1940, she felt that some part of her life had disappeared into the abyss like a landslide and that she was standing "on narrower ground, very crumbly and perilous."[57] She could not believe that there was no news from France and that there was in a sense no France.

By that time she had solved her living problems by taking up temporary residence at Yaddo, the artists' colony in upstate New York. There at the time of the fall of France she was writing her introduction to the new edition of *Flowering Judas and Other Stories,* which was being brought out in a Modern Library edition. Looking back over the past ten years she wrote, "We none of us flourished in those times, artists or not, for art like the human life of which it is the truest voice thrives best by daylight in a green and growing world."[58]

She was quite wrong. The past decade had been her most productive and she would never again rise to such heights of creativity. But she remembered only the pain, and she said there was not one hour of her terrible life that she would want to live over again.

SIXTEEN

A House of My Own

Porter had received a number of the coveted invitations to Yaddo, and in the present crisis it seemed an ideal refuge, solving both material and emotional problems. There was no charge for staying there and it was administered by Elizabeth Ames in a strictly disciplined way which prevented artists from being disturbed, and at the same time from being too isolated. No uninvited visiting was allowed before evening, and those who wished could pick up box lunches after breakfast and work undisturbed until dinner time. Moreover, Yaddo was a beautiful place, consisting of a huge Victorian mansion and some smaller houses and studios on a five-hundred-acre estate. There were woods, formal gardens, and lakes all around. An additional attraction for Porter was its proximity to Saratoga Springs, which her Aunt Annie Gay had visited in its heyday as a fashionable racing center. She felt this gave the place a family connection.[1]

It was a mark of the esteem in which she was held that, when Porter arrived, she was assigned the prized tower room, an enormous boudoir with seventeen mullioned windows forming a semicircle and giving a panoramic view of miles of valley, trees, and hills.

In these idyllic surroundings Porter settled down to contemplate the ruins of her personal life, to recover, and perhaps to write. She brooded a great deal on the collapse of the marriage and wrote constantly to Erskine, telling him that she loved him dearly[2] and reminding him of their first meeting at the Tates', when they watched the full moon and realized that they loved each other.[3]

Years later she expressed astonishment that so many young writers thought they could get married, have children, and live like anyone else.[4] It was clear to her that writing demanded its own discipline and was not compatible with the demands of ordinary domestic life. But she did not reach that conclusion voluntarily and tried for years to combine artistic productivity with marriage. When she left Albert Erskine in the spring of 1940, she said that marriage had meant for her a strange, cruel starvation of the heart, that she now knew that her fortunes in this matter would never change and she would never marry again.[5] But the thought of living alone for the rest of her life filled her with horror. Her mood at the time is conveyed in Mrs. Treadwell's reverie on her fortieth birthday in *Ship of Fools:*

> . . . here she was arrived at that age in human life supposed most to resemble this insect-riddled month . . . when nothing blooms but weeds in the earth, and the soul puts out rank growths, too, according to dreary popular opinion. The lower instincts take alarm for fear they have missed something, are hot for marginal enjoyments. Hearts grow hard and cold, they say, or go overripe and pulpy; women especially, one is told, so often lose their modesty, their grace. They become shrill, or run to fat, or turn to beanpoles, take to secret drinking or nagging their husbands; they get tangled up in disreputable love affairs; they marry men too young for them and get just what they deserve; if they have a little money, they attract every species of parasite, and Lesbians lurk in the offing, waiting for loneliness and fear to do their work.[6]

Given her frame of mind, it is little wonder that she reacted almost with hysteria to the attentions of another woman guest. Carson McCullers was fascinated by Porter's beauty and talent and developed a mooning passion for the older woman, following her around and, on one occasion, lying across the threshold of her bedroom, waiting for her to emerge. Many of the other guests dismissed McCullers' antics as merely childish efforts to get attention.[7] They felt she was indulging in some harmless hero worship rather than developing an erotic attachment. Porter, however, was horrified. She had always had a deep-rooted revulsion for Lesbians and she became seriously disturbed. Elizabeth Ames told her that she could have all her meals in her room and live in retreat, but this was not entirely satisfactory. Eventually she moved to the North Farm, one of the buildings on the estate, consisting of two apartments. This place she shared at one time with the composer David Diamond and at another with Eudora Welty.

Another grief during this period was the collapse of her new bond with her family. She was deeply wounded when her niece, Anna Gay, married and told her aunt the news after the event, while they were sharing a taxicab in New York. Also, the hostility which had long simmered between her two sisters had increased and they were quarreling bitterly about the care of their father, who had suffered a series of debilitating strokes. Each one accused the other of ill treating him and Porter observed that there was "deep division and enmity between her sisters," her quotation of a phrase from *King Lear* suggesting that she identified with Cordelia, the rejected daughter who really loved the old man best.[8] Porter, in spite of her own financial problems, had sent money to Anna Gay and was helping with the expense of nursing her father. It seemed that her generosity was being repaid with ingratitude and contempt. One sister wrote that the other took Porter's money and spent it on herself. The recent reconciliation was swept away by all the dissension and Porter said she remembered again why she had left in the first place. She was astonished to find how vulnerable she still was to being wounded by her family.[9] She always settled the quarrels with her sister Gay and niece Ann, but from this time on she had no further contact with her younger sister, Mary Alice.

Her departure from Baton Rouge, not knowing where she wished to settle, had aggravated her sense of rootlessness. She brooded on her homelessness and at the same time felt guilty for doing so. She said that when so many people had lost their countries, her own personal domestic exile was mild in comparison. Still, her feeling of placelessness grew to the point of desperation; she had to have somewhere to go back to, some geographical point of reference. The time had come for her to find a place where the rug could not be snatched from under her by any old caprice of fortune.[10] She wanted somewhere to put all her books and papers and "dear worthless possessions," and where she could "sleep and work and fuss" for the rest of her days.[11] Of course she had no money for such a place, because the critical acclaim accorded her work had not been matched by financial success and she had earned very little from her writing.

To these assorted miseries was added the horror of the world situation. She listened to the radio and each news bulletin brought news of greater disasters. She had promised the *Southern Review* that she would send in a story and she intended to finish it by December of 1940. It was to be "Season of Fear," the story of her experiences in the North Windham farmhouse in 1924. As she listened to the radio accounts of events in Europe, however, her thoughts turned instead to her months in Berlin in 1931, and it was the story of that time which claimed her attention. She saw that, from her present perspective, she could finish it. By doing so she hoped to solve a number of her problems. She would feel that she had rallied her creative energies once more. The subject matter would be relevant and she hoped she could sell this one story for a very good price. And there was another factor. She had been worrying a great deal about what the artist should do in time of war and, with her strong moral sense, had wondered if her own kind of writing was not somehow irrelevant, inconsequential, in a time of cosmic disaster. The Berlin story was not narrowly personal and, since it dealt with the menace of the Nazi party, she felt that it was a contribution to the war effort.

In her final version she drew on experiences of a widely disparate kind. For the first and only time she made her fictional representative male, a choice which possibly reflects her identification with Eugene Pressly during the Berlin period. For Charles Upton's childhood friend whose German background and German holidays had first stimulated his interest in Germany, she drew on her own memories of Erna Schlemmer, and gave the character a name similar to that of her sister Mary Alice's husband, Kuno Hillendahl. She described him as follows:

> He and Kuno did not remember when they had not known each other. Their first recollection was of standing next each other in a row of children like themselves, singing, or some such nonsense—it must have been kindergarten. . . .
>
> Mr. Hillentafel took his family back to Germany for a few months every two years, and Kuno's post cards, with their foreign stamps, coming from far-off places like Bremen and Wiesbaden and Mannheim and Heidelberg and Berlin, had brought the great world across the sea, the blue silent deep world of Europe, straight to Charles' door.[12]

In depicting the boarders of Rosa Reichl's *pension* she did not change the names but modified the characters, often grafting onto them traits of people she had known elsewhere. Rosa, whom she had really liked, she turned into an unpleasant character. She suppressed her anti-Semitism but heightened other offensive characteristics, making her barely able to mask her hatred for the American whose rich country she believes responsible for the poverty of her own.

Herr Bussen is the closest to the original of her characters and she used the melancholy conversation she had had with him in the hall. For the military gentleman she did not see, she used the character of Hermann Goering. She suppressed what he had said to her about Jews, that they were the ruin of Germany and that once the Hitler regime was established there would not be a Jew left in Germany with any political or cultural or economic power. She did, however, use the Nietzschean views she had heard him express.

For the Polish boarder, Tadeusz Mey, she used the appearance and mannerisms and even whole speeches of Joseph Retinger which she had recorded twenty years earlier in Mexico City. She even gave her character the family name of Retinger's guardian, Zamoyski.[13] When he is introduced he says: "Tadeusz Mey. Polish in spite of the misleading name. Indiscreet grandmother married an Austrian. The rest of my family have names like Zamoisky, lucky devils."[14] And her notes for the story show that she used the memories of another Pole, Janice Tworkov Biala, the companion of Ford Madox Ford:

> The Polish Jews also believe that a Jew must not pass a Catholic Church at midnight, for at that moment the souls of all members of the congregation who have died that year will rush out in the shape of swine and drown him (told to me by Biala [Janice Tworkov], Polish Jewish painter as told from her grandmother).[15]

In this story she used again the symbolic method which had proved so effective in "Flowering Judas." Here the symbolic structure developed from the cheap souvenir of the Leaning Tower of Pisa which Eugene Pressly had crumpled in his hand as they looked at *pensions* in Berlin.

On its simplest level it is a tawdry tourist souvenir, as fragile and insubstantial as the dreams of paradise of all the characters. The history of the original is more significant. The Leaning Tower of Pisa, built in the fourteenth century as a bell tower, is an ornate and impressive structure in white marble, a substance notable for its sturdiness. The sturdiness, however, does not extend to the foundations, for a weakness there caused it to settle and lean. It cannot be used as a bell tower and must receive injections of cement to prevent its collapse. Thus it suggests the Germany that Porter saw, so apparently solid and substantial, and yet undermined by a basic flaw in its foundations.

The Leaning of Tower, furthermore, has sinister overtones from its association with Canto XXXIII of *The Inferno,* in which Dante meets the traitors to their own country. The central figure here is Ugolino of Pisa, who conspired with an enemy party of that city to defeat a rival faction within his own Guelph party. His treachery merely served to weaken his own party, so that he found himself at the mercy of the very enemy with whom he had conspired. He was imprisoned with his children and grandchildren in a tower (not the Leaning Tower, although the story is closely connected with Pisa through Ugolino's imprecation against that city), and the keys were thrown away so that he was forced to watch his children and grandchildren die of hunger before he himself starved to death. Although critics disagree about the meaning of Ugolino's statement that after the death of his children hunger had more power than grief, a frequent conclusion has been that Ugolino resorted to cannibalism. If the Italian does not entirely justify this interpretation, the fact that Ugolino in hell is feeding upon the skull of his enemy suggests that Dante saw such activity as the appropriate fate for those who hope to advance themselves by destroying their own kind and kin.

The account of the chance-gathered occupants of Rosa Reichl's *pension,* all wanderers or defectors from their native lands, is full of images from the Ugolino story. The claustrophobic atmosphere of the *pension* in which they are all shut up, waiting for disaster and with no means of escape (only for Charles Upton is a ship coming from America), is conveyed in images of imprisonment, starvation, cannibalism, death, and hell.

The Leaning Tower of Pisa has always been associated with Galileo because of his birth in that city. One legend has him dropping weights from the tower. Since the story of Galileo evokes and dramatizes the dilemma of the clear-sighted man in a misguided society, it is relevant to the predicament of the man of vision in Nazi Germany.

When Porter was asked about the responsibility of writers in time of war she replied, "The responsibility of the artist toward society is the plain and simple responsibility of any other human being, for I refuse to separate the artist from the human race: his prime responsibility 'when and if war comes' is not to go mad.''[16]

A more detailed answer to the question is contained in "The Leaning Tower." While one cynical artist retreats into the romantic music of Chopin, Charles Upton does not see his art as a refuge or a retreat. He sees very clearly what is going on around him, does not deceive himself, and records the ghastly caricatures of human beings that he sees.

It seems possible that if Porter had settled down quietly at Yaddo and kept on working, the flow of creativity which produced the fine "Leaning Tower" might have been sustained. Instead of doing so, however, she found another major distraction. She decided to solve her problem of homelessness by buying a house in the Saratoga Springs area, and after a few fruitless excursions she found one. It was, like many of her practical decisions, unwise, and her account of her house hunting expedition explains what happened.

The agent drove her around Saratoga Lake, and in a valley she saw an old Colonial house, rather small, in a modified Georgian style. It had a lead roof and several cluttery small porches and sheds.

> "But that is my house," I told him. "That's mine." We struggled around it again knee-deep in snowdrifts, peering through windows. "Let's not bother," I said, "I'll take it." "But you must see inside first," he insisted. "I know what's inside," I said. "Let's go see the owner."[17]

She discovered that she could have the house for $2,000 and that a $200 option would hold it for her until May. That was not a huge amount but it was considerably more than she had. For one thing, the projected sale of "The Leaning Tower" for a large sum of money to *Harper's Bazaar* had fallen through. She had sent in the story and it had been returned to her "most expertly disemboweled" by one of the editors. Porter realized that the story was very long, but she had understood it was to run in two installments. She believed the editors wished to cut it not merely because of the length but because of their pro-German leanings. She reported that one of them, Carmel Snow, had told her over luncheon that she hoped she would manage a good word for the poor dear Germans. Furious, Porter demanded that the story be returned rather than have it appear in a shortened form. She then sent it to the *Southern Review* for a mere $300.[18]

She also ran into trouble with a huge dentist bill. Her teeth had become very bad, the result she said of biting into hot biscuits and cracking open pecans when she was a child, and the cost of fixing them ran to $654. She tried to pay it in installments, but eventually she could not keep up the $100 monthly payments and, having lost the check stubs for the amounts already paid, thought she had been overcharged. In desperation she turned to Glenway Wescott, deploring the fact that he should be involved in anything so unaesthetic as a dentist's bill.[19]

In spite of these financial problems she was determined to have the house, even though it needed extensive repairs. The well was not sufficient to supply water for two small baths and a modern kitchen, the walls turned out to be clapboard filled with rubble (she had thought they were stone), and the roof needed work. In addition, Porter wanted some improvements for her own satisfaction, such as changing the porch into a stone terrace. Not only would these jobs increase the expense but it would be months before she could move in. The contractor she engaged to do the work came to her aid by offering to find a mortgage and she felt that the house was hers.

As well as accepting help from the contractor, Porter tried to raise money herself by persuading her publisher to advance money on future books. Harcourt, Brace had been hoping for some years now for a novel—an expanded version of the story "Promised Land." It now had a new title, "No Safe Harbor,"[20] and Porter had accepted an advance of $2,500 on the book. She had requested an additional advance of $500, and when Donald Brace declined she had asked to terminate their relationship. He had then thought better of his decision and allowed her to "tinker with" her original contract, extending the deadline and providing the extra $500. He also arranged advances on an anthology of short stories she was planning, on her journal, and on the Cotton Mather biography. She felt that her living was thus taken care of for another four years.

During the first part of 1941 she continued to raise money recklessly by drawing up contracts for works not even begun. In July she made contracts with Doubleday for "Erasmus of Basle," to be finished in July 1943, and for "The Trial of Berthe de Fauquemberge," to be finished by July 1, 1942. The advances were $750 for the first and $250 for the second.[21]

Porter had always reacted badly to deadlines, finding herself unable to work under pressure and paralyzed by panic. Now she was stunned by the amount of writing she had to do. She told Glenway Wescott that not only her house but her whole future was mortgaged, and yet she seemed to undertake new works compulsively. In November she signed a contract with Viking Press for an anthology of about twenty-five short stories, to each of which she intended to write an introduction of about three pages. [22]

During the summer of 1941 Eudora Welty returned to Yaddo and again moved in with Porter at North Farm. Porter had met Welty in Baton Rouge, when friends brought her for a visit. Since then Porter had encouraged her and regarded her as a protégée. Now Welty's first collection of short stories was being published and Porter had gladly consented to write an introduction. She told friends that by doing so she would immediately add $10,000 to the book's sales. [23] But before the book finally appeared she added considerably to the mental anguish of both Welty and her publisher. Porter had so much trouble finishing the 3,300-word introduction that publication was delayed by six months.

All this time Porter remained at Yaddo. Work on the house went very slowly and there were constant difficulties with workmen. Nevertheless, owning the place gave her a great deal of satisfaction. All through the spring and summer she made a series of visits there —a ritualistic pilgrimage on her birthday, and numerous trips to show the house to other guests. She began shopping for furniture in Saratoga Springs and her friends were amused at her bizarre taste for gilt, red velvet, and gold fringe. They wondered, too, if she could afford all her purchases. [24]

Not surprisingly she accomplished very little work in 1941, and 1942 brought an unusually large number of interruptions. In January of that year she was deeply affected by the death of her father, which nevertheless came as a relief after his long illness. She said that the news reached her on the day he was to be buried and so she could not attend the funeral. (Later she told people outside the family that he died when she was in Europe.) Her failure to attend this and other family funerals caused some bitterness in the family, but she was not indifferent. She was simply unwilling to expose herself to old hostilities (she especially wished to avoid meeting her younger sister) and to reactivate painful memories of other family funerals. When she received the purple velvet memorial booklet after her father's funeral she felt only revulsion. There were some incorrect spellings (of her name among others) and some erroneous dates. The hymns were "An Old Rugged Cross" and "Abide with Me" (she changed the last two lines). She scrawled across the first page of the booklet, "What a tasteless careless mess!"[25]

Nevertheless, she could not get the death out of her thoughts. She wrote Wescott that she shed tears every day after hearing the news, as if every wound of life had broken open again and flowed tears instead of blood, because her life had been so terribly, mysteriously painful. When she learned that Harrison had become so violent that he had had to have his good hand restrained to prevent him from throwing things, she said she was glad his spirit had not been broken and he had remained to the end his old outrageous and obstreperous self. In a tender, nostalgic tone, she added that her father had been a wonderfully handsome man, intelligent and strangely in advance of his generation in many ways of thinking. Yet he had also been of the old-fashioned eighteenth-century humanistic school. She said that she was his child by temperament and knew all about him by instinct. During the last year his mind had vanished and he had been angry, violent, embittered, and completely alienated. All the women in his life had merged and he had confused his youngest daughter with his wife and mother and sister. It pleased her sense of order that he had died in the house of his daughter on her birthday, the same day that, years ago, her mother had begun to die.[26]

Soon the confused affairs of her own life penetrated her mourning and elegiac mood. When they separated two years before, Porter had wanted to divorce Erskine, who in turn had begged her not to do so (she later attributed his reluctance to his desire not to change his marital status vis à vis the draft). Now he wished to marry again and was urging a quick divorce.[27] Since divorce laws in both Louisiana and New York were stringent, this involved establishing residence in Nevada, where an uncontested divorce could be obtained in six weeks. It would require time and expense which she could ill afford. Later she said that the divorce came at a difficult point and interrupted her work on the novel.[28] But when the trip was imminent she seemed to be looking forward to it, saying that it would take no time at all, that the novel would be finished before she left for Reno and that the residence requirement would give her a welcome breathing space. She could also fit in some lecturing, which would raise some of the money she needed for the house. She was still in a state of suspense about the house and wondered if she had overextended herself, but she said she simply could not face a future as one of those women who lived their lives in hotels and little flats.

The novel was not, of course, finished in spring of 1942 when she set out for Reno, but—seen off in New York by Erskine, who had moved East—she embarked on the journey by train and wrote cheerfully of her arrival. She left the train in broad sunlight, found a pleasant furnished apartment, and went out to see the town with a chance acquaintance who took her to all the night clubs and gambling halls.[29] She was delighted with her lawyer, who turned out to have known her family connections in Kentucky and some of the old people in Texas. As always, the tone of her letters varied according to the recipients. She wrote at the same time to Albert Erskine chiding him for the damage done to her work and saying that he should have been more frank with her in the matter of divorce. He should not have postponed it and finally requested it just when it suited his own convenience.

Donald Brace, expecting the novel in every mail, was chagrined when it not only failed to arrive but in its stead came requests for other projects—a contract for a book of essays and a wish to have parts of the unfinished novel sold in serial form to various well-paying magazines. But he wrote sympathetically and tried to accommodate her with more money, saying she had not had all the advance on *Cotton Mather* and he could send her another $250 any time she liked.[30] After she left Reno she was scheduled to speak at Indiana University at the end of June and the University of Colorado in July. He hoped she could find some time to finish the novel between those two engagements and told her that, while the deadline for all publication was pretty close, they were prepared to perform miracles whenever they got the manuscript. They did not, of course, get the manuscript.

When she returned to Saratoga Springs, her house was ready for occupancy and she was able to leave Yaddo. When she moved in she saw a new moon and the trees were full of owls and whippoorwills. The house sat beautifully in its valley, facing so that the sun came in somewhere every part of the day. The living room was thirty feet long and the old fireplace and bake oven at one end remained untouched. There was a fine chimney that blazed clear and bright in any weather and any wind. There were so many violets blooming in the front yard that the grass looked blue and the fields were full of wild strawberries.[31] She looked forward to having guests most weekends and made plans to entertain and cook for them.

The expected house guests failed to materialize, however, because the house was too far from New York for weekend visits, and this was only one of many disappointments. Owning the house proved to be very much like her experience of marriage. She loved the idea of the place and loved it especially in the abstract, but the day-to-day problems of running it were far too complicated. Her imagination, so alert in many areas, had simply failed when she had planned her life at South Hill. She spent the winter of 1942–43 alone with only a cat for company and three radio stations—Schenectady, Troy, and Albany. It was 40 below zero several times and the furnace broke down twice. Her car was in the garage at Yaddo and a man there who kept her ration book drove out once a week with supplies and messages. She had thought there would be help at hand in the little cabin down the road, but it had deteriorated since she first saw it and no one could live in such a broken-down shack. She was as lonely and isolated as she had been at North Windham (she had turned again to her story "Season of Fear"), and she said she was wintering in a field of snow. By February she knew that she would never spend another winter there.[32]

One guest did appear unexpectedly in the spring of 1943. It was Eugene Pressly, home from his overseas posting and eager to see her. No one had ever replaced her in his affections and he hoped to marry her again. But the visit was not a success. Porter wrote him afterward:

> Dear Gene,
>
> Wasn't it an odd, sixes-and-sevens, all mittens, catch-as-catch-can sort of visit, just our typical old time muddle. . . . No food in the house. A general brouhaha and rushing about. Then a little too much drink for we could never bear to be sober together, and then cross questions and crooked answers as usual, talk in ever widening and separating circles, until we were back at the same old blind alley we used to live in, if it could even be called living.[33]

When fall came around again, and the anniversary of her occupancy of South Hill, she had to make some different plans for the winter. She did not really want to live anywhere else and she could live there quite cheaply on $45 a month and still have enough left over for wine and bourbon. But she decided that it was absurd for her to remain in such complete isolation and human loneliness. She said that doctor bills and taxes had piled up and she was fast reaching the conclusion that she could not make a living doing the kind of writing she wanted to do.[34]

She decided that she must go away somewhere and earn more money. She was pained at the thought of leaving the house but told herself she was not really leaving it, simply going away to earn it, which she should have done earlier.[35] Such plans suggested a long interruption of the work on the novel, but once again friends intervened to provide funds for a retreat to a hotel where she could finish it. The inn in Cold Spring, New York—much nearer the city than Saratoga but still properly isolated—was selected by Glenway Wescott on the advice of Janet Flanner, the *New Yorker*'s Paris correspondent. Most of the financing was undertaken by Barbara Harrison, with Glenway Wescott, George Platt Lynes, and Monroe Wheeler also helping. Porter declared that there had better be a novel and a long literary career at the end of the year or she would have nowhere to put her head except "in a noose," but she really thought that "No Safe Harbor" would get her to dry land at last.[36]

No doubt she hoped, as she always did when she went into retreat, for a resurgence of the creative energy she had experienced in Bermuda and at the Doylestown Inn. This time, however, she was working on a much more unwieldy project, a novel showing the failure of Western society in the twentieth century. It was an ambitious aim for anyone, but for her in particular the difficulties were enormous. It was therefore technical difficulties rather than health problems (although she had another severe bout of influenza) which prevented completion of the novel.

By December she knew that she would not finish the book. Although she was embarrassed at breaking faith with those who had supported her for three months, she felt a certain resignation. She described her appearance to Wescott, saying that she was pale and had a new expression on her face which she could not quite make out, distinctly remote, disengaged, full of mental reservation. She was not restless but, on the contrary, had the same kind of abstracted patience she always had, as to surroundings, people, everyday life, but her nervous system always had been shaky and hard to keep in balance. Yet, she went on, she trusted herself very well and found that the nervous system did not deteriorate. Porter was perhaps expressing what became more apparent over her long life, that under all the instability and frailty there was a certain strength. She told Westcott she was leaving the inn, her reason being simply that a date for finishing the novel had been agreed upon, it was not finished, and she felt she had not kept her side of the bargain. She said she had muffed on a grand scale the whole material question of living, and to set this straight would be her whole concern.[37]

As it happened, an opportunity to solve her financial difficulties came along unexpectedly.[38] Allen Tate was occupying the first Chair of Poetry at the Library of Congress and John Peale Bishop was consultant there. When Bishop's health failed in late 1943, Tate suggested Porter as a replacement to fill out the one-year appointment. Delighted with the honor and with the $3,000 salary the position carried, she accepted immediately.

The friends who had financed the time at Cold Spring never questioned her decision, but Donald Brace, still expecting the novel every day, was somewhat dismayed. Nevertheless, he did the courteous thing and wrote a polite letter of congratulation. The punctiliousness of his gesture was lost on Porter, who scribbled on the letter that she had rarely seen indifference so politely expressed.[39] Brace realized that no more fiction would be forthcoming right away (she had produced only two stories, "The Leaning Tower" and "The Downward Path to Wisdom," in eight years), and the firm decided to make the best of the situation by planning an edition of the remaining uncollected and unpublished stories. They hoped it could include "Season of Fear." Meanwhile, Porter herself made plans to go to Washington, D.C.

SEVENTEEN

The Love of a Lifetime

Washington during the Second World War was a ferment of military and diplomatic as well as literary activity, and when she arrived at Union Station just after midnight on January 21, 1944, Porter thought the huge terminal resembled a madhouse. She spent most of the night consoling a "tired little girl from Alabama" who had come up to see her soldier husband, and trying to telephone the Tates. When they finally got home, they were drunk and not able to pick her up, so she took a cab to their house, where, as she had done twenty years earlier in New York, she was to occupy a room in their basement. Soon after she settled in, she collapsed with a bad attack of flu and spent the next weeks in bed.[1]

When she recovered, a new problem emerged. The Tates shared with another couple, the Tennessee novelist Brainard Cheney and his wife, a house across the Anacostia River in the southeastern part of the District. Friends called the place "The Birdcage" because it was like a nest of singing birds, and it soon proved too small to house birds of such volatile temperament and fine plumage as Caroline Gordon Tate and Porter. Their friendship had endured for twenty years untinged by rivalry, because Gordon was the undisputed superior in education, literary productivity, and talent. Porter's reputation, however, had lately eclipsed Gordon's. Moreover, Porter's more spectacular beauty, charm, and personality caused her to outshine Gordon at every social gathering. Even at home the Cheneys were fascinated by the new arrival and paid far more attention to her than to Gordon.[2]

Various accounts of the "last battle" between Porter and Gordon circulated among their friends. Some thought Allen Tate's admiration for Porter had made Gordon jealous and caused a row.[3] Others remembered hearing of a trivial incident involving some spilled perfume. Allen Tate recalled that Porter read aloud a quotation about the destructive effect of early fame and Gordon gave offense by saying rudely, "Well, that's one thing you need not worry about, Katherine Anne."[4] Whatever the cause, the result was that Gordon had one of her towering rages and flew at Porter tooth and nail, and consequently Porter had to move out of the house. Once she was off the premises, the animosity disappeared. Gordon was quick-tempered but fundamentally generous and the relationship between Porter and both Tates continued on relatively friendly terms. After this incident Porter included Gordon in her list of people she considered insane, but she made certain reservations, adding, "Caroline has something, a quality that redeems her somehow, hard to explain, but with a depth of feeling that appeals to one, no matter how evilly she does."[5]

The flare-up turned out well for Porter, because the new home Allen Tate found for her was highly satisfactory. The Tates had a long-standing friendship with a Tennessee novelist, Anne Goodwin Winslow, and had often visited her plantation home near Memphis. There they had met her daughter-in-law, a young artist named Marcella Comès Winslow. Marcella's husband had recently died in the war and she had settled with her two children in Georgetown, a charming old neighborhood close to the center of Washington. She had worked on portraits of both the Tates and was planning to work on Porter's. When Allen Tate asked her if she would take Porter as a house guest, she was delighted. Not only would Porter's $60 a month help with the rent, she was eager to know better someone her mother-in-law admired more than any other living writer.

For her part, Porter immediately liked the attractive house on the shady brick sidewalk of P Street. It was a narrow, three-story place, with a tiny kitchen, a bright sitting room overlooking the street, and a narrow dining room with a long refectory table. A curving staircase rose to the second floor, where there were two bedrooms and an old-fashioned bathroom with a claw-foot tub. On the third floor were two extra bedrooms, one of which was assigned to Porter. Behind the house was a garden with statuary and flowering trees and shrubs, pleasant for resting and entertaining, especially later in the summer when pale pink roses drifted over the high walls.

Porter was delighted with both the house and the family. She took great interest in the Winslow genealogy, which included Anne Hutchinson, and she never tired hearing of the "big ancestor" whose sword hung in the dining room and who had been commander of the *Kearsarge,* which in the Civil War had sunk the Confederate vessel *Alabama.* In this Catholic household Porter quickly returned to Catholicism. She sent for her rosary and heavy crucifix, and when she poured out her life story to Marcella she spoke so feelingly of her Catholic childhood and convent education—and so disparagingly of converts to the faith—that Marcella never dreamed she was not a "cradle Catholic."[6]

There was no one to share the limelight here, and Porter regaled the family with her stories and became a great favorite, especially with Marcella's children, Mary and John. Marcella was tolerant of Porter's way of life, let her take over the kitchen and never resented the overflowing ashtrays and the ashes that Porter scattered over the house as she chain smoked.

Marcella also began work on a large portrait in oils, and Porter was very cooperative. She went with Marcella to choose a gown for the sittings, and selected a gray dress which accentuated her big eyes and complemented the gray-and-rose color scheme that Marcella planned. Porter herself chose the attitude in which she would pose. One day Marcella imitated Porter's manner of arranging herself, somewhat histrionically with her arms over the back of a chair. Porter was not amused. She might mock herself but never allowed others to hold her up to ridicule, even if it were gently done and kindly meant.

The Comès portrait remains one of the best records of Porter in the middle of her life. She looks younger than fifty-four, but not youthful. At the height of her mature beauty, she has beautifully arranged silver hair, long, tapering fingers, and what Allen Tate described as "her weak chin and noble brow."[7] Above all, the portrait captures Porter's air of infinite sadness.

Besides her work on the portrait, Marcella was so fascinated by her subject that she made a vivid record, in letters to her mother-in-law, of Porter's day-by-day activities.

When Porter came to Washington she had reached an impasse in literary and financial matters. She had decided at last that she must find some more dependable means of supporting herself than by writing. The Library of Congress position provided a steady income, the social life of Washington provided a great deal of excitement, and Porter, enjoying both, did very little writing during the entire year.

When her typewriter broke she sent it to the repair shop and did not retrieve it until the end of the summer. Meanwhile she tried halfheartedly to write by hand.

Marcella described how she spent her time:

> I don't find Katherine Anne a Prima Donna. She wears remarkably well so far and is most considerate in every way. She is too popular for her rather frail person, tho, as the slightest extra exertion knocks her out. She runs high fevers for nothing at all and literally seems to be a too high tension person. You have the feeling the fuse will blow. How she manages to keep her feet so firmly on the earth with all the attention, adulation and emotional strain of her tempestuous life I can't imagine, except that she has a tremendous interest in *everything*. I have hardly hit upon a subject that she doesn't know something about, usually a great deal, from old Colonial silver to astrology. She could run for political office as easily as she could get a chef's job at the Ritz.[8]

Marcella had good reason to mention her guest's cooking, because Porter was reveling in having a kitchen and someone to cook for. She made elaborate meals—onion quiche, chicken in garlic with Worcester sauce to be eaten with sour cream and biscuits, chicken-liver pâté, and a festive Easter dinner of stuffed capon. She also taught Marcella how to bake her own special kind of bread.

For all the pleasure, Porter generated a certain amount of tension in the house. She was very casual about appointments, and Marcella felt responsible when she knew that Porter had to catch a train to an important speaking engagement in New York but was unconcernedly trimming a hat or polishing her Mexican silver jewelry. Usually she would take over, help Porter to bustle her things together, drive her to the station, and get her onto the train breathlessly with minutes to spare. Porter was frequently ill and would then (and sometimes when she simply did not feel like going to work) call the library and say she was ill. When she did go to work she caught her bus to the Library of Congress at the corner of P Street and Wisconsin Avenue. The disadvantage of this arrangement was that the bus stop was in front of an antique shop run for the benefit of the Christ Child Society. The beautiful antiques donated by wealthy Catholics constantly tempted Porter to make purchases far beyond her means. Marcella was astonished when she brought home sets of dishes and glasses which had caught her fancy.

Marcella received an important commission for a painting and, having to leave town for the sittings, asked her mother, Honora, to come and look after the children. A crisis loomed when eleven-year-old Mary Winslow developed mumps. A doctor was called in, and Porter, who was sleeping badly, seized the opportunity to consult him. He prescribed sleeping pills and told her to take one when she went to bed and another if she woke during the night. Porter did wake during the night, not once but several times, and each time she took a pill. By morning she had taken an overdose and could not be roused. Honora feared for her life.

When she recovered Porter explained that she had not attempted suicide. She had taken her prescribed dose and felt so deliciously, dreamily relaxed that she reached out for more and more pills until she was dangerously drugged. Complete recovery took some time, and Honora Comès had the task of climbing up and down two flights of stairs to minister to two invalids.[9]

Ever afterward Porter treasured memories of the time she "caught mumps from Marcella's children," and she reminded Mary Winslow at every meeting of their special bond of having had mumps together.[10]

The incident had another interesting transformation. When Anne Goodwin Winslow's novel Cloudy Trophies was published in 1946, the climax to the novel was the death of the heroine, Laura, caused by an overdose of sleeping pills. Critics were troubled by the ambiguity of the event, which was apparently accidental rather than deliberate suicide. Critics saw the vagueness of motive for the overdose as a weakness of the novel.[11] Once again Porter's eccentric activities had provided the substance not only for her own fiction but for that of her friends.

When winter gave way to spring, Porter felt so much better that she decided to give a party to celebrate her recovery, her new sense of well-being, and what she called her fiftieth birthday. She had a large and distinguished circle of friends in Washington and it pleased her to play the role of Washington hostess. She drew up a guest list of thirty, which, besides the Tates, the Cheneys, some Mexican friends, and Marcella's family, included Archibald MacLeish and his wife, Alexis Léger (who published his poetry under the pen name of St. John Perse), Dennis Devlin, a poet and also the secretary to the Irish Legation to Washington, Attorney General and Mrs. Francis Biddle, the Minister to Finland, Major General and Mrs. Lucius Clay, and several senators. There were also a number of young soldiers from nearby Fort Belvoir.

Porter spent the extravagant sum of $50 on the party and hired a man to arrange everything. She served capon, salad, cake, and good liquor, and her only disappointment was that the bought birthday cake did not quite meet her culinary standards. Everything else was perfect. Allen Tate, who was supposed to be on the wagon, had seven mint juleps and got "quite lit."[12]

A special source of pride was that her niece's ballet company was in Washington, and Porter sent a taxi after the performance to bring Anna Gay to the party. At the end of the evening Ann saw her aunt bidding an affectionate good night to one of the young soldiers and with a now experienced eye suspected that Porter was on the brink of another love affair.[13] Her perception was correct; one reason for Porter's renewed vigor and high spirits was her interest in a young Alabama-born soldier, just back from battles in the South Pacific and stationed at Fort Belvoir.

Charles Shannon and Porter had been introduced by a friend at an art gallery which Caresse Crosby had opened in Washington as her "contribution to the war effort." Shannon, a painter, discussed the exhibition with Porter and they went together to the friend's for drinks afterward. Subsequently he invited Porter to dinner about once a week and she reciprocated by cooking splendid feasts for him at Marcella's house.

The friendship went along slowly for some two months, until Marcella packed up the children and went to spend the summer at Rehoboth Beach, on the Delaware coast. Porter kept the Georgetown house and defrayed the expense by inviting old friends from her Mexican days, Mary Doherty and her sister, to rent the family bedrooms on the second floor. In early July, after he had taken her out to dinner, Shannon asked if he might spend the night instead of returning to camp, and he stayed in the room next to Porter's on the third floor. The next morning they breakfasted together in the garden. It was the beginning of their love affair and the occasion took on a brilliant and romantic aura that she long cherished. A year later she wrote:

> I got up early, had breakfast with coffee, fruit, hot rolls and honey, milk in the tall silver goblet. It was the same breakfast I had with Charles in the garden in Georgetown. . . .

That was the day of the purest happiness I had ever known. He was purely serenely happy too. We gave each other life and joy. It was the last day of our innocence of each other, the beginning of a most terrible end. He loved the cool light on the honey dew melon, the dew on the silver, the honey with the light shining through it, my pale blue gown; I saw how his skin and eyes and hair were all in the tones of the day and the objects catching the morning light. He talked about a painting he would make that would have everything in it that was in that moment with us. I think he will never do that painting.

We went to the National Gallery, and saw Gaddi's Coronation of the Virgin. Saw all the pictures we loved together. . . . At five o'clock we went back to my house in Georgetown and I made a dinner, a beautiful one. Then we talked until midnight, when his pass was up, and when we parted, suddenly with the most infinite tenderness I have ever known in my life, he put his arms around me, gently, gently, and I embraced him around the neck and we touched our faces together for just a moment.[14]

The next weekend, when he stayed overnight, they slept together and the affair was triumphantly under way. When Porter was not in the throes of one of her great passions she could mock (but not regret) her own tendencies and once described them with impressive perspicacity to her nephew:

an Object irrevocably becomes a Subject—in my case, of course, male—which is instantly transfigured with a light of such blinding brilliance all natural attributes disappear and are replaced by those usually associated with archangels at least. They are beautiful, flawless in temperament, witty, intelligent, charming, of such infinite grace, sympathy, and courage, I always wondered how they could have come from such absurdly inappropriate families. . . .

It is no good going into details, for while it lasts there simply aren't any. And when it is over, it is over. And when I have recovered from the shock, and sorted out the damage and put my mangled life in order, I can then begin to remember what really happened. It is probably the silliest kind of love there is, but I am glad I had it. I'm glad there were times when I saw human beings at their best, for I don't think by any means I lent them all their radiance . . . it was there ready to be brought out by someone who loved them.[15]

The description is an exact rendering of her relationship with Charles Shannon. Like someone in a trance of religious ecstasy she transformed him into a godlike being. With sacramental reverence she cherished every detail of their life together. She set up sacred rites and a calendar of anniversaries to be ritualistically observed. The third and fifteenth of every month were to be kept as the time of their first meeting and their first night together. She noted the occasion of receiving her first gardenia from him, a bouquet of white roses, a gift of sea shells from the Pacific.[16]

All other activity was suspended in the great waves of passion that carried her along and were increased by the tantalizing intervals between meetings, by the dramatic last-minute departures and sudden unexpected leaves of wartime. Between meetings, letters, telegrams, flowers, and gifts flew between Washington and Fort Belvoir. For Porter, at least, the love affair was a full-time and totally absorbing occupation.

The Doherty sisters took a very jaundiced attitude to the amorous activity in the house. Since they were paying half the rent, it did not seem right that another guest should make no contribution to the costs, and they were dismayed that their ration books were feeding an extra person. Porter sensed a certain moral disapproval too, and it may account for her later description of Mary Doherty as "one of those Irish girls born with an ingrained fear of sex."[17]

At the time, Porter was impervious to anyone's disapproval as she gloried rapturously in Shannon's physical charms and youthful energy. He was exactly her ideal of masculine beauty and her description of him coincides, as her description of Albert Erskine did eight years before, with the description of Adam in "Pale Horse, Pale Rider." She wrote of Shannon:

> I saw him first in his golden glory. . . . I did love his beauty
> and goldness and savoury sweet-smelling firm body with its
> light down of golden fur like an infant lion. . . . His health
> and hardness and sweetness and his endless pleasure in me
> and my presence and all we did and had and knew together.[18]

Clearly no mere mortal could have lived up to her idealistic image of him and the affair could not have been sustained indefinitely. It was, however, external circumstances which interrupted the idyll.

One day at the end of July, Marcella returned from the beach for a dentist's appointment and witnessed the full impact of the blow upon Porter, whom she found in an old bathrobe, with no make-up, tearful, crushed, swollen-eyed, and smoking even more than usual. Charles was about to be transferred to New York, but, worse than that, he had told her that he was married and that his wife intended to come up from Alabama to join him. Not only was Porter panic-stricken at the idea of losing him, she was shocked at knowing that she had done something as tawdry as having "an affair with a married man," a thing she told Marcella she had never done and never dreamed of or believed herself capable of. As Marcella was trying to console Porter, they both noticed an elegant couple in evening dress coming along the sidewalk. When they approached the house, Porter recognized them as friends she had invited to dinner. They had been invited and let down once before and were now expecting to be recompensed with one of their hostess's celebrated gourmet dinners. Porter was panic-stricken and begged Marcella to head them off, take them to dinner anywhere, but get them out of the house. It was, in fact, too late to do anything. They had to be admitted and they stayed only a short time after sizing up the situation.[19] Once again Marcella wondered how her frail house guest survived the high-tension existence she led, and once again Porter found her life spinning out of control.

Although the first heady weeks of the affair were not recaptured, the relationship did not end with Shannon's revelation. Before he left for New York he went AWOL to spend extra time with her and managed to slip back into Fort Belvoir without being discovered. Now it was the threat of separation which gave intensity to the meetings. After he was transferred Porter joined him in New York on weekends; they were both determined to spend as much of their limited time together as possible. The weekends continued until Porter left Washington for good in early September. For the next two weeks she lived with Charles at the New Weston Hotel, on Madison Avenue, and she described this period, from her arrival until her departure, as a time of the most perfect happiness and joy.[20]

She was joyful too at the publication of *The Leaning Tower and Other Stories,* and Shannon shared with her all the activity that surrounds the launching of a successful book. The publication party was on September 14, and that day a great hurricane flooded the streets and made them impassable. Nothing could have delighted Porter more and appealed to her sense of drama and adventure. She wrote cheerfully that the hurricane began at the hour of the party and that everyone slogged through the wet. After the party there were no taxis and she and Charles had to return on foot to their hotel. She thought it was wonderful walking with Charles through flood and wind for five blocks.[21]

For the occasion Charles gave her white roses, as he always did when he could not find her favorite gardenias. George Platt Lynes gave her an alabaster model of the Leaning Tower of Pisa, and another guest gave her a copy of Virginia Woolf's essays containing the essay "The Leaning Tower." Always sensitive to the idea that she might have borrowed from another writer, Porter said later that this was her first acquaintance with Woolf's essay. In fact, she had recommended it to her nephew in August 1941, soon after it appeared.[22]

She enjoyed the reviews of the book, preferring Glenway Wescott's in the *New York Times Book Review* and Robert Penn Warren's in a Chicago paper. She also liked the review by Edmund Wilson in the *New Yorker,* in which he made his often quoted remark about not being able to take hold of her work in any of the usual ways. She wrote to Monroe Wheeler, "I think Edmund did me proud too, even if he seemed as he said a touch baffled. Our dear Edmund baffles easy where ladies-in-the-arts are concerned; I'm sure he has a feeling that dogs should *not* walk on their hind legs, however expertly, bless him."[23]

The book was successful in other ways too. In two weeks 20,000 copies were sold and Donald Brace had asked for a selection from her three books to be printed in paperback for distribution to the troops overseas. One hundred thousand were to be printed in this special wartime edition, and more if the book went well. She was delighted by the idea even though she stood to gain only one percent royalty per book, a total of $500. Out of the income of this time she paid Monroe Wheeler $300 of the $400 he had lent her seven years before, when she left Pressly and moved to Louisiana.

In spite of the celebrations, the congratulations, the good reviews, and the financial successes, the book was in some ways a disappointment. It was a collection which the publishers had scraped together, in the absence of all the promised works, because nothing had been written for years. Many of the stories in the "Old Order" sequence had been written during the Paris years. "A Day's Work" was written in 1937 and "A Downward Path to Wisdom" was sent to Glenway Wescott in 1939, with apologies for the use of one of his childhood memories. The hoped for "Season of Fear" was not finished and not included. "The Leaning Tower," the strongest story, had been finished in 1940. Porter must have known that the book implied four years of literary silence. True, her translation of *The Itching Parrot,* by José Joaquim Fernandez de Lizardi, had been published by Doubleday in 1942, but it had been finished long before. Moreover, as with her other "translations," she had not so much translated as rewritten a translation. It was Eugene Pressly who had actually translated the book from Spanish into English. Perhaps Porter did not care at this time about her long literary silence, for even more than literary success she now wanted marriage to Charles Shannon. Even as *The Leaning Tower* appeared, the Shannon affair was bitterly running out.

After the publication party, Porter returned to Yaddo and Shannon joined her there for a weekend in early October, staying in the Pine Tree Studio. Unlike the New York meetings, this was not a time of perfect happiness; their hours together were soured by the knowledge of imminent separation. They spoke of his marriage and their situation and a violent and very sudden quarrel blew up, surprising them both by its bitterness and leaving them exhausted and very unhappy. They were both tired and under great strain. Subsequent meetings when Porter went to New York were also strained and filled with quarrels about his unwillingness to divorce and about whether Porter would see him again.[24] The nature of these quarrels is suggested in a marginal note in De Beauvoir's *The Second Sex* beside a passage on marital fidelity: "Poor Ch— and a hundred others I have known!" she wrote. "And some of them would even add 'My experiences will really make me a better husband.' "[25]

Immersed as she still was in the love affair, she found time for some political activity in this election year of 1944. She was working hard for the reelection of Franklin Roosevelt, who was running for his fourth term as President against Thomas Dewey, former governor of New York. By way of justifying her "political existence," as she expressed it to Wheeler, she was to make her debut as a political speaker at a rally at Skidmore College, in nearby Saratoga Springs, on November 1. By making her maiden speech "in this hotbed of Deweyites and Nazi bundsmen" she hoped to do lasting damage to Mr. Dewey and the Republican party.[26]

She studiously avoided mentioning Charles Shannon in her letters to Herbst, but it was probably her anguish about him rather than her political work that undermined her health. On November 9, after her candidate was reelected, she went into the Saratoga hospital and stayed there for two weeks. Charles sent white roses once again and came up for a weekend. There was, however, no way out of their situation. Charles's wife was coming to New York in early December, and Porter went down to the city for a farewell weekend just before she was to arrive.

Their last weekend was incredibly painful. They exchanged gifts. He gave her flowers and a rich leather cigarette case; she gave him a record they had listened to together. They spent their last night together as lovers in the Commodore Hotel. On Monday morning at eight they said good-bye, kissing for the last time as lovers, but his face was so terrible that she called him in the middle of the morning and asked him to come back and have dinner with her. After that, they said good-bye again, more calmly, had a drink to each other's health, and parted at midnight. She noted tersely in her diary for Tuesday, December 5, "She came."

Porter left for a few days with Glenway Wescott and Monroe Wheeler at Stoneblossom, their home in New Jersey, and when she returned to the city on the twelfth she called Charles, who begged to see her. It seemed impossible to sever the relationship completely. They had lunch together and once again they kissed good-bye. When she left for Yaddo in the afternoon, all communication between them finally ceased.

Nine days later, on the shortest day of the year, the winter solstice, Porter had a great *crise de nerfs* and at two in the morning, in a fog of drunkenness and nightmare, she burned all of Charles's letters to her, wishing she could burn everything down to the ground. She had asked Charles to return all her letters to him, and these she burned later, along with a lot of other rubbish, on a day of beautiful winter light. This time she was more serene and said she had no regrets at all.[27]

The ceremonial burning of the letters and tokens they had exchanged was somehow in keeping with the ritualistic, religious tenor of the whole affair.

On January 2, 1945, Porter had tickets for an anti-Franco rally in New York. She took Donald Elder, an editor with Harcourt, Brace, the novelist Jimmie Stern, and Stern's wife, Tania. Charles and his wife were there:

But it was the sight of his wife: the narrow wedding ring on her finger, her sad, forlorn air of frayed pride, his strange conciliatory manner to her, her silence, her face averted from him, a little ordinary girl, thin, rather pretty, but with such a neglected unloved look. . . . I could not face it. I was in a fury with him and with myself. . . . I can't express how she looked to me—like some damageable object that had been left by carelessness out in the rain. . . . I was his accomplice in this criminal negligence. [28]

But this was as harsh as she could ever be about Shannon. She often spoke abusively about former husbands and lovers. John Koontz was "that filthy J.H.," Albert Erskine "that monster," Francisco Aguilera "a silly fraud," Matthew Josephson "a congenital liar." Possibly her relationship with Shannon was too brief to justify revulsion. Perhaps too it was idealized because it took place in the heady atmosphere of "the capital of the free world" in wartime. For a southerner raised on battles long ago, soldiers and military situations had a special attraction. Charles was her Second World War lover as Adam/Alexander was her First World War lover. For more than one reason, then, Charles became established in her imagination as the one man who really, truly loved her. "Entirely too many men have said they loved me," she told her sister, "but this one did." [29] And a year later, when she wrote Wheeler asking for news of Shannon, she still spoke of him as if he were a god who had descended from Olympus to spend a brief spell among the mortals:

A special note to ask something that somehow I was never able to work into a typical letter. I think it is perhaps a weakness, that I am going to ask, but Lord, did I ever promise to be a woman of iron forever?

Do you ever see or hear of Charles, or do you know where he is or what he is doing or what his life is like in the least?

We have not exchanged a line since I left, and though a good many who knew him do write me, not a soul has ever mentioned his name, though they mention freely everybody else. It is as if he were dead or had never been born, or at least had never come among us. [30]

She wrote in her private diary:

Today I do not even know where he is. No one of all the friends we have in common who write me have even mentioned his name. But I kept this anniversary, not meaning, not trying, but that day has lived again in this one, there is even the same brilliant blue sunny weather. And for all I remember the end, and why it came about, and what it meant and all the frightful suffering, still this day one year ago we had pure love and happiness; it was true, and has the right to its own life. And I have a kind of mystical joy, for it was something I believed in, can still believe.

And my life, after its enormous fret and fever and confusion and all the burden and waste and disappointment, has come to this quiet cool clear place, where I am free to remember without rancor or bitterness. I regret my last letter to him. I would ask him to forgive me, but I do not know him well enough now. I would not dare.

I have taken a long sunbath naked in the patio, have washed my hair and bathed and dressed almost ceremonially as if for a feast. Now I shall work on my book, and tonight I shall sleep as I did last night, and as I did not on all these nights last year, with him so near me. I shall put this away with the curious little record of that wonderful deep folly which almost ruined us both, and which I would do again in spite of the end, and I know well that he would too.[31]

She had burned most of his letters and love tokens in the night of wild panic at Yaddo. The tokens that remained—his photograph, an army I.D. card, some cards that had been attached to the bouquets he sent, and her day-by-day account of their time together—she placed in a box that she kept all her life. She wrote in her diary: "I have opened this little box many times this year, but I shall put it away and not open it ever again."

If Wheeler failed to mention the times when he ran into Shannon, it was probably because he thought Porter had already forgotten the affair and because he considered Shannon rather insignificant. Most of Porter's friends felt about him as they did about Pressly, that he was a pale shadow beside her. Mary Doherty remembered him as a "sweet kid." Marcella Winslow had little contact with him but formed a negative opinion when she returned home to find the room he had occupied filled with corked-up bottles of urine. He had not troubled to walk down the one flight of stairs to the bathroom and had left to his hostess the task of disposing of the bottles.[32]

Porter, however, never changed her devoted opinion of him, and when they met years later she was moved by the change in his appearance and the loss of his youthful good looks:

> . . . somewhere on the Gulf Coast probably the first two weeks in August so Charles can do my portrait—to hang on the walls of my library in Austin. Oh God what an end! I never dreamed of it. His wife is most beautiful and we like each other.
>
> I saw him in his golden glory, and he had not changed when I saw him again for the first time after we parted— five years. But that was ten years ago, and that fatal ten years between 35 and 45 is neither youth nor age, the beauty of youth declined and the beauty of age not yet arrived. But I can't tell you how sad it made me, I who never bewept my own youth, I never really knew I had any, nor what it might have been and escaped from it as if from some sort of trap or cheat.
>
> By now both of us know very well what we had, and that it happens once in a long life time if one is very lucky, to most of the human race it never happens at all because they have not been able to imagine love.[33]

Around the same time she told her niece, "I thought then and still do think that if my man was anywhere to be found, he was the one. But, alas alack, another woman had seen him first, and in the end her claim was first with both of us."[34]

The whole affair left her in an altered state of mind which she tried to describe to Glenway Wescott. Just after it ended she wrote him that she had been in love as she never was before and had been loved as never before and that it had somehow loosened her hold on the material world. She had thought of selling her house to relieve herself of the responsibility, financial and otherwise, but the doctor who treated her in Saratoga had warned her against making decisions under stress and so she was trying to be patient and not do anything dramatic and drastic. Still,

> Ever since last winter I have felt like selling my house, giving away my little bits and pieces in which I did take some kind of pleasure; making my will and retiring to a whitewashed cell . . . and finishing up all my books. I too want only to work, and everything else is vanity, vanity. . . .

This too, when for a good while now—it is a split second or a lifetime—I have been in love as I was never and have been loved as I was never, and don't be deceived if anyone tells you that gives you a firm hold on the world of flesh. It does not. It loosens that bond amazingly. It can't end happily, but we knew that. Happiness or unhappiness was not the point.[35]

Her good resolutions were approved by Wescott, who thought the best thing in the world for her would be to relinquish her hold on worldly possessions, go into seclusion, and write. While she was preparing to do this, however, something happened which changed all her plans. Out of a clear sky dropped an offer for her to go to Hollywood as a script writer. The temptation of what—the money? the adventure? the possibility of removing herself from scenes of pain and disappointment?—were too great, and she accepted the offer. She felt that all her problems were solved at one stroke, and she was ready to leave for California by the end of the first week of January 1945.

She stayed in New York the night before she set out for the West Coast. The next day, fifteen minutes before leaving the New Weston to catch her train, she tossed a coin, and when it fell heads she called Charles Shannon and said she could not leave without saying good-bye once more. After a long pause he said, "in a voice of the most terrible coldness and hardness," ". . . Well—good-bye, and good luck." "Good-bye and good luck to you," she said, and hung up.[36]

Monroe Wheeler saw her off at the station and worried afterward because she wept so uncontrollably.[37]

EIGHTEEN

California: "A Perpetual Homesickness for Just Anywhere Else on Earth"

Predictably, when Porter arrived in California in January, she was sick with flu. This time, however, she recovered swiftly and began to enjoy the advantages of the place. First among these was the climate, which suited her perfectly. She responded immediately to the blooming color, the fresh air and sunlight, which were a welcome change from the somber winter she had left behind. She told Josie Herbst in one of her letters from California:

> There's a lovely half-moon tonight, and you should see the light on the almond trees in full bloom. The lemons are budding and the mourning doves are back. Everything that grows here or flies here is something I was used to in Texas and Louisiana and it is just true I have never seen anything I liked better or could live with more comfortably.[1]

She also had the advantage of good medical care, reporting that she had found a doctor who was celebrated for "galvanizing mere corpses." She was put on a regular diet of calcium and vitamins to balance her body chemistry and raise her blood pressure. She said that she now understood why people all around her were "hopping about like grasshoppers" and she hoped to reach that stage herself.[2]

The most dramatic improvement was in her financial status. After all the lean and hungry years of scrimping she now found herself commanding the enormous salary of $1,500 a week. From this she paid roughly $334 in income tax, $200 in additional tax, and $150 to her agent. This left about $800 for herself, of which she put $500 in her Saratoga Springs bank account and reserved $300 for living expenses. She was able now to settle the accumulated debts of the past few years, arrange to have her household effects shipped from Saratoga, live meantime in a pleasant room at the Beverly Hills Hotel, spend $6 a day for taxis, and still have something left over at the end of the week for a few luxury items. These included clothes, naturally, and perfume at $60 an ounce.[3]

Her new wealth also allowed her one of her greatest pleasures, that of dispensing largesse to members of her family who showed promise in the arts. She invited her niece Ann, now divorced, to join her in Hollywood. Ann did so immediately, and at the end of February the two left the Beverly Hills Hotel to set up housekeeping in a small rented house. Porter paid all Ann's expenses, including her ballet lessons, and gave her a generous allowance. She also bought a car, "Ole Honey," which Ann undertook to drive because her aunt's driving was extremely erratic.[4]

Much as she relished her new material security, Porter was quick to note the disadvantages of her situation. She badly missed the "good lively, literary company" of New York and Washington.[5] Many of her letters from California contained accounts of boring parties and people she did not enjoy. She spent an "appalling" evening with Theodore Dreiser, who kept saying "What's the matter with everybody? Can't anybody start some topic we can discuss. Cat got your tongue?" But if anyone did suggest something, he would say, "What a topic!"[6] At Clifford Odets' she met Charlie Chaplin "with his latest child bride." She thought him "an odious little beast, but amiable as hell."[7] Among the people she did enjoy were Greer Garson, "a pretty harmonious-looking creature";[8] Harpo Marx, "sweet and saintly-looking with a wild hazel eye like a startled gazelle";[9] and Judy Garland, who told Porter shyly as a child that she had been a fan of hers "since way back." Porter replied that she was a fan of Judy Garland.[10]

She found the family life of the film people very middle-class and dull:

This whole territory is simply crawling with babies. The most philoprogenitive place I ever saw . . . no matter where you go fond parents trot out a basket of young and everybody takes turns about holding the baby on one side and a

cocktail on the other. . . . This runs along side by side with
the most neo-Victorian domesticity. Celebrated glamour
girls will talk all evening about their infants, their beautiful
false eyelashes quivering with cosy emotions. . . .[11]

On the whole, she found the people involved in the motion-
picture industry to be "vulgar poor-spirited folk" with lots of money.
She said if they had antiques they were purchased without discrimination from dealers who imported them. If they had jewels, they were
"at least as big as your hand."[12] Porter had still wanted to own an
emerald, but she said the sight of the huge, showy jewels of the film
stars had cured her forever of that particular desire.

In the end, it was her work at M-G-M on the screenplay of *Young
Bess,* based on Margaret Irwin's novel about Queen Elizabeth, which
soured her on Hollywood. She said the dialogue was full of "God's
teeth and whiskers" and "wotteths" and "marry-come-ups." Although she had asked the director, Sidney Franklin, to leave the dialogue to her, he refused to do so. She was cleaning it up as best she
could and trying to get into his head that when Elizabeth was not
writing and talking like a Shakespearean queen, her tone and sentences
were as plain and homely as a present-day Kentucky woman's. Exactly the same, in fact, for once she wrote, "I had rather spend the
money on my own folk."[13] Porter would hear herself saying, "For
God's sake, human beings don't talk like that," and Franklin would
turn an alarming scarlet and look as if he were going to have apo-
plexy. Porter disliked him and thought his pictures simply horrible,
"sickeningly fuzzy and sentimental."[14]

Furthermore, the censorship infuriated her. She reached the point
where she felt it was not the corrupt politicians or even the black
marketeers with Fascist tendencies who were running the country but
the women's clubs and the Catholic Church. She said they really did
run things in Hollywood and had a twenty-four-hour patrol on the
job.[15]

She worked thirteen weeks of her three-year contract but even at
the fabulous salary could not bear the work and asked to be released.
After about six weeks she "began gnawing away at her bonds like a
fox with his leg in a trap," and by the thirteenth week she had persuaded Franklin that she was not the woman he needed.[16] Although
he had initially been horrified at her high salary, he then began to
worry about her future. She told him that she was relatively rich and

she was not leaving California, and they parted politely with hand-shakes all round.

Thus ended her first stint as a Hollywood script writer. Her agent, not happy at losing his fee, was eager to have her working again and did, in fact, tempt her back into the industry for a few months in late 1945 and early 1946. This time, for a salary of $2,000 a week, she went to work for Charles Brackett of Paramount (the only producer she respected) on a movie about Madame Sans Gêne, based on a screenplay by Billy Wilder.[17] Although she lived in California more than four years, her actual time as a script writer was less than one, and her work benefited very little from the experience. Nor did she really profit financially, since she spent much of her salary as she went along and spent the rest of it and most of her savings on land speculation. Thinking that she might eventually like to build a house, she bought a beautiful well-watered plot of land on top of a small mountain in San Bernardino County.[18] The house, however, never materialized and the land was sold at a loss.

One of the reasons for her eagerness to quit so soon the only highly paid position she ever held was that she had decided to change her way of life, withdraw from the social scene, and get back to her own writing. This decision was related to the world situation.

For the past year Porter through her family and friends had been closely touched by the war. In Washington she had witnessed the effect on the Winslow household of the death of Marcella's husband and had heard from Charles Shannon about his experiences in the South Pacific, and she was getting regular letters from her nephew, who was in the Field Artillery in the European theater. She also heard from her old friend Erna about her son's military service—Glover Johns, whom Porter had last seen as a baby in Corpus Christi, was a lieutenant colonel in the Allied force that landed at Omaha Beach, in Normandy, on D-Day, June 6, 1944. In addition to these personal involvements, Porter was carefully following the news reports, and she saw the horrifying pictures that sent shock waves around the world when the German concentration camps were liberated in early 1945.

Her reaction was very similar to her response to the outbreak of the war in Europe five years earlier. Then she had turned to her Berlin material and seen it as particularly relevant and important. Now she felt the same way about her account of the journey to Europe in 1931 on the German S.S. *Werra*. She had begun this story as "Promised

Land" and renamed it "No Safe Harbor." She felt at last that she was ready to finish it, and she wanted to retitle it "Ship of Fools."[19]

Her motivation was similar to that which impelled Glenway Wescott to write, as his "contribution to the war effort," *Apartment in Athens,*[20] a novel showing the effects on a Greek family of having a German officer billeted in their home. Porter reviewed the book for the *New York Herald Tribune* on March 4, 1945. Her review, which carried the subhead "A Greek Family Learns the True Nature of Evil and Courage," shows her approval of Wescott's purpose:

> It is a story of the shapeless, immoderate miseries and con-fusions brought by the Germans upon this world for the third time within the memory of living men: it is even "propaganda" against this Germanic savagery, if you like, and if you would call Goya's "Disasters of War" by such a name. Mr. Wescott is said to have remarked that he wrote the book "to show how bad the Germans are"—but he has gone much farther than that. Surely nobody need tell us at this time of day how bad the Germans are: they themselves first told us years ago; and then for years they have demon-strated their meaning precisely. Mr. Wescott has done some-thing much more valuable than that: he has exposed and anatomized that streak of Germanism in the rest of us which made possible the Germany we know today. . . .
>
> They became slaves in their own apartment to a pomp-ous minor god with nasty personal habits and an epileptic instability of temper, the range of whose virtuosity in mean cruelties is endless. Helianos, still "trying to understand the Germans in general by this officer" and comparing notes with his Greek fellow sufferers, begins to grasp little by little that there was nothing unpremeditated in German behavior anywhere. . . . They practiced tortures with various tricks that were like surgery gone wrong, with little up-to-date-mechanical contraptions.[21]

The opinions expressed in this review informed many of the letters she was writing to Josephine Herbst during the spring of 1945. She forgot her sympathetic reactions to the Berliners she had met in 1931 and to the gentle people of the Black Forest region when she and Gene had explored it in 1932. Now she wrote that she had seen Hitler to be "a great national hero and the exact mirror of the popular mind." She wrote angrily that the Germans were "horrible people" and that if there were a few good ones they had no effect on the population as a whole. Her rhetoric as she spoke of the *"sales Boches"* and their "blood-drinking" was that of the anti-German tirades of the First World War, which she had described in "Pale Horse, Pale Rider." In one letter she wrote:

> The Germans have *marched first* in every instance for the past three European wars. If they try to tell me they are duped into making war by other powers I say then let them be punished for their stupidity. I cannot pretend to objectivity: this is my country, my people have been here since the beginning, almost, and I resent from the bottom of my soul that twice in one generation we have sent our men to Europe on account of those god-damned Boches. When I heard that Berlin was being reduced to rubble, I rejoiced. Maybe now they will know a little of what France has suffered, maybe now they will have some gleam in their poor swine-heads what Warsaw and Leningrad went through. They have never had their fields ruined, their houses destroyed. Now they know, and high time, too. . . .
>
> In the meantime, already here their slimy talk about how we mustn't hurt the poor dear wronged Germans is starting up again. The Germans have never been wronged and they have been the curse of the human race long enough. This time I hope they really pay for their periodic binge of blood-drinking. And I hope after this war that all the fake refugees and German sympathizers will be sent out of this country. They poison the air for the rest of us.[22]

Herbst was shocked at the tone and content of Porter's letters and replied to them very carefully, saying that at least Porter was not indifferent, and indifference was the one attitude she could not endure. Nevertheless, she rejected Porter's statements, explaining that she saw no point in national maledictions, since wholesale condemnation did no good after earlier wars and would do no good again. And anyway it seemed a peculiar inversion of the Nazi racial theory.

Porter, however, was less interested in reasons for the outbreak of the war and plans for the future of Europe than she was in condemnation of the Germans. Her recommendations for action were particularly vague. She thought, for example, that the Germans had to be taught a lesson and that "sooner or later those people have got either to belong to the human race or be extinguished."[23]

In May she changed the subject and wrote to Herbst of more personal matters. She mentioned a new pink gabardine dress and her happiness on her birthday, which had brought her "the mystical sense of renewal" that her birthdays always brought. The day had been divinely blue and sunny and, when she reviewed the past year, it seemed that many good things had happened, even though it had been one of the longest and most difficult of her life. She had celebrated with a small dinner party at the Beverly Hills Hotel, planned by Ann and three men they had recently met.[24] Ann and the men had surprised her with the party and with a cake with fifty-one candles, and Ann had given her a watch, the first she had ever owned.[25]

In spite of her horror at the dreadful revelations from Germany, Porter had reason to be cheerful and write to Herbst about the year 1945, "I began to get well as soon as the war ended."[26] Recent events had convinced her that her theme, held since 1919, was of supreme importance. She had stated it several times, in "Magic," "Theft," "Flowering Judas" and other stories. Now it needed to be stated again:

> My book is about the constant endless collusion between good and evil; I believe that human beings are capable of total evil, but no one has ever been totally good: and this gives the edge to evil. I don't offer any solution, I just want to show the principle at work and why none of us has any real alibi in this world.[27]

The propagandistic tone of her letters and reviews did not augur well for the book, but at least she had the impetus to return to work.

She described the book as a "one-draft" work, of which 240 pages had been done in a total writing time of six months, with not a page rewritten. She had worked for two months at Yaddo in 1940, two and a half months at a later time in the same place, and one and a quarter months at South Hill in 1943. Now the story had grown not only into a novel but into a long and ambitious one. One character after another was "screaming to be let in and do his stuff." They were "sprouting at all points like dragon seed" and her difficulty was to "keep my crowd from becoming a mob."[28]

She knew that if she was to get the job done she had to live quietly and keep her life under control. Accordingly, when Ann moved back East, Porter rented another house and lived alone, curtailing her social life and trying to make the outer world "as shadowy as possible." In July 1945 she described her new place as pleasant, "if California," with patios and big windows everywhere. There was a Stromberg-Carlson radio and record player and several thousand records, which made it sound as if a perpetual music festival were going on. In addition, she had her own record collection, piano, and virginal.[29] Such was her life for the next few years.

When she was not working on the novel or listening to music, she relaxed by writing about other people's books. Her friend Russell Lynes, now managing editor of *Harper's Magazine,* asked her for something he could print. She had always thought the magazine dull, but he had published fine pieces by E. M. Forster and V. S. Pritchett, both of whom she admired, and she was eager to fulfill his request.[30] She did so by finishing an essay she had begun years ago on Gertrude Stein. When it appeared in late 1947, "Gertrude Stein: A Self-Portrait" (subsequently titled "The Wooden Umbrella") was so hostile that it became something of a *cause célèbre,* and Porter was "accused of ignoble motives" in writing it.[31]

Porter's animosity to Gertrude Stein had, in fact, been growing decade by decade. Having discovered and enjoyed *Tender Buttons* as early as 1915 in Corpus Christi, she had long been an admirer. She wrote reviews of two of Stein's books in the twenties and, while one was "a parody-review," neither was severely critical. In the early thirties, Porter began her review of two of Kay Boyle's books by stating that Gertrude Stein and James Joyce were the glories of their time and that "many portentous talents had emerged from their shadows."[32]

This admiration had changed abruptly two years later, when Allen Tate and Caroline Gordon took her to visit Stein in the Rue de Fleurus: "Miss Stein and Miss Toklas both were perfectly friendly and courteous, no incident of any kind marked the visit; and my deep feeling of boredom and futility and sense of suffocation came from the atmosphere itself."[33]

The atmosphere might well have displeased her. If, as was her custom, Gertrude Stein conversed with the male visitor (she called him Tate; he called her "Miss Stein") while Alice B. Toklas entertained the women, Porter would have been offended. Moreover, she was suspicious of Lesbians and often spoke harshly of them.

The hostility she felt then was reinforced a decade later, when her nephew, Paul Porter, visited Stein. Stein described in a letter his shock at finding his aunt unknown to her:

> . . . one day a young gentleman called and he sent in a note saying that he was the nephew of Katherine Anne Porter. Then he came in and I said gently and politely, do I know your aunt, I am afraid said he you have never met, and said I politely who is she, and he went quite white and said you know and I said no, and then he decided to take it as a joke, but it was a blow, he had evidently travelled far on his nephewship.[34]

Since Porter was the author of three highly acclaimed volumes of short stories, had met Stein, and had reviewed two of her books, it seems most unlikely that Stein did not remember her and most likely that her description of Paul's visit was malicious. This being so, Porter felt no obligation to curb her own malicious wit. She not only expressed her reservations about Stein's work but wrote a vicious personal attack. She accused Stein of being egocentric, physically repulsive, and morally irresponsible. The portrait is a grotesque caricature, very similar to the picture of Braggioni in "Flowering Judas." Whereas Braggioni had been portrayed as piglike, Stein was depicted as a kind of voracious caterpillar. Porter called her nature "tepid" and "really sluggish, like something eating its way through a leaf,"[35] and she made her, like Braggioni, a compendium of the seven deadly sins. She described her intention to Herbst:

> I do find in the end that she was a kind of huge comedy figure, who, as I mention, practiced with increasing facility and advocated as virtues 5 or 6 of the seven deadly sins, of which avarice became her final favorite. It is a fact that after you read and think her over for a while, you realize that she was a total monster of just plain, pure selfishness, laziness, greed, acedia, avarice, envy and God knows what. She just ate her way through life like a big slug, and digested it all in wads, and called it genius.[36]

Some of Porter's friends, among them Eudora Welty,[37] approved the piece and sent congratulations. Josephine Herbst was among those who were dismayed, and this disagreement put an end at last to the wobbly friendship between Porter and Herbst. Herbst wrote that she liked everything of Porter's she had seen but she had to dissent on the Stein piece. Nevertheless, she ended her letter with assurances of "affection which would survive everything but the atom bomb."[38] Porter could probably have forgiven Herbst's disagreement, but she was annoyed some months later to see Herbst make the quarrel public in a cogent essay in *Partisan Review*. In her essay, which appeared in 1948 and which Porter called an "open letter," Herbst not only defended Stein but attacked Glenway Wescott, who had seemed quite indifferent to the world situation when she met him in 1936. She asked, "By what standard of responsibility is [Gertrude Stein] to be measured? By Silone or Malraux? By Bernard Shaw, H. G. Wells? Is Glenway Westcott's *Apartment in Athens,* which the author acknowledged was his 'contribution to the war effort,' to be the standard, and are we to accept its historical distortions?"[39]

Porter later described the effect of Herbst's essay on their friendship:

We had a long, perfectly good sound good-tempered sort of friendship, and for years; though she was a difficult clamoring sort of creature, she was not so with me but showed a delightful side of her nature, and we must have written tens of dozens of letters to each other during a very tempestuous period of both our lives and the world we lived in. She wrote an indignant open letter to the Partisan Review about my essay on Gertrude Stein, "The Wooden Umbrella," which I ignored; so she did not write to me, nor I to her, and our friendship did not so much perish as it was just abandoned by both of us; and that must be more than ten years, and we haven't exchanged a word since.[40]

Herbst had noted in her essay that Porter condemned Stein on moral grounds, as if she had contributed to the prevailing disorder of the world. This moral condemnation was a feature of much of Porter's literary criticism, for she incorporated into her reviews of other people's books the theme of her own fiction. She believed that a writer who tried to explain, understand, or present sympathetically a morally reprehensible character was in collusion with that character. When Robert Penn Warren's *All the King's Men* appeared, she said she was shocked by it. She called his treatment of Huey Long "a sentimental apology for the worst sort of Fascist demagogue, the most awful slack kind of fatalism." She added that the key was this: Once in a discussion when she had mentioned universal franchise, Warren had said flatly, "I don't believe in universal franchise."[41]

Porter still had a great deal of animosity toward her former husband Albert Erskine. All the same, the two kept up some contact, occasionally lunching together or exchanging letters. Erskine, now an editor in a New York publishing house, sometimes talked with her about books he was publishing. One of these was Malcolm Lowry's *Under the Volcano,* just the kind of book to excite her greatest ire. She wrote:

> There is nothing wrong with the idea, the cast of characters, the writing is consistently good, it has the makings of a masterpiece (Dostoevsky on one hand, Hardy on another, would have known how) but it is a corrupt deathly book and—you know this letter is *only* to you—the corruption is in the mind of the author, the confusion is his, and if I had seen this in ms. I would have advised you not to publish it, because it is an evil book, in a way no true work of art can ever be, because no real artist ever has such confusions. . . .
>
> I really believe that this book will get along because it is the very expression of the kind of debased feeling and thinking that appeals to the public more now than ever. In another way, *Brideshead Revisited* is an example. . . .
>
> Does our author think his physically, spiritually, morally intellectually gelded character really an *hombre noble?* No, Albert, there is a taint in this book I have smelt before and I never could really breathe it easily.[42]

She found many other books, among them some of the most distinguished works of her time, to be similarly tainted. These included novels by Christopher Isherwood, William Faulkner, "that wormy fake Koestler,"[43] and Saul Bellow, about whom she wrote:

> Bellow is an awful writer—all that pity, pity, pity me— ugh! I remember when an excerpt from one of his early novels was published in a literary review, I asked the editor why he took that terrible thing and he said he didn't like it either but it was the coming thing, and he was right. Pity and smut, like Mailer. He writes like a smutty little boy; I can't read him. As for Sartre and de Beauvoir, what a silly pair![44]

The same moral strictures applied even to her lovers. A few years before their friendship ended, Porter wrote to Josephine Herbst about Herbert Schaumann, a young man whom she had met in New York and who had come to visit her in Hollywood in the spring of 1946:

> Do you remember I told you in New York that H.S. was coming to see me. He did and unless I am most fearfully mistaken—I have been, I could be again—that was the beginning of something very new in my life. I think the old painful pattern of self-defeat is broken up. "I want to do the holding," he said. "You have nothing to do but let me love you." (Remember that I told you that he must carry the thing this time because I could not.) My instincts must have been working pretty well. He does, and he will. Four days ago he came to stay here for a month. I am surrounded by friends, observers, a nephew but we manage. He has a room a few blocks away. I have a woman comes in every other day until noon—but the time we spend together is surprising, and we present a united front in our little society. His feelings are so deep and firm and complex I can hardly fathom them but they are right for both of us and I let him make the plans and the directions. Unbelievable how happy we are, but not in any way I ever knew before.[45]

Experience had taught her to be a little suspicious of such felicity, and by now even she recognized her self-destructive tendency to form relationships which were humiliating and degrading. She told Herbst that she knew well that "hell-fire is just under the crust of the flowery meadow."[46] In this instance, the possibility of a happy or lasting relationship was jeopardized not only by the extreme difference in age between the two, but also by the fact that, while Schaumann admired her enormously as a writer, he was not at all sexually attracted to her. Porter had completely misunderstood his intentions and when she realized her mistake she was horrified and said that after a short while she had discovered what in her rage she called "the most warped, perverted, pathological mind and nature I have ever seen." Ignoring the sexual dimension to the collapse of the relationship, she wrote of it in political terms, describing Schaumann's shortcomings as "typical Prussian stupidity," "a total lack of moral sense,"[47] and a set of ideas like those contained in the book *The German Talks Back*.[48] Concluding that the proper place for him was in a prisoner-of-war camp, Porter saw him off on the train, asked for her letters, got them back, burned his and hers, returned every object he had given her, and said she felt as if she should go and have herself disinfected, mind and all.[49]

Porter's description of herself as surrounded by friends, observers, and a nephew is an accurate indication of her failure to withdraw from society for very long. Although she avoided the parties that had bored her in her first days in Hollywood, she had found a circle of old and new friends.

Among her friends was the fashion photographer George Platt Lynes, whom she had known since her Paris days and whom she had tried to make her lover in spite of her knowledge that he was a homosexual. Although she often spoke contemptuously of homosexuality, she was nevertheless generally tolerant of her homosexual friends, such as Lynes and Glenway Wescott (whose letters to her spoke quite frankly of their affairs with other men, as if they were sure of her sympathetic response),[50] and in the course of her life she was more than once drawn to homosexual men whom she found attractive and desirable as lovers. When they did not return her sexual interest in kind, the humiliation she suffered as a result sometimes turned into vicious invective against homosexuality. Lynes was an exception. In spite of her disappointment that she never managed to have a love affair with him, she remained close friends with him, and when he was put in charge of the *Vogue* studio in Hollywood, his presence added pleasantly to her social life and contacts.

Paul Porter had not lost his early admiration for his aunt, and when he got out of the army he went to California to be near her. Relishing the opportunity to foster talent in another young member of the family, she showered him with advice about his reading and university studies. She also seized the opportunity, when it arose, to make more corporeal improvements.

George Platt Lynes had worked out an exchange of professional services with a plastic surgeon who charged as much for his work as Lynes did for his portraits. Lynes photographed the surgeon's wife and in return the surgeon fixed the ears of the young man with whom Lynes was living. A slightly more complicated arrangement was worked out whereby Lynes, as a birthday present to Porter, got the surgeon to perform an "ear-do" on Paul.[51] Porter was pleased with the result but cautioned Paul against perpetuating unattractive physical traits in the family. She wrote her sister that she had told young Paul:

"When you marry pick a girl with fine ears and a
instep, and work this tare out of the strain." It was s
brother with his ears to marry a woman with the same
and flat feet besides, bringing into the family flat feet (w
we all of us in every branch of the family had beau
arches) besides a house full of bat-eared young ones. I thɪɴᴋ
that kind of careless marrying is inexcusable.[52]

What with managing Paul's life, the parties with Lynes, the buying and selling of houses (she made a trip East to dispose of South
Hill), and some intermittent illnesses, Porter was accomplishing very
little on the novel. At the same time she had not lost her sense of
urgency to state her theme. Consequently, when she was invited to
make a cross-country college lecture tour in the spring of 1948, she
thought it might be a good idea. She rationalized that the break from
trying to write would stimulate greater efforts when she returned.
Then she might go back to work "as a starved man eats."[53]

Porter was by now an excellent speaker on certain areas of literature. Her enthusiasm for her subject was stimulating and her devotion to her art contagious. She spoke well on the craft of writing, on
her own work, and on other writers whose work she admired. On
this tour, however, she all but abandoned these subjects and spent
most of her time expounding on her political philosophy and speaking
on such topics as "The Fascist Mind."[54]

It was a subject about which she had more passion than information, and though vehemently anti-Fascist, anti-Communist, and
anti-Nazi, she sometimes reversed herself. On one occasion, not long
after she made this tour, she became embroiled in the controversy
that was aroused when Ezra Pound was awarded the first Bollingen
Prize for Poetry in 1949. Pound had lived in Italy during the war and
had made broadcasts on the Italian radio; many people considered him
not only a great poet but a traitor, and the award caused a literary and
political furor. Porter, as a Fellow of the Library of Congress in
American Letters, had voted in favor of Pound and wrote a lengthy
defense of doing so in the *Saturday Review of Literature*. It is pertinent
to note that her stand on this issue is completely contradictory to her
usual opinions—with, for instance, her vehemence against Nazi sym-
pathizers, real and imaginary. It is also inconsistent with her literary
judgments. She condemned *Under the Volcano, Brideshead Revisited,*
and *All the King's Men,* among other works, because she thought the
writers' sympathies with their morally reprehensible main characters

made the books "evil." She thought the books manifested moral confusions such as no real artist ever has. Yet shortly after expressing these views, she defended an award to Pound which acknowledged the excellence of *The Pisan Cantos*. Her inconsistency was typical of the erratic and often personal nature of her literary opinions. Her list of important twentieth-century authors usually included her friends —Eudora Welty, Edith Sitwell, Glenway Wescott, Caroline Gordon, J. F. Powers, and so on. (Notable exceptions were Virginia Woolf, E. M. Forster, and Richard Hughes, whom she admired but never met.)

Pound (who was indicted for treason along with Jane Anderson and six others) did not stand trial, but was declared mentally incompetent and confined to St. Elizabeth's Hospital, outside Washington, D.C. Porter was to meet him later when Marcella Winslow, who had painted a portrait of Pound, invited Porter to accompany her to the hospital. Porter went eagerly and responded sympathetically to the old man. She was so pleased with the visit that she acknowledged Marcella's part in it with a gift, and also sent Pound a carefully chosen package of cheeses and other delicacies.

But during the spring tour of 1948, her political views had not yet been challenged by the Pound controversy. At this time she was speaking about "the stylish literary communism" of New York and the West Coast, after which she said she found the North and Middle West more like foreign lands than France and Mexico. She compared the people of Nebraska and Indiana with those she knew in California:

> Most of the disturbance on the West Coast is made by people who think they are Communists, but at least they always know what they are up to; but these Midwesterners are Nazis or Fascists (same thing really, only one speaks German and the other Italian), and it comes over me uneasily that they think I am talking about somebody else, never about them. Even when I describe their ways and works, and quote their views back at them, they believe they are all good democratic Republicans.[55]

At Purdue University, in Indiana, she wrote:

> The population here is largely German, the university crawls with them, and they worry night and day about the poor hungry Germans—"Suppose they DID follow Hitler, is that

their fault? Don't they get hungry just like anyone else? Aren't they human beings?" The only answer I can think of, which is much too wicked to say, and is only partly true besides, is that of late I have not found that being human is any great recommendation.[56]

She said the "most incendiary things" and everyone applauded and came around and congratulated her. Even when she described their own "ways and works" they still clapped, perhaps demurring a shade and saying they didn't go all the way with her about the Mundt bill. She would then try to explain that she wanted to do something about Communists and Nazis and Fascists, to say nothing of Franco Spain, but the Mundt bill was not the way.[57]

Porter thoroughly enjoyed her spring tour, which she said had given her, after three years in Hollywood, a "heavenly feeling" of being able to talk and act and feel like a writer again. She felt "fresher in my mind, bolder, more outspoken, incredibly little concerned about the impression I make, determined to speak my mind before forever holding my peace."[58]

She particularly enjoyed the parts of the tour that took her among southerners again. In Kansas she met Caroline Gordon and Allen Tate at a writers' conference, and in Columbia, Missouri, she was the guest of an elderly woman whose family had held on to their money throughout the Civil War.[59] The experience gave her the same sense of homecoming she had felt years before in Louisiana, when she visited the antebellum mansions of St. Francisville.

She concluded that university teaching might fit in well with her writing. It would free her from financial worries and at the same time complement her work. In April, during a five-day series of stops at California universities, she met Wallace Stegner, who successfully combined writing with teaching at Stanford, and indicated to him that she would welcome such work on a part-time basis. A long-time admirer of her work, he set about arranging for her to teach at Stanford University during the academic year 1948–49.[60]

The tour had one ominous interlude. The constant traveling, waiting at airports, disrupted nights and full days, took their toll. Eventually she became so tired that she could no longer hear what was going on around her and had an immense, frightening silence in her head. She felt much as she had when she was on the edge of delirium in the influenza epidemic of 1918. To recover after the tour she took refuge in the Stearns Hotel in Ludington, Michigan. There she regained her health and even worked a little, thinking about her novel and beginning two articles requested by George Davis, the editor of *Flair*. But she had begun a pattern of working herself to the point of collapse which was to be repeated many times during her years of teaching and lecturing.[61] Nevertheless, she was pleased at the thought of leaving Hollywood and getting into university life, and she embarked on her teaching career in a happy, optimistic frame of mind.

Late that summer, when her appointment was confirmed, she went to Palo Alto to find a place to live, imagining at first that she could combine teaching with domesticity and establish a comfortable, interesting household. She wanted a place where she could have all her books and papers and bits and pieces around her—not an easy task, she admitted, in "sunny California for one who hadn't $25,000 to buy a shack with busted plumbing on the wrong side of the tracks."[62] What did appeal to her was a cabin sixteen miles from the campus, up winding mountain trails in an apparently trackless forest full of squirrels and stray cats. It had electricity, an oil burner that smelled, a fireplace that smoked, dust and grime everywhere, and running water of a discouraging tan shade, but it appealed to her and she took it. A schoolboy came up every other day, mopped, swept, and carried out "garbage and verbiage,"[63] and two young men from the English Department sent word they would run errands and take her to town when she wished. She had been in residence just one week, long enough to adopt two cats, when she realized that it was completely impossible. She declared that her pioneer blood had run out and came down the mountain with all her goods heaped on a little truck. She put her books and records and all her loved possessions into storage once again and began her teaching career in what she described as "two pawky little rooms" under someone's garage.[64]

She also began her teaching with a well-developed grudge against the Stanford English Department, which she never forgot. Always sensitive to slights, she was ready to interpret any difference between her treatment and that of the regular faculty members as based on her own lack of academic degrees.[65]

When the appointment was first discussed, Stegner had some difficulty persuading his department to make a regular appointment, since the university was in financial straits and unable to fill three professional appointments. He thought it would be an ideal solution all around to take the money for her salary from contingency funds and to make her classes noncredit. He knew that her course would be popular even without credit and this way she would be spared the chore of examinations and grading papers. He had not reckoned with her sensitivity. Seeing the decision as a vote of nonconfidence, she went out of her way to prove herself up to the job. Stegner had also suggested that she limit her class enrollment to as few as ten students if she wished, but she admitted everyone. As he predicted, the class was the biggest draw on campus, with students sitting on the floor, window ledges, radiators, and each other. Porter was deluged with work. She had class preparation and in addition she had to read papers for some sixty students. By spring she felt she was living in a nightmare, hounded on all sides by students and friends.

Her apartment was not only small and unattractive but far too accessible. When she didn't answer the door visitors would walk around and, having banged on the door, and rung the bell, would then peer through the windows and hearing water running in the shower would call out, "I know you're in there."[66]

She had reservations about the students, too, saying that she was horrified by their opportunism. She had learned that if she praised them a certain hungry look came into their eyes, and the next morning they were asking for letters to editors, letters sponsoring their candidacy for this and that wandering sum of cash. She was amazed by their unconscious cynicism and total lack of scruples and wrote Monroe Wheeler, in a moment of complete disillusionment, that the whole racket sickened her.[67]

She was also disappointed and upset when the Modern Library decided to drop *Flowering Judas and Other Stories* from its list. The blow was not mitigated by the substitution of *Pale Horse, Pale Rider*.[68] Once again disappointment, exhaustion, and the constant demands on her time and energies combined to undermine her health, and she became seriously ill with bronchial pneumonia. The doctor told Wallace Stegner, "She's a very sick old lady" (she was fifty-nine), and Stegner was relieved that she could not hear that diagnosis, knowing full well that she would have risen up and eaten his heart out if she had.[69]

Nevertheless, by late spring she was strong enough to take a brief leave to the South to receive her first honorary doctorate. One reason for her pleasure in the degree, awarded her by the University of North Carolina, was that she hoped it would help her find other teaching positions. It also reinforced some of her reservations about universities. She described the "preliminary skirmishes" between the University of North Carolina and her publisher about who would pay for "the wild-goose chase," and she called them big optimists for expecting her to pay. She said that finally both sides grudgingly decided to divide the damages, and her publisher consented to make an advance on general royalties. The hood alone cost her $400 and cut her to the bone financially, destroying her margin of subsistence for a year at least. There was also some wangling about the degree, which one faction wished to give to a woman writer of "feverish local histories" and powerful political connections. Finally both she and Porter were honored, in what Porter called the "old bill-with-streamer technique."[70]

Porter was back at Stanford in time for its graduation exercises, and, decked out in her newly acquired academic regalia, she walked proudly in the procession. She told friends that female vanity of the more reprehensible kind had prompted her to don her robe and walk in the procession "like a late summer butterfly with her gold doctor's tassel shimmying in the breezes."[71] Wallace Stegner, however, interpreted her red-gowned appearance as inspired by a wicked determination to show that the artist had as good credentials as anyone.

At the end of August, when she gave her last lecture at Stanford, she had no desire either to go on teaching or to remain in California. She wanted to go East and settle down to finish the novel. Looking back on the past few years, she decided they had been mostly wasted time and she was completely soured on California. She wrote Glenway Wescott, "It is just a strange place to me and I suffer a perpetual homesickness for just anywhere else on earth when I am here. . . . It is a place where everything unlovely, crude, corrupt, mindless in our national life is embraced, believed in and practised as a 'way of life.' "[72]

NINETEEN

Disciples Must Be Very Hard
for a Mere Human Being to Endure

With the move back East in the fall of 1949, the parenthetical experience of California ended and certain practical problems were solved. Porter told her publisher that to manage the move and have something left to live on while she finished her novel she needed $500 to $1,000 to begin with and $400 a month for six months. He helped her settle in New York and provided the income for the months that followed.[1]

She had vowed, after the intrusions into her privacy she suffered at Stanford, that she would find a place up three flights of stairs. What she found was a six-story house on East Sixty-fifth Street. She shared it with a family and it was divided so that each got one of the two kitchens, some of the bathrooms, and some of the bedrooms. She had the second and fifth floors and the others had the third floor and basement. The extra rooms were rented to people who did not need kitchens and the arrangement was satisfactory for the moment.[2] It did not, however, entirely solve the problem of protecting her privacy. A vivid account of the kind of interruption she was subjected to is contained in one of her letters during this period.

She wrote the novelist William Goyen about a Mr. Schmucker from Dallas ("Is he one of those wooden-headed Texas Germans? I have never had any good of them ever") who made a nuisance of himself by telephoning and wanting to see her. He wished to pay tribute to her by bringing over a bouquet of roses. She innocently told him to send them. He did and lost no time in phoning again and asking to come and see her.

> Then the telephone rang and it was Mr. Schmucker hell bent on collecting his thanks, and expecting to come straight around to see me. I said, No, I was not very well and was frightfully oppressed with unfinished work. But when he came back next year, to be sure to call me. . . . Bill, what in God's name are certain kind of people really like? I realize more and more that I have no clue at all to certain motives and kinds of behavior. He insisted and insisted, and finally told me that he only wanted to meet personally two writers —Eudora is the other—and he had met Eudora; and he just could not bear to be defeated in his determination to see me in my own house. "It's a challenge," said he, earnestly. I said, "What kind, please? What point can there be to your merely getting into my house, and especially against my wish?" He said, "It is only that I admire you so much!" I said, "But when I tell you I am not well, and should not be disturbed at my work, and cannot see anyone, and do not go anywhere at this moment, if you really do admire me, how can you behave so badly to me?"
>
> And would you believe he dropped a third nickel into the slot and went right on insisting?[3]

She had complained to Glenway Wescott, not quite accurately, that in California she had not made a single friend. In New York, in contrast, she was surrounded by old friends and pleasant new acquaintances, and she had a social life of the literary kind that suited her, although not all the literary gatherings were harmonious.

In 1949, the poet John Malcolm Brinnin had become director of the Poetry Center of the Young Men's–Young Women's Hebrew Association in New York, and one of his first acts was to wire Dylan Thomas an invitation to give a reading. Later he had some misgivings about that decision, since the effect of Thomas's visit proved disastrous. Thomas arrived in February 1950, and two days after his arrival (two days of heavy drinking) he met Porter at a party given by the writer and critic Harvey Breit. He was immediately attracted to her, and after making mumbling, fumbling, and gently rebuffed overtures to her all evening, he approached her as she tried to leave, suggesting that they meet for a drink the next day and announcing that he would take her home right then. She politely refused both offers and Dylan then held her hands and, looking at her in his most engaging baby-owl manner, told her how glad he was to have met her. She was listening indulgently when, quite suddenly, as if she had no more weight than a doll, he lifted her, coat and gloves and all, until her head was within an inch of the ceiling, and kept her there. At this point Brinnin acted and, stepping through the group of half-amused, half-shocked guests, indicated to Dylan that the party was over. Porter, in much greater composure than the other guests, was able to make a final farewell to Dylan and go home, but not before he had followed her halfway downstairs.[4]

The incident itself was trivial but it became very well publicized. Perhaps that was natural, since in it two myths dear to the popular imagination met in a head-on collision. One was that of the rampaging poet-genius on a course of destruction and the other was that of the pale priestess, the literary lady that the public image of Katherine Anne Porter suggested. The same sort of confrontation had occurred years ago between Hart Crane and Porter and it had not ceased to fascinate writers. In the same way, the very brief and inconsequential meeting with Dylan Thomas was blown out of all proportion and subsequently appeared in at least two literary works.

Sidney Michaels' play *Dylan* shows her very flatteringly and has Dylan saying that he loves her short stories and will lift her to the stars where she belongs and that she is head and shoulders over every other woman writer in the world. But Porter always insisted that whoever described the incident got it wrong:

> He was most objectionable, trying to get his hands under my dress, and picking me up, until finally I just had to get out. But they sent me tickets to the play and when I saw it I said I wished they had asked me about it first. Because the woman playing me was about 15 years too young and about 20 pounds too heavy, and I never was a blonde, you know. My hair was black, until I got the plague in 1918 when it all fell out and came back in again all white.
>
> But the worst thing was they had me sitting alone at a bar, which is something I've never done and never would. That made me most annoyed. I suppose even if you didn't know my age you could tell my generation, by the fact that that upset me so.[5]

Another friend who saw the play said there were two things wrong with it: "that is not her shade of pink and that is not her picture hat—when she does sport one she goes all out—the brim cannot be too enormous."[6]

Karl Shapiro's poem "Emily Dickinson and Katherine Anne Porter" included this stanza.

> And when Dylan Thomas was introduced
> To Katherine Anne Porter in a room full of people,
> He stopped and picked her up below the thighs
> And raised her to the ceiling like a drink,
> And held her straight in the slack-jawed smoke-blue air
> Two minutes, five minutes, seven minutes,
> While everybody wondered what it meant
> To toast the lady with her own body
> Or to hold her to the light like a plucked flower.[7]

Besides her literary circle of friends, Porter was able to enjoy once more the younger members of her family who had joined her in California. Paul eventually came East and settled in New York, and Ann lived first in the city and later in the country within easy reach of the city. As in any other family, these close relatives caused Porter some disappointment and anguish, mainly because they failed to live up to her very high expectations of them.

In the spring of 1950 she was acutely disappointed when Ann decided to marry again and eventually give up her dancing career. Ann did not consider her career quite as successful or important as Porter did. She had already given up her position in the New York- and Brazil-based Original Ballets Russes because it was poorly paid and involved a great deal of traveling. For the past year she had been a member of the Radio City Ballet Company. She remained with it for a year following her marriage, and for a while, after her children were born, she ran a ballet school. With the best of intentions Ann sent Porter the last pair of slippers she wore on stage. Porter chose to interpret the gesture as an insult and said that she had supported her niece for ten years and that her help had been treated with complete contempt. Eventually she threw the slippers into the garbage can.

She was extremely protective of her favorite niece and it was with grave misgivings that she saw her marrying for the second time. She showered her with letters of advice and warnings:

> . . . look well and long at any man who proposes to marry
> you. Don't load him down with all the virtues and qualities

you would *wish* him to have, and then be disappointed when it turns out that he hasn't them at all. . . . Remember? Above all find out what a man has in mind for his future and God knows I hope you will marry someone with money enough to make a life for you both, or the capacity for doing this. Any man who does not expect to support you absolutely and without question should be shown the door politely. He is worthless in the grain and will bring you nothing but trouble. . . . Mind you, you may go on with your profession and your earning, but on his part the wish and the ability to take care of you MUST be present, or you are getting another worthless cad. . . . So look out, my sweet angel, tread light.[8]

When Ann was not to be discouraged, Porter nevertheless threw herself into arranging the wedding reception in the house on East Sixty-fifth Street. As she often did, Porter tried to make the present situation approximate a literary description that she had firmly established in her imagination. In her essay "Portrait: Old South" she had described someone's (possibly exaggerated) account of her grandmother Porter's Kentucky wedding, at which the room "was a perfect bower of Southern smilex and white dogwood" and which featured "silver branched candlesticks everywhere, each holding seven white candles, and a crystal chandelier holding fifty white candles, all lighted."[9] Because Ann's wedding was to resemble her great-great-grandmother's as much as possible, Porter, at great expense, had quantities of dogwood sent up from the South. Monroe Wheeler's butler was hired for the occasion and a great crowd of Ann's friends from the ballet were invited.

Porter remembered it as a merry affair, with music and dancing and wedding cake and food and candlelight and white flowers. Fifty of Ann's friends from the ballet were invited and altogether 125 dancers turned up. They had got in from all parts of the globe unexpectedly and, having heard about the party, assumed that they would be welcome, and they were. Another bushel of food and case of champagne was sent out for and the party went on until 3:00 A.M. One guest slept in the basement,[10] although when Porter described the wedding she said ". . . about 10 the next day half a dozen boys and girls straggled up out of the cellar where they had slept on the floor in a blissful fog, and were none the worse for wear! Ah, Youth! as the saying is."[11]

Porter's proprietary feelings toward Ann were indicated by her notation on the wedding photograph. She drew a faint triangle around herself on the front of the picture and wrote on the reverse side, apparently in reference to herself, "Mother of the bride," although her sister Gay, Ann's mother, was also in the picture.[12]

As it happened the marriage turned out to be an unusually happy one. Ann married a boat designer of Swedish descent, an extremely handsome man with many artistic talents. On the unfortunate Walter Heintze, however, Porter heaped all her resentment for Ann's abandoned career. She criticized his failure to provide Ann with a staff of servants, his somewhat conventional (but not unusual) idea of a woman's role, and his adherence to certain Swedish customs. She was particularly outraged when Ann reported that she was having lobster for Christmas dinner and glügg in place of eggnog, seeing these choices as ominous attempts to undermine Ann's native heritage. "So the erosion of her own customs in her own country goes on insidiously and incessantly."[13] In the absence of any conspicuous vices in Walter, Porter declared him, in the face of all evidence to the contrary, to be a colossal bore. A friend described her attitude toward him:

> We always came away from dinner where we had been invited as well as Ann and Walter with the most uncomfortable feeling that we had nearly witnessed murder and if Walter had been anywhere near boring, we had decided that he had been silent mostly in order to avoid any possibility of setting KAP off. One in particular I remember, she was fixing a perfectly marvellous dinner (as usual) and had gotten down to the point of doing steaks; Walter put his head in the kitchen door to see if he could freshen her drink a final time before dinner and the explosion was vast and immediate. I don't think he had even gotten the question out before she was shouting, "Get out, get *out*, get OUT," and then turning to me—still in his hearing saying "Can't he keep out of anything?—Can't he stop interfering with everything I do?"[14]

Although Ann achieved with her husband and sons the close ties of affection that her aunt always yearned for, Porter obstinately referred to the marriage as an unmitigated disaster. When Ann's first son was born, Porter, while expressing disgust to friends and saying that having children was a mug's game,[15] was delighted to be a godmother. And she was as demanding and critical in that role as in her other family relationships. The name Donald Boone was chosen for Ann's younger son and she was furious that Ann had cast aside her family history and refused to name him Daniel Boone.[16]

In spite of all difficulties, Porter remained proud and fond of her family and, chiefly through their forbearance and affection for her, maintained a pleasant relationship with them almost to the end of her life. They cherished the many festive times—birthdays, Christmases, Thanksgiving celebrations—that no one knew better than she how to celebrate.

With Ann engrossed in her domestic life, all Porter's ambitions for the young Porters descended upon Paul. He had a variety of artistic skills and these in combination with his good looks might have led to a successful career in dancing, acting, or the graphic arts. However, since he had first met her in Houston in 1936, when he was sixteen, he had had a consuming veneration for his aunt. Later on friends would tell him that his aunt had ruined his life, and if this was not completely true, she did dominate and influence its course. Now, with her encouragement, he decided to develop his literary skills. She showered him with advice, bombarding him with didactic letters and giving, along with all the advice, some daunting criticism:

> You used to say whole conversations almost word for word back to me, a few days or weeks later and with the air of pure revelation, really believing by then it was all your own. . . . Every individual mind plays its own separate set of tricks on the unfortunate possessor, but for a writer not to assimilate his influences until they become really his own is the worst snare—Be careful—a lot of writers are much more occupied with showing off how well they can write instead of showing off the people and the meaning of the story they are telling. . . . Eudora Welty's latest book is a perfect example of what I mean—technical virtuosity gone into a dizzy spin absolutely drunk on language, a personal showing off as shameless as a slackwire dancer with pinwheels. It is a great pity, and now do you cultivate the virtues of sobriety and truth-telling.[17]

Porter's annoyance with Welty and her dislike of *The Golden Apples* was not entirely dispassionate. Early in 1949 Welty had written a series of articles for the *Atlantic Monthly* on reading and writing.

Porter was astonished and furious to find that her own name was not even mentioned in them. This rankled, and ten years later she was still complaining: "My dear friend and admired colleague Eudora Welty once performed the astonishing feat of writing a three-part essay on the short story without mentioning my name."[18] Moreover, Welty had become a close friend of the English writer Elizabeth Bowen. Porter was jealous of the influence of Bowen, saying that she was a Lesbian and Welty had at last got into very bad company indeed.

Eventually Paul had a story ready for publication and Porter sent it to Kerker Quinn, the editor of *Accent,* who had already published a section of her uncompleted novel. The story was a short four-page fable and it was accepted on condition that certain revisions and changes be made. Porter was highly delighted; her confidence and pride in her nephew was confirmed. Paul, for his part, was horrified when the story appeared to find himself identified in the "Notes on Contributors" simply as "the nephew of Katherine Anne Porter." That description was to dog him annoyingly and unjustly for many years.

A second, longer story appeared in *Accent* and a jubilant Porter told Paul that she already had a publisher for his first novel.[19] By this time, however, Paul had decided that his talents did not justify any great ambitions for a writing career and was looking for a more dependable means of supporting himself. He found a financially rewarding job with a commercial firm that used his practical business skills rather than his artistic talents. The move was one which Porter would have acknowledged as very sensible in anyone else. She herself boasted of giving such advice as Paul had acted upon, saying of one of her protégées:

> I spent seven years struggling with that girl, and finally I said, "You're just wasting your time. You're such a young girl and so pretty and you've got such a nice husband and a good life, why don't you just enjoy it? Writing is a dog's life." And do you know she took it very sensibly, and we're still good friends. I think I saved her marriage, too.[20]

However ready she was to counsel such a decision in others, she did not condone it in a member of her own family. She thought Paul should have shown more determination, matched her own perseverence, and crowned it with literary success. Paul resented the fact that family pride far outweighed any concern for his personal happiness, and so for a time the relationship between aunt and nephew cooled. It did not help that as well as disappointment she felt that the financial help she had given had been wasted and treated once again with contempt.

Paul's decision to abandon a literary career, coming fairly soon after Ann's decision to give up dancing, gave Porter a great sense of despair about her family. She felt that all hope for their producing something worthwhile had run out and that she was the last one who would ever achieve anything. When she observed, as she always did, the birthday of her dead niece Mary Alice, she wrote:

> . . . last December Mary Alice would have been 49 years old . . . she probably would have been the same disappointment that the other children who did stay have turned out to be . . . the line ends with me; that is a strange fate! I thought somehow I might be the beginning of something in our family—a return, a recuperation of forces—a going on —but no, I am the end.[21]

She felt a family bond still with Ann and Paul but often spoke contemptuously of them to her literary friends. One of her charges against her own father had been that he was "the only person she knew who maligned his own children." She reacted to his doing so with the scorn it deserved, and yet she did exactly the same to the next generation. She said frequently that she had molded them out of Texas clay.[22]

Paul, meanwhile, remained devoted to his aunt, and was ready to help or run errands whenever she needed him. There was rarely a time when Porter did not have a friend or lover, but the object of her love never had the time or inclination to provide the services she needed and it was Paul who ran errands and did commissions. Even when she was out of town, instructions came in every mail for purchases and other tasks. She was a great admirer of Mark Twain and when she heard that his house on Lower Fifth Avenue was to be torn down her instructions to Paul were to "get me some scrap, fragment, bit of panelling, wall-paper—of course, if you could get away with the iron front railing, or a whole mantelpiece all the better."[23] He managed a tile from the mantelpiece.

Usually, the enormous job of moving all her belongings from one apartment to another also fell to Paul, and to the end of her life it was he who supervised and arranged all her moves. It was a thankless task; if anything was misplaced, broken, or otherwise went awry he was blamed. Yet his devotion remained steadfast.

When her disciples were not members of her own family the relationship was sometimes easier. With William Humphrey she sustained a relationship for more than twelve years. She first became aware of him after her nephew showed her Humphrey's published short stories and pointed out that they were rewritings of her own. She always read *Accent* and wrote to tell Paul that two recent short stories were rewritings of "The Cracked Looking-Glass" and "A Day's Work," and that the Humphrey who wrote them was from Texas.[24] The stories were "In Sickness and in Health" and "Man with a Family." About a year later Porter received a letter from Humphrey, a young instructor at Bard College, Annandale-on-Hudson, asking her to come and speak at the college, even though they could offer only a little money. She replied that her fee was not high, but $250 with expenses was her minimum, as lecturing had for some time been her one way of making a living.[25]

Humphrey's letters to her were full of warm admiration. He said that she was his one teacher and that he wrote with copies of "Old Mortality," "Noon Wine," "The Cracked Looking-Glass," and "The Old Order" open at his favorite paragraphs. He admitted frankly that he stole his first published story from "A Day's Work." She was the one person whose approval he wanted, and when he published a story he and his wife wondered "if She had seen it." He had his students read her essay on Gertrude Stein, and worried when he heard that Porter's health was poor. The fact that she was from Texas was especially important to him, since it had always seemed to him beforehand that writers had to be from England, France, or New England, and he had thought that being from Texas ruined his hopes. Such admiration was persuasive and Porter undertook the engagement for $50.[26]

At the same time she expressed reservations about his future. She thought he had talents but was likely to smother them to death if he persisted on the road he seemed to be taking. She had found in his first stories a tone of generous warmth, pervasive rather than deep but most hopeful all the same. His first letters to her seemed the same —but after that there was a misunderstanding about his story "The

Fauve." She took it to be a story about a third-rate painter with a bad case of megalomania, a natural-born cad and boor. His wife, also a painter, won an award the "Fauve" thought he should have won, and Porter thought the picture of the filthy nuisance he made of himself was a fine job of satire. Instead, the story was of an unappreciated genius among slick, successful artists, and all Humphrey's cracks at "women's paintings" were in "poisonous earnest." He intended to do a whole series on the theme of the "successful woman," an idea that horrified Porter.

She thought Humphrey's work was being corrupted by some bad internal collision, that he worried about his reputation and was in some kind of conflict with his wife, whom Porter thought older than he, more competent and more experienced. She hoped that he would work through his problems and let himself be a good artist—this depended on his strength and the depth of his intelligence. She wrote:

> When I go to Bard I mean to draw him out and argue with him. At least, I think that is what he wants now; he is teaching, and has no back talk. His wife loves him, and anyway he doesn't respect her opinion. He hasn't anybody to stand up to him and ask him what he means, so I shall do it, and we'll see how it comes out. Above all I wish to ask him why he got that story down so skew-gee—doesn't he know what he wants to say?[27]

Later she decided that her reservations were well founded and that his subsequent commercial success, rather than artistic development, proved her point. In the beginning, however, his admiration won the day. She could rarely resist flattery and the friendship was sealed. She encouraged him with his stories, saying that she had seen nothing she liked better in a long time. She was shocked when she learned that he was rewriting rejected stories, slanting them to appeal to the editorial preferences of certain journals, rather than simply trying to write as best he could.[28]

She read and commented on his stories and his work was steadily published, culminating in the commercially successful *Home from the Hill* in 1958. In his dedication copy of the book he wrote that her life had given him courage and that she had taught him the greatest thing that one writer could teach another, that the place and the life and the speech to which he was born were his place and his subject and his speech.

Initially she hailed the novel with approval, as well she might have, since like his stories it is thematically very close to her own work. The critics, noting the hunting episodes, saw links with Faulkner, a tendency that was reinforced when the movie based on the book was set in Faulkner's home town, Oxford, Mississippi. In fact, the main character of the story, Hannah Hunnicut, is characterized by her failure ever to give way honestly to her hostility, and by a rectitude which ruins many lives. She is closely related to such Porter characters as Granny Weatherall and Mrs. Halloram, and also to the heroines of the melodramas which Porter saw in Denver in 1919.

Eventually Porter demurred about her first judgment that he was a really brilliant and strange talent and concluded that he had gone off. In a panel discussion she said of *Home from the Hill:*

> He is an extremely good short story writer. He preceded that book with a number of good short stories, I think, but he did want to write a successful book if he possibly could, you know, and he got the idea of what is success mixed up with what would be good sales and so he spoiled his book by trying to make it popular.[29]

When the moderator interjected the remark that "he succeeded in that," she said, "He did and good luck to him. He was my student for years and I thought he was going to turn out better than that, I must say." Her friendship with Humphrey survived the success of *Home from the Hill,* but it was damaged, and many years later there would be a final rift.

Of her influence on other writers Porter said:

> I have not yet ever "discovered" or trained a first-rate writer yet. I have talked with and criticized and advised a good number of very fine talents, but whatever they did later was on their own strength, and I have never seen any traces of my "influence." I don't want this, I merely remark that several writing friends I know, really strong ones, have turned out and trained people who do carry their brand the rest of their lives—or up to now; and I always say disciples must be very hard for a mere human being to endure. I think it would be best just to drop them head first down a well.[30]

Her next disciple proved eventually very hard to endure because he became a lover as well as a protégé. In the summer of 1947, when she was still in California, she had received a visit from another young Texan. She was predisposed to like him because he had known some of her family in Houston, having been in the same high school as her niece Ann. He told Porter that her sister Gay had been kind enough to lend him her copy of *Flowering Judas and Other Stories*.[31] Not only was there a family connection but Porter was impressed by his determination to become a serious writer and to dedicate himself to his art. Finally, as with many of her protégés, his unabashed and total admiration of her and tendency to hang on her every word completely disarmed her. He visited her with a friend in August 1947, and later by himself, and wrote letters telling her that whenever he was with her he gained courage.[32] The relationship remained one of successful writer and disciple for some time.

William Goyen was a thirty-five-year-old native of Texas who was at work on his first book, *House of Breath*. When it appeared in August 1950, he wrote in her copy that it had been written with her and her great work as his guiding light.

Porter helped him, not only with advice, but more practically by recommending him for grants and awards. Her *New York Times* review of *House of Breath* was adulatory. With her help, he later won a Guggenheim and also an invitation to Yaddo. Porter herself visited Yaddo in the winter of 1951, while he was there, and it was at this time that Porter's letters to Goyen indicate that the two became lovers.

After she left Yaddo, Goyen joined her in New York. They were still lovers, but she began to be disturbed by his inability to remain with her for longer than brief visits. He preferred to stay for isolated weekends and express his love from a safe distance in long, passionate letters. His excuse was always his dedication to his art and his need for solitude to work out his artistic problems. It was an excuse that Porter found difficult to criticize since she so often expressed the same need.

Nevertheless, she soon suspected that there was something not quite honest and straightforward in Goyen's approach. As early as January 1951 she was writing Paul:

> He would call me or come to see me very seldom, but always to say that he went nowhere, saw no one, did not answer the telephone, and yet was so pursued and embarrassed by attentions . . . then, of course, I would see other

friends and it was plain that Bill was getting all over the literary territory, meeting absolutely every celebrity that hit town, for a modest, extra sensitive young artist of an unworldly heart, he has not missed one single trick on the tricky road to a New York Literary Career.[33]

In spite of her early misgivings, her passion for him increased; she suspended all critical judgment and became totally unaware of the obvious signs of trouble in the relationship. It developed rather like the relationship with Charles Shannon six years earlier, with long separations and short periods together in unusual circumstances, allowing her to live in a romantic haze and treat Goyen as a godlike being. She cut a profile of him from a photograph and hung it above her desk in a silver frame, telling him that she had a "real iconology of you now." Another icon was a photograph of them together, for which she bought the most baroque Victorian silver frame she could find, and she kept that by her bed. The bed he had slept in was shrouded in a "once-virgin white" cover, and she told him she lived with his shadow, his ghost, "a very dear companionable one."[34]

Friends watched with dismay as Porter became more and more engrossed in the love affair. The novelist Eleanor Clark was shocked when she learned of the affair. She tried unsuccessfully to dissuade Porter from her passion for Goyen, but finally realized that she would only arouse Porter's wrath against herself and saw that she could not hope to penetrate Porter's dream image of Goyen. In a way, she admired Porter's capacity for passion: "It must be very hard to be you, Katherine Anne, but worth it, worth it."[35] Other friends watched silently, knowing it would be useless to intervene. Glenway Wescott, shown the picture of Goyen and Porter together, requested a copy, saying very tenderly that it was the most adorable lovers' picture he had seen. He added that everyone who loved her wished her well and cautioned her that it was her own affair and not to let anyone near it.[36]

Goyen continued for a time to play the part of passionate lover kept away from his mistress only by the higher demands of his art. He was sparing of his presence but prodigal of gifts, flowers, and numerous small imaginative attentions, all of which were received and treasured as if they were religious relics—the flowers pressed and kept, the letters tied in bundles, the shells kept close to her bed. That spring, for her sixty-first birthday (he guessed her age at "around fifty"), he gave her a memorial book in which he had painstakingly written out by hand his story "Children of Old Somebody." His dedication said that it was shaped for her when they were together in the months of February and March 1951 and given back to her on her birthday as commemoration and celebration. Sometimes he even managed a visit of a few days, and after he left she was in ecstasy and begged him to return:

> As always when we have been here together, this house for a few days is full of the summer air of our love, a quiver of summer lightning full of rain—remember our storm? I loved and love you better than ever, and there was a kind of brilliance of tenderness in the face you showed me this time, I hope you saw my love and felt it as surely.[37]

> Bill, my angel, if you don't decide very soon just what you will do, or where you will go, maybe you could come here again just a few days even, three or four?[38]

After a long period of separation, even Porter had to acknowledge that something was wrong. Disappointment cleared her vision and she wrote that they should no longer go on deceiving themselves about the nature of the relationship:

> Love that does not touch the whole life of the lovers is nothing. Love that can put itself off until all the other business of life is settled is not love at all, it is a mere convenience of emotion, a few days of excitement to sleep together and think of new ways of making sensation for each other. It is a fair weather holiday, a day at the beach, I despise it and will not have it. I am better than that, and deserve better. I will not have you visit me for three days at intervals when there is nothing else to do, to leave me for any other interest that comes up.[39]

She concluded at last that the relationship was doomed. It was typical of her tendency to gravitate to those least likely to return her love in the way she hoped and most likely to leave her feeling humiliated. It was Goyen's view that Porter always felt unjustifiably betrayed by him and others. In addition, the age difference between them (even though he did not realize how great it was) bothered him and he was alarmed by her demands on him. He remembered that she drank a great deal and, when drunk, would act the role of a Mae West-like seductress. He soon decided, however, that this was a pose she used to cover her anxiety. There was also a kind of insatiable hunger for his attention, admiration and reassurance, and he claimed she was so insecure as an artist that she resented his abilities and became furious when he read his work to her. He concluded that while her writing was full of light, she actually lived in a dark, terrified world that few suspected.[40]

In August, while Goyen was in Houston making excuses for not coming to New York, she told him that she knew perfectly well he was in some sort of relationship with someone there:

> Bill, in the beginning, I knew you . . . could not understand what happens in . . . love. . . . And yet, I did not think it hopeless.
>
> You would not let yourself be taught even a little by me. I do not mean any sexual variations. But you were in such haste you never really knew who you were with, or what it might mean. . . . there are very delicious tendernesses and subtleties in . . . love . . . but that you would not have, you could not wait on that, there was nothing you wished to learn either about love or about me, or my feelings. It is this I should really forgive you for.[41]

Grieved as she was by the realization that the relationship was hopeless and believing that she had been deceived from the beginning about the nature of his affection for her and, later, that he was discussing their affair with his friends, she wrote him furiously:

> From now on, you will please leave my name out of your conversations with your . . . friends. I could even wish that you may not discuss our once-private affairs with Truman Capote. You have given me a partial report of your conversations with Carson McCullers. No word has come in from Tennessee Williams yet, but it is due any minute now.
>
> Now everybody concerned (but me) seems in a high state of dudgeon. I am perfectly calm, having the knack of seeing seven ways through a millstone (except when I am in love. Then I get a little starry-eyed and soft-headed, but a good thrashing can jolt me out of it).[42]

When Porter saw that Goyen had mentioned her name in an interview in the *San Antonio Express,* she wrote him that once again she was put to the public shame of being associated with him. He had said in the interview that he would run twenty miles to get away from "long-hairs" and that he was not "long-haired." She told him that might endear him to certain Texans, the kind she had run several thousand miles to get away from. He had, she said, used her name, decent reputation as an artist, time and energy and faith for everything it could get him, and now, after having treated her with every personal indecency, finally he had repudiated his last shred of decency as an artist.[43]

When Goyen's *In a Farther Country* appeared a few years later she regarded it coldly. On the jacket he disclaimed any affinity with the eccentricities of the Southern School or Gothic bizarreries. Angrily she scribbled in the margin:

Boy! You didn't *need* any Southern eccentricities or Gothic bizarreries, or spurious associations even. You came furnished with your own brand of writers' crookedness, crankiness, perversion, falseness that really made everything of the kind around you seem pale and inert! The most utter liar and traitor in every relation I have ever known.[44]

When her vision cleared, she could become a formidable adversary and repay brutality with brutality. Even so, although she made scathing remarks to and about Goyen, it was a number of years before she relinquished the strong feeling she had for him. When he returned her letters as she requested, she could not bring herself to make a bonfire of them but instead sealed them in a box.[45] She continued to write to Goyen, and while she acknowledged the hopelessness of their relationship she asked him to love her any way he could. When she went to France she went to see the river Goyen in Brittany and brought him back some of its water.[46]

The affair had left her seriously debilitated. In the late fall of 1951 and early winter of 1952, she felt old, ill, and, worst of all, drained of creative energy. She had accomplished very little since she gave up her teaching job, left California, and took the publisher's advance to finish the novel. She had tried to work on "A Vision of Heaven," but once again it was set aside. The publishers were by this time resigned to the postponement of the novel and the absence of more stories and decided to bring out a collection of the critical essays she had produced with the encouragement of editors who were her friends.

Meanwhile she was invited to be part of the American delegation to the conference in Paris of the recently formed Congress for Cultural Freedom. She accepted the invitation and later joined the organization, which in the next few years featured her name among those of other literary figures listed on its letterhead. For all her anti-communist and anti-Fascist tirades of recent years, her motivation in lending her name to an organization that was ostensibly anti-communist is somewhat out of character for someone who had in the past given public speeches and interviews that sometimes indicated political leanings to the left. It seems unlikely that she naively took at face value the Congress's stated purpose of promoting freedom. Was her membership an opportunistic means of protecting herself in the witch hunt atmosphere of the time? Or did she simply welcome the opportunity for some well-funded traveling? Certainly she wrote jubilantly to her nephew that she was as thrilled at the prospect of the trip as when she first set out for Mexico by herself. And she boasted that her first-class fare alone cost $846.[47]

When the speech she gave at the conference in the summer of 1952 was included in her *Collected Essays and Occasional Writings* (long after the Congress had been discredited by disclosures of its CIA funding), she misleadingly designated it as "Opening Speech at Paris Conference (International Exposition of the Arts, 1952)." This, however, may have been the result of the same carelessness that made her list the delegates as "James Farrell, William Faulkner, Katherine Anne Porter, Allen Tate, Robert Penn Warren and Glenway Wescott."[48] Robert Penn Warren did not attend and, while Faulkner gave a speech, he refused to accept funds or be part of the official American delegation. In fact, his aloofness from her party caused Porter some annoyance, as is reported by Faulkner's biographer:

> When the program was over, Wescott took the arm of his friend Katherine Anne Porter and led her with him to the podium, for they both wanted to meet Faulkner. They approached with hands outstretched. Without a glance of recognition, he strolled between them and on out of the auditorium. Wescott just stood and looked. Miss Porter was furious.[49]

Since one member of the official American delegation had to give an address, Porter, as the only woman and as one who would present a colorful appearance, was selected to speak for the group. Her speech was peculiarly rambling and disorganized. She began by making vague remarks about the artist's need for freedom and ended by speaking out against government subdizing of the arts. Her reason was that artists might be "killed by kindness" and that often the great artists were neglected while those "of perfectly second-rate talent, of the overambitious sort," were encouraged. This view was especially surprising since she herself had been the recipient of many grants and had consistently sponsored others for them. Also, because she spoke at the conference, she asked for an extra allowance beyond that which was given to the other delegates. Allen Tate, who thought her address completely inept, was half outraged and half amused; W. H. Auden was heard to mutter that she was an absolute crook.[50]

All in all, the jaunt to Europe was thoroughly enjoyable for Porter. She was surrounded by friends and literary acquaintances. One observed that for the first few days she was constantly getting in and out of taxis with Stephen Spender. On one occasion, she had lunch with Janet Flanner, Glenway Wescott, Virgil Thompson and Cyril Connolly and found that "four of the most opinionated people in the world . . . minded their manners and got along prettily." She invented a new aperitif for Robert Lowell and had a happy reunion with Allen Tate who, though fond of Porter, had few illusions about her.[51] He once said:

> She has few of the ordinary human satisfactions—she can't live in the world, she can't have a deep emotional relationship with anybody, she is always moving: in fact, she is trapped in a cycle of romantic emotions that repeat themselves about every five years. I have watched her through three marriages and divorces, and the pattern in all three is identical. When the human personality suffers repeated failures in a fundamental objective experience, it recoils into self-worship, or at best a refined egoism. . . .[52]

Nevertheless, they were friends of such long standing that, when they got together over the years, their meetings were characterized by an especially warm kind of affection. After this meeting, during which they talked over old times, she wrote to him saying "how positively *quaint* to remember those days when we believed that adultery was the worst sin one could commit."[53]

The atmosphere of these days was so pleasant that she decided to remain in Paris for six months. She settled into the Hotel d'Isly, at 26

Rue Jacob, and worked on the proofs of her collection of critical essays, *The Days Before*. She said she was happy to be back on the Left Bank and to be spending Bastille Day in Paris for the first time in sixteen years. She went to the Basses Pyrénées to visit her translator, Marcelle Sibon, and visited other friends in Brittany.

By fall her spirits were restored, and she felt prepared to face the United States and New York once more. While she was away she had been forced to vacate the house on East Sixty-fifth Street, but Paul had found a new home for her, transferred all her possessions, and arranged everything so that she could move in as soon as she got back. Thus she returned to a place that was not likely to disturb her with memories of the tortured relationship with Bill Goyen.

Soon after she returned from Europe, two friends, Eleanor Clark and Robert Penn Warren, whom she had known separately for some time, were married. She had met Warren in New York in the twenties and had renewed the friendship, in spite of her dislike of his first wife, in Baton Rouge in the late thirties. She met Clark later, liked her personally, and admired her work. After Clark's novel *The Bitter Box* appeared in 1946, Porter had lent her influential support as Clark's sponsor for a grant from the National Institute of Arts and Letters and for a Guggenheim fellowship. When Clark published *Rome and a Villa* in 1952, Porter wrote one of her most unreservedly favorable reviews. Much later, in 1965, when Robert Penn Warren felt it was time his wife was made a member of the National Institute of Arts and Letters, it was Porter whom he asked to make the nomination (threatening at the same time to put arsenic in her bourbon if she ever told that he had asked). And when the Warrens' daughter, Rosanna, was born, they asked Porter to be godmother, a role she thoroughly enjoyed—especially when, as sometimes happened, the godchild was named for her. The marriage of her two loyal friends gave Porter an added satisfaction because she always claimed that they had met each other at one of her Georgetown parties in Marcella Comès Winslow's garden.

The wedding ceremony itself, however, was not a completely happy occasion for Porter. It brought back painful reminders of her last wedding, fourteen years earlier, in Baton Rouge, when Robert Penn Warren had been a witness. These memories were made all the more vivid by the presence of Albert Erskine, now returning the favor and acting as Warren's best man.

Porter also had reservations about the ceremony itself. Soon afterward, when she read in Simone de Beauvoir's *The Second Sex* a criticism of weddings in which women were given in marriage by certain males to other males, she wrote in the margin, "Eleanor's wedding group so very exactly this—consisting of four men—the groom who gave her a ring but did not receive one—the monster, the best man, and her brother-in-law who gave her to the groom— and a beautiful little flower girl for decoration."[54]

After the ceremony Porter reported that Eleanor had thrown her bouquet "rather pointedly" at her. She added, "Please don't think it gave me any silly ideas."[55]

The chief event of Porter's homecoming was, of course, the publication of *The Days Before*. She enjoyed all the publication festivities, the "pleasantly feverish state" of getting a book out.[56] There were letters, telegrams, telephone calls, congratulations, invitations, flowers, dinner parties, cocktail parties, and theater parties. The publication of her book might have given her an added incentive to finish another one, but it did not. After a few months in New York she was ready for a more active kind of work.

TWENTY

University Teaching:
Transmitting Something of Value

One of Porter's favorite axioms, to which she never found an exception, was "There is no such thing as an exact synonym and no such thing as an unmixed motive."[1]

Certainly her own motives were often both mixed and obscure and none more so than when she left New York to teach at the University of Michigan. She said that she took the job because her financial difficulties were beyond control and that she had been going out to lecture, getting enough money to carry her over another paragraph, then coming back so exhausted that she could do nothing for weeks.[2] She told Donald Brace that she never again intended to be without a job in one institution of learning or another—she was trying to get her life on some sort of practical footing and get enough money to have a *margin,* however small.[3]

Years later, when her teaching had ended, Porter looked back on the experience as a grim practical necessity that had kept her from her real work of writing: "The fees from this work were what I used to support my writing which never made a living and I knew early that this was to be true."[4]

Often, however, teaching provided a welcome change in her life and satisfied her need to move on and escape oppressive present circumstances. By the spring of 1953, New York had become unbearable to her. Not only had the bad experience with Goyen soured her on the place, but the novel was evolving so slowly that she felt she was stagnating. Her financial worries became the expression of all her accumulated frustrations and she decided to accept the offer of a year's appointment as visiting professor at the University of Michigan.

Any kind of teaching appealed to her. It had been the work she had turned to most naturally when she left school at fourteen and she returned to it over the years with enthusiasm. She had a deep-rooted didactic impulse, and even when she was not teaching professionally she would teach songs and stories and poems to the children around her. Kitty Barry Crawford summed up this fondness for influencing young people when she said of Porter's teaching career:

> It seemed eminently characteristic of her. She likes people, especially young people, and I feel that she is enormously interested in helping them form good ideals of taste and beauty.
> The "something of value" she transmits may be sent forth by her talks and lectures more truly than by her writing.[5]

Moreover, there was still a great deal of the actress in Porter, and teaching allowed her to use her dramatic skills. When she found herself in front of a microphone on the podium of a large lecture hall full of students, she was inspired not so much to lecture as to give a fine dramatic performance.

In addition, teaching in a university was tempting because it satisfied her pride that, although she had never attended university, she should be asked to teach in one. She frequently boasted that the first time she set foot in a university was as a professor. Her position also confirmed a principle that was very dear to her heart. She believed that the best education was the kind she had received, and which she described in her essay on Henry James as

> all unregulated, to be drawn in with the breath, and absorbed like food . . . in the streets, in theaters . . . at picture galleries, at parties, on boats, in hotels, beaches, at family reunions; by listening, by gazing, dawdling, gaping, wondering, and soaking in impressions and sensations at every pore, through every hair.[6]

All the same, she was still sensitive to slights in her dealings with her employers, and, not surprisingly, her initial negotiations with the Michigan officials were tricky. When there was a delay in confirming her appointment, all her apprehensions about not being treated with full respect because she was not an academic were given weight, and she wrote angrily to release the university from the commitment:

> . . . and I do here and now release them; it would be impossible for me to live and work well among people who have treated me so frivolously. *What* did you have in mind? It is going to take me a good while to repair the damage done to my work and my life by this curious inconsequence and lack of responsibility. Why did you invite me in the first place, if you had not enough interest just to do the simplest routine things to carry the plan through?[7]

When she found out that she was required to sign a card saying that she was not a member of any political party or organization which advocated the overthrow of the constitutional form of government, she wrote, "It is a little embarrassing to me, whose families in many branches came here three-hundred-odd years ago, to have to take a pledge of loyalty to my country."[8]

She profited from her Stanford experience in insisting right at the beginning that her courses be given for credit. She told Dr. Warner Rice, the chairman of the English Department, that she had no college degree because she had left school at seventeen to be married.[9] At that time, she said, she had begun trying seriously to write, and such education as she had she had acquired in that way. She said it made her feel uncomfortable for the students if they received no credits for her class.

There was, in fact, some ground for her feeling that she was being treated with condescension. One of her students, a fervent admirer, was horrified when a member of the English Department said, "It was pretty much of a risk or perhaps a gamble is the better word, for us to invite Miss Porter here to teach. As she herself admits, her education is at best sketchy, and she is, despite being a fine writer, not . . . (ahem) . . . a SCHOLAR."[10]

Finally everything was arranged to her satisfaction and she went to Ann Arbor with a few possessions in a suitcase. She had once said, after her unhappy experience with Charles Shannon, that being so much in love had loosened her hold on the material world.[11] Perhaps she felt so in the wake of the affair with Goyen, because she seemed now to be deliberately divesting herself of material possessions. When

she arrived, she took a room at the Michigan League, a campus building which accommodated alumni and other visitors to the university.
She intended to look for an apartment, but the room, with the convenience of the cafeteria downstairs, was quite adequate for her needs
and she apparently lost her urge for a spacious home. She lived out of
suitcases, and when she received presents of brooches and necklaces
and other trinkets she promptly gave them away to her students.[12]

The university treated her with deference and gave her attractive
working quarters in Angell Hall. The suite, intended as the Avery
Hopwood Award headquarters, included a library, a large seminar
room, a kitchenette, and an office for the director of the awards. The
director agreed to wait a year before he moved into his new office so
that Porter could be accommodated there, and in addition Mary
Cooley, part-time assistant to the director, was given a full-time appointment so that she might act also as receptionist and secretary to
Porter.[13]

The assignment to look after Porter proved to be a difficult one,
and an observer described the relationship between them:

> Mary, in her quiet, conscientious, harried way, is quite an
> incarnation of the negative virtues—who wouldn't be, after
> a life-time of dealing with all those poets? KAP couldn't help
> playing the fairy visitant with her, laughing adorably, win-
> somely forgetful and improvident, and so on—as if she ex-
> pected Mary to be swept off her feet by all this charm. While
> there wasn't one chance in a million that she would be swept
> off her feet. I remember KAP telephoning—consulting her
> notebook, and talking and laughing between *each* digit; with
> Mary looking up at her from under her brows, like a weasel
> from its hole.[14]

Although Mary was indeed case-hardened by years of dealing
with writers, and prejudiced in the first place against southern belles,
it is a testimony to Porter that she completely won Mary over. She
said she detected under Porter's surface charm a keen intelligence and
a great generosity, and for the next year she devoted herself to Porter's
needs, far beyond the requirements of her job.[15]

In retrospect, however, she admitted that the job of being responsible for Porter's academic and personal schedule had made her
extremely tense. It was Mary's duty to warn the English Department
whenever a substitute had to be found. She recalled many occasions

of discomfort as ten o'clock approached and there was no sign of Porter. She feared that if Porter were on her way she would be offended at Mary's warning the office. If she were not on her way, the class would be left without a teacher.[16]

Similarly, Porter would accept far more social commitments than she could fulfill. On one typical occasion she accepted a dinner invitation which Mary felt quite sure she could not manage. Knowing that the hostess was making elaborate preparations and inviting people to meet her, she tried to persuade Porter to warn her hostess that she might not get there. Porter insisted that she would be there—until about six o'clock, when she phoned to ask Mary the name of the "nice people" who had invited her and admitted that she was simply too tired to go out. Mary learned later that she sent them a telegram.[17]

She had another unexpected duty when one of Porter's acquaintances decided she needed a car and lent her a British model. Mary, unfamiliar with foreign cars, undertook to learn to drive it so that she could teach Porter. After her own lessons she took Porter out on a quiet highway outside Ann Arbor. Porter took the wheel and managed to drive along until a car approached from the opposite direction. At this she panicked, pulled to the side of the road, and refused to drive again. The car remained unused all winter, getting bumped in the parking lot, until Mary finally drove it to her own back yard to wait for its owner to retrieve it.[18]

Another problem arose from Porter's casual use of the suite in Angell Hall, which was supposed to be used by other English faculty members. She began to prepare meals for herself in the little kitchenette, and once, to everyone's dismay, the aroma of steak and onions floated down the corridor into the classrooms. On another occasion she adopted a stray kitten and carried it back and forth with her between the League and the Hopwood Room, where she fed it on cream from one of the dean's saucers.[19]

Mary also worried about Porter's finances and was shocked to learn that she had no savings at all. She was beginning to see, however, that it was not possible to change Porter's way of life. When Porter was invited to New York for a fairly lucrative television appearance, Mary thought this would surely solve her problems and provide a little nest egg of a savings account for her. When Porter returned after a few days, she was gleeful because she had spent all the money she earned on a black fox stole she saw in a shop window. She told Mary she thought it would come in handy when she was reduced to sleeping under bridges. A few days later the purchase was delivered to the Hopwood Room while Porter was in conference with a student. Mary saw her immediately unpack it and pirouette about the room, modeling it for the student.[20]

Another time she went to Washington to read the Bill of Rights for the television program "Omnibus." She rehearsed at the Capitol for two exhausting days, and just before the program was to go on, it was canceled because of fear that it might offend Senator Joseph McCarthy, who was in the heyday of his "anti-Communist" crusade and might imagine the reading of the Bill of Rights was aimed at him. The cancellation was a blow, but it was mitigated by the fact that she was paid well and—although Marcella Comès Winslow was out of town—had a pleasant visit with Marcella's mother, Honora. The money she earned from the TV show she spent ahead of time on a beautiful purse she saw in Garfinkel's, borrowing the money from Mrs. Comès.

In spite of all other inconveniences, Mary's biggest worry was always Porter's unreliability in meeting classes. As when she had worked at the Library of Congress ten years earlier, she was incapable of keeping to a regular routine. Sometimes she did not feel well enough to attend class, and sometimes she was simply not mentally prepared. One student, meeting her in a campus restaurant, was embarrassed because he intended to cut class that day. She immediately put him at ease by saying that she intended to cut too.[21]

Conferences with students were another worry. Porter, wishing to devote as much attention as she could to each of her students, would schedule a whole series of individual conferences, but if she did appear for them, she would lose track of time talking to one or another student and the rest would be kept waiting and finally not be able to see her at all. Often the first student to get in was the lucky one; if Porter became interested, the first conference was extended to the exclusion of all the rest.[22]

Her attitude to the curriculum was similarly unorthodox. She was scheduled to teach a course in modern poetry, presumably requiring analysis of modern techniques. She was, however, unused to such careful analysis and reluctant to follow a prescribed method. She solved the problem peremptorily by deciding that the students could not possibly understand modern poetry unless they had read what went before. She therefore turned the class into a historical survey, giving readings, appreciations, and commentaries for her favorite poems from Chaucer down to the present. "I don't suppose they were any the worse for it," commented one faculty member.

Unreliability in practical matters was not as important as the weaknesses in her critical approach to literature. She had a habit of consigning many important writers to the wastebasket, a perfectly understandable and defensible habit when she was in conversation with her peers but a dangerous indulgence when she was instructing impressionable students to think carefully and analytically about literature. She scoffed when one student expressed admiration for *The Catcher in the Rye* ("How right she was," the student said later).[23] Another student reported that Porter became almost strident in her abuse of Evelyn Waugh; she wrote in the margin of one of his papers, "You'll be telling me next that Graham Greene is a great Catholic novelist."[24]

One of her most frequent targets was Faulkner, especially in the second semester, when she taught a course in the modern novel. She had resented his winning the Nobel Prize and had also noted the French admiration of him and his miserable performance at the Paris conference. She described this in one of her lectures and went on to say:

> He does not want to think, he is against the whole thing. Yet he made a wonderful speech about man living by his courage and spirit but still he said nothing about the mind and that is what distresses me. This is the first time I have read him in conjunction with Flaubert's *Madame Bovary,* this led me to "Ward 66" of Chekhov and Turgenev's "Fruit Fly," then Thoreau and James. You know I am shocked at how badly Faulkner holds up beside him. I never realized it before. I hope you are getting some education of this because I certainly am. It really frightens me. For the first time I realized when the artist refused to think and act, that part of their mind and that is where the creative faculty resides, then what are we to say? It has really upset me. You are not to agree with me, you know.[25]

In a private letter to one of her students she wrote:

> Tell you the truth, I wouldn't have dared to be seen reading *Sanctuary* in public anywhere. I think it is a truly scandalous book, scandal in a way that the cheap sensationalists who

don't pretend to offer anything else cannot really be! Yet it is a masterpiece in the way it presents the criminal world and its female camp followers: and surely one of the most utterly gruesomely comic scenes in literature—anywhere!—is the passage where Miss Reba and her lady-friend are drinking beer and talking over the funeral and having a maudlin jag, and Uncle Bud keeps stealing their beer right from under their elbows. It took a real artist to write that book, and yet it is a terrible book, and YET I can't be sorry he wrote it because he does hit a bedrock of the evil in human nature, with a kind of off-hand authority and dead-certain swing that reminded me of Bing Crosby playing golf![26]

The basis of her criticism was, as always, moralistic:

Faulkner also has this extraordinary moral confusion. Brings his characters up to a crisis in their lives where they have to act on a moral issue and they simply do not know what it is and in the end they act out of an inherent convention or in some way crookedly for the reason that they cannot think.[27]

Of *The Sound and the Fury* she said:

Candace is a horror (she is the only kind that interests Faulkner—the only thing his women usually lack is the opportunity). When Faulkner gets a good chance he turns out a Candace. She is no good from the beginning, neither is Quentin. But Q takes upon himself the blackest deed that anyone could perform in that way, which is incest with his sister. Says it was he to save the family pride and not implicate a village boy. Faulkner defends Q's action but it is a perverse action, and an example of perverted morality. . . . I have been reading James and Tolstoy and they do it without preaching too much and you know where they stand. James you know what he thinks and feels about his characters but Faulkner has a moral and human confusion in him as well as in his characters and never has cut himself away and distinguished himself from people he is writing about. He feels kin to them. I think he is confused himself.[28]

Porter's remarks on a student's paper called "Thoughts on Faulkner" illustrate her approach to literature. David Locher wrote:

One can understand how an insane person has lost the power
of distinguishing between good and evil, but no supposedly
sane character in a story can be completely believable or
whole, in my mind, unless he had some idea of how to be
good. There are some people running around the world who
seem to be intrinsically evil and others who have little in the
line of morals, but I know of no place where there have been
so many at once as in Yoknapatawpha County—unless we
count Hollywood as being a real place.[29]

And she singled out that paragraph for the marginal comment, "Very
good." Locher went on to say:

Malcolm Cowley, in his introduction in *The Portable Faulkner,* says, "And Faulkner loves these people created in the
image of the land." I don't believe it. Doesn't love open the
door to pity and sympathy? Where is Faulkner's sympathy?
Where his pity? It is the absence of pity for his characters
that distinguishes Faulkner, artist though he is, from Henry
James. Distinguishes him, and shows him to be a lesser
writer than James. James, for all his faults, is complete in his
understanding of his people; they are human.[30]

Her teaching assistant wrote a marginal note here, saying that Faulkner's sympathy was great and overpowering, but Porter wrote beside
the student's paragraph, "I agree."[31] At the end of the paper the
assistant wrote that it was diffuse and vague and the ideas unsup-
ported. Porter added, "Perhaps, but remember that we asked for
honest and direct opinions."[32]

Although there were few complaints from the students, some
perceptive observers raised eyebrows. Martin Green, a graduate student at the time, has recalled his impressions:

Certainly I believed there was a great deal of performance,
and not much instruction. What one got from her—I went
to one or two public lectures—were some vivid impressions
of her life as a writer and a reader. . . . That rather priggish
word "self-indulgent" was in the air then, I think. Anyway,
that's what I thought she was. On the other hand, she was a
very interesting personality to have around—charming and
graceful and intelligent.
Of course, KAP was a genuinely beautiful woman still

in those days. I used to see her standing in the line for supper at the League, and she looked like a peacock that had fluttered down in a barnyard. But in the tutorials she gave me, she didn't really have anything to say about my writing. She just talked—about her husbands. . . . I remember, too, some long story she told me about some pearls she had just bought—for her 60th birthday, could it have been? Anyhow, it was all about how she had indulged herself with them—"You *deserve* them, I said to myself." With that husky chuckle.[33]

The attitude of most students, however, was just this side of idolatry. One of the faculty dubbed them her "fervents," and ten years later Porter was astonished when she ran into one of her "fervents" in Europe and discovered that he had modeled his entire life and way of thinking on her opinions "as of then."[34]

Few of her students would ever forget the class she taught just after Dylan Thomas died. In spite of their mad encounter, she greatly admired his work and had accompanied some of her students to a reading he gave at Ann Arbor earlier that fall. For her class she read "And Death Shall Have No Dominion," and she told the students that she, Malcolm Cowley, and some other American writers were taking up a collection for Dylan's wife and children.[35]

Another memorable occasion was her public reading of "Flowering Judas" in February. One of her colleagues described it:

When she finished the reading the applause came with the sustained warmth uniquely characteristic, I think, of student audiences. And after she stood and bowed the applause continued until she finally came to the lectern and said she would speak the only poem she still could give from memory. This was the poem, the perfect epigraph for "Flowering Judas":

As Life What Is So Sweet

As life what is so sweet,
What creature would not choose thee?
The wounded hart doth weep
When he is forced to lose thee:
The bruised worm doth strive 'gainst fear of death,
And all choose life with pain 'ere loss of breath.

The dove which knows no guilt
Weeps for her mate a-dying;
And never any blood was spilt
But left the loser crying;
If swans do sing, it is to crave of death
He would not reave them of their happy breath.
                    (Anon., written about 1624?)[36]

One student described Porter as "to generations of women, all over . . . a lively patron saint of literature."[37] Another was staggered by Porter's account of her meeting with Hitler. She told the student that she had met him, recognized his evil, and held herself responsible for the terrible things that happened in the world in the thirties and forties. She said she should have managed to kill him but had not done so. This statement floored the student, who had never thought that individuals could change the course of history; it was a revelation to her that someone would feel guilty about not doing so.[38]

Students' recollections of her classes and conferences give a sense of her lively personality and genuine interest in their lives. One young man was "writing stories for slower high school boys. The whole idea revolted her. She said that educating such people was a waste, but she devoted herself to helping me do what I wanted to do and even gave me some name to which I could submit such writing."[39]

Another student who was not even in any of her classes met her one day in the campus restaurant. The student was trying to write and, burdened by domestic responsibilities, was discouraged and unhappy. She credited the meeting with Porter as changing the whole course of her life. Porter told her "You've a son. . . . You'll write . . . you'll DO." Later this same student invited Porter to a simple family dinner in her home, and this was one engagement Porter kept, reinforcing her support of the young woman.[40]

Perhaps her most successful teaching was in her creative writing classes, for here she combined two of her strengths—her generous interest in individual students and her own experience in writing short stories. In some of the classes there was her usual abdication of pedagogy in favor of personal display, but the entertainment was of very high quality indeed:

The creative writing classes consisted of meetings at various class members' homes or I mean two-room pads, etc. Each student was working on some of his own narrative writing. Excerpts were supposed to be read, but almost all we did was listen to Katherine Anne read and discuss her life and friends.

Some of these sessions were lively to say the least—we heard about her marriages—her friendship with Erskine Caldwell—her stories and her disappointments. She often wore long black leotards and often drank her wine from a champagne glass.

At the slightest word she would assume the middle of the floor and dance in the dance of a slightly aging swan. Her presence was hypnotic. She was always the dainty and delicate bird with a backbone of steel. Each wrinkle had a story which she could expound long and beautifully in that magnificent husky Katherine Anne voice.[41]

And sometimes she was simply too pressed for time and unable to read all the scripts on her desk. Students felt that she had glanced quickly at their work just before they came to discuss it. But one gave this account of her method:

Each week creative writing students had a two-hour session with her in her office in the Hopwood Room. If something you were writing reminded her of something she would pull from her green files a scrap of an unfinished story or a paragraph from an incomplete essay. She took your story to pieces not in the usual technical way, but by reading it aloud to you—putting in it what it had and making you see its imperfection.[42]

For the most part she realized, as every creative writing teacher does, that few of her students had remarkable talent. When she did find a talent she respected, she worked hard and conscientiously to develop it. The comments she made on the entries when she was asked to help judge the manuscripts submitted for the Hopwood Award show that her judgment of unknown talent was much sounder than her judgment of her fellow writers:

What surprises me in a great deal of this work is the technical slickness and the curious lack of character analysis, the strange vagueness about the deeper places of human nature in them. One can hardly say it comes of the youthfulness of the writers—youthful genius has intuitive perception and boldness, a rightness of its own. Also, even in the best of the short stories, there is a disturbing amount of waste motion, aimless space filling conversation, which looks like Hemingway on the page, but is not moving steadily forward with every sentence, as Hemingway's talk does. They seem to me to be following set rules of composition, writing to a formula. This is all very well while one is mastering a craft, perhaps, but it is apprentice work only. I think none of them have come to the point of breaking away from what they have been taught. There is where the test lies, none of them have faced it yet.

I wonder sometimes about the wisdom of our system of driving the young to write by means of awards. I believe it is a good thing for students to practise writing, to study literature, for any knowledge of the arts is good: but perhaps it would be better to train good readers. . . .

[One of the submissions] has many good qualities, wit and good temper and intelligence, she is a beautiful writer, and sustains her superior level of style and point of view throughout: no small achievement. But the material is simply not worth the enormous effort and genuine talent that has been expended on it. . . .

I would say to these writers, condense, condense and again condense. Less than fifty thousand words each would have covered the case in these works.

They all lack depth, as if, instead of studying with Henry James, Flaubert, Tolstoy, and the great poets: as if instead of searching their own hearts and minds they had modelled their style on current saleable fiction.

I chose for potentialities: capacity for absorbing experience, feeling for language, a good balance between seeing and feeling, richness of observation, a prime interest in human beings, awareness on many levels of perception.

Note: how many of the younger writers are engrossed with the theme of the poor boy or girl struggling to break out of a straitened unhappy environment to better things, and how often the better things mean simply better clothes or white leather chairs or a good salary, or the mere chance to "run with the right crowd" . . . And the "college education" they yearn for is only a stepping stone to fulfillment of these little desires, a symbol of social and economic privilege.

Here my personal taste is put to a severe ordeal, for the whole frenetic worship of Jazz and the hip life and the cat psychology and indeed, most of the "music" itself by now bores me to extinction, and I have had a long long long time at it.

I have about got through the mss, reading all day every day—will send you a kind of comment very soon. It's pretty frightfully discouraging, isn't it? They nearly all know how to write, but not how to feel, or to think, or to be and they have really lost their compass, haven't they? It is fantastic to see young university people almost exclusively devoted to the subjects of dope, jazz, gutter sex, and yet with a kind of sentimental wistfulness about virtue like those people in Dante bursting out of a wall of pitch.[43]

Although she had very little imagination and understanding about talents different from her own, she understood her own strengths and discerned them clearly in others. Thus she was able to be very helpful to students and beginning writers whose talents were similar to her own.

Perhaps Porter's lack of experience in university teaching told most of all in her complete underestimation of the demands of the job. Her contract was for five hours of teaching a week, but many more hours were taken up with related tasks. As a visiting professor, she had no administrative duties, but she found her days overburdened with reading endless manuscripts and advising students.[44] That spring she wrote Monroe Wheeler that there were about 24,000 human beings on the campus and she had never seen (except at other universities its size) such "a hellish, leaping, animal vitality." She went home at the end of each day feeling as if she had visited a blood bank. There she took a good stiff swig of bourbon, tidied herself up, had dinner, lolled in a warm bath and went to bed. Ominously she had begun to feel exhausted and crushed with work.[45]

She had two illnesses serious enough to require hospitalization that year, first in Mercy Hospital and later in the University Hospital. The second was the more serious, for she collapsed in front of a class with an attack of angina pectoris, "the kind that can carry you off in one split second or hang around and nag you for forty years."[46]

The New York Times of March 24, 1954, ran an article saying that she had suffered a heart attack. She was not happy at the publicity, which she thought resulted from the campus newspaper with its "flock of young vampire bats" learning to be reporters.[47] One happy result was that she got letters and telegrams from all over the world, and was amazed at the spate of kindness and gentle feeling even from Europe.

After a week of rest she began to feel better and to think about the people she had not heard from. She said she was afflicted by strange silences that had begun to assert themselves, not a word from any writer or colleague except Wescott and Wheeler, or from the entire membership of the National Institute of Arts and Letters, nothing from the Sitwells, from the Warrens or the Tates or Eudora Welty.[48] But she wrote her nephew that she was using the heart attack in her novel—she now understood what Dr. Sacher (an early name for Dr. Schumann) suffered from. She had vaguely described it as a very ordinary form of heart disease, not having the faintest notion of what his trouble might be called. Now she knew.[49]

Later in the spring she had recovered enough to finish her year of teaching feeling happy and optimistic. She marked the end of the year with a party for her students and their husbands and wives. She went to a great deal of trouble and expense for the occasion, helped, as she had been all year, by Mary Cooley. She planned an outdoor party, an elegant picnic with a baron of beef, that staple of Old English hospitality, served up as the main part of the meal. A soft-drink company would supply a hundred pounds of ice to chill the hard and soft drinks—but the snag was that a city ordinance prohibited drinking liquor in city parks, and it was being enforced by police raids. When this was explained, Porter said simply, "But there must be a park where I can have it—and I must give them whiskey." And indeed, the problem was solved when a professor offered his back yard just outside the city limits. Porter cooked two twelve-pound rib roasts in Mary Cooley's kitchen, and saw to it that they were served at just the right temperature, not too hot and not too cold. The party was a huge success.[50]

The University of Michigan expressed its appreciation of her year's work by giving her her second honorary doctorate. This time, she told friends, she was a Doctor of Humane Letters, "no mere doctor of mere letters," and she laid away another gaily colored silk and velvet hood "for the moths."[51] She concluded that her year in Ann Arbor had been unexpectedly happy, quite simply the best year she had known for a long time, and she said that her health was so much better she could not believe it. She had even been able to save a little money, so that she would not have to lecture, give readings, or do odd jobs for a year. And she confided to Wheeler that she was writing.

She had, in fact, managed to complete one small essay which had been commissioned by *Mademoiselle,* and this had been achieved partly through the help of Mary Cooley. When Porter complained that she could not work because of constant interruptions, Mary offered to let Porter use her home and set her up with a typewriter and plenty of paper. The first time she did so was on the day of the weekly Hopwood tea, which Porter usually avoided. On this occasion, however, when Mary thought she was happily at work, Porter turned up at the tea. She explained that she had needed some toothpaste and thought that while she was out she would just stop in the Hopwood Room.[52] In spite of such delaying tactics, the essay, "A Defense of Circe," was finished and sent off to the magazine. But this was probably not what she meant when she wrote that she was at work again.

Porter had brought the manuscript of the novel with her to Ann Arbor. She knew there would be little time for it, but she hoped for a miracle. For most of the year she did little actual writing, but the writing down is, after all, only a part of the creative process. All year long, often without realizing it, as she relaxed after classes, avoided meeting them, or prepared for them, the novel was simmering in her mind. The work was being carried on at a level just below her consciousness, and the part she was working on was the love affair of La Condesa and Dr. Schumann.

The purchase of her strand of pearls during the Ann Arbor year was of extraordinary importance to her, and she talked excitedly about it to everyone, including her students:

> One day she came to our weekly meeting sporting a long string of pearls—down to the knees! Upon hearing us comment, she went into a most unusual explanation about how she had no money except what little she got for teaching at U of M—about how sad she was that she hadn't been able to get her publisher to let her get into pockets, and how while others made money, she lived in poverty on friends to be known as a great writer. She explained the pearls by saying she saw them in a shop window and when she knew they cost almost as much as she was making, she decided to buy them because she had always wanted real pearls in that length.[53]

To her niece she wrote her own version of the "act of extravagance I haven't had the courage to confess to anybody":

> My extravagance is really another little heirloom for you, though that was not in the least the reason I bought it. I bought it for my own joy and pleasure, and it has been that to me every day, and everytime I see it or wear it, and it will be beautiful on you someday too. It is a pearl necklace (cultured of course) of forty-nine pearls about this size: not graduated, a pale rosy pink in tone; some are pinker than others, they are not perfectly matched, they have each one its own little wrinkle of tiny pock, or shade; and the tiniest but perfectly visible differences in size, and so on: it has only a platinum clasp, though I intend one day to have an emerald one: it cost seven hundred and fifty dollars, and would have cost twice as much if they had been absolutely perfectly matched. This is not one of those department store cultured pearl things. It's a serious little piece of jewelry, and it might give a sense of proportion to remember that if it was a natural or Orient necklace, it would cost at present around a hundred and fifty thousand dollars. So leave me not be too proud. . . . They're only cultured, and they bore a gruesome little tag saying *These pearls were grown in living oysters in the sea*. And so they were, and they look and feel it, with that beautiful soft light coming from *inside* them, each one so subtly different you soon learn to know each one separately. As you see, I have had extravagant pleasure from this simple little thing, and have hardly worn anything else around my neck since. I even slept in it in the hospital. It has its white-satin lined case, and hands draped through the leather clasps of the raised lid, and is in fact treated as if it were the queen's own Orients. To me it is. I cannot account for my mysterious happiness in it. I do not believe it is in the least frivolous. I feel quite easy in my mind about *that*, even if I do think it worth mentioning.[54]

It is difficult at first to understand the extravagance of the purchase and the "mysterious happiness" it brought her. The fact was that the pearls were more than a piece of personal adornment. They were properties in the inner drama that Porter was shaping in her imagination. Many of the details of *Ship of Fools* suggest that when she walked about the campus of the University of Michigan a part of her was, in the persona of La Condesa, walking the decks of the S.S. *Werra* with the pearls around her neck. When La Condesa first appears in the ship's dining room it is the necklace which excites comment, just as it did when Porter wore it to class.

The description had already appeared in "The Exile," an extract from the novel, in *Harper's Magazine* in 1950:

> She wore enormous pearls in her ears, around her throat, on two fingers of her left hand. On her right she wore what appeared to be a light-colored much-flawed emerald, big as a robin's egg and surrounded by small diamonds.
>
> "I had never imagined a revolutionist wearing such pearls," said Frau Rittersdorf, who had been thinking her own thoughts. "If, indeed, they are real, which is doubtful."
>
> "When such a lady wears pearls," said little Frau Schmitt, respectfully, "I think we may be confident they are real."[55]

To fully create the woman who wore the pearls and their effect on her fellow passengers, Porter needed to wear them in reality.

Another experience which was transmuted in a different way was her friendship with a young library-science student from Dubuque, Iowa. He was working on the switchboard at Mercy Hospital during Porter's time there and was allowed into her room so that she might autograph a book for him. He found her dressed in a kimono, sitting up in bed surrounded by books and papers, and spent half an hour with her. She was immediately taken with the serious young man, a devout Catholic, who admired her work very much. Later David Locher took her classes and the friendship deepened.

When it was time for him to leave Ann Arbor he went around to the Michigan League to say good-bye. Porter was in bed and unable to see him that afternoon, but she talked to him over the house telephone. He was overwhelmed by the thought that he would never see her again and that this was the end of the friendship. She sensed that he was stricken and responded by telling him, "David, honey, life has few separations that are really complete and entire, and we *will* meet again."[56]

In this instance she was right, for David Locher became one of the most faithful of her devotees. Besides being a bibliophile and a poet he was a skilled craftsman who made large quantities of rosaries to be taken abroad by missionaries. For Porter he made rosaries with special care, and she always carried them with her and kept them at her bedside. The first was of silver with blue moonstones and delicate silver filigree, and later there were others equally beautiful. He supplied her also with relics of the saints and reliquaries, which she counted as her most treasured possessions.

Four years after the Ann Arbor parting, David was surprised to receive two pages which she said were the only two surviving pages from the first draft of her novel. She said that she had typed the first draft at white heat, and later, going back and making corrections and typing a second draft, she destroyed all the pages from the first draft as she went along. The two pages had survived because they got lost on a chair under some magazines.

The passage is from the part of the novel that takes place in the harbor of Santa Cruz de Tenerife and is the farewell scene between Dr. Schumann and La Condesa. It begins with Dr. Schumann entering La Condesa's cabin and ends, " 'Why of course, death,' said La Condesa as if indulging his fancy, 'but not yet!' "[57]

When the passage appeared in the novel Porter had inserted a paragraph not included in the first draft. In this passage La Condesa says of their love:

"It is that innocent romantic love I should have had in my girlhood! But no one loved me innocently, and oh, how I should have laughed at him if he had! . . . Well, here we are. Innocent love is the most painful kind of all, isn't it?"

"I have not loved you innocently," said Dr. Schumann, "but guiltily, and I have done you great wrong, and I have ruined my life. . . ."

"My life was ruined so long ago I have forgotten what it was like before," said La Condesa. "So you are not to have me on your mind. And you must not think of me as sleeping on stone floors and living on bread and water, for I shall not ever—it is not my style. It is not becoming to me. I shall find a way out of everything. And now, now my love, let's kiss again really this time in broad daylight and wish each other well, for it is time for us to say good-bye."[58]

It seems likely that after all her love affairs, all her friendships with the rich and famous, all the adulation of her students, she recognized in David's disinterested and innocent love a quality that moved her very much.

So in the spring of 1954 she was once again immersed in her novel. The time was approaching when she would at last abandon everything else, and sit down and finish it. But there was still another period of traveling, procrastination, and turmoil before she did.

TWENTY-ONE

I Am Really Old Now
and . . . Time Is Running Out

I n *Silences,* Tillie Olsen, accepting Porter's own reasons for the protracted gestation period of her novel, includes her among those who have been unnaturally silenced: "Twenty years went by on the writing of *Ship of Fools,* while Katherine Anne Porter, who needed only two, was 'trying to get to that table, to that typewriter, away from my jobs of teaching and trooping this country and of keeping house.' "[1]

Practical problems were not the only and perhaps not even the main reasons for the delay. There was no reason why Porter, after her year in Ann Arbor, or even before it, should not have withdrawn from public life and finished her novel. Interest in the book was high enough for a number of publishers to be willing to support her for a few years on the chance of bringing out the novel at last. The compelling reason for the delay was in the writer herself, rather than in her circumstances.

The fact was that for more than ten years her creative energy had been very low. She had retained command of her impressive use of language; she was still a master of the short-story technique, which she had developed to a high art; and she still had her theme. But it was in the last area that her chief problem lay. Several years had passed since the ending of the Second World War renewed her confidence in her theme, and she had lost the urgency that comes from having something new and important to say. Her public declarations of her theme were still impassioned, but they were shrill and repetitive rather than convincing.

In addition, the long, ambitious novel, with its huge cast of characters, was giving her trouble. Her particular area of expertise was in the short story. She was perceptive and insightful in depicting characters but she was not able to show them growing, changing, or maturing. Similarly, she could portray incidents that were dramatic and arresting but she was not able to imagine them as causing significant changes in the lives of her characters. Her art was quintessentially that of a short-story writer and within the confinement of that form worked brilliantly. When, however, she tried to work on a huge panoramic canvas and solve the riddle of what had gone wrong with the whole Western world in the twentieth century, she had to weld together all the small incidents and essentially minor characters in such a way that the cumulative effect would achieve significance. It was a daunting technical problem that might well have overwhelmed anyone. In a letter to Glenway Wescott, in which she had been complaining of a series of trivial annoyances, she finally confessed:

> These are not serious matters, not very entertaining either. I suppose I write them to keep from breaking out and saying how I am slogging at this devilish book, and how bored I am with it, because the plan is so finished, there is nothing to do but just type it down to the end, and OH GOD! how I have to beat myself over the head to get started every morning—and even so I am late, and wake every day with my heart sinking, thinking I'll *never* make it. But I must and will, and I shall *never* write another novel, that is flat![2]

When the novel was finished, several critics noted the monotone characteristic that came from the boredom and the sense of mechanical drudgery she felt while writing it.

Given the immensity and variety of her difficulties, it is not surprising that she was an easy prey to distractions, especially when they offered recognition of her work, confirmation of her continued effectiveness, and financial remuneration. When, therefore, at the end of the Michigan year, she was offered another visiting lectureship, this time at the University of Liége, she accepted at once. The job, part of the Fulbright exchange program for American and European scholars, promised prestige and adventure. She told friends that she would be able to see places she had missed before—Rome, Vienna, Florence—and she also loved the idea of the sea voyage. She set out from New York to Rotterdam in a spirit of high adventure. At the back of her mind must have rested the wistful, desperate hope that this trip across the Atlantic would revive her creative power, as her first one had done so many years before.

This time her hopes were dashed the minute she arrived. She disliked Liége instantly on sight (she could hate with the dramatic suddenness with which she fell in love), found the Belgian climate dismal and the atmosphere suffocating to her health and spirits. She fell ill and spent two weeks in bed, and in October she wrote to Glenway Wescott, "I am melancholy to a point I have not known since Germany, Berlin 1931—these heavy dark Northern countries how they oppress me."[3]

It was not only the physical atmosphere that oppressed her. She had a set of problems just the reverse of those she had faced in Ann Arbor. There she had been overwhelmed with invitations, requests for help, and demands on her time. In Liége, where she was not a celebrity with throngs of admirers, and where she had only one one-hour lecture a week, she was completely alone. She felt acutely neglected and lonely and poured out her feelings in desolate letters:

It is five o'clock, I am in a dowdy furnished apartment where the keys don't turn, the gas-cocks stick, the bathroom gadgets work half way, the neighborhood is *tout-petit bourgeois,* the furnishings are from the Belgian branch of Sears Roebuck, the place is suburban, the wild yellow leaves are flying in a high bitter wind under a smoky sky, and I have come to the world's end, and what was my errand here? There is nothing I wish to say to anyone here; does anybody want to listen? But it does look as if here again, with all the unlikeliness, the place and the time had met for me to sit at this table, three and one half feet square, and write something more of my own.

Still, I am here, tethered, if not actually nailed—nails seem more likely for there is a real pain in it . . . and then, I look back and remember, and for how long has life just been for me an endurance contest, how many times have I said, "I will live through this, and to the next thing. . . ." This is really no worse than I have known before. . . . It is only *now,* and the other was *then.*[4]

She could remember other times when she had felt the same desolation in cold climates—in the Connecticut farmhouse in 1924, in Berlin in 1931, in Basle in 1932, and at Yaddo, just after she left Erskine in 1940. Some of these times had yielded rich literary material —Berlin "The Leaning Tower," Basle "Noon Wine," Yaddo the beginning of the novel. Two stories begun in Connecticut twenty years before were still not finished, "Season of Fear" and "A Vision of Heaven," her effort to commemorate the death of her niece.

From the beginning she had had a rough outline of the latter story, which consisted of three episodes from different times telescoped together. These were the child's birth, her death six years later, and the meeting between the child's Aunt Miranda and another child called Alice. The third episode was intended to bring Miranda a climactic revelation about the nature of grief. Porter had gone back to this story frequently over the years—in Berlin, in Basle, at Yaddo. In New York in 1951, at the time of her love affair with Bill Goyen, she felt she had gained control of her theme and grasped the nature of Miranda's revelation about her reaction to the child's death:

> Re-thinking and re-seeing my story, at last I had simply to put away my notes and write a perfectly clear outline, a thing I have never done until now, for I realize that this must be finished now or abandoned. And I cannot abandon it. But I saw—it was like a revelation—that the reason I am so long in finding the meaning and seeing the end of something I know I must tell, is that I have stubbornly refused to accept the shock and the suffering, I *will* not reconcile myself; the memory, instead of staying fluid and going on and changing and living, sets itself and fixes upon that point in time where the shock occurred and cannot be persuaded away from it, and slowly turns to stone. Only a greater shock either of joy or of another suffering, can make it loose its hold. You know what my life has been for the past five years, my whole being resolutely refusing to move from that place where some incurable wrong had been done to that mysterious center in which all my experience seems to take, finally. But the shock *has* occurred that broke up the stony core, and I must re-live with all the courage I have those experiences that I have tried to enclose and hold and yet refuse really to remember to accept. So, my dear love, when I said that being melted is painful, you will see—I feel you have already seen—that your love and my love for you has uprooted me, wrenched me away from that deadened center with such violence.[5]

Bill Goyen was anxious at the time about the critical illness of a child in his family and possibly this caused her to return to her story. She told him:

> You know what the death of a child means to a family, I don't quite know why it leaves such an unhealing wound but it does. I have been living over again all these months that very thing in the *Vision of Heaven*. It is an intolerable blow, I could wish you—and above all the mother—might never feel it. And if it happens remember the mother. It is her grief more than yours, I was selfish, I suffered by myself instead of loving my sister and sharing her trouble. I was wrong and have tried to repair it; but oh things are so badly repaired, no matter what one does.[6]

In Liége, as she sat in the little flat, trying to reconcile herself to her exile, she read her notes on the two stories again and came to an important conclusion. She saw that "Season of Fear" was a part of "A Vision of Heaven." She realized that the two losses, the loss of Mary Alice and the loss, seven years later, of her own baby, were identical and that she had responded to them in the same way. Both incidents had, in fact, embodied her deepest horrors—her fear that everything she touched would die, her sense of loneliness and isolation in an inhuman world. The recognition of this unity was tremendously important to her, and in her notes she recorded it as it happened.[7] It came about between one and half past one in the afternoon. Between that time and half past three, writing about her realization brought such a relief of mind, such a lighting up and warming up of the spirit, that it was a tremendously happy day. She wondered why she had not seen this before and decided she was the same stubborn soul she had always been—it had been too terrible for her to accept the truth of the two experiences. The events followed on the epidemic of 1918 and she had written about that in "Pale Horse, Pale Rider," but there was a residue of truth which she had not told and she thought that now she might be able to do so.

It was not an auspicious sign that she turned from rewriting the stories to writing letters about them to her friends. And, indeed, she had still not entirely solved the technical problems and could not finish the stories, although she never abandoned the hope of doing so. While her sense of displacement in Liége had created the mood in which she turned again to "A Vision of Heaven," she had a more practical incentive for wanting to finish it at this time. It had been especially requested by *Mademoiselle*.

Of all Porter's admirers none was more constant than Cyrilly Abels, managing editor of *Mademoiselle*. An enterprising and energetic woman, she solicited material from Porter persistently, received whatever was offered with boundless enthusiasm, and was able to pay a good price for it. When she was not publishing the work, she kept the friendship alive with lunch invitations, letters, flowers, and gifts —a steady stream of reminders that there was one place where her work was always welcome.

When Porter arrived at the Michigan League in Ann Arbor, for example, one of the first welcoming gifts was a bottle of rare brandy in a splendid case. It was a present from Cyrilly, whose attentions never ceased. They are acknowledged and described in numerous thank-you letters over the years:

> . . . the purple cardigan. . . . Let me just say now it is simply beautiful, just right, and I think such a becoming color for me! Oh what can I do for you? Name something!

> I am simply, as Paul says it, overwhammed at those wonderful sheets and pillow cases. I did not dream you meant to send more, and when I opened that big surprise-party box yesterday I could hardly believe my eyes. . . .
> The book came too—with my pore lil ole check. Cyrilly my angel, do you think it is my birthday?[8]

Although Cyrilly was the busiest of women, with a home and husband and a full schedule of lunches, interviews, and editorial duties, she offered to do errands in New York when Porter was out of town. Never slow to take advantage of such an offer, Porter made constant demands for clothes—evening dresses, purses, and whatever she could not find near at hand. She wrote from Washington, D.C., "Surely someone here sells Delman shoes, but I can't find him. I am sure they are expensive, and I am sending you a check for $25.00 to start, please buy them and have them mailed."[9]

When the two lunched together before Porter's departure for Michigan, Cyrilly had requested "something" for *Mademoiselle*'s annual beauty number and later received the essay "A Defense of

Circe," the one piece of work that Porter finished during the hectic year in Ann Arbor. In this version of the Circe episode in *The Odyssey,* Porter denies that Circe is a wicked witch who turns men into swine, and portrays her instead as a merry-hearted half-goddess whose honeyed food and potent wine merely cause men to reveal themselves for the swine they really are.

The essay appeared in the June 1954 edition of *Mademoiselle* and Porter described it as the only original idea she ever had (actually both Hawthorne and Eudora Welty took similar attitudes to Circe). Porter's version was entirely in keeping with her reading of *The Odyssey.* She heartily disliked Odysseus, and when she read of his conflict with the Cyclops she was firmly on the side of the Cyclops, who she thought was shamefully tricked and robbed of his sheep. Her Circe essay enlarged upon a marginal note she had made in one of her copies of the poem (she thought she owned every English translation ever made): "It is here that I feel not for the first time but most strongly that when Circe attempted to turn Odysseus into the swine that he was, she was right."[10]

In the original, Hermes advises Odysseus to get Circe to swear an oath not to make him "a dastard and unmanned" once she has him stripped and into bed. From this advice Porter draws a firm conclusion:

> This gives us an oblique glimmer of truth about Circe; for these two methodically unreliable beings, strangely enough, never doubt for a moment that Circe can be trusted to honor her oath. It might reasonably be expected that she could not be relied upon any more than any of the other gods once they were set against one; but she could be trusted, it seems, they both knew it and set out cheerfully to take advantage of their knowledge.
>
> Not even a god, having once formed a man, can make a swine of him. That is for him to choose. Circe's honeyed food with the lulling drug in it caused them to reveal themselves. The delicate-minded goddess touched them with her wand, the wand of the transforming truth, and penned the groaning, grunting, weeping, bewildered creatures in the sty back of the hall.[11]

The passage in the Circe episode that Porter loved best was the description of Circe's heating up a mighty caldron of water and bathing Odysseus in it. Porter, saying it "stops my heart with joy," wrote lyrically, ". . . of the goddess herself bathing away weariness of the loved mortal body under her hands; and it celebrates the smoothness of olive oil on the skin, and of fine linen next the flesh, and of good cheer and comfort and sweet smells and savors."[12]

There was usually some source of annoyance in all Porter's publishing ventures, and even *Mademoiselle* cut a whole paragraph near the end of her Circe essay. She considered this "mayhem" and insisted ever afterward that anything she wrote be printed unchanged. But on the whole she thoroughly enjoyed the assignment and the opportunity to write

> something I had in mind for years, but would never have got down on paper if Cyrilly Abels hadn't asked me to contribute to their annual "Beauty Number." The editors seemed to have been astounded at what they got but they printed it after a little backing and filling, skittish mares that they are. . . . I don't mean Cyrilly, she's a love.[13]

In 1955 Harcourt, Brace published *A Defense of Circe* in a limited edition of seventeen hundred numbered copies, intended for friends of the author and the publishers as New Year's greetings. Porter loved giving the copy to friends and often inscribed in it these lines translated from a Pindaric ode:

> Beauty, who creates
> All sweet delights for men,
> Brings honor at will, and makes the false seem true,
> Time and again.[14]

Thus she had generally pleasant associations with writing for Cyrilly. In addition, it was reassuring to see some lesser works appearing when the major task was not progressing. And she liked being paid well. But in spite of these advantages she was a little self-conscious about publishing in a women's fashion magazine and sometimes felt she had to justify herself:

> . . . it is now true that, exactly due to the long war my generation fought for the little magazine, the big fat magazines now will take the kind of thing only the little magazines would print then—and the fat ones pay better, and so

I am just in a way collecting my dues after all those years of giving my work to the literary reviews. . . . I write as I please, as I always did and always will, but now I pick up what I hope is an honest penny for my work whenever I get the chance.[15]

Some time later, when *Encounter,* which had no announced policy against reprints, turned down her "After a Long Journey," giving as a reason the poem's earlier appearance in *Mademoiselle,* she fired off a reply, saying that *Mademoiselle* had published the earliest works of James Purdy, Dylan Thomas, Eudora Welty, and Robert Penn Warren, among others, and that she had published widely "long before either Mr. Spender or Mr. Kristol had published a line anywhere." She lashed out at the *Encounter* editors,

with their talent for occupying fairly safe jobs, their really remarkable sense of career and self-promotion, their real genius for pushing themselves into any situation where they may exercise some power over the writings of others.

It rather chills my blood that a magazine published under your aegis, no doubt having a positive influence in the literary world, should be edited by people who judge a piece of work by where it was published instead of accepting or rejecting it in the light of their own editorial judgment. . . .

I have had very few rejections in a long life of writing, and I have always preferred the honesty and directness of editors who said (1) "I don't like this," or (2) "This is not suitable for us." Perhaps you may suggest very tactfully to your editors that this is a good style to adopt, inoffensive to any sensible author and an effective disguise for their own dubious motives and astounding snobbery.[16]

In *Waiting for the End* the critic Leslie A. Fiedler wrote of Katherine Anne Porter that she had "only in the past few years . . . clearly exposed herself as having gone over to ladies'-magazine fiction." She was so furious that when his picture appeared alongside a review of his book she scribbled around it, "This is what the Jews used to call a Kike—I don't know what that means but this nasty smug conceited smirk is the front for the most indecent mind and the pickiest envy of talent I know and it is pure Jewish as Seymour Kr__ says."[17]

At one of their meetings before Porter went to Belgium, Cyrilly had asked about her "works in progress." She liked the sound of "A Vision of Heaven" and urged Porter to take it along and finish it. At the same time she asked if Porter thought she might contribute again to one of the annual theme issues, this time the "adventure" number planned for the summer of 1955. When "A Vision" did not work out quickly, Porter set it aside for the second request and added her own "adventure" story to the four other articles that appeared, one of them "Adventure in Loafing" by Françoise Sagan.

Taking as her theme a quotation from Yeats which she could never exactly identify and which she had used in her 1941 introduction to Eudora Welty's *A Curtain of Green and Other Stories*, ". . . a type of man considered most unfortunate by W. B. Yeats: one whose experience was more important than he, and completely beyond his powers of absorption,"[18] she began with a short introductory paragraph in which she recalled her own quest for adventure when she tried mountain climbing in Colorado in 1918. (Was she perhaps thinking of Jane Anderson and her disastrous headlong search for adventurous experiences?) Then she used her familiar technique of yoking together two apparently disparate experiences. One was her own reluctant exposure to bullfighting in Mexico; the second came from her favorite bedside text, *The Confessions of St. Augustine*. There she selected the incident of the young man Alypius, who was reluctant to attend the gladiatorial games and discovered to his astonishment that he enjoyed them.

Her intention was to show that she, like Alypius, turned the incident from adventure into experience:

> The difference then between mere adventure and a real experience might be this? That adventure is something you seek for pleasure, or even for profit, like a gold rush or invading a country; for the illusion of being more alive than ordinary, the thing you will to occur; but experience is what really happens to you in the long run; the truth that finally overtakes you.[19]

In technique and language the essay was an embryonic short story. Porter usually began her stories this way and later changed them from first-person narrative to third-person. The trick, she once told Caroline Gordon, was to write about yourself as if you were writing about someone else. Cyrilly loved Porter's essay, bought it, published it, and said that it could not have been done better. Glenway Wescott praised it as a "new art form."[20] Porter herself knew better than to think the story was finished, but she was grateful for his praise:

> Bless you for liking the Adventure. . . . I realize I didn't say enough about Alypius and his career. I am mending that error in the version I mean to send to John Lehmann. . . . I mean to write a number of incidents in my life in that way . . . it is what I can do now, it satisfies me while I am working on it. . . . Not a word was changed this time by any editor, I was so outraged at the mayhem committed on Circe, I made it a matter of life and death that not a word should be changed but I shall add some.[21]

Porter said that she was delighted with the essay and had enjoyed doing it. She intended to expand the incident of Alypius in the later version, and she might well have worked the material into a highly polished story, like "Holiday." All the same, she did no more and "St. Augustine and the Bullfight" remained her sole literary production for the year.

Some relief from the tedium of life in Liége came at Christmas time, when she took a trip to London to read "The Circus" for the B.B.C. She went from there to Paris to buy clothes and celebrate the New Year, but the highlight of her Christmas traveling was her discovery of Rome. New places had always excited her and she reacted to Rome very much as she had to Paris when she discovered it for the first time. A few years later she recalled her first impression:

> I saw Rome for the first time Christmas week 1954, saw all the sights one can see in five days, being handed around by a tireless sightseer—I would have preferred to sit in restaurants with friends and let the sights go by under their own powers—threw a lira in the Trevi Fountain, Denis gave me a cocktail party and it was astounding the number of Princes and Princesses and literary lights turned out on a day's notice! We went to midnight mass Christmas Eve at Ara Coeli, and to the Children's Fair in the Piazza Navona—in fact, did you ever hear of anything more touristy? Then I took the Blue train for Paris for New Year and so back to that awful miserable dark cold smoky dull beastly town of Liége.[22]

And at the time she wrote Glenway Wescott that she was glad she had never seen Rome before, for how could she have dreamed anything so new and fresh could happen just by finding another city? She planned to live there for at least a year after her Liége appointment was finished.[23]

The pleasant interlude was soon forgotten when, shortly after she returned to Liége, she became ill. The trouble was the old villain, influenza, under a new name, La Grippe. She said it was the same trouble she had every year, aggravated by the severe winter and the cold weather. Fulbright staff people came to move her from her cold, squalid flat to a warm hotel and planned to help her move to Brussels, where she could have a better apartment.[24]

She planned a brief holiday in Venice or Antibes but instead found herself in Edith Cavell Hospital in Brussels, in a pleasant room full of flowers sent by people she hardly knew. She had discovered her gall bladder was "as big as a pear." The undertaking of Visiting Fulbright Lecturer at the University of Liége had been a complete disaster. On February 20, released from her teaching contract, she sailed from Cannes on the *Andrea Doria* and returned to New York to recuperate.

Health crises and warnings from her doctors often caused Porter to try, with varying degrees of success, to change her eating, drinking, and smoking habits. In the fall of 1947 she wrote:

For the first time since I was fifteen, I must stop smoking. . . . No coffee. That goes badly, for I love coffee. Have only the finest Bogota bean, ground freshly, pouring boiling water through the coffee once, drinking while perfectly fresh —marvelous, indeed, perfect coffee. Well, goodbye. No alcohol in any form. This will be much easier, except for the automatic habit of bending the elbow when I am in the company of any one else who does, and who do I know that doesn't? I'm glad I have had all these menus plaisirs in abundance, it won't be as if I had really missed anything. All those wines of the good years and the Grands Crus in France and the brandy and bourbon and Irish whiskey and cognac, and champagne and calvados and Marc . . . well, goodbye Paris and Bogota, and Virginia and Carolina leaf . . . It was delightful to have known you, and may we meet again some day . . .

Later the same day she added, "I am smoking a cigarette and a small goblet of very good Bourbon is at my elbow. I haven't the bravura to stop absolutely short in the middle of a sunny afternoon."[25]

Actually, she had given up smoking at that time, but she had not cut down very much on her drinking, and she never could bring herself to give up freshly roasted and ground coffee, of an alarming strength and drunk black.

Her struggles with diet after the Liége trouble were recorded by a friend:

> Gay evening last night with KAP. Just returned from Liége . . . Now recuperating and finds herself trying to follow two contrary medical routines. 1. To eat rich nourishing foods to restore strength and 2. To shun such foods and take antibiotics. Last night we were on the No. 1 routine, no doubt because I was her guest at a popular Italian restaurant on Mulberry street. After an enormous antipasto we scarcely touched the main course—though we did better with the wine.[26]

The wholesale nature of the Liége fiasco had one great benefit. It convinced her at last that she must stop wasting her time and make a change in her life from the very foundation. She knew that if she failed to do that she would never finish her novel and that she herself would be finished as a writer. She wrote Wescott that fall:

> I can tell you one thing—I am really old now and it is not so bad . . . what worries me is that time is running out and I have four more books I want to do, and I wonder about this frantic hope of mine that somehow by taking all these jobs I could save up enough money to get a head start and do them. At this point all other obstructions and obstacles are cleared away, no man will break my bones with his "love," all my vampires have disappeared, I could do it now if only I am given ten years or even less, with enough money to live on without having to go on with this gruesome public sort of life.[27]

She knew at last that her long melancholy and frustration were not rooted in an incurable sickness of the character but in the sheer continued misery of her way of life. This time she made a new start, very much more drastic than her new start when she returned from California to New York.

One important part of her resolution to get her life onto a new footing was the decision to find another publisher. She had long thought that Harcourt, Brace was not doing enough for her, and she felt that

> the worst are the new people—new to me, that is, at Harcourt Brace. I have said and I kept my word after that brouhaha of years ago when I was persuaded against my judgment and feelings to stay on with HBCO, that I would stay until Donald Brace went. . . .
>
> But since I began this, the two new ones, President and Vice-president, have come to me and . . . they conveyed to me that a great many things were going to be different but that I was part of HBCO's history and belonged to that firm, and they would do *anything* I asked to help me start working again, etc. etc. they spoke of having "inherited" me, as well as what they described as a great debt and after all, they owed something to the stockholders! So I asked not for what I really would like to have, of course, my ideas are on the ample side, as you know, but for the minimum of what I need. They at once offered me half. . . . I thought, Poor old Lambert Davis all over again. So I told them with perfect truth that I had an offer three times as good as that, whereat they were indignant, and spoke of the dirty ethics of some publishers trying to get other publishers' property away from them, and I said, "No I told them I wanted to make a change, first. . . ." This really outraged them, and then they came out with their fangs and said, "They aren't after anything but your *name!*" and my jailors said, "They can't sell your books, you just aren't that kind of writer!" and I just said to THEM, "Well, if my name is the only thing I have to peddle, maybe I had better peddle it to the highest bidder while it is still hot!" It was one of the strangest interviews I ever had, with anybody at all, for its strangely mixed motives on the other side . . . determined to keep me, therefore alternatively making the grossest flatteries and sentimental references to our long association, and on the other, belittling my chances of ever getting out of debt to them.[28]

In October 1955, Seymour Lawrence, then an associate editor of the *Atlantic Monthly,* wrote her about her wish to change publishers and suggested that Atlantic, Little, Brown, in Boston, might serve her well. She replied that she did wish most sincerely to make a change but not unless she went to something better. So they began discussions about the terms of the new contract. There was one clause that she took pride in having thought up for herself; she believed she was the first author, at least in the United States, who had won the important point that no books of hers should be allowed to go out of print during her lifetime. She said this had been the secret of her survival at Harcourt, Brace, for they had never advertised her to any extent worth mentioning, or ever departed from their belief that she was a writer's writer who could not expect to have sales.

Eventually the contract was worked out and her total advances of $10,434.93 for three books were taken over by Little, Brown, which also promised an income of $500 a month while she completed the book.

An agreeable side effect of the arrangement was that Porter's early title for the books was at last restored.[29] Some of her friends had objected to "Ship of Fools" on the grounds that it loaded the dice against the characters and conveyed a suggestion of the author's contempt for humanity. Porter told Seymour Lawrence that she had read Sebastian Brandt's *Das Narrenschiff* in Basle, in French or German, and could not remember whether it was ever translated. Lawrence felt it was the right title, and, since no one at Atlantic, Little, Brown objected, it was restored. When the book appeared, it contained a note about the title:

> The title of this book is a translation from the German of *Das Narrenschiff,* a moral allegory by Sebastian Brandt (1458?–1521), first published in Latin as *Stultifera Navis* in 1494. I read it in Basle in the summer of 1932 when I had still vividly in mind the impressions of my first voyage to Europe. When I began thinking about my novel, I took for my own this simple almost universal image of the ship of this world on its voyage to eternity. It is by no means new —it was very old and durable and dearly familiar when Brandt used it; and it suits my purpose exactly. I am a passenger on that ship.[30]

For her work she needed a quiet, fairly isolated place. She found a house on Roxbury Road, in Connecticut, took a three-year lease, and with Paul's help moved and settled down for what she hoped was the final stretch of the novel. The move itself was a massive one, but after it she settled down to work "on guard and secretive and solitary as a woodchuck peeping out of its hidey-hole."[31]

She found that if she had a presentable house in a reasonably good location she could manage without a good many things and discipline herself to work well. She settled down to solitude and to facing the typewriter every morning by eight o'clock if not earlier, on the glassed-in sun deck where she had established her workroom. She described her situation to Wescott:

> Now the days are tremendously long and slow and there is no sense of loneliness or isolation. I can hear the motors on the road . . . the N.Y. bus goes by my driveway, dogs bark, far away—cows go moo from time to time, the birds keep up an intermittent sweet little twitter, but there are thrushes and robins, and now and then, morning and evening, they sing their whole repertoire like opera stars. I love them.
>
> You need to find, somewhere in that house, a work room that no one has occasion to pass through or come near. And no one to ask anything of you until 2 o'clock in the afternoon. You know perfectly well what it takes: uninterrupted meditation and long hours of steady work.[32]

The new regime really worked, and after a few months she was elated because she had accomplished so much and found her affairs much better arranged than they had been for years. She had discovered at last what her requirements were—a house, and in it an inviolable workroom. Uninterrupted meditation and long hours of steady work were the *"impayable"* luxuries. She intended to defend herself tooth and nail against all the familiar threats and she had begun to say a firm NO to invitations.[33]

At this time, she enjoyed a cheerful, relaxed relationship with the members of her family whom she liked. Ann and her family were close by, and Ann's mother, Gay, came up from Texas fairly often. Paul came from New York for weekends and, as always, did numerous practical jobs—burning out hornets' nests, gardening, doing repairs. Birthdays and other family occasions were celebrated at Porter's house. She told a friend that it took her four days to prepare for family parties, one to get ready, one for the day itself, one to clean up the

wreckage, and one to recover. The third day was the worst. For all
the effort, these family occasions were deeply satisfying to her, and
she described one as being filled with all the "dear hullaballoo" such
as only a family can cause. She enjoyed it and felt renewed and re-
freshed afterward.[34]

If she was often nostalgic and sad, this was not only because of
her solitude but because by the latter half of the 1950s so many of her
friends and relatives had died. She was approaching seventy herself
and such losses were inevitable, but she never really easily reconciled
herself to death. She grieved for each one and for all the other deaths
they reminded her of. Her brother died in 1955, her San Antonio
cousin, Lily Cahill, shortly afterward, and then Ann's brother T.H.,
whose birth Porter had attended but whom she had never really
known. Donald Brace's death in 1955 ended their twenty-five year
association, she forgot her resentment of his treatment of her and
mourned. Sylvia Beach wrote her that Adrienne Monnier had died,
and she grieved for the faraway times they had all spent together.[35]
George Platt Lynes's death shocked her by its suddenness, and she
was especially saddened by the equally sudden death of Paul's friend
John Melville, who had a fatal heart attack at the age of thirty-seven.
He was a war hero and had a kind of old-fashioned gallantry that
appealed to Porter. He never forgot any of her special days and anniversaries and she never arrived in New York without finding flowers
from him in her hotel suite. They had had many happy times together, and after his death she wrote to Paul:

> This is a very beautiful sweet smelling green world this
> morning after an enormous storm of wind, rain, lightning
> and thunder that really did sound as if a battle with heavy
> artillery was going on just above the roof. It came up just
> about 2 o'clock, and it continued for nearly the whole hour
> of John's funeral . . . it was dark as twilight, and it was that
> sort of accidental thing that can have the meaning of a mes-
> sage or a revelation. Then it cleared away and became beau-
> tifully clear and cool after these last days of terrible heat, and
> I walked about looking at this world and tried to realize that
> John was no longer in it, and I said goodbye to him; there is
> no greater time of loneliness and feeling of loss for the dead
> than that first night in the grave. Bless his memory, he had
> such beautiful qualities, a kind of fineness of grain with all
> that courage! If there is a place where heroes are received

with honor, he most surely is there by now, safe and sound.[36]

John had left a letter with Paul mentioning a special bequest for Katherine Anne—a small portrait of Mark Twain backed with a flyleaf from a book on which Mark Twain had written a humorous message that much appealed to her: "Let unscrupulous people lie with no motive but let you and I only lie for profit." She treasured the memento and wrote on it the date of John Melville's death, dating her inscription on the day she received it, July 4, 1957.

A year later she wrote,

Added July 4th 1958—This is uncanny. I wrote this note last year to enclose in the Mark Twain frame. Today, July 4th, 1958 I took the picture down to pack it away as I am leaving this house July 31st and noticed for the first time that Mark Twain dated his inscription July 4th 1909—49 years ago today. There's no *point* to all this except the sheer coincidence of these three dates—How did it happen that I took this picture down, noticed the date for the first time, opened the frame meaning to mention the anniversary today. And find I had written a note exactly a year ago today—Nonsense, of course—but it happens to me *too often*.

Later there was another postscript on the flyleaf: "4th July 1964 at 1306 49th Street NW Washington D.C. Looking for this Mark Twain memento I found it again today and read this note!"[37]

Once her sister Gay wrote that she was feeling nostalgic and homesick—not for things that were but for things that should have been. Porter was so struck by this exact expression of her own feelings that she called Gay in Texas to weep along with her. Gay told her that she was having "a very expensive boo-hoo."[38]

For all the solitude and sadness, when the lease on the house ran out, Porter could look back on three years of solid achievement, the longest and most important stretch of her work on the novel. She told Monroe Wheeler on June 29, 1958, that she was slogging away, copying the manuscript, tired to death of it—that nine tenths of the work had been done when she would rather be dead than do it. She knew that time was running out and that every day counted. She felt that if she left before the book was finished she would be abandoning her last chance to finish, and that if she were interrupted now she would never finish.[39]

Nevertheless, she was ready for change and happy to accept invitations to lecture and teach again. She had already in the past year enjoyed taking part in a conference on southern literature in Macon, Georgia, and had particularly liked meeting Flannery O'Connor. For the fall of 1958 she accepted invitations to lecture at the University of Texas in Austin, as well as other places throughout the country, and she planned to teach at the University of Virginia for the first semester and at Washington and Lee University for the second semester.

She always felt that moving was "life in death," and now it was terrifying to be torn up again after three years during which she had "put down roots." Her heart was "swounding down to her toes" at the thought of leaving this phase of her life behind and ending a period that had been largely one of quiet productivity.[40] But she was glad of a change, happy to be going to the universities, and looking forward to everything.

In the fall she had a wonderful homecoming visit to the University of Texas and afterward went to Virginia. Before going to Washington and Lee in early 1959, she felt so confident that the new year would be a success, a truly fabulous year, that she wrote down her hopes for it to Cyrilly Abels:

> Cyrilly darling:
>
> This year is working up to almost too much of a good thing. In this order (1) First Glasgow Professor and first woman on Faculty at Washington and Lee. To know what a dignity this is, you would have to see this place and the way I am treated here. (2) Ford Foundation Grant. (3) Great new Library Center at Austin, University of Texas, to be named for me—in full. (This is top secret, not a word till they say!) Not everybody lives to see his own monument, and I hope I may. . . . (4) To University of California in May to give two lectures on Mark Twain—my choice of subject—at the largest fee I have ever had—$2,500 and expenses. (5) Last but not least, *Ship of Fools*. . . . I am included in that new Whoozwhoozit about women, only 16 thousand-odd names, I believe. Just learned about this. It does look as if my career, such as it was, is getting ready to wind itself up. [41]

TWENTY-TWO

Ship of Fools: *The Last Stretch*

Porter never stopped hoping for a reconciliation with her native state, and in the fall of 1958 it looked as if she might at last achieve her dream. Her visit there could not have been more auspicious. She stayed at the old Driskill Hotel in Austin and saw again the capitol building she had visited as a child. She and her grandmother had gone up in the old water-powered elevator that carried visitors to the dome. It was the first "grand beautiful thing" she had ever seen and she never forgot it. She was happy to see it again and discover that it really was as noble and beautiful as she remembered:

> Palladio did the country a good turn by setting a style, fashion in architecture that will never be ugly or stupid—it just has the innate grandeur of height overhead and light and dignity. . . . His rotunda has never been beaten for grace, and I nearly shed tears of joy and I said, "Well, it wasn't a bad start for a child's first sight of the world."[1]

There were other memories. She had telephone calls from women who had been in school with her and from some who even remembered the farm near Buda. She was not even offended when Erna Glover Johns persisted in calling her "Callie," and she told her niece with some pleasure that a friend had called her by a little name she had forgotten. She felt sure that if she remained in the area she would take Aunt Cat Porter's place as a legendary figure. She was especially gratified that when she gave her lecture/performance at the university there was a young relative in the audience, a granddaughter of her father's cousin Lily Cahill.

She was entertained during her visit by a member of the English Department, William Handy, whose wife had written a master's thesis on Porter's work. Besides looking after her devotedly, the Handys gave her a copy of the thesis as a parting gift. She was interviewed for the *Texas Observer* by another long-standing admirer, a handsome young reporter named Winston Bode, whose mother, like Porter, had been a student at the Thomas School. Bode described Porter for the *Observer*'s readers—she was sporting the fox stole, a rich velvet hat of huge circumference, the pearls, and a lorgnette.[2]

The greatest delight of the visit was the news that Harry Ransom, who was almost single-handedly responsible for collecting the papers that made the university's Humanities Research Center into one of the great repositories of modern American and English literature, wanted to name a building for her. Whether he did in fact offer a library or a room in a library, what he intended and what she thought she heard, has long been obscured, but she left Texas happy in the belief that a large library building would be named for her. She immediately planned to settle nearby, so that she could walk around and see her library and keep an eye on the collections of papers she intended to place in it.

For the next year she described in numerous letters and conversations her plans for the library and her house in Texas. When she met her wartime lover Charles Shannon in the Air Force Library in Alabama they made arrangements for her to sit for her portrait for the library. She also hoped the library would purchase the Marcella Comès Winslow portrait at a "good Texas price." Monroe Wheeler thought it was an excellent idea for Texas to name a library after her, and he had a hunch that, as she was a Texas girl, they should do a great deal more for her, in ways he could suggest.[3]

Porter planned to find near the university an old-fashioned house with big square rooms, French windows, and high ceilings, just right for her old Spanish and Italian and Napoleon III furniture and her Victorian four-poster with its Belgian scarlet damask curtains. It seemed to her a very wonderful and fitting thing to settle within twenty miles of where she was raised, and she intended to have a black sugar fig tree and an Indian cling-peach tree in her yard, such as her grandmother had planted when she owned her farm.[4]

None of these plans ever materialized, nor did the University ever name a library or room for her. Their failure to do so was a great disappointment and humiliation, and it caused a deep rift between her and Texas. The library fiasco was, however, only one in a series of unpleasant after-effects of a visit that seemed at the time to have been completely harmonious.

It was only after she left Austin that Porter found time to read Deirdre Handy's master's thesis, and when she did she was transfixed with fury. Often her initial pride in being the subject of an essay or review turned to rage if the interpretation was even mildly critical. This time she was especially angry because there was some criticism of the character of Sophia Jane Rhea, the character based on Porter's grandmother. Porter started to make marginal comments on the thesis itself, but gave up and instead wrote an angry letter:

> I began to make a few notes on the margins, but gave it up, as the entire argument and point of view was so intricately netted with your own personal prejudices against a whole social system, the traditional Southern one, and was so closely argued on the basis that a moral system that does not work outside of a certain environment—see your note on the grandmother's influence and teaching as corrupt and evil —I gave up in despair, seeing that it would take another essay of the same length to refute this. . . . I want to ask only one question: Does the rejection and denial of a Christian and moral idea of life by the lowest elements of the population (which began taking over some time ago, and has now got our society debased beyond recognition) prove that system to have been evil and corrupt, or has it been simply cast aside by the evil and corrupt powers of our society. This is, I think, pragmatism in a very dangerous form . . . good is not turned to evil merely because it has, apparently at least, lost the battle. Things are not per se good simply because they are in power.[5]

The house-hunting venture also ended badly, partly because the real estate agent she was referred to, imagining her to be rich, seemed bent on selling her a very high-priced house. Possibly he was following standard selling techniques, but Porter began to see his approach as a further symptom of the corruption of the whole place.

Furthermore, she had subscribed to the *Texas Quarterly* since its inception in 1958 and, always particular about keeping complete sets of such journals, was chagrined when she was not notified that her subscription had run out and when she had difficulty obtaining the missing issues. Since academic journals tend to err in hounding subscribers rather than letting them go, it seems likely that Porter's frequent changes of address caused the lapse, but she was angry all the same.[6] She even decided in retrospect that there had been something she resented in the phone calls from old friends. They were not really interested in her work, but in the vulgar idea of a local girl making good.

Of course her chief grudge was against the university for not naming a library for her, and it seemed strange to her that an episode promising to be so pleasant should have drifted away into a rather murky cloud of humiliation and disappointment for her. When a newspaper tried to make something of her resentment, she denied it but wrote at the same time to Harry Ransom:

> . . . after a lecture engagement in Austin you had written me a very cordial letter which I still have as a pleasant memento, saying, in effect, that the U was building a new library center and that you would like to name some part or section or room, I forgot exactly which and it doesn't seem important, for me. I was entirely delighted, it was a splendid surprise and honor. I accepted rather fulsomely, perhaps. You also offered me a key to a private room in the library as a kind of office in which to see students. . . . Then I wrote to you offering my books, papers, all literary estate I might have at my death. *From that day to this I have not received an answer to that letter.*[7]

Her negative feelings about Texas were reinforced some years later by yet another incident. Winston Bode, who had charmed her when he interviewed her, had just finished a book of his own, and he sent her a copy. The subject was her old rival, the favorite son of Texas, J. Frank Dobie. The gift was not one that she could greatly relish, but she did the courteous thing and acknowledged the book with routine words of thanks, saying that it could hardly have been done better. Somewhat naïvely, Bode applied at once for permission to use her words for advertising purposes. This happened to be a subject on which she had very strong views. It had been a rule of her life never to write anything for a jacket or advertisement of any book, even for her best friends or the people whose work she admired most.

She detested the whole system, and had been so embarrassed by eulogies on the jackets of her own books that for many years she had always refused to give blurbs, although she had an average of fifty requests a year. The only exception was when James Laughlin, the head of New Directions, asked her to write something about a collection of James Purdy's short stories he was publishing. Laughlin persuaded her to do it by saying that Purdy was in dire straits and having great trouble getting published, and, against her better judgment, she agreed. Since then her principle had been proved correct: Purdy, three books and two publishers later, was still using the paragraph she had written on the jackets of books she had never seen.[8] (Another exception occurred in the last year of her life, when she was physically incapacitated: Seymour Lawrence used her informal praise of Tillie Olsen's *Silences* in an advertisement in the *New York Times Book Review*.) When she received Bode's well-intentioned request to quote her words, she regarded as pure exploitation his desire to use praise she had given casually and amicably for a commercial enterprise that would bring money for him. She sent off a very angry telegram and the episode ended with ill will all around.

One pleasant experience of this Texas trip was not obliterated—the resumption of her childhood friendship with Erna Johns. This relationship was strengthened later, for when Porter was settled in at Washington and Lee University for the spring semester of 1959, she discovered that Erna's son, the Second World War hero, was commandant at the nearby Virginia Military Institute. Erna often came east to visit her son, her daughter-in-law, Rita, and her two grandsons. On these occasions she and Porter had happy reunions, full of childhood reminiscences and laughter. The friendship had stood the test of time very well; Porter was proud of her association with the Glover Johns family and loved to speak of her connection with them. In 1961 she saw in *Life* magazine prominent pictures of Glover Johns, Jr., leading American troops to face the Russians in the initial confrontation at Check Point Alpha in West Germany, and later at Check Point Charlie. She wrote to Erna that it was no small thing to know that her "dear life-long friend's sole irreplaceable life's treasure was lately standing up in a jeep leading troops through enemy territory."[9] To Cyrilly Abels she wrote:

Did you happen to see that big photograph I think in LIFE of a helmeted American officer standing in a jeep—well, in this

photograph mostly only his head and shoulders show, leading his troops through East Berlin into the West? Col.
Glover Steiner Johns? That is the only child of my only
childhood friend, we don't remember when we first saw
each other, she is still living and beautiful—three months
younger than I am—in Austin, Texas. . . . They are German by origin, very high-born (hochwohlgeboren!!!) titled
Junkers in the old country, and Glover reverted to type, is
more German than the Germans, looks like a medieval
Knight-Crusader on his way to the Holy Sepulchre, but let's
remember it was his class and kind that put up the only really
bitter resistance to Hitler. . . . I just thought darling, if you
saw the picture—I thought it very brilliant—you might be
entertained to know that those are my oldest friends, the
only people who have known me from the cradle (that is,
the mother has) and with luck will see me to the grave.[10]

The Johns family, in turn, were proud of Porter. She was considerably more flamboyant and unconventional than they were, but they
accepted her with indulgent amusement. On one occasion Porter arrived at one of Rita's luncheon parties and was horrified to find that
it was a ladies' luncheon. She stood in the doorway, aghast, and asked
Rita, "But where are all the men?" She was so genuinely outraged
that Rita expected her to stomp out, but the women gave her a great
deal of attention and eventually she was mollified.[11] Erna was greatly
amused, as they both approached seventy, at her friend's flirtatious-
ness. "Writing wasn't the only thing she had a genius for," she said.[12]

In spite of the pleasant times with the Johnses and the distinction
of her position as the first woman to be visiting professor at Washington and Lee University, the early part of 1959 was not a success.
Unable to pace herself, she had worked too hard the previous fall. In
addition to her work at the University of Virginia, during which she
underestimated the time required for meeting students and reading
papers, she had undertaken extensive speaking engagements and had
toured the country from Portland, Oregon, to Auburn, Alabama,
with side trips to Oklahoma and New York. She was also leading a
full social life that included being "squired around" by a young naval
lieutenant whom she had met during a visit to Cornell, so that when
she was at Washington and Lee University, she was ill most of the
time and able to give only one lecture before she left.

Her time in the South, however, had convinced her that she felt more at home there than anywhere else.[13] It was a useful piece of knowledge, because she was ready to settle again for the last period of work on the novel and needed to choose a place to live. She was supported by a generous grant from the Ford Foundation now, and could live almost where she pleased. She decided to finish the book in Washington, D.C.

At first she stayed in the Jefferson Hotel, recovering from the previous year, resting a little, and working on the novel, copying out certain sections and finishing others. After a time her nest-building urge revived and she looked for a house to rent. The one she found was in Georgetown, on Q Street, just a street away from Marcella Comès Winslow's home, where she had been so happy with Charles Shannon fifteen years before. She loved the narrow white house and said it was better than any house she had had—even better than the ones in Paris, Baton Rouge, and Saratoga Springs.[14] It had an elegant parlor, a dining room overlooking an enclosed garden with gingko trees, and a high-ceilinged drawing room. The place was admirably suited to house her furniture—the pieces from Rue Notre Dame des Champs, the Mexican folk art, the refectory table she had bought in New York, and the sixteenth-century cupboard from Avila. She acquired a new table for the dining room, a huge round slab of Vermont marble which cost her a mere $28, though the shipping bill added another $149 and she had to find a base for it too.[15]

The obvious disadvantage of living in Washington was that it was one of the places where isolation would be extremely difficult. Porter had many old friends there, and the city was full of interesting people coming and going. There were constant temptations in the form of invitations to social gatherings, and perhaps she anticipated them when she vowed not to let a soul in Washington know she was there. She did not, of course, keep her vow, and once she had her pleasant house, she began entertaining. One of the first people she looked up was Marcella Winslow, who once more recorded her impressions in letters, this time to her daughter in Italy:

> I had a day with Katherine Anne Saturday. She had me to lunch which she cooked herself—a wonderful soup which she starts with bouillon of beef and then adds potatoes, a lobster, shrimp dish in scalloped shells, and home made rolls. She can make 6 kinds of bread. Her house is lovely and she wants to buy it and live here always—but she always starts off that way. She bought my Siena fruit picture for

$100 and she gave me $50 now. Also has a frame already for a head which she wants me to do. A small one. She says her novel is FINISHED which is hard to believe but I had to. She expects to make a fortune on it—movie rights and so on. She is so conscious of HER fame and HER charm. Too much so! After lunch we walked Massa a bit and then went to the Caledonia to see her painting (mine) in the window and then to the Early American Shop and the Door Store and the Pottery Fair. I restrained her in all of them but she bought a table at the Caledonia and 15 long stemmed wine glasses at the Pottery place for $2 each. She is living on a Ford Foundation Grant of $25,000 for 2 years or something of the sort. Talk about money burning holes![16]

The Princes and I had a typical KAP evening at her house last night. It consists of everyone (there was a man who has apt below hers too) sitting around and listening to her talk about herself. Once in a while she stops and says she shouldn't go on like that but goes right ahead just the same. It makes her feel she has stopped after she says that. The rules of the game are that you don't interrupt and no one talks of anyone else. You have delicious Jack Daniels whiskey and a marvellous dinner which she does all herself, including home-baked bread. Good wine, good coffee and liqueurs. Then you listen to a letter—2 pages closely written that is a photostat of one she wrote to someone who sold it before he died and she got a copy and just loves it. Then she autographs a photograph of herself for each one all around the margin saying "To Marcella a souvenir of the house in Q Street" all dated and everything to make it easier for you to sell, if you can bear to part with it later on. She will be here another year she says. . . . A few months ago she wanted to buy her house, now she doesn't like it. It is hard to believe that in her 70th year she still feels herself a femme fatale but she does and she has got some little clever Italian doctor picking up the big checks.

Since she is 69 years old, I doubt if you could believe this. She is having a real raging affair with, believe it or not, her Italian eye doctor. Utterly incredible but there it is—she is so sure of her charm. She had the nerve to get into this and what's more altho he is 49 he seems smitten. Is this just being Italian or what? He can't even read her books. She says the first man who has loved her for herself alone and the only man who is as good in his field as she is in hers. "Two champions" she kept saying.[17]

Marcella's words sound harsh, but Porter had by this time progressed from being simply talkative to being downright garrulous. Eudora Welty found visits difficult because Porter used her as a sounding board, talked without stopping, and Welty developed headaches from listening.[18] Some friends laughed at this mannerism, as Porter herself did. Once, when a friend apologized for interrupting her, Porter said, "That's all right. It's the only way you'll get a word in."[19]

Another opportunity for conviviality arose from an unexpected source. Soon after she moved into the house on Q Street she was surprised to find a young man sitting in the garden at the back of the house. When she approached him she learned for the first time that the downstairs apartment was rented and the garden shared with its tenant.

The situation was potentially inflammatory. It became even more so when she was invited to a party downstairs, drank too much, and made advances to the young man, calling him Adam, the hero of "Pale Horse, Pale Rider."[20]

In spite of the tempestuous beginning, the relationship remained amicable and was a great source of strength to her in the last stages of the novel. That it did remain unbroken was largely due to the unshakable good nature of the young man. Rhea Johnson was a soft-spoken, self-effacing Texan who worked for the State Department. Although neither of them ever realized this, he was distantly related to Porter and, coincidentally, bore the name of her fictional family. Rhea was thirty-three years old, unmarried, and very much interested in music —his cat was named Béla Bartók. When Porter took over his life, she adopted both his musical interests and Béla. Happily, she had stumbled on a situation which satisfied her instincts for domesticity without the danger of amorous involvement, and the two households merged in cheerful camaraderie. She loved having someone to look after and immediately put a stop to Rhea's bachelor habit of subsisting on convenience foods. "You live like an insect," she told him, and not only cooked for him but taught him how to cook for himself. He was taught the art of bread making and other culinary skills and said often, "She changed my whole life."

The two met every day for cocktails and frequently for dinner;

he fell in easily with her plans and was happy to assist her in any way. He escorted her on outings, because she never liked to go out in the evening unaccompanied by a man. He also drove her on shopping expeditions, did various errands, and eventually helped her with her work, sorting papers, copying sections of the novel, reading proof.

It was Johnson's efforts to impose some order on the boxes of manuscript in the house that resulted in the appearance of some long-forgotten stories. He uncovered the three versions of "Holiday" which had been set aside in 1924. Porter read them, saw how the story should go, triumphantly finished it, sent it to the *Atlantic Monthly,* and won an O. Henry Award. She gave the three manuscript versions to Johnson who later sent them to the Humanities Research Center at the University of Texas.[21]

Another find was "The Fig Tree," which had been finished in 1929 and subsequently lost. As she told Glenway Wescott in 1960,

> I have managed at last to get into mss. and papers that I have not seen since I packed them up and left them in South Hill in 1942. And I have discovered two very strange short stories I wrote, one in 1928 [sic] in Bermuda and the other dated Basle October 4 1932. One is completely finished about a little madman in an insane asylum, who thinks that everyone there is merely one of his other selves. The second is finished but I kept all the notes for it, and I left out things that I see now should have gone in and am going to start copying it today. It actually belongs with that series of stories linked together in *The Leaning Tower,* another going-to-the-country-for-the-summer story, but about Miranda instead of her Grandmother.[22]

This story was eventually included in *The Collected Stories of Katherine Anne Porter* and almost appeared in the *New Yorker*. She told an interviewer in 1975 about its near-publication there:

> Well, Harold Ross and that lovely Mrs. White took me to the Algonquin and asked me why I didn't have anything for them. Then that nice William Maxwell and dear Frank O'Connor kept trying to persuade me. One day I found a whole packet of unpublished manuscripts I had written and in it was "The Fig Tree." . . . That was only 5 or 6 years ago. I sent it off to Maxwell and didn't hear anything for

two or three weeks. I didn't like this and besides I had my suspicions. Finally he wrote me a letter and sent the story back and said, "Everybody loved the story and we did want to publish it. You know, it was nearly perfect and we thought if we could just get you to change some points it would be more perfect." Well, to me, people who say something can be "more perfect" I can do without.[23]

What astonished her about these stories was that she had totally forgotten them, and for years, when editors asked her for material, she had thought she had nothing. Now she decided there were a number of stories she could finish—"Lucid Interval," the story about the madman; "The Darling Buds of May," about a group of young people and their chaperone at a picnic; and, again, "A Vision of Heaven." The publication of some stories and the thought of finishing others provided momentary satisfaction while she struggled on with the novel. The nature of that effort is perhaps best indicated by some of the notes she pushed under Rhea Johnson's door:

Jan 14, 1960   Dear Rhea
. . . P.S. come up at 6:30 if you are not engaged, for a drink and roast beef and onion tart, specialité de la maison.

Jan 21, 1960   Dear Rhea,
Getting better slowly but still it is very painful to move—nothing to be done except live along with it, it will pass.
    Thank you for the S.R. *[Saturday Review]*—I wonder if everybody else's sketch of the C.R. is as stupid as mine—left out nearly everything of interest (except the play) and got address wrong, but what the hell? as Mehitabel so aptly remarked.
    Here are the books written in, I am afraid not brilliantly, but really with best wishes.
            Your K.A.P.

Feb 15, 1960   Have gone to bed
Dear Rhea—
Would you mind dropping this in the Post box on the corner for me _now_. Even if you do mind, please do this for it's important and I can't get out —sore throat.

Oct 31, 1960 Dear Rhea

Please use one of these to hear Robert Lowell or maybe someone may go with you. I am utterly exhausted and must go to bed, it is a great disappointment.

Dec 21, 1960 Dear Rhea

I am too tired, and can't have a drink with you today after all. Sorry. Here are some stray cards. This time I looked at the name before opening them.

 This is St. Lucy's Day, shortest day of the year—but I've been up since 5 this morning and it seems long to me. à bientôt K.A.P.

Dec 27, 1960 If you get home in time, please post these at the corner. One is important. Thank you. Didn't see Battling Bela all day! He's launched, looks like!

May 5, 1961 Dear Rhea

I didn't bring Battling Bela up until about 2:30 this afternoon. He drank a little milk and ate a half gram of scrambled egg. He does not eat well with me. He is merry and full of fox-fire—I leave this cellophane because he loves it—has played ever since he got here in it. I am leaving him now because I am tired and must go to bed. (now exactly 4:30 p.m.).

May 6, 1961 Dear Rhea,

Please mark this and sign my name and mail it for me—I can't go anywhere on Sunday. Too far in arrears with my jobs KAP (Saturday).

 Gave Battling Bela chicken broth and then he boxed the whole afternoon.[24]

Before her seventieth birthday, in May 1960, she at last reconciled herself to her exact age, saying that there were really only three ages—"young, mature and remarkable." She now announced to friends something they may have guessed—that she was seventy. Forgetting the time long ago when she gave as her birth date the "last possible year" she could have been born in, she said that she had never intended to lie about her age at all. There was once a typographical error and she had simply never had the courage to correct it. She had never expected to live so long, but now she was full of interest and curiosity to see what would happen in the next decade.[25]

The spring of 1960 also brought a severe emotional shock—a disaster she had not dreamed of.[26] She had to brace herself for the possibility of losing her niece, Ann, the person she was closest to and who had replaced her older sister, Mary Alice, in Porter's affections. Ann's life was threatened by cancer: she had been told by her doctor that she had five years to live. Porter decided she must now spend as much time with her niece as possible. Invited to Mexico on a speaking engagement for the State Department, she asked Ann to go along. Ann needed a holiday after having undergone extensive surgery and chemotherapy, and she accepted, paying her own way. She and Porter were very compatible as traveling companions, since Ann could help out when Porter "went to pieces" as she tended to do over confused schedules and problems with exchanging money. They received a wonderful reception—in Monterrey there were placards in all the windows with "Bienvenida KAP" on them—and Porter was consoled for her disappointment over the University of Texas library. Having young sons to look after, Ann left Mexico before her aunt did, and as they sat over their last breakfast together, the two made a pact to defend each other from the "routine tortures and last-minute operations" performed in hospitals on dying people. Porter had never been closer to Ann, and it seemed to her that Ann's terrible experience had brought out her character; she had a new courage and *"presence."*[27]

When Porter returned to Washington, she felt more harassed than ever and complained that she had not had one quiet, uninterrupted day since she moved into the house. She worried about Ann, quarreled with Paul, and alternated between feeling irritated by Rhea Johnson and dependent on his help with minor errands and his company when she was lonely. She was in despair about ever finishing the book and reported that her publisher Seymour Lawrence shared her despair. He was now pulling out his teeth, having long ago finished his hair.[28]

As the pressures built up, her life became steadily more chaotic. Her drinking had increased over the years, and a situation described by David Locher became a recurrent happening. He came for a brief visit during the last week of August 1960, and she had planned to make him two memorable meals. He had a dinner engagement, however, so Porter made a salad for lunch and they reminisced about Ann Arbor and talked about her present work. She said that she simply had to finish *Ship of Fools* because time was running out; she had received a great deal of money to complete it and the publisher was getting nasty.

As the conversation took this worrisome turn, she decided they needed a drink and began to make strong and copious Daiquiris (at the same time giving lessons in pronunciation—dah-queer-ee, not dakkeree). They were wonderful but David was late for his dinner engagement. He got back after his hostess had gone to bed, and the next morning he was shocked to see a long cut, wide open, on her left temple. She told him, "I'm all right, but I should know better than to drink anything when I am taking medication to help me sleep. I don't know how this happened, but I must have fallen in the bathroom during the night."[29] David had to leave for the airport that morning, and Porter at the same time took a cab to Georgetown University Medical Center to find a doctor who would stitch her up. When David called later she told him she was "like half again as good as new."[30]

As always when the heat was on, she accepted all sorts of invitations to leave town and distract herself. In October 1960 she took part in a panel discussion on "Recent Southern Fiction" at Wesleyan College, in Macon, Georgia. The other panelists were Flannery O'Connor, Caroline Gordon, and Madison Jones; the moderator was Louis D. Rubin, Jr. She was in a somewhat arch mood, her calm statements in striking contrast to Caroline Gordon's impassioned remarks and comments. When Gordon railed against the northern publishers because they could bear only one image of the southerner and would publish only novels full of white columns and magnolias, Porter replied that the very place right this minute was absolutely filled to the chin with moonlight and magnolias. "All you have to do is look outside."[31]

Perhaps the most memorable part of the occasion for Porter was that she was able to see Flannery O'Connor again. O'Connor gave her own account of the meeting:

Katherine Anne remembered to inquire about a chicken of mine that she had met here two years before. I call that really having a talent for winning friends and influencing people when you remember to inquire for a chick that you met two years before. She was so sorry that it was night and she wouldn't get to see him again as she had particularly wanted to. I call that social grace.[32]

In January 1961 there was the excitement of the Kennedy Inauguration. She was "invited to everything" and delighted to be included, for she loved "the dear beautiful Kennedys." Asked to take in a visiting literary person, she was dismayed when it turned out to be Tennessee Williams. She tried to get out of it and was relieved when he wired that he was not well and would not be coming. She was "saved by the eyelashes."[33]

In February she was off to California, which she found "as wonderful as ever." She was tempted to stay and raise camellias, almonds, peaches, figs, and jacaranda and orange trees in the back yard. She had been invited to give the Regents' Lecture at the Riverside campus of the University of California. However, the part of the trip that she liked most was not her Regents' Lecture but a side trip to La Jolla, where she spoke to a group of oceanographers. She read her "Defense of Circe" to them and thought it charming that these men of science should be so touched by poetry and enjoy hearing about Odysseus. It made her think it was time for the arts, sciences, and religion to work together as they had in ancient times.[34] Back East again, she went up to New York in May for the spring festivities of the National Institute of Arts and Letters, of which Glenway Wescott was now president.

But these travels were simply diversions from the main task in hand, her final work on *Ship of Fools*. It now seemed to her that the steady concentration needed for the last stretch would not be achieved in Washington, where even the presence of steady, patient Rhea Johnson became ever more annoying to her. As her irritability reached fever pitch, she turned on him, referring to him as "the slack-a-daisical young man in the basement . . . who comes with the house . . . and whose presence I never make any attempt to explain; I only know I wish to God he was anywhere else at all."[35] Johnson became the target of such violent explosions that onlookers began to suspect there was something masochistic in his loyalty to her.

Porter had already, as she told Ann, "fallen out with my Italian beau, you'll be glad to hear. Really for good this time." And she added firmly, "I simply have no patience with men, never had much and now have none at all."[36] Eventually, she and her "Italian beau" were reconciled, for in 1974 he arranged a party at which she might receive the President's Medal, awarded to her (when she was ill) by St. John's College High School for her "contribution to Christian education."

Almost the only person with whom she did not have a row was

her beloved Cyrilly Abels, but she managed to work up a healthy grudge against Cyrilly's husband, who admired Porter as devotedly as his wife did. She wrote to Cyrilly:

> We never see each other except in the wild hubbub of dear Jerome, who WON'T let anybody talk, not even to him: I always feel baffled, but what to do? I think it is the lawyer in him—he is going to win his case, no matter what. . . . I talk too much of course, but I'm not trying to beat anybody, I'm just wanting to tell.[37]

Above all, her hatred of the Q Street house knew no bounds. It was difficult to keep down cockroaches in the old Georgetown neighborhood and they became an obsession with her. Her plants did not thrive and she saw this as an ominous sign that the house was unfit for anything living. Looking back over her whole life of gardening in all ways, from pots on window sills to groves of camellias, roses, and irises, she said she had never known anything like the mortality rate at Q Street.[38]

There was clearly only one course open to her if she was to keep her sanity and sobriety and finish the novel. She needed a few weeks of Bermuda-like seclusion. Her Boston publisher helped by finding a quiet hotel in Pigeon Cove, on Cape Ann, Massachusetts. She flew to Boston, where John Malcolm Brinnin met her and drove her to the Yankee Clipper Inn. She knew very well that the expenses of the place, including all her "so-called collect" telephone calls to the publisher, would in time be paid by herself out of the earnings from the book. Nevertheless, she was grateful for the change of scene, the soothing coastal setting, and the seclusion. She wrote to Johnson in a happier mood:

> 1 June 1961—Looking into the sea! It is heavenly
>
> Dear Rhea
>
> . . . I am working nearly all day really alone, really happy and hopeful. I dread coming back to Q Street, even for a day, but when I do, I will have got to the end of my difficulties and will be free to pack and go in some kind of order—Or so I hope. I intend to go somewhere to coast line, close to the sea, give my usual kiss on his top knot to

Battling Bela; I know he thrives and grows—He certainly was doing both when I saw him last.[39]

7 June 1961 5 p.m.

I get up at 6, work, eat, gaze at the sea, go for walks—everything in bloom—and—surprise—a completely teetotally non-alcoholic life, not a drop of anything for nine days and it's fun! This place is strictly local option and it works! It is so pleasant I am toying with the idea of taking the pledge! Well, we'll see. It wouldn't be fair now when I am so easy and happy. Wait till Hell rolls over me again in Georgetown! Wish me luck.[40]

9th June 1961

Dear Rhea

The arrows mark my porch overlooking the cove and the Atlantic and if it wasn't for my sweat about the finish I'd think I was in Celestial Paradise, not an earthly one. I'd love to live here but shan't make any reckless decisions. I haven't seen or heard of a [drawing of a cockroach] since I landed! *That alone* makes it nearly perfect.[41]

15th June 1961

Dear Rhea,

I didn't like to inflict my handwriting on you, but I have an unfinished page in the Olivetti and am superstitious about taking one out of the machine. It *must* stay there until finished.

This is wonderful beyond words—breakfast on tray around 8—coffee and little snack at 12:30—I work all day til 5, bathe, dress, dinner at six thirty, walk 45 minutes, to bed, read, sleep like a log—*no* bufferin, no nothing!—and repeat next day. . . . I'll know where to run next time! I am staying a week longer than I expected. *Hate* to leave. . . .

I have a great curiosity to see Battling Bela again, and whether the plants are surviving.[42]

20th June 1961

Pigeon Cove, Facing the blue sea looking over rocks and greenery, with the flag snapping in the high wind at the top of its tall pole . . . the one time I was out driving we saw the ambulance beside the road of the Underwater rescue force, with men diving, we learned, for a skin diver who had stayed down. And every day helicopters fly in patrol over this calm looking little cove, which has I am told a very dangerous undertow. On clear days the whole sea is filled with little sailboats, and a father and small son were drowned nearby and so on. . . . As to Battling Bela, you must expect a little awkwardness from adolescent tom cats, as well as any other kind of adolescent. They're all feet and curiosity for a while, but they learn. Don't hit him with anything except a folded paper and not very hard. Speak harshly to him at the same time. He'll catch on. If you don't like him better than . . . a coffee or a bottle of gin, you are a mere summer-soldier as a cat-lover—which reminds me, have you had him wormed, given his anti-distemper shots, and a shot or two of vitamins? He is at the right age now to begin such things. Also have his ears looked into for ear mites. And chuck him under the chin for me, he was such a sweet wildcat of a kitten, I shall miss him when I see the big bully he is no doubt becoming.[43]

On June 15, 1961, at 10:27 A.M. and just a month after her seventy-first birthday, she wrote to herself:

Note: *Ship of Fools* came out of this voyage and these notes, now destroyed unless Caroline Gordon has kept her copy of it. . . . I did not copy my original notes, but wrote her a long account in letter form, working in some of the episodes from my notes, putting in others. I did not keep copies for myself. I should like so much to think that they still exist, I should like to have seen them for use in the novel. . . . But all this is over now, I need not think of it again.[44]

It was a great moment and she savored it to the full.

Her dramatic statement that she need not think of the novel again was of course an exaggeration—rewriting, correcting, copying, and proofreading were still to be done—but the essential task was finished. Many people, sometimes including herself, had doubted that she could do it, but, after twenty-two years, she had triumphed.

She returned to Georgetown, to the Q Street house where everything was "stacked *against* living," but she soon went back to Pigeon

Cove for the rest of a serene, productive summer, "the first good summer I have had since my lovely Roxbury Road." That fall she delivered the complete manuscript to her publisher. *Ship of Fools* really was finished.

Publication was timed, "like Melville's *The Confidence Man*," with its "flock of fools on this ship of fools with its captain of fools," for All Fools' Day. On Sunday April 1, 1962, Katherine Anne Porter was the heroine of the hour. Both the *New York Times Book Review* and the *New York Herald Tribune* book section carried on their front pages immensely favorable reviews. In the opening paragraph of his review for the *Times,* Mark Schorer wrote:

> This novel has been famous for years. It has been awaited through an entire literary generation. Publishers and foundations, like many once hopeful readers, long ago gave it up. Now it is suddenly, superbly here. It would have been worth waiting for for another thirty years if one had had any hope of having them. It is our good fortune that it comes at last still in our time. It will endure, one hardly risks anything in saying, far beyond it, for many literary generations.[45]

Louis Auchincloss ended his *Herald Tribune* review with:

> Miss Porter supplies a passenger list to which it is necessary to make frequent references in reading her early chapters. But, as in the case of the big Victorian novels, the effort involved in meeting the characters pays off in the richness of illusion created. The reader feels that he has been on board the Vera for the twenty six days of her voyage, but unlike his fellow passengers, he is reluctant to disembark.[46]

Howard Moss wrote in the *New Yorker* for April 28, "There is not an ounce of weighted sentiment in it. Its intelligence lies not in the profundity of its ideas but in the clarity of its viewpoint; we are impressed not by what Miss Porter says but by what she knows."[47]

Porter herself, in the interviews that accompanied the *Times* and *Tribune* reviews, was jubilant and euphoric; she did not dwell on past difficulties. She told one interviewer that she had just got back from Connecticut, where she had been sledding on a sort of flying saucer, a metal thing like the top of a garbage can on which she whizzed down hills. She said that people who didn't know her were stunned

but not her friends.[48] She went on to say that upstairs in her workroom she had forty stories that were interrupted one way and another,
and that she was going on vacation to Ireland and Rome and Paris
and then coming back to finish the short stories. She could hardly
wait. The novelist Elizabeth Janeway, reporting all this in the *Times
Book Review* interview, added her own description of Porter:

> Perhaps this is one way to say what she is: imagine a most
> delicate and sensitive apparatus constructed a world or two
> ago in West Texas, when the Civil War and its aftermath
> were still remembered and operative forces, an apparatus set
> to read the truth of events in our time. Its housing is a
> beautiful, merry little person skilled in traditional female
> arts; who is, none the less, first and foremost the priestess of
> this seismographic machine. To it, she will sacrifice any-
> thing without a moment of hesitation. She is its guardian
> and its servant; but a most charming and exquisite dragon,
> Chinese porcelain of the best period, with the purr of an
> affectionate tiger; unless you encroach on her treasure, her
> talent. ("If I have that," she says, "I have everything, and if
> I don't, I have nothing.")[49]

She had been buoyed up before by the pleasantly feverish euphoria attendant on publication of a book. This time she had a prolonged extravaganza of celebration and adulation. There were parties
in New York and in Washington. The "dear beautiful Kennedys"
were in the White House, and when Ernest Hemingway's widow,
Mary Hemingway, sat beside the President at dinner and tried to talk
about Cuba, his response was to ask if she had read *Ship of Fools*.[50]

With the book so gloriously launched, it seemed at last that Porter had at seventy-two set her world in order. With calm seas and
auspicious gales, she could now embark in her final years on a new
life of peace and ease.

TWENTY-THREE

The Aftermath of Ship of Fools:
I Was Happier Before

Porter was fond of quoting Mark Twain's response when he was asked to say something in favor of tight shoes. He replied that they make you forget your other troubles. Now she felt exactly the same about *Ship of Fools*. Once the novel was published, she was overwhelmed by other troubles.

It was only reasonable that after the months of cumulative pressure—finishing and proofreading the book, and worrying about its reception—she should have a delayed nervous reaction. In May, as the publication festivities tapered off, Glenway Wescott very sensibly suggested that she go into a hospital incommunicado for a checkup and a complete rest,[1] but like most of his excellent practical advice it went ignored, although the following winter she did acknowledge to David Locher that she was on the brink of a total breakdown:

> Dear David, I have been very near to going over the edge altogether. There can come a time when too much goes on for too long and though for me it took years, still the time came. I have the worst kind of nervous breakdown, the walking kind when one is able to get up and give signs of life for a little while so that everyone says "Why, there's nothing wrong with you! You look *wonderful!*" and begins to make plans for me. Then I would fall on my face and instead of feeling a little sympathy, they would be outraged at the way I had failed them.[2]

One of the reasons for her mental anguish was that she felt bedeviled by the sudden complication of her life; she had an agent, two publishers, a lawyer, and an accountant, and at least fifteen charitable and political organizations were hounding her. Her mail was full of demands—writers sent manuscripts, publishers sent her books to read, fans asked for autographs, institutions asked her to lecture, and organizations wanted to send her on what she considered wild-goose chases. She hated the "hyena newspaper columnists" and "coyote camera men" who besieged her. "Have you ever," she asked a friend, "tried ignoring a wasp in your car when you are driving, or a bee tangled in your hair?" She said that when people told her, "That is the price of fame," she wanted to smack them but she knew it would not stop the next fool from saying the same thing.[3]

Her chief cause of misery, surprisingly enough, was her financial situation. This time it differed from the chronic financial difficulties of all her previous years, for now she was a very rich woman. But she had little experience with financial matters and had an uneasy feeling that the control of her affairs was out of her hands and her money was being drained away. She felt that she was being exploited by all those who tried to protect her income, and she could not understand why she could not have immediate and complete access to the money to spend exactly as she wished. She described her frustrations to David Locher:

> The bringing out of the book was a real shambles, the most senseless interminable ordeal of my life, as it came at the time when I had nearly reached breaking point anyway and it may be that some day I'll remember something pleasant or at least painless about it, but I haven't yet. Can you imagine any book of mine being a "best seller"? There is one good thing about it, it made quite a lot of money, with a good deal more to come. I can't have it because the Revenooers will move in and take 91 percent of it—so I have to be content with a fair but not extravagant income for the rest of my life, and *that* is no misfortune, is it?
>
> It is a very strange custom, one I can't explain, but the government may take that money, or my publishers can keep it for me and dole out a fixed income, meanwhile using it, investing it and making more money on it but I who furnished the pretext, you might say, for the money, without me it would not have come into their hands, am not

allowed to have it or even a decent share of it. I think it would have been fun to invest part of it, give away part, make presents, buy charming things I like, live easily and amply—but no, that will not be! Its all *perfectly* legal, perfectly customary since our confiscatory system of taxation began, and I am the only one in my particular set-up of publisher and Revenue office who seems to find any fault with it![4]

Among the charming things she wanted immediately were jewels, a house, and a holiday abroad. Westcott had counseled her that such big purchases all at once were not feasible, that even millionaires would shrink from buying a house and an emerald in the same month, and he had told her that if she made her publishers pay her more than $3,000 a month she would find herself in a calamitous tax situation that might cost her perhaps $50,000 or $75,000. He suggested that she borrow from the bank for her immediate purposes, get a good lawyer to handle her affairs, and postpone her traveling for a time.[5]

Westcott's financial advice was scorned, as her remarks in the many interviews she gave that spring indicate. When she was asked why she had taken so long to finish the book, she included in her list of obstacles the friends who had got in her way when she wanted to do anything: "Telephone calls, those friends I mentioned, the necessity to earn money by going on speaking tours and public reading engagements, and housekeeping chores."[6] Now she had her eye on a house in Washington she wanted to buy, but every time she made up her mind to do something, friends seemed to jump up from every corner of the world saying, "Don't! Don't!" and stamp the life out of the project. She loved her friends, she was not mad at them, but they made it impossible for her to live where they were.[7]

She put off buying a house, but she was not to be deterred from her other plans. The first major purchase she made was a ring with a huge square-cut emerald set all around with diamonds. She had wanted one since she was a girl looking at her Aunt Ione's jewels, and she had described La Condesa in *Ship of Fools* as wearing a diamond-set emerald the size of a robin's egg. Her own ring was larger than La Condesa's, and at $20,000 it was not a wise purchase but a hurried choice. Nevertheless, it was a source of immense satisfaction to her. It was the idea of the ring, rather than the actual object, that she cherished; it became the symbol of her success and the subject of numerous anecdotes. She loved repeating her reply to Barbara Wescott, who had said, "Katherine Anne, you have been poor all your life, is that the only thing you could think of to buy?" To which she said, "It was the only thing I did want."[8] As Matthew Josephson escorted her up the stairs at a meeting of the National Institute of Arts and Letters, she held out her hand to show him the huge ring and said, "I did it all for this!"[9] She told of someone asking if it were a gift, and of her own reply, "No, I'm the unlucky woman who had to buy her own emerald."[10] She told of another friend who commented on its prodigious size and deep color by saying, "I know you wanted a ring, but did you have to buy a swimming pool?" And she told of being warned that she would be a sure target for thieves and of promising to give any thief who tried to snatch it the busiest fifteen minutes of his life. When she visited the College of Notre Dame of Maryland, she had the nuns try on the ring. One wrote, "As we sisters sat and listened, she turned to the sister at her side, and—taking off the emerald ring—said, 'Wouldn't you like to try it on?' Of course, we all did. And we enjoyed the sight of the huge stone on fingers that had not had rings on for some time."[11] And when Father Raymond Roseliep was poet in residence at Georgetown University, in Washington, and spent an evening with her, he wore it the entire time and mentioned it frequently in the poems he wrote to her.[12]

Besides buying the emerald, she also went off on a holiday to Europe, traveling once more with Ann, whose expenses she paid. Ann had made a good recovery from her surgery and therapy; in spite of the grim prognosis she had received a few years earlier, both she and Porter felt optimistic that she would survive her illness (which she in fact did), and they enjoyed their holiday, resting, eating well, and taking pictures of each other. They visited Sicily and stayed in an old monastery in Taormina. In the evenings they sat on their balcony and watched Mount Etna as it smoked and rumbled. Later they went to Rome and to Naples, where Porter watched an elaborate funeral procession. She wrote a description of it to Glenway Wescott:

> I saw at Naples what no-one had ever told me of—a pompe funebre like nothing I have ever seen in this world (and remember, I come from a region and a time and a society whose dead were conveyed to their last home in a glass and black lacquer hearse with four black horses wearing large black plumes on their heads. So the Naples funeral should not have been such a delightful surprise but it was). A great motor coach, all gold and black, swooped around the curve and down the long hill, and through the great panes of glass

I saw an enormous baroque gilded kind of cradle frame containing a black and gold cut velvet coffin, with flower wreaths on the lid. Just behind came an ornamental sort of truck, also black lacquered, with a mere forest of greenery, flowers of all colors, the woods of Dunsinane on the move! Why has no one, writing about Naples, ever told us what charming funerals they have.[13]

In spite of the rest and all the diverting sights, the traveling, as Wescott had predicted, tired Porter. It also prevented her from being present to make important decisions about the handling of her affairs and did nothing to alleviate the problems that were "the price of fame."

To these problems was added a new source of irritation. Her work had from the beginning led a charmed life among the critics. Regardless of their gender, commentators on her work had often adopted the attitude of knights defending a gallant lady, vying in the extravagance of their praise. The novel, however, disappointed some of her former admirers and offered a new and larger target to those who had never liked her work in the first place. One observer described the tone of the early reviews as "a little cracked and breathless with excitement,"[14] like that of an elated witness to a unique personal triumph. But soon after the initial chorus, the unfavorable reviews started to come in. Porter began to feel "as if I had tripped into a tankful of piranhas, you know, those man-eating fish. They say a small school of them can strip one in thirty seconds and I think it may be true."[15]

Of course there were dissenting voices at the very beginning, too. Stanley Kauffman, for example, writing in the *New Republic* on April 2, 1961, compared the book unfavorably with Porter's earlier work, speaking of "somewhat more labor and slightly less certainty." He described the style as "more of an enameled richness with paradoxical lapses which like cracks in the table reveal the veneer."[16] He thought the characters shallow and made a criticism that was to recur in most of the unfavorable reviews—that the characters did not grow, that after their first appearances all that Porter had to say about them was known. Kauffman concluded that the book was less tragic than satiric and added that satire about a huge complex of civilizations ceases to be satire and becomes misanthropy. He summed up with the verdict that the whole effect was smaller than could have been anticipated from Miss Porter's other work.

No review was more devastating than the one by Theodore So-

lotaroff in his *Commentary* essay, " 'Ship of Fools' and the Critics."
"No effective principle of change operates on the action or on the
main characters or on the ideas," he wrote, "and hence the book has
virtually no power to sustain, complicate, and intensify any real re-
sponsiveness to it. . . . Miss Porter's narrative technique betrays at
almost every point the hand of the unreconstructed short-story
writer." He then went on to attack the gallery of characterizations
that other reviewers had applauded. The relationship of La Condesa
and Dr. Schumann was "a kind of higher soap opera," and La Condesa herself was "little more than a stock theatrical crooning voice or
shrieking in the wilderness inhabited by the fallen ladies of literature."
After reading fifty pages he had found the characters predictable and
less revealing of human nature than of Miss Porter's remarkably shallow design and sensibility.[17]

The chief focus of his criticism was the portrayal of the salesman
Julius Lowenthal, which he called a "caricature of Jewish vulgarity"
and one more example of Porter's compulsive tendency to simplify
and close her characters and issues, to look down upon life from the
perspective of a towering arrogance, contempt, and disgust. He concluded that there was nothing "majestic" or "terrible" about Miss
Porter's image of human failure.

His opinion of Lowenthal was shared by Porter's old friend Josephine Herbst, who, although she wrote no formal criticism of the
book, wrote to a friend, "There are even nasty things in this book.
She poses her one Jew as the least appetizing of mortals. He is a
stereotyped 'Jew,' wants to be sociable but has too many aggressive
faults, etc."[18]

The charge of anti-Semitism was to recur in discussions of Porter's work, especially when in an interview a few years later she
criticized one idiom in American writing:

> These others have fallen into a curious kind of argot more
> or less originating in New York, a deadly mixture of aca-
> demic, guttersnipe, gangster, fake-Yiddish, and dull old
> worn-out dirty words—an appalling bankruptcy in lan-
> guage, as if they hate English and are trying to destroy it
> along with all other living things they touch.[19]

The charge was not unfounded, and comments in the margins of
some of her books show that her virulent anti-Semitism was part of a

general racism. On the jacket of *Portrait of a Jew,* by Albert Memmi, a book she bought in Georgetown in 1962, she wrote beside the author's photograph, "This writer is completely typically Jewish, nose and mouth especially—But it is not a question of features. It is a *look,* an expression, a manner, that identifies them. And it is not a question of ugliness."[20] In the book itself she wrote, "Everybody except the Jews knows the Jews are not chosen but are a lot of noisy, arrogant, stupid, pretentious people and then what?" This was more than a reaction to a personal attack, which she had recorded when Fiedler criticized her. She also made a note in Memmi's book that in the United States Jews made up 4 percent of the population but about 60 percent of the criminals, Negroes about 10 percent of the population but about 25 percent of the criminals. She did not of course give any sources for her statistics.

Her remarks were not limited to tirades scrawled in books when she was barely sober, but were sometimes made in very public places. On November 20, 1958, four years after the *Brown* v. *Board of Education* decision by the Supreme Court, the *Richmond News Leader* carried the following story:

> Katherine Anne Porter said here today the Supreme Court acted "recklessly and irresponsibly" in the school desegregation decision.
>
> "I belong to the school of thought that believes the Supreme Court reacted recklessly and irresponsibly in precipitating this crisis at the worst possible time when we already had enough crises on hand."
>
> In the midst of saying it, the famous novelist paused to add "I wonder what kind of trouble this may get me in, but I don't care."
>
> Miss Porter said she believed the justices "acted with moral irresponsibility because apparently they are ignorant of the true situation.
>
> "That thing was taking care of itself very well," she added.
>
> "The down-trodden minorities," she said, "are organized into tight little cabals to run the country so that we will become the down-trodden vast majority if we don't look out.
>
> "The only things that make the world interesting," she said, "are the differences in nations and people. Why destroy that?"[21]

In letters to friends she consistently expressed the same objection to school desegregation. When she was living on Roxbury Road she had a cleaning woman whom she described to Glenway Wescott as "a big black brash-mouthed North Carolina field Negro" and whose conversation she reported thus:

> Desegregation or (as she calls it) "segregation" has about thrown her off her center of gravity if she ever had any, and she can talk of nothing if I am in hearing distance, but of the horrors of being a negro anywhere at all—worse here with the Yankees, she says, than in the South because there if they don't want you they let you know it, and here they pretend . . . her poor brain is just simply one boiling seething smoking mass of molten lava.[22]

Porter was moved by the woman's singing, a sound with which all her childhood and youth were associated, but she was dismayed to have the Negro question bounce back into her life after she had left her native land to get away from it.

After Porter was quoted in *Time* magazine on July 28, 1961, as referring to "wonderful old slaves" and "companions" in her family, she received a letter of protest from Pauline Young, of the National Association for the Advancement of Colored People, who said she could not reconcile the two terms. Porter then did a partial turnabout, and expressed horror that black people should have had to resort to riots "to gain something they should have had all along." Her letter also clarifies the way she substituted fantasies and fictions for the facts of her own life:

> Perhaps I am among the last few persons of my class and kind who were brought up in the house with two former slaves, who had remained with my grandmother—of the original number of 39 in Kentucky, none of whom left her at once, but stayed on until she found places for them and helped them get at least a little settled before she went to Texas.
>
> My Aunt Jane and Uncle Jimbilly came right along with her and stayed with her until she died, and then stayed on with us until they died. And believe me, anybody who mistakes that for servility or "Uncle Tomism"—a vulgar phrase I was never guilty of pronouncing or writing until now—

has just simply lost sight of a most important element of human life—that there were and are and I believe always will be people of virtue and goodness and strength of courage and the capacity for love, and I believe this because I saw it lived and exemplified in these old people, my grandmother and her former slaves, who behaved to each other with such grace and kindness and ease of manner, they taught me all the manners and morals I know, I feel pretty sure. And they did this in the midst of a custom of society so wrong, so basically evil, so hard on all of them, and so apparently incurable, it is a matter of pure wonder to me even now, who saw it in its last phase and lived with it.

The reporter brought up the subject of the present miserable condition of affairs between the races in this country now, and I said I was horrified at the Negro people in this country having to riot to gain something they should have had all along. I wonder at the pig-headedness of custom, I never stop being appalled by the obstinacy and selfishness of those who will not give way an inch ever when it would be for everybody's good if they did. And I said, there are many different kinds of colored people as there are of any other race, and I have always been lucky to know the best kind—and I don't mean "best" because they were convenient help and pleasant to be around, I mean really self-respecting, intelligent people, besides some wonderful artists and religious leaders.[23]

At first glance it seems that in public she would express an opinion that she felt would be acceptable to the audience at hand and in private and among friends who shared her opinions she was frankly racist. On the other hand, *Ship of Fools* is perhaps the accurate expression of the ambivalence of her attitudes. She could not depict a likable Jewish character and yet the book consciously shows the irrational, mindless, dangerous nature of such prejudice and, by implication, its devastating course toward the Holocaust.

Criticism of the novel focused on other areas besides anti-Semitism. In her private letter Herbst described some of the other limitations that critics noted:

> *Ship of Fools* finally drove me out of my mind, I got sick of it. I first admired the way it went, the language, for instance, very much. But things happen with the monotony of a tic.

It is finally all resolved on the personal antagonisms engendered and yet she herself sets the scale to a social view. Her very people from Mexico, from Cuba and those Spaniards in the steerage have roots in social happenings yet it is all resolved on private lives. It becomes too much. Instead of doing as Proust does, taking a subjective view from inside and working out to a world, she hints and only hints at the world and then draws it all back inside individuals. . . .

I am hopelessly tired of these lion-tamers of prose who never have anything really new to say. We all know it is awful, people can be terrible, but show me a first-rate writer who doesn't manage to throw in a more diversified view. . . .

I question all of her moral attitudes. They are based on manners as morals and there is a basic snobbishness which comes through. There is no love—absence of love is dramatized by what love is not. That's O.K.—I could get around that too—except that she is kind of smug about it too. Only see how candid I am—admitting that the whole sexual business isn't worth a damn.

It's all overschematized—this is 1931, she centers it on the Germans and there is only one question—the Jewish question. Her Germans have never heard of the Weimar republic, its glories or its disgraces. The issues that even Hitler had to hurdle before he could get around to the Jewish question are not present, none of the actors that Isherwood documents in the Berlin Stories. But then, of course, she puffs it all up as allegory—I am tired of this stuff . . . .

I think Porter gives too much to the triumphs of this world.[24]

Some of Porter's friends, aware of the overall limitations of the work, still expressed admiration for its stylistic virtues. Flannery O'Connor wrote, "I am over two thirds the way across the Atlantic with Katherine Anne. It [Ship of Fools] may not be a great book but it is in many ways a fine one. It has a sculptured quality. I admire the bulldog in the same way I would admire a bulldog carved to perfection. Essence of bulldog."[25] And Father Roseliep in a litany of his favorite contemporary writers included "Katherine Anne Porter, for Ship of Fools, bearing what must be some of the most beautiful writing in the world."[26]

Like the voice of reason after the shrill chorus of the professional reviewers came the balanced view of Porter's earliest critic, Lodwick Hartley. In his opinion the basic frustration is the book's refusal to shape up either dramatically or thematically to the point where the reader can take hold of it with assurance. If the majesty of human failure was missing from Miss Porter's picture, he wrote, the terror was powerfully and hypnotically revealed. If it did not show, as some of the greatest tragedies do, the possibility of universal order above the chaos, at least it showed the dark chaos of life itself.[27]

Porter's English publisher, Secker and Warburg, had told her that the book had created a tremendous impression among a host of new and appreciative British readers who had been beguiled and shaken. Nevertheless, the reviews that followed the book's publication in England provided little evidence of appreciation. Porter scorned them by saying that the old taste for blood sports was in full cry. She said mostly they were dull, thick, full of prejudices and hatreds of their own character—she wanted to usher some of them up the gangplank with the other fools. She felt that the redeeming joy and light were Raymond Mortimer and Sybille Bedford, both of whom had come forward with criticism-with-a-view, warm and generous but with their own reservations and questions.[28]

Sybille Bedford wrote in the *Spectator:*

Katherine Anne Porter has written a tremendous novel. It took twenty years. One might pause for an instant to imagine this. Twenty years. The courage, the discipline, the fortitude; the cost of every kind, the pressures involved in bearing what must have been at times an almost intolerable burden. And here it is at last, the legend become print: the book has been out (in the United States) for barely half a year and already something of its substance has eaten itself into the marrow of those who read it. The Great American Novel has appeared; ironically, it has turned out to be a great universal novel.[29]

At the end of the otherwise approving review Bedford looked for faults and decided that the book might have been even more effective, more stunning, for less length, since bulk, whatever its quality, blunts. She also felt that the grotesques might have been done more lightly. "Did the only Jew on board have to be such an utter wretch? Did he *have* to trade in rosaries?" She thought the most serious flaw the novel's static quality, the fact that the characters move "on tramlines towards crescendoes not development," and that there was accumulation but "no choice, no crossroads, no turning point." She concluded that Porter had brought forth a Brueghel: "We hope, but cannot be sure, that it is less than a Piero della Francesca."[30]

The unsigned review in the *Time Literary Supplement* in November 1962 granted the book moments of great power and compassion but thought its achievements were those of a great short-story writer. They glittered like passages of subtle, concentrated brushwork on a canvas too thinly composed. This reviewer thought the novel lacked a dramatic center, and added, "One cannot help wondering whether she *knows* enough—of German history, of the sources of modern anti-semitism, of European middle-class speech and values—or whether that knowledge has penetrated the exquisite, but very special range of her feelings."[31]

Porter's reaction to the harsher criticisms was to suspect the reviewers of personal malice. When she was told she was on the short list for the Nobel Prize, she attributed her failure to win to the judges' annoyance at the unpleasant Swedish character in the novel. In a *McCall's* "Celebrity Register" interview by Cleveland Amory, she said, "I'm writing about real people in the real world, people who are either unable to see what's going on around them or unable to face up to it, people who get into trouble and come through the best they can. And a lot of my people are nicer than some of the critics who reviewed the book."[32]

When she failed to win the 1962 National Book Award, she said that her publisher was furious, but she had tried to prepare him for the outcome. She had explained why she would never get any more awards or prizes in the United States: too many people who had resented her for years were getting into the act; she had had her share of love and praise and fine criticism and had to expect a reaction, especially when she hit a million-dollar jackpot as she had; there were people who hated her writing and her reputation, and when they were joined by the people who hated her having that money it made quite a mob.[33]

As the pressures mounted steadily in the months after the publication of the novel, and as new sources of annoyance arrived in every mail, her drinking, which had been uncontrollable for some periods in the past years, grew worse. In the fall of 1962 she had one of her most serious accidents. Rhea Johnson was in his apartment downstairs one evening when he heard a terrific crash. He rushed upstairs and found Porter collapsed at the foot of the long flight of stairs that led to the second floor. The fall had sobered her a little, but she resisted going to the hospital until she was more sober. Three hours later Johnson carried her to his car and drove her to the hospital, where it was discovered that she had broken six ribs.[34] Later she could not remember the fall, nor the blow, but just Rhea's anxious face as he bent over her.[35] While she was recovering in the hospital, she decided that she could stand the United States no longer, and that as soon as she got on her feet she would spend the next year in Italy. Ever since her Christmas there in 1954 she had vowed some day to return to live. Now was the time.

On November 5, she set sail for Italy aboard the *Leonardo da Vinci,* seen off by Ann, now much recovered from her illness. Once in Rome, Porter settled first in the Hotel d'Inghilterra, where she and Ann had stayed in the summer. She could not completely abandon her problems this time either, and many of them followed her. Letters came from her lawyers and accountants and she learned that she had to pay still more income tax. She hoped that this $2,500 they "chiseled" from her would be the last, and she was not consoled when her CPA told her that she was not in the 65 percent income bracket of the privileged class. Just the same, she told herself that no matter how much they grabbed she did have enough left to live in fair comfort and enough to send her sister Gay about $300 a month, so that none of them need worry about money ever again.[36]

She was now trying to plan for the disposal of her papers and literary estate, and that was another problem. In a spontaneous gesture of generosity she had given large amounts of her material to the Library of Congress. Soon, however, she became annoyed by their handling of the material, and hearing that an American university had paid $42,000 for the papers of her English friend Edith Sitwell did not help. Porter had held an honorary position at the Library of Congress, and when she resigned from this "Library of Congress chore," she asked that her papers be returned as soon as possible and placed in storage in Washington with the Security Storage Company. Not understanding the work involved in such matters, she took no account of the time and expense that had already gone into arranging her papers at the Library of Congress. Before she left, a plan was already under way to have a show of her papers and books and a reception for her, but when she received a letter in Rome in December reminding her of this, she considered it a complete disregard of her instructions. For a time she despaired of ever getting the matter straightened out, but ultimately the Library of Congress did send the papers on to her storage company.

During these months too, as *Ship of Fools* sold out one printing after another, she undertook the task of correcting proofs over and over again. She agonized over the mistakes she found each time and readily paid for the corrections from her own money. By the time she had corrected for the ninth American printing and the third printing in England she thought she would go crazy from the constant close work,[37] and the paperback editions were still to come.

In these circumstances, Christmas in Rome was neither festive nor peaceful. She did not find the hotel as pleasant as it had seemed before and she did not enjoy Christmas, though she granted that perhaps she did not have the holiday spirit. All the same, she announced that she had drifted to the conclusion that life in Rome was more possible than elsewhere and she intended to stick it out for about a year. She took action by moving to the Hotel Eden on the Via Ludovisi, where she had a little suite and the sun shone in all day.

While she was at the Eden, Porter decided that she might like to rent accommodations more suited to her new affluence, so she house hunted a little, which she always enjoyed anyway. She fell in love with a palazzo, "a fifteenth-century Florentine daydream of gold leaf everywhere it would stick on," the whole place "a pure riot of gold, silver and brocade." A vivid letter to Barbara Wescott explains why, alas, the deal fell through:

My agent and I went back the next day to see the owner and sign the lease. By now I had an interpreter from the hotel, as my Sicilian agent knew just enough English to say that he did not speak it, and neither did the owner, a certain Marchesa Venaro. She showed up under the great entrance in her pram-sized car, a good-looking blonde woman in early middle life, very healthy and full of zing, with a lovely smiling face, huge gray eyes, wearing good-looking country clothes. She turned out to have the flat just above the one I was until then regarding as mine, but spent most of her time out of town somewhere.

Well, the brocades and gold cloth were stripped from the bed, with plain white counterpanes in their place. Gone were the silver, gold, porcelain, silk and linen, and the gold leaf chairs were covered with plain, dull, red stuff, and indeed after a good look around, I asked one question: "Is this really the same place I saw yesterday?" As La Marchesa talked, and my interpreter asked her some searching questions, her manner changed—she showed the high spirits, bad temper and senseless excitement of a badly-trained horse, and that good-looking face was tough as a boot. What she wanted and would have, besides all that rent, was a deposit of $2,000 against possible wear and tear or damage and loss, two months' rent in advance. . . . I would have to supply my own linen . . . everything movable [from the kitchen] was gone. . . . She seemed entirely unconscious of my total silence; I was letting the agent, the interpreter and La Marchesa do the talking, but my mind had been severely made up for a good while. "Of course, you will need two servants at least," she said, and the interpreter handed this remark on to me with a hasty addition of his own—"Don't you sign anything until you've seen a lawyer," running the sentence together until it sounded like one word. I said, "Don't worry, I'm not going to sign anything. Tell the lady we will let her know tomorrow."[38]

In the same letter she described another episode in an entirely different tone, her visit to the room where Keats died in a tall house to the right of the Spanish Steps. Porter was infinitely moved by the tiny room with its narrow little bed beside the fireplace, and the sight of the small treasures, keepsakes, and other humble little objects. She knew from Keats's letters that he had almost no possessions and that it was cold in that room in February when he died. She felt that the visit confirmed some of her own feelings which in the aftermath of success had been forced underground:

. . . I walked back to the hotel, up that hill, slowly and happily with my entire being warmed and softened, a kind of gratitude of tears that the roots of my feelings and my beliefs that I have lived by were not dead, but just somehow beaten unconscious for a while by the savage forces that were nearly too much for me. The presence of that bravery and that genius and that love flourishing in the narrow room, in the very face of a hard life and a long death, has touched and changed me, turned me back into my path, has restored me to my own life. I was suffering more than I knew, as if I had lost everything and yet could not name it or tell when it began to go.[39]

The letter, with its two episodes, might have been turned into a short story, for it shows the kind of seriousness and honesty that comes out in her fiction. She had always wavered between her attraction to the ascetic life necessary to her creative work and her fondness for a lavish social life in luxurious surroundings. So far she had achieved the first far more often than the second, not always by choice; but whenever she had been able to live a luxurious life, as in Hollywood in the 1940s, she had soon tired of it and returned to the more profound pleasure of artistic work in austere surroundings. The letter contained a very central truth about her present circumstances. She was sickened by all the hubbub and luxury and she needed badly to get back to her own kind of work.

She did not stay in Italy as long as she had planned. She found herself unable to take pleasure in any of her usual interests—the ballet, the theater, music, paintings—and she did not even go to the Etruscan Museum.[40] She traveled a little in the spring, first to Venice and later to Paris, but in October she wrote to Rhea Johnson, "Guess where I'm off to, after all? No place I've planned to—not England, nor Spain—not Greece, not back to Italy, nonono: Guess again."[41] She went on to explain that she was to be back in Washington on October 31, and that she decided she had had her year's leave of absence from the horrors of life in her dear native land. It was high time she got back and shouldered again her share of the white man's burden.

Soon after she returned, the whole country, and particularly the city of Washington, was stunned by the assassination of President John Kennedy. Once again she was witnessing one of the momentous events of the century, and because of her friendship and admiration for the Kennedys—and perhaps because it occurred in Texas—it touched her very keenly. Soon afterward she wrote an essay on Jacqueline Kennedy for the *Ladies' Home Journal*.[42] For once her mood was in harmony with that of the country.

She was happy to be back, and in the future she never moved very far from Washington. She found temporary quarters in the Jefferson Hotel and began to look around for a house in the area. She was invited to the White House by the new President, as she had been during the Kennedy time, and if she had reservations about Johnson and his policies, she had none about his wife. She thoroughly enjoyed Lady Bird Johnson and her daughters and savored the attention she received from this Texas family.

There were still moments of bitterness. When she was invited to

Harvard as the first woman ever to receive an award from Signet, the all-male undergraduate literary society, she was deeply offended by the rowdy crowd of students. What was worse, the award speech tactlessly emphasized how honored she should feel at receiving it.[43]

Porter was looking very beautiful, dressed all in white and carrying a single red rose, and she was the only woman in the room, a circumstance that would normally have delighted her. But the tone of the occasion was so antifeminist that she did a slow burn throughout the ceremony and, when it was her turn to speak, without showing excessive anger she coldly conceded that it was indeed a man's world and told her male audience she was glad of it. She wanted no part of it and they could have it.

Nevertheless, Porter's feminist sentiments had been considerably modified over the years. She no longer railed, as she had to Josephine Herbst and Caroline Gordon, about the condescension and patronage of the masculine literary establishment in general, and against Malcolm Cowley, Paul Rosenfeld, and Ford Madox Ford in particular. Nor did she often speak of her early struggles to be an artist and being told to stay home, write letters, and fix up her hair. In 1956, when she picked up again the copy of Virginia Woolf's *A Room of One's Own* which she had bought in 1929 she had written in it: "I read this book again, all through, on the night of January 6 1956—long after Virginia Woolf is dead, and Donald Brace is dead and that time— 1929—is dead and so much has changed—but it is still freshly full of truth, of energy and life—her lovely intelligence and generosity."[44] But she did not feel the same admiration for the feminist writers of the fifties and sixties. One of her interviews when *Ship of Fools* was published exemplifies her change of heart, or at least change of public attitude:

> No, I've never felt that the fact of being a woman put me at a disadvantage, or that it's difficult being a woman in a "man's world." The only time men get a little tiresome is in love—oh, they're OK at first, but they do tend, don't they, to get a little bossy and theological about the whole business?[45]

There were a number of reasons for the change. One was that the pleasures of success sometimes made her forget her early difficulties. Another was that she was a little threatened by the well-educated, well-informed, articulate women who were now speaking out. And then, quite simply, there was the fact that she often spoke for effect, and gauged what opinions would go down well with her audience. She was fond of quoting Mrs. Patrick Campbell's line that she didn't care what women did as long as they didn't do it in the street and frighten the horses. On a later occasion, when two women interviewers asked if she was ready to join the women's liberation movement, she laughed "uproariously" and replied:

> "Certainly not. . . . I don't agree with them. I told them, 'I will not sit down with you and hear you tell me men have abused you.'
>
> "Any man who ever did wrong to me got back better than he gave.
>
> "And I don't care about any rights. Rights never did me any good. I want my privileges (I haven't always gotten those).
>
> "There is something lacking there. I just can't read any more about them. I don't care what they do, just so they don't do it in the streets and scare the horses.
>
> "I felt that way, too, about Betty Friedan's book when it was sent to me to read. While I was going through it, I thought, 'Oh, Betty, why don't you go and mix a good cocktail for your husband and yourself and forget about this business.' "[46]

Porter was pleased to be back in Washington, and she felt that she knew at last where her home was. Christmas 1963 was one of those she called "the happiest Christmas of my life." She spent it with Monroe Wheeler, Glenway Wescott, and Barbara Wescott in New Jersey, and Paul, with whom she was once again on affectionate terms, was invited also. Surrounded by some of her oldest and most loved friends, she was radiant as light, and her good looks seemed as timeless as ever. Everyone thought she must amaze even herself. She was, at last, adjusting to success.

TWENTY-FOUR

Two Kinds of Success

Since Porter's career had finally culminated in the appearance of a novel, it now seemed to the academic critics that it was possible to assess her entire career. A number of full-length critical studies began to come out.

The first of these appeared in 1963—a monograph by Ray West in the University of Minnesota series on American writers.[1] It served to indicate the pitfalls which awaited critics of Porter's work, in that, while the personal nature of her fiction invited some commentary on her own life, the biographical information available was extremely unreliable. Professor West took at face value Porter's description of her Catholic upbringing, and, having thus recorded much erroneous information, was later forced to retract and correct it. His experience served notice to others that biographical data could not be accepted without question from Porter herself but must be gained from other sources.

The second book-length critical work was *Katherine Anne Porter and the Art of Rejection,* a version of a doctoral dissertation by Brother William Nance. The nature of the book is indicated in this summary paragraph at the end:

The principle of rejection which impelled Katherine Anne Porter into art, while it severely restricted that art both in quantity and in scope, nevertheless enabled her to give form to a limited area of human experience in such a way that she

463

has provided for her contemporaries a penetrating insight into the dark reality that faces them. Miss Porter's technical ability deserves the ample praise it has received. Her pursuit of truth, while severely limited in its success, yet contains elements of honesty and courage which demand respect. The fact of her life and work—of this proud but flawed achievement so intricately wrought out of blended courage and fear, vision and blindness—stands as a compelling reminder of the mystery that lies at the center of man, of woman, and of art. If her works seem to express grave doubts about the possibility of human achievement, those very works constitute an achievement that contradicts that doubt.[2]

Like many another of her critics, Nance assumed that his criticisms would not offend, since they were outweighed by his strong admiration and praise of his subject. He therefore sent her a copy of the book with an inscription expressing his gratitude. Porter had a heyday of marginal scribbling with this book. Beside the inscription she wrote that whoever had this fellow's gratitude did not need a pet viper, and that she preferred the good free-swinging hatchet jobs of some of the reviewer "critics" to the one drop of arsenic to ten drops of syrup that this friar used.[3] She told Caroline Gordon that his Alpha-Beta-cum-mildewed-Freudian method and theory was worn out years ago,[4] and against his final comment on her instinct for rejection, she wondered what instinct had caused the little brother to run to the cover of the cowl and monastery and speculated that it was his fear of sex, marriage, and family life.[5]

Caroline Gordon wrote an essay-review of Nance's book, scorning the "Procrustean couch upon which the Freudian literary critic prefers to stretch his author, rather than to contemplate her work." She made a claim for the cohesiveness of Porter's work and stated that "Miss Porter's 'comédie humaine' is a 'divine comedy.' "[6] Porter was grateful for the effort, although she told Gordon that she feared Nance was well past praying for. She added that he quoted and admired all the third-rate hacks whom she had despised ever since she read their stuff—Granville Hicks, Lodwick Hartley, Ray West, Vernon Young—and that he passed "rather tetchily" by Allen Tate and Robert Penn Warren. She said it was critics like this who had caused her, if not compelled her, to try to explain her point of view, her art, and, to a certain extent, her life. It was all words wasted, and fools like Nance would go on forever.[7]

Perhaps the book that annoyed her most was written by George Hendrick for the Twayne series,[8] a series with a prescribed format that includes a biographical survey and a general survey, in chronological order, of the fiction. As the earliest full-length biography of Porter, it was well done. Professor Hendrick did original biographical research in Texas and drew on some theses and dissertations which had also been based on original research. He therefore corrected some biographical errors that had circulated about Porter and added new biographical facts to the record.

When she read the book, Porter was ecstatic with rage. What caused her the most anguish was that her childhood name "Callie" was made public for the first time. She wrote in the book that her name had originally been Katherine Anne Maria Callista Russell Porter, hence Callie, and ever afterward with some variations she gave that list as her real name.[9] Sometimes Veronica was added along the way, and sometimes Katherine Anne was dropped and she admitted that she had chosen it herself out of respect for her grandmother's memory, but she always maintained that Callie was a shortened version of Callista. Against the accurately reported facts, such as that she had worked as a reporter for the *Fort Worth Critic* in 1917, she wrote "silly," and against the detail that in 1919 she went to New York and did hack work and ghost writing, she scribbled "nonsense."[10]

She made accurate corrections too. When Hendrick reported that she had been divorced after three years in her first marriage, although she had often said just that in interviews, she gave the correct length of time and said that the marriage ended after nine years.

She objected strongly to Hendrick's praise of the symbolic associations of her characters' names. He linked Miranda's brother, Paul, with St. Paul, saw Ellen Thompson of "Noon Wine" as an ironic, mock-heroic version of Helen of Troy, and commented on the name Gabriel in "Old Mortality." Porter noted angrily that her brother really was named Paul, that Mrs. Thompson was indeed named Ellen, and that her uncle really was Gabriel Gay.[11]

Her anger in this matter was exceeded only by that aroused when critics suggested that she had been influenced by other writers. Even when she herself had acknowledged that she had been influenced by them, she was still annoyed. She rejected Hendrick's suggestion that she had been influenced by Sir Walter Scott, and said that she had never read a page of Scott's poetry or prose in her life. She said also that she had never read more than four poems by Whitman and that she detested him and always had. When Hendrick compared the ending of "Holiday" with Frost's "Stopping by Woods on a Snowy Evening," she simply let out a marginal shriek, "wow wow wow jesus jesus." And when Hendrick mentioned her association with Ford Madox Ford she wrote that he didn't know anything and couldn't guess right and should keep his grubby little paws off her life and shut up. "Another bloody monkey mind" was her final comment on the book.[12]

In more balanced moments she recognized that she had detractors and strong supporters and she learned to accept both. Writing to David Locher about a review of Hendrick's book, she was resentful at the praise of Hendrick but took stock of all the critics of her work whom she appreciated:

> Such critics and artists as Glenway Wescott, V. S. Pritchett, Sybille Bedford, Cyril Connolly, Louis Auchincloss, Robert Penn Warren, Caroline Gordon, Jay Featherstone (New Republic)—oh a list of them—have written with intelligence and knowledge of my work and they do not perpetuate silly gossip about my personal life, and when they are not sure of their facts, they ask me, and get, above all, a candid straight answer. Sister Joselyn's remark about "the somewhat less than candid first lady of American letters" insults me personally on two counts: she calls me a liar by inference, and I find that "first lady" thing somewhat more than vulgar: I resent its use deeply in reference to me. But there is a whole subnormal squirm of little people—the absurd Brother Nance, the more absurd Hendrick, and a dreadful little fellow whose name I cannot now remember who wrote a nasty little pamphlet on my work to go in a series got out by the University of Minnesota some time ago. . . . Samuel Butler once wrote: "I don't mind lying, but I detest inaccuracy." I detest both and I propose to protect myself from both so far as I can.[13]

A new interest in Porter's life was the filming of *Ship of Fools*. Interest in buying the movie rights had been high, and David O. Selznick had written to bid on them even before he finished reading the book. He did not, however, get the rights, which were sold to United Artists for $400,000 a month after the novel came out. The movie was to be directed by Stanley Kramer and the screenplay written by Abby Mann. Work on the movie got under way early in 1963 and Abby Mann went to Rome to talk to Porter about it. She said afterward that she saw him for dinner or drinks or something every day for three weeks and that he asked silly questions like "Who did Mrs. Treadwell sit with at her table on the 'Werra.' "[14]

In spite of her disparaging remarks, she was flattered at having a movie made of her work and took a great interest in the casting. Since she firmly resisted even slight changes in her stories, it is surprising that she was always cooperative and interested when dramatizations of them were done, a process that necessarily meant taking liberties with the original text. Her interest in the film version of *Ship of Fools* remained high, and, besides allowing Abby Mann to interview her extensively, she gave advice and information by letter while he was at work on the screenplay. When she returned to Washington, the letters continued back and forth. She wrote details about the clothes she wore in 1931, obviously condoning the link being made between herself and Jenny Brown. She told Mann that she had worn slacks and riding breeches as early as 1923, and also the backless sun dresses and evening dresses which were high style at the time. She said that in 1930 those "ugly hermaphrodite skirt-pants" came in and she was fool enough to wear them too.[15]

Most of her advice concerned the characters, and here she often defended them against the more severe judgment of Abby Mann. She wrote that Jenny Brown was not a bitch, that she was not going to have the usual kind of luck, not the conventional future, but that she was not as beaten down as she seemed when she first arrived in Germany.[16] She was just then at the beginning of her life.

She also defended Mrs. Treadwell against Mann's impression that she was "she-wolfish." Porter explained that she was a tenderly brought up woman who had made a bad marriage; she had sustained shocks of cruelty which had frightened her into a retreat from life and a fear of people and experience and yet her heart remained, in a way, tender. She was easily moved and her first impulse was to a kind of impersonal friendliness—her second a drawing away with a kind of cynical remembrance of past entanglements. When attacked with threats of rape and bone-breaking by a drunken thug, she defends herself with an accumulated rage against the brutalities in all life, not just her own. Porter added that she had been shocked because reviewers of the book had loudly condemned Mary Treadwell for her coldness and for her action in beating Denny with the heel of her slipper when he attacked her, although no word had been spoken against Denny for his attempted rape.[17] She said if she had ever found herself in the same position she would have done the same, and she hoped she would have had a more effective weapon.

Porter was gratified that so many talented actors and stars were considered for the parts—Sir Laurence Olivier for Dr. Schumann, Marlene Dietrich for La Condesa (it was thought eventually that she would be too predictable in the part and that a better person for the role would be someone whose strength was as an actress rather than as a personality), and Katharine Hepburn for Mrs. Treadwell.

In fact, the casting was one of the strong points of the movie. Stanley Kramer well understood the links between the various sets of characters which critics had noticed. A number of essays had traced the links of Jenny Brown, Mrs. Treadwell, and La Condesa and between the various couples. To Kramer the characters were all aspects of Katherine Anne Porter herself and of what she felt and responded to, and all the couples were a single couple seen at various stages of life and in various countries.[18]

His understanding of the characters informed his technique of building sequences and cutting from scene to scene and also affected his casting. He considered only two actresses for the part of Mrs. Treadwell—Katharine Hepburn and Vivien Leigh—and Leigh played the role. Giving one of the strongest performances in the movie, she used her own contradictory personality in the role, becoming both a grande dame with impeccable manners and a wild, uninhibited street girl. It was no coincidence that Leigh's best roles, Scarlett O'Hara and Blanche DuBois, had been portrayals of southern belles who combined the two extremes. Her personal life too was being torn apart by the conflicting parts of her personality.[19]

These two sides were also present in Porter, though they did not conflict nearly so tragically as in Vivien Leigh. The two women had a great deal in common, both possessing, quite apart from their talent, an overpowering charm and "star quality" that brought them a train of devoted admirers. There was even a close physical resemblance between the English actress, in her fifties when she played forty-six-year-old Mary Treadwell, and Porter in her younger days. They shared a lean, dark, feline quality, a kittenishness that could indeed sometimes turn to she-wolfishness. Stanley Kramer allowed Leigh a great deal of freedom in her interpretation of the part, and consequently all the traits she shared with Porter came fully into play.

Elizabeth Ashley, who played Jenny Brown, shared a physical resemblance with Porter and Leigh. She looked like a plausible younger version of Mrs. Treadwell and something of a mother-daughter relationship developed between the two women.

In a different way Simone Signoret brought to the role of La Condesa certain personality links with author and character. She had a history of political engagement and a fierce will to survive not by compromise but through a kind of determined integrity and maturity. Some of her dialogue seems to come not so much from the book as from the descriptions Porter had given Mann about her early life—as when La Condesa talks of persuading her little brother to eat lye.

Another actor with a natural affinity for the part he played was Lee Marvin. Coming onto the set to play William Denny, the rough, ignorant Texan, he was often drunk and exhaling stale-scotch breath so strongly that Vivien Leigh refused to act with him.[20]

A departure from the book's description was the casting of Dr. Schumann as a much younger man. The part was played by the forty-three-year-old Viennese actor Oskar Werner, who was slightly built and looked even younger than his actual age. Critics considered his performance brilliant and pointed out that he was prepared for it by his experience in classical roles such as *Hamlet*.[21]

The greatest change in the whole movie was in the character of Herr Lowenthal, the stereotyped Jew whose presence in the novel had aroused some critics' anger. He was changed from an unpleasant character into a wonderfully benign elderly gentleman with understanding and good will for all. In the movie he is a war hero, proud of his Iron Cross award, and he says that he is a German first and a Jew second. When he hears a Strauss waltz, his comment is, "Doesn't that give you a special feeling about being German?"

This character was played by the noted German actor Heinz Ruehann, who had been a star in pre-Hitler Germany. Not Jewish himself, he felt a great burden of guilt for the whole Jewish nation. When Kramer told him he was looking for someone to play a Jew, Ruehann said, "I'm your man."[22]

In his case, it was not the casting but the changing of the character in the script that was particularly revealing. The change reduces the whole story to melodrama—a simple sharp conflict between the villainous Germans (represented by Herr Rieber, the Captain, Lizzie Spockenkeiker) and the saintly Jew (represented by Herr Lowenthal). The movie version shows how dangerously close to melodrama the whole conception of the novel was, and it suggests that there Porter had an artistic reason for making the Jewish character unpleasant. That helped to keep the book from being obviously melodramatic.

Critics were quick to point out the elementary-school moralizing that runs through the movie from the beginning, when the dwarf, brilliantly played by Michael Dunn, tells the audience, "My name is Herr Glocken and this is a ship of fools . . . the ship is full of them, if you look closely enough you might find yourself," to the end, when he says, "What has all this to do with us today? Why, nothing at all!" —this last sentence delivered with a knowing smile.

Nearly all the ironies of the movie are based on hindsight. As one Nazi shouts inanities, another German says, "Every time I listen to him I know that no one will support his party." When the kindly Herr Lowenthal is asked about the projected uprooting of the Jews, he says genially, "There are nearly a million Jews in Germany. What are they going to do, kill us all?" And when Herr Rieber, temporarily won over by Lowenthal's kindness to him while he is seasick, asks "Why don't you go back to your own country?" Lowenthal explains (without animosity), "My father was born in Germany." The irony of that remark is increased by the fact that Rieber's father was born not in Germany but in Austria. Referring to some of these clumsy speeches, one critic called the film "the shoddiest example of fakery since the days of Ann Corio's Monogram epics."[23] It should be remembered, however, that the novel itself contains many similar ironies, like Captain Thiele's reverie of power, violence, and suppression, and Herr Rieber's suggestion for solving the problem of the itinerant sugar workers:

> Herr Rieber and Lizzi Spockenkeiker pranced onto the deck, and Lizzi screamed out to little Frau Otto Schmitt, whose tender heart was plainly to be surmised in her soft pink face: "Oh, what do you think of this dreadful fellow? Can you guess what he just said? I was saying, 'Oh these poor people, what can be done for them?' and this monster"—she gave a kind of whinny between hysteria and indignation—"he said, 'I would do this for them: I would put them all in a big oven and turn on the gas!' Oh," she said weakly, doubling over with laughter, "isn't that the most original idea you ever heard?"[24]

Porter was fond of telling her literary friends that she had never seen the movie, that she had no interest in seeing it and knew only what people told her about it—and she had heard that some terrible things were done to the book. She would have liked to maintain such aloofness, no doubt, but her curiosity got the better of her. The outing was arranged, at her request, by the obliging Rhea Johnson.

Although he was no longer a part of Porter's ménage, Rhea frequently visited her at the house she was now renting in Spring Valley, a suburb of Washington. He was still the target of rages but still, to the amazement of her family, continued the relationship. There were compensations. She still liked to cook elaborate meals for him, she was a vastly entertaining companion, and she rewarded his devotion with gifts of papers, photographs, books, and sometimes gifts from other friends that she thought more appropriate for him. Sometimes her generosity was of an inconvenient kind. One evening when they had enjoyed a fine dinner and much good wine, she insisted on giving him a chair he had long admired. He resisted at first but finally succumbed to her persuasion and took the chair home in his car. The next morning she called him up and said, "We did have a good time, didn't we, honey? The only thing is I can't find that green chair anywhere." He hastily put it back in the car and returned it.[25]

He was still as accommodating as ever in running errands and providing escort service when needed. He had taken Porter to the movies before, and the experience was usually unnerving because of her habit of talking loudly throughout the film, as if no one else were in the theater. In turn, people in neighboring seats made a good deal of noise shushing her. When Johnson was asked to take her to see *Ship of Fools,* he winced. They had nearly been thrown out of *Tom Jones* just the week before. He tried to avoid a similar embarrassment by taking her in the afternoon of the last day *Ship of Fools* was being shown in Washington, when the movie house was less likely to be crowded. Time off from his job was a small price to pay.

Porter's reaction to the movie was very favorable. She had been told that Dr. Schumann died before the end, and she threatened often and loudly to leave if he did, but she remained in her seat to the end. She even admired some of Abby Mann's additions to the dialogue. In one scene Dr. Schumann asks La Condesa if she likes German music and she replies, "Ye-es, I like Cherman music. . . . It's just that a little Cherman music goes a long way with me." "God, I wish I'd thought of that line," cried Porter.[26]

All in all, her greatest delight in the movie was the large amount of money it brought in. And the one constant in her life now was that the money came flowing in from all sides, steadily and effortlessly. It did not, however, bring her complete satisfaction, for to be content it was necessary to be writing, or at least to feel that she was writing. She spoke a true word when she said that if she had her art she had everything and if she lost that she had nothing.

> I had really believed that this money *Ship of Fools* brought me would bring leisure and freedom with it, but oh, God, it has not, it has not! . . . Yet I assure you I am not altogether whupped, as my native Southern dialect has it: I mean even yet at this late day to find my way out of this senseless muddle, and try to finish some writing I have in mind.[27]

In Italy she had been frustrated by her inability to work and she had determined to rally her resources as soon as possible. She had written:

> . . . age, real age, can play dreadful tricks on the mind and spirit; Gluttony I do not practice; in fact, I eat less and less, but it is my lassitude, just laissez faire, which translates nicely into Lazy. That worries me. I shall put myself on a sterner regime. . . . I want to work. . . . My mind is painfully distracted by all the hundreds of things irrelevant to anything I am doing, and it must end.[28]

Once back in the United States she made a determined effort to carry out her resolution, and she was helped in this by a great stroke of good fortune: she had at last found the perfect literary agent. She wrote her French translator:

> Cyrilly Abels, my good friend, who used to be the managing editor of Mademoiselle, has founded her own agency, and allelulia, at last I have an agent who not only could read my work, but liked it, and was able to handle it for me and has done wonders so far and is going to do more and better.[29]

Few business associations were lastingly satisfying to Porter, but she now entered upon one which was wholly so. When Cyrilly Abels went into business for herself as an agent, Porter had someone acting for her who really put her interests first and whom she trusted absolutely. In the next few years her faith and affection for Abels never wavered. Now, not only did the stream of gifts continue—red roses at Christmas, "Pink Perfection" camellias for her birthday (these gifts were often arranged through the obliging offices of Rhea Johnson, whom Cyrilly had befriended as she had Paul Porter)—but also a stream of checks, the results of Cyrilly's tireless efforts to sell any available material of Porter's.

Through her efforts the *Ladies' Home Journal* had commissioned the article on Jacqueline Kennedy and later published "The Spivvelton Mystery," which Porter described as "her first and last mystery story." She had written it in the late twenties, submitted it for publication, had it rejected, and set it aside when Malcolm Cowley told her that it was "not so hot" and correctly diagnosed that it had three separate themes which she had not integrated to make the story cohesive.[30] Although Cowley's judgment was correct, in the wake of *Ship of Fools* the story was not only eagerly accepted and published but won an award from the Mystery Writers of America. Years earlier, when she was fifty, Porter had boasted that the magazines would publish her laundry lists if she let them but had added soberly that most of her writing went into the wastebasket where it belonged. At that time she exerted a severe control over what she allowed to appear in print. Now, in her mid-seventies, she relaxed a little and enjoyed selling and publishing whatever she could.

Cyrilly was also energetic in selling Porter's work abroad, and this provided a steady revenue. Porter no longer needed these relatively small sums of money, but they were eagerly received, both for themselves and as reassurances that her work was sought after.

When essays and stories and articles were not forthcoming, Cyrilly turned to Porter's plentiful letters. The letter from Italy to Barbara Wescott was sent to the American Express magazine, *Travel and Leisure*. The editor wrote that the letter intrigued him, although he did not immediately see how he could squeeze it in, since the style was odd for the magazine.[31] But he did manage it, and a check for $1,000 went to Cyrilly. Two letters to Paul were sold for $700 and Cyrilly began to think about a book of Porter's letters to Glenway Wescott and Monroe Wheeler, and perhaps a collection of her letters to Donald Elder.

Porter also changed publishers. Seymour Lawrence, who had overseen the publication of *Ship of Fools,* had decided to leave the Atlantic Monthly Press and start his own publishing house in Boston. He hoped Porter would go with him for her future works. At first the idea of changing publishers upset Porter, as any change did, and though she was slightly influenced in favor of Lawrence by his enthusiasm for her work, she expressed her frustration in a letter to Cyrilly:

> My time is shortening; even if I live to be a hundred I cannot presume on my creative faculties holding out forever—I must have quiet and leisure NOW, and if the worst comes to the worst, I shall simply call off the whole thing, and do my writing without any fixed publisher. I am no longer able to sustain and recover from the shocks of this preposterous situation, as I have in the past. There is no time!
>
> I will tell you what I have in mind: (1) The Collection of Occasional writings (2) A Collection of short stories, but I do not want to be bedevilled about this by any publisher. I will write them as I can, and sell them to magazines as I write them, and that is that, utterly. I don't want to hear a word about what editors want or anybody thinks I should give a particular magazine, (3) The Cotton Mather Study.[32]

The balance tipped in Lawrence's favor when Cyrilly argued for him against Peter Davison of Atlantic Monthly: ". . . Peter is a pretty decent chap. I *know* he and Little Brown are truly eager for you to stay . . . however! The only thing I can say against Peter is that he doesn't have Sam's strength (or is the word 'gumption,' or doggedness or some combination of all three)."[33]

In the spring of 1965 she finally signed a two-book contract which Seymour Lawrence had drawn up. The books were to be a collection of essays and occasional writings and the long-neglected biography of Cotton Mather. The total advance was a staggering $82,000, $10,000 on signing the contract, $10,000 on delivery of the manuscript of the essays, and $25,000 on delivery of *Cotton Mather*. The collection of essays was the least worrisome task because she intended to use the ones published in 1952 in *The Days Before* and add to them some of the essays, reviews, poems, and letters she had written before and after that edition. Since the task was one of collecting and selecting rather than writing, the proposed delivery date was October 1, 1965. *The History of Cotton Mather* was a heavier commitment, because nine of the twenty chapters still remained to be completed. Nevertheless, the proposed delivery date for that book was set for October 1, 1966, and agreed to by Porter, who earlier, in the midst of contract negotiations, had begun to experience again her old author's panic in the face of deadlines. She told Cyrilly:

The only thing is after all the fanfare and trumpet voluntaries and cash on the barrel-head, I face a future looking at pages in a typewriter alternated by frenzied glances at the blank wall, for as far as I can see, the rest of my natural life. But it won't be so bad with all that wonderful money rolling in. . . .

The Fall deadline for the occasional writing is perhaps good enough, and, if I can work every day, I might by miracle be able to produce the Cotton Mather book by Fall of 1966, God knows I should like to. If they do not press too much for an exact deadline, let these dates stand. The trouble is publishers always begin to harass me when I show signs of lagging, and, no matter what psychologists might be able to make of this, pressure of that sort simply throws me into a catatonic state, paralyzes my will, muddles my mind, and hurts my feelings. Let's hope that if I don't quite make the deadlines they will not begin to harass me about it; it will just delay things.[34]

The dates did stand for the moment. By now, missing deadlines and fretting about contracts had become a way of life, and the present ones caused less anguish than had earlier ones. She was seventy-five and her reputation was established. Neither it nor her income depended on future publications.

That year she had the pleasure of seeing a fine new edition of her stories published. In the fall of 1965 Harcourt brought out *The Collected Stories of Katherine Anne Porter,* containing all the stories which had been published over the years in separate collections and the new stories which had appeared recently. "The Fig Tree" was in its appropriate place and so was "Holiday." She sent the new collection on its way with a new preface, in which she took a slap at Matthew Josephson and others who had claimed to launch her. She insisted that the credit for "discovering" her belonged squarely to Carl Van Doren. She urged readers to avoid calling her stories novellas or novelettes and asked them to use the simple adequate English words: short stories, long stories, short novels, long novels. And she concluded: "To part is to die a little, it is said (in every language I can read), but my farewell to these stories is a happy one, a renewal of their life, a prolonging of their time under the sun, which is what any artist most longs for."[35]

TWENTY-FIVE

The Rewards of Success

I f one lives long enough, everything will come,"[1] Katherine Anne Porter told a cousin, and sure enough, when she was in her mid-seventies, she at last achieved much that she had spent her life striving for. The immediate nuisances of bestsellerdom faded away, and although serenity was not quite in character for her, the next ten years were good ones.

Even the literary prizes that had eluded *Ship of Fools* now came effortlessly. *The Collected Stories of Katherine Anne Porter* won both the National Book Award and the Pulitzer Prize. She had often scorned the latter as a mere newspaperman's prize, but when she heard over the telephone that she had won she said, "Oh, I'm so excited! I'm so happy! I get $500? Well, I'll pay my income tax with it."[2]

When she made her acceptance speech at the American Academy of Arts and Letters for the National Institute's Gold Medal for Fiction, she spoke of her long struggle and her satisfaction now that it was won:

> I had at first thought everything was going to come very easy, but it was a long war, and an exhausting one, and I have a feeling now that this medal is a little bit like a laurel leaf put around my brow to show that I nearly won, you know. But just the same, I wouldn't have missed the life that I've had, just as it was, for anything. . . . I read lately an observation by Anthony Trollope: "Success is a necessary misfortune of life, but it is only to the very unfortunate that it comes early." . . .

I have avoided a career as long as I possibly could, and distrusted Success, in the way that we know it here, all my life. But I worked at my vocation and late in my life, by total hazard, by no design of my own whatever, I wrote a novel that became a modest bestseller.[3]

She was told that she had won the medal by a very narrow squeak and said that gave it the exhilaration of a good horse race. Naturally, she was not really pleased to hear that she had only barely won. Years later she wrote beside the speech in her copy of the Collected Essays that on the first vote she tied with Vladimir Nabokov, and on the second vote she won by a narrow margin but no one would tell by how much or how little. She added that Glenway Wescott had remarked with his usual venom that Nabokov would most probably have refused the medal.[4]

She also grew accustomed to wealth and could now afford the kind of home she had always wanted. The Spring Valley house was just such a home. Described by Robert Penn Warren as a "mansion," it had twelve rooms and a lush lawn on a tree-shaded street in the suburbs—"the last place I ever expected to find myself," she said. It was supposed to be Jacobean, she said, but she called it "1905 American Stratford-on-Avon."[5] She settled there with a secretary, housekeeper, maid, and gardener.

In spite of her depreciating remarks, she adored being the chatelaine of such an establishment; like her emerald ring, it became a triumphant symbol of her success. She happily conducted visitors on tours of the house, describing her acquisitions and explaining where and how each one had been chosen. All the old pieces were displayed to advantage, and there were new ones from her recent trips. She had told Rhea Johnson when she was in Italy that she was going broke on "gold leaf furniture, heavy white silk curtains and Venetian glass."[6]

She now had two immense chandeliers, a Waterford one and a new one from the Murano glass works. She had brought this from Venice with matching glass sconces, and all had made the journey without a crack. In the living room, above the mantelpiece, was a massive baroque mirror bought at auction in Belgium, and in the same room an eleven-foot Louis Quinze sofa she had found sitting outside a Brussels store in the rain. There was a group of seventeenth-century French marquetry-and-brass tables, a rosewood desk ("for bill paying, not for writing"), and her Avila cupboard that dated back to 1600. In the dining room one chandelier hung over the Vermont marble table. In an adjacent room was an eighteenth-century drafts-man's table under an engraving of General Lee on his horse Traveller. There was an ornate crystal and silver epergne from the Christ Child Opportunity Shop and described as one of her "joke things."[7] Her bed had a headboard of Venetian gilt and was upholstered in peacock blue; beside was a table thought to have belonged to Madame de Pompadour.

When visitors were dazzled by all the gilt and crystal, she ex-plained that she had lived out of a suitcase for so long that she finally decided, if she was to live under one roof like everyone else she would not have anything that was not good. "Everything here is original. It looks good and expensive and it is."[8]

In comparison with the luxury of the other rooms, her work-room was austere except for the fifteenth-century Fiesole monastery table with heart-shaped carving which she said was the only table long enough to hold all her papers when she worked. Her proudest exhibit here was the part of her library that housed the 126 editions of her work translated into thirty-two languages.

To add to her sense of putting down roots and setting her house in order, she at last found a home for her literary estate.

In 1966 the University of Maryland wanted to award her the honorary degree of Doctor of Humane Letters. She had already re-ceived half a dozen such honors and was no longer excited by them. She felt she could not continue to run around receiving them, and anyway she wondered what a degree was worth if it depended on the presence of the honoree. Accordingly, she told the University of Maryland officials that she was not well enough to be present at the ceremony.

The president of the University, Dr. Wilson Elkins, then wrote and asked permission to present the degree to her at home when she felt strong enough. The ceremony, which took place during a week-end visit from Ann and Walter, could not have delighted Porter more. She looked out her window and saw a parade of twelve or thirteen cars coming down the street, then about twenty-five people, univer-sity officials, faculty members, and students, piled out and into the house. They had brought one of the most beautiful hoods she had ever seen, and she proudly put it on for the ceremony. Afterward she served champagne and home-baked rolls and everyone sat around drinking the wine and listening to her talk. Dr. Elkins was, like Porter, from a small Texas town, and she felt an immediate warmth for him and for his attractive wife, Dorothy. At the end of the visit she declared it was the most charming thing that had ever happened to her.

After the degree ceremony she visited the university and said, "Now I know what my university is. I'm going to give my papers and some of my belongings to the University of Maryland."[9] In turn, the university promised to set aside in its fine McKeldin Library a suite of rooms to house her gift that would be known as the Katherine Anne Porter Room.

It disappointed some of Porter's admirers that the Humanities Research Center, in Austin, Texas, which housed so many of the great literary archives of the twentieth century, including many from England, was not also the repository of the papers of Katherine Anne Porter, born just a few miles away. And yet the University of Maryland, closer to the center of her activities in her later years, was also an appropriate place. After all, she had never liked to be one of a group, even a distinguished literary group.

The University of Maryland's arrangements could not have been more attractive. The three-room suite on the third floor of the McKeldin Library overlooked a broad view of the campus. The entrance to the building was flanked by two huge magnolia trees, and on the floor above the Porter Room was the Maryland Room, housing the state archives. The place was near enough to her home so that she could look forward to visiting her room and looking at the possessions she had placed there.

The project of setting up the Katherine Anne Porter Room and deciding on the disposition of her literary estate now took on an excitement far beyond the ordinary, for adding piquancy to the happiness of these years was the fact that once again, now for the last time, she had fallen in love.

Elijah Barrett Prettyman, Jr., a Washington lawyer thirty-five years her junior, had something of the appeal for her that Matthew Josephson had had long ago. On the surface he appeared conventional —a member of a prominent family (his father had been a distinguished judge) and the product of St. Albans, Yale, and the University of Virginia Law School. He had been a special assistant to Attorney General Robert Kennedy, and lived with his pretty wife and two children in the wealthy suburb of Chevy Chase, Maryland. At the same time he was restless in his family life and his successful legal career. He had literary inclinations and craved some occupation that would take him out of the legal and political world and into literary circles. He collected first editions, rare books, and copies of books autographed by their authors.

Prettyman had found some outlet for his writing skills by working on his own book, *Death and the Supreme Court,* a series of case histories selected and put together in such readable form that it won the Mystery Writers of America Award for the best fact-crime book of 1961. When *Ship of Fools* appeared, his admiration for the book and its author was unbounded, and he sent her a copy asking her to sign it for his collection. At the same time he sent her a copy of his book with the inscription:

For Katherine Anne Porter—

With envy, the greatest respect,
and every best wish from an enthusiastic traveler—
Barrett Prettyman, Jr.[10]

She acknowledged the gift courteously but it was not until some years later that the two met.

She had always approached the business of appointing a literary executor in a mood of high seriousness tinged with assumed modesty. At different times over the years she had written Glenway Wescott, William Goyen, and William Humphrey asking them to undertake the job and assuring them of her complete understanding if they were not able to. She knew, of course, that she was offering a high honor that would be eagerly accepted. In recent years Rhea Johnson had been included as someone who might help the executor. She had written to William Humphrey, "What I ask of you, William, is will you be my literary executor and editor if Glenway does not outlive me?"[11] and had added that Rhea Johnson would assist the executor.

Shortly after they met, a similar request went out to Barrett, asking him to act as her lawyer:

Dear Mr. Prettyman,

For several months I have been meditating on what I am about to ask you. . . . I wish to ask for your professional advice about making my will. . . .

    If for any reason you do not care to undertake this matter, I shall understand perfectly. But I have my hopes.[12]

Barrett, of course, was delighted to act as attorney for so distinguished a writer and went out to see her. When they met to discuss business they were enchanted with each other. He was fascinated not only by her stature as a writer but by her peerless conversation, her wit and vivacity, the whole magical fabric of her life. She in turn was delighted by his boyish good looks, for he seemed younger than forty as he rode up to her house on his motorcycle. As she remembered it, each was a little in awe of the other at first, and inhibited slightly by the great age difference. Looking back on this initial awkwardness she wrote him:

But I wish you could have seen how serious I was, and would have given me signals instead of saying you were serious and did not think I was! You were right not to take it too seriously at first, and I am catching up not to take it too seriously now, but happily, easily. Winter is coming, darling. Let's sit in the sunlight a little. Once I asked you, years and years ago in Spring Valley, "But what are we going to do?" And you answered instantly and gently, "I don't know, but let it be together." What a hope!

Love you in Hell's despite.[13]

What they mostly did together was to work on a series of legal projects connected with the Katherine Anne Porter Room and the drawing up of the will. The spirit of these endeavors was not at all dry and legalistic but quite festive, with guests and a generous flow of champagne. On December 4, 1966, she gave a will-signing party to ratify her gift to the university. There were about a dozen guests, including Rhea Johnson and Barrett's wife, and she described the evening to Barbara Wescott as

the rite of incorporating my little Foundation which intends to give useful sums of money to serious writers who practise literature as an art and therefore have to spend half their lives and energies doing other jobs to live.

This has called for several gatherings supposedly of a legal and businesslike nature, but a little of that goes far with me and I always turn it into a party with small foods and champagne—usually my own homemade bread with sweet butter, hot and crusty, and plain old non-vintage Moët et Chandon. So, day before yesterday, the last round with TV and other cameras, 18 press reps, Pres and Mrs. Elkins of the University, tape recorders and all, we went through a spontaneous unrehearsed ritual of handing over the ms. of *Ship of Fools* as token of my gift to them of all my books, papers, ms. Dear Barbara in the midst of all this I take pain-pills for each occasion and go back to bed for a rest when it is over.[14]

Once the basic will was drawn up, other festive occasions presented themselves in the numerous changes and codicils she made. Barrett wrote in her guest book, "Many, many codicils."[15] She signed her letters to him, "Your adoring client."

In the past Porter's tendency to mix business and social events, professional relationships and friendships, had sometimes proved disastrous. There had been an unpleasant row a few years earlier when a Washington friend who was a real estate agent had tried to arrange the sale of a house with her. The episode had ended with mutual recriminations, much bitterness, and a broken friendship. She seemed incapable of entering into even a business relationship unless there was total devotion to her, quite beyond the normal requirements of professional services.

In the relationship with Barrett there was the odd circumstance that for all the festive meetings, the cheerful drawing up of codicils, she was being charged a substantial fee for his professional services. Prettyman explained that this was not his wish, but the policy of his law firm would not permit him to do otherwise.[16] Porter gave the matter little thought. She was ecstatically in love, ready to worship; for her the association was perfect.

Meanwhile, behind the scenes, work began on the less visible but really important part of her gift to the university—the papers. These were sorted, arranged, and catalogued. The transfer of her furniture went on simultaneously and the Katherine Anne Porter Room became an attractive reality.

The curtains at the windows duplicated the ones in Porter's house, carrying out the rose color scheme of the upholstery of the Louis Quinze sofa and the big oriental rug. On three sides of the room was her library, in glass cases and arranged according to her instructions—the translations of her works in one section, English-language publications—magazines and books—in another, books by her friends, and then her own collections—a large section on witch-craft, one on the Middle Ages, the lives of the saints, books on cats, on growing camellias, and many more.

There was the long Fiesole table, the eighteenth-century drafts-man's table, the spinet with the little gold chair of the kind she had in her dining room. And among them and in the bookcases were the souvenirs of a lifetime—the Buddha given to her when she was four-teen by her brother who was in the navy; the crucifix from her early days in Mexico and various pieces of Mexican pottery; the little stamp machine she had bought in Italy; the heavy brass vase bought from her guide in Pompei.

All around, on walls, desks, and bookcases, were photographs. These provided a record of Porter's life: a baby picture when she was two, a picture from her acting days in Fort Worth in 1922, pictures of her in Mexico, in Paris, and in Hollywood, from snapshots to elaborate studio portraits by Henri Cartier-Bresson and George Platt Lynes. There were pictures of her family—of her mother as a young woman, of her father in middle age and old age, of her niece and nephew and friends: Robert Penn Warren, Marcelle Sibon, Eudora Welty. Some of the pictures were taken by Porter herself with the Mexican photographer Tina Modetti's camera—of Hart Crane in her garden in Mexico and Ford Madox Ford in her hotel in Basle. There were pictures of the actresses who had appeared in dramatic versions of her stories, pictures of many of her cats, and several pictures of Barrett Prettyman.

There were tributes, awards, medals, citations, and gowns and hoods from universities; the certificate of her marriage to Eugene Pressly with its array of signatures; the page with Mark Twain's inscription left to her by John Melville; and the desk used by Barrett Prettyman's father, with a metal plaque to designate it as such.

For the dedication ceremony of the Katherine Anne Porter Room, friends and family converged on the University of Maryland. Among the guests were Glenway Wescott, Monroe Wheeler, Eudora Welty, and Ann (whose pleasure was somewhat lessened when she saw that the Fiesole table, which she had been promised, was included in the furniture). It was a gala occasion and Barrett was never far from her elbow.

He loved such public occasions—escorting her to the spring meeting of the American Academy of Arts and Letters and seeing the impressive gathering of writers and other artists, and being included in social occasions where he could meet her distinguished friends. Once, fascinated, he overheard a conversation between Porter and Iris Murdoch. And on quieter occasions he enjoyed simply listen-ing to Porter talk about her life.

They met for the holidays. She cooked Thanksgiving dinner for his family and sometimes spent the holidays with them, and year after year Barrett and his wife were guests at her Twelfth Night party.

At Christmas 1967 he was on a trip to Saigon, but his gift to her was a pair of wineglasses with which he hoped they would toast every occasion, including those they just made up. She was forbidden to use them with anyone else. She was in the hospital just before that Christmas and he brought her photographs signed "For Katherine Anne, with happy memories of lovely, relaxed, fiery, reminiscent afternoons of good talk in the best of company—and with love."[17]

And a year later he rededicated his first gift to her—the copy of his book, *Death and the Supreme Court*—with a new inscription:

> For Katherine Anne—
> A subsequent postscript because time, fortunately, changes things, and so now I wish you love and happiness and all things good, and I thank you for all the good times —which are all the times we've had together—and I say good for the past and good for the future and good for us.[18]

For Porter there was in this relationship an added romance in the bittersweet knowledge that this was almost inevitably her last love, an aspect she never forgot:

> I am not your first love, and I will not be the last by a long shot, but you *are* my last, and you must wait until you get there to know what a miracle of reconciliation and tenderness and joy it can be. But meantime, love me as long as you can, and as you may: and if I could, I would bring you the happiness you deserve. If I bring you respite and a little joy for a while, that gives me happiness. I love you.[19]

And she exulted always in his good looks, writing him when she was seventy-eight:

> My love and my darling, you are most certainly harassed a good deal beyond the call of duty: if you are neurotic, I must be a full-fledged lunatic. If you are homely,—well, I take that badly, because you are saying that I don't know a good looking man when I see one: to me you are the most delightfully attractive man I ever knew, and I love every feature of

your face, and your expressions, all, all, and I do not accept your hint that I have not good taste in these important matters. So there. In a word, you have style, and it shows up even more so when you are with other people, and I don't mean people such as we were with yesterday, who don't really count as people.[20]

Flaunting her sexual exploits was part of Porter's *femme fatale* guise. When she was seventy she had boasted to her nephew about the new sexual techniques she was learning from her Italian lover (Paul was skeptical since he could not imagine that his aunt had anything new to learn on that subject). To her nun and priest friends in Washington she hinted that she had not always been a saint. When she was old her favorite toast was the Mexican one:

> Salud y pesetas
> Y mas fuerza a las brazos
> Y muchos amores escondidos
> Y tiempo para gozarlos.

For her biographer she wrote her own "Texas American Translation":

> Health and Money!
> And More power to your elbow—
> Many hidden love affairs
> And Time to enjoy them!

And she added, "That last line is the joker. The trick—nobody has time enough even for *one* love affair, hidden or played out on T.V."

Now she told Paul that her current love was unconsummated. Sometimes she said it remained so by her wish and that Barrett accepted the fact. At other times she said that Barrett thought their becoming lovers would spoil the relationship.[21] Certainly Barrett, with his commitments to his family, had every reason for not wishing to become more involved. And so the relationship remained platonic and Porter seemed content with the idealized romantic nature of their attachment. She often said that between Alexander in 1918 and Barrett there had been no lover who really counted. At last she had the kind of relationship that was most satisfying to her—a handsome, youthful admirer, full of flattering attentions, who made no other demands.

She could go on being a *femme fatale* with none of the complications. She enjoyed telling a reporter that she usually had champagne, not for lunch but for late breakfast, or what she called her "second breakfast," and that she had homemade bread and snails and invited one friend— always a man—because men had more command of their time.[22] To Prettyman himself she once wrote a playful note:

> If you remember the story I told you about the lady who had snails and champagne for breakfast with her most favorite guest in the world, and she asked this marvellous man if he had ever had breakfast before with a lady in a black lace nightgown and an emerald necklace and being a famous attorney he did not answer Yes or No. I forgot to say that the lady had never had such a moment before and I like to think it was rather a delightful exchange of virginities which naturally grow fewer and fewer as time passes.[23]

Thus occupied, she lived in Spring Valley longer than in any other place, longer than on Rue Notre Dame des Champs, Roxbury Road, or the birdcage in Santa Monica. In retrospect, it appears to have been most surely her home, just as Pressly seems to have been most durably her husband. But her restlessness was, to use one of her favorite words, "cureless," and she began to turn against this house too and to look for one she could own. The project was another that was enlivened by Barrett's assistance. After a visit to a house in Annapolis, she wrote:

> My Dear. In my excitement at talking to you, just after reading your so wise and exact and loving letter, I failed to say the one thing important about this house thing. I said I'd rather have the emeralds than the house. And when I consider your wild life, and your remarking that any Washington friend I should like to see would have to take at least half a day for it, and how we have never been able to manage a half day together even when I am in Spring Valley, I can only say I had rather be near you than to have either emeralds or the house. True.
>
> I am smitten with something like awe at the thoroughness and explicitness of your examination of that house, even to the slowness of the hot water to rise: and you must have surmised my horror at Mrs. G's suggestion that my neighbors would be glad to do things for me. That was the first

moment I wavered in my obstinate hope to contemplate that water every day: I cannot imagine anything more terrifying to my soul than to have to ask favors of strangers. It is painful even to take the help of generous and loved persons: you lectured me about this once, so I won't bring it on myself again, but I promised you I would try to reform, and I have. But not to such an extent as our realtoress imagines.[24]

The idea of moving suddenly solved itself when she had another of her serious accidents. She reported to David Locher that she was tripped up by her kittens, Juniper and Jennifer, and fell down a long flight of stairs. This time there was no Rhea Johnson to help and she lay unconscious for some time. When she was taken to the hospital, she had injuries to her head, vertebrae, ribs, spine, and right arm.[25] It seemed clear to everyone that the huge house in Spring Valley was not the place for her, and while she was recovering Paul came down from New York, found a town house for her in College Park, Maryland, and moved her possessions there. It was not a palatial place, but it was compact and pleasant and near the Katherine Anne Porter Room.

The following year the news came of the death from cancer on January 28, 1969, of her old friend Josephine Herbst. Their lives and accomplishments had diverged very much. Josie had continued to write, but fame with its accompaniment of adulation, fortune, admiration, and flocks of friends had not been accorded to her. She still lived in Erwinna, in the Pennsylvania countryside, and like Porter she was still a talker, but with age she had increased in wisdom. Younger writers of impressive stature had sought out Herbst to learn what she had to teach them. Among them were Saul Bellow, the poet Jean Garrigue, and critics such as Alfred Kazin and Hilton Kramer.[26] After the death Porter spoke elegiacally of Herbst:

Josephine Herbst was in many ways a remarkable person and had an extraordinary kind of misled and misused life. In order to explain this, I suppose I should have to write a book myself about the strange career of hers, for her career was never so much in her life as a writer as it was in her private misadventures and her personal human life.

It was a lamentable life in more ways than one and disastrous in more than one way yet she had a marvelous sense of humor and of the bawdy, of low life lived for fun.

There was no evil in it because the people she fought with fought back and deserved the worst she could do to them though I'm sorry to say she didn't win as often as she would have liked, and I as well.[27]

In private, did Porter think of her own fame, her house, her clothes and jewels, and did she wonder for a moment what Josie would have thought if she had looked at them with her sad, circled eyes? (Herbst had written, after she read *Ship of Fools,* that she thought Porter set too much store by the things of this world.[28]) Perhaps Porter recalled that years ago, when she had worried about the age difference between herself and Pressly, it was Josie who reminded her of George Eliot and Hester Thrale Piozzi, scolded her for being anxious, and told her she would probably have followers at seventy and eighty.[29] Certainly Josie was the one person to whom she might happily have confided her excitement over Barrett.

In 1970, Porter was in the hospital again for her eightieth birthday, having "pulled that classical old Granny trick" of breaking her hip.[30] Before that happened, however, she was able to celebrate the appearance of *The Collected Essays and Occasional Writings*. There was the usual round of parties, all the more enjoyable this time because Barrett was there to share them with her. In March there was a gala reception in the Katherine Anne Porter Room, for which she wore one of her favorite Geoffrey Beene outfits, a double strand of pearls with a diamond-and-emerald clasp, a diamond-and-emerald spray pin, and her twenty-two carat emerald ring. She carried a bouquet of roses from Cyrilly Abels' husband and she was flanked in the receiving line by Prettyman and her publisher, Seymour Lawrence.[31] The highlight of the evening was a short concert by the university's madrigal singers under the direction of Rose Marie Grentzer, which concluded with four songs from Katherine Anne Porter's French song book: "Marion's Song," "Full Moon," "Three Sailors," and "Marlborough." After the reception Lawrence gave a dinner for her at the university's Adult Education Center.[32]

The new book carried an affectionate dedication:

> To E. Barrett Prettyman, Jr.
> Faithful friend, able and
> fearless counselor, gifted writer,
> and joyful company, who has guided me

through a rain-forest in these
past rather terrible years.
Yet we can laugh together
and we know what to laugh at.[33]

The reference was to Virginia Woolf's essay on William Cowper
in which she says that the best thing about having a sure moral sense
is that you know what you can laugh at. In Barrett's own copy Porter
wrote below the dedication:

For God's sake, let us sit upon the ground
And tell sad stories of the death of kings
And old, unhappy far-off things
And battles long ago.[34]

In acknowledgment of the dedication the Prettymans gave a dinner party at the F Street Club, and the friends who attended were
invited to contribute to a gift—a two-volume copy of *Adam Bede*
which Henry James had given to the English novelist Rhoda Broughton in 1894. The inscription to Porter read:

Presented to Katherine Anne Porter by her friends and admirers as she enters her 80th year and on the publication of
her Collected Essays and Occasional Writings. As was said
of Rhoda Broughton, to whom these books were given by
Henry James, "She possesses a clean lash of words, a crisp
habit, a fund of human wisdom and wit, and an ease and
liberality in her Victorianism." But more than that she is
poetry and genius combined for the benefit of us all.
At dinner
March 26th 1970
1925 F St Club[35]

Among those who contributed were Rhea Johnson, Monroe
Wheeler, Glenway Wescott, and Roger Mudd, the television news-
caster; Mudd and his wife had been invited by Prettyman. Both Porter
and Barrett loved ceremonial inscriptions, dedications, and ritual exchanges of autographed gifts. Two years later Porter gave the volumes of *Adam Bede* back to Barrett, rededicated:

Barrett, my love—I wrote in these books as you asked me
to when we were driving to Virginia the other day—my

darling, you came late to me, but I am glad I lived to know you—it was worth everything else! my love again and for always

Katherine Anne 10 May 1972 5:30 p.m.

added—
and afternoon May 10th 1972, within 5 days of my 82nd birthday—with happiest memories of that dream—like evening and of the love it celebrated, real as day, and for life.[36]

Apart from the celebrations of its appearance, *The Collected Essays and Occasional Writings* did not bring unmitigated pleasure. When she saw the published book she was mortified. It had been completed while she herself was ill and unable to make the final selections of what should go in or to do the proofreading. Friends had helped, and had been acknowledged in the book: "The publishers wish to express profound appreciation to Robert A. Beach, Jr., George Core, William Humphrey, Rhea Johnson, and Glenway Wescott for their help and guidance in the preparation of this volume."[37]

Porter wrote angrily in her copy refuting this acknowledgment, and for the rest of her life took pleasure in doing the same in every copy she could find. Autograph hunters at her public appearances were urged to send up their copies for her comments on the acknowledgment page, and were often delighted to get not merely the sought-after signature but bursts of indignation:

This piece of impudence was committed without my knowledge and consent by advice of the publisher, Seymour Lawrence. He is morally irresponsible, but what induced this group to think they could guide or help me? K.A.P.[38]

The author of this book is outraged.

This preposterous piece of impudence was committed without my permission or knowledge by a publisher who knew better. Damn their eyes, one and all! K.A.P. June 28, 1976

The damndest piece of impudence I ever encountered in my long war with such idiots as Seymour Lawrence. In this group of five misled men, there is not one I would have ever in all my life asked for a word about my work. K.A.P.

It's a pity the "help and guidance" of the strange group named two pages on didn't do a job of proofreading.[39]

As she approached eighty and passed it, Porter was fond of quoting Mark Twain's remark: she did not want to be an octogenarian but the alternative was too unpleasant.[40] She decided, looking back over the past ten years, that if she had died when she was seventy she would have missed some of the pleasantest experiences of her life. "I think I'll hang on till ninety and see how it goes," she said.[41]

These days the center of her life was always Barrett Prettyman, as her notes over the years show:

For me, you are the center of my life, my one love, and it grows more difficult every day to live—is this living—so far away from you.

Please remember now and then with that also enviable selective memory of yours, how I have loved you and love you now and shall love you. . . . Distance and silence and separation finally do become a natural part of life.[42]

Her great disappointment was that she did not see more of Prettyman. He could always be counted on for the gala occasions—her Twelfth Night parties with their impressive guest list, and the annual meeting of the American Academy of Arts and Letters—but she really wanted to involve him in some kind of domestic life. She loved to cook for him and arrange little dinners and lunches and breakfasts for just the two of them. He explained carefully that this was not possible. Besides his professional work he was busy with numerous volunteer organizations. He was on the board of directors of Georgetown University, a trustee of American University, attorney for the National Council on Crime and Delinquency, a corporate member of Children's Hospital, and a member of the advisory board of the Salvation Army. The demands on his time were very heavy,[43] and, like many another of Porter's friends, he had discovered that her demands on his time and attention were endless, excessive and insatiable.

She consoled herself by shopping thoughtfully for gifts of a wifely kind—shirts from the Custom Shop in Washington, lapis-lazuli-and-gold cufflinks from Cartier in New York. But most of all she longed to be serving delicious meals and giving memorable banquets. She made countless menus like the following:

breakfast for Barrett 8:30 Friday 13 1974

French orange juice
coffee with half and half '
Omelette with Bacon
Huevos Rancheros Florentine KAP
Clover leaf rolls KAP
optional glass of muscatel wine

lunch for Barrett 5th Jan 1973

KAP Fresh pea soup
Delmonico steak poivade saude—spiced yam puree
popovers
avocado with lettuce, sauce—onion juice, fresh tomato,
    lemon juice, salt
Anjou pear baked in orange blossom honey, orange juice,
    grated orange peel
Romanee merlcourt 1966

Fresh green pea-chicken broth silver bowls gold spoons
smoked pheasant barely warm
Fresh tomato aspic, small peas with butter
country home-made rolls
vanilla ice cream crushed sweetened strawberries in Grand
    Marnier

Some of the menus were used but many others awaited the time "when Barrett is able to get out of his incredibly harassed life."[44]

The situation sometimes led to quarrels between them. He wrote to say that he resented the implication in her letters that if he really wanted to see her, he would try harder. He asked her, in what he called almost biblical terms, to approach him not only with love but with understanding and forgiveness and faith. Another time, after he read an interview in a Washington paper in which she said, "I never met anybody in the world who didn't want the use of me," he wrote her very tartly that many people knew he acted for her and this was embarrassing.[45]

In the fall of 1973 she became, at least momentarily, reconciled to the situation:

I am not missing you more than I have always for absences and missing have been from the first nominated in the bond; but there is in our nature—blessed be—a slow moving deep merciful healing power for all our griefs, and missing you perpetually I find doesn't hurt as much as it did. And—this being my incorrigible personal twist of temperament, the less I suffer because of you, or more exactly, because of our cureless predicament, the more I am able to love you and so . . .

And so . . . you see, Yours inescapably, God-Awfully, forever.[46]

In spite of her loneliness for Prettyman, and her diminished energy and recurrent physical problems, she still found many diversions and consolations. She visited the Katherine Anne Porter Room and sometimes traveled farther afield. She even went back to Bermuda, where she looked for Hilgrove but could not remember exactly where it was. Each year she gave her wonderful Twelfth Night parties, renting tables and chairs, hiring sailors from a naval base to do the serving and cleaning, filling the house with poinsettias which she gave to the departing guests. And she made another reconciliation in her life. Through a friendship which developed between her and the nuns of the College of Notre Dame of Maryland, in Baltimore, she turned once again to the Church.

The college had wanted to give her an honorary degree at the 1973 commencement, but she had been at Lehman College in New York City that spring and could not attend the ceremony. Like the University of Maryland, the College of Notre Dame waived the usual procedure and delighted her by coming to her house for a private and moving little ceremony of the kind she most enjoyed. The degree was bestowed upon her in her apartment by Sister Maura and Sister Kathleen, who was president of the college. Porter was dressed all in white —openwork shoes, slacks, ribbed sweater. Sister Maura read the citation she had written:

Titles like "Flowering Judas," "Pale Horse, Pale Rider," "Noon Wine" and "Ship of Fools" linger in the mind like bell sounds in quiet sunlight. Her fiction—exploring man's enduring themes—links her with the great company of classic story tellers. She believes in the young. Because she is young of heart, she invited us all to timelessness in God, she is our flowering branch, our spring renewal.[47]

Porter, of course, served refreshments: cookies and a punch of tea, ginger ale, and fruit juice.

The association with the nuns continued to the end of her life and was deeply satisfying to her. At a late afternoon liturgy in the college chapel, on the Feast of the Immaculate Conception, she walked slowly back from receiving holy communion at the altar, leaning on Sister Kathleen's arm. Tears were streaming down her cheeks. It was a moment of deep emotion for her, to be back in a convent chapel receiving holy communion on the Feast of the Immaculate Conception.

She still enjoyed extremes, and she also accepted an assignment from *Playboy* magazine to go to Florida and write a piece on a moon shot at Cape Canaveral. She had a wonderful time, and in December 1972, when she next spoke to students in the Katherine Anne Porter Room, she made her Cape Canaveral experience the subject of her talk:

> It looked as if it were limping, you know, and suddenly, it just soared and the fire burst through the center and then the whole world was illuminated with the light I never saw— not even in daylight.
> . . . it disappeared in seven minutes looking like a great flaming bird. The flames looked like wings and at the base of it was a deep—like a transparent lapis lazuli blue, but transparent, french parrot and the great flames like wings. I thought of a great bird—some fantastical magic bird, don't you know, that had a thousand wings. That's what I thought of. And it just disappeared like that and, as it disappeared, it became a circle then and it was golden and deep blue and outside a brilliant scarlet and then out.[48]

She yoked the experience with the story of the flight of Icarus, thinking of Brueghel's painting and seeing it as man's aspiration always to leave the earth—"the perfectly innocent and natural and human aspiration, you know, to get into the great blue sky that's so much nicer than where we live"[49]—and she described in detail Brueghel's painting, everyone going about his business and paying no attention as Icarus fell into the sea, "his little pink leg disappearing into the water." Then she linked this with the moon shot:

> The most tremendous thing that could ever possibly happen in the world was going on and they are fishing and plowing

and mounting their sails and plowing the field and the lovely
landscape all around them, and it has been like that, all the
time. We never have changed a bit and so on this boat, you
know, they were playing shuffleboard and chess and poker
and heaven knows what and sitting up until four o'clock in
the morning and dancing and eating and talking and laugh-
ing and just having a wonderful time you know.[50]

The speech was a masterful performance, and the linking of her
Cape Canaveral experience with her favorite painting, Brueghel's *Fall
of Icarus,* might have been turned into one of her successful short
stories. Indeed, she told her audience she was going to write about it
but had to "cool down" first. But the short story was not written,
nor was the essay *Playboy* had commissioned. There were no new
stories and no old stories finished, although she did not abandon her
writing and cherished the hope that she would still produce some
fiction. She was spending longer hours in bed—resting, reading, listening to music, thinking about the past and sorrowing for the loss of
family and friends. All her brothers and sisters had died, and it was
hard to accept the death, from cancer, of her friend and agent Cyrilly
Abels in 1975. And always she hoped that Barrett would come and
see her. One of her last notes to him celebrates an occasion when he
did:

LOVE, LOVE, LOVE! FOREVER AND EVER That's a long time isn't
it? Not half long enough. There doesn't seem to be anything
just now worth saying, except that you are my dear love
and you left me very light-hearted because after all we are
not so very far away from each other: but if you come here
again (I don't mean to our spring shindig at the Academy I
mean here in my sordid cell) I shall not let you choose your
lunch. You should have had, instead of that woohoofus of a
tinned crab and tuna—I can still see it wallowing around on
our plates—a beautiful fresh slab of rare beef, with creamed
potatoes, and your fruit bowl. I *knew* this and yet let you
have a horrid lunch. Shame on me. Just the same it was a
happy little time wasn't it?[51]

"The sordid cell" was in fact a rather lavish apartment in a high-
rise building in College Park. The town house in its turn had proved
too much for her and a new home was found nearby. She
took two apartments at the end of a corridor on the fifteenth floor of
the building, and had the wall between them removed so that she had

a place large enough for all her possessions. When the two apartments were joined she had two kitchens, four bathrooms, three bedrooms (one for herself and one each for Ann and Paul when they visited), a sorting room for mail and manuscripts, a workroom, and two sizable living rooms. From her bedroom she could see across the miles to Washington and on clear days could see the outline of the buildings on Capitol Hill. The only drawback was that she was not allowed to keep cats. All her life she had had a cat to keep her company—Rufus in Bermuda, Skipper in Paris, Jennifer and Juniper and numerous others, and she felt the lack of a pet very keenly, but she consoled herself by filling her rooms with huge pots of flowering shrubs and plants.

The apartment in Westchester Towers was her last home, and she lived there quietly through the late 1970s. She traveled a bit, entertained, cooked enthusiastically for old friends and new ones, and tried to write, but everything was at a slower pace and she thought a great deal about death. She purchased a mail-order coffin from Arizona and stored it upright in a hall closet, loving to shock her guests by displaying it and sometimes standing inside it. For all this, she had lived so long that she said she didn't think she would ever die. She boasted that she had a heart like an ox and it scared her sometimes. She wondered what it would take to kill her. "There's such a thing," she said, "as staying on after the party's over."[52]

TWENTY-SIX

The Final Chapter

T
his has been the happiest year of my life," Porter
often said during her eighty-seventh year, and for the most part that
was true. The chief reason for the serenity of her last active year was
her happy discovery of an assistant with the rare combination of skills
for that demanding job. He was a forty-seven-year-old retired naval
officer, Lieutenant Commander William Raymond Wilkins.[1]

Porter was looking for a new assistant in early 1976 and Wilkins
wrote to ask if he might come and discuss the position. When he
arrived she took an immediate liking to him: "My god, honey, can
you start tomorrow?" she said.[2]

The tasks facing any amanuensis of Porter's were overwhelming
in their diversity, and her demands grew greater as her physical
strength waned. It was necessary to cope with a huge volume of
incoming mail, provide companionship and moral support, escort her
on forays to doctors' offices and supermarkets, and accompany her to
parties and receptions. When she gave a dinner party help was often
needed in the kitchen, and there was always the overriding task of
assisting with the "works in progress."

Bill Wilkins was perhaps the one person who could juggle all
these jobs and at the same time find the company so stimulating that
he never wearied of her conversation, and never resented the long
hours and the relatively small salary. "There's nothing I wouldn't do
for that woman,"[3] he often said. He was a sympathetic listener,
skilled in such practical jobs as mending phonographs and framing

497

pictures, and amid all the distractions he found time to answer letters and to impose an impressive order on the hampers of jumbled letters, manuscripts, and photographs.

Once again, as when she lived in the Q Street house with Rhea Johnson, she could feel that she had a ménage. There was someone to cook for and fuss over, and although Wilkins complained that he was supposed to be watching his weight, he really enjoyed the festive meals, even when they were marked by culinary disasters:

> We had been invited down to enjoy a roast goose—something she had been wanting to tackle for a long time, but had not done because "honey—if you ain't got a gaggle of friends around, it just ain't worth the time worrying about a goose." To save time, she had baked bread earlier in the week and when the then current daily had gone home on Friday night, she had taken the keys to the freezer and the wine as well. She made do with some nice rolls from the deli downstairs and she did manage to find a couple of splits of fairly decent red wine which she allowed would be acceptable. Then to sort of put the cap on the pile of confusion standing in her way, something had gone wrong with the oven. We did not know what had happened, because the goose, when put on the beautifully laid table was, as far as we knew, roasted to perfection, stuffed with pâté and white grapes. After she had cut a slice or two and served the stuffing with a lovely silver spoon, she noted that the closer she got to the center of the critter, the rawer it looked. She quietly put down the silver spoon, looked around her—appearing for a moment as if she might fly into one of the great fulminating Porter rages—and then settling down said, "Well, babies, we got store-bought bread, and we ain't got but half enough wine and now this here bird seems to have come out half done and I just pray," as she reached into the innards of the bird, grabbed a handful of the stuffing and splatted it onto a plate, "that the Good Lord, or whoever is running this God Damned show, will shortly put an end to it." All of this had been delivered by that lovely showpiece who was dressed to the nines, was perfectly coiffed and made up and garnished with several yards of pearls and the Porter emeralds. We all caught the fun of it instantly and someone, I forget who, raced out, bought some champagne, and we still had one hell of a night of it. There was, of course, enough of everything to go round. Not even providence dared to mess around with KAP in those days.[4]

Other occasions were quieter times that she and Bill made for themselves:

> I do so clearly remember and with some loving tenderness, how she would send for catalogue after catalogue of expensive, beautiful things for which there was little real need, but for which there would be a little use. She would pore over them for days on end and then finally make her selections and send off for whatever. The day things arrived was always a festival. When I brought up the boxes—and mind you this is not a ton of things foolishly ordered but a hundred dollars or so of gourmet things that we'd all enjoy using—we'd have to stop whatever we might be doing and pour a glass of wine and *then* open. Each object was lovingly considered and very often consigned to a new owner right then and there—sometimes it was off to the kitchen to try something out—but she *did* love to buy those fripperies. Very often it would be a truly beautiful book for anywhere from $35 to $100 and we'd have to call everything to a halt, make coffee and consider it for an hour.[5]

Bill's companionship consoled her for Prettyman's absences, and as with Rhea Johnson, this relationship was all the more harmonious for not being complicated by sexual overtones. Questioned on the nature of their warmly affectionate friendship, Bill would comment simply that he included his wife in their social occasions as much as possible. His doing so also created a bond between Porter and his wife and daughter. His wife sent in pies and other treats, and Porter gave young Robin the substantial gift of a pearl necklace.

Perhaps Bill's greatest asset was that he had enough literary ability and academic training to help Porter with her writing. This was especially important, because her sense of well-being still depended upon her being able to continue working or at least maintain the illusion that she was.

Almost immediately Bill started work on the notes Porter had assembled on her experiences during the Sacco-Vanzetti protest in 1927. Over the years she had picked them up and set them aside again. She had tried to finish the essay in time to publish it on the twenty-fifth anniversary of the death of Sacco and Vanzetti and now she was trying again to do so in time for the fiftieth anniversary. Atlantic–Little, Brown had become interested as soon as Owen Laster, Porter's new agent, approached them in November 1976. Glenway Wescott had returned her notes, perhaps as they went to him, in something of a muddle. Bill put them in order, taking them home with him and working on them in the evening, since the camaraderie of the day made that kind of work impossible. When he had a rough outline she went to work, but the notes got confused again and he and Porter started from the beginning once more.[6] Bill considered it a rare privilege to be entrusted with the project and Porter had a sustained sense of purpose. They talked also of another project, beyond this one—the completion of the Cotton Mather biography.

At the same time Porter mustered the energy to make a last round of visits to places that had figured importantly in her life. Some were carefully planned, and others seemed to happen spontaneously.

In early spring she was invited to Skidmore College to receive an honorary degree and to give the annual Frances Steloff Lecture, named in honor of the founder of New York's famous bookstore, the Gotham Book Mart. This occasion provided the opportunity for her to visit South Hill, the house she had not been able to afford, and had hardly lived in, but which had remained in her imagination as the closest she ever came to owning a home of her own.

In the fall she made another excursion, this time to read one of her stories at the Poetry Center of the YM-YWHA, where she had often appeared before. This visit was almost a family occasion. Bill went with her up to New York and she was fêted there by Monroe Wheeler and Glenway Wescott. Ann and Paul were in the audience and Barrett Prettyman too was on hand for the performance.

Between these two trips she made the most important pilgrimage, a visit to Texas. For some time Porter had been courted by Howard Payne University, in Brownwood, near her Indian Creek birthplace. The president had sent her a rubbing of the inscription on her mother's tombstone and a copy of the inscription, and she had a great desire to visit his campus. She wrote him:

> I am 85 years old, so I have a great feeling that it is time for
> me to gather up a great many of these scattered memories
> and all the mementos I can find to leave as a part of a possible
> biography . . .
> I wish that you would help me make a plan and if you
> say you would like, I would be pleased to visit your school
> or give a public speech in any place you find appropriate.[7]

In the spring semester of 1976 the school offered a course devoted to Porter's works and ended it with a conference to which Porter scholars from all over the United States and Canada were invited. Porter was invited, of course, and was offered an honorary degree.

She yearned, as always, for a reconciliation with her native state, and the return to her birthplace at this point in her life promised a deeply satisfying completion of a pattern. She took little note of the fact that the institution she was going to was an odd choice for someone who had said, "Politically my bent is to the left," and had rejected the "petty middle class of fundamentalists." Payne was a fundamentalist Baptist college and a very right-wing institution. A *Texas Observer* writer who covered Porter's visit described its Hall of Christian Civilization, which was part of the General Douglas A. MacArthur Academy of Freedom: the Magna Carta Hall, a would-be replica of a medieval castle, Independence Hall, a replica of the room in which the Declaration of Independence had been signed, and an eight-foot bronze statue of MacArthur by the same artist who did the Texas Ranger on display in the terminal lobby at Love Field in Dallas:

> What most shocks the uninitiated visitor is the superserious-
> ness of it all. The rigidity to the underlying tone of this
> rightist planetarium prevents it from having any kind of
> broad appeal, but it is nonetheless wonderfully indicative of
> the conservative, pious and unquestioning patriotism that is
> still the majority of political ethic in the hinterlands. The
> whole place is frightening to an egalitarian sensitivity, to
> anyone who cares about duty, honor, country, but who
> would serve the cause of enlightenment first.[8]

Unaware of these hazards, Porter found her frail health the chief obstacle to the trip. Her doctor was reluctant to agree to her undertaking such a long journey and such a heavy schedule at the end of it. In the face of her determination, however, he relented. She flew to Dallas and was met by the Howard Payne faculty and driven back to Brownwood. There she attended the graduation ceremony, accepted her honorary degree, and handed out diplomas. There was considerable nervousness about her health: some of her hosts feared that perhaps she had come home to die. A photograph shows Porter in her academic robes flanked by the chancellor and the president. The fourth person in the picture was a doctor assigned not to let her out of his sight, his real purpose disguised by his academic dress.

It was probably Porter's frailty that spared her an inspection of the Academy of Freedom. She did not see enough of the campus to depress her and held on to her jaunty mood, holding court in her motel room and dispensing champagne to her hosts, who sipped it warily, conscious that they were violating college rules against alcohol. The next day she went to visit the grave of her mother and brother. It was an anniversary in many ways because it happened to be May 8, the exact day when in 1936 she had returned from Paris and visited the cemetery.[9] She had hoped to have a picnic lunch and celebrate her birthday with a cake in the cemetery; the picnic lunch took place, but the cake was saved for a more orthodox setting. She had also wanted to do as her father had done earlier, and place a blanket of talisman roses on the grave. Instead, to her chagrin, a bouquet of pink roses had been purchased for her.[10]

But on the whole the visit gave her great satisfaction. She had been born in Indian Creek, had traveled all over the world, and now she was home again. Feeling that she had at last made her reconciliation with Texas, she decided that when she died she would have her body brought back to the Indian Creek cemetery to lie beside her mother's.

After each of these trips she had to spend days in bed recovering. Her eyes bothered her too, and her memory was beginning to play tricks on her. She forgot a great deal, and she joked that once she woke up in the night and, unable to remember her own name, tried to look it up in the telephone book.

In early December she entered Johns Hopkins Medical Center for a checkup. She was still there at Christmas and enjoyed the celebration anyway. She had a private room and her visiting hours were not restricted. She chatted with the staff, received her own visitors, and saw other patients who had heard about her and wanted to meet her. Bill came daily, bringing the mail, running errands, keeping her company. He reported that she looked magnificent, was satisfied that she was getting an honest estimate of her condition, and felt it was better than she had expected. She would spend the days sociably and then, after the night nurse came on duty, would get out her papers and try to work. In January she felt so confident that she planned two new projects. The Sacco-Vanzetti essay had been completed, and so she turned Bill loose on the notes for the remaining chapters of *Cotton Mather*. She also engaged a translator to make an English version of an old French murder mystery she wanted to work on.

By mid-January she was becoming restive with the hospital routine, but she was elated at the results of her tests:

I was born on Thursday May 15, 1890 Reborn on Thursday 1977 Allelulia

Today at 11 minutes to 12 p.m. Dr. Tumulty came to tell me that tremendous news—my blood oxygen is not just normal, but high normal. This is what all this testing and rule and discipline has been about. I am at ease all over for the first time in 74 years. I have lived on the law of Miracle all my life.[11]

The idea of being born again had always been precious to her, and she left the hospital in a buoyant mood. But she had been at home only a day when she fell and had to return to Johns Hopkins. Soon afterward, still in the hospital, she had the first of a series of debilitating strokes. The first seizure affected her speech, destroyed the use of her right arm, and frightened her very badly. She never regained the use of her arm and never reconciled herself to its loss and to the fact that she could no longer write. She had to be fed intravenously and to have a constant supply of oxygen. Moreover, the sudden decline in her condition was the signal for renewed series of tests. Once, she and Ann had agreed to prevent such "tortures" on each other, but Ann, having survived her crisis and now at her aunt's bedside, was powerless to prevent all the X-rays and spinal taps. Protests were met with the firm response that patients could not simply be let alone, "especially not in a teaching hospital."[12]

In less than a week Porter suffered another stroke. The staff, who had overruled all the visitors' protests, now discovered that they had a more formidable adversary in Porter herself. She asserted her will, resisted treatment, and determined to die in her own way. She had all the life-sustaining oxygen and food disconnected, and she dismissed the doctors with one word, "Out!"—accompanied by an imperious gesture of her good arm. She said that her death belonged to her and to no one else, and she gathered around her Bill, Paul, Ann, and her biographer, making sure that they understood exactly the arrangements to be made for her burial and memorial service and for her monument.

Having done all that, she improved. She once more asserted her will and in mid-spring 1977 decided to go home. With Bill's help, she did, and was taken back to her apartment to be looked after by nurses around the clock. She seemed to regain a little of her strength and take an interest in life. Her speech improved. On good days she would get up and be wheeled through the rooms to look at her precious possessions.

The improvement, however, was more illusory than real. She had suffered considerable brain damage. Her speech control was affected and she suffered from aphasia. Her left eye was almost useless and her right eye was confused by the impairment of the left. Her right arm remained paralyzed. But most serious of all was her increasing paranoia. As her father and sisters had done before they died, she was growing hostile, furious, and at times violent. The targets of her rage were those who had been closest to her, and among these the first victim was Bill, who had been at her side constantly during the past months. She accused him of robbing and abusing her, of bringing his women (the nurses) into her house, and of ruining her work. He described the experience in a letter:

> You cannot imagine the scope of the wild fulminating rage into which she flew as she swore, called me everything under the sun and declared unto God Almighty and whoever else might be in the audience that she had told me one thousand and six times that the book was not to be worked on any longer—that it was to be sent in as it was. . . . I know that it is the illness speaking, that my Katherine Anne is not there any more, but the utter futility of trying to be a helper, a bolster, or whatever, suddenly struck me with the force of a sledgehammer. It is not me nor any other person who can do handy things she needs right now. It is her nurses and maybe a body-slave or two. It is a sort of madness that afflicts her now, this paranoia, the constant suspicion that someone is trying to rob her, that everyone is trying to kill her. I strongly suspect that she has lost all real concept of time for the most part and very often does not really know who individuals are. At other times, few and far between, there is stunning clarity of speech and lucidity of thought. But never for long and it must be hell to have one's mind and thoughts for those brief times and then be pulled back into that strange nether world of not remembering or understanding or being able to articulate those things that are so important to her. At any rate, I just got up after that tirade and quietly said I thought it had all been a mistake, that we had found out before that we could not work together and that we should have left things as they were . . . and left.[13]

Having to leave her when she badly needed him caused Bill a great deal of anguish, but he was able to write:

> Do you know, it is not a rough time about KAP any longer. I think I did for her whatever it was I was supposed to do and muddling around in her life and moaning about my lost position as dear friend and confidant and psychological lover (I ain't stupid, kid) will do nothing for me, and certainly not for her. I know a great deal more about the whole thing. I feel that the first hassle we had was when she came out of hospital the second time and was angry that I had not brought her a large silver something that she claims I promised to buy for her. The dear Lord knows what was going through her mind, but from time to time she would say that she could not "go on living here with you this way—I must get back to my own home and get to work."[14]

The Sacco-Vanzetti book on which Bill had worked so hard was now about to be published. In acknowledgment of his help, Porter had dedicated *The Never-Ending Wrong* to him, and he worried that the dedication might spoil her pleasure in the book. He was reassured by her family that the dedication had been written when Porter's mind was sound and that it should remain. He asked that a sentence indicating that the book would not have been finished without his help be deleted and this was done. When Porter received her advance copies, she furiously tore out the dedication pages in each of these and all other copies she came across.

The next target of her anger was Ann, who was working as an occupational therapist and had taken time off from her job to be with her aunt. When Porter turned on Ann, she left quietly and returned to Connecticut.

Porter now imagined that she was being punished for her participation in the Sacco-Vanzetti protest and for what she had written about that situation. She believed that she had been in another prison (the hospital) and had escaped from there with the help of Barrett Prettyman.

While she was in the hospital she had wanted to see Barrett, but he was on an extended leave from his law firm and was water skiing in Tahiti. The only message from him was a post card of a piranha, which had been pinned to the notice board beside her hospital bed.

He was the person she most longed to see, and on her eighty-seventh birthday she dictated a letter to him, one of the last she wrote:

Barrett my dear,

I'm writing to you by a different hand, my pleasant young nurse.

I take now my own words to ask of you, please for the love of God, talk to me, write to me, see me, for I'm very sick and need to see you one more time.

I need desperately to ask of you many questions and put my mind at ease. I will wait now till I hear from you with great anxiety.

Love and anxiety.[15]

The people close to Porter also hoped for his return, so that something could be done about a situation becoming increasingly difficult. The main problem was that with Bill gone, there was no one to take charge of the apartment, the rotating group of nurses, and Porter herself. People who had never been invited to the apartment as guests now seized the opportunity to visit. Others, welcome friends from earlier years, still took away gifts which Porter gave them. In spite of warnings that she was not in her right mind, and was giving away possessions which she needed, which had been willed to others, or which might have to be sold for her support, visitors carried away valuable books, pictures, furniture. Over the telephone she told some people from Howard Payne University to come with a moving van and remove the furniture, and they prepared to do so. Paul intervened in time and prevented the place from being stripped still further.

She begged to have her emeralds returned from the vault where they had been stored. When this was not done, because the nurses could not accept the responsibility of having them in the house, Porter was convinced that they had been stolen. She turned against Paul, and when Barrett returned and could not do any of the things she requested—get her out of "prison," return her jewels—she turned against him too and decided he was part of an elaborate plot to kill her.

In the fall of 1977 Paul and Barrett filed a legal petition asking that a guardian be appointed to watch over her affairs. The hearing was reported in the local newspaper:

Famed writer Katherine Anne Porter, a long-time resident of the College Park area, was quietly ruled incapable of managing her own affairs in an Upper Marlboro courtroom last week. . . .

The appointment of a guardian to watch over her affairs was requested by a nephew, Paul Porter of New York, and Chevy Chase lawyer E. Barrett Prettyman Jr., a friend and former attorney for the author. . . .

Court records paint a picture of a partially paralyzed, bedridden woman who is often hard to understand and must be attended by nurses 24 hours a day.

The two physicians told to examine Miss Porter were Carl H. Keller, chief of psychiatry at Prince Georges General Hospital in Cheverly, and Gustave J. Weiland, hospital vice-chief of psychiatry. . . .

Although he said he found Miss Porter "in a bright mood" Keller said it was "often difficult to follow the line of her thought because she seems to be easily distracted. . . ." He said she is "often unable to recall words to express her thoughts and substitutes other words and phrases and often substitutes words of her own creation."

He said Miss Porter knows she is the author of five books but "she no longer follows television nor current events nor does she have access to her previous fund of information."[16]

The request was granted. The court records revealed that her chief personal property amounted to more than $100,000 in paintings, antiques, and furnishings, $25,000 worth of books and manuscripts, and jewelry valued at more than $50,000. The only regular income was a monthly social security check and a monthly check from Little, Brown for deferred royalties on *Ship of Fools*.

Paul was appointed guardian, and although he had little actual contact with his aunt, he supervised the running of the apartment, the hiring of the nurses, and all Porter's financial matters.

The arrangement was not completely satisfactory. Inevitable changes of nursing staff upset Porter and interrupted the smooth running of the apartment. Intruders still managed to gain admittance and books and photographs continued to disappear. Porter herself sometimes gave books away as gifts, once to the priest who ministered to her. In her advanced years, she simply forgot that these books, which were worth hundreds of dollars, had been willed to the Katherine

Anne Porter Room.[17] But at least she was in her familiar surroundings and kept as comfortable as possible. She was often fretful and unhappy but was sometimes distracted by visitors and amused by their gifts and anecdotes. She showed flashes of her old spirit. When Seymour Lawrence sent her a ham for Christmas she told her nurse, "I don't like that man. But we'll keep the ham."[18]

When her apartment building was converted into condominiums, she could no longer remain there, and in late March 1980 Paul arranged one last move as he had done many times before. She returned to the outskirts of Washington, D.C., and spent her remaining months in the Carriage Hill Nursing Center in Silver Spring, Maryland.

During the last years, when she was "very much taken up with dying," Porter found her greatest consolation in the Church. She had never attended Mass regularly and her attitude toward her chosen faith was often playful. She told Rhea Johnson once that she was "charmed" by Catholicism.[19] Yet she chose her words advisedly and this one was apt. She delighted in the rituals and observances of the Catholic Church; she cherished the beautiful rosaries from her Dubuque friends David Locher and Raymond Roseliep; she loved the High Masses at Christmas and Easter; and she enjoyed the literary qualities of the prayers and the saints' lives. Best of all she liked confession. The sense of unburdening herself, confessing her sins, and gaining forgiveness brought her serenity and peace. (No doubt her fondness for telling stories about her life also added to her pleasure and made her one of the livelier occupants of the confessional.) And she was always soothed by the presence of priests and the gentle nuns.

Knowing this, Paul asked Sister Kathleen and Sister Maura of the College of Notre Dame of Maryland to visit. They did so faithfully and also brought a priest who regularly heard her confession and gave her the Eucharist. Besides this, she received telephone calls from Father Roseliep that never failed to make her happy.

Flannery O'Connor had long before sensed a terrible need under her friend's bantering remarks about the Church. Now as Porter neared death that need became more evident. She longed to believe in God and in life after death. She told Sister Maura, "Death is beautiful. I long to die. I love God. I know that he loves me."[20] And when Father Roseliep assured her that eternity would be better than this world she told him, "Oh yes, I know that." He said that those five words expressed the Christian faith of Katherine Anne Porter as he had known it: "A faith as indestructible as the love."[21] Clearly she yearned deeply for the promise of life after death, but whether that yearning was ever transformed into true faith before she died, it is impossible to say.

She lived to be over ninety, and in doing so outlived most of the people she had known, many of them younger than she. Gone were old critics and adversaries, as well as former lovers and friends—Matthew Josephson, Lodwick Hartley, Allen Tate, Josephine Herbst, Elizabeth Ames of Yaddo, Cyrilly Abels, and the devoted patron Barbara Wescott. Of her contemporaries a few women, indomitable as herself, remained—Mildred Koontz, Erna Glover Johns, and Kitty Barry Crawford in Texas; Mary Doherty and Caroline Gordon, both in Mexico.

So much of Porter's life had been transmuted into her fiction—into the stories and into *Ship of Fools* with its freight of passengers drawn from her own life—Eugene Pressly, John Koontz, and her own younger selves. Now, in turn, it seemed that the fiction had foreshadowed her own ending, and she lay like Granny Weatherall visited by the shadows and scenes of her vanishing past. There were moments for memories to come and fade in her mind before the gathering darkness: her grandmother's death in Marfa; midnight Mass in Inez; the funeral of John Koontz's father; the vigil in Boston on the night of the execution of Sacco and Vanzetti, when she stood on the cobblestones looking up at the little point of light in the prison tower; the visit to her mother's grave in Indian Creek . . . And all the merry times: like Jenny Brown she had danced perhaps twice around the globe . . . the tea dances in Fort Worth, with Felipe Puerto Carillo in Mexico City, with Matthew Josephson up in Harlem . . . And all the exciting times: splashing through the storm with Charles Shannon after the launching of *The Leaning Tower,* seeing Rome for the first time, watching the movie of *Ship of Fools* . . . And the quiet, happy times: listening to music with Ann . . . watching Paul burn out a hornets' nest . . . and the last years of happiness and laughter and Barrett . . .

At the very end she lay, like La Condesa on the *Vera,* drugged and demented, bereft of her home and her jewels, but defiant until the last moment when on September 18, 1980, the little point of light flickered and failed.

Epilogue

In 1956, Katherine Anne Porter wrote: "I believe, I hope I shall have my place in the story of American literature; even at this point how could they write it and leave me out?"[1] Her reputation gained very little from the novel or from the stories that appeared subsequently, but it was already assured, as she had guessed, by the short fiction written in the first half of her life.

For years these stories were the standard fare offered to college freshmen in literary anthologies. Generations of students were nurtured on "The Grave," "The Jilting of Granny Weatherall," "Flowering Judas," and "Noon Wine." Lately her stories have been displaced, not by better stories but by more current favorites. Porter does not deserve to be dislodged by the whims of fashion. As her fame was once exaggerated by her theatrical stage presence, so the present decline in her popularity is an error of judgment.

Porter's work, moreover, has woven itself into the fabric of American literature by its influence on other writers. Many have expressed their debt to Porter. Among the earliest to do so were Eudora Welty and Kay Boyle. Besides a host of Texas writers, Carson McCullers and Truman Capote at one time idolized her.[2] Tillie Olsen revered her[3] and that reverence is evident in *Tell Me a Riddle*. Flannery O'Connor professed an influence which Porter claimed not to see, but which is apparent when "The Displaced Person" is compared with "Noon Wine."

Besides the phrase "a writer's writer," the other label that at-

510

tached itself to Porter was that of "preeminent stylist." This she deplored: "I've been called a stylist until I really could tear my hair out."[4] In spite of her objections, the praise is apt, for she forged out of the soft rhythms of southern speech and the racy idioms of her native Texas a unique style, at once elegant and tough, lyrical and vigorous, formal and witty, truly a classical style for all seasons. That accomplishment is not, as she seemed to think, to be scorned as a minor achievement. She has quite simply done what every significant artist does, left her medium the richer for her having used it. All those coming after her who use the English language artfully must be indebted to her, as everyone must who uses the genre that was truly hers, the short story.

And what of her other creation, the fabrication of a life meant to appear as elegant and structured as the short stories? How successful was the phenomenon of Katherine Anne Porter—aristocratic first lady of American letters, linguist, musician, *femme fatale,* forced to spurn many lovers because of her greater devotion to her art, her "standing engagement with a higher power"; the raconteur whose conversation was as dazzling as her stories because it was often equally fictitious, crafted, and rehearsed? It was a wonderful work of art, but did it convince her that she had amounted to something? Did it succeed in repairing the damage sustained in the earliest years by this most delicate of sensibilities?

It almost did. She had learned in the beginning that flight into an assumed persona could provide escape from her personal demons. On public occasions, when she was in the spotlight, center stage, dressed in her lovely costumes and jewels, with her admirers, the bit players in her personal drama, hanging on to her every word and giving her back her own desired image of herself, she felt cherished and even lovable.

But she could not remain always in public. Inevitably she had to return to her private world and face who she really was and what her life and loves had been. Occasionally overzealous researchers reminded her. Sometimes another young lover left her and she relived the nightmares of other rejections. And sometimes, waking alone in the middle of the night, she must have remembered and understood. . . .

And there was one thing which produced the most grueling self-revelations of all—the act of writing, that occupation so demanding of honesty and self-knowledge and apt to produce unexpected moments of self-confrontation. She knew this well, for as she had once cautioned Pressly, "Don't be afraid of giving yourself away either, for if you write, you must. And if you can't face that, better not write."[5]

She did face it herself, and her best fictions are full of instances of her artistic courage—her portrayal of sexual terror in "The Grave," of Granny Weatherall's never-ending humiliation, of Frau Rittersdorf's terrifying ambush by her childhood memories, of Mrs. Treadwell's reaction to the brutalities of a lifetime. These are the real toads in Porter's imaginary gardens.

Is it any wonder that the production of her fiction through the exploration of its sources was a slow, agonizing process, a kind of self-torture, or that her tendency to procrastinate was legendary? But in spite of the almost superhuman effort it required, she never abandoned her battle to "wangle the sprawling mess of . . . existence in this bloody world into some kind of shape."[6] It was a lonely, desperate battle, costly to herself and to the people she sacrificed in her determination to be somebody and to create something lasting, beautiful, and orderly. But who can deny that it was a valiant effort, a most brave voyage?

Notes

PROLOGUE

1 Katherine Anne Porter to Paul Porter, 20 June 1957, McKeldin Library, University of Maryland, College Park, Maryland.
Gioia Diliberto, "Setting Sail 'Ship of Fools,'" *Times Record* (Saratoga Springs), 18 April 1976.
2 Katherine Anne Porter, *The Collected Essays and Occasional Writings of Katherine Anne Porter* (New York: Delacorte Press, 1970), p. 160.
3 Barbara Thompson, "Katherine Anne Porter: An Interview," *Paris Review*, No. 29 (1963), pp. 87–114. Reprinted in *Writers at Work: "The Paris Review" Interviews* (New York: Viking Penguin, 1963), pp. 137–163.
4 Thompson, "Katherine Anne Porter: An Interview," p. 4.
5 *Collected Essays*, p. 229.
6 Lady Bird Johnson to Joan Givner, 1 December 1977, collection of author.
7 Raymond Roseliep to Joan Givner, 19 November 1978, collection of author.
8 Andrew Lytle to Joan Givner, 6 July 1979, collection of author.
9 Malcolm Cowley, interview in Sherman, Connecticut, 18 June 1977.
10 Katherine Anne Porter, *Ship of Fools* (Boston: Atlantic–Little, Brown, 1962), p. 370.
11 Edward Burns, ed., *Staying on Alone: Letters of Alice B. Toklas* (New York: Liveright, 1973), p. 294.
12 Thompson, "Katherine Anne Porter: An Interview," p. 10.
13 KAP to Gay Porter Holloway, undated, McKeldin.
14 Paul Rosenfeld, "An Artist in Fiction," *Saturday Review of Literature*, 1 April 1939, p. 7.
15 Thompson, "Katherine Anne Porter: An Interview," p. 8.
16 *Collected Essays*, p. 93.
17 Thompson, "Katherine Anne Porter: An Interview," p. 8.
18 Katherine Anne Porter, notes, undated, McKeldin.
19 *Collected Essays*, p. 474.
20 Thompson, "Katherine Anne Porter: An Interview," p. 4.
21 Katherine Anne Porter, "And to the Living, Joy," *McCall's*, December 1971, p. 76.

513

22 KAP to Josephine Herbst, 16 April 1930, the Beinecke Rare Book Library, Yale University.

23 Paul Porter, interview in New York, 15 March 1978.

24 Matthew Josephson to Joan Givner, 11 October 1974, collection of author.

25 Eudora Welty to Joan Givner, 8 March 1975, collection of author.

26 Glenway Wescott, "Katherine Anne Porter Personally," in *Katherine Anne Porter: A Critical Symposium.*

27 *Ship of Fools,* p. 384.

28 KAP to Glenway Wescott, 23 October 1954, McKeldin.

29 Marginal notes in George Hendrick, *Katherine Anne Porter* (New York: Twayne, 1965), McKeldin, p. 145.

30 KAP to Edward Schwartz, 1 July 1956, McKeldin.

31 Katherine Anne Porter, *Outline of Mexican Popular Arts and Crafts* (Mexico City: S.I.C.yT., 1922), p. 4.

32 KAP to Joan Givner, 29 September 1976, collection of author.

33 Katherine Anne Porter, untitled lecture given at the Katherine Anne Porter Room, McKeldin Library, College Park, Maryland, November 1972.

34 Porter summoned me to visit her with a telegram 3 October 1976. Another telegram sent 22 November 1976 asked me to set a date during my visit to her at which I might meet "the four people most concerned with the brave voyage we are planning together [by which she meant the retelling of her life]—my assistant, my attorney, and the director of the Katherine Anne Porter Room."

1: THE PORTER FAMILY HISTORY

1 Thompson, "Katherine Anne Porter: An Interview," p. 6.

2 KAP to Harrison Boone Porter, 22 March 1933, McKeldin.

3 Harrison Boone Porter to KAP, 4 March 1933, McKeldin.

4 KAP to Harrison Boone Porter, undated, McKeldin.

5 KAP to Harrison Boone Porter, 16 February 1928, McKeldin.

6 KAP to Gay Porter Holloway, 6 December 1955, McKeldin.

7 KAP to Harrison Boone Porter, 16 February 1928, McKeldin.

8 KAP to Harrison Boone Porter, 12 February 1928, McKeldin.

9 KAP to Gay Porter Holloway, 15 July 1934, McKeldin.

10 KAP to Gay Porter Holloway, 8 April 1957, McKeldin.

11 KAP to Harrison Boone Porter, 21 January 1933, McKeldin.

12 KAP to Harrison Boone Porter, undated letter, McKeldin.

13 KAP to Gay Porter Holloway, 22 March 1934, McKeldin.

14 KAP to Gay Porter Holloway, 29 March 1956, McKeldin.

15 Katherine Anne Porter, "History for Boy and Girl Scouts," *New Republic,* 10 November 1926, p. 353.

16 Thompson, "Katherine Anne Porter: An Interview," p. 6.

17 John F. Vallentine, U.S. Genealogical Research Services, to Joan Givner, 6 May 1978, collection of author.

18 Anne Markle, former president of the History Club, Marfa, Texas, to Joan Givner, 25 January 1978. Alfred Steinberg, *Sam Johnson's Boy* (New York: Macmillan Company, 1968), p. 7.

19 KAP to Gay Porter Holloway, 15 July 1934, McKeldin.

20 1850 Slave Census, Warren County, Kentucky.

21 1860 Census, Warren County, Kentucky.

22 Will of James Skaggs, Courthouse, Warren County, Kentucky.

23 1850 Census, Warren County, Kentucky.

24 *Collected Essays,* p. 162.

25 Mildred Kilpatrick to Joan Givner, 14 June 1978, collection of author.

26 Vida Vliet, "The Shape of Meaning: A Study of the Development of Katherine Anne Porter's Fictional Form" (Ph.D. dissertation, Pennsylvania State University, 1968), pp. 21–22.

27 Harrison Boone Porter to KAP, 4 March 1933, McKeldin.

28 *Collected Essays,* p. 160.

29 Harrison Boone Porter to Gay Porter Holloway, 11 December 1936, collection of Breckenridge Porter, Sr., Houston, Texas.

30 Harrison Boone Porter to KAP, 4 March 1933, McKeldin.

31 Harrison Boone Porter to KAP, 4 March 1933, McKeldin.

32 *Collected Essays,* p. 161.

33 "Travis Guards and Rifles," in *Handbook of Texas* (Austin: Texas State Historical Association, 1952), vol. 2, p. 797.

34 *Collected Essays,* p. 161.

35 Vida Vliet, "The Shape of Meaning," pp. 21–23.

36 Katherine Anne Porter, *The Collected Stories of Katherine Anne Porter* (New York: Harcourt, Brace & World, Inc., 1965), p. 335.

37 Katherine Anne Porter, *Collected Stories,* p. 337.

38 Mrs. Fannie Manlove, "Mountain City," *Kyle News,* 20 April 1928, sec. 1, p. 4.

39 Mrs. Roberta Belvin Pritchett, "1866 Coronal Institute 1918," *Kyle News,* 20 April 1928, sec. 4, p. 5.

40 Mary Alice Jones, "Does the Bible Teach Everlasting Punishment?" valedictory address given at Coronal Institute, undated, McKeldin.

41 Sallie Crawford Willson to KAP, undated, McKeldin.

42 Mary Alice Jones to Harrison Boone Porter, 20 August 1880, McKeldin.

43 Mildred Kilpatrick to Joan Givner, 14 June 1978, collection of author.

44 Mary Alice Jones to Harrison Boone Porter, 19 November 1880, McKeldin.

45 Harrison Boone Porter to Mary Alice Jones, 22 January 1881, McKeldin.

46 Harrison Boone Porter to KAP, 4 March 1933, McKeldin.

47 Jeanette James, " 'Callie' Recalled at Indian Creek," *Brownwood Bulletin,* 22 April 1962.

48 Tevis Clyde Smith, "The Reverend Noah Byars—Figures in Texas History," *Pecan Valley News,* 22 December 1976.

49 Gay Porter Holloway to KAP, 14 December 1955, McKeldin.

50 T. R. Havins, *Something About Brown: A History of Brown County, Texas* (Brownwood: Banner Printing Company, 1958), p. 75.

51 Lex Johnston, "Brown County Pioneers Able to Quench Thrists [sic]," *Brownwood Bulletin,* 1977.

52 Breckenridge Porter, Sr., interview in Houston, 5 September 1977.

53 Gay Porter Holloway to KAP, 14 December 1955, McKeldin.

54 Harrison Boone Porter to Mary Alice Jones, 22 January 1881, McKeldin.

55 Gay Porter Holloway to KAP, 22 April 1955, McKeldin.

56 Cora Annie McBride to Joan Givner, 1 October 1973, collection of author.

57 Gay Porter Holloway to KAP, 14 December 1955, McKeldin.

58 KAP to Cora Posey, 12 July 1957, McKeldin.

59 Gay Porter Holloway to KAP, 26 February 1956, McKeldin.

60 Gay Porter Holloway to KAP, 14 December 1955, McKeldin.

61 Gay Porter Holloway to KAP, 26 February 1956, McKeldin.

62 KAP to Harrison Boone Porter, 28 February 1935, McKeldin.

63 KAP to L. O. Porter, 11 November 1964, McKeldin.

64 Gay Porter Holloway to KAP, undated, McKeldin.

65 KAP to Harrison Boone Porter, undated, McKeldin.

66 Marginal notes in George Hendrick, Katherine Anne Porter (New York: Twayne, 1965), McKeldin, p. 19.

67 KAP to Gay Porter Holloway, 5 December 1955, McKeldin.

68 Harrison Boone Porter to KAP, 11 December 1936, collection of Breckenridge Porter, Sr., Houston, Texas.

69 Photograph, McKeldin.

70 Gay Porter Holloway to KAP, 14 December 1955, McKeldin.

71 Harrison Boone Porter to Cora Posey, 29 April 1893, McKeldin.

72 KAP to Gay Porter Holloway, 5 December 1955, McKeldin.

73 Harrison Boone Porter, notes, undated, McKeldin.

74 Lady Bunton Terry to Joan Givner, 11 May 1978, collection of author.

75 Jeanette James, " 'Callie' Recalled at Indian Creek," Brownwood Bulletin, 22 April 1962.

76 Annie May Miller, "The History of Kyle, Texas" (M.A. thesis, Southwest Texas State Teachers' College, San Marcos, Texas, 1950), p. 34.

77 KAP to Eugene Pressly, May 1936, McKeldin.

78 Katherine Anne Porter, "Notes on the Texas I Remember," Atlantic, March 1975, p. 103.

79 Katherine Anne Porter, completed questionnaire, McKeldin.

80 Katherine Anne Porter, notes, undated, McKeldin.

81 Katherine Anne Porter, marginal notes in Joseph Grasset, The Semi-Insane and the Semi-Responsible (Demifou et Demiresponsable), authorized American edition, trans., Scott Smith Jelliffe (New York: Funk & Wagnalls Company, 1907), p. 10.

2: BORN TO THE PRACTICE OF LITERATURE

1 KAP to Dr. R. L. Brooks, President, Howard Payne University, Brownwood, Texas, 7 October 1975, McKeldin.

2 Leslie Stephen, Hours in a Library, 4 vols. (New York: G. P. Putnam's Sons, 1904; reprint ed., Scholar's Press, Grosse Pointe, Michigan, 1968), vol. III, p. 284.

3 Undated fragment, McKeldin.

4 Undated fragment, McKeldin.

5 Vida Vliet to William Nance, 27 July 1964, collection of author.

6 KAP to Gay Porter Holloway, 13 November 1961.

7 KAP to Erna Glover Johns, 23 December 1938, collection of Erna Glover Johns, Austin, Texas.

8 Collected Stories, p. 57.

9 Collected Stories, p. 56.

10 KAP to Mary Alice Porter, 1921, McKeldin.

11 Katherine Anne Porter, "Pull Dick—Pull Devil," notes toward a memoir of her childhood, undated, McKeldin.

12 Breckenridge Porter, Sr., interview in Houston, Texas, 5 September 1977.

13 Harrison Boone Porter to KAP, undated, McKeldin.

14 KAP to Gay Porter Holloway, 30 January 1932, McKeldin. Porter describes

herself as "mystified by his cold attitude to us, towards life . . . so death-like and despairing and inert and will-less, and talking from his forty-fifth birthday about being old."

[15] KAP to Eugene Pressly, May 1936, McKeldin.

[16] KAP to Cora Posey, 21 October 1952, McKeldin.

[17] Katherine Anne Porter, "Pull Dick—Pull Devil."

[18] Mary Alice Jones to Harrison Boone Porter, 7 December 1880, McKeldin.

[19] Mary Alice Jones to Harrison Boone Porter, 19 November 1880, McKeldin.

[20] Photograph, McKeldin.

[21] KAP to Paul Porter, 20 June 1957, McKeldin.

[22] Harrison Paul Porter to Gay Porter Holloway, 14 February 1942, McKeldin.

[23] KAP to Gay Porter Holloway, 14 February 1942, McKeldin.

[24] Katherine Anne Porter, "Pull Dick—Pull Devil."

[25] Mabel Kilpatrick to Joan Givner, 14 June 1978, collection of author.

[26] KAP to Erna Glover Johns, 29 March 1937, collection of Erna Glover Johns.

[27] *Collected Stories*, p. 278.

[28] KAP to Gay Porter Holloway, 6 June 1933, McKeldin.

[29] KAP to Gay Porter Holloway, 14 February 1942, McKeldin.

[30] Erna Glover Johns to KAP, 3 May 1931, collection of Erna Glove Johns.

[31] *Collected Stories*, p. 337.

[32] *Collected Stories*, p. 471.

[33] George Hendrick, *Katherine Anne Porter* (New York: Twayne, 1965), p. 17.

[34] Katherine Anne Porter, marginal note in George Hendrick, *Katherine Anne Porter* (New York: Twayne, 1965), p. 17.

[35] Mrs. Lex Word, interview in Kyle, Texas, 6 September 1975.

[36] Katherine Anne Porter, "Notes on the Texas I Remember," *Atlantic*, March 1975, p. 103.

[37] Mildred Kilpatrick to Joan Givner, 14 June 1978, collection of author.

[38] Katherine Anne Porter, "Pull Dick—Pull Devil."

[39] Erna Glover Johns, interview in Austin, Texas, 9 September 1975.

[40] KAP to Paul Porter, transcription of taped telephone conversation, undated, McKeldin.

[41] Katherine Anne Porter, "Pull Dick—Pull Devil."

[42] Thompson, "Katherine Anne Porter: An Interview," p. 9.

[43] Undated fragment, McKeldin.

[44] Undated fragment, McKeldin.

[45] KAP to Gay Porter Holloway, 13 November 1961, McKeldin.

[46] KAP to Gay Porter Holloway, 8 April 1957, McKeldin.

[47] *Collected Stories*, p. 177.

[48] Gay Porter Holloway, marginal notes in *Pale Horse, Pale Rider: Three Short Novels* (New York: Harcourt, Brace and Company, 1939), p. 10, McKeldin.

[49] KAP to Harrison Boone Porter, 1936, McKeldin.

[50] KAP to Rhea Johnson, 23 March 1963, McKeldin.

[51] Kitty Barry Crawford, interview in Arlington, Texas, 31 May 1978.

[52] Erna Victoria Schlemmer Johns, *To Whom It May Concern*, vol. 1, *The Schlemmers* (Austin, Texas: privately printed, 1975).

[53] KAP to Erna Glover Johns, 20 December 1939, collection of Erna Glove Johns, Austin, Texas.

54 KAP to Erna Glover Johns, 29 March 1937, collection of Erna Glover Johns, Austin, Texas.

55 Erna Glover Johns to KAP, 3 May 1939, collection of Erna Glover Johns, Austin, Texas.

56 Erna Glover Johns to Joan Givner, 15 June 1976, collection of author.

57 Erna Glover Johns, interview in Austin, Texas, 8 September 1975.

58 Erna Glover Johns to Joan Givner, 1 May 1979, collection of author.

59 Katherine Anne Porter, interview in College Park, Maryland, 25 June 1977.

60 *Collected Stories,* p. 438.

61 Katherine Anne Porter, notes, undated, McKeldin.

62 KAP to Erna Glover Johns, 29 March 1937, collection of Erna Glover Johns, Austin, Texas.

63 Katherine Anne Porter, marginal notes in Joseph Grasset, *The Semi-Insane and the Semi-Responsible (Demifou et Demiresponsable),* authorized American edition, trans., Scott Smith Jelliffe (New York: Funk & Wagnalls Company, 1907), p. 10.

3: ADOLESCENCE

1 Katherine Anne Porter, interview in College Park, Maryland, 25 June 1977.

2 Katherine Anne Porter, "Notes on the Texas I Remember," *Atlantic,* March 1975, p. 104.

3 KAP to Gay Porter Holloway, 8 April 1957, McKeldin.

4 *Collected Stories,* p. 340.

5 Katherine Anne Porter, interview in College Park, Maryland, 24–26 June 1977.

6 Erna Glover Johns, interview in Austin, Texas, 3 September 1975.

7 *San Antonio Daily Express,* 6 October 1901.

8 *Collected Stories,* p. 362.

9 KAP to Gay Porter Holloway, 30 January 1932.

10 Kitty Barry Crawford, interview in Arlington, Texas, 31 May 1978.

11 Katherine Anne Porter, marginal notes in Deirdre C. Handy, "The Family Legend in the Stories of Katherine Anne Porter" (M.A. thesis, University of Oklahoma, 1953), Humanities Research Center, Austin, Texas.

12 Katherine Anne Porter, notes, undated, McKeldin.

13 Paul Porter, interview in New York, 15 March 1978.

14 Katherine Anne Porter, notes, undated, McKeldin.

15 Robert Penn Warren, ed., *Katherine Anne Porter: A Collection of Critical Essays* (Englewood Cliffs, New Jersey: Prentice-Hall, Inc., 1979), p. 2.

16 Katherine Anne Porter, notes, undated, McKeldin.

17 *Collected Stories,* p. 365

18 *Collected Stories,* p. 367.

19 Paul Porter, interview in New York, 11 December 1979.

20 Edmund Wilson, "Katherine Anne Porter," *New Yorker,* 30 September 1944, pp. 72–75.

21 KAP to Josephine Herbst, 1928, Beinecke.

22 *Collected Stories,* p. 327.

23 *Collected Stories,* p. 27.

24 *Collected Stories,* p. 327.

25 Erna Glover Johns, interview in Austin, Texas, 3 September 1975. Mabel Kilpatrick to Joan Givner, 14 June 1978, collection of author.

26 KAP to Ann Holloway Heintze, 29 October 1928, McKeldin.
27 Mabel Kilpatrick to Joan Givner, 14 June 1978, collection of author.
28 Gay Porter Holloway to KAP, 5 February 1957, McKeldin.
29 Lady Bird Johnson to Joan Givner, 1 December 1977, collection of author.
30 Mabel Kilpatrick to Joan Givner, 14 June 1978, collection of author.
31 Mabel Kilpatrick to Joan Givner, 14 June 1978, collection of author.
32 Mabel Kilpatrick to Joan Givner, 14 June 1978, collection of author.
33 Breckenridge Porter to Joan Givner, 31 July 1979, collection of author.
34 *Collected Stories*, p. 233.
35 *Collected Stories*, p. 229.
36 *Collected Stories*, p. 229.
37 Mark Schorer, Afterword to *Pale Horse, Pale Rider* (New York: Signet Modern Classic, 1967), p. 172.
38 Mabel Kilpatrick to Joan Givner, 14 June 1978, collection of author.
39 *Collected Essays*, p. 480.
40 Andy Moore, "Regional Imagery: A 'Right Smart' Device in Katherine Anne Porter's *Noon Wine*," paper presented at Katherine Anne Porter Symposium, Brownwood, Texas, 8 May 1976.
41 *Collected Essays*, p. 468.
42 Mrs. Lex Word, interview in Kyle, Texas, 2 September 1975.
43 *Collected Essays*, p. 471.
44 KAP to Gay Porter Holloway, 8 October 1956, McKeldin.
45 *Collected Essays*, pp. 478, 481.
46 Mabel Kilpatrick to Joan Givner, 14 June 1978, collection of author.
47 Mabel Kilpatrick to Joan Givner, 14 June 1978, collection of author.
48 Vida Vliet, "The Shape of Meaning: A Study of the Development of Katherine Anne Porter's Fictional Form," p. 30.
49 Mabel Kilpatrick to Joan Givner, 14 June 1978, collection of author.
50 KAP to Ann Holloway Heintze, 29 October 1928, McKeldin.
51 Katherine Anne Porter, entry in Erna Glover Johns's book, collection of author.
52 Erna Victoria Schlemmer Johns, *To Whom It May Concern*, vol. 1, *The Schlemmers* (Austin, Texas: privately printed, 1975), pp. 66, 67, collection of author.
53 *Collected Essays*, p. 355.
54 KAP to Mrs. Thomas Gossett, 6 December 1964, Humanities Research Center, University of Texas, Austin, Texas. KAP to Gerald Ashford, 22 March 1966, collection of author.
55 KAP to Mrs. Thomas Gossett, 6 December 1964, Humanities Research Center, University of Texas, Austin, Texas.
56 KAP to Gerald Ashford, 22 March 1966, collection of author.
57 George Hendrick, *Katherine Anne Porter* (New York: Twayne, 1965), p. 18.
58 *Twenty-second Annual Catalogue: The Thomas School for Girls 1922–1923*, collection of author.
59 Mildred Whiteaker, "Glimpses of San Antonio at Turn of Century" (San Antonio) *Express and News*, 21 January 1973.
60 Katherine Anne Porter, note, undated, McKeldin.
61 KAP to Monroe Wheeler, 1940, McKeldin.
62 Mrs. Stella Conway to Action Line (San Antonio) *Light*, 11 August 1975.
63 A. A. Thomas to student ("Dear friend"), 21 March 1921, collection of author.
64 Katherine Anne Porter, notes, undated, McKeldin.

[65] KAP to Gay Porter Holloway, 1927, McKeldin.
[66] Katherine Anne Porter, marginal notes in Simone de Beauvoir, *The Second Sex* (New York: Knopf, 1953), p. 345, McKeldin.
[67] Maggie Mae Bode to Joan Givner, 4 February 1978, collection of author.
[68] *Ship of Fools,* p. 303.
[69] Katherine Anne Porter, notes, undated, McKeldin.
[70] Paul Porter, interview in New York, 12 December, 1979.
[71] KAP to Joan Givner, 10 December 1979, collection of author.
[72] Mildred Whiteaker, "Glimpses of San Antonio at Turn of Century" (San Antonio) *Express and News,* 21 January 1973.
[73] Katherine Anne Porter, "Pull Dick—Pull Devil," McKeldin.
[74] *Collected Essays,* p. 113.
[75] KAP to Margarita Porter Folks, 3 September 1976, collection of Margarita Porter Folks, San Antonio, Texas.

4: THAT PREPOSTEROUS FIRST MARRIAGE

[1] KAP to Gay Porter Holloway, 10 October 1930, McKeldin.
[2] Roy Newquist, "An Interview with Katherine Anne Porter," *McCall's,* August 1965, p. 138.
[3] Erna Glover Johns, interview in Austin, Texas, 8 September 1975.
[4] Kitty Barry Crawford to Joan Givner, 9 January 1978, collection of author.
[5] Roy Newquist, "An Interview with Katherine Anne Porter," p. 139. *International Herald Tribune,* 5 June 1974.
[6] *Collected Essays,* p. 121.
[7] *300 Years in Victoria County,* ed., Roy Grimes (Victoria: Advocate Publishing Co., 1968). Leopold Morris, *Pictorial History of Victoria and Victoria County* (San Antonio: Clemens Printing Co., 1953).
[8] Mildred Koontz, interview in Inez, Texas, 4 September 1977.
[9] Marriage License 87, Angelina County, Texas, 20 June 1906.
[10] KAP to Gay Porter Holloway, 14 June 1956, McKeldin. KAP to Gay Porter Holloway, 10 October 1930, McKeldin.
[11] KAP to Paul Porter, 20 June 1956, McKeldin.
[12] Certified Copy of Divorce Judgment no. 19893-C, Katherine Porter Koontz vs. J. H. Koontz, filed 20 May 1915, with Matt. L. Cobb, District Clerk, Dallas Co., Texas.
[13] Roy Newquist, "An Interview with Katherine Anne Porter."
[14] *Ship of Fools,* p. 208.
[15] Katherine Anne Porter, "American Critics Discredit Fetish of Foreign Artists," *Rocky Mountain News,* 8 June 1919, p. 13.
[16] Katherine Anne Porter, review of *Distressing Dialogues,* by Nancy Boyd, in *New York Herald Tribune,* 28 December 1924.
[17] (Lafayette, Louisiana) *Daily Advertiser,* 17, 24, 31 July, 7, 14 August, 1907.
[18] Katherine Anne Porter, interview in College Park, Maryland, 30 November 1976.
[19] Mary Koontz Lowery, interview in Victoria, Texas, 4 September 1977.
[20] Mildred Whiteaker, "Glimpses of San Antonio at Turn of the Century" (San Antonio) *Express and News,* 21 January 1973.
[21] Katherine Anne Porter to Ann Holloway Heintze, 8 December 1963.
[22] Katherine Anne Porter, notes, undated, McKeldin.
[23] Erna Glover Johns, interview in Austin, Texas, 8 September 1975.

[24] *Ship of Fools,* p. 330.
[25] Katherine Porter Koontz, "Texas: By the Gulf of Mexico," *Citrus Fruit Grower,* Houston, Texas, undated:

> Ye shivering ones of the frozen North, list to my happy song
>   Of the seventh heaven nestled here below,
> In our rich, fertile valleys, midst sunkissed fruits and flowers
>   In Texas, by the Gulf of Mexico.
>
> For here, lieth without measure, peaceful rest and gold
>   enstore;
>   So to quiet the vague longing of your mind,
> Come build yourself a cottage, plant roses by the door,
>   Then forget the sleet and snow you left behind.
>
> For the man who knows his business—yea, the man who's
>   wondrous wise—
>   Knows that Texas is a paradise. I trow,
> Far better than a palace 'neath the frozen northern skies
>   Is an orange grove around a bungalow.
>
> In all this song and flight of bird beneath skies of clearest
>   blue
>   Above the fluttering jessamine trees that sway
> To every wanton breeze that waft their fragrance sweet to
>   you,
>   You'll find a fresh delight for each new day.
>
> But there's other things as perfect as this ever changing
>   scene,
>   Where homes spring up as flowers on a hill—
> For your garden grows on gaily through the winter, fresh
>   and green,
>   Bringing bright and jingling coins into your till.
>
> So, lock the door and call the dog, and catch the nearest train
>   That departs to where the sunset's golden glow
> Is a forecast of the money you will seek, and not in vain—
>   In Texas, by the Gulf of Mexico.

[26] KAP to Erna Glover Johns, 17 March 1914, collection of Erna Glover Johns.
[27] "This Book Mart Grew with City" (Corpus Christi) *Caller-Times,* 7 September 1941. "Move to Kaffie Building Marks New Chapter for Firm," *Caller-Times,* 9 July 1950. "Pioneer Merchant Gunst Will Close Book on Firm," *Caller-Times,* 8 October 1960.
[28] *Collected Essays,* p. 32.
[29] KAP to Gay Porter Holloway, 5 March 1928, McKeldin.
[30] *Collected Stories,* p. 407.
[31] KAP to Erna Glover Johns, 29 March 1937, collection of Erna Glover Johns, Austin, Texas.
[32] KAP to Gay Porter Holloway, 10 October 1930, McKeldin.
[33] George Hendrick, *Katherine Anne Porter* (New York: Twayne, 1965), p. 23. This description very likely came from Kitty Barry Crawford.

[34] Katherine Anne Porter, marginal note in George Hendrick, *Katherine Anne Porter* (New York: Twayne, 1965), McKeldin, p. 23.

[35] Katherine Anne Porter, notes, undated, McKeldin.

[36] Reverend Msgr. Anton J. Frank, Pastor, Annunciation Church, Houston, Texas, to Joan Givner. Letter with enclosure of pages copied from historical brochure of his church. Collection of author.

[37] George Plimpton, ed., *American Journey: The Times of Robert Kennedy:* Interviews by Jean Stein (New York: Harcourt Brace Jovanovich, 1970), p. 62, McKeldin.

[38] Paul Porter, Sr., to Mrs. K. R. Koontz, 23 March 1909, McKeldin.

[39] Katherine Anne Porter, marginal notes in Henry Charles Lea, *History of the Inquisition of the Middle Ages,* vol. I (New York: Harper, 1900), p. 400, McKeldin.

[40] Katherine Anne Porter, marginal notes in St. Jerome, *Selected Letters,* English translation, F. A. Wright.

[41] Katherine Anne Porter, marginal notes in R. E. L. Masters, *Eros and Evil: The Sexual Psychopathology of Witchcraft* (New York: Julian Press, Inc., 1962), p. 168, McKeldin.

[42] Katherine Anne Porter, marginal notes in *A History of the Inquisition of the Middle Ages,* vol. III.

[43] KAP to Rhea Johnson, 23 March 1963, McKeldin.

[44] Ann Holloway Heintze, interview in Pound Ridge, New York, 10 December 1979.

[45] Erna Glover Johns to Joan Givner, 26 January 1976, collection of author.

[46] Flannery O'Connor, *Habit of Being,* ed., Sally Fitzgerald (New York: Farrar, Straus and Giroux, 1979), p. 275.

[47] *Collected Stories,* p. 220.

[48] Glenway Wescott, "Katherine Anne Porter Personally," p. 27.

[49] KAP to Harrison Boone Porter, 1920, McKeldin.

5: THE UNGODLY STRUGGLE

[1] Elaine Showalter, *A Literature of Their Own* (Princeton: Princeton University Press, 1977), p. 53.

[2] *Collected Essays,* p. 121.

[3] KAP to Erna Glover Johns, 17 March 1914, collection of Erna Glover Johns, Austin, Texas.

[4] KAP to Erna Glover Johns, 13 April 1914, collection of Erna Glover Johns, Austin, Texas.

[5] KAP to Erna Glover Johns, 13 April 1914, collection of Erna Glover Johns, Austin, Texas.

[6] Thompson, "Katherine Anne Porter: An Interview," p. 8. Katherine Anne Porter, Essanay Studios, notes, undated, McKeldin.

[7] *Collected Essays,* p. 121.

[8] Thompson, "Katherine Anne Porter: An Interview," p. 8.

[9] Kitty Barry Crawford, interview in Arlington, Texas, 31 May 1978.

[10] Glenway Wescott, "Katherine Anne Porter Personally," p. 47.

[11] "Song in the Dark," *Moving Picture World,* 6 June 1914, p. 1434, Library of Congress.

[12] KAP to Erna Glover Johns, 17 March 1914, collection of Erna Glover Johns, Austin, Texas.

[13] Breckenridge Porter, Sr., interview in Houston, Texas, 6 September 1977.

[14] KAP to Paul Porter, 8 November 1951, McKeldin.

[15] Virginia Woolf, *A Room of One's Own* (London: Hogarth Press, 1949), p. 8.

[16] *English and Scottish Popular Ballads,* ed., Francis James Child, vol. III (New York: Dover, 1965), p. 379.

[17] Katherine Anne Porter, taped telephone conversation with Paul Porter, undated, McKeldin.

[18] Mildred Koontz, interview in Inez, Texas, 5 September 1977.

[19] KAP to Lon Tinkle, 19 August 1976, McKeldin.

[20] Kitty Barry Crawford, interview in Arlington, Texas, 1 June 1978.

[21] Ora Lee Griggs to Joan Givner, 14 January 1978, collection of author.

[22] Howard E. Smith, *Texas Tuberculosis Highlights,* booklet issued by Texas Department of Health Resources.

[23] Kitty Barry Crawford to George Hendrick, 20 November 1961, collection of author.

[24] Kitty Barry Crawford to Joan Givner, 21 December 1977, collection of author.

[25] Jane Anderson, "The Gift of the Hills," *Harper's Weekly,* 21 October 1911. Jane Anderson, "The Keeper of the Well," *Harper's Weekly,* 23 April 1910. Jane Anderson, "The Burying of Lil," *Harper's Weekly,* 13 August 1910. Jane Anderson, "The Spur of Courage," *Harper's Weekly,* 13 January 1912. Jane Anderson, "El Valiente," *Harper's Weekly,* 22 June 1912.

[26] Jane Anderson to Kitty Barry Crawford, July 1917, collection of Kitty Barry Crawford, Arlington, Texas.

[27] *Letters: Joseph Conrad to Richard Curle,* introd., notes, and ed., Richard Curle (New York: Crosby Gaige, 1928), p. 37.

[28] "What One Woman Is Doing to Help Children," *Dallas Morning News,* 16 December 1916.

[29] KAP to Gay Porter Holloway, 8 December 1916, McKeldin.

[30] KAP to Gay Porter Holloway, 8 December 1916, McKeldin.

[31] (Fort Worth) *Critic,* 15 September 1917.

[32] Katherine Anne Porter, "It's Easy to Be Mad Nowadays and M.D.'s List You as Genius," *Rocky Mountain News,* 13 July 1919.

[33] Pauline Naylor, "Katherine Anne Porter's Fort Worth Days Recalled" (Fort Worth) *Star-Telegram,* 10 April 1966, sec. 5.

[34] Kitty Barry Crawford to Joan Givner, 21 December 1977, collection of author.

[35] Kitty Barry Crawford to Joan Givner, 21 December 1977, collection of author.

[36] Katherine Anne Porter, "American Critics Discredit Fetish of Foreign Artists," *Rocky Mountain News,* 8 June 1919.

[37] Jane Anderson was one of eight people, including Ezra Pound, indicted for treason in 1943 (*New York Times,* 27 July 1943) for broadcasting propaganda from Germany and Italy against the United States and its wartime allies. The charges against Anderson were dropped in 1947 because of insufficient evidence (*New York Times,* 28 October 1947). Porter wrote of Anderson in 1949:

Just a year or two ago there was exonerated in an American Court another, a woman, who had no talents except for political intrigue of a low kind. She did for Hitler, by radio from Berlin, exactly the same work that Pound did for Mussolini in Italy. . . . She is living no doubt comfortably in Spain, and the judge in freeing her in absentia remarked in effect that even if she was working for Nazism, the great point was that she was defending religion and morality. I have heard no complaints about this case, and though she seemed to suffer a debased form of religious mania, I have never heard her called insane. (*Collected Essays*, pp. 212–213.)

[38] *Collected Essays*, p. 92.

6: DEATH AND REBIRTH IN DENVER

[1] KAP to Margaret Harvey, 15 September 1965, McKeldin.

[2] Lucile Clayton Robinson to KAP, 12 December 1930, McKeldin.

[3] Erna Glover Johns, *To Whom It May Concern*, vol. 1, *The Schlemmers* (Austin, Texas: privately printed, 1975), p. 72, collection of Erna Glover Johns, Austin, Texas.

[4] KAP to Margaret Harvey, 15 September 1965, McKeldin.

[5] Kitty Barry Crawford, interview in Arlington, Texas, 21 May 1978.

[6] Harrison Boone Porter to Gay Porter Holloway, 23 October 1918, McKeldin.

[7] Thompson, "Katherine Anne Porter: An Interview," p. 10.

[8] KAP to Gay Porter Holloway, 29 March 1956, McKeldin.

[9] *Denver Post*, 22 March 1956, p. 29C.

[10] John Dorsey, "Katherine Anne Porter On" (Baltimore) *Sun Magazine*, 26 October 1969.

[11] Katherine Anne Porter, "Recollection of Rome," *Travel and Leisure*, January 1974, p. 4.

[12] John Dorsey, "Katherine Anne Porter On," *op. cit.*

[13] Kathryn Adams Sexton, "Katherine Anne Porter's Years in Denver" (M.A. thesis, University of Colorado, 1961).

[14] "Let's Shop with Suzanne," *Rocky Mountain News*, 8 June 1919.

[15] Katherine Anne Porter, "American Critics Discredit Fetish of Foreign Artists," *Rocky Mountain News*, 8 June 1919.

[16] Katherine Anne Porter, "Why Does a 'Genius' Lose Pep As Soon As the Coin Rolls in?" *Rocky Mountain News*, 17 August 1919.

[17] Katherine Anne Porter, "Denver Players Offer Delightful Program," *Rocky Mountain News*, 22 May 1919.

[18] Katherine Anne Porter, "The Week at the Theatres," *Fort Worth Critic*, 15 September 1917.

[19] Katherine Anne Porter, "Beauty Unadorned Attracts When War Hero Is Passed By," *Rocky Mountain News*, 4 May 1919.

[20] Katherine Anne Porter, "American Critics Discredit Fetish of Foreign Artists," *Rocky Mountain News*, 8 June 1919.

[21] Katherine Anne Porter, "Theatergoers Like to Shiver Over Sins of Stage Heroes," *Rocky Mountain News*, 23 February 1919.

[22] Katherine Anne Porter, "Beauty Unadorned Attracts When War Hero Is Passed By," *Rocky Mountain News*, 4 May 1919.

[23] Katherine Anne Porter, "Theatergoers Like to Shiver Over Sins of Stage Heroes," *Rocky Mountain News*, 23 February 1919.

[24] Katherine Anne Porter, "American Critics Discredit Fetish of Foreign Artists," *Rocky Mountain News*, 8 June 1919.

[25] Editorial, unsigned, untitled, *Rocky Mountain News,* 28 July 1919.

[26] Katherine Anne Porter, "Beauty Unadorned Attracts When War Hero Is Passed By," *Rocky Mountain News,* 4 May 1919.

[27] James Ruoff and Del Smith, "Katherine Anne Porter on *Ship of Fools,*" *College English,* February 1963, pp. 396–397.

[28] *Ship of Fools,* p. 294.

[29] *Ship of Fools,* p. 294.

[30] Thompson, "Katherine Anne Porter: An Interview," p. 21.

[31] James Ruoff and Del Smith, "Katherine Anne Porter on *Ship of Fools,*" *College English,* February 1963, pp. 396–397.

[32] Thompson, "Katherine Anne Porter: An Interview," p. 18.

[33] Katherine Anne Porter, notes, undated, McKeldin.

[34] KAP to Gay Porter Holloway, Denver, 1919, incomplete letter, McKeldin.

[35] KAP to Gay Porter Holloway, 1 April 1920, McKeldin.

[36] Katherine Anne Porter, "Poem for Dead Mary Alice," undated, McKeldin.

[37] Katherine Anne Porter, inscription in *A Christmas Story* (New York: Delacorte Press, 1967), collection of David Locher, Dubuque, Iowa.

[38] Katherine Anne Porter, notes, undated, McKeldin.

[39] KAP to Gay Porter Holloway, Denver, 1919, incomplete letter, McKeldin.

7: GREENWICH VILLAGE AND MEXICO CITY

[1] *Collected Essays,* p. 180.

[2] Kitty Barry Crawford, interview in Arlington, Texas, 31 May 1978.

[3] KAP to the Porter family ("To my bunch"), 3 January 1920, McKeldin.

[4] KAP to Donald Stalling, 28 March 1956, McKeldin.

[5] KAP to the Porter family ("To my bunch"), 3 January 1920, McKeldin.

[6] Thompson, "Katherine Anne Porter: An Interview," p. 9.

[7] Katherine Anne Porter, "Charles Ray," *Motion Picture Magazine,* vol. 20, no. 9 (October 1920), p. 36, Library of Congress.

[8] KAP to Mary Alice Hillendahl, 14 June 1920, McKeldin.

[9] KAP to the Porter family ("To my bunch"), 3 January 1920, McKeldin.

[10] Thompson, "Katherine Anne Porter: An Interview," p. 17.

[11] KAP to the Porter family ("To my bunch"), 3 January 1920, McKeldin.

[12] Katherine Anne Porter, "The Shattered Star," *Everyland,* January 1920, pp. 422–423, Widener Library, Harvard University.

[13] Katherine Anne Porter, "The Faithful Princess," *Everyland,* February 1920, pp. 42–43, Widener Library, Harvard University.

[14] Katherine Anne Porter, "The Magic Earring," *Everyland,* March 1920, pp. 86–87, Widener Library, Harvard University.

[15] "Hadji: A Tale of a Turkish Coffee-House," retold by Katherine Anne Porter, *Asia,* August 1920, pp. 683–684.

[16] "Hadji: A Tale of a Turkish Coffee-House," retold by Katherine Anne Porter, *Asia,* August 1920, pp. 683–684.

[17] Donald A. Mackenzie, *Indian Myth and Legend* (London: Gresham Publishing Co., 1913).

[18] Hank Lopez, "A Country and Some People I Love," *Harper's,* September 1965, pp. 58–68.

[19] KAP to Gay Porter Holloway, 29 March 1956, McKeldin.

[20] KAP to Harrison Boone Porter, 3 May 1930, McKeldin.

[21] Transcriptions of taped interviews with Hank Lopez, McKeldin.

[22] KAP to Gay Porter Holloway, 29 March 1956, McKeldin.

[23] Katherine Anne Porter, note, Yaddo, 1941, McKeldin.

[24] *Collected Essays,* p. 356.

[25] Hank Lopez, "A Country and Some People I Love," p. 58.

[26] M.T.F., *My Chinese Marriage* (New York: Asia Publishing Co., 1921), Houghton Library, Harvard University, McKeldin.

[27] *Collected Essays,* p. 94.

[28] Katherine Anne Porter, notes, undated, McKeldin.

[29] Katherine Anne Porter, notes, undated, McKeldin.

[30] Marya Fforde to Joan Givner, 9 November 1977, collection of author.

[31] Katherine Anne Porter, lecture in the Katherine Anne Porter Room, fall 1972.

[32] Katherine Anne Porter, lecture in the Katherine Anne Porter Room, fall 1972.

[33] KAP to Lodwick Hartley, 4 May 1940, collection of author. Katherine Anne Porter, lecture in Katherine Anne Porter Room, fall 1972. Thomas Walsh to Joan Givner, interview by telephone, 6 June 1982.

[34] KAP to Josephine Herbst, 18 March 1933, Humanities Research Center, Austin, Texas.

[35] Enrique Hank Lopez, *Conversations with Katherine Anne Porter: Refugee from Indian Creek* (Boston: Little, Brown and Company, 1981), pp. 65–67.

[36] *Collected Stories,* p. 101.

[37] *Collected Essays,* p. 399.

[38] KAP to Paul Hanna, 19 April 1921, McKeldin.

[39] Katherine Anne Porter, notes, undated, McKeldin.

[40] Kitty Barry Crawford, interview in Arlington, Texas, 31 May 1978.

[41] Jane Anderson Jenkins, interview in Arlington, Texas, 31 May 1978.

[42] Kitty Barry Crawford to George Hendrick, 20 November 1961, collection of author.

[43] "Let's Go Shopping with Marie" (Fort Worth) *Record,* 4, 25 September, 2 October, 9 November 1921.

[44] Ida Belle Hicks, "Twenty Years Ago Today the Little Theater Got Its Start in Fort Worth," newspaper clipping, 12 October 1941, collection of author.

[45] Jane Anderson Jenkins, interview in Arlington, Texas, 31 May 1978.

[46] (Fort Worth) *Record,* 9 November 1921.

[47] Jane Anderson Jenkins, interview in Arlington, Texas, 31 May 1978.

[48] KAP to Joseph Retinger, undated, McKeldin.

[49] Kitty Barry Crawford to Joan Givner, 17 January 1978, collection of author.

[50] Mary Doherty to KAP, undated, McKeldin.

[51] John Dorsey, "Katherine Anne Porter On," p. 18.

[52] *Collected Essays,* p. 426.

[53] Conversations with Katherine Anne Porter, p. 71.

[54] Conversations with Katherine Anne Porter, p. 72.

[55] *Collected Essays,* p. 398.

[56] John Dorsey, "Katherine Anne Porter On," p. 18.

8: GETTING READY TO BE A WRITER

[1] Robert L. Beare, interview in Lexington, Massachusetts, 18 September 1978.

[2] KAP to Harrison Boone Porter, 27 July 1922, McKeldin.

[3] Hank Lopez, "A Country and Some People I Love," p. 62.

[4] Katherine Anne Porter, *Outline of Mexican Popular Arts and Crafts* (Mexico City: S.I.C.yT., 1922), p. 38.

[5] *Collected Essays,* p. 355.

[6] *Collected Essays,* p. 356.

[7] Hank Lopez, "A Country and Some People I Love," p. 62.

[8] Charles Sumner Williams to KAP, undated, McKeldin.

[9] KAP to Ann Holloway Heintze, 4 October 1958, McKeldin.

[10] Francisco Aguilera to KAP, undated, McKeldin.

[11] Francisco Aguilera to KAP, undated, McKeldin.

[12] KAP to Gay Porter Holloway, undated, McKeldin.

[13] Katherine Anne Porter, note scribbled on enveloped postmarked 31 March 1924, 1937, McKeldin.

[14] KAP to Edward G. Schwartz, Ash Wednesday, 1958, McKeldin.

[15] KAP to Delafield Day Spier, 17 February 1931, collection of Delafield Day Spier, Victoria, British Columbia.

[16] KAP to Genevieve Taggard, 14 November 1924, McKeldin, New York Public Library.

[17] KAP to Genevieve Taggard, 28 November 1924, McKeldin, New York Public Library.

[18] KAP to Genevieve Taggard, 18 December 1924, McKeldin, New York Public Library.

[19] John Thompson to Joan Givner, 21 November 1977, collection of author.

[20] Katherine Anne Porter, notes, undated, McKeldin.

[21] KAP to Genevieve Taggard, 14 November 1924, McKeldin, New York Public Library.

[22] Enrique Hank Lopez, *Conversations with Katherine Anne Porter: Refugee from Indian Creek* (Boston: Little, Brown and Company, 1981), p. 83.

[23] Molly Luce Burroughs, telephone interview, 10 July 1979.

[24] KAP to Genevieve Taggard, undated, McKeldin, New York Public Library.

[25] Josephine Herbst, "A Man of Steel," *American Mercury,* January 1934, pp. 32–40.

[26] KAP to Josephine Herbst, 5 May 1928, Beinecke.

[27] Katherine Anne Porter, notes, undated, McKeldin.

[28] KAP to Genevieve Taggard, 3 June 1926, McKeldin, New York Public Library.

[29] Molly Luce Burroughs, telephone interview, 10 July 1979. Molly Luce Burroughs to Joan Givner, 15 July 1979, collection of author.

[30] *Collected Stories,* p. 42.

[31] Josephine Herbst, "A Man of Steel," p. 35.

[32] Ann Holloway Heintze, interview in Baltimore, Maryland, 22 February 1977.

[33] KAP to Josephine Herbst, undated, Beinecke. Molly Luce Burroughs, telephone interview, 10 July 1979. Peggy Bacon, telephone interview, 9 July 1979.

[34] KAP to Peggy Cowley, 1931, McKeldin.

[35] KAP to Eugene Pressly, 1934, McKeldin.

[36] KAP to Genevieve Taggard, 10 May 1924, McKeldin, New York Public Library.

[37] KAP to Genevieve Taggard, 14 November 1924, McKeldin, New York Public Library.

[38] KAP to Genevieve Taggard, 9 October 1924, McKeldin, New York Public Library.

[39] Katherine Anne Porter, interview in College Park, Maryland, 3 December 1976.

[40] Josephine Herbst, "A Year of Disgrace," *Noble Savage*, no. 3, 1961, pp. 128–160.

[41] KAP to Josephine Herbst, 7 July 1932, Beinecke.

[42] Katherine Anne Porter, notes, 6 October 1975, McKeldin.

[43] Elinor Langer to Joan Givner, 26 October 1978, collection of author.

[44] Allen Tate, interview in Nashville, Tennessee, 3 June 1978.

[45] Josephine Herbst, *Rope of Gold* (New York: Harcourt, Brace & Company, 1937), pp. 21, 47.

[46] KAP to Genevieve Taggard, 3 June 1926, McKeldin, New York Public Library.

[47] Katherine Anne Porter, review of *Nothing Is Sacred,* by Josephine Herbst, *New York Herald Tribune,* 7 October 1928.

[48] Katherine Anne Porter, review of *Money for Love,* by Josephine Herbst, in *New Masses,* November 1928, p. 19.

[49] KAP to Genevieve Taggard, 3 June 1926.

[50] Thompson, "Katherine Anne Porter: An Interview," p. 9.

9: THE FOREIGN LAND OF MASSACHUSETTS

[1] Rob Roy Purdy, ed., *Fugitives' Reunion: Conversations at Vanderbilt* (Nashville: Vanderbilt University Press, 1959), p. 209.

[2] *Collected Essays,* p. 472.

[3] Katherine Anne Porter, notes, undated, McKeldin.

[4] Katherine Anne Porter, notes, undated, McKeldin.

[5] Katherine Anne Porter, "Notes on the Texas I Remember," p. 102.

[6] Katherine Anne Porter, "Beauty Unadorned Attracts When War Hero Is Passed By," *Rocky Mountain News,* 4 May 1919, p. 11.

[7] Book jacket for unpublished work, Katherine Anne Porter, *The Devil and Cotton Mather* (New York: Horace Liveright). The original jacket on deposit in the McKeldin Library was destroyed. Photostat copies remain in the collections of David Levin, Department of English, University of Virginia, and the author.

[8] Doris Grumbach, "The Katherine Anne Porter Watch: After Sacco and Vanzetti, What? 'The Devil and Cotton Mather,' " *Village Voice,* 26 January 1976.

[9] Walter Gilmer, *Horace Liveright: Publisher of the Twenties* (New York: David Lewis, 1970), p. 189.

[10] Katherine Anne Porter, notes, undated, McKeldin.

[11] *Collected Essays,* p. 88.

[12] Walter Gilmer, *Horace Liveright: Publisher of the Twenties,* pp. 190, 191.

[13] KAP to Glenway Wescott, 24 December 1935, McKeldin.

[14] *Collected Essays,* p. 141.

[15] David Levin, *Cotton Mather: The Young Life of the Lord's Remembrancer* (Cambridge, Mass.: Harvard University Press, 1978), p. xiii.

[16] KAP to Josephine Herbst, 1928, Beinecke.

[17] *Collected Essays,* p. 313.

[18] David Levin, *In Defense of Historical Literature* (New York: Hill and Wang, 1967), p. 41.

[19] Katherine Anne Porter, *The Never-Ending Wrong* (Boston, Atlantic-Little, Brown, 1977), p. 13.

[20] *Ship of Fools,* p. 164.

[21] *The Never-Ending Wrong,* p. 44.

[22] Glenway Wescott, "Katherine Anne Porter Personally," p. 35.

[23] *Collected Stories,* p. 311.

[24] John Leonard, review of *Justice Crucified,* by Roberta Strauss Feverlicht, and *The Never-Ending Wrong,* by Katherine Anne Porter, *New York Times,* 25 August 1977.

[25] Eudora Welty, review of *The Never-Ending Wrong,* by Katherine Anne Porter, *New York Times Book Review,* 21 August 1977, pp. 9–29.

[26] *The Never-Ending Wrong,* p. 49.

[27] *The Never-Ending Wrong,* p. 6.

[28] *The Never-Ending Wrong,* p. 55.

[29] KAP to Gay Porter Holloway, 5 March 1928, McKeldin.

[30] Katherine Anne Porter, notes, 1928, McKeldin.

[31] KAP to Josephine Herbst, 1928, Beinecke.

[32] Robert Penn Warren, "Uncorrupted Consciousness: The Stories of Katherine Anne Porter," *Yale Review,* LV, 1966, pp. 280–290.

[33] Hank Lopez, "A Country and Some People I Love," p. 67.

[34] Nathaniel Hawthorne, *The House of Seven Gables* (Columbus: Ohio State University Press, 1965), p. 66.

[35] *Hawthorne's Short Stories,* ed., Newton Arvin (New York: Vintage Books, 1960), p. 356.

[36] *Collected Stories,* p. 41.

[37] Katherine Anne Porter, notes, undated, McKeldin.

[38] KAP to Glenway Wescott, 5 January 1960, McKeldin.

[39] Katherine Anne Porter, notes, undated, McKeldin.

[40] *Collected Essays,* p. 38.

[41] KAP to Josephine Herbst, 1928, Beinecke.

10: THE FABULOUS YEAR

[1] Matthew Josephson, *Life Among the Surrealists* (New York: Holt, Rinehart and Winston, 1962), p. 352.

[2] Matthew Josephson, diary, Beinecke.

[3] Matthew Josephson, interview in Sherman, Connecticut, 18 June 1977.

[4] KAP to Rebecca Crawford, 7 April 1929, McKeldin.

[5] Thompson, "Katherine Anne Porter: An Interview," p. 20.

[6] Matthew Josephson, *Life Among the Surrealists,* p. 353.

[7] Katherine Anne Porter, notes, 24 June 1948, McKeldin.

[8] Thompson, "Katherine Anne Porter: An Interview," p. 16.

[9] Matthew Josephson, *Life Among the Surrealists,* p. 356.

[10] Matthew Josephson, interview in Sherman, Connecticut, 18 June 1977.

[11] Matthew Josephson, diary, Beinecke.

[12] KAP to Matthew Josephson, 7 January 1931, Beinecke.

[13] Matthew Josephson, diary, Beinecke.

[14] *Ship of Fools,* p. 374.

[15] *Collected Stories,* p. 63. Matthew Josephson, interview in New York, 7 December 1974.

[16] Katherine Anne Porter, lecture at the Katherine Anne Porter Room, McKeldin Library, November 1972.

[17] Rebecca Crawford to KAP, 12 June 1929, McKeldin.
[18] Josephine Herbst to KAP, 15 June 1938, McKeldin.
[19] Matthew Josephson to Joan Givner, 26 October 1974, collection of author.
[20] KAP to Josephine Herbst, 18 March 1929, Beinecke.
[21] KAP to Monroe Wheeler, 23 March 1935, McKeldin.
[22] KAP to Josephine Herbst, 18 March 1929, Beinecke.
[23] KAP to Josephine Herbst, 18 March 1929, Beinecke.
[24] KAP to Josephine Herbst, 29 April 1929, Beinecke.
[25] Amy Clendenning, interview in Bermuda, 25 February 1974.
[25] KAP to Delafield Day Spier, undated, collection of Delafield Day Spier, Victoria, British Columbia.
[27] KAP to Josephine Herbst, 29 April 1929, Beinecke.
[28] Amy Clendenning, interview in Bermuda, 25 February 1974. Katherine Anne Porter, interview in College Park, Maryland, 1 December 1976.
[29] *Collected Essays,* p. 470.
[30] KAP to Andrew Lytle, 14 May 1931, Vanderbilt University.
[31] *Collected Stories,* p. 326.
[32] KAP to Josephine Herbst, 21 May 1929, Beinecke.
[33] KAP to Rebecca Crawford, 7 April 1929, McKeldin.
[34] KAP to Rebecca Crawford, 15 April 1929, McKeldin.
[35] KAP to Rebecca Crawford, 21 May 1929, McKeldin.
[36] KAP to Delafield Day Spier, 14 July 1929, collection of Delafield Day Spier, Victoria, British Columbia.
[37] KAP to Josephine Herbst, 14 July 1929, Beinecke.
[38] KAP to Delafield Day Spier, undated, collection of Delafield Day Spier, Victoria, British Columbia.
[39] Walter Gilmer, *Horace Liveright: Publisher of the Twenties,* p. 190.
[40] J. V. Cunningham, "The 'Gyroscope' Group," *The Bookman,* V, 75, November 1932, pp. 703–705.
[41] Thompson, "Katherine Anne Porter: An Interview," p. 20.
[42] KAP to Rebecca Crawford, undated, McKeldin.
[43] *Collected Stories,* p. 97.
[44] Thompson, "Katherine Anne Porter: An Interview," p. 20.

11: FAREWELL TO MEXICO

[1] Matthew Josephson to Harcourt, Brace, 17 July 1929, Harcourt, Brace correspondence file.
[2] KAP to Allen Tate, January 1962, McKeldin.
[3] Edmund Wilson, *Letters on Literature and Politics 1912–1972,* ed., Elena Wilson (New York: Farrar, Straus and Giroux, 1977), p. 196.
[4] KAP to Delafield Day Spier, 17 February 1931, collection of Delafield Day Spier, Victoria, British Columbia.
[5] Matthew Josephson, telegram, 3 July 1929, McKeldin.
[6] Matthew Josephson, diary, Beinecke.
[7] Matthew Josephson, interview in Sherman, Connecticut, 18 June 1977. Susan Jenkins Brown, interview in Sherman, Connecticut, 18 June 1977.
[8] Malcolm Cowley, *And I Worked at the Writer's Trade* (New York: Viking Press, 1978), pp. 82–87. Malcolm Cowley, interview in Sherman, Connecticut, 18 June 1977. David Shi to Joan Givner, 30 October 1979, collection of author.

⁹ Matthew Josephson, *Life Among the Surrealists,* p. 376. Matthew Josephson, interview in Sherman, Connecticut, 18 June 1977.
¹⁰ Walter Frank to KAP, 16 April 1930, McKeldin.
¹¹ KAP to Delafield Day Spier, 7 June 1930, collection of Delafield Day Spier, Victoria, British Columbia. KAP to Josephine Herbst, 6 June 1930, Beinecke.
¹² KAP to Josephine Herbst, 12 July 1930, Beinecke.
¹³ KAP to Josephine Herbst, 28 April 1930, Beinecke.
¹⁴ KAP to Eugene Pressly, 5 May 1934, McKeldin.
¹⁵ KAP to Eugene Pressly, 5 May 1934, McKeldin.
¹⁶ *Ship of Fools,* p. 144.
¹⁷ KAP to Matthew Josephson, 7 January 1931, Beinecke.
¹⁸ KAP to Matthew Josephson, undated, Beinecke.
¹⁹ KAP to Matthew Josephson, 7 January 1931, Beinecke.
²⁰ KAP to Malcolm Cowley, 5 November 1931, McKeldin.
²¹ KAP to Josephine Herbst, 11 February 1931, Beinecke.
²² KAP to Matthew Josephson, 7 January 1931, Beinecke.
²³ Malcolm Cowley to KAP, 30 November 1930, McKeldin.
²⁴ KAP to Josephine Herbst, 11 February 1931, Beinecke.
²⁵ KAP to Josephine Herbst, 11 February 1931, Beinecke.
²⁶ Malcolm Cowley to KAP, 9 April 1931, McKeldin.
²⁷ Katherine Anne Porter, review of *Plagued by the Nightingale* and *Wedding Day,* by Kay Boyle, *New Republic,* 22 April 1931, pp. 279–280.
²⁸ KAP to Edward G. Schwartz, 10 April 1952, McKeldin.
²⁹ KAP to Josephine Herbst, 11 February 1931, Beinecke.
³⁰ KAP to Josephine Herbst, 11 March 1931, Beinecke.
³¹ KAP to Josephine Herbst, 7 April 1931, Beinecke.
³² David Locher to Joan Givner, 25 July 1980, collection of author.
³³ KAP to Kenneth Burke, 6 October 1930, Pennsylvania State University Library.
³⁴ KAP to Josephine Herbst, 7 April 1931, Beinecke. KAP to Malcolm Cowley, 25 February 1931, McKeldin.
³⁵ KAP to Josephine Herbst and John Herrmann, 20 February 1931, Beinecke.
³⁶ KAP to Josephine Herbst, 7 April 1931, Beinecke.
³⁷ KAP to Malcolm Cowley, 17 June 1930, McKeldin.
³⁸ KAP to Susan Jenkins Brown, 13 May 1931, collection of author.
³⁹ KAP to Susan Jenkins Brown, 13 May 1931, collection of author.
⁴⁰ John Unterecker, *Voyager: A Life of Hart Crane* (New York: Farrar, Straus and Giroux, 1969), p. 666.
⁴¹ KAP to Susan Jenkins Brown, 13 May 1931, collection of author.
⁴² Matthew Josephson, interview in Sherman, Connecticut, 18 June 1977.
⁴³ John Unterecker, *Voyager,* p. 670.
⁴⁴ John Unterecker, *Voyager,* p. 672.
⁴⁵ KAP to Josephine Herbst, 1 June 1931, Beinecke.
⁴⁶ Hank Lopez, "A Country and Some People I Love," p. 61.
⁴⁷ KAP to Caroline Gordon, 14 December 1931, McKeldin.
⁴⁸ KAP to Edward G. Schwartz, 11 March 1958, McKeldin.
⁴⁹ KAP to Kenneth Burke, 6 October 1930, Pennsylvania State University Library.
⁵⁰ Marginal notes in Katherine Anne Porter, *Hacienda* (New York: Harrison of Paris, 1934), Humanities Research Center, University of Texas, Austin, Texas.

⁵¹ *Collected Stories,* p. 142.
⁵² *Collected Stories,* p. 168.
⁵³ *Collected Stories,* p. 165.
⁵⁴ Marginal notes in Katherine Anne Porter, *Hacienda* (New York: Harrison of Paris, 1934), Humanities Research Center, University of Texas, Austin, Texas.
⁵⁵ KAP to Caroline Gordon, 28 August 1931, Princeton University Library.
⁵⁶ KAP to Caroline Gordon, 28 August 1931, Princeton University Library.

12: THE GERMAN EXPERIENCE

¹ James Ruoff and Del Smith, "Katherine Anne Porter on *Ship of Fools,*" *College English,* February 1963, pp. 396–397.
² KAP to Erna Glover Johns, 20 December 1939, collection of Erna Glover Johns, Austin, Texas.
³ KAP to Caroline Gordon, 28 August 1931, Princeton University Library.
⁴ KAP to Caroline Gordon, 28 August 1931, Princeton University Library.
⁵ KAP to Josephine Herbst, 1 June 1931, Beinecke.
⁶ John Dorsey, "Katherine Anne Porter On," p. 21.
⁷ KAP to Caroline Gordon, 28 August 1931, Princeton University Library.
⁸ *Ship of Fools,* p. 42.
⁹ KAP to Caroline Gordon, 28 August 1931, Princeton University Library.
¹⁰ *Ship of Fools,* p. 40.
¹¹ *Ship of Fools,* p. 52.
¹² *Ship of Fools,* p. 375.
¹³ *Ship of Fools,* p. 264.
¹⁴ *Ship of Fools,* p. 497.
¹⁵ KAP to Caroline Gordon, 28 August 1931, Princeton University Library.
¹⁶ KAP to Caroline Gordon, 28 August 1931, Princeton University Library.
¹⁷ KAP to Caroline Gordon, 28 August 1931, Princeton University Library.
¹⁸ KAP to Caroline Gordon, 28 August 1931, Princeton University Library.
¹⁹ KAP to Caroline Gordon, 28 August 1931, Princeton University Library.
²⁰ KAP to Caroline Gordon, 28 August 1931, Princeton University Library.
²¹ Mary Anne Dolan, "Almost Since Chaucer with Miss Porter," *Washington Star,* 11 May 1975.
²² KAP to Delafield Day Spier, 28 September 1931, collection of Delafield Day Spier, Victoria, British Columbia.
²³ KAP to Kenneth Burke, 27 September 1931, Pennsylvania State University Library.
²⁴ *Collected Essays,* p. 491.
²⁵ Notes in response to essay on "The Leaning Tower," by Kay Boyle, undated, McKeldin.
²⁶ KAP to Eugene Pressly, 4 December 1931, McKeldin.
²⁷ Caroline Gordon to KAP, undated, McKeldin.
²⁸ Malcolm Cowley to KAP, 1931, McKeldin.
²⁹ KAP to Malcolm Cowley, 5 November 1931, McKeldin.
³⁰ KAP to Glenway Wescott, 6 July 1949, McKeldin.
³¹ KAP to Malcolm Cowley, 5 November 1931, McKeldin.
³² KAP to Caroline Gordon, 14 December 1931, McKeldin.
³³ KAP to Eugene Pressly, 26 December 1931, McKeldin.
³⁴ KAP to Josephine Herbst, 21 December 1931, Beinecke.

35 KAP to Eugene Pressly, 26 January 1936, McKeldin.
36 Notes, undated, McKeldin.
37 Herbert Klein to Joan Givner, 25 March 1978, collection of author.
38 Herbert Klein to Joan Givner, 11 April 1978, collection of author.
39 KAP to Josephine Herbst, 16 January 1932, Beinecke.
40 Sigrid Schultz to Joan Givner, 10 March 1978, collection of author.
41 KAP to Josephine Herbst, 16 October 1933, Beinecke.
42 Note, November 1931, McKeldin.
43 Enrique Hank Lopez, *Conversations with Katherine Anne Porter: Refugee from Indian Creek* (Boston: Little, Brown and Company, 1981), p. 189.
44 Transcriptions of taped interviews, McKeldin.
45 Mary Anne Dolan, "Almost Since Chaucer with Miss Porter," *Washington Star,* 11 May 1975.
46 KAP to Eugene Pressly, 18 November 1931, McKeldin.
47 KAP to Eugene Pressly, 26 January 1932, McKeldin.
48 Herbert Klein to Joan Givner, 25 March 1978, collection of author.
49 KAP to Eugene Pressly, 22 January 1932, McKeldin.
50 Notes, undated, McKeldin.
51 KAP to Eugene Pressly, 5 January 1932, McKeldin.

13: PARIS, MADRID, BASLE, PARIS

1 KAP to Josephine Herbst, 1 July 1932, McKeldin.
2 KAP to William Harlan Hale, 14 February 1932, McKeldin.
3 KAP to William Harlan Hale, 14 February 1932, McKeldin.
4 KAP to Josephine Herbst, 1 July 1932, Beinecke.
5 KAP to Eugene Pressly, 8 March 1932, McKeldin.
6 KAP to William Harlan Hale, 5 March 1932, McKeldin.
7 KAP to William Harlan Hale, 14 February 1932, McKeldin.
8 KAP to William Harlan Hale, 11 May 1932, McKeldin.
9 KAP to Eugene Pressly, 8 November 1932, McKeldin.
10 Robert L. Beare, interview in Lexington, Massachusetts, 18 September 1978.
11 KAP to Eugene Pressly, 8 March 1932, McKeldin.
12 Jean Rhys, *Quartet* (New York: Simon and Schuster, 1929).
13 KAP to Eugene Pressly, 10 March 1932, McKeldin.
14 KAP to Eugene Pressly, 21 May 1932, McKeldin.
15 KAP to Eugene Pressly, 21 May 1932, McKeldin.
16 Eugene Pressly to KAP, 21 November 1932, McKeldin.
17 KAP to Eugene Pressly, 21 May 1932, McKeldin.
18 Eugene Pressly to KAP, 21 November 1932, McKeldin.
19 KAP to Eugene Pressly, 5 August 1935, McKeldin.
20 *Collected Essays,* p. 229, McKeldin.
21 Sy M. Kahn, "Glenway Wescott: A Critical and Biographical Study" (Ph.D. dissertation, University of Wisconsin, 1957), pp. 1–17.
22 Matthew Josephson to Joan Givner, 26 November 1975, collection of author.
23 Thomas Daniel Young and John J. Hindle, eds., *The Republic of Letters in America: The Correspondence of John Peale Bishop and Allen Tate* (Kentucky: The University Press of Kentucky, 1981), pp. 172–173.
24 James T. Farrell to Joan Givner, 30 December 1978, collection of author.

[25] KAP to Josephine Herbst, 1 July 1932, Beinecke.
[26] KAP to Josephine Herbst, 3 August 1932, Beinecke.
[27] Notes, undated, McKeldin.
[28] KAP to Eugene Pressly, 18 November 1932, McKeldin.
[29] *Collected Essays*, p. 473.
[30] KAP to Eugene Pressly, p. 1 missing, 1932, McKeldin.
[31] KAP to Eugene Pressly, 3 November 1932, McKeldin.
[32] Katherine Anne Porter, notes, undated, McKeldin.
[33] KAP to Eugene Pressly, 9 December 1932, McKeldin.
[34] KAP to Gay Porter Holloway, 2 March 1933, McKeldin.
[35] KAP to Josephine Herbst, 18 March 1933, Humanities Research Center, University of Texas, Austin, Texas.

14: PARIS

[1] KAP to Josephine Herbst, 29 April 1945, Beinecke.
[2] KAP to Ione Porter, spring 1933, McKeldin.
[3] *Ship of Fools,* p. 212.
[4] KAP to Ione Porter, spring 1933, McKeldin.
[5] Ford Madox Ford, *It Was the Nightingale* (London: William Heinemann Ltd., 1934).
[6] KAP to the Porter family, 8 December 1933.
[7] Katherine Anne Porter, undated, collection of author.
[8] *Collected Essays,* p. 107.
[9] *Collected Essays,* p. 106.
[10] KAP to Philip Horton, notes, undated, McKeldin.
[11] KAP to Monroe Wheeler, 25 February 1935.
[12] Katherine Anne Porter, notes, undated, McKeldin.
[13] KAP to Eugene Pressly, 4 May 1934, McKeldin.
[14] Eugene Pressly to KAP, 11 May 1934, McKeldin.
[15] Stella Brown, *Drawn From Life: Reminiscences* (London: Collins Publishers, 1941), p. 88.
[16] KAP to Paul Porter, 1952, McKeldin.
[17] Eugene Pressly to KAP, 11 September 1935, McKeldin.
[18] KAP to Eugene Pressly, 5 August 1935, McKeldin.
[19] Josephine Herbst, *Somewhere the Tempest Fell* (New York: Charles Scribner's Sons, 1947), pp. 180–181.
[20] KAP to William Harlan Hale, 3 September 1932, McKeldin.
[21] KAP to Josephine Herbst, 25 July 1935, McKeldin.
[22] Katherine Anne Porter, marginal notes in *Oliver Cromwell,* by John Buchan, 26 February 1936, McKeldin. The dedication translates as: To my dearest wife, companion in (my) labors, (my) studies, (my) joys.
[23] Caroline Gordon to KAP, undated, McKeldin.
[24] KAP to Eugene Pressly, May 1936, McKeldin.
[25] KAP to Eugene Pressly, May 1936, McKeldin.
[26] Notes, 8 May 1936, McKeldin.
[27] KAP to Eugene Pressly, May 1936, McKeldin.

15: PENNSYLVANIA, NEW YORK, LOUISIANA, TEXAS

[1] Matthew Josephson, interview in Sherman, Connecticut, 18 June 1977.
[2] KAP to Josephine Herbst, 31 October 1936, Beinecke.
[3] KAP to Monroe Wheeler, 24 November 1936, McKeldin.
[4] KAP to Monroe Wheeler, 24 November 1935, McKeldin.
[5] KAP to Monroe Wheeler, 6 December 1936, McKeldin.
[6] Katherine Anne Porter, notes, undated, McKeldin.
[7] KAP to Eugene Pressly, 28 November 1936, McKeldin.
[8] KAP to Josephine Herbst, 30 January 1937, Beinecke. KAP to Monroe Wheeler, 6 January 1937, McKeldin.
[9] KAP to Eugene Pressly, 20 September 1937, McKeldin.
[10] KAP to Eugene Pressly, 21 December 1931, McKeldin.
[11] KAP to Eugene Pressly, 11 May 1934, McKeldin.
[12] Katherine Anne Porter, *Ship of Fools* (Boston: Atlantic–Little, Brown, 1962), p. 357. Porter makes clear in her letters that Pressly served as the basis for the character of David in *Ship of Fools*.
[13] John Dorsey, "Katherine Anne Porter On" (Baltimore) *Sun Magazine,* 26 October 1969.
[14] Eugene Pressly to KAP, 8 April 1937, McKeldin.
[15] KAP to Monroe Wheeler, 24 September 1937, McKeldin.
[16] KAP to Erna Glover Johns, 23 December 1938, collection of Erna Glover Johns, Austin, Texas.
[17] KAP to Erna Glover Johns, 23 December 1938, collection of Erna Glover Johns, Austin, Texas.
[18] Allen Tate to KAP, 23 October 1932 or 1936 (date illegible), McKeldin.
[19] KAP to Josephine Herbst, 15 August 1937, Beinecke.
[20] Caroline Gordon to KAP, 12 May 1936, McKeldin.
[21] KAP to Albert R. Erskine, 18 October 1940, McKeldin.
[22] Allen Tate, interview in Nashville, Tennessee, 3 June 1978.
[23] KAP to Monroe Wheeler, 24 September 1937, McKeldin.
[24] KAP to Josephine Herbst, 22 September 1937, Beinecke.
[25] KAP to Monroe Wheeler, 29 September 1937, McKeldin.
[26] KAP to Josephine Herbst, 22 September 1937, Beinecke.
[27] KAP to Glenway Wescott, 23 March 1938, McKeldin.
[28] KAP to Josephine Herbst, 22 October 1937, Beinecke.
[29] KAP to Eugene Pressly, 21 October 1937, McKeldin.
[30] KAP to Albert R. Erskine, 28 October 1937, McKeldin.
[31] KAP to Albert R. Erskine, 25 December 1937, McKeldin.
[32] KAP to Albert R. Erskine, 15 December 1937, McKeldin. KAP to Albert R. Erskine, 23 December 1937, McKeldin.
[33] Breckenridge Porter, interview in Houston, Texas, 6 September 1977.
[34] Breckenridge Porter, interview in Houston, Texas, 6 September 1977.
[35] KAP to Albert R. Erskine, 1 March 1938, McKeldin.
[36] KAP to Albert R. Erskine, 21 March 1938, McKeldin.
[37] KAP to Albert R. Erskine, 5 April 1937, McKeldin.
[38] Paul Porter, interview in New York, 11 December 1979.
[39] KAP to Robert Penn Warren, 9 April 1965, McKeldin.
[40] KAP to Albert R. Erskine, 18 April 1959, McKeldin.
[41] Allen Tate, interview in Nashville, Tennessee, 3 June 1978.

[42] KAP to Albert R. Erskine, 18 June 1940, McKeldin.

[43] Katherine Anne Porter, notes, undated, McKeldin.

[44] Marginal note in Simone de Beauvoir, *The Second Sex*, McKeldin.

[45] KAP to Glenway Wescott, 5 September 1939, McKeldin.

[46] KAP to Albert R. Erskine, 20 July 1938, McKeldin. KAP to Albert R. Erskine, 28 July 1938, McKeldin.

[47] KAP to Erna Glover Johns, 13 December 1938, collection of Erna Glover Johns, Austin, Texas.

[48] KAP to Monroe Wheeler, 7 November 1938, McKeldin.

[49] KAP to Glenway Wescott, 16 November 1938, McKeldin.

[50] Ralph Thompson, review of *Pale Horse, Pale Rider,* by Katherine Anne Porter, in *New York Times,* 30 March 1939.

[51] Lewis Gannett, review of *Pale Horse, Pale Rider,* by Katherine Anne Porter, in *New York Herald Tribune,* 30 March 1939.

[52] Paul Rosenfeld, review of *Pale Horse, Pale Rider,* by Katherine Anne Porter, in *Saturday Review of Literature,* XIX, 1 April 1937, p. 7.

[53] Clifton Fadiman, review of *Pale Horse, Pale Rider,* by Katherine Anne Porter, in *New Yorker,* 1 April 1939, pp. 69–70.

[54] Glenway Wescott, review of *Pale Horse, Pale Rider,* by Katherine Anne Porter, in *Southern Review,* V, 1939, pp. 161–173.

[55] Wallace Stegner, review of *Pale Horse, Pale Rider,* by Katherine Anne Porter, in *Virginia Quarterly Review,* XV, 1939, pp. 443–447.

[56] KAP to Albert Erskine, 12 May 1939, McKeldin.

[57] KAP to Glenway Wescott, 28 June 1940, McKeldin.

[58] *Collected Essays,* p. 456.

16: A HOUSE OF MY OWN

[1] KAP to Albert R. Erskine, 4 June 1940, McKeldin.

[2] KAP to Albert R. Erskine, 21 October 1940, McKeldin.

[3] KAP to Albert R. Erskine, 4 June 1940, McKeldin.

[4] Thompson, "Katherine Anne Porter: An Interview," p. 11.

[5] KAP to Albert R. Erskine, 7 January 1941, McKeldin.

[6] *Ship of Fools,* p. 253.

[7] KAP to Albert R. Erskine, 8 July 1940, McKeldin.

[8] KAP to Albert R. Erskine, 28 March 1938, McKeldin.

[9] KAP to Glenway Wescott, 21 January 1941, McKeldin.

[10] KAP to Glenway Wescott, 23 January 1941, McKeldin.

[11] KAP to Josephine Herbst, 16 November 1940, McKeldin.

[12] *Collected Stories,* p. 463.

[13] Joseph Retinger, *Memoirs of an Eminence Grise,* ed., John Pomian (Sussex: The University Press, 1972), p. 3.

[14] *Collected Stories,* p. 463.

[15] Katherine Anne Porter, notes, undated, McKeldin.

[16] *Collected Essays,* p. 456.

[17] *Collected Essays,* p. 176.

[18] KAP to Glenway Wescott, 21 January 1941, McKeldin.

[19] KAP to Glenway Wescott, 7 April 1942, McKeldin.

[20] Donald Brace to KAP, 11 December 1940, McKeldin.

[21] Donald Brace to KAP, 4 December 1940, McKeldin.

[22] Contracts, McKeldin.

[23] Marcella Comès Winslow, interview in Center Sandwich, New Hampshire, 30 August 1978.

[24] Eudora Welty, interview in Jackson, Mississippi, 19 February 1975.

[25] Memorial booklet, McKeldin.

[26] KAP to Glenway Wescott, 5 February 1942, McKeldin.

[27] Albert R. Erskine to KAP, 31 July 1942, McKeldin. By late July, Erskine had already been married to his second wife for about a month. This letter touches upon the events of the previous spring—his and Porter's plans to obtain a quick divorce and Porter's subsequent trip to Reno.

[28] Katherine Anne Porter, notes on above letter, McKeldin.

[29] KAP to Glenway Wescott, 15 May 1942, McKeldin.

[30] Donald Brace to KAP, 10 June 1942, McKeldin.

[31] KAP to Josephine Herbst, 28 December 1943, McKeldin.

[32] KAP to Monroe Wheeler and George Platt Lynes, 6 February 1943, McKeldin.

[33] KAP to Eugene Pressly, 6 April 1943, McKeldin.

[34] KAP to Monroe Wheeler, 23 August 1942, McKeldin. KAP to Glenway Wescott, 20 September 1943, McKeldin.

[35] KAP to Monroe Wheeler, 29 September 1943, McKeldin.

[36] KAP to Monroe Wheeler, 25 November 1945, McKeldin.

[37] KAP to Glenway Wescott, 27 December 1943, McKeldin.

[38] KAP to Monroe Wheeler, 10 November 1943, McKeldin.

[39] Donald Brace to KAP, 3 February 1944, McKeldin.

17: THE LOVE OF A LIFETIME

[1] KAP to Honora Comès, 19 January 1946, collection of Marcella Comès Winslow, Washington, D.C.

[2] Allen Tate, interview in Nashville, Tennessee, 3 June 1978.

[3] Marcella Comès Winslow, interviews in Center Sandwich, New Hampshire, 30 August 1978; Washington D.C., 17 April 1979; Lexington, Massachusetts, 11 June 1979.

[4] Allen Tate, interview in Nashville, Tennessee, 3 June 1978.

[5] KAP to Paul Porter, 3 September 1949, McKeldin.

[6] KAP to Marcella Comès Winslow, 1 January 1948, collection of Marcella Comès Winslow, Washington D.C.

[7] Marcella Comès Winslow to Joan Givner, 12 September 1978, collection of author.

[8] Marcella Comès Winslow to Anne Goodwin Winslow, 23 April 1944, collection of Marcella Comès Winslow, Washington D.C.

[9] Marcella Comès Winslow to Anne Goodwin Winslow, 13 April 1944, collection of Marcella Comès Winslow, Washington D.C.

[10] KAP to Marcella Comès Winslow, 16 January 1950, collection of Marcella Comès Winslow, Washington D.C.

[11] Orville Prescott, review of Cloudy Trophies, by Anne Goodwin Winslow, in New York Times Book Review, 21 June 1946.

[12] Marcella Comès Winslow to Mary C. Chapman, 11 June 1944, collection of Marcella Comès Winslow, Washington D.C.

[13] Ann Holloway Heintze, interview in Pound Ridge, New York, 8 December 1979.

[14] Notes, 9 July 1945, McKeldin.

[15] *Collected Essays,* p. 111.
[16] Notes, undated, McKeldin.
[17] Hank Lopez, "A Country and Some People I Love," p. 59.
[18] KAP to Glenway Wescott, 3 April 1959, McKeldin.
[19] Marcella Comès Winslow, interview in Washington, D.C., 17 April 1979.
[20] Notes, McKeldin.
[21] KAP to Marcella Comès Winslow, 4 October 1944, collection of Marcella Comès Winslow, Washington, D.C.
[22] Paul Porter to KAP, 24 September 1941, McKeldin.
[23] KAP to Monroe Wheeler, 27 August 1944, McKeldin.
[24] Notes, McKeldin.
[25] Marginal note in Simone de Beauvoir, *The Second Sex,* McKeldin.
[26] KAP to Monroe Wheeler, 27 August 1944, McKeldin.
[27] KAP to Charles Shannon, 21 December 1944, unmailed letter, McKeldin.
[28] Notes, McKeldin.
[29] KAP to Gay Porter Holloway, 11 July 1957, McKeldin.
[30] KAP to Monroe Wheeler, 23 August 1945, McKeldin.
[31] Katherine Anne Porter, notes, undated, McKeldin.
[32] Marcella Comès Winslow, interview in Washington D.C., 17 April 1979.
[33] KAP to Glenway Wescott, 21 May 1959, McKeldin.
[34] KAP to Ann Holloway Heintze, 6 January 1959, McKeldin.
[35] KAP to Glenway Wescott, 27 November 1944, McKeldin.
[36] Katherine Anne Porter, notes, undated, McKeldin.
[37] KAP to Monroe Wheeler, 4 January 1946, McKeldin.

18: CALIFORNIA

[1] KAP to Josephine Herbst, 30 January 1947, Beinecke.
[2] KAP to Glenway Wescott, 26 February 1945, McKeldin.
[3] KAP to Monroe Wheeler, 25 February 1945, McKeldin.
[4] Ann Holloway Heintze, interview in Pound Ridge, New York, 8 December 1979.
[5] KAP to Monroe Wheeler, 25 February 1945, McKeldin.
[6] KAP to Monroe Wheeler, 25 February 1945, McKeldin.
[7] KAP to Monroe Wheeler, 3 December 1945, McKeldin.
[8] KAP to Glenway Wescott, 26 February 1945, McKeldin.
[9] KAP to Monroe Wheeler, 20 September 1945, McKeldin.
[10] KAP to Monroe Wheeler, 3 December 1945, McKeldin.
[11] KAP to Monroe Wheeler, 3 December 1945, McKeldin.
[12] KAP to Monroe Wheeler, 25 February 1945, McKeldin.
[13] KAP to Glenway Wescott, 26 February 1945, McKeldin.
[14] KAP to Monroe Wheeler, 25 April 1945, McKeldin.
[15] KAP to Monroe Wheeler, 25 April 1945, McKeldin.
[16] KAP to Monroe Wheeler, 26 April 1945, McKeldin.
[17] KAP to Monroe Wheeler, 30 October 1945, McKeldin.
[18] KAP to Gay Porter Holloway, 14 April 1946, McKeldin.
[19] KAP to Josephine Herbst, 23 January 1946, Beinecke.
[20] Glenway Wescott, *Apartment in Athens* (New York: Harper and Brothers, 1945).
[21] Katherine Anne Porter, review of *Apartment in Athens,* by Glenway Wescott, in *New York Herald Tribune Books,* 4 March 1945.

22 KAP to Josephine Herbst, 29 April 1945, Beinecke.
23 KAP to Josephine Herbst, 29 April 1945, Beinecke.
24 KAP to Josephine Herbst, 17 May 1945, Beinecke.
25 Ann Holloway Heintze, interview in Pound Ridge, New York, 8 December 1979.
26 KAP to Josephine Herbst, 13 January 1946, Beinecke.
27 KAP to Josephine Herbst, 23 January 1946, Beinecke.
28 KAP to Josephine Herbst, 7 July 1947, Beinecke.
29 KAP to Monroe Wheeler, 9 July 1945, McKeldin.
30 KAP to Josephine Herbst, 20 July 1947, Beinekce.
31 *Collected Essays,* p. 271.
32 Katherine Anne Porter, review of *Wedding Day* and *Plagued by the Nightingale,* by Kay Boyle, in *New Republic,* 22 April 1931, pp. 279–280.
33 *Collected Essays,* p. 274.
34 *Collected Essays,* p. 272. Stein's letter was written to Donald Sutherland.
35 *Collected Essays,* p. 262.
36 KAP to Josephine Herbst, 20 July 1947, Beinecke.
37 Eudora Welty to KAP, 25 June 1948, McKeldin.
38 Josephine Herbst to KAP, 8 January 1948, Beinecke.
39 Josephine Herbst, "Miss Porter and Miss Stein," *Partisan Review,* May 1948, pp. 568–572.
40 KAP to Edward Schwartz, Ash Wednesday 1958, McKeldin.
41 KAP to Josephine Herbst, 17 May 1945, Beinecke.
42 KAP to Albert Erskine, 4 January 1947, McKeldin.
43 KAP to Josephine Herbst, 20 July 1947, Beinecke.
44 Alice Denham, "Katherine Anne Porter: Washington's Own Literary Lioness," *Washingtonian,* May 1965, p. 33.
45 KAP to Josephine Herbst, 16 April 1946, Beinecke.
46 KAP to Josephine Herbst, 30 January 1947, Beinecke.
47 KAP to Josephine Herbst, 30 January 1947, Beinecke.
48 Heinrich Hauser, *The German Talks Back* (New York: Henry Holt and Company, 1945). It is most unlikely that Schaumann, an ex-G.I., sympathized completely with the ideas expressed in this book.
49 KAP to Josephine Herbst, 30 January 1947, Beinecke.
50 George Platt Lynes to KAP, 29 October 1947 and 24 November 1948, McKeldin. Glenway Wescott to KAP, 24 February 1947 and 15 March 1947, McKeldin.
51 KAP to Gay Porter Holloway, 22 March 1948, McKeldin.
52 KAP to Gay Porter Holloway, 22 March 1948, McKeldin.
53 KAP to Monroe Wheeler, 18 December 1948, McKeldin.
54 KAP to Ann Holloway Heintze, 22 February 1946, McKeldin.
55 *Collected Essays,* p. 113.
56 *Collected Essays,* p. 113.
57 *Collected Essays,* p. 113.
58 KAP to Glenway Wescott, 9 May 1948, McKeldin.
59 KAP to Monroe Wheeler, 11 July 1948, McKeldin.
60 Wallace Stegner to Joan Givner, 11 January 1978, collection of author.
61 Monroe Wheeler to KAP, 22 March 1948, McKeldin. Wheeler asked if she hadn't collapsed after the last tour. She wrote on his letter, "Yes and one after that and after that and after that until 1964. Then I retired. K.A.P. 3 August 1965."
62 KAP to Monroe Wheeler, 16 January 1949, McKeldin.

[63] KAP to Monroe Wheeler, 16 January 1949, McKeldin.
[64] KAP to Monroe Wheeler, 16 January 1949, McKeldin.
[65] Wallace Stegner to Joan Givner, 31 October 1977, collection of author.
[66] KAP to Donald Brace, 12 September 1949, McKeldin.
[67] KAP to Monroe Wheeler, 6 July 1949, McKeldin.
[68] Donald Brace to KAP, 5 May 1946, McKeldin. KAP to Donald Brace, 9 May 1946, McKeldin.
[69] Wallace Stegner to Joan Givner, 11 January 1978, collection of author.
[70] KAP to Monroe Wheeler, 6 July 1949, McKeldin.
[71] KAP to Monroe Wheeler, 6 July 1949, McKeldin.
[72] KAP to Glenway Wescott, 10 August 1949, McKeldin.

19: DISCIPLES MUST BE VERY HARD
FOR A MERE HUMAN BEING TO ENDURE

[1] KAP to Donald Brace, 12 September 1949, McKeldin.
[2] KAP to Marcella Comès Winslow, 16 January 1950, collection of Marcella Comès Winslow, Washington, D.C.
[3] KAP to William Goyen, 18 July 1951, McKeldin.
[4] John Malcolm Brinnin, *Dylan Thomas in America* (London: Dent, 1956), p. 15.
[5] John Dorsey, "Katherine Anne Porter On," p. 40.
[6] Raymond Roseliep to Joan Givner, 1 May 1979, collection of author.
[7] Karl Shapiro, "Emily Dickinson and Katherine Anne Porter," *Poetry* April 1961.
[8] KAP to Ann Holloway Heintze, 14 March 1949, McKeldin.
[9] *Collected Essays,* p. 161.
[10] Ann Holloway Heintze, interview in Pound Ridge, New York, 8 December 1979.
[11] KAP to David Locher, 25 February 1965, McKeldin.
[12] Photograph, collection of Paul Porter, New York.
[13] KAP to Gay Porter Holloway, 18 January 1959, McKeldin.
[14] William R. Wilkins to Joan Givner, 27 January 1980, collection of author.
[15] KAP to Paul Porter, undated, McKeldin.
[16] Gay Porter Holloway to Lady Bunton, 7 March 1956, collection of author.
[17] KAP to Paul Porter, 2 August 1949, McKeldin.
[18] KAP to Cyrilly Abels, 15 June 1963, McKeldin.
[19] KAP to Paul Porter, 29 November 1951, McKeldin.
[20] John Dorsey, "Katherine Anne Porter On," p. 41.
[21] Katherine Anne Porter, notes, 31 May 1961, McKeldin.
[22] William R. Wilkins, interview in College Park, Maryland, 1 December 1976.
[23] KAP to Paul Porter, 15 April 1954, McKeldin.
[24] KAP to Paul Porter, 11 March 1949, McKeldin.
[25] KAP to William Humphrey, 26 September 1950, McKeldin.
[26] William Humphrey to KAP, 28 September 1950, McKeldin.
[27] KAP to William Goyen, 19 October 1950, McKeldin.
[28] KAP to William Humphrey, 1951, McKeldin.
[29] "Recent Southern Fiction: A Panel Discussion," pamphlet issued by Wesleyan College, Macon, Georgia, 1960, p. 8.

[30] KAP to David Locher, Lady Day 1961, collection of David Locher, Dubuque, Iowa.

[31] KAP to Gay Porter Holloway, 6 December 1955, McKeldin.

[32] William Goyen to KAP, 26 August 1947, McKeldin.

[33] KAP to Paul Porter, 13 January 1951, McKeldin.

[34] KAP to William Goyen, 19 April 1951, McKeldin.

[35] KAP to William Goyen, 11 July 1951, McKeldin.

[36] KAP to William Goyen, 30 May 1951, McKeldin. This picture appears in Enrique Hank Lopez, *Conversations with Katherine Anne Porter: Refugee from Indian Creek* (Boston: Little, Brown, 1981), p. 216. There it has the caption: "Miss Porter with her third husband, Albert Erskine."

[37] KAP to William Goyen, 3 May 1951, McKeldin.

[38] KAP to William Goyen, 30 May 1951, McKeldin.

[39] KAP to William Goyen, 19 June 1951, McKeldin.

[40] William Goyen, telephone interview, 12 April 1982, in New York.

[41] KAP to William Goyen, 12 June 1951, McKeldin.

[42] KAP to William Goyen, 7 November 1951, McKeldin.

[43] KAP to William Goyen, June 1952, not sent, McKeldin.

[44] William Goyen, *In a Farther Country* (New York: Random House, 1955), McKeldin.

[45] McKeldin.

[46] KAP to William Goyen, 11 July 1952, McKeldin.

[47] KAP to Paul Porter, 21 March 1952, McKeldin.

[48] *Collected Essays,* pp. 216–219.

[49] Joseph Blotner, *Faulkner: A Biography* Vol. II (New York: Random House, 1974), p. 1422.

[50] Allen Tate, interview in Nashville, Tennessee, 3 June 1978.

[51] KAP to William Goyen, 2 June 1952, McKeldin.

[52] Thomas Daniel Young and John J. Hindle, eds., *The Republic of Letters in America: The Correspondence of John Peale Bishop and Allen Tate* (Kentucky: University Press of Kentucky, 1981), pp. 172–173.

[53] KAP to Allen Tate, 18 June 1952, McKeldin.

[54] Katherine Anne Porter, marginal note in Simone de Beauvoir, *The Second Sex,* McKeldin.

[55] KAP to Paul Porter, 19 December 1952, McKeldin.

[56] KAP to Paul Porter, 19 December 1952, McKeldin.

20: UNIVERSITY TEACHING

[1] *Collected Essays,* p. 225.

[2] KAP to Glenway Wescott, 26 September 1953, McKeldin.

[3] KAP to Donald Brace, 9 September 1952, McKeldin.

[4] KAP to Joan Givner, 29 September 1976, collection of author.

[5] Kitty Barry Crawford to George Hendrick, 20 November 1961, collection of George Hendrick, Urbana-Champaign, Illinois.

[6] *Collected Essays,* p. 242.

[7] KAP to Professor Louis I. Bedvold, 6 August 1953, University of Michigan Library.

[8] KAP to Professor Louis I. Bedvold, 22 August 1953, University of Michigan Library.

[9] KAP to Dr. Warner G. Rice, 3 June 1953, University of Michigan Library.

542 / NOTES

10 Jeanne Rockwell to Joan Givner, 12 January 1978, collection of author.
11 KAP to Glenway Wescott, November 1944, McKeldin.
12 Elizabeth Uhr to Joan Givner, 17 February 1978, collection of author.
13 Mary Cooley to Joan Givner, 3 November 1977, collection of author.
14 Martin Green to Joan Givner, 12 March 1978, collection of author.
15 Mary Cooley to Joan Givner, 23 November 1977, collection of author.
16 Mary Cooley to Joan Givner, 23 November 1977, collection of author.
17 Mary Cooley to Joan Givner, 23 November 1977, collection of author.
18 Mary Cooley to Joan Givner, 27 February 1978, collection of author.
19 Elizabeth Uhr to Joan Givner, 17 February 1978, collection of author.
20 Mary Cooley to Joan Givner, 23 November 1977, collection of author.
21 David Locher to Joan Givner, 4 June 1979, collection of author.
22 Mary Cooley to Joan Givner, 23 November 1977, collection of author.
23 Elizabeth Uhr to Joan Givner, 17 February 1978, collection of author.
24 David Locher, class notes, 14 May 1954, collection of David Locher, Dubuque, Iowa.
25 Elizabeth Davenport, class notes, 3 May 1954, collection of Elizabeth Davenport, Ann Arbor, Michigan.
26 KAP to David Locher, 30 December 1957, collection of David Locher, Dubuque, Iowa.
27 Elizabeth Davenport, class notes, 3 May 1954, collection of Elizabeth Davenport, Ann Arbor, Michigan.
28 Elizabeth Davenport, class notes, 3 May 1954, collection of Elizabeth Davenport, Ann Arbor, Michigan.
29 David Locher, "Thoughts on Faulkner," 14 May 1954, collection of David Locher, Dubuque, Iowa.
30 David Locher, "Thoughts on Faulkner," 14 May 1954, collection of David Locher, Dubuque, Iowa.
31 David Locher, "Thoughts on Faulkner," 14 May 1954, collection of David Locher, Dubuque, Iowa.
32 David Locher, "Thoughts on Faulkner," 14 May 1954, collection of David Locher, Dubuque, Iowa.
33 Martin Green to Joan Givner, 12 March 1978, collection of author.
34 KAP to Ann Holloway Heintze, 8 December 1962, McKeldin.
35 Richard Colewell to Joan Givner, 8 February 1971, collection of author.
36 Professor Carlton F. Wells to Joan Givner, 19 December 1977, collection of author.
37 Jeanne Rockwell to Joan Givner, 22 February 1978, collection of author.
38 Elizabeth Uhr to Joan Givner, 17 February 1978, collection of author.
39 Richard Colewell to Joan Givner, 8 February 1971, collection of author.
40 Jeanne Rockwell, "The Magic Cloak," *Michigan Quarterly Review,* 5, 1966, pp. 283–284. Jeanne Rockwell to Joan Givner, 12 January 1978, collection of author.
41 Richard Colewell to Joan Givner, 8 February 1971, collection of author.
42 Richard Colewell to Joan Givner, 8 February 1971, collection of author.
43 KAP to Professor Cowden, 14 May 1954, University of Michigan Library.
44 KAP to Glenway Wescott, 18 February 1953, McKeldin.
45 KAP to Monroe Wheeler, 1 April 1954, McKeldin.
46 KAP to Monroe Wheeler, 1 April 1954, McKeldin.
47 KAP to Monroe Wheeler, 1 April 1954, McKeldin.
48 KAP to Glenway Wescott, 18 February 1953, McKeldin.
49 KAP to Paul Porter, 13 April 1954, McKeldin.

50 Mary Cooley to Joan Givner, 23 November 1977, collection of author.
51 KAP to Monroe Wheeler, 17 June 1954, McKeldin.
52 Mary Cooley to Joan Givner, 27 February 1978, collection of author.
53 Richard Colewell to Joan Givner, 8 February 1971, collection of author.
54 KAP to Ann Holloway Heintze, 15 June 1954, McKeldin.
55 *Ship of Fools,* p. 106.
56 David Locher to Joan Givner, 4 June 1979, collection of author.
57 KAP to David Locher, 12 June 1958, collection of David Locher, Dubuque, Iowa.
58 *Ship of Fools,* p. 59.

21: I AM REALLY OLD NOW
AND . . . TIME IS RUNNING OUT

1 Tillie Olsen, *Silences* (New York: Delta/Seymour Lawrence, 1978), p. 13.
2 KAP to Glenway Wescott, 5 July 1956, McKeldin. .
3 KAP to Glenway Wescott, 23 October 1954, McKeldin.
4 KAP to Glenway Wescott, 23 October 1954, McKeldin.
5 KAP to William Goyen, 8 April 1951, McKeldin.
6 KAP to William Goyen, 19 June 1951, McKeldin.
7 Katherine Anne Porter, notes, 20 October 1954, McKeldin.
8 KAP to Cyrilly Abels, 3 November 1961, McKeldin. KAP to Cyrilly Abels, 13 November 1962, McKeldin.
9 KAP to Cyrilly Abels, 2 May 1960, McKeldin.
10 Marginal notes in *The Odyssey,* McKeldin.
11 *Collected Essays,* p. 135.
12 *Collected Essays,* p. 137.
13 KAP to Monroe Wheeler, 17 June 1954, McKeldin.
14 *Collected Essays,* p. 291.
15 KAP to David Locher, 6 December 1957, McKeldin.
16 KAP to Mr. Warburg, 8 January 1958, McKeldin.
17 Katherine Anne Porter, note, undated, McKeldin.
18 *Collected Essays,* p. 289.
19 *Collected Essays,* p. 92.
20 Glenway Wescott to KAP, 14 July 1955, McKeldin.
21 KAP to Glenway Wescott, 4 August 1955, McKeldin.
22 KAP to Honora Comès, 20 December 1957, collection of Marcella Comès Winslow, Washington, D.C.
23 KAP to Glenway Wescott, 27 December 1954, McKeldin.
24 KAP to Monroe Wheeler, 26 January 1955, McKeldin.
25 Katherine Anne Porter, notes, 21 October 1947, McKeldin.
26 Angna Enters, *Artist's Life* (New York: Coward, McCann, 1958). This particular extract is dated 2 April 1955.
27 KAP to Glenway Wescott, 23 October 1955, McKeldin.
28 Katherine Anne Porter, letter fragment, 23 December 1955, McKeldin.
29 KAP to Glenway Wescott, 7 July 1956, McKeldin.
30 *Ship of Fools.*
31 KAP to Glenway Wescott, 4 August 1955, McKeldin.
32 KAP to Glenway Wescott, 4 August 1955, McKeldin.
33 KAP to Glenway Wescott, 4 August 1955, McKeldin.

[34] KAP to David Locher, 20 April 1958, McKeldin.
[35] KAP to Glenway Wescott, 21 Feburary 1956, McKeldin.
[36] KAP to Paul Porter, 20 June 1957, McKeldin.
[37] Katherine Anne Porter, inscriptions, McKeldin.
[38] Gay Porter Holloway to Lady Bunton, 7 March 1950, collection of author.
[39] KAP to Monroe Wheeler, 29 June 1958, McKeldin.
[40] KAP to Monroe Wheeler, 29 June 1958, McKeldin.
[41] KAP to Cyrilly Abels, undated, McKeldin.

22: SHIP OF FOOLS: *THE LAST STRETCH*

[1] KAP to Ann Holloway Heintze, 29 October 1958, McKeldin.
[2] Winston Bode, "Miss Porter on Writers and Writing," *Texas Observer,* 31 October 1958, pp. 6–7.
[3] Monroe Wheeler to KAP, 15 February 1959, McKeldin.
[4] KAP to Ann Holloway Heintze, 5 January 1959, McKeldin.
[5] Katherine Anne Porter, notes on Deirdre Handy, "The Family Legend in the Stories of Katherine Anne Porter" (M.A. thesis, University of Oklahoma, 1953), Humanities Research Center, University of Texas, Austin, Texas.
[6] KAP to Harry Ransom, 20 January 1967, McKeldin.
[7] KAP to Harry Ransom, 20 January 1967, McKeldin.
[8] KAP to David Locher, 18 January 1961, collection of David Locher, Dubuque, Iowa.
[9] KAP to Erna Glover Johns, 31 August 1961, McKeldin.
[10] KAP to Cyrilly Abels, 20 October 1961, McKeldin.
[11] Rita Johns, interview in Austin, Texas, 10 May 1976.
[12] Erna Glover Johns, interview in Austin, Texas, 10 May 1976.
[13] KAP to Glenway Wescott, 10 June 1959, McKeldin.
[14] KAP to Monroe Wheeler, 4 January 1960, McKeldin.
[15] Ann Holloway Heintze, interview in Pound Ridge, New York, 8 December 1979.
[16] Marcella Comès Winslow to Mary Winslow Poole, 17 November 1959, collection of Marcella Comès Winslow, Washington, D.C.
[17] Marcella Comès Winslow to Mary Winslow Poole, 22 March 1960, collection of Marcella Comès Winslow, Washington, D.C.
[18] Eudora Welty to Joan Givner, interview, in Jackson, Mississippi, 19 February 1955.
[19] KAP, interview in College Park, Maryland, 2 December 1976.
[20] Rhea Johnson, interview in Washington, D.C., 24 June 1977.
[21] Rhea Johnson, interview in Washington, D.C., 24 June 1977.
[22] KAP to Glenway Wescott, 5 January, 1960, McKeldin.
[23] Mary Anne Dolan, "Almost Since Chaucer with Miss Porter," *Washington Star,* 11 May 1975.
[24] KAP to Rhea Johnson, all notes dated by KAP, collection of Rhea Johnson, Washington, D.C.
[25] KAP to Eleanor Clark, 21 April 1960, McKeldin.
[26] KAP to Eleanor Clark, 21 April 1960, McKeldin.
[27] KAP to Eleanor Clark, 21 April 1960, McKeldin.
[28] KAP to Monroe Wheeler, 4 January 1960, McKeldin.
[29] David Locher to Joan Givner, 31 March 1979, collection of author.
[30] David Locher to Joan Givner, 31 March 1979, collection of author.

[31] "Recent Southern Fiction: A Panel Discussion," pamphlet issued by Wesleyan College, Macon, Georgia, 1960.

[32] Flannery O'Connor, *The Habit of Being,* ed., Sally Fitzgerald (New York: Farrar, Straus and Giroux, 1979), p. 416.

[33] KAP to David Locher, 18 January 1961, collection of David Locher, Dubuque, Iowa.

[34] KAP to David Locher, Lady Day 1961, collection of David Locher, Dubuque, Iowa.

[35] KAP to Cyrilly Abels, 30 May 1961, McKeldin.

[36] KAP to Ann Holloway Heintze, 16 August 1960, McKeldin.

[37] KAP to Cyrilly Abels, 30 May 1961, McKeldin.

[38] KAP to Rhea Johnson, 20 June 1961, collection of Rhea Johnson, Washington, D.C.

[39] KAP to Rhea Johnson, 1 June 1961, collection of Rhea Johnson, Washington, D.C.

[40] KAP to Rhea Johnson, 7 June 1961, collection of Rhea Johnson, Washington, D.C.

[41] KAP to Rhea Johnson, 9 June 1961, collection of Rhea Johnson, Washington, D.C.

[42] KAP to Rhea Johnson, 15 June 1961, collection of Rhea Johnson, Washington, D.C.

[43] KAP to Rhea Johnson, 20 June 1961, collection of Rhea Johnson, Washington, D.C.

[44] Katherine Anne Porter, note, 15 June 1961, McKeldin.

[45] Mark Schorer, review of *Ship of Fools,* by Katherine Anne Porter, in *New York Times Book Review,* 1 April 1962, p. 1.

[46] Louis Auchincloss, review of *Ship of Fools,* by Katherine Anne Porter, in *New York Herald Tribune,* 1 April 1962, pp. 3, 11.

[47] Howard Moss, review of *Ship of Fools,* by Katherine Anne Porter, in *New Yorker,* 28 April 1962, pp. 165–173.

[48] Elizabeth Janeway, "For Katherine Anne Porter, 'Ship of Fools' Was a Lively Twenty-two Year Voyage," *New York Times Book Review,* 1 April 1962, pp. 4–5.

[49] Elizabeth Janeway, "For Katherine Anne Porter, 'Ship of Fools' Was a Lively Twenty-two Year Voyage," *New York Times Book Review,* 1 April 1962, pp. 4–5.

[50] Mary Hemingway, *How It Was* (New York: Alfred A. Knopf, 1976), p. 514.

23: THE AFTERMATH OF SHIP OF FOOLS

[1] Glenway Wescott to KAP, 4 May 1962, McKeldin.

[2] KAP to David Locher, 13 December 1962, collection of David Locher, Dubuque, Iowa.

[3] KAP to David Locher, 25 June 1964, collection of David Locher, Dubuque, Iowa.

[4] KAP to David Locher, 13 December 1962, collection of David Locher, Dubuque, Iowa.

[5] Glenway Wescott to KAP, 4 May 1962, McKeldin.

[6] Maurice Dolbier, "I've Had a Good Run for My Money," *New York Herald Tribune Books,* 1 April 1962, pp. 3, 11.

[7] Cleveland Amory, "Celebrity Register," *McCall's,* April 1973.

[8] Katherine Anne Porter, lecture, McKeldin Library, December 1972.

[9] Matthew Josephson, interview in New York, December 1974.

[10] Katherine Anne Porter, interview in College Park, Maryland, 3 December 1976.

[11] Sister Maura to Joan Givner, 12 February 1979, collection of author.

[12] Raymond Roseliep to Joan Givner, 23 October 1978, collection of author.

[13] Glenway Wescott to KAP, 26 November 1962, McKeldin.

[14] Theodore Solotaroff, " 'Ship of Fools' and the Critics," *Commentary*, 24 October 1962, pp. 277–286.

[15] *Collected Essays*, p. 228.

[16] Stanley Kauffman, "Katherine Anne Porter's Crowning Work," *New Republic*, 2 April 1962, pp. 23–25.

[17] Theodore Solotaroff, " 'Ship of Fools' and the Critics," *Commentary*, 24 October 1962, pp. 277–286.

[18] Josephine Herbst to Daniel Curley, 26 April 1962, Beinecke.

[19] Hank Lopez, "A Country and Some People I Love," p. 68.

[20] Katherine Anne Porter, marginal notes in Albert Memmi, *Portrait of a Jew*, trans., Elizabeth Abbott (New York: Orion Press, 1962), p. 23, McKeldin.

[21] Katherine Anne Porter, interview in *Richmond News Leader*, 20 November 1958.

[22] KAP to Glenway Wescott, 30 July 1956, McKeldin.

[23] KAP to Pauline Young, 4 November 1961, McKeldin.

[24] Josephine Herbst to Daniel Curley, 26 April 1962, Beinecke.

[25] Flannery O'Connor, *Habit of Being*, ed., Sally Fitzgerald (New York: Farrar, Straus and Giroux, 1979), p. 484.

[26] Raymond Roseliep, "Devilish Wine," in *Voyages to the Inland Sea* (La Crosse, Wisconsin: University of Wisconsin Press, 1974), p. 59.

[27] Lodwick Hartley, "Dark Voyagers: A Study of Katherine Anne Porter's *Ship of Fools*," *University Review*, XXX, 1963, pp. 83–94.

[28] KAP to Glenway Wescott, 26 November 1962, McKeldin.

[29] Sybille Bedford, "Voyage to Everywhere," *Spectator*, 16 November 1962, pp. 763–764.

[30] Sybille Bedford, "Voyage to Everywhere," *Spectator*, 16 November 1962, pp. 763–764.

[31] "On the Good Ship Vera," *Times Literary Supplement*, 2 November 1962, p. 837.

[32] Cleveland Amory, "Celebrity Register," *McCall's*, April 1963.

[33] *Collected Essays*, p. 119.

[34] Rhea Johnson, interview in Washington, D.C., 24 June 1977.

[35] KAP to Glenway Wescott, 6 September 1962, McKeldin.

[36] KAP to Paul Porter, 9 February 1963, McKeldin.

[37] KAP to Glenway Wescott, 23 April 1963, McKeldin.

[38] Katherine Anne Porter, "Recollection of Rome," *Travel and Leisure*, January 1974, pp. 4–9.

[39] Katherine Anne Porter, "Recollection of Rome," *Travel and Leisure*, January 1974, pp. 4–9.

[40] *Collected Essays*, p. 42.

[41] KAP to Rhea Johnson, 17 October 1963, collection of Rhea Johnson, Washington, D.C.

[42] *Collected Essays*, p. 304.

[43] Robert Kiely, interview in Cambridge, Massachusetts, 7 February 1979.

[44] KAP, marginal note, 6 January 1956, in Virginia Woolf, *A Room of One's Own*. Porter's copy is dated: "Brooklyn December 1929."

[45] Maurice Dolbier, "I've Had a Good Run for My Money," *New York Herald Tribune Books,* 1 April 1962, p. 11.

[46] Josephine Novak and Elise Chisholm, "Don't Scare the Horses, Miss Porter Tells Liberation Women," *Baltimore Evening Sun,* 23 March 1970, p. C1.

24: TWO KINDS OF SUCCESS

[1] Ray B. West, Jr., *Katherine Anne Porter* in University of Minnesota Pamphlets on American Writers, No. 28 (Minneapolis: University of Minnesota Press, 1963).

[2] William L. Nance, S.M., *Katherine Anne Porter and the Art of Rejection* (Chapel Hill, N.C.: University of North Carolina Press, 1964).

[3] Katherine Anne Porter, marginal notes in William L. Nance, S.M., *Katherine Anne Porter and the Art of Rejection* (Chapel Hill, N.C.: University of North Carolina Press, 1964).

[4] KAP to Caroline Gordon, 30 September 1964, McKeldin.

[5] Katherine Anne Porter, marginal notes in William L. Nance, S.M., *Katherine Anne Porter and the Art of Rejection* (Chapel Hill, N.C.: University of North Carolina Press, 1964).

[6] Caroline Gordon, "Katherine Anne Porter and the ICM," *Harper's,* November 1964, pp. 146–148.

[7] KAP to Caroline Gordon, 30 September 1964, McKeldin.

[8] George Hendrick, *Katherine Anne Porter* (New York: Twayne, 1965).

[9] KAP to Vida Vliet, 11 September 1965, McKeldin.

[10] Katherine Anne Porter, marginalia in George Hendrick, *Katherine Anne Porter* (New York: Twayne, 1965).

[11] Katherine Anne Porter, marginalia in George Hendrick, *Katherine Anne Porter* (New York: Twayne, 1965).

[12] Katherine Anne Porter, marginalia in George Hendrick, *Katherine Anne Porter* (New York: Twayne, 1965).

[13] KAP to David Locher, 25 August 1966, collection of David Locher, Dubuque, Iowa.

[14] Carl Schoettler, "Katherine Anne Porter Reigns for Students," *Baltimore Evening Sun,* 15 April 1974.

[15] KAP to Abby Mann, 11 May 1964, McKeldin.

[16] KAP to Abby Mann, 11 May 1964, McKeldin.

[17] KAP to Abby Mann, 11 May 1964, McKeldin.

[18] Donald Spoto, *Stanley Kramer Film Maker* (New York: G. P. Putnam's Sons, 1978), pp. 264–271.

[19] Anne Edwards, *Vivien Leigh* (New York: Simon and Schuster, 1977).

[20] Anne Edwards, *Vivien Leigh* (New York: Simon and Schuster, 1977).

[21] Bosley Crowther, review of movie, *Ship of Fools, New York Times.* Richard L. Cow, review of movie, *Ship of Fools, Washington Post,* 21 October 1965.

[22] Donald Spoto, *Stanley Kramer Film Maker* (New York: G. P. Putnam's Sons, 1978), pp. 264–271.

[23] Donald Spoto, *Stanley Kramer Film Maker* (New York: G. P. Putnam's Sons, 1978), pp. 264–271.

24 *Ship of Fools,* p. 58.
25 Rhea Johnson, interview in Washington, D.C., 24 June 1977.
26 Rhea Johnson, interview in Washington, D.C., 24 June 1977.
27 KAP to Cyrilly Abels, 5 November 1964, McKeldin.
28 *Collected Essays,* p. 119.
29 KAP to Marcelle Sibon, 20 July 1964, McKeldin.
30 Malcolm Cowley to KAP, 14 January 1931, McKeldin.
31 Caskie Stinnett to Cyrilly Abels, 12 July 1973, McKeldin.
32 KAP to Cyrilly Abels, 5 November 1964, McKeldin.
33 Cyrilly Abels to KAP, 23 March 1965, McKeldin.
34 KAP to Cyrilly Abels, 19 March 1965, McKeldin.
35 *Collected Stories,* p. vi.

25: THE REWARDS OF SUCCESS

1 *Collected Essays,* p. 293.
2 *San Antonio Express,* 3 May 1966.
3 *Collected Essays,* p. 228.
4 Katherine Anne Porter, marginal notes in *Collected Essays,* McKeldin.
5 *Potomac Magazine,* section of *Washington Post,* 14 November 1965.
6 KAP to Rhea Johnson, 17 October 1963, McKeldin.
7 KAP to Rhea Johnson, 17 October 1963, McKeldin.
8 KAP to Rhea Johnson, 17 October 1963, McKeldin.
9 Josephine Novak, "Miss Porter Returns to 'Lovely Funny Treasures,' " *Baltimore Evening Sun,* March 1969.
10 Barrett E. Prettyman, inscription in *Death and the Supreme Court,* Mc-Keldin.
11 KAP to William Humphrey, 2 March 1965, McKeldin.
12 KAP to Barrett E. Prettyman, 28 May 1966, McKeldin.
13 Katherine Anne Porter, undated fragment, McKeldin.
14 KAP to Barbara Wescott, 16 December 1966, McKeldin.
15 Barrett Prettyman, inscription in Katherine Anne Porter's visitors' book, 3 December 1966, McKeldin.
16 Paul Porter, interview in New York, 15 March 1978.
17 Barrett Prettyman, inscription on photograph, 8 December 1967, Mc-Keldin.
18 Barrett Prettyman, inscription in *Death and the Supreme Court,* McKeldin.
19 KAP to Barrett Prettyman, 10 October 1968, McKeldin.
20 KAP to Barrett Prettyman, 10 October 1968, McKeldin.
21 Paul Porter, interview in New York, 15 March 1978.
22 "Sick Transit," *Women's Wear Daily,* 18 March 1970, McKeldin.
23 KAP to Barrett Prettyman, 16 February 1968, McKeldin.
24 KAP to Barrett Prettyman, 10 October 1968, McKeldin.
25 KAP to David Locher, 23 December 1968, McKeldin.
26 Elinor Langer, "If in Fact I Have Found a Heroine," *Mother Jones,* May 1981, pp. 36–46.
27 KAP to Joan Givner, 6 July 1976, collection of author.
28 Josephine Herbst to Daniel Curley, 26 April 1962, Beinecke.
29 Josephine Herbst, 14 July 1931, Beinecke.
30 Judith Martin, "Porter at 80," *Washington Post,* 15 May 1970.
31 "Don't Scare the Horses, Miss Porter Tells Liberation Women," *Baltimore Evening Sun,* 23 March 1970.

[32] "Don't Scare the Horses, Miss Porter Tells Liberation Women," *Baltimore Evening Sun,* 23 March 1970.

[33] *Collected Essays,* McKeldin.

[34] Katherine Anne Porter, inscription in *Collected Essays,* McKeldin.

[35] Inscriptions in George Eliot, *Adam Bede.*

[36] Inscriptions in George Eliot, *Adam Bede.*

[37] *Collected Essays.*

[38] Inscription in *Collected Essays,* collection of author.

[39] Inscription in *Collected Essays,* collection of Paul Porter.

[40] KAP to Glenway Wescott, 6 September 1962, McKeldin.

[41] Judith Martin, "Porter at 80," *Washington Post,* 15 May 1970.

[42] KAP to Barrett Prettyman, 22 November 1974, McKeldin.

[43] Barrett Prettyman to KAP, 30 December 1970, McKeldin.

[44] Katherine Anne Porter, notes, undated, McKeldin.

[45] Barrett Prettyman to KAP, 1975, McKeldin.

[46] KAP to Barrett Prettyman, 19 September 1973, McKeldin.

[47] Carl Schoettler, "Katherine Anne Porter Reigns for Students," *Baltimore Evening Sun,* 15 April 1974.

[48] Katherine Anne Porter, lecture, Katherine Anne Porter Room, December 1972.

[49] Katherine Anne Porter, lecture, Katherine Anne Porter Room, December 1972.

[50] Katherine Anne Porter, lecture, Katherine Anne Porter Room, December 1972.

[51] Katherine Anne Porter, notes, undated, McKeldin.

[52] Ralph Henderson, "Author Sees Disorder but Refuses to Despair," *Baltimore Evening Sun,* 26 February 1976.

26: THE FINAL CHAPTER

[1] Katherine Anne Porter, interview in College Park, Maryland, 3 December 1976.

[2] William R. Wilkins to Joan Givner, 16 August 1977, collection of author.

[3] William R. Wilkins, interview in College Park, Maryland, 5 December 1976.

[4] William R. Wilkins to Joan Givner, 13 July 1980, collection of author.

[5] William R. Wilkins to Joan Givner, 2 February 1978, collection of author.

[6] William R. Wilkins to Joan Givner, 16 August 1977, collection of author.

[7] KAP to Roger L. Brooks, 7 October 1975, McKeldin.

[8] James Stanley Walker, "Dougout Doug and Drugstore Blitz," *Texas Observer,* 2 December 1977.

[9] Joan Givner, "A Fine Day of Homage to Porter," *Dallas Morning News,* 23 May 1976.

[10] Katherine Anne Porter, interview in College Park, Maryland, 3 December 1976.

[11] Katherine Anne Porter, notes, 13 January 1977, McKeldin.

[12] Interview with medical staff, Johns Hopkins Hospital, 21 February 1977.

[13] William R. Wilkins to Joan Givner, 9 June 1977, collection of author.

[14] William R. Wilkins to Joan Givner, 18 May 1977, collection of author.

[15] KAP to Barrett Prettyman, 15 May 1977, McKeldin.

[16] Art Jaeger, "Celebrated Writer Assigned Guardian," (Prince Georges County) *Journal,* 5 October 1977.

[17] Joseph Gallagher, "Katherine Anne Porter: The Last Candle Is Out," *Baltimore Evening Sun,* 30 September 1980.

[18] Paul Porter to Joan Givner, 27 December 1978, collection of author.

[19] KAP to Rhea Johnson, 23 March 1963, McKeldin.

[20] Sister Maura to Joan Givner, 12 February 1978, collection of author.

[21] Raymond Roseliep to Joan Givner, 23 October 1978, collection of author. Raymond Roseliep to Joan Givner, 15 October 1981, collection of author.

EPILOGUE

[1] KAP to Edward G. Schwartz, 1 July 1956, McKeldin.

[2] Truman Capote, inscription in uncorrected proof of *Other Voices, Other Rooms,* 4 December 1947, McKeldin.

[3] Tillie Olsen, conversation in Cambridge, Massachusetts, 15 March 1979.

[4] Thompson, "Katherine Anne Porter: An Interview," p. 18.

[5] *Collected Essays,* p. 443.

[6] *Collected Essays,* p. 93.

Index

About the Author

Joan Givner, who has written extensively on the work and life of Katherine Anne Porter for over a decade, was born in Manchester, England, in 1936. After receiving her B.A. from the University of London, she emigrated to the United States and became a U.S. citizen in 1962. She obtained her M.A. from Washington University in St. Louis, Missouri, and her Ph.D. from the University of London. She has been affiliated with the University of Regina in Saskatchewan, Canada, since 1965, and currently holds the position of Professor of English. She is also the editor of *Wascana Review*. Among the awards she has received are fellowships from the National Endowment for the Humanities and from the Mary Ingraham Bunting Institute of Radcliffe College.

Joan Givner lives in Regina, Saskatchewan, with her husband and is the mother of two teenage daughters.

Outstanding Paperback Books from the Touchstone Library

☐ **Maugham: A Biography**
by Ted Morgan
This full-scale biography of one of
the most fascinating and secretive
literary figures of this century was an
American Book Award nominee in
1981. "One dare not skip a word of
Morgan's text. And just as well for it
is an amazing account he has put
together of all that Maugham was."
The New York Times
50581-5 $12.95

☐ **Mr. Clemens and Mark Twain**
by Justin Kaplan
From the winner of the National
Book Award and the Pulitzer Prize,
a brilliant portrait of the towering
figure whose dual personae
symbolized the American conflict
between morality and success.
47071-X $8.95

☐ **Attorney for the Damned**
edited by Arthur Weinberg
with Foreword by Justice
William O. Douglas
The collection of lectures, court
summations and articles that
portray the highlights of Clarence
Darrow's career, bringing back the
resonant voice of one of this
country's greatest defense
attorneys.
49251-9 $9.95

☐ **Hitchcock**
by Francois Truffaut
A series of intriguing dialogues
between the legendary Hitchcock
and his renowned admirer Truffaut.
With detailed histories of all of his
films and 472 photographs, this is the
most comprehensive book on the
master ever published.
20346-0 $11.95

☐ **Mornings on Horseback**
by David McCullough
The American Book Award-winning
biography of Theodore Roosevelt,
this stunning volume brings into vivid
focus the childhood of one of
America's most outstanding political
figures.
44754-8 $9.95

☐ **Churchill: Young Man in a Hurry
1874–1915**
by Ted Morgan
"Mr. Morgan's is essentially a story of
action, richly detailed, constructed in
the highly readable paragraphs of
the expert reporter." (*The New York
Times*) Morgan draws on a wealth of
archival documents to present an
intimate account of Churchill's early
decades.
25304-2 $10.95

------------- MAIL COUPON TODAY—NO-RISK 14 DAY FREE TRIAL ------------

Simon & Schuster, Inc.
Simon & Schuster Building, 1230 Avenue of the Americas,
New York, N.Y. 10020, Mail Order Dept.TB4

Please send me copies of the books checked above.
(If not completely satisfied, you may return for full refund within 14 days.)
☐ Save! Enclose full amount per *copy* with this coupon: publisher pays
postage and handling: or charge my credit card.

☐ Master Card   ☐ Visa

My credit card number is_____Card expires_____

Signature_____

Name_____
                              (Please Print)

Address_____

City_____State_____Zip Code_____
or available at your local bookstore   Prices subject to change without notice.